Identity Fraud

Committed by the Government Against the People

by Thomas Marvin; Maxwell
and Ken Gullekson

HEISENBERG PRESS
Post Office Box 1178
Glendale, California

Print on Demand Edition
Copyright ©2002

Maxwell, Thomas Marvin.
   Identity fraud: committed by the government against
the people / by Thomas Marvin; Maxwell and Ken
Gullekson. 1st ed.
   p. cm.
   Includes index.
   LCCN 2002110937
   ISBN 0-9653136-2-X   19.95

   1. Civil rights—United States—History. 2. Human
rights—United States—History. 3. Constitutional law—
United States. 4. Liberty. 5. Conspiracies—United
States—History. 6. United States—Politics and
government.   I. Gullekson, Ken. II. Title.

JC599.U5M39 2002   323.49'0973
                                 QBI33-701

Heisenberg Press
Post Office Box 1178
Glendale, California

Acknowledgment and thanks to Richard McDonald, whose research first opened my eyes in 1993 and set me on a path, which ultimately led to the writing of this book.

Thomas Marvin; Maxwell

"We hold these truths to be self-evident, that all men are created equal, that they are endowed by their Creator with certain unalienable Rights, that among these are Life, Liberty and the pursuit of Happiness.

That whenever any Form of Government becomes destructive of these ends, it is the Right of the People to alter or to abolish it,...

IN CONGRESS, JULY 4, 1776.

The unanimous Declaration of the thirteen united States of America,

When in the Course of human events, it becomes necessary for one people to dissolve the political bands which have connected them with another, and to assume among the powers of the earth, the separate and equal station to which the Laws of Nature and of Nature's God entitle them, a decent respect to the opinions of mankind requires that they should declare the causes which impel them to the separation. ———— We hold these truths to be self-evident, that all men are created equal, that they are endowed by their Creator with certain unalienable Rights, that among these are Life, Liberty and the pursuit of Happiness.—That to secure these rights, Governments are instituted among Men, deriving their just powers from the consent of the governed, —That whenever any Form of Government becomes destructive of these ends, it is the Right of the People to alter or to abolish it, and to institute new Government, laying its foundation on such principles and organizing its powers in such form, as to them shall seem most likely to effect their Safety and Happiness. Prudence, indeed, will dictate that Governments long established should not be changed for light and transient causes; and accordingly all experience hath shewn, that mankind are more disposed to suffer, while evils are sufferable, than to right themselves by abolishing the forms to which they are accustomed. But when a long train of abuses and usurpations, pursuing invariably the same Object evinces a design to reduce them under absolute Despotism, it is their right, it is their duty, to throw off such Government, and to provide new Guards for their future security.—Such has been the patient sufferance of these Colonies; and such is now the necessity which constrains them to alter their former Systems of Government. The history of the present King of Great Britain is a history of repeated injuries and usurpations, all having in direct object the establishment of an absolute Tyranny over these States. To prove this, let Facts be submitted to a candid world. He has refused his Assent to Laws, the most wholesome and necessary for the public good.

He has forbidden his Governors to pass Laws of immediate and pressing importance, unless suspended in their operation till his Assent should be obtained; and when so suspended, he has utterly neglected to attend to them.

He has refused to pass other Laws for the accommodation of large districts of people, unless those people would relinquish the right of Representation in the Legislature, a right inestimable to them and formidable to tyrants only.

He has called together legislative bodies at places unusual, uncomfortable, and distant from the depository of their public Records, for the sole purpose of fatiguing them into compliance with his measures.

He has dissolved Representative Houses repeatedly, for opposing with manly firmness his invasions on the rights of the people.

He has refused for a long time, after such dissolutions, to cause others to be elected; whereby the Legislative powers, incapable of Annihilation, have returned to the People at large for their exercise; the State remaining in the mean time exposed to all the dangers of invasion from without, and convulsions within.

He has endeavoured to prevent the population of these States; for that purpose obstructing the Laws for Naturalization of Foreigners; refusing to pass others to encourage their migrations hither, and raising the conditions of new Appropriations of Lands.

He has obstructed the Administration of Justice, by refusing his Assent to Laws for establishing Judiciary powers.

He has made Judges dependent on his Will alone, for the tenure of their offices, and the amount and payment of their salaries.

He has erected a multitude of New Offices, and sent hither swarms of Officers to harrass our people, and eat out their substance.

He has kept among us, in times of peace, Standing Armies without the Consent of our legislatures.

He has affected to render the Military independent of and superior to the Civil power.

He has combined with others to subject us to a jurisdiction foreign to our constitution, and unacknowledged by our laws; giving his Assent to their Acts of pretended Legislation:

For Quartering large bodies of armed troops among us:

For protecting them, by a mock Trial, from punishment for any Murders which they should commit on the Inhabitants of these States:

For cutting off our Trade with all parts of the world:

For imposing Taxes on us without our Consent:

For depriving us in many cases, of the benefits of Trial by Jury:

For transporting us beyond Seas to be tried for pretended offences

For abolishing the free System of English Laws in a neighbouring Province, establishing therein an Arbitrary government, and enlarging its Boundaries so as to render it at once an example and fit instrument for introducing the same absolute rule into these Colonies:

For taking away our Charters, abolishing our most valuable Laws, and altering fundamentally the Forms of our Governments:

For suspending our own Legislatures, and declaring themselves invested with power to legislate for us in all cases whatsoever.

He has abdicated Government here, by declaring us out of his Protection and waging War against us.

He has plundered our seas, ravaged our Coasts, burnt our towns, and destroyed the lives of our people.

He is at this time transporting large Armies of foreign Mercenaries to compleat the works of death, desolation and tyranny, already begun with circumstances of Cruelty & perfidy scarcely paralleled in the most barbarous ages, and totally unworthy the Head of a civilized nation.

He has constrained our fellow Citizens taken Captive on the high Seas to bear Arms against their Country, to become the executioners of their friends and Brethren, or to fall themselves by their Hands.

He has excited domestic insurrections amongst us, and has endeavoured to bring on the inhabitants of our frontiers, the merciless Indian Savages, whose known rule of warfare, is an undistinguished destruction of all ages, sexes and conditions.

In every stage of these Oppressions We have Petitioned for Redress in the most humble terms: Our repeated Petitions have been answered only by repeated injury. A Prince whose character is thus marked by every act which may define a Tyrant, is unfit to be the ruler of a free people.

Nor have We been wanting in attentions to our Brittish brethren. We have warned them from time to time of attempts by their legislature to extend an unwarrantable jurisdiction over us. We have reminded them of the circumstances of our emigration and settlement here. We have appealed to their native justice and magnanimity, and we have conjured them by the ties of our common kindred to disavow these usurpations, which, would inevitably interrupt our connections and correspondence. They too have been deaf to the voice of justice and of consanguinity. We must, therefore, acquiesce in the necessity, which denounces our Separation, and hold them, as we hold the rest of mankind, Enemies in War, in Peace Friends.

We, therefore, the Representatives of the united States of America, in General Congress, Assembled, appealing to the Supreme Judge of the world for the rectitude of our intentions, do, in the Name, and by Authority of the good People of these Colonies, solemnly publish and declare, That these United Colonies are, and of Right ought to be Free and Independent States; that they are Absolved from all Allegiance to the British Crown, and that all political connection between them and the State of Great Britain, is and ought to be totally dissolved; and that as Free and Independent States, they have full Power to levy War, conclude Peace, contract Alliances, establish Commerce, and to do all other Acts and Things which Independent States may of right do. And for the support of this Declaration, with a firm reliance on the protection of divine Providence, we mutually pledge to each other our Lives, our Fortunes and our sacred Honor.

CONSTITUTION *of the* UNITED STATES. 163

The conſtitution framed for the united ſtates of America, by a con-
vention of deputies from the ſtates of New-Hampſhire, Maſſachu-
ſetts, Connecticut, New York, New Jerſey, Pennſylvania, De-
laware, Maryland, Virginia, North-Carolina, South Carolina,
and Georgia, at a ſeſſion begun May 25, and ended September
17, 1787.

WE the people of the united ſtates, in order to form a more
perfect union, eſtabliſh juſtice, inſure domeſtic tranquillity, provide for the common defence, promote the general welfare, and ſecure the bleſſings of liberty to ourſelves and our poſ-
terity, do ordain and eſtabliſh this conſtitution for the united
ſtates of America.

A R T I C L E   I.

S E C T I O N   I.

ALL legiſlative powers herein granted, ſhall be veſted in a con-
greſs of the united ſtates, which ſhall conſiſt of a ſenate and houſe
of repreſentatives.

S E C T I O N   II.

1. The houſe of repreſentatives ſhall conſiſt of members choſen every ſecond year, by the people of the ſeveral ſtates : and the
electors, in each ſtate, ſhall have the qualifications requiſite for
electors of the moſt numerous branch of the ſtate legiſlature.

2.. No perſon ſhall be a repreſentative, who ſhall not have attained to the age of twenty-five years, and been ſeven years a
citizen of the united ſtates ; and who ſhall not, when elected, be
an inhabitant of that ſtate in which he ſhall be choſen.

Taken from a 1791 printing of the Constitution of the United States with the
following publishing information:

PHILADELPHIA
FROM THE PRESS OF CAREY, STEWART, AND CO.
M,DCC,XCI [1791]

This clearly demonstrates the original "lower case" spelling of "united ſtates."
The printing style of the day used a different character for the lower case "s" within
a word. In fact, in that day, the "s" that we now use exclusively was only used when
the "s" was the last letter of the word. Otherwise an "ſ" was used.

Table of Contents

Preface

In this book, we reveal and discuss racial biases that are engrained in current and long-standing law. For this reason, our perspective with regard to race could easily be misunderstood. Therefore, we wish to make it clear that we are not racists. We do not harbor any racial biases. Nothing in this book will support the views of anyone who is racist, especially as it applies to equal protection under the law.

Though some progress has been made with regard to racial equality in America, "racism" is still very much alive in this country—where "freedom and justice for all" is supposed to prevail—and it can still be a divisive issue, even when it is due to nothing more than a misunderstanding. We sincerely want to avoid any possibility of misunderstanding here.

So, as you read this book, we want it clearly understood that we firmly believe that, regardless of race, religion, creed, gender, or ethnic heritage, every one of us is truly created equal and has an unquestionable right to be treated equally under the law.

Of course, the actual application of equality is in the "eye of the beholder." Therefore, there are perspectives of equality that will not be addressed in this book, because our primary concern is that everyone has a right to be treated equally under the law. We believe that this one issue must be addressed and resolved before any other efforts to achieve equal treatment can be wholly effective. When the time comes that everyone is truly equal under the law, it will then be much more difficult for other forms of prejudice and inequality to be defended or justified for any reason whatsoever.

Foreword

The crime of "identity fraud" features prominently in the news these days, and most people are horrified to realize that their identity can be surreptitiously "stolen" by criminal entrepreneurs. In response, we look to the government to protect us from this kind of crime.

But would it surprise you to learn that the government itself has been the greatest perpetrator of identity fraud on the American people? This claim may seem too preposterous to be true, but this book will document it beyond any doubt.

The result of the identify fraud committed by the government against the people has been the flagrant theft of the inalienable rights we hold so dear and believe—despite growing evidence to the contrary—that we still enjoy. Even as this book is being prepared, the United States Supreme Court has ruled that warrantless arrests and searches do not violate a person's rights. This appears to fly in the face of the most cherished provisions of the federal Constitution . . . until you understand the underlying principle revealed in this book. Once you understand that principle, the apparent insanity becomes all too clear.

It behooves every American who cherishes his or her freedom to study and grasp this principle.

Ken Gullekson

Introduction

In this book, we cite various court cases to prove our thesis. As the reader, you will need to understand how to decipher the code used to identify and refer to these cases. Readers encountering this code for the first time may be intimidated by what appears to be hidden meaning. However, rest assured, it is deceptively simple.

For example, court cases are typically referenced in the following manner: *Walther v. Rabolt*, 30 Cal. 185. The first name listed, "Walther" in this example, is the appellant (the party who brought the case to the court that made the ruling). The second name, "Rabolt" here, refers to the respondent. The numbers and abbreviations that follow the names represent, respectively, the volume number, court abbreviation (or publication series), and page number of the volume in which the case is published. In this example, the case of *Walther v. Rabolt* is published in volume 30 of the California Reports (California Supreme Court) beginning on page 185. Sometimes a second page number will be given in the manner of *Walther v. Rabolt*, 30 Cal. 185, 188. This is simply a reference to a particular page within the cited case, page 188 in this example.

Statutes are identified in a similar manner. For examples: 66 Stat. 163 means volume 66 of the United States Statutes at Large, page 163; and Stats 1872, ch. 350, means Statutes of California, legislative year 1872, chapter 350. The volumes of any given series, whether court cases or statutes, are typically found all together in numerical order on the shelves of a law library.

Sometimes with court cases, the abbreviations for the different courts or publication series will sometimes vary. The differences are usually just a style preference of the writer. For example, "Cal.," the California Reporter (California Supreme Court) is sometimes simply "C"; and "Cal.App.," the California Appellate Reports (California Court of Appeal) is sometimes listed as "C.A." or "CA."

We have included a legend beginning on page 90 with which you will be able to find the full identification of all the court cases or statutes that we have referenced in this book.

❧ CHAPTER 1 ❧

Identifying the Problem

❧❧❧❧❧❧❧❧❧❧❧❧❧❧❧❧❧❧❧❧

The most common token of identity is one's name. But we like to identify ourselves by other characteristics as well. Gender, ethnic background, creed, sexual orientation, race, and nationality are the most recognized. We have even come to use a variety of numbers to allegedly add a level of security or uniqueness to our identity.

"Nationality" is that expression of identity that connects us with the country to which we pledge allegiance. Another word for nationality is "citizenship." In other words, our "citizenship" identifies us in relation to our country. It is our citizenship which distinguishes Americans from the inhabitants of all other countries.

When asked about their citizenship, most Americans will tell you that they are a "U.S. citizen" or a "citizen of the United States." In fact, this response is almost automatic. But when asked what "U.S. citizenship" or "citizenship of the United States" actually means, most people get it wrong, or cannot articulate a definition at all. And when told the true meaning of these terms, most Americans respond in disbelief.

The problem can be simply stated. According to federal statute law and numerous court rulings, there are two distinct classes

1

of citizenship in the united states of America[1]: "state citizenship" and "citizenship of the United States." One class carries with it the unalienable[2] rights our Founding Fathers fought to secure for us as stated in the Declaration of Independence, as enumerated in the Bill of Rights amended to the Constitution of the United States, and as included in the Declaration of Rights[3] found in many of the state constitutions. The other class of citizenship carries no such rights.

If you have not already guessed from the preceding language, the "U.S. citizenship" or "citizenship of the United States" automatically claimed by most Americans is the class of citizenship which does not carry with it the rights envisioned as unalienable by our Founding Fathers in the Declaration of Independence. Respectively, it is state citizenship which carries those unalienable rights we hold so dear. The problem is that we have been systematically coerced into renouncing our native state citizenship (and the unalienable rights which it carries) and adopting "citizenship of the United States" (which carries no unalienable rights).

For all of you reading this right now who are certain that you enjoy the protection of these unalienable rights, we offer the following caution: Unless you have knowingly and deliberately taken steps to preserve or reclaim your native state citizenship *you have been coerced into unwittingly waiving your unalienable rights by claiming "U.S. citizenship."* Yes, this means you. And since it is the government[4] that has coerced you into misidentifying yourself as a "U.S. citizen" and unwittingly waiving your unalienable rights, we believe it is fair and accurate to say that the government is therefore perpetrating "identity fraud" on the people of this country. As this fraud reaches into the lives of practically every American man, woman, and child, it can be

---

[1] The lower case "u" and "s" are consistent with the writing on the original Constitution of the United States. See the illustration on page *vi*.
[2] In the Declaration of Independence, the spelling is "unalienable." In many state constitutions, the spelling is "inalienable," though some do use "unalienable." *Black's Law Dictionary* considers the two words to be synonymous. In this book, we will typically use the spelling from the source to which we are making reference.
[3] Some state constitutions have a "Bill of Rights" rather than a "Declaration of Rights."
[4] We use the generic term "the government" here because both the federal government and the various state governments have been party to the coercion we describe.

fairly characterized as one of the most massive frauds ever perpetrated on mankind[5].

In this book, we carefully document the current existence and validity of the "lost" state citizenship, and expose the fraudulent efforts of both the federal government and most state governments to deprive us of our unalienable rights by requiring all Americans to identify themselves as "U.S. citizens"[6] or "citizens of the United States" in order to participate in certain activities.

As part of the fraud, Congress wants us to believe that the federal government is the driving force behind a genuine effort to create equal rights for everyone. This simply isn't true. In fact, the federal government is deliberately creating an illusion of equality in order to deny us the unalienable rights we all hold so dear, as expressed in the Bill of Rights and the various declarations of rights that appear in each of the state constitutions—rights which are truly ours by birthright. In service of this illusion of equality, and in contravention of the facts, government officials typically insist—in conversation, correspondence, and court arenas—that "citizenship of the United States" is the only valid citizenship and that state citizenship has been subsumed and nullified by it. This scandalous lie and the breach of faith behind it is a substantive part of the identity fraud that will be exposed within these pages. (See pages 92–93 for the complete definition of "fraud" from *Bick's Law Dictionary*, 7th Edition.)

Our presentation of this information, though certain to be controversial, is not merely rhetorical. As you read, you will see that each point is supported by unassailable documentation. In explaining the documentation, we try to keep it as simple as possible, although sometimes that is difficult, because the issue itself is complicated by many layers of government deception.

We have included in the Appendix complete renditions of virtually all the documentation we reference. We've done this for the simple reason that we want you to be able to review, in its

---

[5] Another such massive fraud is the debt-based economy which the Federal Reserve System has perpetrated on the United States of America and other countries. But that's another story.

[6] The terms "U.S. citizen" and "U.S. citizenship" are not expressly defined in any recognized body of law. They are doppelgangers of the legally defined terms "citizen of the United States" and "citizenship of the United States," respectively. However, both the federal government and the various state governments use these terms as though they had legal meaning. As you read, you will discover how this fits right into the identity fraud exposed by this book.

entirety, the same documentation by which we support our thesis—to have an opportunity to make your own assessment and decide for yourself whether or not we are right. We don't want a single reader to "just take our word for it." This is too important.

If we have failed to explain anything clearly enough for you to be completely comfortable with your understanding, please feel free to address your questions to us by e-mail.

hsc@blaquemoor.com

∞ CHAPTER 2 ∞

Defining the Problem

It is the resulting deprivation of unalienable rights occasioned by this "identity fraud" that makes the deception committed by the government so heinous. To understand how this identity fraud actually denies us our unalienable rights, we must understand the definition of "rights."

Although you may not realize it, there *are* two categories of rights. There are "unalienable rights," such as we have already mentioned, and there are "civil rights." As you may be aware, we hear the term "civil rights" bandied about in political and media circles rather regularly, yet the term "unalienable rights" is used quite rarely, if ever. So, what are "civil rights," and how do they differ from "unalienable rights?"

In order to keep this all in perspective, we first need to realize that the Declaration of Independence makes specific reference to "certain *unalienable Rights*, that among these are Life, Liberty and the pursuit of Happiness." This inevitably raises the question: Are *civil rights* the same as, or equal to, the *unalienable rights* recognized in the Declaration of Independence? The answer is: No. *Unalienable rights* are a distinctly different class of rights than *civil rights*.

According to the ideology of the Founders, as expressed in their Declaration of Independence, unalienable rights are those rights which we deem to have been granted to mankind by the Creator. Although it does not define either "inalienable rights" or "unalienable rights," *Bouvier's Law Dictionary* (Third Revision, 1914) does provide definitions for "inalienable" and "unalienable." Note that these two entries are effectively synonymous, and contain references to certain "rights" that are considered unalienable/inalienable.

> **inalienable.** A word denoting the condition of things the property in which cannot be lawfully transferred from one person to another. Public Highways and rivers are inalienable. There are also many rights which are inalienable, as the rights of liberty or speech.

> **unalienable.** Incapable of being transferred. Things which are not in commerce, as, public roads, are in their nature unalienable. Some things are unalienable in consequence of particular provisions in the law forbidding their transfer; as, pensions granted by the government. The natural rights of life and liberty are unalienable.

Black's Law Dictionary (7th Edition, 1999), lends support to these definitions with its interpretation of "inalienable right":

> **inalienable right.** A right that cannot be transferred or surrendered; esp., a natural right such as the right to own property.

As should be evident from these definitions, the governing concept behind unalienable rights is the proposition that men and women—"mere mortals," if you will—cannot take from each other that which has been granted to us by our Creator. As such, rights recognized as "unalienable" cannot be abrogated by any legislature in its enactments, or by the police in their law enforcement activities.

Now let's look at two definitions of "civil rights." *Black's Law Dictionary* (7th Edition) provides the most current definition of the term:

> **civil right.** (*usually plural*) 1. The individual rights of personal liberty guaranteed by the Bill of Rights and by the 13th, 14th, 15th and 19th Amendments, as well as by

legislation such as the Voting Rights Act. Civil rights include especially the right to vote, the right of due process, and the right of equal protection under the law.

Note that this definition names certain amendments to the federal constitution, along with the Bill of Rights, as being the guarantors of "civil rights." As it can be argued that *Black's Law Dictionary* is a tool of the government that has perpetrated this identity fraud upon us, it's useful to review an earlier definition of the term in a less politically motivated lexicon. From *Bouvier's Law Dictionary* (Third Revision, 1914):

> **civil rights.** A term applied to certain rights secured to *citizens of the United States* by the 13th and 14th Amendments to the constitution, and by various acts of congress made in pursuance thereof. [*emphasis* added]

Note that no reference is made to the Bill of Rights in this definition, but two other amendments to the federal constitution and various acts of Congress are deemed the guarantors of "civil rights." Thus, whereas the Creator grants "unalienable rights", "civil rights" are granted by legislation, either as an amendment to the federal constitution, or a statute passed by Congress. This is an extremely important distinction, because any right *granted* by legislation *can be taken away by legislation*! Thus, civil rights do not compare with *unalienable rights*, which, having been granted by the Creator, no man or woman can lawfully take them away from you.

In a sense, the identity fraud that is the subject of this book is evident in the *Black's Law Dictionary* definition of "civil rights" because it neglects to disclose to whom the different rights apply, or more importantly, to whom they *do not* apply. Note that the 1914 Edition of *Bouvier's* defines "civil rights" as "certain rights secured to *citizens of the United States*...." Thus, according to this definition, civil rights do not apply to state citizens. This definition is directly supported by decisions of the United States Supreme Court[7], which has ruled that the Bill of Rights *does not* apply to the citizen of the United States, and the 14th Amendment applies *only* to the citizen of the United States. Yet this is *not* disclosed in *Black's Law Dictionary*, nor to the public at large

---

[7] To be cited in subsequent chapters.

when someone is asked to declare his status of citizenship. This is the *foundation* of the identity fraud being committed by the government against the people. And, it only gets worse from there.

As we will learn in subsequent chapters, the distinction between unalienable rights and civil rights is central to the question of national identity. For this reason, it is useful to review two of the items listed in the definition for civil rights—the 13th and 14th Amendments—and see how and where they apply and, equally important, where they do not apply.

As we all know, the purpose of the 13th Amendment was to abolish slavery.[8] However, you might not realize that it was not necessary to *apply* this Amendment in *all* of the states. That is not to say that it did not *encompass* an abolition of slavery within *all* of the several states of the union, because it certainly did. However, it was not *necessary* in all the states because, even prior to the Civil War, some states had already expressly abolished slavery. For example, California *began* its statehood, fifteen years before the 13th Amendment was adopted in 1865, with an abolition of slavery provided for within its state constitution, as follows:

> **Article I, Section 18.** Neither slavery, nor involuntary servitude, unless for punishment of crime, shall ever be tolerated in this state.

Other states included similar provisions within their constitutions.

Unfortunately, even with the abolition of slavery, there was still no provision for the freed slaves to acquire citizenship. Thus, in 1868, the 14th Amendment was added to the federal Constitution, granting "citizenship of the United States" to the freed slaves. But like the 13th Amendment before it, certain elements of the 14th Amendment weren't really necessary in all the states. From Section 1 of the 14th Amendment:

> **Section 1.** ...No state shall make or enforce any law which shall abridge the privileges and immunities of citizens of the United States; *nor shall any state deprive*

---

[8] Section 1. Neither slavery nor involuntary servitude, except as a punishment for crime whereof the party shall have been duly convicted, shall exist within the United States, or any place subject to their jurisdiction. (See page 114 for the complete text of the amendment.)

any person of life, liberty, or property without due process
of law; nor deny to any person within its jurisdiction the
equal protection of the laws. [emphasis added] (See page
114 for more text of the amendment.)

This passage contains what is commonly known as the "due
process clause" of the 14th Amendment. Note that this provision
was already stipulated in the Constitution of the State of California, adopted in 1850, eighteen years earlier:

Article I, Section 8. ...No person shall...be deprived
of life, liberty or property, without due process of law;...

Given that the 13th and 14th Amendments deal with matters
that were already provided for in at least some of the state constitutions, we must ask ourselves what was the purpose of these
amendments? In states whose constitutions already contained
similar provisions, to whom did these new amendments apply?
Since 1868, numerous court rulings have appeared to embrace the
14th Amendment as though it applied to *everyone* in the several
states. Does the 14th Amendment *really* include *everyone*? The
answers to these questions—examined in the chapters to follow—
may surprise you. Our hope is that they will shock you.

By the way, none of the rights recognized within the federal
constitution, including the Bill of Rights, are expressly described
in that document as being *unalienable* or *inalienable*, and only
twenty-six of the constitutions of the several states expressly
recognize the rights listed therein as unalienable or inalienable
(refer to page 94 for the list of the states).

As an example of one of the twenty-six states that do recognize the rights enumerated in its constitution as inalienable, the
original Constitution of the State of California declares at Article
I, Section 1:

All men are by nature free and independent and have
certain inalienable rights, among which are those of
enjoying and defending life and liberty; acquiring,
possessing, and protecting property; and pursuing and
obtaining safety, and happiness.

One hundred fifty-one years later, these rights remain recognized as inalienable in the current Constitution of the State of

California,[9] with the wording amended to encompass women as well as men, and the addition of "privacy" to the list:

> All people are by nature free and independent and have inalienable rights. Among these are enjoying and defending life and liberty, acquiring, possessing, and protecting property, and pursuing and obtaining safety, happiness, and privacy. (See page 94.)

The remaining twenty-four states *do not* recognize the rights listed within their respective constitutions[10] as unalienable or inalienable (refer to page 99 for the list of the states). *Think about it!* The citizens of twenty-four states do not have express constitutional protection of the unalienable rights upon which this country was founded. If their rights were violated by an agency of the state government, it would be much more difficult to claim and prove damages. This, in and of itself, is a major flaw in the protection of the rights of the people of those twenty-four states.

In the final analysis, the most important thing to understand is that through the fraud of deceiving people into falsely identifying themselves, the government coerces state citizens into waiving direct access to their "inalienable rights" and accepting substitute civil rights, which the government then regulates and chips away at ever so slowly so that the people hardly even notice that their rights are diminishing.

---

[9] After the Civil War, in 1879, California adopted a second constitution to accommodate the newly freed slaves declared "citizens of the United States" by the 14th Amendment. Many other states did the same. It should be noted that in most cases, if not in all cases, these "second constitutions" applied only to 14th Amendment citizens and did not repeal the original constitutions, which remain in effect to date.

[10] Some of the 24 state constitutions do recognize "inherent rights"; however, the definition of "inherent" does not specify that the rights cannot be transferred, surrendered, or otherwise taken away.

❧ CHAPTER 3 ❧

Two Classes of Citizenship

Prior to the 14th Amendment, the term "citizen of the united states"[11] was used in the federal constitution *without definition*, as in Article II, Section 1, Clause 5:

> No person except a natural born citizen, or a *citizen of the united states*, at the time of the adoption of this Constitution...." [*emphasis* added]

This term was understood without definition because, at that time, the people were *always* recognized as being citizens of one of the several states.[12] This is further explained by a California Supreme Court opinion published in 1855 which, in effect, finally provided a pre-14th Amendment definition of the term "citizen of the united states":

> A citizen of any one of the States of the Union, is held to be, and called a citizen of the United States, although technically and abstractly *there is no such thing.* To conceive a citizen of the United States who is not a citizen of some one of the States, is totally foreign to the

---

[11] The lower case "u" and "s" are consistent with the writing on the original Constitution of the United States. See the illustration on page *vi*.

[12] See "the people of the united states," as referred to in the Preamble to the Constitution of the United States, and the "citizens of the several states," as referred to in Article IV, Section II, clause 1.

> idea, and inconsistent with the proper construction and common understanding of the expression as used in the Constitution, which must be deduced from its various other provisions. — *Ex parte Frank Knowles*, 5 Cal. 300, 302. [*emphasis* added] (See page 216 for this passage. Refer to page 215 for the complete text of the case.)

Thus, within the context of the Constitution of the United States prior to 1868, the term "citizen of the united states" can only be construed as a general, descriptive term referring to only *one* class of citizens, that being the citizens of the several states of the Union.

Then, in 1868, the 14th Amendment introduced a curious wrinkle into the citizenship question. Section 1 of the amendment declared that:

> All persons born or naturalized in the United States, and subject to the jurisdiction thereof, are *citizens of the United States* and of the state wherein they reside. [*emphasis* added] (See page 114 for additional text of the amendment.)

On the surface, the wording used in the 14th Amendment can easily be misconstrued as referring to the same "citizen of the united states" (a citizen of one of the several states) that is recognized in Article II of the federal constitution. However, that is not the case. As one example, in 1966 the Maryland Supreme Court issued a ruling in which they stated:

> Citizenship of the United States is defined by the Fourteenth Amendment ..." — *Crosse v. Board of Elections*, 243 Md. 555, 558. (See page 190)

Therefore, *Crosse v. Board of Elections* combined with *Ex parte Frank Knowles*, clearly demonstrates that the 14th Amendment did, *in fact*, create an *entirely new definition* of the term "citizen of the United States." And, in fact, the "citizenship of the United States" created by the 14th Amendment is a distinct and separate class of citizenship, with different, *inferior* "rights." Thus, the use of the same wording—"citizen of the United States"—as redefined in the 14th Amendment, becomes the origin of the identity fraud that this book exposes.

To complicate matters further, with the language "and of the state wherein they reside," the 14th Amendment also creates a pseudo-state citizenship. This is not the true state citizenship of the people, with unalienable rights protected by the various state constitutions. It is a charlatan, which serves only to deceive the unwary. Not everyone agrees with this assertion, preferring to believe that 14th Amendment "state citizenship" is true state citizenship. But our thesis can be substantiated with case law and, for the benefit of the skeptics, we will do so in the next chapter.

Now, to fully understand the identity fraud that this book exposes, we need to go back two more years, to the Civil Rights Act of 1866. This legislation marks the true beginning of the creation of the second class of citizenship in the United States of America, even though subsequent court rulings will typically refer only to the 14th Amendment.

On April 9, 1866, Congress passed a Statute at Large, found at 14 Stat. 27,[13] entitled "CHAP. XXXI.—*An act to protect all Persons in the United States in their Civil Rights, and furnish the Means of their Vindication"* (refer to page 103 for the complete text of the statute).

The first thing we wish to bring to your attention is what the title of this Act does not say. It does not say, "*An Act to protect all People....*" It says, "*An Act to protect all Persons....*" This distinction goes unnoticed by most readers. However, in legal terminology, such distinctions are almost always significant, very rarely arbitrary, despite appearances to lay readers. So is this distinction meaningful in *this* case? Why, after "people" had been the word of choice for the framers of the federal constitution as well as the various state constitutions, is the legislature suddenly using the word "persons" in the Civil Rights Act? Is there a legal difference between "all people" and "all persons?" If so, who are "the people" and who are "the persons?" In 1866, the California Supreme Court defined "the people" as follows:

> The people are such as are *born upon the soil*, by whom and for whom in the first place the Government was ordained.... — *Walther v. Rabolt,* 30 Cal. 185, 189 (1866).[14] [*emphasis* added] (See page 356.)

---

[13] 14 Stat. 27 came right "on the heels" of the 13th Amendment, which was ratified on December 6, 1865

[14] Though this is a California Supreme Court case, it is applicable in all 50 states. "Full faith and credit shall be given in each state to the... judicial proceedings of every other state." — Constitution of the United States, Article IV, §1.

In this ruling, the California Supreme Court is defining "the people" as those who are "born upon the soil." In California, as it is in all of the states, the state constitution and state laws are enacted to protect "the people" of the *state*. That said, then who are the "persons" that the Civil Rights Act of 1866 is purported to protect? Part of the answer to this question can be found in Section 1 of the Act.

> *Be in enacted by the Senate and House of Representatives of the United States of America in Congress assembled,* That all persons <u>born in the United States</u> and not subject to any foreign power, excluding Indians not taxed, are hereby declared to be citizens of the United States; and such citizens, of every race and color, without regard to any previous condition of slavery or involuntary servitude...shall have the same right, in every State and Territory in the United States...as is enjoyed by white citizens.... — 14 Stat. 27, §1. [emphasis added] (See page 103.)

The first clue to the difference between "people" and "persons," then, is where they are born. The California court stated that the *people* are "born upon the *soil*." This statute uses the language "born *in the United States*." Again, though this distinction may elude lay readers, it is *legally* significant.

By 1866, *people* had been born upon the soil in each of the several states for almost 80 years since the Constitution of the United States was written, and for 90 years since the Declaration of Independence. There had *never* been any question as to the status of the citizenship of these people. So why is it that, all of the sudden, in 1866, Congress is passing a statute "declaring" that "*persons* born in the United States" are citizens of the United States? And why does the 1866 statute name "persons" and not "people?" This brings us back to the question: Who were these "persons?"

The answer is: They were the slaves freed after the Civil War. Although the Act does not expressly name freed slaves, the language of the first paragraph makes it clear that the "persons" to which the statute refers were individuals "of every race and color, without regard to any previous condition of slavery or involuntary servitude." Remember, up to that time in our history, only white people were counted as citizens. Thus, this language was a direct reference to non-whites, who were, at the time, predominately freed slaves of African heritage.

Furthermore, the rights conferred upon these "persons" by this statute are being equated to the rights of "white citizens." If the term "persons" were intended to include white citizens, the equation of their rights to those of white citizens would be unnecessary and meaningless. And since, by maxim, the law never does anything unnecessary, these "persons" *had* to be non-whites—again, the freed slaves of African heritage.

Certainly, 14 Stat. 27 *was* a step in the right direction. However, for all the good intentions that may have lain behind the origin of this statute, the United States Supreme Court would rule in the *Civil Rights Cases*, 109 U.S. 3, some seventeen years later in 1883,[15] that the federal constitution did not grant the federal government any jurisdiction to enact or enforce a statute such as 14 Stat. 27 inside the boundaries of any of the several states.

The difficulty in enforcing this new statute apparently did not escape Congress, as it was on June 13, 1866, only two months after passage of the Civil Rights Act, that the 14th Amendment was proposed. In order to create an illusion of validity for the 1866 Civil Rights Act, the federal government *needed* the 14th Amendment.

However, even the 14th Amendment was not "enforceable" by the federal government within the boundaries of any of the several states. An opinion issued by the California Supreme Court in 1870, two years after the 14th Amendment was allegedly ratified,[16] demonstrates how very little power the 14th Amendment had over the states. At issue in this case was a California statute that prevented a man of Chinese descent from testifying in a state court. The California court handed down the following decision:

> Section 14 of the Act of this State concerning crimes and punishments, as amended in 1863, reads as follows: "No person having one half or more Indian blood, or Mongolian or Chinese, shall be permitted to give evi-

---

[15] *The Civil Rights Cases*, 109 U.S. 3 is discussed in more detail in Chapter 4.

[16] For those of you believe that the 14th Amendment was not lawfully ratified, we will not be arguing that point here. For purposes of this book, the 14th Amendment is in the Constitution, it is being used, and it is at the heart of the fraud that this book exposes. Even if the argument that it was not lawfully ratified could be proven, it is not needed to prove our point here. For that reason, it is not a part of this text. However, for the record, we do not believe it was lawfully ratified.

dence in favor of, or against, any white man." — *People v. Brady*, 40 Cal. 198. (See page 251 for this passage. Refer to page 247 for the complete text of the case.)

The 14th Amendment would *seem* to have granted a Chinese man the needed citizenship to testify in a state court, but the California court found that it did *not* have the power to reach into state affairs. One of the "headnotes" in that case reads as follows:

> The Fourteenth Amendment to the Constitution of the United States *does not conflict* with the power of the Legislature in the exercise of its discretion *to exclude Chinamen from the right to testify* in the State Courts. — *People v. Brady*, supra. [*emphasis* added] (See page 247 for this passage.)

As if to confirm the ruling by the California Supreme Court, only four years after the 14th Amendment was added to the Constitution, the United States Supreme Court rendered it a "practical nullity" by its ruling in the *Slaughter-House Cases*, 16 Wall (83 U.S.) 36 (1872).

On page 77 of the *Slaughter-House Cases* the court reveals the limitations of the 14th Amendment by drawing a parallel between it and Article IV, Section 2 of the federal constitution. Describing the limitations of Article IV, Section 2, the court said:

> The constitutional provision there alluded to *did not create those rights*, which it called privileges and immunities of citizens of the States. It threw around them in that clause *no security for the citizen of the State* in which they were claimed or exercised. *Nor did it profess to control the power of the State governments* over the rights of its own citizens. (See page 278.)
>
> Its sole purpose was to declare to the several States, that whatever those rights, as you grant or establish them to your own citizens, or as you limit or qualify, or impose restrictions on their exercise, the same, neither more nor less, shall be the measure of the rights of citizens of other States within your jurisdiction. (See page 278.)
>
> It would be the vainest show of learning to attempt to prove by citations of authority, that up to the adoption of the recent amendments, no claim or pretence was set up that those rights depended on the Federal government for their existence or protection, beyond the very few express limitations which the Federal Constitution imposed upon the States—such, for instance, as the prohibition against ex post facto laws, bills of attainder, and laws impairing

the obligation of contracts. But with the exception of these and a few other restrictions, *the entire domain of the privileges and immunities of citizens of the States, as above defined, lay within the constitutional and legislative power of the States,* and without that of the Federal government. *Was it the purpose of the fourteenth amendment,* by the simple declaration that no State should make or enforce any law which shall abridge the privileges and immunities of citizens of the United States,[17] *to transfer the security and protection of all the civil rights which we have mentioned, from the States to the Federal government?* And where it is declared that Congress shall have the power to enforce that article, *was it intended to bring within the power of Congress the entire domain of civil rights heretofore belonging exclusively to the States?* (See page 278.)

> ...

> We are convinced that no such results were intended by the Congress which proposed these amendments, nor by the legislatures of the States which ratified them. — *Slaughter-House Cases,* 16 Wall (83 U.S.) 36. [*emphasis* added] (See page 279. Refer to page 259 for the complete text of the case.)

As the preceding citation is rather "long winded," even for those accustomed to reading court cases, allow us to help make sense of it. This ruling recognized and reasserted the fact that the rights of the citizens of any one of the several states came under the exclusive control of state law. Then, by demonstrating that the 14th Amendment in no way modified that provision, the court showed that the amendment did not and could not grant the federal government any new power over the rights of state citizens. Thus, by way of this parallel construction, the United States Supreme Court clearly established in the *Slaughter-House Cases* that the 14th Amendment:

1. *Did not* create any rights for citizens of the United States.
2. *Did not* provide any security for the citizens of any of the several states.

---

[17] "Section 1. ...No state shall make or enforce any law which shall abridge the privileges and immunities of citizens of the United States...." This clause is known as the "privileges and immunities" clause of the 14th Amendment. See page 114 for additional text of the amendment.

3. *Did not* provide for any new federal control over the powers of the state governments.
4. *Did not* change the fact that the entire domain of the rights of citizens of a state lay within the power of the state.

The *Slaughter-House Cases* clearly demonstrate that, notwithstanding its language, the 14th Amendment did not confer any new power upon the federal government, and therefore the amendment could not and cannot grant or provide any rights that can be enforced upon the states by the federal government.

As a testament to its validity, the *Slaughter-House Cases* stood firm until 1935, when the United States Supreme Court tried to change the direction of things with *Colgate v. Harvey*, 296 U.S. 403 (refer to page 155 for the complete text of the case). In this case, the Court ordered the enforcement of privileges and immunities pursuant to the 14th Amendment within the state of Vermont. However, *Colgate v. Harvey* was short lived and was overturned in 1939 when the Court reversed itself again in *Madden v. Kentucky*, 309 U.S. 83 (refer to page 239 for the complete text of the case), effectively reaffirming its ruling in the *Slaughter-House Cases*. Since *Madden*, the federal courts have stood firm on the rulings in the *Slaughter-House Cases* with regard to the privileges and immunities clause of the 14th Amendment.

In addition to the statements cited above, the *Slaughter-House Cases* revealed other details that have been forgotten and are not well known today. On page 73, for example (see page 276), it clearly states, "That its main purpose was to establish the citizenship of the negro [sic] can admit of no doubt." The phraseology is odd, but the meaning is nevertheless clear. The specific intent of the 14th Amendment was to confer a form of citizenship on the freed slaves.

On page 79 of the *Slaughter-House Cases* (see page 278) there is a somewhat rambling statement attempting to describe what some of the privileges and immunities of a citizen of the United States might be. As you read through them, it is pretty clear that what is being discussed falls within the powers that were granted to the federal government by the Constitution of the United States at Article I, Section 8, and nothing more.

However, we need not rely on the *Slaughter-House Cases* to know the limitations of the privileges and immunities granted by the 14th Amendment to citizens of the United States. A more specific listing can be found in *Twining v. New Jersey*, 211 U.S. 78, 97 (1908), as follows:

> Thus, among the rights and privileges of national citizenship recognized by this court are the right to pass freely from state to state; the right to petition Congress for a redress of grievances; the right to enter public lands; the right to vote for national officers; the right to be protected against violence while in the custody of a United States marshal; and the right to inform the United States authorities of violations of its laws. — *Twining v. New Jersey*, 211 U.S. 78, 97. (See page 308-309. Refer to page 303 for the complete text of the case.)

Where is the right to life, liberty and the pursuit of happiness? Where is the right to private property that we value so highly? Where is the right to free speech and religion? Where is the right to a speedy trial by jury? The answer to these questions is: They are *not* part of *this* deal. Those rights are protected *only* by the constitutions of the states that include them in their respective Declarations of Rights.

Where does our sacred Bill of Rights fit in for the citizen of the United States, the 14th Amendment federal citizen? The answer is: It doesn't. Does that surprise you? It surprises *most* people. However, this *has* been the ruling of the courts over the last 130 years. In the next chapter, we will take you through some of those court cases. You will see that the court decisions have been consistent over the years. That said, after you have read what these cases have to say, you may wonder how it is that the government has been able to keep it a secret from you.

✍ CHAPTER 4 ✍

The Courts Have Upheld
the Two Classes of Citizenship

✍✍✍✍✍✍✍✍✍✍✍✍✍✍✍✍✍✍✍✍✍

In reading the first three chapters of this book, if you were surprised by the existence of the two classes of citizenship, you may also be surprised to see how consistently the courts have upheld these two classes of citizenship, all the while keeping it secret from most Americans.

In this chapter, we will take you through a series of court cases in chronological order, so that you can see that the courts have truly been consistent over time on this issue since its introduction in 1866 after the Civil War. The one exception to chronological order will be *Jones v. Temmer*, 829 F.Supp. 1226, a recent case from 1993, to firmly establish in your mind that what we are talking about here is truly *still* the position taken by the courts in the present.

> The privileges and immunities clause of the Fourteenth Amendment *protects very few rights* because *it neither incorporates any of the Bill of Rights* nor protects all rights of individual citizens. See *Slaughter-House Cases*, 83 U.S. (16 Wall.) 36, 21 L.Ed. 394 (1873). Instead, this provision *protects only those rights peculiar to being a citizen of the federal government*; it does not protect those rights which relate to state citizenship. — *Jones v. Temmer*, 829 F.Supp. 1226, 1232 (D. Colo.

1993). [*emphasis* added] (See page 227 for this passage. Refer to page 223 for complete text of the case.)

It is noteworthy that, one hundred twenty-one years after the *Slaughter-House Cases*, this federal court is *still* citing that landmark ruling. Notice that the court in this case makes it clear that the privileges and immunities clause of the 14th Amendment *does not incorporate any of the rights itemized in the Bill of Rights.* We will touch upon this again later in this chapter. Note also that this court recognizes the 14th Amendment citizen as a "citizen of the federal government." The following quotation, also from *Jones v. Temmer*, may seem redundant, but it is important to see how this same court makes a subtly different, yet parallel statement, only a few paragraphs later.

> The privileges and immunities clause of the Fourteenth Amendment protects very few rights. To my knowledge, in the history of the United States Supreme Court, only one decision determined that a state violated this provision and that decision was overruled within a few years. *Colgate v. Harvey*, 296, U.S. 404, 56 S.Ct. 252, 80 L.Ed. 299 (1935) overruled in *Madden v. Commonwealth of Kentucky*, 309 U.S. 83, 60 S.Ct. 406, 84 L.Ed. 590 (1940). In the *Slaughter-House Cases*, 83 U.S. (16 Wall.) 36, 21 L.Ed. 394 (1873), the Supreme Court held that *this clause neither incorporates the Bill of Rights* nor protects all rights of individual citizens. Rather the provision *protects only those rights peculiar to being a citizen of the United States*; it does not protect those rights which relate to state citizenship. — *Jones v. Temmer*, 829 F.Supp. 1226, 1233 (D. Colo. 1993). [*emphasis* added] (See page 228 for this passage. Refer to page 223 for complete text of the case.)

Note that in our first quotation cited from *Jones v. Temmer*, the court says: "...this provision protects only those rights peculiar to being a citizen of the *federal government.*" In the second quotation, the court uses essentially identical language, with one telling exception: "...the provision protects only those rights peculiar to being a citizen of the *United States.*" By its use of this parallel phrasing, the court *equated* the term "citizen of the federal government" with the term "citizen of the United States." Thus, these two nearly identical passages from *Jones v. Temmer* make it clear that the "citizen of the United States," as created by the 14th Amendment, is actually a *"citizen of the federal government!"*

For anyone who has doubted that "citizenship of the United States" is actually different from "state citizenship," a comparison of these two paragraphs should erase that doubt. Now let's review the rest of the court cases beginning shortly after the Civil War.

In 1872, four years after the 14th Amendment was added to the Constitution, the California Supreme Court heard the case of *Van Valkenburg v. Brown*, 43 Cal. 43. Dated in January, eleven months before the *Slaughter-House Cases* ruling in December of 1872, *Van Valkenburg v. Brown* is one of the first court decisions to address the implications of the 14th Amendment. The case is about a woman who sued for the right to vote pursuant to the privileges and immunities clause of the 14th Amendment. On page 47 of the *Van Valkenburg* case, the California Supreme Court makes a clear and decisive ruling:

> No white person born within the limits of the United States, and subject to their jurisdiction, or born without those limits, and subsequently naturalized under their laws, owes the status of citizenship to the recent amendments to the Federal Constitution. The history and aim of the Fourteenth Amendment is well known, and the purpose it had in view in its adoption well understood. That purpose was to confer the status of citizenship upon a numerous class of persons domiciled within the limits of the United States, who could not be brought within the operation of the naturalization laws because native born, and whose birth, though native, had at the same time left them without the status of citizenship. These persons were not white persons, but were, in the main, persons of African descent, who had been held in slavery in this country, or, if having themselves never been held in slavery, were the native-born descendants of slaves. Prior to the adoption of the Fourteenth Amendment it was settled that neither slaves, nor those who had been such, nor the descendants of these, though native and free born, were capable of becoming citizens of the United States.
> — *Van Valkenburg v. Brown*, 432 Cal. 43, 47. (See page 351 for this passage.)

In the very first sentence of this passage, the court makes it clear that the 14th Amendment was not responsible for the status of citizenship enjoyed by white people who were the citizens of their state. The court goes on to explain in detailed terms that the purpose of the amendment was to confer a form of citizenship upon the recently freed slaves. Not surprisingly, the racial distinctions and biases prevalent even within the courts in the 1870's are readily apparent in this ruling, and this case gives us a "base line" upon which to build a complete understanding of the fraud and chicanery that has taken place in the years since.

There is one more detail in *Van Valkenburg* that stands out as very important to understanding the provisions of the 14th Amendment. The amendment uses the language "...born or naturalized within the United States and subject to *the* jurisdiction thereof...." *Van Valkenburg* uses the language "...born within the limits of the United States, and subject to *their* jurisdiction...." Do you see the difference? *Van Valkenburg*, is referring to a *plurality* of jurisdictions, obviously meaning the collection of the individual jurisdictions of the several states with regard to their citizens. The 14th Amendment mentions only *one* jurisdiction, obviously meaning the federal government as it relates to the citizens of the United States. Soundly confirming this, the United States Supreme Court, in the *Slaughter-House Cases* as we cited in Chapter 3, uses the language "subject to *its* jurisdiction"[18] — utilizing a definitively singular possessive pronoun—in referring to the jurisdiction to which citizens of the United States are subject. This detail is the *first* hint that "citizens of the United States" are really citizens of the federal government, as confirmed in 1993 by *Jones v. Temmer* (see page 21).

The next judicial ruling made in this chronology was that of the *Slaughter-House Cases* in December of 1872. A few pages before the passages we quoted in Chapter 3 (see pages 16-17), the *Slaughter-House* court said:

> [T]he *distinction* between citizenship of the United States and citizenship of a State is clearly recognized and established. ...
>
> It is quite clear, then, that there is a citizenship of the United States, and a citizenship of a State, which are *distinct* from each other, and which depend upon *different characteristics or circumstances* in the individual. — *Slaughter-House Cases,* 16 Wall (83 U.S.) 36, 73-74.

---

[18] [The first clause of the first section of the 14th Amendment] overturns the Dred Scott decision by making *all persons* born within the United States and subject to its jurisdiction citizens of the United States. — *Slaughter-House Cases*, 16 Wall (83 U.S.) 36, 73. [*italics emphasis* supplied, underscore emphasis added]

[*emphasis* added] (See page 276 for this passage. Refer to page 259 for the complete text of the case.)

This case makes clear for the first time that there is a distinction between citizenship of the United States and citizenship of a state—that they *are not the same*, though our government officials of today would have us believe otherwise. Remember, before the 14th Amendment, the only class of citizenship recognized in the federal and state constitutions was that of state citizenship.

Barely two years after the *Slaughter-House Cases*, in November of 1874, the Supreme Court of Indiana heard the case of *Cory v. Carter*, 48 Ind. 327, where it examined the rights, pursuant to the 14th Amendment, of black children seeking admission into a school exclusively for whites. Quoting the first section of the amendment, the decision states in pertinent part:

> First. "All persons born or naturalized in the United States, and subject to the jurisdiction thereof, are citizens of the United States and of the state wherein they reside."
>
> In the *Slaughter-House Cases*, the Supreme Court of the United States say, this is a declaration "that persons may be citizens of the United States without regard to their citizenship of a particular state, and it overturns the Dred Scott decision by making all persons born within the United States and subject to its jurisdiction citizens of the United States. That its main purpose was to establish the citizenship of the negro [sic] can admit of no doubt. ... It is quite clear, then, that there is a citizenship of the United States, and a citizenship of a state, which are distinct from each other, and which depend upon different characteristics or circumstances in the individual." ...
>
> Second. "No state shall make or enforce any law which shall abridge the privileges or immunities of citizens of the United States."
>
> This clause does not refer to citizens of the states. It embraces only citizens of the United States. ... It places the privileges and immunities of citizens of the United States under protection of the Federal Constitution, and leaves the privileges and immunities of citizens of a state under protection of the state constitution. This is fully shown by the recent decision of the Supreme Court of the United States in the *Slaughter-House Cases*, 16 Wall. 36.
> — *Cory v. Carter*, 48 Ind. 327, 349-350. (See page 180 for this passage. Refer to page 171 for the complete text of the case.)

Cory v. Carter confirms the basic purpose of the 14th Amendment as stated in *Van Valkenburg v. Brown* and the *Slaughter-House Cases*. It also provides further explanation of the limitations of the 14th Amendment as expressed in those two cases, and again recognizes citizenship of the United States as distinct from state citizenship.

In combination, these three cases establish two foundational principles with respect to the 14th Amendment:

1. The citizens of the several states—which were only the whites in that day—*did not* owe their status of citizenship to the 14th Amendment.
2. The 14th Amendment *did*, in fact, confer a *new* and distinct status of citizenship upon the freed slaves and their descendants, a status of citizenship *not* in existence before that time and *not* the same as citizenship of a state.

In light of these revelations, it is not unreasonable to conclude that, because of the racial biases that existed in that day, the 14th Amendment was probably *not* a sincere attempt to create true equality for the freed slaves.

Following *Cory v. Carter* by only one year, the United States Supreme Court ruled again on this subject in 1875, in the case of *United States v. Cruikshank*, 92 U.S. 542. This case analyzed the appropriateness of a criminal indictment based upon the distinction between the two classes of citizenship and how jurisdiction over them is obtained. In that case, the highest Court stated:

> We have in our political system a government of the United States and a government of each of the several States. Each one of these governments is distinct from the others, *and each has citizens of its own who owe it allegiance*, and whose rights, within its jurisdiction, it must protect. — *United States v. Cruikshank*, 92 U.S. 542, 549. [*emphasis* added] (See page 325 for this passage. Refer to page 323 for the complete text of the case.)

Here, the United States Supreme Court is confirming that the federal government has citizens *exclusive* of the states. There is a different *allegiance* with different *rights* unique to each jurisdiction. We emphasize the term "allegiance" here because we will revisit this concept in Chapter 6.

We suspect that Congress wanted people to *think* the 14th

Amendment provided a guarantee and protection of rights for all Americans. However, it is clear from just these few cases that, right from the beginning, the highest courts in our country were upholding the two separate classes of citizenship and recognizing that the 14th Amendment provided *nothing* of any *real value* to the freed slaves.

A good example of the complete uselessness of the 14th Amendment can be seen in the evolution of 18 Stat. 335, entitled the "Civil Rights Act," passed in 1875. Note that this legislation comes only nine years after the Civil Rights Act of 1866. That Congress was attempting to legislate still *more* "rights" makes clear the fact that the Civil Rights Act of 1866, combined with the 14th Amendment, simply did not guarantee the broad scope of unalienable rights recognized by the Bill of Rights and the declarations of rights embodied in most state constitutions. To wit, Section 1 of the Civil Rights Act stated:

> *Be it enacted by the Senate and House of Representatives of the United States of America in Congress assembled,* That all persons within the jurisdiction of the United States shall be entitled to the full and equal enjoyment of the accommodations, advantages, facilities, and privileges of inns, public conveyances on land or water, theaters, and other places of public amusement; subject only to the conditions and limitations established by law, and applicable alike to citizens of every race and color, regardless of any previous condition of servitude. — 18 Stat. 335, §1. (Refer to page 107 for the complete text of the statute.)

Note the mundane nature of the "rights" granted in this act: "accommodations, advantages, facilities," etc. This is the extent of the scope of this legislation! Section 2 of the statute merely provided penalties for violations of Section 1. This lends further proof of the impotence of the 14th Amendment and previous civil rights legislation.

Interestingly, notwithstanding the 14th Amendment, the United States Supreme Court ruled in 1883, in the *Civil Rights Cases*, 109 U.S. 3, that Sections 1 and 2 of The Civil Rights Act of 1875 were *unconstitutional*! However, it is important to realize and understand that it was not the "subject matter" of the statute that was found unconstitutional. The court ruled that it was unconstitutional because the federal government did not have constitutional authority to enact such a statute. The 14th Amendment alleged to prohibit a state from enacting a law that abridged the privileges and immunities of the citizens of the United States, but it *did not* authorize Congress to pass legislation creating rights for the citizen of the United States.

Next, we move forward in time to 1908 and revisit the United States Supreme Court case of *Twining v. New Jersey*, 211 U.S. 78. You will recall that our previous look at Twining (page 18-19) revealed the anemic list of rights that the 14th Amendment allegedly guaranteed to the citizens of the United States. *Twining* probably makes the most lasting impression concerning the in-alienable rights that we value so highly, yet which are unavailable to the citizen of the United States. Here is what *Twining* says about the 5th Amendment right against self-incrimination.

> [At pg. 91] The exemption from testimonial compul-sion, that is, from disclosure as a witness of evidence against oneself, forced by any form of legal process, is universal in American law... (See page 305.)

> [At pg. 97] If, then, it be assumed, without deciding the point, that an exemption from compulsory self-incrimination is what is described as a fundamental right belonging to all who live under a free government, and in-capable of impairment by legislation or judicial decision, it is, so far as the states are concerned, a fundamental right inherent in state citizenship, and is a privilege and immunity of that citizenship only. Privileges and immunities of citizens of the United States, on the other hand, are only such as arise out of the nature and essential character of the national government...." (See page 308.)

> [At pg. 99] We conclude, therefore, that *the exemp-tion from compulsory self-incrimination is not a privilege or immunity of national citizenship* guaranteed by this clause of the 14th Amendment against abridgment by the states. — *Twining v. New Jersey*, 211 U.S. 78. [*emphasis* added] (See page 309.)

In other words, the *Twining* court is saying that the 14th Amendment does *not* guarantee to citizens of the United States the right of immunity from self-incrimination recognized by the 5th Amendment. We have already seen from *Jones v. Temmer*, citing the *Slaughter-House Cases*, that the 14th Amendment did not incorporate the Bill of Rights. This passage from *Twining* certainly supports that ruling. However, *Twining* has more to say about the application of the Bill of Rights with regard to "citizens of the United States."

> [At pg. 98] The right of trial by jury in civil cases, guaranteed by the 7th Amendment (*Walker v. Sauvinet*, 92 U.S. 90, 23 L. ed. 678), and the right to bear arms, guaranteed by the 2d Amendment (*Presser v. Illinois*, 110 U.S. 252, 29 L. ed. 615, 6 Sup. Ct. Rep. 580), have been distinctly held not to be privileges and immunities of citizens of the United States, guaranteed by the 14th Amendment against abridgment by the states, and in effect the same decision was made in respect of the guaranty against prosecution, except by indictment of a grand jury, contained in the 5th Amendment (*Hurtado v. California*, 110 U.S. 516, 28 L. ed. 232, 4 Sup. Ct. Rep. 111, 292), and in respect to the right to be confronted with witnesses contained in the 6th Amendment (*West v. Louisiana*, 194 U.S. 258, 48 L. ed. 965, 24 Sup. Ct. Rep. 650). — *Twining v. New Jersey*, 211 U.S. 78. (See page 308. Refer to page 303 for the complete text of the case.)

What *Twining* is saying in this quotation is that the rights recognized in the 2nd, 5th, 6th and 7th Amendments are not possessed by citizens of the United States. In short, the citizen of the United States is truly without the protection afforded by the Bill of Rights. How many of the people who refer to themselves as a "U.S. citizen" or a "citizen of the United States" realize and understand that by making such a claim, they are effectively waiving access to the Bill of Rights? For all practical purposes, it is not far from the truth to say that *no one* understands that. Of course, this is the reason that we have written this book.

In 1909, just one year after *Twining*, the Alabama Supreme Court, in *Gardina v. Board of Registrars* 160 Ala. 155, 48 S.Rep. 788, further confirmed the existence of the two classes of citizenship:

> There are, then, under our republican form of government, two classes of citizens, one of the United States and one of the state. — *Gardina v. Board of Registrars*, 160 Ala. 155, 48 S.Rep. 788, 791. (See page 221 for this passage. Refer to page 219 for the complete text of the case.)

In 1927, the California Supreme Court weighed in with another ruling on this subject when it heard *K. Tashiro et al. v. Jordan*, 201 Cal. 236, 256 P. 545, affirmed the following year by the United States Supreme Court in *Jordan v. Tashiro*, 278 U.S. 123, 73 L.Ed. 214, 49 S.Ct. 47 (1928):

> That there is a citizenship of the United States and a citizenship of state, and the privileges and immunities of one are not the same as the other is well established by the decisions of the courts of this country. The leading cases upon the subjects are those decided by the Supreme Court of the United States and reported in 16 Wall. 36, 21 L.Ed. 394, and known as the *Slaughter-House Cases*. — *K. Tashiro et al. v. Jordan*, 201 Cal. 236, 246. (See page 237 for this passage. Refer to page 233 for the complete text of the case.)

Clearly, in this case, the California Supreme Court, citing the *Slaughter-House Cases*, again verified that the two classes of citizenship, and their rights, are different.

In 1940, in addition to striking down *Colgate v. Harvey*, the U.S. Supreme Court, in *Madden v. Kentucky*, 309 U.S. 83, added to the list of "rights" not granted by the 14th Amendment to U.S. citizens:

> We think it quite clear that the right to carry out an incident to a trade, business or calling such as the deposit of money in banks is not a privilege of national citizenship. — *Madden v. Kentucky*, 309 U.S. 83. (See page 242.)

In this quotation, the term "national citizenship" refers to 14th Amendment citizenship of the United States. This denial of a right claimed pursuant to the 14th Amendment stands in stark contrast to the unalienable right to life, liberty and the pursuit of happiness, which naturally includes the use of a bank account.

The consistency of the rulings by the courts continues into 1966 with the Maryland Supreme Court.

> Both before and after the Fourteenth Amendment to the federal Constitution, it has not been necessary for a person to be a citizen of the United States in order to be a citizen of his state. *United States v. Cruikshank*, 92 U.S. 542, 549 (1875); *Slaughter-House Cases*, 83 U.S. (16 Wall.) 36, 73-74 (1873); and see *Short v. State*, 80 Md. 392, 401-02, 31 Atl. 322 (1895). — *Crosse v. Board of Electors*, 243 Md. 555. (See page 190.)

And finally, in 1993, less than a decade prior to this writing, *Jones v. Temmer* (see pages 21-22) again confirms the earlier rulings and, as demonstrated earlier, equates "citizenship of the United States" with "citizenship of the federal government."

Thus, from 1872 through 1993, the courts have consistently confirmed the distinction between the two classes of citizenship. Furthermore, they have made clear the fact that citizens of the United States are not protected by either the Bill of Rights, nor the declarations of rights found in most state constitutions. We are certain most Americans would shudder at this fact, were they only aware of it.

With the foregoing as background, let us now revisit our assertion that the "state citizenship" created by the 14th Amendment is not true state citizenship with inalienable rights, but a "pseudo-state citizenship" without them. As we indicated in Chapter 3, this thesis is in dispute by some skeptics. It is our intention to put that dispute to rest.

The first hint that 14th Amendment "state citizenship" is not true state citizenship is evident in the mechanism for acquiring 14th Amendment "state citizenship": Whereas true state citizenship is acquired as a result of being "born on the soil" in one of the states of the Union,[19] this pseudo-state citizenship is acquired when a 14th Amendment "citizen of the United States" becomes a "resident" of one of the several states.[20] Again, this sort of distinction is almost always *legally* significant, and we contend that it is significant here.

Yet, even as we observe this distinction, the *Slaughter-House* court *seems* to support an opposing view, only a few pages after the passage we quoted in Chapter 3:

> [A] citizen of the United States can, of his own volition, become a citizen of any State of the Union by a *bonâ fide* residence therein, with the same rights as other citizens of that State. — *Slaughter-House Cases*, 16 Wall (83 U.S.) 36, 80. [emphasis added] (See page 279 for this passage. Refer to page 259 or the complete text of the case.)

---

[19] *Walther v. Rabolt*, 30 Cal. 185, 189 (1866). See page 13 of Chapter 3.
[20] "[A]n important element is necessary to convert [a citizen of the United States] into [a citizen of a State]. He must reside within the State to make him a citizen of it." — *Slaughter-House Cases*, 83 U.S. 36, 74. See page 276 in the Appendix of this text.

Note that this statement *seems* to suggests that a citizen of the United States, in becoming a citizen of a state by virtue of residence therein, secures the unalienable rights of true state citizens. This may be the basis for skepticism on the part of those who believe that 14th Amendment "state citizenship" is the same as true state citizenship. However, this is ill considered, both by the skeptics and the court.

The language of the 14th Amendment—"citizens of the United States *and* of the State wherein they reside"—suggests that a person can *simultaneously* be a citizen of the United States and a citizen of the state in which he resides. However, several of the decisions listed above make it clear that state citizenship and citizenship of the United States *do not* simultaneously exist within a single individual. These court cases *do not* refer a person being a state citizen *at the same time* that he is a citizen of the United States. The courts are referring to state citizens who are *different* people than those who are citizens of the United States. To wit:

> [T]his provision *protects only those rights peculiar to being a citizen of the federal government*; it does not protect those rights which relate to state citizenship. — *Jones v. Temmer*, 829 F.Supp. 1226, 1232 (D. Colo. 1993). [*emphasis* added]

In assessing the rights protected by the 14th Amendment, the federal court in this case is clearly referring to a "citizen of the federal government" as an individual possessing only that class of citizenship, as distinguished from state citizens.

> [The privileges and immunities clause] places the privileges and immunities of *citizens of the United States* under protection of the Federal Constitution, and leaves the privileges and immunities of *citizens of a state* under protection of the state constitution. — *Cory v. Carter*, 48 Ind. 327, 350. [*emphasis* added]

This passage clearly treats "citizens of the United States" and "citizens of a state" as different individuals.

> Each one of these governments is distinct from the others, and *each has citizens of its own* who owe it allegiance, and whose rights, within its jurisdiction, it must protect. — *United States v. Cruikshank*, 92 U.S. 542, 549. [*emphasis* added]

Again, this passage distinctly recognizes the citizens of the different jurisdictions as *different* people, *not* the *same* people simultaneously possessing the two classes of citizenship.

> There are, then, under our republican form of government, two classes of citizens, one of the United States and one of the state. — *Gardina v. Board of Registrars*, 160 Ala. 155, 48 S.Rep. 788, 791.

This ruling declares explicitly that there are "two classes of *citizens*"—not merely two classes of "citizenship" (which could hypothetically dwell within a single individual at the same time). In other words, the state citizen is simply not the same individual as the citizen of the United States.

It is noteworthy that not one of these rulings presumes *both* classes of citizenship to occupy the same individual at the same *time*. Yet this is the circumstance that *must* prevail if what the skeptics say is true. This turns out to be a logical impossibility that the courts have not acknowledged, and may not even have contemplated.

Consider this: If the 14th Amendment were intended to create both citizenship of the United States and true state citizenship in a single individual *at the same time*, as suggested by the word "and" in the first sentence of the amendment, such person would—*at the same time*—both *have* unalienable rights as a state citizen, and *not have* unalienable rights as a citizen of the United States. This, of course, would be impossible: If his state citizenship gave him unalienable rights, then he would have them as a citizen of the United States. Conversely, if his citizenship of the United States denied him unalienable rights, then he would not have them as a state citizen. In light of the maxim that denies the law impossibilities,[21] this could not be what is intended by the 14th Amendment.

Further, in order to apply the prescription given in the *Slaughter-House Cases* for acquiring the unalienable rights that go with true state citizenship (by taking up bona fide residence in a state), *a person would have to renounce his citizenship of the United States* in order rid himself of the "rightless" condition of that class of citizenship. In such event, of course, citizenship of the

---

[21] *Lex non cogit impossibilia.* The law requires nothing impossible. Co. Litt. 231, b; 1 Bouv. Inst. n. 951.

United States and true state citizenship would *not* occupy a single person at the same time, as we have observed above. (So far as we are aware, this circumstance has never been tested in court.)

Likewise, if the 14th Amendment had intended to offer an alternative to citizenship of the United States, as seems to be suggested by the one statement in the *Slaughter-House Cases*, it would have used the word "or" instead of "and" in the first sentence of Section 1, i.e.: "...citizens of the United States *or* of the State wherein they reside." *That* would have reflected what the *Slaughter-House* ruling seems to be saying. But the 14th Amendment used "and," clearly intending for both classes of citizenship to dwell within a single person at the same time. As such, the "state citizenship" created by the 14th Amendment *cannot* be true state citizenship with unalienable rights. It can only be a *pseudo*-state citizenship if the unalienable rights are not included. We therefore believe, that the statement in the *Slaughter-House Cases* as we have cited on page 31, *cannot* be taken literally, because a literal interpretation of that statement *is not supported* by any of the remainder of that case, nor any other case law cited in this book.

Finally, in at least three of the cases we have cited, the courts make it clear that the federal government did not have the authority to dictate to the individual governments of the states regarding issues of state citizenship. In *People v. Brady*, the California Supreme Court found the 14th Amendment powerless to decide who would be its citizens:

> The Fourteenth Amendment to the Constitution of the United States *does not conflict* with the power of the [California] Legislature in the exercise of its discretion *to exclude Chinamen from the right to testify* in the State Courts. — *People v. Brady*, 40 Cal. 198. [*emphasis* added] (See page 247 for this passage.)

In the *Slaughter-House Cases,* the United States Supreme Court said:

> [W]hen, the effect is to fetter and degrade the State governments by subjecting them to the control of Congress, in the exercise of powers heretofore universally conceded to them of the most ordinary and fundamental character; when in fact it radically changes the whole theory of the relations of the State and Federal govern-

ments to each other and of both these governments to the people; the argument has a force that is irresistible, in the absence of language which expresses such a purpose too clearly to admit of doubt.

We are convinced that no such results were intended by the Congress which proposed these amendments, nor by the legislatures of the States which ratified them. — *Slaughter-House Cases*, 16 Wall (83 U.S.) 36. [*emphasis* added] (See page 279.)

In *Cory v. Carter*, the Indiana Supreme Court observed, in reference to the 10th Amendment, that:

[T]he power to fix the qualifications of the citizen of the state, and to establish his rights in the state, is one of the powers expressly reserved to the state by this amendment....*Cory v. Carter*, 48 Ind. 327, 353. (See page 179 for this passage.)

And seven pages later, the Indiana Supreme Court went on to conclude that:

The fourteenth amendment contains *no new grant of power* from the people, who are the inherent possessors of all power, to the Federal Government. *It did not enlarge the powers of the Federal Government, nor diminish those of the states.* — *Cory v. Carter*, supra, 353. [*emphasis* added] (See page 182 for this passage. Refer to page 171 for the complete text of the case.)

Clearly, the federal government does not have the authority to dictate to a state who can become its citizens. Thus, the "state citizenship" created in the 14th Amendment *cannot* be the true state citizenship of the people of the several states. The significance of all of this will become evident in Chapter 9.

While the court cases presented in this chapter do not comprise a complete list of the rulings confirming the existence of and distinction between the two classes of citizenship, they surely provide a compelling one.[22] Yet, compelling as the list may be, how many people are aware of these cases? Certainly, the vast

---

[22] There are many other court rulings that cite the *Slaughter-House Cases* with regard to the distinction of two classes of citizenship. A few more examples are: *Boyd v. Nebraska*, 143 U.S. 135 (1892); *McPherson v. Blacker*, 146 U.S. 1 (1892); Duncan v. Missouri, 152 U.S. 377 (1894); *Maxwell v. Dow*, 176 U.S. 581 (1900); *Maxwell v. Bugbee*, 250 U.S. 525 (1919); *Prudential Ins. Co. v. Cheek*, 259 U.S. 530 (1922); *Hamilton v. Regents*, 293 U.S. 245 (1934).

majority of lay people are not. Are attorneys and lower court judges aware of the tenets established by these rulings? If they are, attorneys certainly don't advocate them in favor of your rights, and judges do not currently refer to these cases in their rulings.

At practically every turn of your life—from opening a bank account, to applying for a job, to obtaining a driver's license—you are being required to claim that you are a "U.S. citizen" or a "citizen of the United States"—*a misidentification of your true nationality*. Once you have claimed that you are the citizen of the United States, the government can now treat you as a "federal citizen" under the 14th Amendment—stripped of the rights guaranteed by the Bill of Rights and the declarations of rights in the various state constitutions. *This is* the identity fraud. In the next chapter we will learn the essence of *how* this fraud is committed upon us.

∾ CHAPTER 5 ∾

The Requirement to Misidentify Ourselves

∾∾∾∾∾∾∾∾∾∾∾∾∾∾∾∾∾∾∾∾∾

The first four chapters of this book have clearly demonstrated the reality of and distinction between the two classes of citizenship. We have seen, on the one hand, how the "citizens of the several states" have solid protection of rights under their respective state constitutions and the Bill of Rights in the federal constitution. We have learned on the other hand how the "citizens of the United States" under the 14th Amendment have very few rights, and none of them are unalienable. When at every turn of our lives we are being required to misidentify ourselves as "U.S. citizens," under penalty of perjury in many cases, one begins to wonder if there is a concerted government effort afoot to have us effectively waive all access to our unalienable rights as citizens of our respective states, and accept what few "civil rights" the government is willing to dole out to citizens of the United States. In this chapter, we'll pull back the curtain to reveal the deception the government uses to dupe us into adopting citizenship of the United States and surrendering our unalienable rights.

There is no plainer example of identity fraud than the application for a California Driver's License. Prior to August of 2001, in order to obtain a driver's license in California, an applicant had to swear to being either a U.S. citizen or an alien. Section 7, on the front of the form, required the applicant to "certify under penalty of perjury" that he had read all the certifications on the back and made no false statements (see page 368). On the back of the form, the fourth item in the "Certifications" section was the preprinted statement, "I certify that I am a U.S. citizen or a qualified alien...." (see page 369). Obviously the Department of Motor Vehicles did not intend for this preprinted information to be changed. Therefore, by signing the application, the applicant was swearing under penalty of perjury to be a citizen of the United States pursuant to the 14th Amendment.

After various efforts on our part, including law suits alleging that officials of the California Department of Motor Vehicles were suborning perjury[23] by requiring state citizens to misidentify themselves as U.S. citizens in order to obtain a license, the certifications on the application were changed on August 2001, and as of this writing no longer require an applicant to swear to being a U.S. citizen. However, an even more insidious requisite to obtaining a driver's license in California still obligates an applicant to effectively claim U.S. citizenship by way of the requirement to furnish a Social Security Number. We will show, later in this chapter, how this requirement is the functional equivalent to swearing to being a U.S. citizen.[24]

In similar manner, the California Voter Registration Form presents a "damned-if-you-do, damned-if-you-don't" dilemma. Right at the top of the form you are asked "Are you a U.S. citizen?" You are given checkbox options labeled "Yes" and "No." Following the "No" option is the caveat: "If No, Don't Fill Out Or Mail This Form." Thus, in California, there is currently no way for a state citizen to make his voice heard through the venerable "American way" of voting, without first adopting "U.S. citizenship" and waiving his unalienable rights. The clerks who process voter registration forms are as unaware of the two classes of citizenship as the vast majority of Americans. Therefore, the administrative and clerical mechanisms which allow federal

---

[23] *Black s Law Dictionary*, 6th Edition, defines subornation of perjury as "The offense of procuring another to take such a false oath as would constitute perjury in the principle." It is a felony and carries the same penalties as perjury itself.

[24] As federal influence has forced a certain amount of consistency between the various states with regard to the requirement of U.S. citizenship on driver's license applications, this waiver of rights is required in every state, in one way or another.

citizens to join the register of voters simply do not exist for state citizens. If someone were to attempt to register to vote as a citizen of the state but *not* a 14th Amendment U.S. citizen, the poor clerk would not have a clue! Though we have not reviewed voter registration forms in states other than California, this is certain to be the case in other states as well.

The fraud exposed in these examples even extends to the state constitution. In Article I of the Constitution of the State of California, entitled the Declaration of Rights, Section 2 originally stated:

> All political power is inherent in the people. Government is instituted for the protection, security and benefit of the people, and they have the right to alter or reform the same whenever the public good may require it.

Note that this section correctly identifies the *people* as the source of all political power in the state, and it is located right up front, in Article I, second only to Section 1 that declares our inalienable rights. But on November 5, 1974, the voters in California were duped into repealing that Section 2 from its original position in the Declaration of Rights and replacing it as Section 26. Then, one and a half years later, on June 8, 1976, the section was further renumbered as Section 1 of Article II, the article which deals with *voting*. Originally in the Declaration of Rights, it was an "all inclusive" statement that the political power belonged to the people. Now, since 1976, it serves merely as a description of the "right to vote," and nothing more. Thus, in California, even the political power of the people has been diluted.

It is beyond outrageous that these acts of deception have effectively *silenced* the voice of the people in the affairs of government. It is even more astonishing to think that this fraud has been perpetrated on us in the United States of America—where the voice of the people is held to be sacrosanct.

At the federal level, the Application for a Social Security Card, Form "SS-5" (see pages 375), also tricks unsuspecting state citizens into claiming federal citizenship and waiving their constitutionally protected rights. Though not readily apparent, there are several tipoffs to this artifice. First, on page three of the current form, it says:

> US CITIZENSHIP: We can accept most documents that show you were *born in the* U.S. [*emphasis* added] (See page 373.)

The fact that this passage echoes the language used in the 14th Amendment—"born in the U.S." (with the minor substitution of "U.S." for "United States")—makes clear the fact that the form does not apply to anyone "born upon the soil"—the state citizen.

Next, for question 3, "Citizenship," on page 5 of the form, the applicant is given a choice, with a series of checkboxes, of claiming that he is either a "U.S. citizen," a "Legal Alien Allowed To Work," a "Legal Alien Not Allowed To Work," or "Other" (see page 375). The first checkbox looks innocent enough:

☐ U.S. Citizen.

But for all the reasons that have been discussed throughout this book, the "U.S. citizen" option does not apply to a "citizen of a state." You will recall that, on page 77 of its ruling on the *Slaughter-House Cases*, the United States Supreme Court said, "The constitutional provision there alluded to...threw around them in that clause *no security for the citizen of the State* in which they were claimed or exercised." Though this statement was directly referring to Article IV, Section 2 of the federal constitution, the court concluded a few paragraphs later that the 14th Amendment also did not make any such provision. While this case predates the Social Security Act by many decades, it correctly observes that the federal constitution, including the 14th Amendment, makes no provision for extending *"security,"* such as Social *"Security,"* to the state citizen. Thus, the option of "U.S. citizen" on the SS-5 *cannot* legitimately include a "citizen of a state" that is not a descendant of a freed slave. As a result, when a state citizen checks "U.S. citizen" on an Application for a Social Security Card, he unwittingly waives all of his rights under both his state constitution and the Bill of Rights, and accepts the very limited "protection" provided by the privileges and immunities clause of the 14th Amendment. Unfortunately, the average American will check "U.S. citizen," not knowing the real meaning of the term or the consequential loss of rights attendant with getting the Social Security Number.

The next two checkboxes, "Legal Alien Allowed To Work" and "Legal Alien Not Allowed To Work," are not relevant to our discussion, as they apply only to aliens.

Then there is the last box:

☐   Other (See Instructions On Page 1).

One might think this option would allow a state citizen to obtain a Social Security Number without waiving his rights. But note that it is followed by the parenthetical direction, "See Instructions On Page 1" (refer to page 371 for "Page 1" of Form SS-5). These instructions expressly confine the "Other" applicant to one applying for a federal "benefit or service." But because only federal citizens and qualified aliens[25] are eligible for federal benefits, the "Other" option is *not* a provision available to a citizen of a state. This is further clarified by Title 20 of the Code of Federal Regulations (C.F.R.), which demonstrates conclusively that state citizens aren't even eligible for a Social Security Number:

> **20 C.F.R. § 422.104.   To whom Social Security numbers are assigned.**
>
> (a) *Persons with evidence of age, identity, and U.S. citizenship or alien status.* A Social Security number may be assigned to an applicant who meets the evidence requirements in § 422.107, if the applicant is:
>
> (1) A U.S. citizen;
>
> (2) An alien lawfully admitted to the United States for permanent residence or under other authority of law permitting him or her to work in the United States (see § 422.105 regarding presumption of authority of nonimmigrant alien to work); or
>
> (3) An alien who is legally in the United States but not under authority of law permitting him or her to engage in employment, but only for a valid nonwork purpose. (See § 422.107.)

Obviously, the state citizen is not in the list of those eligible for a Social Security Number. In many respects, the Application for a Social Security Card is the primary tool of deception by which the government induces state citizens to adopt 14th Amendment citizenship of the United States and waive their constitutionally protected rights. Further, each use of a Social Security Number on both federal and state forms, such as the

---

[25] Such as an "illegal alien" with a child born in the United States applying for a number in order to receive AFDC

Driver's License Application, reaffirms the misidentification of U.S. citizenship, and the waiver of unalienable rights that goes along with it. And because this misidentification is hidden in the Social Security agreement, the unwary user doesn't realize he is waiving his rights each time he uses the number. It is unfortunate that the distinction between the two classes of citizenship is not more widely known. If it were, the Application for a Social Security Card would not be so successful in deceiving state citizens into accepting U.S. citizenship.

It should come as no surprise that the application for a United States passport also requires the applicant to claim U.S. citizenship or nationality of the United States.[26] These examples represent just a few of the circumstances in which state citizens are required to waive their rights and adopt the inferior status of federal citizenship. They lurk in practically every government form we are asked to fill out.

To give you an idea of how serious this is, and just how much power the government has over 14th Amendment citizens of the United States, consider a ruling handed down in 1884 by the United States Supreme Court in *Elk v. Wilkins*, 112 U.S. 94. In reference to the 14th Amendment, the Court said:

> This section contemplates two sources of citizenship, and two sources only: birth and naturalization. The persons declared to be citizens are 'all persons born or naturalized in the United States, and subject to the jurisdiction thereof.' The evident meaning of these last words is, not merely subject in some respect or degree to the jurisdiction of the United States, but completely subject to their political jurisdiction, and owing them direct and immediate allegiance. — *Elk v. Wilkins,* 112 U.S. 94, 101-102. (See page 196)

Note that this ruling states that persons declared citizens by the 14th Amendment are "subject to" the jurisdiction of the United States. At first blush, this language may not be too alarming. But consider how *Black's Law Dictionary* defines "subject to":

> **Subject to.** Liable, subordinate, subservient, inferior, obedient to; ...[27]

---

[26] "National of the United States" is expalined in Chapter 6.
[27] *Black's Law Dictionary*, 6th Edition, pg. 1425.

42

Already, this definition begins to reveal the implications of the ruling in *Elk v. Wilkins*: The 14th Amendment citizen of the United States is clearly considered by the court to be subordinate, subservient, and inferior. This stands in stark contrast to state citizens who comprise the sovereign—the most superior status—of each state. That the court would so readily reveal this harsh truth may be surprising, but back in 1884, a century before the advent of political correctness, the government did not yet feel so desperate to cover up this truth as it does today.

But remember, the court used the language *"completely subject to..."* and this has yet deeper implications. Let's look at another definition from *Black's*:

> **Slave.** A *person* who is *wholly subject to* the will of another; one who has no freedom of action, but whose person and services are wholly under the control of another....[28] [*emphasis* added]

Note first that this definition uses the word "person," the term we examined earlier that is used instead of "people" in the 14th Amendment and civil rights legislation. Given the difference in meaning between "people" and "persons," the use of "person" in this definition sheds additional light on its meaning in said amendment and legislation. But there's more. According to this definition, a slave is "wholly subject to" another. As standard English dictionaries typically equate "wholly" and "completely," we can conclude from *Elk v. Wilkins*—which states that 14th Amendment citizens of the United States are *"completely* subject to" the jurisdiction of the United States—that the status and "rights" of the 14th Amendment citizen are no greater than those of a slave. This is proof positive that "citizenship of the United States" is little more than a fancy label to conceal the horrible truth that the freed slaves were never recognized as equal to white people and have to this day been denied the status of state citizen with all attendant unalienable rights.

Please take note of the fact that the definitions of "subject to" and "slave" given above were quoted from the 6th Edition of *Black's Law Dictionary*. This is in contrast to our usual quotation from the 7th Edition, the latest in the series, as of this writing. The

---

[28] Black's Law Dictionary, 6th Edition, pg. 1388.

reason we have quoted from the 6th Edition is because these definitions have been *removed* from the 7th Edition. This does not mean that those terms are no longer meaningful; it only means that the truth they reveal is being deliberately *hidden* from us. This is identity fraud in action!

George Washington, our nation's first president, is quoted as saying, "Government is not reason; it is not eloquence; it is force! Like fire, it is a dangerous servant and a fearful master."[29] How prophetically true his words ring in light of these revelations about the 14th Amendment! Clearly, our Founders recognized from day one the dangers with which government is fraught, and it behooves us to be likewise alert.

Given the hidden meanings of the words in the 14th Amendment, it is horrifying to realize that, over the years, the vast majority of Americans—people born as citizens of their respective states, with all the unalienable rights that their constitutions guaranteed to them—have been deceived into renouncing their state citizenship and adopting 14th Amendment "citizenship of the United States." Of course, some Americans actually *are* descendants of the slaves freed after the Civil War. Therefore, we must ask ourselves a very important question: In light of our modern understanding and sensibilities about racial equality, is it not *also* fraud to *still* require actual descendants of former slaves to claim the *unquestionably inferior* federal citizenship of the United States? The only responsible answer is: *Yes, it is* fraud. "*All* [people] are created equal...." There is no longer any valid argument for *requiring* this second class of citizenship for *anyone*.

In the following chapters, we will explore "The Requirement to Claim Citizenship of the United States"—simply referred to hereafter as "The Requirement"— from various perspectives. In the end, we'll discuss a solution to the pervasive use of "The Requirement" and the identity fraud that it represents.

---

[29] G. Edward Griffin, *The Fearful Master: A Second Look at the United Nations* (Western Islands, 1964), p. ii.

✌ CHAPTER 6 ✍

The Requirement is Controverted by Law

✌✌✌✌✌✌✌✌✌✍✍✍✍✍✍✍✍✍

As we established in Chapter 5, the primary manifestation of the identity fraud committed by the government against the people is the *requirement* imposed by government officials upon state citizens to claim "citizenship of the United States." The existence of "state citizenship" is virtually unknown to almost everyone, including government officials and clerks, even though the two classes of citizenship *are* clearly recognized in a long parade of court cases. For this reason, it would help our thesis if the existence of the two classes of citizenship could be found within federal statutes. Fortunately, current federal statutory law *does* recognize the two classes of citizenship. Unfortunately, Congress has been very creative, if not deceptive, in hiding the distinction between them within some very convoluted language.

Appropriately, the two classes of citizenship, which we have established as being expressly recognized by the courts, can be found within current federal law in the Immigration and Nationality Act, 66 Stat. 163.[30] Section 101(a) of the Immigration

---

[30] This statute replaced the Nationality Act of 1940, 54 Stat. 1137, where the definitions we have referenced in this chapter first appeared in federal law. The definitions cited here from 66 Stat. 163 were brought forward verbatim from this earlier statute.

and Nationality Act gives us four important definitions.[31] (Refer to page 109 for the complete text of 66 Stat. 163 §101(a).[32]) Of primary interest at this point are the definitions of "national" and "national of the United States."

> §101(a)(21) The term "national" means a person owing permanent *allegiance* to a *state*. [*emphasis* added] (See page 111.)

> §101(a)(22) The term "national of the United States" means (A) a citizen of the United States, or (B) a person who, though not a citizen of the United States, owes permanent allegiance to the United States. (See page 111.)

Although these definitions don't clarify state citizenship and federal citizenship directly, they do clarify a promising distinction between the "national" and the "national of the United States."

Note that while the term "national of the United States" has a broader meaning than merely "citizen of the United States," the definition given in §101(a)(22) clearly embraces the "citizen of the United States." As such, it would be a natural leap of logic to conclude that the definition for "national" given in §101(a)(21) embraces the "state citizen." But §101(a)(21) is not so express as to come right out and say the "national" is a "state citizen." This is where Congress has taken pains to hide the distinction between the two classes of citizenship. In order to be sure that the "national" is the "state citizen," and that the two classes of citizenship are indeed reflected in this statute, we need to do some analysis. Be forewarned: The Powers That Be have done their level best to disguise the truth, so sorting it out will be complex and challenging.

We start by noting that §101(a)(21) does, indeed, attach the "national" to a "state." To the honest observer, it's obvious that this language could easily serve to define "state citizen." However, the clarity of this appears to scare some government

---

[31] These same definitions are found in current 8 U.S.C. §1101(a)(14), (21), (22) and (36). Because we are citing 66 Stat. 163, which was enacted in 1952, we wish to assure you that these definitions are currently valid. Title 8 U.S.C. is implemented by Title 8, Code of Federal Regulations (8 C.F.R.). *Current* 8 C.F.R 1.1(a) states: "The terms defined in section 101 of the Immigration and Nationality Act (66 Stat. 163) shall have the meanings ascribed to them in that section and as supplemented, explained, and further defined in this chapter." Thus, these definitions *are currently in effect.*

[32] The complete statute is over 120 pages in the original volume. The subject matter of the statute is, for the most part, exclusively about immigration and naturalization.

personnel. In an effort to obtain passports as state citizens, we cited this definition to Sharon E. Palmer-Royston, a lawyer for the U.S. State Department, as proof that a state citizen is recognized in the statute. Instead of convincing her, this seemed to raise her defenses and she averred that the word "state" in §101(a)(21) refers only to *foreign* states, rendering the "national" a *foreigner*. While we considered this merely an attempt on her part to enforce the *requirement* to laim "citizenship of the United States," the *possibility* that it might be correct must still be examined. This is done by studying the definition of "foreign state," which is given at §101(a)(14), as follows:

> §101(a)(14) The term "foreign state" includes outlying possessions of a foreign state, but self-governing dominions or territories under mandate or trusteeship shall be regarded as separate foreign states. (See page 110.)

In addition to twice violating the rule that forbids the use within a definition of the term being defined, this provision says nothing to suggest that "state" in §101(a)(21) refers to a "foreign state." Further, pursuant to rules of statutory construction, all of the definitions within a particular statute *must work in harmony with each other*; one definition cannot conflict with another. Therefore, §101(a)(21) cannot be in conflict with §101(a)(14). In order for the definition of "national" to refer *only* to citizens of foreign states, it would have to expressly read: "The term 'national' means a person owing permanent allegiance to a *foreign* state." This is not what it says. Thus, the term "state" in §101(a)(21) *cannot* mean only a foreign state.

But to be sure of our interpretation of §101(a)(21), we still need to find a way to verify that "state" in that definition refers to the several states of the Union. This is done by looking for support in case law. As it turns out, we don't have to look far. Note that in §101(a)(21) the "national" is attached to the "state" by way of "allegiance." This is a word we've seen before. In Chapter 3, we promised to revisit *United States v. Cruikshank*, the case in which the United States Supreme Court connected citizens to their body politic through "allegiance." As you will recall, the *Cruikshank* court stated:

> We have in our political system a government of the United States and a government of each of the *several*

> *States.* Each one of these governments is distinct from the others, and *each has citizens of its own who owe it allegiance,* and whose rights, within its jurisdiction, it must protect. — *United States v. Cruikshank,* 92 U.S. 542, 549. [*emphasis* added] (See page 325.)

In this passage, the Court is expressly recognizing that the government of each of the *several states* has citizens who "owe it allegiance." This language, which is paraphrastically reflected in §101(a)(21), verifies that the word "state" in that definition does—or at least *can*—mean the several states of the Union, and clearly equates the "national" with the "state citizen." This would seem to put the matter to rest once and for all, until we factor in the definition of "State" given at §101(a)(36). It says:

> §101(a)(36) The term "State" includes (except as used in section 310(a) of Title III) Alaska, Hawaii, the District of Columbia, Puerto Rico, Guam, and the Virgin Islands of the United States.[33] (See page 113.)

Note that the language of this definition does not expressly include the several states of the Union. This would seem to set us back, as we cannot rely on it to define "state" to our satisfaction in §101(a)(21). Does it finally mean that "state" in §101(a)(21) does not refer to the several states? No. Layered with obsurity, §101(a)(36) may be the best illustration of Congress' deception in this statute. This does make things more difficult for us, however, please bear with us as we try to make sense of it.

First, note that §101(a)(36) purports to define as "States" only the District of Columbia and a number of territorial possessions of the U.S. government. But the District of Columbia and the U.S. territories constitute the domain under exclusive jurisdiction of the federal government. This is the domain to which "citizens of the United States" are subject. So if the "state" in §101(a)(21) were really the "State" defined in §101(a)(36), then the "national" defined in §101(a)(21) would be the "national of the United States." But that term is separately defined in §101(a)(22)! There would be no point in defining "national" separately from "national of the United States" if they were one

---

[33] This is the original language of the statute. Of course, the current condition of this definition in 8 U.S.C. §1101(a)(36) does not list Alaska and Hawaii, which joined the Union after 1952.

and the same. Since they *are* defined separately, the "state" in §101(a)(21) cannot be the "State" defined in §101(a)(36). This yields the very odd situation of a word used in a statute having a meaning *other* than that given in the *definition* of that word, provided in the same statute. Given that this is "law," this state of affairs seems to defy comprehension, until we examine the parenthetical expression, "except as used in section 310(a) of Title III," near the beginning of §101(a)(36).

To begin with, the very fact that there is an exception to this definition of "State" suggests that there *can* be instances of states in the statute *other* than the federal "States" expressly identified in the body of the definition. In fact, such an instance appears in the section named in the exception clause, "§310(a) of Title III." For reasons of length and relevance, we have not included the complete text of the Immigration and Nationality Act beyond the definitions in §101(a). Therefore, we need to quote the text of Title III, Chapter 2, §310(a), which states:

> Sec. 310. (a) Exclusive jurisdiction to naturalize persons as citizens of the United States is hereby conferred upon the following specified courts: District courts of the United States now existing, or which may hereafter be established by Congress in any *State*, District Courts of the United States for the Territories of Hawaii and Alaska, and for the District of Columbia and for Puerto Rico, the District Court of the Virgin Islands of the United States, and the District Court of Guam; also all courts of record in any *state* or Territory now existing, or which may hereafter be created, having a seal, a clerk, and jurisdiction in actions at law or equity, or law and equity, in which the amount in controversy is unlimited. The jurisdiction of all the courts herein specified to naturalize persons shall extend only to such persons resident within the respective jurisdictions of such courts, except as otherwise specifically provided in this title. [*emphasis* added]

Note in the foregoing quotation that in *one* instance, the word in question is capitalized—"State"—and in the *other* instance it is not—"state." To the lay reader, the matter of capitalization may not seem significant, but capitalization differences within the same statute, and particularly within the same section, *are* significant. The harmony rule assures this. Thus, the mere fact that Congress chose to capitalize it in one place and not another within *this* section (not to mention throughout §101(a)) means that

"State" and "state" have different meanings. This cannot be chalked up to sloppiness or inconsistency, as that could potentially void the law for reasons of vagueness. No, this difference is significant and it reveals the undefined "state" that appears in §101(a)(21). Ultimately, this exception clause finally proves that there *are* instances of "state" in the statute that fall outside of the definition of "State" given at §101(a)(36).

The united states of America consists of *only* the individual states. The *U.S. government* owns the *U.S. territories* (federal "States") named in §101(a)(36), exclusive of the jurisdiction of any of the individual states. Given that the language in §310(a)— "all courts of record in any *state* or Territory"—offers the alternatives of either "state" *or* "Territory," this use of "state" cannot be a reference to the territories listed in §101(a)(36); it can only refer to the several states of the Union.

Further proof of this can be found in *Ex parte Frank Knowles*, which states:

> By the third section of the Act of 1802, it is enacted "that every Court of Record in any *individual State*, having common law jurisdiction and a seal, and clerk or prothonotary, shall be considered as a District Court within the meaning of this Act." *Ex parte Frank Knowles*, 5 Caql 300, 305 [*emphasis* added.] (See page 217)

Note the similarity of the language in an earlier statute from 1802 regarding naturalization, and the pertinent portion of §301(a) in question in our discussion. Section 3 of the Act of 1802 referenced in *Ex parte Frank Knowles* is clearly referring to the individual states. With the similarity of language used in §301(a), how can anyone argue that "state" in the current statute is not a specific reference to the individual states as opposed to the federal territories defined as "States?" The term "state" *is* the exception listed in the definition of "State." The term within the definition of "national" is "state," not "State."

Thus, the "national" defined in §101(a)(21) is in fact a national of one of the several states, and the ruling in *U.S v. Cruikshank* confirms that the "national" is a "state citizen."

After diligently following Congress' Machiavellian maze to its conclusion, we finally have confirmation that the state citizen is recognized in 66 Stat. 163 at §101(a)(21).

After all of this, we believe that it is important to take note of the fact that Congress is perfectly willing and able to specify the "several states" in its definitions of "State" when it wants to. In 31 U.S.C. (Money and Finance), for example, the "several States" are expressly included in the definition of "State":

§6720(a)(4) "State" means any of the *several States* and the District of Columbia. [*emphasis* added]

The four *current* statutory definitions found in §101 of the Immigration and Nationality Act, when viewed together and in harmony with each other, *are consistent* with and support all the case law identifying and distinguishing the *two* classes of citizenship. Therefore, these definitions clearly support our position that "The Requirement to Claim Citizenship of the United States" is a *fraudulent* imposition which deceives the citizens of the several states into misidentifying themselves and waiving the fundamental rights that belong to them under their respective constitutions and laws.

By way of final, and perhaps inadvertent, confirmation of this from a source outside of 66 Stat. 163, the U.S. Government Printing Office *Style Manual*, published as recently as 2000, forty-eight years after the enactment of the Immigration and Nationality Act, gives us §5.23 under the heading "Nationalities, etc." It says:

5.23. In designating the natives of the *several States,* the following forms will be used. [*emphasis* added]

Alabamian	Indianian	Nebraskan	South Carolinian
Alaskan	Iowan	Nevadan	South Dakotan
Arizonan	Kansan	New Hampshirite	Tennessean
Arkansan	Kentuckian	New Jerseyan[35]	Texan
Californian	Louisianian	New Mexican	Utahn
Coloradan	Mainer	New Yorker	Vermonter
Connecticuter	Marylander	North Carolinian	Virginian
Delawarean	Massechusettsan	North Dakotan	Washingtonian
Floridian	Michiganian[34]	Ohioan	West Virginian
Georgian	Minnesotan	Oklahoman	Wisconsinite
Hawaiian	Mississippian	Oregonian	Wyomingite
Idahoan	Missourian	Pennsylvanian	
Illinoisan	Montanan	Rhode Islander	

---

[34] Published as "Michiganite" in 1984 edition of the GPO Style Manual.
[35] Published as "New Jerseyite" in 1984 edition of the GPO Style Manual.

Note that these nationalities are identified by word forms of the names of the several states, and that the list *does not include* *"citizen of the United States!"*

The *effect* of the fraud is real. The rights you have given up as a result of this government deception are *not* included in the "privileges and immunities" of the U.S. citizen. You are left only with the generosity of the government, which can be diminished merely by bureaucratic whim. And this government generosity has been vanishing at a slow but steady pace which goes unnoticed by most Americans. In the next chapter, you will see an actual example of the loss of an inalienable right due to the *effect* of the requirement of claiming U.S. citizenship.

∝ CHAPTER 7 ∾

The Effect of The Requirement

As we have observed earlier, the government seems expressly intent upon *avoiding* its constitutional mandate to protect our *inalienable rights*, and the California Supreme Court has provided us with an excellent example of this. It is accomplished by simply *allowing* a state citizen to erroneously claim that he is a "citizen of the United States" pursuant to the 14th Amendment. The case is *Escobedo v. State of California*, 35 Cal.2d 870 (1950).

In this case, Mr. Escobedo's driver's license was revoked by the Department of Motor Vehicles when it was discovered that he had not made a security deposit establishing financial responsibility following a collision with another vehicle. Mr. Escobedo sued the state for violating both his right to due process of law under Article I, §13 of the state constitution and his right to equal protection under the 14th Amendment to the federal constitution. On page 875 of its ruling, the court states:

> Fundamentally it must be recognized that in this country "Highways are for the use of the traveling public, and all have . . . the right to use them in a reasonable and proper manner, and subject to proper regulations as to the manner of use." (13 Cal.Jur. 371, § 59.) "*The streets of a city belong to the people of the state*, and the use thereof is an *inalienable right* of every citizen, subject to

legislative control or such reasonable regulations as to the traffic thereon or the manner of using them as the legislature may deem wise or proper to adopt and impose." (19 Cal.Jur. 54, § 407.) "Streets and highways are established and maintained primarily for purposes of travel and transportation by the public, and uses incidental thereto. Such travel may be for either business or pleasure . . . *The use of highways* for purposes of travel and transportation *is not a mere privilege, but a common and fundamental right*, of which the public and individuals cannot rightfully be deprived . . . [A]ll persons have an equal right to use them for purposes of travel by proper means, and with due regard for the corresponding rights of others." — *Escobedo v. State of California*, 35 Cal.2d 870. [*emphasis* added] (See page 209. Refer to page 207 for the complete text of the case.)

Note how the court expressly states that the streets belong to "the *people*," then goes on to affirm that the use of the streets is an "*inalienable* right." This is consistent with the California state constitution which declares that "All *people* are by nature free and independent and have *inalienable* rights." The court further states that this "use of the highways...is not a mere privilege but a common and fundamental right."

This all sounds pretty solid, right? After all, "inalienable" *does mean* that the right cannot be taken away *at all—ever*! Then how is it that the government is able to take away the inalienable right to use the public highways, such as was done in *Escobedo*, and to do so on a daily basis? It is really very simple. All the government has to do to remove your inalienable rights is to *allow* you to claim, or to *deceive* you into claiming, that you are the 14th Amendment "citizen of the United States." Remember, according to the rulings of the court cases we have studied in this book, a 14th Amendment "citizen of the United States" does not possess the inalienable rights recognized by our Founders and protected by the state constitutions. The proof of this is disclosed by the court in *Escobedo* in the *very next sentence* following the above quotation:

Notwithstanding such general principles characterizing the primary right of the individual, it is equally well established (as is recognized in the texts above cited) that usage of the highways is subject to reasonable *regulation for the public good. In this connection,* the constitutionality of various types of financial responsibility laws has been often upheld against contentions that they violated the due process clause of *the Fourteenth Amendment.* — *Escobedo v. State of California*, 35 Cal.2d 870. [*emphasis* added] (See page 209.)

Note that, according to this, "regulation for the public good" is authorized "[i]n...connection" with "the Fourteenth Amendment." Based upon the principles we have studied in the preceding chapters, the courts can deny an *inalienable* right to a person who claims 14th Amendment citizenship, or alleges a violation of the 14th Amendment. In California, this capability was given to the courts in previous years by an applicant's declaration of "U.S. citizenship" on his Driver License Application.[36]

Note that, in addition to claiming that the state had violated his right to equal protection under the 14th Amendment, Mr. Escobedo also claimed deprivation of due process of law under Article I, §13 of the state constitution. It is disturbing to recognize that once the court ruled that the suspending of Mr. Escobedo's driver's license did not violate the 14th Amendment, the fact that he also claimed protection of rights under the state constitution *is never discussed in the ruling.* This demonstrates that once a petitioner invokes the 14th Amendment, the court is no longer required to justify why or how an *inalienable* right, or due process under the *state* constitution, can be denied without remedy. Of course, this is consistent with the rulings cited in Chapter 3 where the "rights" of a "citizen of the United States" are protected only by federal law and the federal constitution. It is also important to note that the ruling in *Escobedo*, with four justices concurring, is followed by two dissenting opinions. Yet, even the dissenting opinions *did not raise the issue of the protection of rights under the state constitution!*

Just as there is no variation in the equation of 2+2=4, there is no variation in the government's justification for denying rights to U.S. citizens. The justification is always that the denial of the right does not violate the privileges and immunities clause of the 14th Amendment.

We doubt that there are many people who have not heard the

---

[36] As noted in Chapter 5, the most obvious aspect of this requirement was removed from the California Driver License Application in August of 2001. See page 38.

long-standing maxim of law: "Ignorance of the law is no excuse." The saying *is* true. The government relies on *your* ignorance of the law to *deprive you of your rights.*

We would be willing to bet money, without ever having met Mr. Escobedo, that he was not a descendant of a slave freed after the Civil War. Yet, out of pure, unadulterated ignorance, Mr. Escobedo allowed his lawyer to claim a violation of protection afforded by the 14th Amendment, thus *canceling out* his other claim of a violation of rights under the state constitution. We will never know if the lawyer was equally ignorant about the effects of claiming deprivation of rights under the 14th Amendment, or whether he knowingly raised a 14th Amendment issue to assist the court in its ruling.

If it strikes you as odd that we raise the possibility that a lawyer might undermine his own client's interests, you must first understand that lawyers are "officers of the court." It is in fact stated in *Corpus Juris Secundum* (1980 edition), §4, Attorney & Client, "His first duty is to the courts and the public, not to the client, and wherever the duties to his client conflict with those he owes as an officer of the court in the administration of justice, the former must yield to the latter."

Still, we dare any court, at least in California, to argue that the court *did not* have a constitutional obligation to provide protection for Mr. Escobedo's rights. In *O'Connell v. Judnich*, 71 Cal.App. 386, the California Court of Appeal stated:

> One of the prime objects of the courts is to protect the constitutional rights of the citizen. ... If by legislation a right vouchsafed by the constitution could be so abridged or limited, the right would not be an absolute or inalienable one but a mere privilege revocable at the will of the law-making body. — *O'Connell v. Judnich*, 71 Cal.App. 386, 388. (See page 245.)

These statements do not require an explanation. In *Escobedo*, the court recognized the right to travel as inaleinable, yet their ruling treated that right as if it were a mere revocable privilege. In light of this ruling in *O'Connell v. Judnich*, the court was certainly required to inform Mr. Escobedo that his claim of deprivation of rights under the 14th Amendment was *not appropriate.*

If you remember, in *Van Valkenburg v. Brown*, the California Supreme Court denied Ms. Van Valkenburg's claim of rights under the 14th Amendment because she was not a descendant of a slave.[37] So, why didn't the court deny Mr. Escobedo claim under the 14th Amendment for the very same reason? Are we seeing an inconsistency between these rulings? No. In both cases, the court ruled against these petitioners. Ms. Van Valkenburg was *correctly* denied benefit of the 14th Amendment and thereby *her case was denied.* Mr. Escobedo was *allowed* to *erroneously* allege the violation of a benefit under the 14th Amendment in order for the court to be able to *deny his case*!

Therein lies the substance of the damage the government can do to us as a result of the identity fraud we reveal in this book. The United States Court of Appeal, Fifth Circuit, explains a principle that applies to this identity fraud in *United States v. Prudden*, 424 F.2d 1021, which states:

> Silence can only be equated with fraud where there is a legal or moral duty to speak or where an inquiry left unanswered would be intentionally misleading. — *United States v. Prudden*, 424 F.2d 1021, 1032. (See page 346. Refer to page 337 for the complete text of the case.)

The *Escobedo* court's legal duty to speak is demonstrated in *O'Connell v. Judnich.* In *Escobedo*, the court *fraudulently* left the inquiry of violation of rights under the state constitution *unanswered*! We feel that this clearly demonstrates that the government does seem expressly *intent* upon avoiding its constitutional mandate to protect our inalienable rights.

---

[37] See Chapter 4, page 23, and page 351 for the full text of the case—*Van Valkenburg v. Brown,* 43 Cal. 43.

✑ CHAPTER 8 ✑

The Illusion of Equality

❧❧❧❧❧❧❧❧❧❧❧❧❧❧❧❧❧❧❧❧

At the heart of our thesis of identity fraud is the waiver of unalienable rights that a state citizen is required to make when coerced by various government agencies into claiming citizenship of the United States. In an attempt to disguise this waiver of unalienable rights, Congress has provided an *illusion of equality* by legislating "civil rights" which they would have us believe protect the rights of all Americans, pursuant to the 14th Amendment. Title 42, Chapter 21 of the United States Code (U.S.C.)—entitled "Civil Rights"—is the portion of federal law which is purported to enforce the 14th Amendment. However, we already understand from the United States Supreme Court ruling in the *Slaughter-House Cases* that the 14th Amendment is a "practical nullity." That means Congress cannot legislate enforcement of the 14th Amendment.[38] Even the courts, for the most part, have not used this amendment as a tool to achieve any substantive protection of rights for the citizen of the United States. So, why does Title 42, Chapter 21 exist at all? (See page 115.)

---

[38] Remember, the attempt at legislating rights for 14th Amendment citizens of the United States through the Civil Rights Act in 1875 was ruled unconstitutional by the Supreme Court in the *Civil Rights Cases* in 1883.

As a matter of law, Title 42, Chapter 21 does not exist by any Constitutional authority provided to Congress to legislate for the several states. The federal government has very limited authority when enacting legislation for the several states of the Union. In fact, the 14th Amendment is the *only* provision of the federal constitution which could *possibly* authorize the application of Title 42, Chapter 21 within the several states. However, the United States Supreme Court *has already ruled* that the 14th Amendment *does not provide any such authorization.* This was made abundantly clear in the *Civil Rights Cases* in 1883 when the court stated, in reference to the 14th Amendment:

> It does not authorize congress to create a code of municipal law for the regulation of private rights; but to provide modes of redress against the operation of state laws, and the action of state officers, executive or judicial, when these are subversive of the fundamental rights specified in the amendment. Positive rights and privileges are undoubtedly secured by the fourteenth amendment; but they are secured by way of prohibition against state laws and state proceedings affecting those rights and privileges, and by power given to congress to legislate for the purpose of carrying such prohibition into effect; and such legislation must necessarily be predicated upon such supposed state laws or state proceedings, and be directed to the correction of their operation and effect. A quite full discussion of this aspect of the amendment may be found in *U. S. v. Cruikshank*, 92 U.S. 542; *Virginia v. Rives*, 100 U.S. 313, and *Ex parte Virginia,* Id. 339. — *Civil Rights Cases*, 109 U.S. 3, 11-12. (See page 131.)

In short, this passage is saying that the amendment grants Congress the authority *only* to prohibit states from impairing the rights of U.S. citizens, *not* to *grant* rights for U.S. citizens within the several states. That said, *can* Title 42, Chapter 21 create any rights? When the actual text of it is examined with that question in mind, the answer is obviously "no." Yet, it is commonly presumed that it does create rights, or at least a protection of rights. We are not convinced it actually does either. As far as it relates to the jurisdictions of each of the several states, it is as unenforceable as the 14th Amendment itself. Let's analyze Title 42, Chapter 21 to see if the equality it purports to assure is anything more than mere illusion.

The very first section, §1981, is entitled *"Equal rights under the law."* The first paragraph reads:

> (a) Statement of equal rights
> All persons within the jurisdiction of the United States shall have the same right in every State and Territory to make and enforce contracts, to sue, be parties, give evidence, and to the full and equal benefit of all laws and proceedings for the security of persons and property as is enjoyed by white citizens, and shall be subject to like punishment, pains, penalties, taxes, licenses, and exactions of every kind, and to no other.

Note that this provision applies *only* to "persons *within* the jurisdiction of the United States."[39]   Now, we know such "persons" to be the 14th Amendment citizens of the United States. Therefore, this paragraph does not apply to the citizens of a *state* because the federal government does not control the power of the state governments over the rights of *its own citizens*, as ruled in the *Slaughter-House Cases*, 83 U.S. 36, 77 (see page 277).

Section 1981 then goes on to state that these persons "...shall have the same right in every State and Territory...as is enjoyed by *white citizens*...." First of all, by comparing the rights of citizens of the United States with the rights of "white citizens," this paragraph again confirms the fact that *the law* considers white citizens to be *different* from citizens of the United States—i.e., white citizens are not citizens of the United States. If white citizens were "citizens of the United States," there would be no basis for setting the rights of citizens of the United States equal to the rights of white citizens. This, of course, is consistent with *Van Valkenburg v. Brown*, in which the California Supreme Court ruled that white people do not owe their status of citizenship to the 14th Amendment, and with everything else we have studied thus far. We feel the fact that this racial distinction is made in current, published law is outrageous. If you ask us, it is counterproductive to the achievement of truly equal rights under the law.

---

[39] The term "United States," in many of its appearances in the United States Code, is defined as the District of Columbia and the U.S. territories and possessions, *not* the several states of the Union. See, for instance, 18 U.S.C. 3077(4) and 26 U.S.C. 7701(a)(9). Even state codes reflect this meaning. For example, current California Commercial Code §9307(h) declares, "The United States is located in the District of Columbia."

Next, the federal government pretends, in §1981, to grant these rights "in every State." But how can it do this when the United States Supreme Court, in the *Slaughter-House Cases*, has already ruled that it cannot "control the power of the State governments over the rights of its own citizens?"

Finally, let's look at the first item in the "list" of rights that §1981 alleges to confer: "to make and enforce contracts." On this matter, the United States Supreme Court has already ruled as, follows[40]:

> Take the subject of contracts, for example. The constitution prohibited the states from passing any law impairing the obligation of contracts. *This did not give to congress power to provide laws for the general enforcement of contracts*; nor power to invest the courts of the United States with jurisdiction over contracts, so as to enable parties to sue upon them in those courts. — *Civil Rights Cases*, 109 U.S. 3, 12. [*emphasis* added] (See page 131.)

Pursuant to this ruling, the provision in §1981 alleged to grant the U.S. citizen the right "to make and enforce contracts" almost certainly cannot be enforced.

The next section, Title 42, §1982, deals specifically with "Property rights of citizens." It states:

> All citizens of the United States shall have the same right, in every State and Territory, as is enjoyed by white citizens thereof to inherit, purchase, lease, sell, hold, and convey real and personal property. (See page 117.)

Again, a federal law is *highlighting* a racial distinction and emphasizing that white citizens have property rights that citizens of the United States otherwise do not. Does the *emphasis* on the racial distinction assist in the implementation of racial equality? Our view is that it does not. To our knowledge, there are no longer any laws in any of the states that allege rights or privileges "for whites only." So why does the language of these federal laws still make these distinctions, as if there are still "whites only" laws that must be overcome? Of course, we know that the property rights of white citizens are *unalienable*, while the "civil rights" of

---

[40] *The Civil Rights Cases* (*U.S. v. Singleton*) 109 U.S. 3, is cited in the note of 42 U.S.C. §1984 (see page 118), confirming that the ruling in the *Civil Rights Cases* is still considered valid.

citizens of the United States can be taken away at the whim of Congress. We believe that *this* is the purpose for this distinction. Isn't it time that the property rights of *all* people be acknowledged as unalienable, regardless of race, or any other distinction? We believe it is.

The most puzzling section in Title 42, Chapter 21 may be §2000a, "Prohibition against discrimination or segregation in places of public accommodation." This section states:

> (a) Equal access
> All persons shall be entitled to the <u>full and equal enjoyment of the goods, services, facilities, privileges, advantages, and accommodations of any place of public accommodation,</u> as defined in this section, without discrimination or segregation on the ground of race, color, religion, or national origin. [<u>emphasis</u> added] (See page 124.)

To make the necessary point here we need to revisit, and make a direct comparison with the text of the first section of the 1875 Civil Rights Act, 18 Stat. 335, which states:

> *Be it enacted by the Senate and House of Representatives of the United States of America in Congress assembled,* That all persons within the jurisdiction of the United States shall be entitled to the <u>full and equal enjoyment of the accommodations, advantages, facilities, and privileges of inns, public conveyances on land and water, theaters, and other places of public amusement;</u> subject only to the conditions and limitations established by law, and applicable alike to citizens of every race and color, regardless of any previous condition of servitude. [<u>emphasis</u> added] (See page 107.)

The similarity between the 1875 Civil Rights Act and 42 U.S.C §2000a is unmistakable. The notes under Title 42 §1984, acknowledge that Section 1 of the 1875 Civil Rights Act was ruled *unconstitutional* by the *Civil Rights Cases*, 109 U.S. 3 (see page 118). How, then, can Title 42, §2000a, in effect, repeat what was stated in 18 Stat. 335, §1 without also being unconstitutional?! If, as we have shown above, the subject matter of Title 42, Chapter 21 is no more *constitutionally* enforceable than earlier attempts to apply the 14th Amendment, how can the current application of Title 42, Chapter 21 be taking place?!

The answer to this is really quite simple and fits right into the context of all that we have revealed in this book. Notwithstanding the apparent unconstitutionality of Title 42, Chapter 21, virtually *everyone* who has ever been deemed in violation of its provisions has claimed to be a "citizen of the United States" and therefore *placed himself* within the jurisdiction of these sections of federal law.

We must therefore conclude that a "citizen of a state" who understands how to effectively establish that he is *not* a 14th Amendment "citizen of the United States" would be able to violate Title 42, Chapter 21, challenge the constitutionality of the law by citing the *Civil Rights Cases*, and have any case against him dismissed. Of course, we are not advocating that anyone do this. We say this only to demonstrate that Title 42, Chapter 21 does not provide any true grant or protection of rights for those it purports to assist.

The illusion of equality created by Title 42, Chapter 21 can be summarized as follows:

A) It does not actually create any rights.
B) It *emphasizes* racial distinctions that are purported as having long since been erased.
C) It presumes that, without this law, non-whites do not have the same rights as "white citizens."
D) It is no more constitutional within the several states of the Union than the Civil Rights Act of 1875, 18 Stat. 335.

Thus, the "two classes of citizenship" that exist as a result of the 14th Amendment actually *prevent* the realization of true equality under the law. And Title 42, Chapter 21 creates nothing more than an *illusion of equality*.

Having demonstrated that the subject matter of Title 42, Chapter 21 does not stand up to constitutional scrutiny, we now revisit the question we asked at the head of this chapter: Why does Chapter 21 of this title exist at all? One would think, because the subject matter is clearly outside the legislative authority granted to Congress by the Constitution, that Chapter 21 would have long ago been struck down by the United States Supreme Court. Recognizing that is hasn't, our question now becomes "Why not?"

The short answer is: Title 42 is "law" only within the District of Columbia, and *not* within the several states of the Union. In other words, Title 42 "gets away with" these unconstitutional provisions because it isn't intended to apply within the several states of the Union, and therefore is not subject to standard constitutional constraints.

If this isn't immediately understandable, reference to Title 1, Section 204(a), should provide clarification. Of the fifty titles of the United States Code, some twenty-two apply in the several states of the Union. The rest govern only the District of Columbia and the U.S. territories and possessions. Section 204(a) sets forth which titles of the code apply where throughout the land:

> **Sec. 204.—Codes and Supplements as evidence of the laws of United States and District of Columbia; citation of Codes and Supplements**
>
> In all courts, tribunals, and public offices of the United States, at home or abroad, of the District of Columbia, and of each State, Territory, or insular possession of the United States—
>
> (a) United States Code.—[1] The matter set forth in the edition of the Code of Laws of the United States current at any time shall, together with the then current supplement, if any, establish *prima facie the laws of the United States*, general and permanent in their nature, in force on the day preceding the commencement of the session following the last session the legislation of which is included: Provided, however, That [2] *whenever titles of such Code shall have been enacted into positive law* the text thereof shall be legal evidence of the laws therein contained, in all the courts of the United States, the *several States*, and the Territories and insular possessions of the United States. [*emphasis* added]

This language is very challenging to understand at first blush, but can be sorted out by examining it clause by clause. In clause [2] of paragraph (a) above, note that titles enacted into positive law[41] represent legal evidence of the law in three different places: "the United States," "the several States," and "the Territories and insular possessions of the United States." The first thing we notice here is that both "the United States" and "the several States" are mentioned in this list of places. This makes clear the fact that the "United States" is different from the "several States,"

---

[41] Positive law. Law actually and specifically enacted or adopted by proper authority for the government of an organized jural society. — *Black's Law Dictionary*, 6th Edition, page 1162.

at least in this code section. If they were one and the same, they would not both be mentioned. For those who had not, up to this point, recognized this distinction, a review of the ruling by the United States Supreme Court in *Hooven & Allison Co. v. Evatt*[42] should provide enlightenment. It held that the term "United States" can refer to federal territory (i.e. the District of Columbia and the U.S. possessions) as distinct from the several states of the Union. As we noted in footnote 39, "United States" is expressly defined as federal territory in several sections of the United States Code, and also in the California Code. This distinction will play an important role in a moment.

Now look at clause [1] of paragraph (a) above. By a somewhat odd (and perhaps intentionally deceptive) construction, it describes all the titles which have *not* been enacted into positive law: They constitute merely "prima facie"[43] law, and apply only in one place: "the United States." Of course, we know from examining clause [2] that "United States" in this code section means the District of Columbia, not the several states of the Union.

With this in mind, we now need only determine into which clause of paragraph (a) above Title 42 falls. For this we refer to the "Notes on Sec. 204," which tell us which titles have been enacted into positive law. These notes are too voluminous to quote here, but the Preface of the United States Code gives a succinct list of these titles. It says:

> Titles 1, 3, 4, 5, 9, 10, 11, 13, 14, 17, 18, 23, 28, 31, 32, 35, 37, 38, 39, 44, 46, and 49 have been revised, codified, and enacted into positive law and the text thereof is legal evidence of the laws therein contained. *The matter contained in the other titles of the Code is prima facie evidence of the laws.* [emphasis added]

Note that Title 42 is *not* amongst the list of titles enacted into

---

[42] "The term 'United States' may be used in any one of several senses. It may be merely the name of a sovereign occupying the position analogous to that of other sovereigns in the family of nations. It may designate the territory over which the sovereignty of the United States extends, or it may be the collective name of the states which are united by and under the Constitution." — *Hooven & Allison Co. v. Evatt*, 324 U.S. 652, 671 (1944)

[43] **Prima facie**. Lat. At first sight; on the first appearance; on the face of it; so far as can be judged from the first disclosure; presumably; a fact presumed to be true unless disproved by some evidence to the contrary. — *Black's Law Dictionary*, 6th Edition, page 1189. "Prima facie law" only appears to be law "at first sight" or "on the face of it"; a court could require proof of the statutes (positive law) underlying prima facie law.

positive law. It must, therefore, be one which is merely "prima facie" law. Thus, it applies only in "the United States"—i.e. the District of Columbia. In other words, it is not even purported by the United States Code itself to be law in the "several States!" That's why it can contain provisions that would clearly be unconstitutional in the several states without risk of being struck down. It also confirms that Title 42, Chapter 21 does not and cannot be construed to govern state citizens in the several states of the Union, and makes clear once again that the equality purported by this title is merely an illusion.

∽ CHAPTER 9 ∾

Opposing The Requirement

There is no doubt that the government has intentionally and specifically engineered the requirement to claim citizenship of the United States.   Through various actions at law, we have personally mounted opposition to this requirement, and have been met with formidable resistance by both government attorneys and the judges in the courts. In order to illustrate just how strenuously the government fights anyone trying to oppose "The Requirement," the following section chronicles a test case initiated by Thomas Marvin; Maxwell.

Thomas Marvin; Maxwell v. Steven Grouley[44]

On April 12, 2000, I filed suit against Steven Grouley, Director of Motor Vehicles in California, challenging the requirement to claim "U.S. citizenship" on the Driver License Application.   My cause of action alleged "subornation of

---

[44] This account is presented for educational purposes only. Do not attempt this, or any other legal action, without appropriate training and expertise.

perjury," because the California Driver's License Application at that time required an applicant to declare "U.S. citizenship" *under penalty of perjury.*[45] For myself, a citizen of California who is not a descendant of a former slave, if I declared that I am a "U.S. citizen," it would be a false statement. Therefore, such a declaration under penalty of perjury would be a serious violation of law—a felony. The case number was BC228126 in the superior court for Los Angeles county, California (refer to pages 357-410 for complete documentation of this case).

The term "perjury" is commonly used and understood to mean "making a false statement under oath," which includes any such statement in writing. However, because "*subornation of perjury*" is not a common term, a little explanation is in order. For this, I refer to the California Penal Code, which provides a functional definition:

> §127. Every person who willfully procures another person to commit perjury is guilty of subornation of perjury, and is punishable in the same manner as he would be if personally guilty of the perjury so procured.

Thus, in California, anyone who willfully induces another to commit perjury has committed the felony of subornation of perjury. All of the citizens of California who are *not* 14th Amendment U.S. citizens, who have been deceived into claiming U.S. citizenship on a Driver's License Application, have unwittingly committed perjury, feloniously "suborned" by the California Department of Motor Vehicles in its processing of the application.

As the first step in initiating this court case, I applied for a California Driver's License using a Driver's License Application which I had altered to reflect my state citizenship. I did this by deleting certain parts of the form with "white out" and typing in information which I could honestly declare as true under penalty of perjury. Changes of this kind were

---

[45] As indicated in Chapter 5, in the wake of this case, and, we believe, as a result of our various other efforts against the DMV, as of August 2001, the California Driver's License Application no longer required an applicant to make direct certification that he or she is a "U.S. citizen." However, the application still requires a Social Security Number, which still directly imposes "The Requirement." All references to the California Driver License Application in this chapter will be to the older form as illustrated in the appendix.

required on both the front and the back of the form.[46] I have included a copy of the actual altered application in the appendix on pages 366 & 367.

On the front of the application, at the far right, in section 2, I whited out "Social Security Number" and replaced it with "N/A for national." I will explain this change in greater detail a little later, but as you will recall from Chapter 5, only "U.S. citizens" are eligible for a Social Security Number.

Again, on the front of the application, at the far right of the third line of section 2, in the box for the number and street where I lived at that time, I whited out the words "Residence Address" and replaced them with "Home Location." As discussed in Chapter 4, U.S. citizens must establish "residence" in a state in order to claim the pseudo-state citizenship created by the 14th Amendment.[47] When an applicant enters information as a "residence address," the government makes the presumption that he "knows" his citizenship is based upon that "residency," and that he owes his allegiance to the United States government, rather than to the state within which he lives. As a citizen of California, I do not have a "residence address" because I do not *need* to establish *residency*. My state citizenship is a birthright.

Eliminating the references to the "Social Security Number" and "Residence Address" was important, but the most critical change was made on the back of the form in the last paragraph of the "Certifications" section. The original language of this paragraph stated:

> I certify that I am a U.S. citizen or a qualified alien....[48] (Refer to page 369 for an original unaltered application.)

I replaced that wording with the following:

> I certify that I am a national as defined in the

---

[46] Some of the changes on the Driver's License application are not directly relative to the subject matter of this book and therefore will not be specifically referenced or discussed.

[47] See page 31, to review the complete discussion of 14th Amendment pseudo-state citizenship.

[48] (Continued from above) ...pursuant to the Personal Responsibility and Work Opportunity Reconciliation Act of 1996 (8 U.S.C. §1621 et seq.) and therefore eligible for a commercial license, a noncommercial fire fighter license, a special certificate, a training document, or a clearance document.

Nationality Act of 1940, 54 Stat. 1137,[49] and 8 U.S.C. §1101(a)(21), and that I am expressly not a citizen of the United States as created by and defined in the Fourteenth Amendment to the federal constitution (See page 367)

With these three pieces of information changed, I could then sign the application without falsely identifying myself as a 14ᵗʰ Amendment citizen of the United States and committing perjury.

When I took this application to the Department of Motor Vehicles, I expressly disclosed these changes to the clerk, expecting the application to be rejected *because* of the changes. As it turned out, the manager at the DMV office accepted the application because it was, in his words, "an attempt to comply."

The acceptance of this application on which I had not only correctly identified my state citizenship, but expressly stated that I was *not* the U.S. citizen, was a real step forward.[50] However, even after accepting an application that correctly identified me as a "state citizen" rather than a "U.S. citizen,"[51] the DMV still refused to issue the driver license without a Social Security Number, and would only issue a "temporary permit" (see page 370). As we saw in Chapter 5, *only* U.S. citizens and qualified aliens are eligible for a Social Security Number. Therefore, as a state citizen, I can neither obtain a Social Security Number nor provide the DMV with one without adopting U.S. citizenship and waiving the inalienable rights guaranteed to me by my state constitution.

In pursuing an action such as this, it is very important to establish certain things in the complaint. On the caption page at lines 10-11 (see page 357), I clarify that I am "one of the people of California," with a footnote citing the *Walther v. Rabolt* case (see page 357) that defines the people as those "born on the soil."

In paragraph 2 of the complaint (see pages 357-358), I include a detailed description of who I am, a statement that I live "on the Land" ("soil") in California, and a statement by which I reserve all of my rights. With these items expressly declared in the complaint, the defendant would now have to expressly prove at trial that these statements are not true in order to treat me as if I were a U.S. citizen under the 14th Amendment.

Paragraphs 4-9 (see pages 358-359) comprise a "statement of facts" establishing the circumstances with regard to my Driver License Application.

Paragraphs 10-11 (see pages 359-360) cite and briefly describe some of the court cases that were previously discussed in this book, establishing the foundation in law of the existence of the two classes of citizenship.

Finally, paragraphs 17-20 (see page 362) establish the details of the Social Security application.[52]

In response to my complaint, the defendant Steve Grouley, Director of Motor Vehicles, filed a demurrer[53] (refer to pages 377-383 for the complete document). This demurrer does a very artful dance around the issues, never directly addressing my assertions concerning the two classes of citizenship, even though they are the foundation of my complaint. Note that on page 5 of the demurrer (see page 381), within all of his argument relative to the Social Security Number, not once does he address the citizenship issue nor try to controvert my position, nor do the court cases he cites deal with the citizenship issues that I raised. In other words, Mr. Grouley's demurrer is written as if I had not raised the issue of citizenship in the complaint at all. Yet this was the central issue of my complaint!

Without addressing the issue of the two classes of citizenship, at the bottom of page 4 of his demurrer, Mr. Grouley cites California Vehicle Code §1653.5(a) (see page 380), and though he does not quote the actual language of the code section, he claims it to be the statutory authority for the requirement of the Social Security Number on the Driver's License Application.

On page 3 of my Opposition to the Demurrer (see page 387), I do quote the language of §1653.5, as follows:

> 1653.5(a) Every form prescribed by the department for use by an applicant for the issuance or

> renewal by the department of a driver's license or identification card pursuant to Division 6 (commencing with Section 12500) shall contain a *section* for the applicant's social security account number. [*emphasis* added]

Note that this section only requires the form to have a *space* for the number. There is no language requiring an applicant to have the number. Remember, this is the code section Mr. Grouley cited as his authority to require a Social Security Number *from the applicant*, and it is completely impotent in that regard. However, to be fair and complete, there is more to §1653.5 than just the paragraph (a) cited by Mr. Grouley. The balance of the section states:

> (b) Every form prescribed by the department for use by an applicant for the issuance, renewal, or transfer of the registration or certificate of title to a vehicle shall contain a section for the applicant's driver's license or identification card number.

> (c) Any person who submits to the department a form that, pursuant to subdivision (a), contains a section for the applicant's social security account number, or pursuant to subdivision (b), the applicant's driver's license or identification card number, if any, shall furnish the appropriate number in the space provided.

> (d) *The department shall not complete any application that does not include the applicant's social security account number or driver's license or identification card number as required by subdivision (c).* [*emphasis* added]

> (e) An applicant's social security account number shall not be included by the department on any driver's license, identification card, registration, certificate of title, or any other document issued by the department.

> (f) Notwithstanding any other provision of law, information regarding an applicant's social security account number, obtained by the department pursuant to this section, is not a public record and shall not be disclosed by the department except for any of the following purposes:

> (1) Responding to a request for information from

an agency operating pursuant to, and carrying out the provisions of, Part A (Aid to Families with Dependent Children), or Part D (Child Support and Establishment of Paternity), of Subchapter IV of Chapter 7 of Title 42 of the United States Code.

(2) Implementation of Section 12419.10 of the Government Code.

(3) Responding to information requests from the Franchise Tax Board for the purpose of tax administration.

Paragraphs (c) and (d) above require close scrutiny. Note that the wording in these paragraphs *could* lead an applicant to presume that a Social Security Number is required, but that is *not* what it *actually* says. Paragraph (c) contains the qualifier "if any," allowing for the possibility that an applicant may not have any of these numbers to furnish. Lest you think that "if any" refers only to "the applicant's driver's license or identification card number," careful analysis of the sentence structure will show that it applies equally to the "social security account number." Further, the "mandatory" statement in this text merely requires that the applicant "shall furnish the *appropriate* number in the space provided." However, if the applicant is a state citizen who doesn't and cannot have a Social Security Number, then such a number would *not* be *appropriate*, and thus not required by this code section.

After all that, paragraph (d) *appears* to unconditionally prevent the DMV from accepting an application that does not contain these numbers. But even that is illusory, as it depends upon paragraph (c), which does not apply to the state citizen. As is evident, although the language in this section does not expressly require a Social Security Number, it is craftily worded to induce the lay reader to presume that everyone is required to provide the number on the application.

Ultimately, the judge sustained Mr. Grouley's demurrer and dismissed the suit, in clear violation of the law and my rights as one of the people of California. Nevertheless, the case is instructive, and I urge you to take the time to read through the remainder of the documents I filed in it (see pages 391-406), as well as the transcript of the hearing on the demurrer (see page 407-410.) They clearly demonstrate complete and consistent "stonewalling" on the issues I have raised. You will see first hand just how aggressively the government resists the efforts of anyone who tries to "escape" the inferior U.S. citizenship.

My research has continued, and I have discovered further foundation for my position on these issues, which will be presented in a new case against the California DMV: The driver's license application alleges that "the authority to collect the social security number is 42 U.S.C. §405." However, the Privacy Act of 1974, as codified in 5 U.S.C. §552a, *prohibits* the requirement of a Social Security Number unless there was a law in place prior to January 1, 1975 establishing such a requirement. There was no such law in place in California prior to January 1, 1975. Further, 31 C.F.R.[54] §1.36 lists all the government agencies that are exempt from the Privacy Act of 1974. The California DMV is not in the list. Nor is the DMV for any other state. Additionally there are no federal regulations implementing the requirement of Social Security Numbers on driver's license applications as alleged in 42 U.S.C. §405. You will recall from Chapter 8 that Title 42 is not "positive law." Title 5, the title that restricts the requirement of a Social Security Number, *is* positive law. The alleged "authority" in 42 U.S.C. §405, supposedly requiring a Social Security Number for a California driver license, is pure "smoke and mirrors."

* * * * *

The elements argued in this test case are supported by two key factors: 1) There is no law requiring the acquisition of a Social Security Number. We challenge *anyone* to prove us wrong on this point. Any such requirement would, of necessity, have to be a *federal* law, since Social Security is a *federal program*. The

Social Security Administration itself will tell you that the acquisition of an SSN is purely *voluntary*. In fact, it *must* be voluntary, because getting the number requires the applicant to waive his unalienable rights as well as other inherent and vested rights, and such a waiver of rights *must* be voluntary or it is null and void.[55] And 2) Although the California Code does not *expressly* acknowledge the true state citizenship that pre-existed the 14th Amendment, one part of the Code does distinguish "the people" from "persons." This distinction serves as further statutory confirmation of the two classes of citizenship. Unfortunately, if you don't already understand the fraud, you would not recognize it.

This distinction is found in the California Government Code. However, it must be assembled in pieces like a jig-saw puzzle. The first piece can be found at §100, which states:

> §100. The Sovereignty of the State resides in the *people* thereof, and all writs and process shall issue in their name. [*emphasis* added]

Note that this section identifies "the people" as the source of the state's sovereignty. Remember, the California state constitution recognizes that it is "the *people*" that possess the inalienable rights acknowledged in Article I, Section 1; and Article II, Section 1 declares that "All political power is inherent in the *people*." The next piece of the puzzle is §240 which remains consistent with §100 when it states:

> §240. The *people*, as a political body, consist of:
>
> (a) Citizens who are electors.
>
> (b) Citizens not electors. [*emphasis* added]

Note that the term "persons" is not used in either of these two sections. However, "persons" is the only term used in California Government Code at §241, which states:

> §241. The citizens of the State are:
>
> (a) All *persons born* in the State and *residing* within it, except the children of transient aliens and of alien public ministers and consuls.

> (b) All *persons born* out of the State who are citizens of the United States and *residing* within the State. [*emphasis* added]

The appearance of the words "citizens of the State" in this code section may seem to contradict what we stated above—that the California Code does not expressly acknowledge true state citizenship—but it does not. Remember, true "state citizens" are "the people," and the subparagraphs of this section refer only to "persons," even though the word "people" *would have been grammatically correct.* This use of "persons" instead of "people" tips us off to the fact that the "citizens of the State" alluded to in this code section are merely 14th Amendment citizens. In this regard, the stated place of birth and the fact that the word "residing" accompanies the word "persons" become significant. To best appreciate this significance, we need to make a parallel comparison of §241 with the 14th Amendment:

✔ 14th Amendment:

> All persons *born...in the United States...*and of the state wherein they *reside...*

✔ Government Code §241:

> (a) ...persons *born in the State* and *residing within it...*
> (b) ...persons *born out of the State...*and *residing...*

First, you will recall from *Walther v. Rabolt* (see page 356) that the *people*—true state citizens—are those "born on the soil." Though the "persons" in Government Code §241(a) are specified as "born in the State," the use of the word "person" is a clear indication that they are not "the people." And the fact that §241(b) openly states that "citizens of the State" can also be "citizens of the United States" (who happen to have been born elsewhere) confirms that what is being defined here are 14th Amendment citizens.

Next, the qualification imposed by §241 of "residing within" the State, as provided originally by the 14th Amendment, clearly identifies such persons as 14th Amendment citizens.

In law, the people of a state are not referred to as residents!

There is a reason for that. Being "born on the soil," their *citizenship* is a *birthright*. They do not need to *earn* their state citizenship by establishing *residency*. In contrast, as we have already observed, the citizen of the United States gains such pseudo-state citizenship *only by establishing residency* pursuant to the 14th Amendment.

Finally, the phrase "in the State" has a peculiar and telling meaning. It is defined in the California Revenue and Taxation Code at §§6017 and 11205 as follows:

> 6017. "In this State" or "in the State" means within the exterior limits of the State of California and *includes all territory within these limits owned by or ceded to the United States of America.*[56] [emphasis added]

When the haze of legalese clears, you realize that "in the State" refers only to federal territory (which we have learned is called the "United States") not to the land ("soil") of the state. Thus, "born *in the State*" is equivalent to "born in the United States," and the "citizens of the State" defined in §241 are not "the people," but federal "citizens of the United States." If you have found the process of deciphering these provisions of the California Code to be mind-numbingly complicated, recognize that the Code was designed to discourage you from understanding it and learning the truth. This is more evidence of the identity fraud we expose in this book, hidden by convoluted language.

We are so confident that our analysis is completely correct that we challenge *anyone* to find a court case or statute, be it federal or state, that expressly controverts the statements we have made concerning the use of *"the people"* and *"persons"* as they apply to the two distinct classes of citizenship.

The bottom line is that the government has engineered things like the Social Security Number and Driver License Application to coerce and require everyone to give up all their rights, just to be able to function within society. In order to get a driver license in California, you are required to claim that you are the *inferior* U.S. citizen. To get a bank account, you must divulge a Social Security Number and claim to be the *inferior* U.S. citizen. The same thing goes for business licenses, contractor's licenses, registering to vote, and many other activities that people would consider necessary in their lives. Parents are even coerced into depriving their children of all their unalienable rights *at birth* by the fiction that a Social Security Number is *required* for their child. The children are never given a choice. Their rights are gone from day one, and they grow up without a clue.

We believe this trend can be reversed, but our efforts alone are not enough correct this problem. We urge those of you who read this book to learn all you can about your unalienable rights and become part of the effort to end the fraud and reverse the pattern before it is too late. We are not ready to abandon what began with the Declaration of Independence:

> "We hold these truths to be self-evident, that all men are created equal, that they are endowed by their Creator with certain unalienable Rights, that among these are Life, Liberty and the pursuit of Happiness. ... That whenever any Form of Government becomes destructive of these ends, it is the Right of the People to alter or to abolish it,...

Therefore, the next chapter is our proposal for a real solution to end the fraud.

❧ CHAPTER 10 ❧

The Solution

On the cover of this book, we wrote, "We the People of the united states of America are being deprived of the vision that began with the Declaration of Independence."

That vision, as Thomas Jefferson expressed it in that brave document, is:

> "We hold these truths to be self-evident, *that all men are created equal*, that they are endowed by their Creator with certain unalienable Rights, that among these are Life, Liberty and the pursuit of Happiness." [*emphasis* added]

In the 21st Century, we believe it is time to recognize that Mr. Jefferson's words—"all men"—are intended to include every member of the human species, irrespective of gender or race, and we propose to spark that recognition within the legal document that founded this nation.

In the first nine chapters of this book, we have shown how the government has, in effect, *prevented* the realization of true equality for all people through identity fraud made possible by the 14th Amendment.

When the government acts with clear disregard for the ideals expressed by Thomas Jefferson, as it has in perpetrating the identity fraud we reveal in these pages, do we not have a remedy for that? We believe that we do. Mr. Jefferson went on to write:

> "That whenever any Form of Government becomes *destructive of these ends*, it is the *Right of the People to alter or to abolish it.*" [*emphasis* added]

We are *certain* that government officials would argue that the loss of rights that occur as a result of the identity fraud is balanced out by the resulting "public safety" for which the government so publicly proclaims responsibility.

In answer to that, we remind you of the words spoken over two hundred years ago by a brilliant American sage named Benjamin Franklin: "They that can give up essential liberty to obtain a little temporary safety deserve neither liberty nor safety."[57] As we have seen, the government hopes you will give up the unalienable rights Thomas Jefferson envisioned for you in exchange for a little temporary safety.

On August 28, 1963, Martin Luther King, Jr gave his famous "I Have A Dream" speech in Washington, DC. Do you remember what he said on that day?

> I have a dream that one day this nation will rise up and live out the true meaning of its creed: "We hold these truths to be self-evident, that all men are created equal."

On January 20, 1960, two and a half years before Martin Luther King, Jr spoke those memorable words, John F. Kennedy said at his inaugural address:

> [T]he same revolutionary beliefs for which our fore-bears fought are still at issue around the globe, the belief that the rights of man come not from the generosity of the state but from the hand of God. *We dare not forget* today that we are the heirs of that first revolution. Let the word go forth from this time and place, to friend and foe alike, that the torch has passed to a new generation of Americans, born in this century, tempered by war, disciplined by a hard and bitter peace, proud of our ancient heritage, and *unwilling to witness or permit the slow undoing of those human rights* to which this nation has always been committed and to which we are still committed today at home and around the world. [*emphasis* added]

---

[57] From An Historical Review of the Constitution and Government of Pennsylvania.

John F. Kennedy was taken from us 1000 days later—less than three months after Martin Luther King, Jr's speech—and it would seem that we have all forgotten! We the people of the united states of America have allowed our unalienable rights to be *slowly undone.* For the most part, the government has merely taken advantage of our indifference and ignorance of the law.

Our rights are still there, waiting to be *reclaimed.* But in order to redeem these rights—our *birthrights*—we first must remember them and what they mean to us. Only then can we demand them. We also must know that, in order to demand our rights, *we* must first identify ourselves as "the *people.*"

The key word here is *"we."* Unless a great number of people wake up and start demanding the unalienable rights with which they were born, the destruction of those rights may very well become permanent. The government's resistance to our claim of fundamental rights is steadfast and formidable, but *only* because *so few people* are demanding them.

We believe there is a solution. The "ideal" solution, of course, would be to simply repeal the first section of the 14th Amendment and be done with it. However, that would be too disruptive. The 14th Amendment, and all the federal welfare that has been put in place in connection with it, has been with us for far too long. Too many lives depend on things like Social Security and other federal programs that are designed exclusively for the 14th Amendment citizen of the United States. Therefore, we must find a solution that does not upset or destroy people's lives.

The solution we propose requires an entirely new amendment to the federal constitution that is consistent with the rest of that document and accomplishes two objectives: *First,* this new amendment must provide *full disclosure* of the two *different* classes of citizenship; *Second,* it must provide a truly level playing field for everyone, so there is real equality under the law for all without exception.

The amendment we propose comprises eight sections, each having an express purpose and function. Below is the text of the proposed amendment, broken down section by section, with commentary on the purpose and function of each individual section. The complete, consecutive text of the proposed amendment, as we envision it, can be found on pages 412-413 of the Appendix. The amendment would, of necessity, begin by repealing the first section of the 14th Amendment:

> SECTION 1. The first section of the fourteenth article of amendment to the Constitution of the United States is hereby repealed.

With this blight excised, we can begin rebuilding. A review of the Constitution of the United States will show that nowhere in that founding document are the rights it protects identified as "unalienable." In the federal arena, this word is found only in the Declaration of Independence. But the Declaration of Independence, as venerable as that document is, is not law in and of itself, nor does it provide a foundation for any law. As a result, a constitutional guarantee of *unalienable* rights has never been established for the United States. We intend to correct this omission with Section 2 of our proposed amendment, and we aim to include *all* Americans in its embrace:

> SECTION 2. We hold these truths to be self-evident, that all people are created equal, that they are endowed by their Creator with certain unalienable rights, that among these are life, liberty, privacy, and the pursuit of happiness. All people born or naturalized in one of the several states are expressly so endowed with these unalienable rights, and shall enjoy citizenship of the state in which they are born or make their permanent abode, with rights protected by the constitution and laws of that state, as well as the Bill of Rights amended to this constitution, and with all other rights preserved to the states or to the people by this constitution, subject to the provisions of Section 3 of this Amendment.

Now, because government benefits have become so entrenched in our society and so many people have become utterly dependent upon them, the new amendment must contain provisions to allow a "status quo" for those who are financially "stuck" with national (federal) citizenship and the welfare it provides, so as not to disrupt their lives. These provisions would allow those who prefer the "relative security" of national citizenship to take advantage of the safety net of government benefits and welfare programs available to them. However, anyone making this *choice* would be required to willingly and knowingly waive access to their unalienable rights in order to have this "relative security." Sections 3 of the proposed amendment would contain these provisions:

> SECTION 3. Upon reaching the age of majority, all people born or naturalized in one of the several states shall have the right to a voluntary choice of either: a) citizenship of the state in which he or she is born or makes his or her permanent abode; or, b) national citizenship of the United States whose rights shall be exclusively protected by this constitution and applicable federal law.

People born in the District of Columbia are not state citizens because they were not born on the land within the boundaries of one of the several states, and therefore they have no lawful means of claiming or acquiring the unalienable rights attendant with state citizenship. Section 4 of the proposed amendment would remedy this problem:

> SECTION 4. All people born within the boundaries of the District of Columbia shall be deemed as citizens of one of the states which ceded the land to form the seat of the federal government.

The citizenship of the inhabitants of the U.S. territories and possessions would also be fully disclosed, and the opportunity for state citizenship and access to unalienable rights would be made available to them by Section 5:

> SECTION 5. All people born within the boundaries of Puerto Rico, Guam, the Virgin Islands of the United States or any other applicable federal territory, shall have national citizenship of the United States, and shall be qualified to apply for naturalization as a citizen of one of the several states upon establishing permanent residency therein.

Because Section 1 of the proposed amendment repeals the first section of the 14th Amendment, our amendment must replace the prohibitions against abridgement by the states of the rights of national citizens. However, the new amendment must overcome certain problems encountered by the 14th Amendment. If you'll recall, the "privileges and immunities" clause of the 14th Amendment was unenforceable in part due to the complete lack of specificity as to what those "privileges and immunities" were. The new amendment must contain sufficient specificity to overcome these enforcement problems, and Section 6 is designed to do that with a clause equivalent to the 14th Amendment's "privileges and immunities" clause. This section would also expressly recognize the source of protection of the rights of state citizens:

> SECTION 6. Each of the several states shall retain sovereign control over the protection of the rights of its citizens. No state shall make or enforce any law that abridges the privileges and immunities of national citizenship of the United States, although particular privileges and immunities of national citizenship, as may be established by law, shall of necessity depend upon the establishment of permanent residency within a particular state.

Although the specificity we have placed in the prohibitions of the new amendment should translate into improved "privileges and immunities" for the national citizen, it is just a simple fact of life that "there is no such thing as a free lunch." Having a "guarantee" that the government is going to "take care of you" has a price. That price is a loss of some of the personal freedom and independence you could otherwise enjoy as a state citizen.

In addition to replacing the "privileges and immunities" clause of the 14th Amendment, we would need to replace the "due process" and "equal protection" clauses of that amendment. Section 7 would do this with equivalent clauses, again with enhanced specificity.

> SECTION 7. No state shall deprive any citizen of life, liberty, or property, without due process of law; nor shall any state make any law respecting any race, creed, ethnic background, or gender, so that each citizen of any one of the several states shall have equal protection under the laws of that state, including unfettered access to any declaration of rights or bill of rights applicable within that state, as well as unfettered access to all rights protected by this constitution within the federal jurisdiction where they are applicable.

Finally, the new amendment would have to contain an assurance that it is not meant to alter any other provision of the Constitution, plus enforcement and application clauses. This is supplied by Section 8:

> SECTION 8. Nothing in this Amendment shall be construed as amending or altering the effect of Article IV, Section 2, clause 1, of this constitution. The provisions of this Amendment shall apply to all people to whom it

> expressly applies that are born or naturalized after the ratification thereof as well as those who are alive at the time of its ratification. Congress shall have power to enforce, by appropriate legislation, the provisions of this article.

We must credit our Founding Fathers for having constructed such a sound instrument for the protection of our private rights. Think about it. This protection is so sound that in over two hundred years, the *only* way the "powers that be" who seek to rob us of our unalienable rights have been able to accomplish their objective has been to trick and deceive us into *"voluntarily" giving them up*! The foundation of our birthright is still there for us to reclaim . . . for now! How much longer will it be there if we do not do something to ensure its preservation? The question is more pressing than ever before.

Before reading this book, you probably *did not know* that you had waived all your unalienable rights. Now that you do, we encourage you to speak up and become part of an effort to amend the federal constitution. We need to keep alive the vision that began with the signing of the Declaration of Independence!

We urge you to write letters, make phone calls, and send faxes or e-mails to your representatives in Congress. Send them a copy of the amendment we have proposed and demand that they participate in the restoration and preservation of our rights. After all, that is what they were elected to do!

Appendix

The vast majority of the documents in this appendix are electronic versions, either downloaded from the Internet, or scanned and converted with OCR software. We have applied considerable diligence to ensure the accuracy of this reference material. If there are any typographical errors, they are likely to be obvious, and the actual word or correct spelling can easily be determined from the context. If you discover any such errors, we would certainly appreciate being informed so that we can make corrections in future printings.

In the following documents, you will occasionally see numbers in brackets, such as "**[100]**" or "**[109 U.S. 3, 47]**." The first of these represents the current page number in the original published volumes; the second represents both the court cite and the current page number. You will find such numbers throughout the court cases published on the Internet, and in secondary publications of the references.

We have used **bold** type to emphasize the passages of the court cases cited within the book in order to make them easy to locate in this appendix. However, we urge you to read as much of the complete texts of these court cases as you can possibly tolerate. We have found them to be very informative regarding the attitudes and thinking of the judges of earlier times and helpful in fully understanding their intentions with regard to many of their rulings. We do understand that "legal" writings have acquired a reputation for being "boring." However, when it comes to the subject of the preservation of our rights, we cannot allow it to be boring. It is our hope that you won't either.

Statute & Court Case Legend

જ્ઞે જ્ઞે જ્ઞે જ્ઞે જ્ઞે જ્ઞે જ્ઞે જ્ઞે જ્ઞે જ્ઞે જ્ઞે જ્ઞે જ્ઞે જ્ઞે જ્ઞે જ્ઞે

Statutes at Large   14 Stat. 27

United States Statutes at Large, Volume 14, page 27

Statutes at Large   18 Stat. 335

United States Statutes at Large, Volume 18, page 335

Statutes at Large   66 Stat. 163 §101(a)

United States Statutes at Large, Volume 66, page 163

42 U.S.C.

Title 42 of the United States Code

Civil Rights Cases, 109 U.S. 3 (1883)

United States Supreme Court Reports, Volume 109, page 3

Colgate v. Harvey, 296 U.S. 404 (1935)

United States Supreme Court Reports, Volume 296, page 404

Cory et al. v. Carter, 48 Ind. 327 (1874)

Indiana Reporter, Volume 48, page 327

Crosse v. Board of Elections, 243 Md. 555 (1966)

Maryland Reports, Volume 243, page 555

Escobedo v. State of California, 35 Cal.2d 870 (1950)

California Reports, Second Series, Volume 35, page 870

Ex Parte—Frank Knowles, 5 Cal. 300 (1855)

California Reports, Volume 5, page 300

Gardina v. Board of Registrars 160 Ala. 155 (1909)

Alabama Reporter, Volume 160, page 155

Jones v. Temmer, 829 F.Supp. 1226 (1993)

Federal Supplement, Volume 829, page 1226

K. Tashiro v. Jordan, 201 Cal. 236 (1927)

California Reports, Volume 201, page 236

Madden v. Kentucky, 309 U.S. 83 (1940)

United States Supreme Court Reports, Volume 309, page 83

People v. Brady, 40 Cal. 198 (1870)

California Reports, Volume 40, page 198

O'Connell v. Judnich , 71 Cal.App. 386 (1925)

California Appellate Reports, Volume 71, page 386

The Slaughter-House Cases, 83 U.S. 36 (1872)

United States Supreme Court Reports, Volume 83, page 36

Twining v. New Jersey, 211 U.S. 78 (1908)

United States Supreme Court Reports, Volume 211, page 78

U S v. Cruikshank, 92 U.S. 542 (1875)

United States Supreme Court Reports, Volume 92, page 542

United States v. Prudden, 424 F.2d 1021 (1970)

Federal Reporter, Second Series, Volume 424, page 1021

Van Valkenburg v. Brown, 43 Cal. 43 (1872)

California Reports, Volume 43, page 43

Walther v. Rabolt, 30 Cal. 185 (1866)

California Reports, Volume 30, page 185

Black s Law Dictionary, 7th Edition

[670]

fraud, *n.* 1. A knowing misrepresentation of the truth or concealment of a material fact to induce another to act to his or her detriment. • Fraud is usu. a tort, but in some cases (esp. when the conduct is willful) it may be a crime. 2. A misrepresentation made recklessly without belief in its truth to induce another person to act. 3. A tort arising from a knowing misrepresentation, concealment of material fact, or reckless misrepresentation made to induce another to act to his or her detriment. 4. Unconscionable dealing; esp., in contract law, the **[671]** unconscientious use of the power arising out of the parties' relative positions and resulting in an unconscionable bargain. — **fraudulent,** *adj.*

"[T]he use of the term fraud has been wider and less precise in the chancery than in the common-law courts. This followed necessarily from the remedies which they respectively administered. Common law gave damages for a wrong, and was compelled to define with care the wrong which furnished a cause of action. Equity refused specific performance of a contract, or set aside a transaction, or gave compensation where one party had acted unfairly by the other. Thus 'fraud' at common law is a false statement ... : fraud in equity has often been used as meaning unconscientious dealing — 'although, I think, unfortunately,' a great equity lawyer has said." William R. Anson, *Principles of the Law of Contract* 263 (Arthur L. Corbin ed., 3d Am. ed. 1919).

actual fraud. A concealment or false representation through a statement or conduct that injures another who relies on it in acting. — Also termed *fraud in fact; positive fraud; moral fraud.*

civil fraud. 1. FRAUD (3). 2. *Tax.* An intentional — but not. Willful — evasion of taxes. • The distinction between all intentional (i.e., civil) and willful (i.e., criminal) fraud is not always clear, but civil fraud carries only a monetary, non criminal penalty. Cf. *criminal fraud*; TAX EVASION.

common-law fraud. 1. See *promissory fraud.*

constructive fraud. 1. Unintentional deception or misrepresentation that causes injury to another. — Also termed *legal fraud; fraud in contemplation of law; equitable fraud.* 2. See *fraud in law.*

"The layman would probably rather be found guilty of fraud, for he can then say the court was wrong, than be found guilty of 'constructive fraud,' for he does not know what that means and he may doubt whether the court does either." Lon L. Fuller, Anatomy of the Law 12 (1968).

criminal fraud. 1. *Tax.* The willful evasion of taxes accomplished by filing a fraudulent tax return. • *Criminal fraud* subjects the offender to criminal penalties such as fines and imprisonment. Cf. *civil fraud*; TAX EVASION. 2. *Larceny by trick* under LARCENY.

election fraud. See ELECTION FRAUD.

extrinsic fraud. 1. Deception that is collateral to the issues being considered in the case; intentional misrepresentation or deceptive behavior outside the transaction itself (whether A contract or a lawsuit), depriving one party OF informed consent or full participation. • For example, a person might engage in extrinsic fraud by convincing a litigant not to hire counsel or answer by dishonestly saying the matter will not be pursued. — Also termed *collateral fraud.* 2. Deception that

92

prevents a person from knowing about or asserting certain rights.

fraud in contemplation of law. See *constructive fraud.*

fraud in fact. See *actual fraud.*

fraud in law. Fraud that is presumed under the circumstances, as when a debtor transfers assets and thereby impairs creditors' efforts to collect sums due. — Also termed constructive fraud.

fraud in the factum. Fraud occurring when a legal instrument as actually executed differs from the one intended for execution by the person who executes it, or when the instrument may have had no legal existence. • Compared to fraud in the inducement, fraud in the factum occurs only rarely, as when a blind person signs a mortgage when misleadingly told that it's just a letter. — Also termed *fraud in the execution; fraud in the making.* Cf. *fraud in the inducement.*

fraud in the inducement. Fraud occurring when a misrepresentation leads another to enter into a transaction with a false impression of the risks, duties, or obligations involved; an intentional misrepresentation of a material risk or duty reasonably relied on, thereby injuring the other party without vitiating the contract itself esp. about a fact relating to value. Cf. *fraud in the factum.*

fraud in the making. See *fraud in the factum.*

fraud on the court. A lawyer's or party's misconduct in a judicial proceeding so serious that it undermines or is intended to undermine the integrity of the proceeding. • Examples are bribery of a juror and introduction of fabricated evidence.

fraud on the market. 1. Fraud occurring when an issuer of securities gives out misinformation that affects the market price of stock, the result being that people who buy or sell are effectively misled even though they did not rely on the statement itself or anything derived from it other than the market price. 2. The securities-law claim based on such fraud. See FRAUD-ON-THE-MARKET PRINCIPLE.

insurance fraud. Fraud committed against an insurer, as when an insured lies on a policy application or fabricates a claim.

intrinsic fraud. Deception that pertains to an issue involved in an original action. • Examples include the use of fabricated evidence) a false return of service, perjured testimony [672], and false receipts or other commercial documents.

legal fraud. See *constructive fraud.*

mail fraud. An act of fraud using the U.S. Postal Service, as in making false representations through the mail to obtain an economic advantage. is USCA §§ 1341-1347.

moral fraud. See *actual fraud.*

positive fraud. See *actual fraud.*

promissory fraud. A promise to perform made when the promisor had no intention of performing the promise. — Also termed *common-law fraud.*

tax fraud. See TAX EVASION.

wire fraud. An act of fraud using electronic communications, as by making false representations on the telephone to obtain money. • The federal Wire Fraud Act provides that any artifice to defraud by means of wire or other electronic communications (such as radio or television) in foreign or interstate commerce is a crime. 18 USCA § 1343.

States Which Include Unalienable/Inalienable Rights In the State Constitutions

Alabama Article I, Section 1. Equality and rights of men. That all men are equally free and independent; that they are endowed by their Creator with certain **inalienable rights;** that among these are life, liberty and the pursuit of happiness.

Arkansas Article II, Section 2. All men are created equally free and independent, and have certain inherent and **inalienable rights**, amongst which are those of enjoying and defending life and liberty; of acquiring, possessing and protecting property and reputation, and of pursuing their own happiness. To secure these rights governments are instituted among men, deriving their just powers from the consent of the governed.

California Article I, Section 1. All people are by nature free and independent and have **inalienable rights**. Among these are enjoying and defending life and liberty, acquiring, possessing, and protecting property, and pursuing and obtaining safety, happiness, and privacy.

Colorado Article II, Section 3. Inalienable rights. All persons have certain natural, essential and **inalienable rights**, among which may be reckoned the right of enjoying and defending their lives and liberties; of acquiring, possessing and protecting property; and of seeking and obtaining their safety and happiness.

Florida Article I, Section 2. All natural persons, female and male alike, are equal before the law and have **inalienable rights**, among which are the right to enjoy and defend life and liberty, to pursue happiness, to be rewarded for industry, and to acquire, possess and protect property; except that the ownership, inheritance, disposition and possession of real property by aliens ineligible for citizenship may be regulated or prohibited by law. No person shall be deprived of any right because of race, religion, national origin, or physical disability.

Hawaii Article I, Section 2. All persons are free by nature and are equal in their inherent and **inalienable rights**. Amoung these rights are the enjoyment of life, liberty and the pursuit of happiness, and the acquiring and possessing of property. These rights cannot endure unless the people recognize their corresponding obligations and responsibilities.

Idaho Article I, Section 1. All men are by nature free and equal, and have certain **inalienable rights**, among which are enjoying and defending life and liberty; acquiring, possessing and protecting property; pursuing happiness and securing safety.

Illinois Article I, Section 1. All men are by nature free and independent and have certain inherent and **inalienable rights** among which are life, liberty and the pursuit of happiness. To secure these rights and the protection of property, governments are instituted among men, deriving their just powers from the consent of the governed.

Indiana Article 1. Section 1. We Declare, That all people are created equal; that they are endowed by their creator with certain **inalienable rights**; that among these are life, liberty, and the pursuit of happiness; that all power is inherent in the People; and that all free governments are, and of right ought to be, founded on their authority, and instituted for their peace, safety, and well-being. For the advancement of these ends, the People have, at all times, an indefeasible right to alter and reform their government.

Iowa Article I, Section 1. All men and women are, by nature, free and equal, and have certain **inalienable rights**—among which are those of enjoying and defending life and liberty, acquiring, possessing and protecting property, and pursuing and obtaining safety and happiness.

Kansas Kansas Bill of Rights, § 1. Equal rights. All men are possessed of equal and **inalienable** natural **rights**, among which are life, liberty, and the pursuit of happiness.

Kentucky All men are, by nature, free and equal, and have certain inherent and **inalienable rights**, among which may be reckoned:

> **First**: The right of enjoying and defending their lives and liberties.
> **Second**: The right of worshipping Almighty God according to the dictates of their consciences.
> **Third**: The right of seeking and pursuing their safety and happiness.
> **Fourth**: The right of freely communicating their thoughts and opinions.
> **Fifth**: The right of acquiring and protecting property.

Sixth: The right of assembling together in a peaceable manner for their common good, and of applying to those invested with the power of government for redress of grievances or other proper purposes, by petition, address or remonstrance.

Seventh: The right to bear arms in defense of themselves and of the State, subject to the power of the General Assembly to enact laws to prevent persons from carrying concealed weapons.

Louisiana Article I, Section 1. All government, of right, originates with the people, is founded on their will alone, and is instituted to protect the rights of the individual and for the good of the whole. Its only legitimate ends are to secure justice for all, preserve peace, protect the rights, and promote the happiness and general welfare of the people. The **rights enumerated in this Article are inalienable** by the state and shall be preserved inviolate by the state.

Maine Article I, Section 1. Natural rights. All people are born equally free and independent, and have certain natural, inherent and **unalienable rights**, among which are those of enjoying and defending life and liberty, acquiring, possessing and protecting property, and of pursuing and obtaining safety and happiness.

Massachusetts Article CVI. Article I of Part the First of the Constitution is hereby annulled and the following is adopted:- All people are born free and equal and have certain natural, essential and **unalienable rights**; among which may be reckoned the right of enjoying and defending their lives and liberties; that of acquiring, possessing and protecting property; in fine, that of seeking and obtaining their safety and happiness. Equality under the law shall not be denied or abridged because of sex, race, color, creed or national origin.

Montana Article II, Section 3. All persons are born free and have certain **inalienable rights**. They include the right to a clean and healthful environment and the rights of pursuing life's basic necessities, enjoying and defending their lives and liberties, acquiring, possessing and protecting property, and seeking their safety, health and happiness in all lawful ways. In enjoying these rights, all persons recognize corresponding responsibilities.

Nebraska CI-1 Statement of rights. All persons are by nature free and independent, and have certain inherent and **inalienable rights**; among these are life, liberty, the pursuit of happiness, and the right to keep and bear arms for security or defense of self, family, home, and others, and for lawful common defense, hunting, recreational use, and all other lawful purposes, and such rights shall not be denied or infringed by the state or any subdivision thereof. To secure these rights, and the protection of property, governments are instituted among people, deriving their just powers from the consent of the governed.

Nevada Article I, Section. 1. Inalienable rights. All men are by Nature free and equal and have certain **inalienable rights** among which are those of enjoying and defending life and liberty; Acquiring, Possessing and Protecting property and pursuing and obtaining safety and happiness.

New Jersey Article I, Section 1. All persons are by nature free and independent, and have certain natural and **unalienable rights**, among which are those of enjoying and defending life and liberty, of acquiring, possessing, and protecting property, and of pursuing and obtaining safety and happiness.

New Mexico Article II, Section 4. All persons are born equally free, and have certain natural, inherent and **inalienable rights**, among which are the rights of enjoying and defending life and liberty, of acquiring, possessing and protecting property, and of seeking and obtaining safety and happiness.

North Carolina Article I, Section 1. The equality and rights of persons. We hold it to be self-evident that all persons are created equal; that they are endowed by their Creator with certain **inalienable rights**; that among these are life, liberty, the enjoyment of the fruits of their own labor, and the pursuit of happiness.

North Dakota Article I, Section 1. All individuals are by nature equally free and independent and have certain **inalienable rights**, among which are those of enjoying and defending life and liberty; acquiring, possessing and protecting property and reputation; pursuing and obtaining safety and happiness; and to keep and bear arms for the defense of their person, family, property, and the state, and for lawful hunting, recreational, and other lawful purposes, which shall not be infringed.

Ohio § 1.01 Inalienable Rights (1851) All men are, by nature, free and independent, and have certain **inalienable rights**, among which are those of enjoying and defending life and liberty, acquiring, possessing, and protecting property, and seeking and obtaining happiness and safety.

Pennsylvania Article I, Section 1. All men are born equally free and independent, and have certain inherent and **indefeasible rights**,[1] among which are those of enjoying and defending life and liberty, of acquiring, possessing and protecting property and reputation, and of pursuing their own happiness.

Utah Article I, Section 1. All men have the inherent and **inalienable right** to enjoy and defend their lives and liberties; to acquire, possess and protect property; to worship according to the dictates of their consciences; to assemble peaceably, protest against wrongs, and petition for redress of grievances; to communicate freely their thoughts and opinions, being responsible for the abuse of that right.

Vermont Chapter I. Article 1. That all persons are born equally free and independent, and have certain natural, inherent, and **unalienable rights**, amongst which are the enjoying and defending life and liberty, acquiring, possessing and protecting property, and pursuing and obtaining happiness and safety; therefore no person born in this country, or brought from over sea, ought to be holden by law, to serve any person as a servant, slave or apprentice, after arriving to the age of twenty-one years, unless bound by the person's own consent, after arriving to such age, or bound by law for the payment of debts, damages, fines, costs, or the like.

---

[1] The definition of "indefeasible" is substantially the same as "inalienable."

States Which Do *Not* Include Unalienable/ Inalienable Rights In the State Constitutions

The following list is based upon how these state constitutions read **today**. There may have been protection of "inalienable or unalienable" rights in an earlier version of the constitution that was subsequently removed, or if the protection was **never there at all**.

Alaska Article I, Section 1. This constitution is dedicated to the principles that all persons have a natural right to life, liberty, the pursuit of happiness, and the enjoyment of the rewards of their own industry; that all persons are equal and entitled to equal rights, opportunities, and protection under the law; and that all persons have corresponding obligations to the people and to the State.

Arizona Article II, Section 1. A frequent recurrence to fundamental principles is essential to the security of individual rights and the perpetuity of free government.

Connecticut Article I, Section 1. All men when they form a social compact, are equal in rights; and no man or set of men are entitled to exclusive public emoluments or privileges from the community.

Delaware [No rights of life, liberty and pursuit of happiness.]

Georgia Article 1. Section I. Paragraph I. No person shall be deprived of life, liberty, or property except by due process of law.[1] Paragraph III. Each person has the natural and **inalienable right** to worship God, each according to the dictates of that person's own conscience; and no human authority should, in any case, control or interfere with such right of conscience.

Maryland Declaration of Rights, Article 1. That all Government of right originates from the People, is founded in compact only, and instituted solely for the good of the whole; and they have, at all times, the **inalienable right**[2] to alter, reform or abolish their Form of Government in such manner as they may deem expedient.

---

[1] Though in "Paragraph III" the religious freedom is listed as being inalienable, note that in "Paragraph I" that life, liberty, or property are not listed as being inalienable.

[2] Here "inalienable" does not expressly include rights to life, liberty and pursuit of happiness.

Michigan Article I, Sec. 2. No person shall be denied the equal protection of the laws; nor shall any person be denied the enjoyment of his civil or political rights or be discriminated against in the exercise thereof because of religion, race, color or national origin. The legislature shall implement this section by appropriate legislation.

Minnesota Article I, Sec. 2. No member of this state shall be disfranchised or deprived of any of the rights or privileges secured to any citizen thereof, unless by the law of the land or the judgment of his peers. There shall be neither slavery nor involuntary servitude in the state otherwise than as punishment for a crime of which the party has been convicted.

Mississippi Article 3, Sec. 6. The people of this state have the inherent, sole, and exclusive right to regulate the internal government and police thereof, and to alter and abolish their constitution and form of government whenever they deem it necessary to their safety and happiness; Provided, such change be not repugnant to the constitution of the United States.

Missouri Article I, Section 2. That all constitutional government is intended to promote the general welfare of the people; that all persons have a natural right to life, liberty, the pursuit of happiness and the enjoyment of the gains of their own industry; that all persons are created equal and are entitled to equal rights and opportunity under the law; that to give security to these things is the principal office of government, and that when government does not confer this security, it fails in its chief design.

New Hampshire [Art.] 2. All men have certain natural, essential, and inherent rights - among which are, the enjoying and defending life and liberty; acquiring, possessing, and protecting, property; and, in a word, of seeking and obtaining happiness. Equality of rights under the law shall not be denied or abridged by this state on account of race, creed, color, sex or national origin.

[Art.] 4. Among the natural rights, some are, in their very nature **unalienable**,[3] because no equivalent can be given or received for them. Of this kind are the Rights of Conscience.

New York Bill of Rights, Section 1. No member of this state shall be disfranchised, or deprived of any of the rights or

---

[3] Though the term "unalienable" is used here, note that there is no specific list of rights, such as "unalienable right to Life, Liberty and the pursuit of Happiness."

privileges secured to any citizen thereof, unless by the law of the land, or the judgment of his peers, except that the legislature may provide that there shall be no primary election held to nominate candidates for public office or to elect persons to party positions for any political party or parties in any unit of representation of the state from which such candidates or persons are nominated or elected whenever there is no contest or contests for such nominations or election as may be prescribed by general law.

Oklahoma Article II, Section 2: Inherent rights. All persons have the inherent right to life, liberty, the pursuit of happiness, and the enjoyment of the gains of their own industry.

Oregon Article I, Section 1. We declare that all men, when they form a social compact are equal in right: that all power is inherent in the people, and all free governments are founded on their authority, and instituted for their peace, safety, and happiness; and they have at all times a right to alter, reform, or abolish the government in such manner as they may think proper.

Rhode Island Article I, Section 2. All free governments are instituted for the protection, safety, and happiness of the people. All laws, therefore, should be made for the good of the whole; and the burdens of the state ought to be fairly distributed among its citizens. No person shall be deprived of life, liberty or property without due process of law, not shall any person be denied equal protection of the laws. No otherwise qualified person shall, solely by reason of race, gender or handicap be subject to discrimination by the state, its agents or any person or entity doing business with the state. Nothing in this section shall be construed to grant or secure any right relating to abortion or the funding thereof.

South Carolina Article I, Section 3. The privileges and immunities of citizens of this State and of the United States under this Constitution shall not be abridged, nor shall any person be deprived of life, liberty, or property without due process of law, nor shall any person be denied the equal protection of the laws.

South Dakota Article VI, § 1. Inherent rights. All men are born equally free and independent, and have certain inherent rights, among which are those of enjoying and defending life and liberty, of acquiring and protecting property and the pursuit of happiness. To secure these rights governments are instituted among men, deriving their just powers from the consent of the governed.

Tennessee Article I, Section 1. That all power is inherent in the people, and all free governments are founded on their authority, and instituted for their peace, safety, and happiness; for the advancement of those ends they have at all times, an **unalienable and indefeasible right**[4] to alter, reform, or abolish the government in such manner as they may think proper.

Texas Article 1, Section 3. All free men, when they form a social compact, have equal rights, and no man, or set of men, is entitled to exclusive separate public emoluments, or privileges, but in consideration of public services. Section 3a. Equality under the law shall not be denied or abridged because of sex, race, color, creed, or national origin.

Virginia Article I, Section 1. That all men are by nature equally free and independent and have certain inherent rights, of which, when they inter into a state of society, they cannot, by any compact, deprive or divest their posterity; namely, the enjoyment of life and liberty, with the means of acquiring and possessing property, and pursuing and obtaining happiness and safety.

Washington Article I, Section 1. All political power is inherent in the people, and governments derive their just powers from the consent of the governed, and are established to protect and maintain individual rights. Section 3. No person shall be deprived of life, liberty, or property, without due process of law.

West Virginia CON 3-1. All men are, by nature, equally free and independent, and have certain inherent rights, of which, when they enter into a state of society, they cannot, by any compact, deprive or divest their posterity, namely: The enjoyment of life and liberty, with the means of acquiring and possessing property, and of pursuing and obtaining happiness and safety.

Wisconsin Article I, Section 1. All people are born equally free and independent, and have certain inherent rights; among these are life, liberty and the pursuit of happiness; to secure these rights, governments are instituted, deriving their just powers from the consent of the governed.

Wyoming Article I, Section 2. In their inherent right to life, liberty and the pursuit of happiness, all members of the human race are equal.

---

[4] Note that this use of "unalienable and indefeasible" does not expressly include "unalienable right to Life, Liberty and the pursuit of Happiness."

United States
Statutes at Large — 14 Stat. 27

Chap. XXXI. — An Act to protect all Persons in the United States in their Civil Rights, and furnish the Means of their Vindication.

Be it enacted by the Senate and House of Representatives of the United States of America in Congress assembled, That all persons born in the United States and not subject to any foreign power, excluding Indians not taxed, are hereby declared to be citizens of the United States; and such citizens, of every race and color, without regard to any previous condition of slavery or involuntary servitude, except as punishment for a crime whereof the party shall have been convicted, shall have the same right, in every State and Territory in the United States, to make and enforce contracts, to sue, be parties, and give evidence, to inherit, purchase, lease, sell, hold, and convey real property, and to full and equal benefit of all laws and proceedings for the security of person and property, as is enjoyed by white citizens, and shall be subject to like punishment, pains, and penalties, and to none other, any law, statute, ordinance, regulation, or custom, to the contrary notwithstanding.

Sec. 2. *And be it further enacted,* That any person who, under color of any law, statute, ordinance, regulation, or custom, shall subject, or cause to be subjected, any inhabitant of any State or Territory to the deprivation of any right secured by this act, or to different punishment, pains, and penalties, on account of such person having at any time been held in a condition of slavery or involuntary servitude, except as punishment for a crime whereof the party shall have been duly convicted, or by any reason of his color or race, than is prescribed for the punishment of white persons, shall be deemed guilty of a misdemeanor, and, on conviction, shall be punished by fine not exceeding one thousand dollars, or imprisonment not exceeding one year, or both, in the discretion of the court.

Sec. 3. *And be it further enacted,* That the district courts of the United States, within their respective districts, shall have, exclusively of the courts of the several States, cognizance of all crimes and offences committed against the provisions of this act, and also, concurrently with the circuit courts of the United States, of all causes, civil and criminal, affecting persons who are denied or cannot enforce in the courts or judicial tribunals of the State of locality where they may be any of the rights secured to them by the first section of this act; and if any suit or prosecution, civil or criminal, has been or shall be commenced in any State court, against any such person, for any cause whatsoever, or against any officer, civil or military, or other person, for any arrest or imprisonment, trespasses, or wrong done or committed by virtue or under color of authority derived from this act or the act establishing a Bureau for the relief of Freedmen and Refugees, and all acts amendatory thereof, or for refusing to do any act upon ground that it would be inconsistent with this act, such defendant shall have the right to remove such cause for trial to the proper district or circuit court in the manner prescribed by the "Act relating to habeas corpus and regulating proceedings in certain cases," approved March three, eighteen hundred and sixty-three, and all acts amendatory thereof. The jurisdiction in civil and criminal matters hereby conferred on the district and circuit courts of the United States shall be exercised in conformity with the laws of the United States, so far as such laws are suitable to carry the same into effect; but in all cases where such laws are not adapted to the object, or are deficient in the provisions necessary to furnish suitable remedies and punish offenders against the law, the common law, as modified and changed by the constitution and statutes of the State wherein the court having jurisdiction of the cause, civil or criminal, is held, so far as the same is not inconsistent with the Constitution and laws of the United States, shall be extended to and govern said courts in the trial and disposition of such cause, and, if of a criminal nature, in the infliction of punishment on the party found guilty.

[28] Sec. 4. *And be it further enacted*, That the district attorneys, marshals, and deputy marshals of the United States, the commissioners appointed by the circuit and territorial courts of the United States, with powers of arresting, imprisoning, or bailing offenders against the laws of the United States, the officers and agents of the Freedmen's Bureau, and every other officer who may be specially empowered by the President of the United States, shall be, and they are hereby, specially authorized and required, at the expense of the United States, to institute proceeding against all and every person who shall violate the provisions of this act, and cause him or them to be arrested and imprisoned, or bailed, as the case may be, for trial before such court of the United States or territorial court as by this act has cognizance of the offence. And with a view to affording reasonable protection to all persons in their constitutional rights of equality before the law, without distinction of race or color, or previous condition of slavery or involuntary servitude, except as a punishment for crime, whereof the party shall have been duly convicted, and to the prompt discharge of the duties of this act, it shall be the duty of the circuit courts of the United States and the superior courts of the Territories of the United States, from time to time, to increase the number of commissioners, so as to afford a speedy and convenient means for the arrest and examination of persons charged with a violation of this act; and such commissioners are hereby authorized and required to exercise and discharge all the powers and duties conferred on them by this act, and the same duties with regard to offences created by this act, as they are authorized by law to exercise with regard to other offences against the laws of the United States.

Sec. 5. *And be it further enacted*, That it shall be the duty of all marshals and deputy marshals to obey and execute all warrants and precepts issued under provisions of this act, when to them directed; and should any marshal or deputy marshal refuse to receive such warrant or other process when tendered, or to use all proper means diligently to execute the same, he shall, on conviction thereof, be fined a sum of one thousand dollars, to the use of the person upon whom the accused is alleged to have committed the offence. And the better to enable the said commissioners to execute their duties faithfully and efficiently, in conformity with the Constitution of the United States and the requirements of this act, they are hereby authorized and empowered, within their counties respectively, to appoint, in writing, under their hands, any one or more suitable persons, from time to time, to execute all such warrants and other process as may be issued by them in the lawful performance of their respective duties; and the persons so appointed to execute any warrant or process as aforesaid shall have authority to summon and call to their aid the bystanders or posse comitatus of the proper county, or such portion of the land or naval forces of the United States, or of the militia, as may be necessary to the performance of the duty with which they are charged, and to insure a faithful observance of the clause of the Constitution which prohibits slavery, in conformity with the provisions of this act; and said warrants shall run and be executed by said officers anywhere in the State or Territory within which they are issued.

Sec. 6. *And be it further enacted*, That any person who shall knowingly and willfully obstruct, hinder, or prevent any officer, or other person charged with the execution of any warrant or process issued under the provisions of this act, or any person or persons lawfully assisting him or them, from arresting any person for whose apprehension such warrant or process may have been issued, or shall rescue or attempt to rescue such person from the custody of the officer, other person or persons, or those lawfully assisting as aforesaid, when so arrested pursuant to the authority herein given and declared, or shall aid, abet, or assist any person so arrested as aforesaid, directly or indirectly, to escape from custody of the officer or other person legally authorized as aforesaid, or shall harbor or [29] conceal any person for whose arrest a warrant or process have been issued as aforesaid, so as to prevent his discovery and arrest after notice or knowledge of the fact that a warrant has been issued for the apprehension of such person, shall, for either of said offences, be subject to a fine not exceeding one thousand dollars, and imprisonment not exceeding six months, by indictment and conviction before the district court of the United States for the district in which said offence may have been committed, or before the proper court of criminal jurisdiction, if committed within one of the organized Territories of the United States.

Sec. 7. *And be it further enacted,* That the district attorneys, the marshals, their deputies, and the clerks of the said district and territorial courts shall be paid for their services the like fees as may be allowed to them for similar services in other cases; and in all cases where the proceedings are before a commissioner, he shall be entitled to a fee of ten dollars in full for his services in each case, inclusive of all services incident to such arrest and examination. The person or persons authorized to execute the process to be issued by such commissioners for the arrest of offenders against the provisions of this act shall be entitled to a fee of vie dollars for each person he or they may arrest and take before any such commissioner as aforesaid, with such other fees as may be deemed reasonable by such commissioner for such other additional services as may be necessarily performed by him or them, as such attending examination, keeping the prisoner in custody, and providing him with food and lodging during his detention, and until the final determination of such commissioner, and in general for performing such other duties as may be required in the premises; such fees to be made up in conformity with the fees usually charged by the officers of the courts of justice within the proper district or county, as near as may be practicable, and paid out of the Treasury of the United States on the certificate of the judge of the district within which the arrest is made, and to be recoverable from the defendant as part of the judgment in case of conviction.

Sec. 8. *And be it further enacted,* That whenever the President of the United States shall have reason to believe that offences have been or are likely to be committed against the provisions of this act within any judicial district, it shall be lawful for him, in his discretion, to direct the judge, marshal, and district attorney of such district to attend such place within the district, and for such time as he may designate, for the purpose of the more speedy arrest and trial of persons charged with a violation of this act; and it shall be the duty of every judge or other officer, when any such requisition shall be received by him, to attend at the place and for the time therein designated.

Sec. 9. *And be it further enacted,* That it shall be lawful for the President of the United States, or other such person as he may empower for that purpose, to employ such part of the land or naval forces of the United States, or of the militia, as shall be necessary to prevent the violation and enforce the due execution of this act.

Sec. 10. *And be it further enacted,* That upon all question of law arising in any cause under the provisions of this act a final appeal may be taken to the Supreme Court of the United States.

SCHUYLER COLFAX,
Speaker of the House of Representatives.
LA FAYETTE S. FOSTER,
President of the Senate, pro tempore.

(There is further text with regard to this Bill being passed by two thirds of the Senate, and two thirds of the House of Representative, subsequent to a veto by the President, that is omitted here in this text as it is not pertinent to the subject matter of this book.) * * * [30]* * *

United States
Statutes at Large — 18 Stat. 335

Chap. 114. — An Act to protect all citizens in their civil and legal rights.

Whereas, it is essential to just government we recognize the equality of all men before the law, and hold that it is the duty of government in its dealings with the people to mete out equal and exact justice to all, of whatever nativity, race, color or persuasion, religious or political; and it being the appropriate object of legislation to enact great fundamental principles into law: Therefore, [336]

Be in enacted by the Senate and House of Representatives of the United States of America in Congress assembled , That all persons within the jurisdiction of the United States shall be entitled to the full and equal enjoyment of the accommodations, advantages, facilities, and privileges of inns, public conveyances on land and water, theaters, and other places of public amusement; subject only to the conditions and limitations established by law, and applicable alike to citizens of every race and color, regardless of any previous condition of servitude.

Sec. 2. That any person who shall violate the foregoing section by denying to any citizen, except for reasons by law applicable to citizens of every race and color, and regardless of any previous condition of servitude, the full enjoyment of any of the accommodations, advantages, facilities, or privileges in said section enumerated, or by aiding or inciting such denial, shall, for every such offense, forfeit and pay the sum of five hundred dollars to the person aggrieved thereby, to be recovered in an action of debt, with full costs; and shall also, for every such offense be deemed guilty of a misdemeanor, and, upon conviction thereof, shall be fined not less than five hundred dollars nor more than one thousand dollars, or shall be imprisoned not less than thirty days nor more than one year: *Provided* , That all persons may elect to sue for the penalty aforesaid or to proceed under their rights at common law and by State statutes; and having so elected to proceed in the one mode or the other their right to proceed in the other jurisdiction shall be barred. But this proviso shall not apply to criminal proceedings, either under this act or the criminal law of any State: *And provided further* , That a judgment for the penalty in favor of the aggrieved party, or a judgment upon an indictment, shall not bar to either prosecution respectively.

Sec. 3. That the district and circuit courts of the United States shall have, exclusive of the courts of the several States, cognizance of all crimes and offenses against, and violations of, the provisions of this act; and actions for the penalty given by the proceeding section may be prosecuted in the territorial, district, or circuit courts of the United States wherever the defendant may be found, without regard to the other party; and the district attorneys, marshals, and deputy marshals of the United States, and commissioners appointed by circuit and territorial courts of the United States, with powers of arrest and imprisoning or bailing offenders against the laws of the United States, are hereby specially authorized and required to institute proceedings against every person who shall violate the provisions of this act, and cause him to be arrested and imprisoned or bailed, as the case may be, for trial before such court of the United States, or territorial courts, as by law has cognizance of the offense, except in respect of the right of action accruing to the person aggrieved; and such district attorneys shall cause such proceedings to be prosecuted to their termination as in other cases: *Provided* , That nothing contained in this section shall be construed to deny or defeat any right of civil action accruing to any person, whether by reason of this act or otherwise; and any district attorney who shall willfully fail to institute and prosecute the proceedings herein required, shall, for every such offense, forfeit and pay the sum of five hundred dollars to the person aggrieved thereby, to be recovered by an action of debt with full costs, and shall, on conviction thereof, be deemed guilty of a misdemeanor, and be fined not less than one thousand dollars or more than five thousand dollars: *Ad provided further* , That a judgment for the penalty in favor of the party aggrieved against any such district attorney, or a judgment upon indictment against any such district attorney, shall bar to either prosecution respectively.

Sec. 4.   That no citizen possessing all other qualifications which are or may be prescribed by law shall be disqualified for service as grand or petit juror in any court of the United States, or of any State, on account of race, color, or previous condition of servitude; and any officer or other person charged with any duty in the selection or summoning of jurors who shall exclude or fail to summons any citizen for the cause [337] aforesaid shall, on conviction thereof, be deemed guilty of a misdemeanor, and be fined nor more than five thousand dollars.

Sec. 5.   That all cases arising under the provisions of this act in the courts of the United States shall be reviewable by the Supreme Court of the United States, without regard to the sum in controversy, under the same provisions and regulations as are now provided by law for the review of other causes in said court.

Approved, March 1, 1875

United States
Statutes at Large — 66 Stat. 163 §101(a)

An Act

To revise the laws relating to immigration, naturalization, and nationality; and for other purposes.

Be in enacted by the Senate and House of Representatives of the United States of America in Congress assembled, That this Act, divided into titles, chapters, and sections according to the following table of contents, may be cited as the "Immigration and Nationality Act".

TABLE OF CONTENTS (omitted)

[166]
TITLE I — GENERAL
definitions

Section 101. (a) As used in this Act —

(1) The term "administrator" means the administrator of the Bureau of Security and Consular Affairs of the Department of State.

(2) The term "advocates" includes, but is not limited to, advises, recommends, furthers by overt act, and admits belief in.

(3) The term "alien" means any person not a citizen or national of the United States.

(4) The term "application for admission" has reference to the application for admission into the United States and not to the application for the issuance of an immigrant or nonimmigrant visa.

(5) The term "Attorney General" means the Attorney General of the United States.

(6) The term "border crossing identification card" means a document of identity bearing that designation issued to an alien who is lawfully admitted for permanent residence, or to an alien who is a resident in foreign contiguous territory, by a consular officer or an immigration officer for the purpose of crossing over the borders between the United States and foreign contiguous territory in accordance with such conditions for its issuance and use as may be prescribed by regulations.

(7) The term "clerk of court" means a clerk of a naturalization court.

(8) The terms "Commissioner" and "Deputy Commissioner" mean the Commissioner of Immigration and Naturalization and a Deputy Commissioner of Immigration and Naturalization, respectively.

(9) The term "consular officer" means any consular, diplomatic, or other officer or employee of the United States designated under regulations prescribed under authority contained in this Act, for the purpose of issuing immigrant or nonimmigrant visas. In the cases of aliens, in the [167] Canal Zone and the outlying possessions of the United States, the term "consular officer" means an officer designated by the Governor of the Canal Zone, or the governors of the outlying possessions, for the purpose of issuing immigrant or nonimmigrant visas under this Act.

(10) The term "crewman" means a person serving in any capacity on board a vessel or aircraft.

(11) The term "diplomatic visa" means a nonimmigrant visa bearing that title and issued to a non immigrant in accordance with such regulations as the Secretary of State may prescribe.

(12) The term "doctrine" includes, but is not limited to, policies, practices, purposes, aims, or procedures.

(13) The term "entry" means any coming of an alien into the United States, from a foreign port or place or from an out lying possession, whether voluntarily or otherwise, except that an alien having a lawful permanent residence in the United States shall not be regarded as making entry into the United States for the purposes of the immigration laws if the alien proves to the satisfaction of the Attorney General that his departure to a foreign port or place or to an outlying possession was not intended or reasonably to be expected by him or his presence in a foreign port or place or outlying possession was not voluntary: Provided, That no person whose departure from the United States was occasioned by deportation proceedings, extradition, or other legal process shall be held to be entitled to such exception.

(14) The term "foreign state" includes outlying possessions of a foreign state, but self-governing dominions or territories under mandate or trusteeship shall be regarded as separate foreign states.

(15) The term "immigrant" means every alien except an alien who is within one of the following classes of nonimmigrant aliens -

(A) (i) an ambassador, public minister, or career diplomatic or consular officer who has been accredited by a foreign government, recognized de jure by the United States and who is accepted by the President or by the Secretary of State, and the members of the alien's immediate family; (ii) upon a basis of reciprocity, other officials and employees who have been accredited by a foreign government recognized de jure by the United States, who are accepted by the Secretary of State, and the members of their immediate families; and (iii) upon a basis of reciprocity, attendants, servants, personal employees, and members of their immediate families, of the officials and employees who have a nonimmigrant status under (i) and (ii) above;

(B) an alien (other than one coming for the purpose of study or of performing skilled or unskilled labor or as a representative of foreign press, radio, film, or other foreign information media coming to engage in such vocation) having a residence in a foreign country which he has no intention of abandoning and who is visiting the United States temporarily for business or temporarily for pleasure;

(C) an alien in immediate and continuous transit through the United States, or an alien who qualifies as a person entitled to pass in transit to and from the United Nations Headquarters District and foreign countries, under the provisions of paragraphs (3), (4), and (5) of section 11 of the Headquarters Agreement with the United Nations (61 Stat. 758);

(D) (i) an alien crewman serving in good faith as such in a capacity required for normal operation and service on board a vessel (other than a fishing vessel having its home port or an operating base in the United States), or aircraft, who intends to land temporarily and solely in pursuit of his calling as a crewman **[168]** and to depart from the United States with the vessel or aircraft on which he arrived or some other vessel or aircraft;

(E) an alien entitled to enter the United States under and in pursuance of the provisions of a treaty of commerce and navigation between the United States and the foreign state of which he is a national, and the spouse and children of any such alien if accompanying or following to join him: (i) solely to carry on substantial trade, including trade in services or trade in technology, principally between the United States and the foreign state of which he is a national; or (ii) solely to develop and direct the operations of an enterprise in which he has invested, or of an enterprise in which he is actively in the process of investing, a substantial amount of capital;

(F) an alien having a residence in a foreign country which he has no intention of abandoning, who is a bona fide student qualified to pursue a full course of study and who seeks to enter the United States temporarily and solely for the purpose of pursuing such a course of study at an established institution of learning or other recognized place of study in the United States, particularly designated by him and approved by the Attorney General after consultation with the Office of Education of the United States, which institution or place of study shall have agreed to report to the Attorney General the termination of attendance of each nonimmigrant student, and if any such institution of learning or place of study fails to make reports promptly the approval shall be withdrawn;

(G) (i) a designated principal resident representative of a foreign government recognized de jure by the United States, which foreign government is a member of an international organization entitled to enjoy privileges, exemptions, and immunities as an international organization under the International Organizations Immunities Act (59 Stat. 669), accredited resident members of the staff of such representatives, and members of his or their immediate family; (ii) other accredited representatives of such a foreign government to such international organizations, and the members of their immediate families; (iii) an alien able to qualify under (i) or (ii) above except for the fact that the government of which such alien is an accredited representative is not recognized de jure by the United States, or that the government of which he is an accredited representative is not a member of such international organization; and the members of his immediate family; (iv) officers, or employees of such international organizations, and the members of their immediate families; (v) attendants, servants, and personal employees of any such representative, officer, or employee, and the members of the immediate families of such attendants, servants, and personal employees;

(H) an alien having a residence in a foreign country which he has no intention of abandoning (i) who is of distinguished merit and ability and who is coming temporarily to the United States to perform temporary services of an exceptional nature requiring such merit and ability; or (ii) who is coming temporarily to the United States to perform other temporary services or labor, if unemployed persons capable of performing such service or labor cannot be found in this country; or (iii) who is coming temporarily to the United States as an industrial trainee;

(I) upon a basis of reciprocity, an alien who is a bona fide representative of foreign press, radio, film, or other foreign information **[169]** media, who seeks to enter the United States solely to engage in such vocation, and the spouse and children of such a representative, if accompanying or following to join him;

(16) The term "immigrant visa" means an immigrant visa required by this chapter and properly issued by a consular officer at his office outside of the United States to an eligible immigrant under the provisions of this Act.

(17) The term "immigration laws" includes this chapter and all laws, conventions, and treaties of the United States relating to the immigration, exclusion, deportation, expulsion, or removal of aliens.

(18) The term "immigration officer" means any employee or class of employees of the Service or of the United States designated by the Attorney General, individually or by regulation, to perform the functions of an immigration officer specified by this Act or any section thereof.

(19) The term "ineligible to citizenship," when used in reference to any individual, means, notwithstanding the provisions of any treaty relating to military service, an individual who is, or was at any time permanently debarred from becoming a citizen of the United States under section 3(a) of the Selective Training and Service Act of 1940, as amended (54 Stat. 885; 55 Stat. 844), or under section 4(a) of the Selective Service Act of 1948, as amended (62 Stat. 605; 65 Stat. 76), or under any section of this Act, or any other Act, or under any law amendatory of, supplementary to, or in substitution for, any of such sections or Acts.

(20) The term "lawfully admitted for permanent residence" means the status of having been lawfully accorded the privilege of residing permanently in the United States as an immigrant in accordance with the immigration laws, such status not having changed.

(21) The term "national" means a person owing permanent allegiance to a state.

(22) The term "national of the United States" means (A) a citizen of the United States, or (B) a person who, though not a citizen of the United States, owes permanent allegiance to the United States.

(23) The term "naturalization" means the conferring of nationality of a state upon a person after birth, by any means whatsoever.

(24) The term "naturalization court", unless otherwise particularly described, means

a court authorized by section 310 (a) of title III to exercise naturalization jurisdiction.

(25) The term "noncombatant service" shall not include service in which the individual is not subject to military discipline, court martial, or does not wear the uniform of any branch of the armed forces.

(26) The term "nonimmigrant visa" means a visa properly issued to an alien as an eligible nonimmigrant by a competent officer as provided in this Act.

(27) The term "nonquota immigrant" means —

(A) an immigrant who is the child or the spouse of a citizen of the United States;

(B) an immigrant, lawfully admitted for permanent residence, who is returning from a temporary visit abroad;

(C) an immigrant who was born in Canada, the Republic of Mexico, the Republic of Cuba, the Republic of Haiti, the Dominican Republic, the Canal Zone, or an independent country of Central or South America, and the spouse or the child of any such immigrant, if accompanying or following to join him;

(D) an immigrant who was a citizen of the United States and may, under section 324 (a) or 327 of title III, apply for reacquisition of citizenship;

[170]

(E) an immigrant included within the second proviso to section 349(a)(1) of title III,

(F) (i) an immigrant who continuously for at least two years immediately preceding the time of his application for admission to the United States has been, and who seeks to enter the United States solely for the purpose of carrying on the vocation of minister of a religious denomination, and whose services are needed by such religious denomination having a bona fide organization in the United States; and (ii) the spouse or the child of any such immigrant, if accompanying or following to join him; or

(G) an immigrant who is an employee, or an honorably retired former employee, of the United States Government abroad, and who has performed faithful service for a total of fifteen years, or more, and his accompanying spouse and children: Provided, That the principal officer of a Foreign Service establishment, in his discretion, shall have recommended the granting of nonquota status to such alien in exceptional circumstances and the Secretary of State approves such recommendation and finds that it is in the national interest to grant such status.

(28) The term "organization" means, but is not limited to, an organization, corporation, company, partnership, association, trust, foundation or fund; and includes a group of persons, whether or not incorporated, permanently or temporarily associated together with joint action on any subject or subjects.

(29) The term "outlying possessions of the United States" means American Samoa and Swains Island.

(30) The term "passport" means any travel document issued by competent authority showing the bearer's origin, identity, and nationality if any, which is valid for the admission of the bearer into a foreign country.

(31) The term "permanent" means a relationship of continuing or lasting nature, as distinguished from temporary, but a relationship may be permanent even though it is one that may be dissolved eventually at the instance either of the United States or of the individual, in accordance with law.

(32) The term "quota immigrant" means any immigrant who is not a nonquota immigrant. An alien who is not particularly specified in this Act as a nonquota immigrant or a nonimmigrant shall not be admitted or considered in any manner to be either nonquota immigrant or a nonimmigrant notwithstanding his relationship to any individual who is so specified or by reason of being excepted from the operation of any other law regulating or forbidding immigration.

(33) The term "residence" means the place of general abode; the place of general abode of a person means his principal, actual dwelling place in fact, without regard to intent. Residence shall be considered continuous for the purpose of sections 350 and 352 of title III where there is a continuity of stay but not necessarily an uninterrupted physical presence in a

112

foreign state or states or outside the United States.

(34) The term "Service" means the Immigration and Naturalization Service of the Department of Justice.

(35) The term "spouse", "wife", or "husband" do not include a spouse, wife, or husband by reason of any marriage ceremony where the contracting parties thereto are not physically present in the presence of each other, unless the marriage shall have been consummated.

(36) The term "State" includes (except as used in section 310 (a) of title III) Alaska, Hawaii, the District of Columbia, Puerto Rico, Guam, and the Virgin Islands of the United States.

(37) The term "totalitarian party" means an organization which advocates the establishment in the United States of a totalitarian [171] dictatorship or totalitarianism. The terms "totalitarian dictatorship" and "totalitarianism" mean and refer to systems of government not representative in fact, characterized by (A) the existence of a single political party, organized on a dictatorial basis, with so close an identity between such party and its policies and the governmental policies of the country in which it exists, that the party and the government constitute an indistinguishable unit, and (B) the forcible suppression of opposition to such party.

(38) The term "United States", except as otherwise specifically herein provided, when used in a geographical sense, means the continental United States, Alaska, Hawaii, Puerto Rico, Guam, and the Virgin Islands of the United States.

(39) The term "unmarried", when used in reference to any individual as of any time, means an individual who at such time is not married, whether or not previously married.

(40) The term "world communism" means a revolutionary movement, the purpose of which is to establish eventually a Communist totalitarian dictatorship in any or all the countries of the world through the medium of an internationally coordinated Communist political movement.

(The foregoing definitions are taken from United States Statutes at Large, 66 Stat. 163-171, §§101(a)(1)-(40) — the balance of that statute continues on page 171 through page 281. Some of the definitions in this statute have been amended, repealed, and several new definitions added as found in current Title 8 United States Code §1101(a). I have not researched these changes which I do not consider pertinent to the issues presented in this book. The definitions that are pertinent to this text, 14, 21, 22, and 36, remain word-for-word the same as found in this statute.)

Sam Rayburn,
Speaker of the House of Representatives.
Alben W. Barkley,
President of the Senate.

13th and 14th Amendments

Thirteenth Amendment

SECTION 1. Neither slavery nor involuntary servitude, except as a punishment for crime whereof the party shall have been duly convicted, shall exist within the United States, or any place subject to their jurisdiction.

SECTION 2. Congress shall have the power to enforce this article by appropriate legislation.

Fourteenth Amendment

SECTION 1. All persons born or naturalized in the United States, and subject to the jurisdiction thereof, are citizens of the United States and the State wherein they reside. No State shall make or enforce any law which shall abridge the privileges and immunities of the citizens of the United States; nor shall any State deprive any person of life, liberty, or property, without due process of law; nor deny to any person within its jurisdiction the equal protection of the laws.

SECTIONS 2-4[1]

SECTION 5. Congress shall have the power to enforce, by appropriate legislation, the provisions of this article.

---

[1] Sections 2-4 deal with apportionment of representation, disqualification for public office, and guarantee of public debt. They are not included here as they are not dealt with or referred to in the text of this book.

Title 42 United States Code — Chap. 21

§1981 - §2000a-6[1]

Sec. 1981. Equal rights under the law

♦ (a) *Statement of equal rights*

All persons within the jurisdiction of the United States shall have the same right in every State and Territory to make and enforce contracts, to sue, be parties, give evidence, and to the full and equal benefit of all laws and proceedings for the security of persons and property as is enjoyed by white citizens, and shall be subject to like punishment, pains, penalties, taxes, licenses, and exactions of every kind, and to no other.

♦ (b) *Make and enforce contracts defined*

For purposes of this section, the term "make and enforce contracts" includes the making, performance, modification, and termination of contracts, and the enjoyment of all benefits, privileges, terms, and conditions of the contractual relationship.

♦ (c) *Protection against impairment*

The rights protected by this section are protected against impairment by nongovernmental discrimination and impairment under color of State law.

Sec. 1981a. Damages in cases of intentional discrimination in employment

♦ (a) *Right of recovery*

♦ (1) *Civil rights*

In an action brought by a complaining party under section 706 or 717 of the Civil Rights Act of 1964 (42 U.S.C. 2000e-5, 2000e-16) against a respondent who engaged in unlawful intentional discrimination (not an employment practice that is unlawful because of its disparate impact) prohibited under section 703, 704, or 717 of the Act (42 U.S.C. 2000e-2, 2000e-3, 2000e-16), and provided that the complaining party cannot recover under section 1981 of this title, the complaining party may recover compensatory and punitive damages as allowed in subsection (b) of this section, in addition to any relief authorized by section 706(g) of the Civil Rights Act of 1964, from the respondent.

♦ (2) *Disability*

In an action brought by a complaining party under the powers, remedies, and procedures set forth in section 706 or 717 of the Civil

---

[1] The balance of 42 U.S.C., Chapter 21 – Civil Rights, §2000b - §2000h-6 can be reviewed on the Internet at http://www4.law.cornell.edu/uscode/42/ch21.html, or in the hard bound volumes in your local law library.

Rights Act of 1964 (42 U.S.C. 2000e-5, 2000e-16) (as provided in section 107(a) of the Americans with Disabilities Act of 1990 (42 U.S.C. 12117(a)), and section 794a(a)(1) of title 29, respectively) against a respondent who engaged in unlawful intentional discrimination (not an employment practice that is unlawful because of its disparate impact) under section 791 of title 29 and the regulations implementing section 791 of title 29, or who violated the requirements of section 791 of title 29 or the regulations implementing section 791 of title 29 concerning the provision of a reasonable accommodation, or section 102 of the Americans with Disabilities Act of 1990 (42 U.S.C. 12112), or committed a violation of section 102(b)(5) of the Act, against an individual, the complaining party may recover compensatory and punitive damages as allowed in subsection (b) of this section, in addition to any relief authorized by section 706(g) of the Civil Rights Act of 1964, from the respondent.

◆ (3) *Reasonable accommodation and good faith effort*

In cases where a discriminatory practice involves the provision of a reasonable accommodation pursuant to section 102(b)(5) of the Americans with Disabilities Act of 1990 (42 U.S.C. 12112(b)(5)) or regulations implementing section 791 of title 29, damages may not be awarded under this section where the covered entity demonstrates good faith efforts, in consultation with the person with the disability who has informed the covered entity that accommodation is needed, to identify and make a reasonable accommodation that would provide such individual with an equally effective opportunity and would not cause an undue hardship on the operation of the business.

◆ (b) *Compensatory and punitive damages*

◆ (1) *Determination of punitive damages*

A complaining party may recover punitive damages under this section against a respondent (other than a government, government agency or political subdivision) if the complaining party demonstrates that the respondent engaged in a discriminatory practice or discriminatory practices with malice or with reckless indifference to the federally protected rights of an aggrieved individual.

◆ (2) *Exclusions from compensatory damages*

Compensatory damages awarded under this section shall not include backpay, interest on backpay, or any other type of relief authorized under section 706(g) of the Civil Rights Act of 1964 (42 U.S.C. 2000e-5(g)).

◆ (3) *Limitations*

The sum of the amount of compensatory damages awarded under this section for future pecuniary losses, emotional pain, suffering, inconvenience, mental anguish, loss of enjoyment of life, and other nonpecuniary losses, and the amount of punitive damages awarded under this section, shall not exceed, for each complaining party -

◆ (A) in the case of a respondent who has more than 14 and fewer than 101 employees in each of 20 or more calendar weeks in the current or preceding calendar year, $50,000;

♦   (B) in the case of a respondent who has more than 100 and fewer than 201 employees in each of 20 or more calendar weeks in the current or preceding calendar year, $100,000; and

♦   (C) in the case of a respondent who has more than 200 and fewer than 501 employees in each of 20 or more calendar weeks in the current or preceding calendar year, $200,000; and

♦   (D) in the case of a respondent who has more than 500 employees in each of 20 or more calendar weeks in the current or preceding calendar year, $300,000.

♦   (4) *Construction*

Nothing in this section shall be construed to limit the scope of, or the relief available under, section 1981 of this title.

♦   (c) *Jury trial*

If a complaining party seeks compensatory or punitive damages under this section -

♦   (1) any party may demand a trial by jury; and (2) the court shall not inform the jury of the limitations described in subsection (b)(3) of this section.

♦   (d) *Definitions*

As used in this section:

♦   (1) Complaining party

The term "complaining party" means -

♦   (A) in the case of a person seeking to bring an action under subsection (a)(1) of this section, the Equal Employment Opportunity Commission, the Attorney General, or a person who may bring an action or proceeding under title VII of the Civil Rights Act of 1964 (42 U.S.C. 2000e et seq.); or

♦   (B) in the case of a person seeking to bring an action under subsection (a)(2) of this section, the Equal Employment Opportunity Commission, the Attorney General, a person who may bring an action or proceeding under section 794a(a)(1) of title 29, or a person who may bring an action or proceeding under title I of the Americans with Disabilities Act of 1990 (42 U.S.C. 12111 et seq.).

♦   (2) *Discriminatory practice*

The term "discriminatory practice" means the discrimination described in paragraph (1), or the discrimination or the violation described in paragraph (2), of subsection (a) of this section.

Sec. 1982. Property rights of citizens

All citizens of the United States shall have the same right, in every State and Territory, as is enjoyed by white citizens thereof to inherit, purchase, lease, sell, hold, and convey real and personal property.

Sec. 1983. Civil action for deprivation of rights

Every person who, under color of any statute, ordinance, regulation, custom, or usage, of any State or Territory or the District of Columbia, subjects, or causes to be subjected, any citizen of the United States or other person within the jurisdiction thereof to the deprivation of any rights, privileges, or immunities secured by the Constitution and laws, shall be liable to the party injured in an action at law, suit in equity, or other proper proceeding for redress, except that in any action brought against a judicial officer for an act or omission taken in such officer's judicial capacity, injunctive relief shall not be granted unless a declaratory decree was violated or declaratory relief was unavailable. For the purposes of this section, any Act of Congress applicable exclusively to the District of Columbia shall be considered to be a statute of the District of Columbia.

Sec. 1984. Omitted -COD- CODIFICATION Section, act Mar. 1, 1875, ch. 114, Sec. 5, 18 Stat. 337, which was formerly classified to section 46 of Title 8, Aliens and Nationality, related to Supreme Court review of cases arising under act Mar. 1, 1875. Sections 1 and 2 of act Mar. 1, 1875 were declared unconstitutional in [the *Civil Rghts Cases*] *U.S. v. Singleton*, 109 U.S. 3, and sections 3 and 4 of such act were repealed by act June 25, 1948, ch. 645, Sec. 21, 62 Stat. 862.

Sec. 1985. Conspiracy to interfere with civil rights

♦   (1) *Reventing officer from performing duties*

If two or more persons in any State or Territory conspire to prevent, by force, intimidation, or threat, any person from accepting or holding any office, trust, or place of confidence under the United States, or from discharging any duties thereof; or to induce by like means any officer of the United States to leave any State, district, or place, where his duties as an officer are required to be performed, or to injure him in his person or property on account of his lawful discharge of the duties of his office, or while engaged in the lawful discharge thereof, or to injure his property so as to molest, interrupt, hinder, or impede him in the discharge of his official duties;

♦   (2) *Obstructing justice;intimidating party, witness, or juror*

If two or more persons in any State or Territory conspire to deter, by force, intimidation, or threat, any party or witness in any court of the United States from attending such court, or from testifying to any matter pending therein, freely, fully, and truthfully, or to injure such party or witness in his person or property on account of his having so attended or testified, or to influence the verdict, presentment, or indictment of any grand or petit juror in any such court, or to injure such juror in his person or property on account of any verdict, presentment, or indictment lawfully assented to by him, or of his being or having been such juror; or if two or more persons conspire for the purpose of impeding, hindering, obstructing, or defeating, in any manner, the due course of justice in any State or Territory, with intent to deny to any citizen the equal protection of the laws, or to injure him or his property for lawfully enforcing, or attempting to enforce, the right of any person, or class of persons, to the equal protection of the laws;

♦   (3) *Depriving persons of rights or privileges*

If two or more persons in any State or Territory conspire or go in disguise on the highway or on the premises of another, for the purpose of depriving, either directly or indirectly, any person or class of persons of the equal protection of the laws, or of equal privileges and immunities under the laws; or for the purpose of preventing or hindering the constituted authorities of any State or Territory from giving or securing to all persons within such State or Territory the equal protection of the laws; or if two or more persons conspire to prevent by force, intimidation, or threat, any citizen who is lawfully entitled to vote, from giving his support or advocacy in a legal manner, toward or in favor of the election of any lawfully qualified person as an elector for President or Vice President, or as a Member of Congress of the United States; or to injure any citizen in person or property on account of such support or advocacy; in any case of conspiracy set forth in this section, if one or more persons engaged therein do, or cause to be done, any act in furtherance of the object of such conspiracy, whereby another is injured in his person or property, or deprived of having and exercising any right or privilege of a citizen of the United States, the party so injured or deprived may have an action for the recovery of damages occasioned by such injury or deprivation, against any one or more of the conspirators.

Sec. 1986. Action for neglect to prevent

Every person who, having knowledge that any of the wrongs conspired to be done, and mentioned in section 1985 of this title, are about to be committed, and having power to prevent or aid in preventing the commission of the same, neglects or refuses so to do, if such wrongful act be committed, shall be liable to the party injured, or his legal representatives, for all damages caused by such wrongful act, which such person by reasonable diligence could have prevented; and such damages may be recovered in an action on the case; and any number of persons guilty of such wrongful neglect or refusal may be joined as defendants in the action; and if the death of any party be caused by any such wrongful act and neglect, the legal representatives of the deceased shall have such action therefor, and may recover not exceeding $5,000 damages therein, for the benefit of the widow of the deceased, if there be one, and if there be no widow, then for the benefit of the next of kin of the deceased. But no action under the provisions of this section shall be sustained which is not commenced within one year after the cause of action has accrued.

Sec. 1987. Prosecution of violation of certain laws

The United States attorneys, marshals, and deputy marshals, the United States magistrate judges appointed by the district and territorial courts, with power to arrest, imprison, or bail offenders, and every other officer who is especially empowered by the President, are authorized and required, at the expense of the United States, to institute prosecutions against all persons violating any of the provisions of section 1990 of this title or of sections 5506 to 5516 and 5518 to 5532 of the Revised Statutes, and to cause such persons to be arrested, and imprisoned or bailed, for trial before the court of the United States or the territorial court having cognizance of the offense.

Sec. 1988. Proceedings in vindication of civil rights

♦ (a) *Applicability of statutory and common law*
The jurisdiction in civil and criminal matters conferred on the district courts by the provisions of titles 13, 24, and 70 of the Revised Statutes for the protection of all persons in the United States in their civil rights, and for their vindication, shall be exercised and enforced in conformity with the laws of the

United States, so far as such laws are suitable to carry the same into effect; but in all cases where they are not adapted to the object, or are deficient in the provisions necessary to furnish suitable remedies and punish offenses against law, the common law, as modified and changed by the constitution and statutes of the State wherein the court having jurisdiction of such civil or criminal cause is held, so far as the same is not inconsistent with the Constitution and laws of the United States, shall be extended to and govern the said courts in the trial and disposition of the cause, and, if it is of a criminal nature, in the infliction of punishment on the party found guilty.

♦   (b) *Attorneys' fees*

In any action or proceeding to enforce a provision of sections 1981, 1981a, 1982, 1983, 1985, and 1986 of this title, title IX of Public Law 92-318 (20 U.S.C. 1681 et seq.), the Religious Freedom Restoration Act of 1993 (42 U.S.C. 2000bb et seq.), title VI of the Civil Rights Act of 1964 (42 U.S.C. 2000d et seq.), or section 13981 of this title, the court, in its discretion, may allow the prevailing party, other than the United States, a reasonable attorney's fee as part of the costs, except that in any action brought against a judicial officer for an act or omission taken in such officer's judicial capacity such officer shall not be held liable for any costs, including attorney's fees, unless such action was clearly in excess of such officer's jurisdiction.

♦   (c) *Expert fees*

In awarding an attorney's fee under subsection (b) of this section in any action or proceeding to enforce a provision of section 1981 or 1981a of this title, the court, in its discretion, may include expert fees as part of the attorney's fee.

Sec. 1989. United States magistrate judges; appointment of persons to execute warrants

The district courts of the United States and the district courts of the Territories, from time to time, shall increase the number of United States magistrate judges, so as to afford a speedy and convenient means for the arrest and examination of persons charged with the crimes referred to in section 1987 of this title; and such magistrate judges are authorized and required to exercise all the powers and duties conferred on them herein with regard to such offenses in like manner as they are authorized by law to exercise with regard to other offenses against the laws of the United States. Said magistrate judges are empowered, within their respective counties, to appoint, in writing, under their hands, one or more suitable persons, from time to time, who shall execute all such warrants or other process as the magistrate judges may issue in the lawful performance of their duties, and the persons so appointed shall have authority to summon and call to their aid the bystanders or posse comitatus of the proper county, or such portion of the land or naval forces of the United States, or of the militia, as may be necessary to the performance of the duty with which they are charged; and such warrants shall run and be executed anywhere in the State or Territory within which they are issued.

Sec. 1990. Marshal to obey precepts; refusing to receive or execute process

Every marshal and deputy marshal shall obey and execute all warrants or other process, when directed to him, issued under the provisions of section 1989 of this title. Every marshal and deputy marshal who refuses to receive any warrant or other process when tendered to him, issued in pursuance of the provisions of this section, or refuses or neglects to use all proper means diligently to execute the same, shall be liable to a fine in the sum of $1,000, for the benefit of the party aggrieved thereby.

Sec. 1991. Fees; persons appointed to execute process

Every person appointed to execute process under section 1989 of this title shall be entitled to a fee of $5 for each party he may arrest and take before any United States magistrate judge, with such other fees as may be deemed reasonable by the magistrate judge for any additional services necessarily performed by him, such as attending at the examination, keeping the prisoner in custody, and providing him with food and lodging during his detention, and until the final determination of the magistrate judge; such fees to be made up in conformity with the fees usually charged by the officers of the courts of justice within the proper district or county, as near as may be practicable, and paid out of the Treasury of the United States on the certificate of the judge of the district within which the arrest is made, and to be recoverable from the defendant as part of the judgment in case of conviction.

Sec. 1992. Speedy trial

Whenever the President has reason to believe that offenses have been, or are likely to be committed against the provisions of section 1990 of this title or of section 5506 to 5516 and 5518 to 5532 of the Revised Statutes, within any judicial district, it shall be lawful for him, in his discretion, to direct the judge, marshal, and United States attorney of such district to attend at such place within the district, and for such time as he may designate, for the purpose of the more speedy arrest and trial of persons so charged, and it shall be the duty of every judge or other officer, when any such requisition is received by him to attend at the place and for the time therein designated

Sec. 1993. Repealed. Pub. L. 85-315, pt. III, Sec. 122, Sept. 9, 1957, 71 Stat. 637

Sec. 1994. Peonage abolished

The holding of any person to service or labor under the system known as peonage is abolished and forever prohibited in any Territory or State of the United States; and all acts, laws, resolutions, orders, regulations, or usages of any Territory or State, which have heretofore established, maintained, or enforced, or by virtue of which any attempt shall hereafter be made to establish, maintain, or enforce, directly or indirectly, the voluntary or involuntary service or labor of any persons as peons, in liquidation of any debt or obligation, or otherwise, are declared null and void.

Sec. 1995. Criminal contempt proceedings; penalties; trial by jury

In all cases of criminal contempt arising under the provisions of this Act, the accused, upon conviction, shall be punished by fine or imprisonment or both: Provided however, That in case the accused is a natural person the fine to be paid shall not exceed the sum of $1,000, nor shall imprisonment exceed the term of six months: Provided further, That in any such proceeding for criminal contempt, at the discretion of the judge, the accused may be tried with or without a jury: Provided further, however, That in the event such proceeding for criminal contempt be tried before a judge without a jury and the sentence of the court upon conviction is a fine in excess of the sum of $300 or imprisonment in excess of forty-five days, the accused in said proceeding, upon demand therefore, shall be entitled to a trial de novo before a jury, which shall conform as near as may be to the practice in other criminal cases. This section shall not apply to contempts committed in the presence of the court or so near thereto as to interfere directly with the administration of justice nor to the misbehavior, misconduct, or disobedience, of any officer of the court in respect to the writs, orders, or process of the court. Nor shall anything herein or in any other provision of law be construed to deprive courts of their power, by civil contempt proceedings, without a jury, to secure compliance with or to prevent obstruction of, as distinguished from punishment for violations of, any lawful writ, process, order, rule, decree, or command of the court in accordance with the prevailing usages of law and equity, including the power of detention.

Sec. 1996. Protection and preservation of traditional religions of Native Americans

On and after August 11, 1978, it shall be the policy of the United States to protect and preserve for American Indians their inherent right of freedom to believe, express, and exercise the traditional religions of the American Indian, Eskimo, Aleut, and Native Hawaiians, including but not limited to access to sites, use and possession of sacred objects, and the freedom to worship through ceremonials and traditional rites.

Sec. 1996a. Traditional Indian religious use of peyote

♦ (a) *Congressional findings and declarations*

The Congress finds and declares that -

♦ (1) for many Indian people, the traditional ceremonial use of the peyote cactus as a religious sacrament has for centuries been integral to a way of life, and significant in perpetuating Indian tribes and cultures;

♦ (2) since 1965, this ceremonial use of peyote by Indians has been protected by Federal regulation;

♦ (3) while at least 28 States have enacted laws which are similar to, or are in conformance with, the Federal regulation which protects the ceremonial use of peyote by Indian religious practitioners, 22 States have not done so, and this lack of uniformity has created hardship for Indian people who participate in such religious ceremonies;

♦ (4) the Supreme Court of the United States, in the case of Employment Division v. Smith, 494 U.S. 872 (1990), held that the First Amendment does not protect Indian practitioners who use peyote in Indian religious ceremonies, and also raised uncertainty whether this religious practice would be protected under the compelling State interest standard; and

♦ (5) the lack of adequate and clear legal protection for the religious use of peyote by Indians may serve to stigmatize and marginalize Indian tribes and cultures, and increase the risk that they will be exposed to discriminatory treatment.

♦ (b) *Use, possession, or transportation of peyote*

♦ (1) Notwithstanding any other provision of law, the use, possession, or transportation of peyote by an Indian for bona fide traditional ceremonial purposes in connection with the practice of a traditional Indian religion is lawful, and shall not be prohibited by the United States or any State. No Indian shall be penalized or discriminated against on the basis of such use, possession or transportation, including, but not limited to, denial of otherwise applicable benefits under public assistance programs.

♦ (2) This section does not prohibit such reasonable regulation and registration by the Drug Enforcement Administration of those persons who cultivate, harvest, or distribute peyote as may be consistent with the purposes of this section and section 1996 of this title.

♦ (3) This section does not prohibit application of the provisions of section 481.111(a) of Vernon's Texas Health and Safety Code Annotated, in effect on October 6, 1994, insofar as those provisions pertain to the cultivation, harvest, and distribution of peyote.

♦ (4) Nothing in this section shall prohibit any Federal department or agency, in carrying out its statutory responsibilities and functions, from promulgating regulations establishing reasonable limitations on the use or ingestion of peyote prior to or during the performance of duties by sworn law enforcement officers or personnel directly involved in public transportation or any other safety-sensitive positions where the performance of such duties may be adversely affected by such use or ingestion. Such regulations shall be adopted only after consultation with representatives of traditional Indian religions for which the sacramental use of peyote is integral to their practice. Any regulation promulgated pursuant to this section shall be subject to the balancing test set forth in section 3 of the Religious Freedom Restoration Act (Public Law 103-141; 42 U.S.C. 2000bb-1).

♦ (5) This section shall not be construed as requiring prison authorities to permit, nor shall it be construed to prohibit prison authorities from permitting, access to peyote by Indians while incarcerated within Federal or State prison facilities.

♦ (6) Subject to the provisions of the Religious Freedom Restoration Act (Public Law 103-141; 42 U.S.C. 2000bb-1) (42 U.S.C. 2000bb et seq.), this section shall not be construed to prohibit States from enacting or enforcing reasonable traffic safety laws or regulations.

♦ (7) Subject to the provisions of the Religious Freedom Restoration Act (Public Law 103-141; 42 U.S.C. 2000bb-1), this section does not prohibit the Secretary of Defense from promulgating regulations establishing reasonable limitations on the use, possession, transportation, or distribution of peyote to promote military readiness, safety, or compliance with international law or laws of other countries. Such regulations shall be adopted only after consultation with representatives of traditional Indian religions for which the sacramental use of peyote is integral to their practice.

♦ (c) *Definitions*
For purposes of this section -
♦ (1) the term "Indian" means a member of an Indian tribe;

♦ (2) the term "Indian tribe" means any tribe, band, nation, pueblo, or other organized group or community of Indians, including any Alaska Native village (as defined in, or established pursuant to, the Alaska Native Claims Settlement Act (43 U.S.C. 1601 et seq.)), which is recognized as eligible for the special programs and services provided by the United States to Indians because of their status as Indians;

♦ (3) the term "Indian religion" means any religion -

♦ (A) which is practiced by Indians, and (B) the origin and interpretation of which is from within a traditional Indian culture or community; and

♦ (4) the term "State" means any State of the United States, and any political subdivision thereof.

♦ (d) *Protection of rights of Indians and Indian tribes*

Nothing in this section shall be construed as abrogating, diminishing, or otherwise affecting -

♦ (1) the inherent rights of any Indian tribe;

♦ (2) the rights, express or implicit, of any Indian tribe which exist under treaties, Executive orders, and laws of the United States;

♦ (3) the inherent right of Indians to practice their religions; and

♦ (4) the right of Indians to practice their religions under any Federal or State law.

Sec. 1996b. Interethnic adoption

♦ (1) *Prohibited conduct*

A person or government that is involved in adoption or foster care placements may not -

♦ (A) deny to any individual the opportunity to become an adoptive or a foster parent, on the basis of the race, color, or national origin of the individual, or of the child, involved; or

♦ (B) delay or deny the placement of a child for adoption or into foster care, on the basis of the race, color, or national origin of the adoptive or foster parent, or the child, involved.

♦ (2) *Enforcement*

Noncompliance with paragraph (1) is deemed a violation of title VI of the Civil Rights Act of 1964 (42 U.S.C. 2000d et seq.).

♦ (3) *No effect on the Indian Child Welfare Act of 9*

This subsection shall not be construed to affect the application of the Indian Child Welfare Act of 1978 (25 U.S.C. 1901 et seq.).

Sec. 2000a. Prohibition against discrimination or segregation in places of public accommodation

♦ (a) *Equal access*

All persons shall be entitled to the full and equal enjoyment of the goods, services, facilities, privileges, advantages, and accommodations of any place of public accommodation, as defined in this section, without discrimination or segregation on the ground of race, color, religion, or national origin.

♦ (b) *Establishments affecting interstate commerce or supported in their activities by State action as places of public accommodation; lodgings; facilities principally engaged in selling food for consumption on the premises; gasoline stations; places of exhibition or entertainment; other covered establishments*

Each of the following establishments which serves the public is a place of public accommodation within the meaning of this subchapter if its operations affect commerce, or if discrimination or segregation by it is supported by State action:

♦ (1) any inn, hotel, motel, or other establishment which provides lodging to transient guests, other than an establishment located within a building which contains not more than five rooms for rent or hire and which is actually occupied by the proprietor of such establishment as his residence;

♦ (2) any restaurant, cafeteria, lunchroom, lunch counter, soda fountain, or other facility principally engaged in selling food for consumption on the premises, including, but not limited to, any such facility located on the premises of any retail establishment; or any gasoline station;

♦ (3) any motion picture house, theater, concert hall, sports arena, stadium or other place of exhibition or entertainment; and

♦ (4) any establishment (A)(i) which is physically located within the premises of any establishment otherwise covered by this subsection, or (ii) within the premises of which is physically located any such covered establishment, and (B) which holds itself out as serving patrons of such covered establishment.

♦ (c) *Operations affecting commerce; criteria; "commerce" defined*

The operations of an establishment affect commerce within the meaning of this subchapter if (1) it is one of the establishments described in paragraph (1) of subsection (b) of this section; (2) in the case of an establishment described in paragraph (2) of subsection (b) of this section, it serves or offers to serve interstate travelers or a substantial portion of the food which it serves, or gasoline or other products which it sells, has moved in commerce; (3) in the case of an establishment described in paragraph (3) of subsection (b) of this section, it customarily presents films, performances, athletic teams, exhibitions, or other sources of entertainment which move in commerce; and (4) in the case of an establishment described in paragraph (4) of subsection (b) of this section, it is physically located within the premises of, or there is physically located within its premises, an establishment the operations of which affect commerce within the meaning of this subsection. For purposes of this section, "commerce" means travel, trade, traffic, commerce, transportation, or communication among the several States, or between the District of Columbia and any State, or between any foreign country or any territory or possession and any State or the District of Columbia, or between points in the same State but through any other State or the District of Columbia or a foreign country.

♦ (d) *Support by State action*

Discrimination or segregation by an establishment is supported by State action within the meaning of this subchapter if such discrimination or segregation (1) is carried on under color of any law, statute, ordinance, or regulation; or (2) is carried on under color of any custom or usage required or enforced by officials of the State or political subdivision thereof; or (3) is required by action of the State or political subdivision thereof.

♦ (e) *Pvate establishments*

The provisions of this subchapter shall not apply to a private club or other establishment not in fact open to the public, except to the extent that the facilities of such establishment are made available to the customers or patrons of an establishment within the scope of subsection (b) of this section.

Sec. 2000a-1. Prohibition against discrimination or segregation required by any law, statute, ordinance, regulation, rule or order of a State or State agency

All persons shall be entitled to be free, at any establishment or place, from discrimination or segregation of any kind on the ground of race, color, religion, or national origin, if such discrimination or segregation is or purports to be required by any law, statute, ordinance, regulation, rule, or order of a State or any agency or political subdivision thereof.

Sec. 2000a-3. Civil actions for injunctive relief

♦ (a) *Prsons aggrieved; intervention by Horney Gneral; legal representation;commencement of action without payment of fees, costs, or security*

Whenever any person has engaged or there are reasonable grounds to believe that any person is about to engage in any act or practice prohibited by section 2000a-2 of this title, a civil action for preventive relief, including an application for a permanent or temporary injunction, restraining order, or other order, may be instituted by the person aggrieved and, upon timely application, the court may, in its discretion, permit the Attorney General to intervene in such civil action if he certifies that the case is of general public importance. Upon application by the complainant and in such circumstances as the court may deem just, the court may appoint an attorney for such complainant and may authorize the commencement of the civil action without the payment of fees, costs, or security.

♦ (b) *Horneys' fees;liability of United States for costs*

In any action commenced pursuant to this subchapter, the court, in its discretion, may allow the prevailing party, other than the United States, a reasonable attorney's fee as part of the costs, and the United States shall be liable for costs the same as a private person.

♦ (c) *State or local enforcement proceedings;notification of State or local authority;stay of Federal proceedings*

In the case of an alleged act or practice prohibited by this subchapter which occurs in a State, or political subdivision of a State, which has a State or local law prohibiting such act or practice and establishing or authorizing a State or local authority to grant or seek relief from such practice or to institute criminal proceedings with respect thereto upon receiving notice thereof, no civil action may be brought under subsection (a) of this section before the expiration of thirty days after written notice of such alleged act or practice has been given to the appropriate State or local authority by registered mail or in person, provided that the court may stay proceedings in such civil action pending the termination of State or local enforcement proceedings.

♦ (d) *Rferences to Community Rlations Service to obtain voluntary compliance;duration of reference;extension of period*

In the case of an alleged act or practice prohibited by this subchapter which occurs in a State, or political subdivision of a State, which has no State or local law prohibiting such act or practice, a civil action may be brought under subsection (a) of this section: Provided, That the court may refer the matter to the Community Relations Service established by subchapter VIII of this chapter for as long as the court believes there is a reasonable possibility of obtaining voluntary compliance, but for not more than sixty days: Provided further, That upon expiration of such sixty-day period, the court may extend such period for an additional period, not to exceed a cumulative total of one hundred and twenty days, if it believes there then exists a reasonable possibility of securing voluntary compliance.

Sec. 2000a-4. Community Relations Service; investigations and hearings; executive session; release of testimony; duty to bring about voluntary settlements

The Service is authorized to make a full investigation of any complaint referred to it by the court under section 2000a-3(d) of this title and may hold such hearings with respect thereto as may be necessary. The Service shall conduct any hearings with respect to any such complaint in executive session, and shall not release any testimony given therein except by agreement of all parties involved in the complaint with the permission of the court, and the Service shall endeavor to bring about a voluntary settlement between the parties.

Sec. 2000a-5. Civil actions by the Attorney General

♦ (a) *Complaint*

Whenever the Attorney General has reasonable cause to believe that any person or group of persons is engaged in a pattern or practice of resistance to the full enjoyment of any of the rights secured by this subchapter, and that the pattern or practice is of such a nature and is intended to deny the full exercise of the rights herein described, the Attorney General may bring a civil action in the appropriate district court of the United States by filing with it a complaint (1) signed by him (or in his absence the Acting Attorney General), (2) setting forth facts pertaining to such pattern or practice, and (3) requesting such preventive relief, including an application for a permanent or temporary injunction, restraining order or other order against the person or persons responsible for such pattern or practice, as he deems necessary to insure the full enjoyment of the rights herein described.

♦ (b) *Three-judge district court for cases of general public importance: hearing, determination, expedition of action, review by Supreme Court; single judge district court:hearing, determination, expedition of action*

In any such proceeding the Attorney General may file with the clerk of such court a request that a court of three judges be convened to hear and determine the case. Such request by the Attorney General shall be accompanied by a certificate that, in his opinion, the case is of general public importance. A copy of the certificate and request for a three-judge court shall be immediately furnished by such clerk to the chief judge of the circuit (or in his absence, the presiding circuit judge of the circuit) in which the case is pending. Upon receipt of the copy of such request it shall be the duty of the chief judge of the circuit or the presiding circuit judge, as the case may be, to designate immediately three judges in such circuit, of whom at least one shall be a circuit judge and another of whom shall be a district judge of the court in which the proceeding was instituted, to hear and determine such case, and it shall be the duty of the judges so designated to assign the case for hearing at the earliest practicable date, to participate in the hearing and determination thereof, and to cause the case to be in every way expedited. An appeal from the final judgment of such court will lie to the Supreme Court.

In the event the Attorney General fails to file such a request in any such proceeding, it shall be the duty of the chief judge of the district (or in his absence, the acting chief judge) in which the case is pending immediately to designate a judge in such district to hear and determine the case. In the event that no judge in the district is available to hear and determine the case, the chief judge of the district, or the acting chief judge, as the case may be, shall certify this fact to the chief judge of the circuit (or in his absence, the acting chief judge) who shall then designate a district or circuit judge of the circuit to hear and determine the case.

It shall be the duty of the judge designated pursuant to this section to assign the case for hearing at the earliest practicable date and to cause the case to be in every way expedited.

Sec. 2000a-6. Jurisdiction; exhaustion of other remedies; exclusiveness of remedies; assertion of rights based on other Federal or State laws and pursuit of remedies for enforcement of such rights

♦ (a) The district courts of the United States shall have jurisdiction of proceedings instituted pursuant to this subchapter and shall exercise the same without regard to whether the aggrieved party shall have exhausted any administrative or other remedies that may be provided by law.

♦ (b) The remedies provided in this subchapter shall be the exclusive means of enforcing the rights based on this subchapter, but nothing in this subchapter shall preclude any individual or any State or local agency from asserting any right based on any other Federal or State law not inconsistent with this subchapter, including any statute or ordinance requiring nondiscrimination in public establishments or accommodations, or from pursuing any remedy, civil or criminal, which may be available for the vindication or enforcement of such right.

United States Supreme Court
Civil Rights Cases, 109 U.S. 3 (1883)

United States v. Stanley. [On a Certificate of Division in Opinion between the Judges of the Circuit Court of the United States for the District of Kansas.]

United Statesv. Ryan. [In Error to the Circuit Court of the United States for the District of California.]

United Statesv. Nichols. [On a Certificate of Division in Opinion between the Judges of the Circuit Court of the United States for the Western District of Missouri.]

United Statesv. Singleton. [On a Certificate of Division in Opinion between the Judges of the Circuit Court of the United States for the Southern District of New York.]

Robinson and wife v. Memphis & Charleston R. Co. [In Error to the Circuit Court of the United States for the Western District of Tennessee.]

October 15, 1883

Sol. Gen. Phillips, for plaintiff, the United States.

No counsel for defendants, Stanley, Ryan, Nichols, and Singleton. **[109 U.S. 3, 4]** These cases are all founded on the first and second sections of the act of congress known as the "Civil Rights Act," passed March 1, 1875, entitled "An act to protect all citizens in their civil and legal rights." 18 St. 335. Two of the cases, those against Stanley and Nichols, are indictments for denying to persons of color the accommodations and privileges of an inn or hotel; two of them, those against Ryan and Singleton, are, one an information, the other an indictment, for denying to individuals the privileges and accommodations of a theater, the information against Ryan being for refusing a colored person a seat in the dress circle of Maguire's theater in San Francisco; and the indictment against Singleton being for denying to another person, whose color is not stated, the full enjoyment of the accommodations of the theater known as the Grand Opera House in New York, "said denial not being made for any reasons by law applicable to citizens of every race and color, and regardless of any previous condition of servitude." The case of Robinson and wife against the Memphis & Charleston Railroad Company was an action brought in the circuit court of the United States for the western district of Tennessee, to recover the penalty of $500 **[109 U.S. 3, 5]** given by the second section of the act; and the gravamen was the refusal by the conductor of the railroad company to allow the wife to ride in the ladies' car, for the reason, as stated in one of the counts, that she was a person of African descent. The jury rendered a verdict for the defendants in this case upon the merits under a charge of the court, to which a bill of exceptions was taken by the plaintiffs. The case was tried on the assumption by both parties of the validity of the act of congress; and the principal point made by the exceptions was that the judge allowed evidence to go to the jury tending to show that the conductor had reason to suspect that the plaintiff, the wife, was an improper person, because she was in company with a young man whom he supposed to be a white man, and on that account inferred that there was some improper connection between them; and the judge charged the jury, in substance, that if this was the conductor's bona fide reason for excluding the woman from the car, they might take it into consideration on the question of the liability of the company. The case is brought here by writ of error at the suit of the plaintiffs. The cases of Stanley, Nichols, and Singleton come up on certificates of division of opinion between the judges below as to the constitutionality of the first and second sections of the act referred to; and the case of Ryan, on a writ of error to the judgment of the circuit court for the district of California sustaining a demurrer to the information.

[109 U.S. 3, 7] Wm. M. Randolph, for plaintiffs in error, Robinson and wife.

[109 U.S. 3, 8] W. Y. C. Humes, for defendant in error, the Memphis & Charleston R. Co. Bradley, J.

It is obvious that the primary and important question in all [109 U.S. 3, 9] the cases is the constitutionality of the law; for if the law is unconstitutional none of the prosecutions can stand.

The sections of the law referred to provide as follows:

"Section 1. That all persons within the jurisdiction of the United States shall be entitled to the full and equal enjoyment of the accommodations, advantages, facilities, and privileges of inns, public conveyances on land or water, theaters, and other places of public amusement; subject only to the conditions and limitations established by law, and applicable alike to citizens of every race and color, regardless of any previous condition of servitude.

"Sec. 2. That any person who shall violate the foregoing section by denying to any citizen, except for reasons by law applicable to citizens of every race and color, and regardless of any previous condition of servitude, the full enjoyment of any of the accommodations, advantages, facilities, or privileges in said section enumerated, or by aiding or inciting such denial, shall, for every such offense, forfeit and pay the sum of $500 to the person aggrieved thereby, to be recovered in an action of debt, with full costs; and shall, also, for every such offense, be deemed guilty of a misdemeanor, and upon conviction thereof shall be fined not less than $500 nor more than $1,000, or shall be imprisoned not less than 30 days nor more than one year: Provided, that all persons may elect to sue for the penalty aforesaid, or to proceed under their rights at common law and by state statutes; and having so elected to proceed in the one mode or the other, their right to proceed in the other jurisdiction shall be barred. But this provision shall not apply to criminal proceedings, either under this act or the criminal law of any state: And provided, further, that a judgment for the penalty in favor of the party aggrieved, or a judgment upon an indictment, shall be a bar to either prosecution respectively."

Are these sections constitutional? The first section, which is the principal one, cannot be fairly understood without attending to the last clause, which qualifies the preceding part. The essence of the law is, not to declare broadly that all persons shall be entitled to the full and equal enjoyment of the accommodations, advantages, facilities, and privileges of inns, [109 U.S. 3, 10] public conveyances, and theaters; But that such enjoyment shall not be subject to any conditions applicable only to citizens of a particular race or color, or who had been in a previous condition of servitude. In other words, it is the purpose of the law to declare that, in the enjoyment of the accommodations and privileges of inns, public conveyances, theaters, and other places of public amusement, no distinction shall be made between citizens of different race or color, or between those who have, and those who have not, been slaves. Its effect is to declare that in all inns, public conveyances, and places of amusement, colored citizens, whether formerly slaves or not, and citizens of other races, shall have the same accommodations and privileges in all inns, public conveyances, and places of amusement, as are enjoyed by white citizens; and vice versa. The second section makes it a penal offense in any person to deny to any citizen of any race or color, regardless of previous servitude, any of the accommodations or privileges mentioned in the first section.

Has congress constitutional power to make such a law? Of course, no one will contend that the power to pass it was contained in the constitution before the adoption of the last three amendments. The power is sought, first, in the fourteenth amendment, and the views and arguments of distinguished senators, advanced while the law was under consideration, claiming authority to pass it by virtue of that amendment, are the principal arguments adduced in favor of the power. We have carefully considered those arguments, as was due to the eminent ability of those who put them forward, and have felt, in all its force, the weight of authority which always invests a law that congress deems itself competent to pass. But the responsibility of an independent judgment is now thrown upon this court; and we are bound to exercise it according to the best lights we have.

The first section of the fourteenth amendment,—which is the one relied on,—after declaring who shall be citizens of the United States, and of the several states, is prohibitory in its character, and prohibitory upon the states. It declares that [109 U.S. 3, 11] "no state shall make or enforce any law which shall abridge the privileges or immunities of citizens of the United States; nor shall any state deprive any person of life, liberty, or property without due process of law; nor deny to any person within its jurisdiction the equal protection of the laws." It is state action of a particular character that is prohibited. Individual invasion of individual rights is not the subject- matter of the amendment. It has a deeper and broader scope. It nullifies and makes void all state legislation, and state action of every kind, which impairs the privileges and immunities of citizens of the United States, or which injures them in life, liberty, or property without due process of law, or which denies to any of them the equal protection of the laws. It not only does this, but, in order that the national will, thus declared, may not be a mere *brutum fulmen*, the last section of the amendment invests congress with power to enforce it by appropriate legislation. To enforce what? To enforce the prohibition. To adopt appropriate legislation for correcting the effects of such prohibited state law and state acts, and thus to render them effectually null, void, and innocuous. This is the legislative power conferred upon congress, and this is the whole of it. It does not invest congress with power to legislate upon subjects which are within the domain of state legislation; but to provide modes of relief against state legislation, or state action, of the kind referred to. **It does not authorize congress to create a code of municipal law for the regulation of private rights; but to provide modes of redress against the operation of state laws, and the action of state officers, executive or judicial, when these are subversive of the fundamental rights specified in the amendment. Positive rights and privileges are undoubtedly secured by the fourteenth amendment; but they are secured by way of prohibition against state laws and state proceedings affecting those rights and privileges, and by power given to congress to legislate for the purpose of carrying such prohibition into effect; and such legislation must necessarily be predicated upon such supposed state laws or state proceedings, and be directed to the correction [109 U.S. 3, 12] of their operation and effect. A quite full discussion of this aspect of the amendment may be found in *U. S. v. Cruikshank*, 92 U.S. 542 ; *Virginia v. Rives*, 100 U.S. 313 , and *Ex parte Virginia*, Id. 339.**

An apt illustration of this distinction may be found in some of the provisions of the original constitution. **Take the subject of contracts, for example. The constitution prohibited the states from passing any law impairing the obligation of contracts. This did not give to congress power to provide laws for the general enforcement of contracts; nor power to invest the courts of the United States with jurisdiction over contracts, so as to enable parties to sue upon them in those courts.** It did, however, give the power to provide remedies by which the impairment of contracts by state legislation might be counteracted and corrected; and this power was exercised. The remedy which congress actually provided was that contained in the twenty-fifth section of the judiciary act of 1789, giving to the supreme court of the United States jurisdiction by writ of error to review the final decisions of state courts whenever they should sustain the validity of a state statute or authority, alleged to be repugnant to the constitution or laws of the United States. By this means, if a state law was passed impairing the obligation of a contract, and the state tribunals sustained the validity of the law, the mischief could be corrected in this court. The legislation of congress, and the proceedings provided for under it, were corrective in their character. No attempt was made to draw into the United States courts the litigation of contracts generally, and no such attempt would have been sustained. We do not say that the remedy provided was the only one that might have been provided in that case. Probably congress had power to pass a law giving to the courts of the United States direct jurisdiction over contracts alleged to be impaired by a state law; and, under the broad provisions of the act of March 3, 1875, giving to the circuit courts jurisdiction of all cases arising under the constitution and laws of the United States, it is possible that such jurisdiction now exists. But under that or any other law, it must appear, as [109 U.S. 3, 13] well by allegation as proof at the trial, that the constitution had been violated by the action of the state legislature. Some obnoxious state law passed, or that might be passed, is necessary to be assumed in order to lay the foundation of any federal remedy in the case, and for the very sufficient reason that the constitutional prohibition is against state laws impairing the obligation of contracts.

And so in the present case, until some state law has been passed, or some state action through its officers or agents has been taken, adverse to the rights of citizens sought to be protected by the fourteenth amendment, no legislation of the United States under said amendment, nor any proceeding under such legislation, can be called into activity, for the prohibitions of the amendment are against state laws and acts done under state authority. Of course, legislation may and should be provided in advance to meet the exigency when it arises, but it should be adapted to the mischief and wrong which the amendment was intended to provide against; and that is, state laws or state action of some kind adverse to the rights of the citizen secured by the amendment. Such legislation cannot properly cover the whole domain of rights appertaining to life, liberty, and property, defining them and providing for their vindication. That would be to establish a code of municipal law regulative of all private rights between man and man in society. It would be to make congress take the place of the state legislatures and to supersede them. It is absurd to affirm that, because the rights of life, liberty, and property (which include all civil rights that men have) are by the amendment sought to be protected against invasion on the part of the state without due process of law, congress may, therefore, provide due process of law for their vindication in every case; and that, because the denial by a state to any persons of the equal protection of the laws is prohibited by the amendment, therefore congress may establish laws for their equal protection. In fine, the legislation which congress is authorized to adopt in this behalf is not general legislation upon the rights of the citizen, but corrective legislation; that is, such as may be necessary and proper for counteracting such laws as the states may [109 U.S. 3, 14] adopt or enforce, and which by the amendment they are prohibited from making or enforcing, or such acts and proceedings as the states may commit or take, and which by the amendment they are prohibited from committing or taking. It is not necessary for us to state, if we could, what legislation would be proper for congress to adopt. It is sufficient for us to examine whether the law in question is of that character.

An inspection of the law shows that it makes no reference whatever to any supposed or apprehended violation of the fourteenth amendment on the part of the states. It is not predicated on any such view. It proceeds *ex directo* to declare that certain acts committed by individuals shall be deemed offenses, and shall be prosecuted and punished by proceedings in the courts of the United States. It does not profess to be corrective of any constitutional wrong committed by the states; it does not make its operation to depend upon any such wrong committed. It applies equally to cases arising in states which have the justest laws respecting the personal rights of citizens, and whose authorities are ever ready to enforce such laws as to those which arise in states that may have violated the prohibition of the amendment. In other words, it steps into the domain of local jurisprudence, and lays down rules for the conduct of individuals is society towards each other, and imposes sanctions for the enforcement of those rules, without referring in any manner to any supposed action of the state or its authorities.

If this legislation is appropriate for enforcing the prohibitions of the amendment, it is difficult to see where it is to stop. Why may not congress, with equal show of authority, enact a code of laws for the enforcement and vindication of all rights of life, liberty, and property? If it is supposable that the states may deprive persons of life, liberty, and property without due process of law, (and the amendment itself does suppose this,) why should not congress proceed at once to prescribe due process of law for the protection of every one of these fundamental rights, in every possible case, as well as to prescribe equal privileges in inns, public conveyances, and theaters. The truth is that the implication of a power to legislate in this manner is based [109 U.S. 3, 15] upon the assumption that if the states are forbidden to legislate or act in a particular way on a particular subject, and power is conferred upon congress to enforce the prohibition, this gives congress power to legislate generally upon that subject, and not merely power to provide modes of redress against such state legislation or action. The assumption is certainly unsound. It is repugnant to the tenth amendment of the constitution, which declares that powers not delegated to the United States by the constitution, nor prohibited by it to the states, are reserved to the states respectively or to the people.

We have not overlooked the fact that the fourth section of the act now under consideration has been held by this court to be constitutional. That section declares "that no citizen, possessing all other qualifications which are or may be prescribed by law, shall be disqualified for service as grand or petit juror in any court of the United States, or of any state, on account of race, color, or previous condition of servitude; and any officer or other person charged with any duty in the selection or summoning of jurors who shall exclude or fail to summon any citizen for the cause aforesaid, shall, on conviction thereof, be deemed guilty of a misdemeanor, and be fined not more than five thousand dollars." In *Ex parte Virginia*, 100 U.S. 339 , it was held that an indictment against a state officer under this section for excluding persons of color from the jury list is sustainable. But a moment's attention to its terms will show that the section is entirely corrective in its character. Disqualifications for service on juries are only created by the law, and the first part of the section is aimed at certain disqualifying laws, namely, those which make mere race or color a disqualification; and the second clause is directed against those who, assuming to use the authority of the state government, carry into effect such a rule of disqualification. In the Virginia case, the state, through its officer, enforced a rule of disqualification which the law was intended to abrogate and counteract. Whether the statute-book of the state actually laid down any such rule of disqualification or not, the state, through its officer, enforced such a rule; and it is against such state action, through its officers and agents, that the last clause of the section is directed. **[109 U.S. 3, 16]** This aspect of the law was deemed sufficient to divest it of any unconstitutional character, and makes it differ widely from the first and second sections of the same act which we are now considering.

These sections, in the objectionable features before referred to, are different also from the law ordinarily called the "Civil Rights Bill," originally passed April 9, 1866, and re-enacted with some modifications in sections 16, 17, 18, of the enforcement act, passed May 31, 1870. That law, as re-enacted, after declaring that all persons within the jurisdiction of the United States shall have the same right in every state and territory to make and enforce contracts, to sue, be parties, give evidence, and to the full and equal benefit of all laws and proceedings for the security of persons and property as is enjoyed by white citizens, and shall be subject to like punishment, pains, penalties, taxes, licenses, and exactions of every kind, and none other, any law, statute, ordinance, regulation, or custom to the contrary notwithstanding, proceeds to enact that any person who, under color of any law, statute, ordinance, regulation, or custom, shall subject, or cause to be subjected, any inhabitant of any state or territory to the deprivation of any rights secured or protected by the preceding section, (above quoted,) or to different punishment, pains, or penalties, on account of such person being an alien, or by reason of his color or race, than is prescribed for the punishment of citizens, shall be deemed guilty of a misdemeanor, and subject to fine and imprisonment as specified in the act. This law is clearly corrective in its character, intended to counteract and furnish redress against state laws and proceedings, and customs having the force of law, which sanction the wrongful acts specified. In the Revised Statutes, it is true, a very important clause, to-wit, the words "any law, statute, ordinance, regulation, or custom to the contrary not-withstanding," which gave the declaratory section its point and effect, are omitted; but the penal part, by which the declaration is enforced, and which is really the effective part of the law, retains the reference to state laws by making the penalty apply only to those who should subject **[109 U.S. 3, 17]** parties to a deprivation of their rights under color of any statute, ordinance, custom, etc., of any state or territory, thus preserving the corrective character of the legislation. Rev. St. 1977, 1978, 1979, 5510. The civil rights bill here referred to is analogous in its character to what a law would have been under the original constitution, declaring that the validity of contracts should not be impaired, and that if any person bound by a contract should refuse to comply with it under color or pretense that it had been rendered void or invalid by a state law, he should be liable to an action upon it in the courts of the United States, with the addition of a penalty for setting up such an unjust and unconstitutional defense.

In this connection it is proper to state that civil rights, such as are guarantied by the constitution against state aggression, cannot be impaired by the wrongful acts of individuals, unsupported by state authority in the shape of laws, customs, or judicial or executive proceedings. The wrongful act of an individual, unsupported by any such authority, is simply a private wrong, or a crime of that individual; an invasion of the rights of the injured party, it is true, whether they affect his person, his property, or his reputation; but if not sanctioned in some way by the state, or not done under state authority, his rights remain in full force, and may presumably be vindicated by resort to the laws of the state for redress. An individual cannot deprive a man of his right to vote, to hold property, to buy and to sell, to sue in the courts, or to be a witness or a juror; he may, by force or fraud, interfere with the enjoyment of the right in a particular case; he may commit an assault against the person, or commit murder, or use ruffian violence at the polls, or slander the good name of a fellow-citizen; but unless protected in these wrongful acts by some shield of state law or state authority, he cannot destroy or injure the right; he will only render himself amenable to satisfaction or punishment; and amenable therefor to the laws of the state where the wrongful acts are committed. Hence, in all those cases where the constitution seeks to protect the rights of the citizen against discriminative and unjust laws of the state by prohibiting such laws, it is not individual offenses, but abrogation and [109 U.S. 3, 18] denial of rights, which it denounces, and for which it clothes the congress with power to provide a remedy. This abrogation and denial of rights, for which the states alone were or could be responsible, was the great seminal and fundamental wrong which was intended to be remedied. And the remedy to be provided must necessarily be predicated upon that wrong. It must assume that in the cases provided for, the evil or wrong actually committed rests upon some state law or state authority for its excuse and perpetration.

Of course, these remarks do not apply to those cases in which congress is clothed with direct and plenary powers of legislation over the whole subject, accompanied with an express or implied denial of such power to the states, as in the regulation of commerce with foreign nations, among the several states, and with the Indian tribes, the coining of money, the establishment of post-offices and post-roads, the declaring of war, etc. In these cases congress has power to pass laws for regulating the subjects specified, in every detail, and the conduct and transactions of individuals respect thereof. But where a subject is not submitted to the general legislative power of congress, but is only submitted thereto for the purpose of rendering effective some prohibition against particular state legislation or state action in reference to that subject, the power given is limited by its object, and any legislation by congress in the matter must necessarily be corrective in its character, adapted to counteract and redress the operation of such prohibited state laws or proceedings of state officers.

If the principles of interpretation which we have laid down are correct, as we deem them to be,—and they are in accord with the principles laid down in the cases before referred to, as well as in the recent case of *U. S. v. Harris*, decided at the last term of this court, [1 SUP. CT. REP. 601,]—it is clear that the law in question cannot be sustained by any grant of legislative power made to congress by the fourteenth amendment. That amendment prohibits the states from denying to any person the equal protection of the laws, and declares that congress shall have power to enforce, by appropriate legislation, the provisions of the amendment. The law in question, without any reference to adverse state legislation on the subject, [109 U.S. 3, 19] declares that all persons shall be entitled to equal accommodation and privileges of inns, public conveyances, and places of public amusement, and imposes a penalty upon any individual who shall deny to any citizen such equal accommodations and privileges. This is not corrective legislation; it is primary and direct; it takes immediate and absolute possession of the subject of the right of admission to inns, public conveyances, and places of amusement. It supersedes and displaces state legislation on the same subject, or only allows it permissive force. It ignores such legislation, and assumes that the matter is one that belongs to the domain of national regulation. Whether it would not have been a more effective protection of the rights of citizens to have clothed congress with plenary power over the whole subject, is not now the question. What we have to decide is, whether such plenary power has been conferred upon congress by the fourteenth amendment, and, in our judgment, it has not.

We have discussed the question presented by the law on the assumption that a right to enjoy equal accommodations and privileges in all inns, public conveyances, and places of public amusement, is one of the essential rights of the citizen which no state can abridge or interfere with. Whether it is such a right or not is a different question, which, in the view we have taken of the validity of the law on the ground already stated, it is not necessary to examine.

We have also discussed the validity of the law in reference to cases arising in the states only; and not in reference to cases arising in the territories or the District of Columbia, which are subject to the plenary legislation of congress in every branch of municipal regulation. Whether the law would be a valid one as applied to the territories and the district is not a question for consideration in the cases before us; they all being cases arising within the limits of states. And whether congress, in the exercise of its power to regulate commerce among the several states, might or might not pass a law regulating rights in public conveyances passing from one state to another, is also a question which is not now before us, as the sections in question are not conceived in any such view. **[109 U.S. 3, 20]** But the power of congress to adopt direct and primary, as distinguished from corrective, legislation on the subject in hand, is sought, in the second place, from the thirteenth amendment, which abolishes slavery. This amendment declares "that neither slavery, nor involuntary servitude, except as a punishment for crime, whereof the party shall have been duly convicted, shall exist within the United States, or any place subject to their jurisdiction;" and it gives congress power to enforce the amendment by appropriate legislation.

This amendment, as well as the fourteenth, is undoubtedly self- executing without any ancillary legislation, so far as its terms are applicable to any existing state of circumstances. By its own unaided force and effect if abolished slavery, and established universal freedom. Still, legislation may be necessary and proper to meet all the various cases and circumstances to be affected by it, and to prescribe proper modes of redress for its violation in letter or spirit. And such legislation may be primary and direct in its character; for the amendment is not a mere prohibition of state laws establishing or upholding slavery, but an absolute declaration that slavery or involuntary servitude shall not exist in any part of the United States.

It is true that slavery cannot exist without law any more than property in lands and goods can exist without law, and therefore the thirteenth amendment may be regarded as nullifying all state laws which establish or uphold slavery. But it has a reflex character also, establishing and decreeing universal civil and political freedom throughout the United States; and it is assumed that the power vested in congress to enforce the article by appropriate legislation, clothes congress with power to pass all laws necessary and proper for abolishing all badges and incidents of slavery in the United Stated; and upon this assumption it is claimed that this is sufficient authority for declaring by law that all persons shall have equal accommodations and privileges in all inns, public conveyances, and places of public amusement; the argument being that the denial of such equal accommodations and privileges is in itself a subjection to a species of servitude within the meaning of the amendment. Conceding the major proposition to be true, that that **[109 U.S. 3, 21]** congress has a right to enact all necessary and proper laws for the obliteration and prevention of slavery, with all its badges and incidents, is the minor proposition also true, that the denial to any person of admission to the accommodations and privileges of an inn, a public conveyance, or a theater, does subject that person to any form of servitude, or tend to fasten upon him any badge of slavery? If it does not, then power to pass the law is not found in the thirteenth amendment.

In a very able and learned presentation of the cognate question as to the extent of the rights, privileges, and immunities of citizens which cannot rightfully be abridged by state laws under the fourteenth amendment, made in a former case, a long list of burdens and disabilities of a servile character, incident to feudal vasslage in France, and which were abolished by the decrees of the national assembly, was presented for the purpose of showing that all inequalities and observances exacted by one man from another, were servitudes or badges of slavery, which a great nation, in its effort to establish universal liberty, made haste to wipe out and destroy. But these were servitudes imposed by the old law, or by long custom which had the force of law, and exacted by one man from another without the latter's consent. Should any such servitudes be imposed by a state law, there can be no doubt that the law would be repugnant to the fourteenth, no less than to the thirteenth, amendment; nor any greater doubt that congress has adequate power to forbid any such servitude from being exacted.

But is there any similarity between such servitudes and a denial by the owner of an inn, a public conveyance, or a theater, of its accommodations and privileges to an individual, even through the denial be founded on the race or color of that individual? Where does any slavery or servitude, or badge of either, arise from such an act of denial? Whether it might not be a denial of a right which, if sanctioned by the state law, would be obnoxious to the prohibitions of the fourteenth amendment, is another question. But what has it to do with the question of slavery? It may be that by the black code, (as it was called,) in the times when slavery prevailed, the proprietors of inns and public **[109 U.S. 3, 22]** conveyances were forbidden to receive persons of the African race, because it might assist slaves to escape from the control of their masters. This was merely a means of preventing such escapes, and was no part of the servitude itself. A law of that kind could not have any such object now, however justly it might be deemed an invasion of the party's legal right as a citizen, and amenable to the prohibitions of the fourteenth amendment.

The long existence of African slavery in this country gave us very distinct notions of what it was, and what were its necessary incidents. Compulsory service of the slave for the benefit of the master, restraint of his movements except by the master's will, disability to hold property, to make contracts, to have a standing in court, to be a witness against a white person, and such like burdens and incapacities were the inseparable incidents of the institution. Severer punishments for crimes were imposed on the slave than on free persons guilty of the same offenses. Congress, as we have seen, by the civil rights bill of 1866, passed in view of the thirteenth amendment, before the fourteenth was adopted, undertook to wipe out these burdens and disabilities, the necessary incidents of slavery, constituting its substance and visible from; and to secure to all citizens of every race and color, and without regard to previous servitude, those fundamental rights which are the essence of civil freedom, namely, the same right to make and enforce contracts, to sue, be parties, give evidence, and to inherit, purchase, lease, sell, and convey property, as is enjoyed by white citizens. Whether this legislation was fully authorized by the thirteenth amendment alone, without the support which it afterwards received from the fourteenth amendment, after the adoption of which it was re-enacted with some additions, it is not necessary to inquire. It is referred to for the purpose of showing that at that time (in 1866) congress did not assume, under the authority given by the thirteenth amendment, to adjust what may be called the social rights of men and races in the community; but only to declare and vindicate those fundamental rights which appertain to the essence of citizenship, and the enjoyment or deprivation of which constitutes the essential distinction between freedom and slavery. **[109 U.S. 3, 23]** We must not forget that the province and scope of the thirteenth and fourteenth amendments are different: the former simply abolished slavery: the latter prohibited the states from abridging the privileges or immunities of citizens of the United States, from depriving them of life, liberty, or property without due process of law, and from denying to any the equal protection of the laws. The amendments are different, and the powers of congress under them are different. What congress has power to do under one, it may not have power to do under the other. Under the thirteenth amendment, it has only to do with slavery and its incidents. Under the fourteenth amendment, it has power to counteract and render nugatory all state laws and proceedings which have the effect to abridge any of the privileges or immunities which have the effect to abridge any deprive them of life, liberty, or property without due process of law, or to deny to any of them the equal protection of the laws. Under the thirteenth amendment the legislation, so far as necessary or proper to eradicate all forms and incidents of slavery and involuntary servitude, may be direct and primary, operating upon the acts of individuals, whether sanctioned by state legislation or not; under the fourteenth, as we have already shown, it must necessarily be, and can only be, corrective in its character, addressed to counteract and afford relief against state regulations or proceedings.

The only question under the present head, therefore, is, whether the refusal to any persons of the accommodations of an inn, or a public conveyance, or a place of public amusement, by an individual, and without any sanction or support from any state law or regulation, does inflict upon such persons any manner of servitude, or form of slavery, as those terms are understood in this country? Many wrongs may be obnoxious to the prohibitions of the fourteenth amendment which are not, in any just sense, incidents or elements of slavery. Such, for example, would be the taking of private property without due process of law; or allowing persons who have committed certain crimes (horse-stealing, for example) to be seized and hung by the posse comitatus without regular trial; or denying to any person, or class of persons, the right to pursue any peaceful **[109 U.S. 3, 24]** avocations allowed to others. What is called callous legislation would belong to this category, and would be obnoxious to the prohibitions of the fourteenth amendment, but would not to the prohibitions of the fourteenth when not involving the idea of any subjection of one man to another. The thirteenth amendment has respect, not to distinctions of race, or class, or color, but to slavery. The fourteenth amendment extends its protection to races and classes, and prohibits any state legislation which has the effect of denying to any race or class, or to any individual, the equal protection of the laws.

Now, conceding, for the sake of the argument, that the admission to an inn, a public conveyance, or a place of public amusement, on equal terms with all other citizens, is the right of every man and all classes of men, is it any more than one of those rights which the states by the fourteenth amendment are forbidden to deny to any person? and is the constitution violated until the denial of the right has some state sanction or authority? Can the act of a mere individual, the owner of the inn, the public conveyance, or place of amusement, refusing the accommodation, be justly regarded as imposing any badge of slavery or servitude upon the applicant, or only as inflicting an ordinary civil injury, properly cognizable by the laws of the state, and presumably subject to redress by those laws until the contrary appears?

After giving to these questions all the consideration which their importance demands, we are forced to the conclusion that such an act of refusal has nothing to do with slavery or involuntary servitude, and that if it is violative of any right of the party, his redress is to be sought under the laws of the state; or, if those laws are adverse to his rights and do not protect him, his remedy will be found in the corrective legislation which congress has adopted, or may adopt, for counteracting the effect of state laws, or state action, prohibited by the fourteenth amendment. It would be running the slavery argument into the ground to make it apply to every act of discrimination which a person may see fit to make as to the guests he will entertain, or as to the people he will take into his coach or cab or car, or admit to his concert or theater, or deal with in **[109 U.S. 3, 25]** other matters of intercourse or business. Innkeepers and public carriers, by the laws of all the states, so far as we are aware, are bound, to the extent of their facilities, to furnish proper accommodation to all unobjectionable persons who in good faith apply for them. If the laws themselves make any unjust discrimination, amenable to the prohibitions of the fourteenth amendment, congress has full power to afford a remedy under that amendment and in accordance with it.

When a man has emerged from slavery, and by the aid of beneficent legislation has shaken off the inseparable concomitants of that state, there must be some stage in the progress of his elevation when he takes the rank of a mere citizen, and ceases to be the special favorite of the laws, and when his rights as a citizen, or a man, are to be protected in the ordinary modes by which other men's rights are protected. There were thousands of free colored people in this country before the abolition of slavery, enjoying all the essential rights of life, liberty, and property the same as white citizens; yet no one, at that time, thought that it was any invasion of their personal status as freemen because they were not admitted to all the privileges enjoyed by white citizens, or because they were subjected to discriminations in the enjoyment of accommodations in inns, public conveyances, and places of amusement. Mere discriminations on account of race or color were not regarded as badges of slavery. If, since that time, the enjoyment of equal rights in all these respects has become established by constitutional enactment, it is not by force of the thirteenth amendment, (which merely abolishes slavery,) but by force of the fourteenth and fifteenth amendments.

On the whole, we are of opinion that no countenance of authority for the passage of the law in question can be found in either the thirteenth or fourteenth amendment of the constitution; and no other ground of authority for its passage being suggested, it must necessarily be declared void, at least so far as its operation in the several states is concerned.

This conclusion disposes of the cases now under consideration. In the cases of *U. S. v. Ryan, and of Robinson v. Memphis & C.* **[109 U.S. 3, 26]** *R. Co.*, the judgments must be affirmed. In the other cases, the answer to be given will be, that the first and second sections of the act of congress of March 1, 1875, entitled "An act to protect all citizens in their civil and legal rights," are unconstitutional and void, and that judgment should be rendered upon the several indictments in those cases accordingly. And it is so ordered.

HARLAN, J., dissenting.

The opinion in these cases proceeds, as it seems to me, upon grounds entirely too narrow and artificial. The substance and spirit of the recent amendments of the constitution have been sacrificed by a subtle and ingenious verbal criticism. "It is not the words of the law but the internal sense of it that makes the law. The letter of the law is the body; the sense and reason of the law is the soul." Constitutional provisions, adopted in the interest of liberty, and for the purpose of securing, through national legislation, if need be, rights inhering in a state of freedom, and belonging to American citizenship, have been so construed as to defeat the ends the people desired to accomplish, which they attempted to accomplish, and which they supposed they had accomplished by changes in their fundamental law. By this I do not mean that the determination of these cases should have been materially controlled by considerations of mere expediency or policy. I mean only, in this form, to express an earnest conviction that the court has departed from the familiar rule requiring, in the interpretation of constitutional provisions, that full effect be given to the intent with which they were adopted.

The purpose of the first section of the act of congress of March 1, 1875, was to prevent race discrimination. It does not assume to define the general conditions and limitations under which inns, public conveyances, and places of public amusement may be conducted, but only declares that such conditions and limitations, whatever they may be, shall not be applied, by way of **[109 U.S. 3, 27]** discrimination, on account of race, color, or previous condition of servitude. The second section provides a penalty against any one denying, or aiding or inciting the denial, to any citizen that equality of right given by the first section, except for reasons by law applicable to citizens of every race or color, and regardless of any previous condition of servitude.

There seems to be no substantial difference between my brethren and myself as to what was the purpose of congress; for they say that the essence of the law is, not to declare broadly that all persons shall be entitled to the full and equal enjoyment of the accommodations, advantages, facilities, and privileges of inns, public conveyances, and theaters, but that such enjoyment shall not be subject to any conditions applicable only to citizens of a particular race or color, or who had been in a previous condition of servitude. The effect of the statute, the court says, is that colored citizens, whether formerly slaves or not, and citizens of other races, shall have the same accommodations and privileges in all inns, public conveyances, and places of amusement as are enjoyed by white persons, and vice versa.

The court adjudges that congress is without power, under either the thirteenth or fourteenth amendment, to establish such regulations, and that the first and second sections of the statute are, in all their parts, unconstitutional and void.

[109 U.S. 3, 28] *Before considering the particular language and scope of these amendments it will be proper to recall the relations which, prior to their adoption, subsisted between the national government and the institution of slavery, as indicated by the provisions of the constitution, the legislation of congress, and the decisions of this court. In this mode we may obtain keys with which to open the mind of the people, and discover the thought intended to be expressed.

In section 2 of article 4 of the constitution it was provided that "no person held to service or labor in one state, under the laws thereof, escaping into another, shall, in consequence of any law or regulation therein, be discharged from such service or labor, but shall be delivered up on claim of the party to whom such service or labor may be due." Under the authority of that clause congress passed the fugitive slave law of 1793, establishing the mode for the recovery of a fugitive slave, and prescribing a penalty against any person knowingly and willingly obstructing or hindering the master, his agent or attorney, in seizing, arresting, and recovering the fugitive, or who should rescue the fugitive from him, or who should harbor or conceal the slave after notice that he was a fugitive.

In *Prigg v. Com.* 16 Pet. 539, this court had occasion to define the powers and duties of congress in reference to fugitives from labor. Speaking by Mr. Justice STORY, the court laid down these propositions: That a clause of the constitution conferring a right should not be so construed as to make it shadowy, or unsubstantial, or leave the citizen without a remedial power adequate for its protection, when another mode, equally accordant with the words and the sense in which they were used, would enforce and protect the right so granted; that congress is not restricted to legislation for the exertion **[109 U.S. 3, 29]** of its powers expressly granted; but, for the protection of rights guarantied by the constitution, it may employ, through legislation, such means, not prohibited, as are necessary and proper, or such as are appropriate, to attain the ends proposed; that the constitution recognized the master's right of property in his fugitive slave, and, as incidental thereto, the right of seizing and recovering him, regardless of any state law, or regulation, or local custom whatsoever; and that the right of the master to have his slave, so escaping, delivered up on claim, being guarantied by the constitution, the fair implication was that the national government was clothed with appropriate authority and functions to enforce it.

The court said:

"The fundamental principle, applicable to all cases of this sort, would seem to be that when the end is required the means are given, and when the duty is enjoined the ability to perform it is contemplated to exist on the part of the functionary to whom it is intrusted."

Again:

"It would be a strange anomaly and forced construction to suppose that the national government meant to rely for the due fulfillment of its own proper duties, and the rights which it intended to secure, upon state legislation, and not upon that of the Union. A fortiori, it would be more objectionable to suppose that a power which was to be the same throughout the Union should be confided to state sovereignty, which could not rightfully act beyond its own territorial limits."

The act of 1793 was, upon these grounds, adjudged to be a constitutional exercise of the powers of congress.

It is to be observed, from the report of *Prigg's* Case, that Pennsylvania, by her attorney general, pressed the argument that the obligation to surrender fugitive slaves was on the states and for the states, subject to the restriction that they should not pass laws or establish regulations liberating such fugitives; that the constitution did not take from the states the right to determine the status of all persons within their respective jurisdictions; that it was for the state in which the alleged fugitive was found to determine, through her courts, or in such modes as she prescribed, whether the person arrested was, in fact, a freeman or a fugitive slave; that the sole power **[109 U.S. 3, 30]** of the general government in the premises was, by judicial instrumentality, to restrain and correct, not to forbid and prevent in the absence of hostile state action; and that, for the general government to assume primary authority to legislate on the subject of fugitive slaves, to the exclusion of the states, would be a dangerous encroachment on state sovereignty. But to such suggestions this court turned a deaf ear, and adjudged that primary legislation by congress to enforce the master's right was authorized by the constitution.

We next come to the fugitive slave act of 1850, the constitutionality of which rested, as did that of 1793, solely upon the implied power of congress to enforce the master's rights. The provisions of that act were far in advance of previous legislation. They placed at the disposal of the master seeking to recover his fugitive slave, substantially, the whole power of the nation. It invested commissioners, appointed under the act, with power to summon the posse comitatus for the enforcement of its provisions, and commanded "all good citizens" to assist in its prompt and efficient execution whenever their services were required as part of the posse comitatus. Without going into the details of that act, it is sufficient to say that congress omitted from it nothing which the utmost ingenuity could suggest as essential to the successful enforcement of the master's claim to recover his fugitive slave. And this court, in *Ableman v. Booth*, 21 How. 526, adjudged it to be, "in all of its provisions, fully authorized by the constitution of the United States."

The only other decision prior to the adoption of the recent amendments, to which reference will be made, is *Dred Scott v. Sandford*, 19 How. 393. That suit was instituted in a circuit court of the United States by Dred Scott, claiming to be a citizen of Missouri, the defendant being a citizen of another state. Its object was to assert the title of himself and family to freedom. The defendant pleaded in abatement to the jurisdiction of the court that Scott-being of African descent, whose ancestors, of pure African blood, were brought into this country, and sold as slaves-was not a citizen. The only matter in issue, said the court, was whether the descendants of slaves so imported [109 U.S. 3, 31] and sold, when they should be emancipated, or who were born of parents who had become free before their birth, are citizens of a state in the sense in which the word "citizen" is used in the constitution of the United States.

In determining that question the court instituted an inquiry as to who were citizens of the several states at the adoption of the constitution, and who, at that time, were recognized as the people whose rights and liberties had been violated by the British government. The result was a declaration by this court, speaking through Chief Justice **TANEY**, that the legislation and histories of the times, and the language used in the Declaration of Independence, showed "that neither the class of persons who had been imported as slaves, nor their descendants, whether they had become free or not, were then acknowledged as a part of the people, nor intended to be included in the general words used in that instrument:" that "they had for more than a century before been regarded as beings of an inferior race, and altogether unfit to associate with the white race, either in social or political relations, and so far inferior that they had no rights which the white man was bound to respect, and that the negro might justly and lawfully be reduced to slavery for his benefit;" that he was "bought and sold, and treated as an ordinary article of merchandise and traffic, whenever a profit could be made by it;" and that "this opinion was at that time fixed and universal in the civilized portion of the white race. It was regarded as an axiom in morals as well as in politics, which no one thought of disputing, or supposed to be open to dispute; and men in every grade and position in society daily and habitually acted upon it in their private pursuits, as well as in matters of public concern, without for a moment doubting the correctness of this opinion."

The judgment of the court was that the words "people of the United States" and "citizens" meant the same thing, both describing "the political body who, according to our republican institutions, form the sovereignty and hold the power and conduct the government through their representatives;" that "they are what we familiarly call the 'sovereign people,'" and [109 U.S. 3, 32] every citizen is one of this people and a constituent member of this sovereignty;" but that the class of persons described in the plea in abatement did not compose a portion of this people, were not "included, and were not intended to be included, under the word 'citizens' in the constitution;" that, therefore, they could "claim none of the rights and privileges which that instrument provides for and secures to citizens of the United States;" that, "on the contrary, they were at that time considered as a subordinate and inferior class of beings, who had been subjugated by the dominant race, and, whether emancipated or not, yet remained subject to their authority, and had no rights or privileges but such as those who held the power and the government might choose to grant them."

Such were the relations which, prior to the adoption of the thirteenth amendment, existed between the government, whether national or state, and the descendants, whether free or in bondage, of those of African blood who had been imported into this country and sold as slaves.

The first section thereof provides that "neither slavery nor involuntary servitude, except as a punishment for crime, whereof the party shall have been duly convicted, shall exist within the United States, or any place subject to their jurisdiction." Its second section declares that "congress shall have power to enforce this article by appropriate legislation." This amendment was followed by the civil rights act of April 9, 1866, which, among other things, provided that "all persons born in the United States, and not subject to any foreign power, excluding Indians not taxed, are hereby declared to be citizens of the United States." 14 St. 27. The power of congress, in this mode, to elevate the race thus liberated to the plane of national citizenship, was maintained, by the supporters of the act of 1866, to be as full and complete as its power, by general statute, to make the children, being of full age, of persons naturalized in this country, citizens of the United States without going through the process of naturalization. The act of 1866, in this respect, was also likened to that of 1843, in which congress declared "that the Stockbridge tribe of Indians, and each and every one of them, shall be deemed to be, and are hereby declared to be, citizens of the United States to **[109 U.S. 3, 33]** all intent and purposes, and shall be entitled to all the rights, privileges, and immunities of such citizens, and shall in all respects be subject to the laws of the United States." If the act of 1866 was valid, as conferring national citizenship upon all embraced by its terms, then the colored race, liberated by the thirteenth amendment, became citizens of the United States prior to the adoption of the fourteenth amendment. But, in the view which I take of the present case, it is not necessary to examine this question.

The terms of the thirteenth amendment are absolute and universal. They embrace every race which then was, or might thereafter be, within the United States. No race, as such, can be excluded from the benefits or rights thereby conferred. Yet it is historically true that that amendment was suggested by the condition, in this country, of that race which had been declared by this court to have had, according to the opinion entertained by the most civilized portion of the white race at the time of the adoption of the constitution, "no rights which the white man was bound to respect," none of the privileges or immunities secured by that instrument to citizens of the United States. It had reference, in a peculiar sense, to a people which (although the larger part of them were in slavery) had been invited by an act of congress to aid, by their strong right arms, in saving from overthrow a government which, theretofore, by all of its departments, had treated them as an inferior race, with no legal rights or privileges except such as the white race might choose to grant them.

These are the circumstances under which the thirteenth amendment was proposed for adoption. They are now recalled only that we may better understand what was in the minds of the people when that amendment was being considered, and what were the mischiefs to be remedied, and the grievances to be redressed.

We have seen that the power of congress, by legislation, to enforce the master's right to have his slave delivered up on claim was implied from the recognition and guaranty of that right in the national constitution. But the power conferred by the thirteenth amendment does not rest upon implication or **[109 U.S. 3, 34]** inference. Those who framed it were not ignorant of the discussion, covering many years of the country's history, as to the constitutional power of congress to enact the fugitive slave laws of 1793 and 1850. When, therefore, it was determined, by a change in the fundamental law, to uproot the institution of slavery wherever it existed in this land, and to establish universal freedom, there was a fixed purpose to place the power of congress in the premises beyond the possibility of doubt. Therefore, *ex industria*, the power to enforce the thirteenth amendment, by appropriate legislation, was expressly granted. Legislation for that purpose, it is conceded, may be direct and primary. But to what specific ends may it be directed? This court has uniformly held that the national government has the power, whether expressly given or not, to secure and protect rights conferred or guarantied by the constitution. *U. S. v. Reese,* 92 U.S. 214 ; *Strauder v. West Virginia,* 100 U.S. 303 . That doctrine ought not now to be abandoned, when the inquiry is not as to an implied power to protect the master's rights, but what may congress do, under powers expressly granted, for the protection of freedom, and the rights necessarily inhering in a state of freedom.

The thirteenth amendment, my brethren concede, did something more than to prohibit slavery as an institution, resting upon distinctions of race, and upheld by positive law. They admit that it established and decreed universal civil freedom throughout the United States. But did the freedom thus established involve nothing more than exemption from actual slavery? Was nothing more intended than to forbid one man from owning another as property? Was it the purpose of the nation simply to destroy the institution, and then remit the race, theretofore held in bondage, to the several states for such protection, in their civil rights, necessarily growing out of freedom, as those states, in their discretion, choose to provide? Were the states, against whose solemn protest the institution was destroyed, to be left perfectly free, so far as national interference was concerned, to make or allow discriminations against that race, as such, in the enjoyment of those fundamental rights that inhere in a state of freedom? [109 U.S. 3, 35] Had the thirteenth amendment stopped with the sweeping declaration, in its first section, against the existence of slavery and involuntary servitude, except for crime, congress would have had the power, by implication, according to the doctrines of *Prigg v. Com.*, repeated in *Strauder v. West Virginia,* to protect the freedom thus established, and consequently to secure the enjoyment of such civil rights as were fundamental in freedom. But that it can exert its authority to that extent is now made clear, and was intended to be made clear, by the express grant of power contained in the second section of that amendment.

That there are burdens and disabilities which constitute badges of slavery and servitude, and that the express power delegated to congress to enforce, by appropriate legislation, the thirteenth amendment, may be exerted by legislation of a direct and primary character, for the eradication, not simply of the institution, but of its badges and incidents, are propositions which ought to be deemed indisputable. They lie at the very foundation of the civil rights act of 1866. Whether that act was fully authorized by the thirteenth amendment alone, without the support which it afterwards received from the fourteenth amendment, after the adoption of which it was re-enacted with some additions, the court, in its opinion, says it is unnecessary to inquire. But I submit, with all respect to my brethren, that its constitutionality is conclusively shown by other portions of their opinion. It is expressly conceded by them that the thirteenth amendment established freedom; that there are burdens and disabilities, the necessary incidents of slavery, which constitute its substance and visible form; that congress, by the act of 1866, passed in view of the thirteenth amendment, before the fourteenth was adopted, undertook to remove certain burdens and disabilities, the necessary incidents of slavery, and to secure to all citizens of every race and color, and without regard to previous servitude, those fundamental rights which are the essence of civil freedom, namely, the same right to make and enforce contracts, to sue, be parties, give evidence, and to inherit, purchase, lease, sell, and convey property as is enjoyed by white citizens; that under the thirteenth amendment congress has to do with slavery and [109 U.S. 3, 36] its incidents; and that legislation, so far as necessary or proper to eradicate all forms and incidents of slavery and involuntary servitude, may be direct and primary, operating upon the acts of individuals, whether sanctioned by state legislation or not. These propositions being conceded, it is impossible, as it seems to me, to question the constitutional validity of the civil rights act of 1866. I do not contend that the thirteenth amendment invests congress with authority, by legislation, to regulate the entire body of the civil rights which citizens enjoy, or may enjoy, in the several states. But I do hold that since slavery, as the court has repeatedly declared, was the moving or principal cause of the adoption of that amendment, and since that institution rested wholly upon the inferiority, as a race, of those held in bondage, their freedom necessarily involved immunity from, and protection against, all discrimination against them, because of their race, in respect of such civil rights as belong to freemen of other races. Congress, therefore, under its express power to enforce that amendment, by appropriate legislation, may enact laws to protect that people against the deprivation, on account of their race, of any civil rights enjoyed by other freemen in the same state; and such legislation may be of a direct and primary character, operating upon states, their officers and agents, and also upon, at least, such individuals and corporations as exercise public functions and wield power and authority under the state.

By way of testing the correctness of this position, let us suppose that, prior to the adoption of the fourteenth amendment, a state had passed a statute denying to freemen of African descent, resident within its limits, the same rights which were accorded to white persons, of making or enforcing contracts, or of inheriting, purchasing, leasing, selling, and conveying property; or a statute subjecting colored people to severer punishment for particular offenses than was prescribed for white persons, or excluding that race from the benefit of the laws exempting homesteads from execution. Recall the legislation of 1865-66 in some of the states, of which this court, in the *Slaughter-* [109 U.S. 3, 37] *house Cases,* said that it imposed upon the colored race onerous disabilities and burdens; curtailed their rights in the pursuit of life, liberty, and property to such an extent that their freedom was of little value; forbade them to appear in the towns in any other character than menial servants; required them to reside on and cultivate the soil, without the right to purchase or own it; excluded them from many occupations of gain; and denied them the privilege of giving testimony in the courts where a white man was a party. 16 Wall. 57. Can there by any doubt that all such legislation might have been reached by direct legislation upon the part of congress under its express power to enforce the thirteenth amendment? Would any court have hesitated to declare that such legislation imposed badges of servitude in conflict with the civil freedom ordained by that amendment? That it would have been also in conflict with the fourteenth amendment, because inconsistent with the fundamental rights of American citizenship, does not prove that it would have been consistent with the thirteenth amendment.

What has been said is sufficient to show that the power of congress under the thirteenth amendment is not necessarily restricted to legislation against slavery as an institution upheld by positive law, but may be exerted to the extent at least of protecting the race, so liberated, against discrimination, in respect of legal rights belonging to freemen, where such discrimination is based upon race.

It remains now to inquire what are the legal rights of colored persons in respect of the accommodations, privileges, and facilities of public conveyances, inns, and places of public amusement.

1. As to public conveyances on land and water. In *New Jersey Steam Nav. Co. v. Merchants' Bank,* 6 How. 382, this court, speaking by Mr. Justice NELSON, said that a common carrier is "in the exercise of a sort of public office and has public duties to perform, from which he should not be permitted to exonerate himself without the assent of the parties concerned." To the same effect is *Munn v. Illinois,* 94 U.S. 113 . In *Olcott v. Sup'rs,* 16 Wall. 694, it was ruled that [109 U.S. 3, 38] railroads are public highways, established, by authority of the state, for the public use; that they are none the less public highways because controlled and owned by private corporations; that it is a part of the function of government to make and maintain highways for the conveyance of the public; that no matter who is the agent, and what is the agency, the function performed is that of the state; that although the owners may be private companies, they may be compelled to permit the public to use these works in the manner in which they can be used; that upon these grounds alone have the courts sustained the investiture of railroad corporations with the state's right of eminent domain, or the right of municipal corporations, under legislative authority, to assess, levy, and collect taxes to aid in the construction of railroads. So in *Town of Queensbury v. Culver,* 19 Wall. 91, it was said that a municipal subscription of railroad stock was in aid of the construction and maintenance of a public highway and for the promotion of a public use. Again, in *Township of Pine Grove v. Talcott,* 19 Wall. 676: "Though the corporation [railroad] was private, its work was public; as much so as if it were to be constructed by the state." To the like effect are numerous adjudications in this and the state courts with which the profession is familiar. The supreme judicial court of Massachusetts, in *Inhabitants of Worcester v. Western R. Corp.* 4 Metc. 566, said, in reference to a certain railroad:

"The establishment of that great thoroughfare is regarded as a public work, established by public authority, intended for the public use and benefit, the use of which is secured to the whole community, and constitutes, therefore, like a canal, turnpike, or highway, a public easement. ... It is true that the real and personal property necessary to the establishment and management of the railroad is vested in the corporation; but it is in trust for the public."

In *Erie & N. E. R. Co. v. Casey*, 26 Pa. St. 287, the court, referring to an act repealing the charter of a railroad, and under which the state took possession of the road, said, speaking by Black, J.:

"It is a public highway, solemnly devoted to public use. When the lands were taken it was for such use, or they could not have been taken at all. ... Railroads established [109 U.S. 3, 39] upon land taken by the right of eminent domain by authority of the commonwealth, created by her laws as thoroughfares for commerce, are her highways. No corporation has property in them, though it may have franchises annexed to and exercisable within them."

In many courts it has been held that because of the public interest in such a corporation the land of a railroad company cannot be levied on and sold under execution by a creditor. The sum of the adjudged cases is that a railroad corporation is a governmental agency, created primarily for public purposes, and subject to be controlled for the public benefit. It is upon that ground that the state, when unfettered by contract, may regulate, in its discretion, the rates of fares of passengers and freight. And upon this ground, too, the state may regulate the entire management of railroads in all matters affecting the convenience and safety of the public; as, for example, by regulating speed, compelling stops of prescribed length at stations, and prohibiting discriminations and favoritism. If the corporation neglect or refuse to discharge its duties to the public, it may be coerced to do so by appropriate proceedings in the name or in behalf of the state.

Such being the relations these corporations hold to the public, it would seem that the right of a colored person to use an improved public highway, upon the terms accorded to freemen of other races, is as fundamental in the state of freedom, established in this country, as are any of the rights which my brethren concede to be so far fundamental as to be deemed the essence of civil freedom. "Personal liberty consists," says Blackstone, "in the power of locomotion, of changing situation, or removing one's person to whatever place one's own inclination may direct, without restraint, unless by due course of law." But of what value is this right of locomotion, if it may be clogged by such burdens as congress intended by the act of 1875 to remove? They are burdens which lay at the very foundation of the institution of slavery as it once existed. They are not to be sustained, except upon the assumption that there is still, in this land of universal liberty, a class which may yet be discriminated against, even in respect of rights of a character [109 U.S. 3, 40] so essential and so supreme, that, deprived of their enjoyment, in common with others, a freeman is not only branded as one inferior and infected, but, in the competitions of life, is robbed of some of the most necessary means of existence; and all this solely because they belong to a particular race which the nation has liberated. The thirteenth amendment alone obliterated the race line, so far as all rights fundamental in a state of freedom are concerned.

2. As to inns. The same general observations which have been made as to railroads are applicable to inns. The word "inn" has a technical legal signification. It means, in the act of 1875, just what it meant at common law. A mere private boarding-house is not an inn, nor is its keeper subject to the responsibilities, or entitled to the privileges of a common innkeeper. "To constitute one an innkeeper, within the legal force of that term, he must keep a house of entertainment or lodging for all travelers or wayfarers who might choose to accept the same, being of good character or conduct." Redf. Carr. 575. Says Judge STORY:

"An innkeeper may be defined to be the keeper of a common inn for the lodging and entertainment of travelers and passengers, their horses and attendants. An innkeeper is bound to take in all travelers and wayfaring persons, and to entertain them, if he can accommodate them, for a reasonable compensation; and he must guard their goods with proper diligence. ... If an innkeeper improperly refuses to receive or provide for a guest, he is liable to be indicted therefor. ... They [carriers of passengers] are no more at liberty to refuse a passenger, if they have sufficient room and accommodations, than an innkeeper is to refuse suitable room and accommodations to a guest." Story, Bailm. 475, 476.

Said Mr. Justice **COLERIDGE**, in *Rex v. Ivens*, 7 Car. & P. 213, (32 E. C. L. 495:)

"An indictment lies against an innkeeper who refuses to receive a guest, he having at the time room in his house; and either the price of the guest's entertainment being tendered to him, or such circumstances occurring as will dispense with that **[109 U.S. 3, 41]** tender. This law is founded in good sense. The innkeeper is not to select his guests. He has no right to say to one, you shall come to my inn, and to another you shall not, as every one coming and conducting himself in a proper manner has a right to be received; and for this purpose innkeepers are a sort of public servants, they having in return a kind of privilege of entertaining travelers and supplying them with that they want."

These authorities are sufficient to show a keeper of an inn is in the exercise of a quasi public employment. The law gives him special privileges, and he is charged with certain duties and responsibilities to the public. The public nature of his employment forbids him from discriminating against any person asking admission as a guest on account of the race or color of that person.

3. As to places of public amusement. It may be argued that the managers of such places have no duties to perform with which the public are, in any legal sense, concerned, or with which the public have any right to interfere; and that the exclusion of a black man from a place of public amusement on account of his race, or the denial to him, on that ground, of equal accommodations at such places, violates no legal right for the vindication of which he may invoke the aid of the courts. My answer to that argument is that places of public amusement, within the meaning of the act of 1875, are such as are established and maintained under direct license of the law. The authority to establish and maintain them comes from the public. The colored race is a part of that public. The local government granting the license represents them as well as all other races within its jurisdiction. A license from the public to establish a place of public amusement, imports, in law, equality of right, at such places, among all the members of that public. This must be so, unless it be-which I deny-that the common municipal government of all the people may, in the exertion of its powers, conferred for the benefit of all, discriminate or authorize discrimination against a particular race, solely because of its former condition of servitude.

I also submit whether it can be said—in view of the doctrines of this court as announced in *Munn v. Illinois*, **[109 U.S. 3, 42]** U. S. 123, and reaffirmed in *Peik v. Chicago & N. W. Ry. Co.* 94 U.S. 178 — that the management of places of public amusement is a purely private matter, with which government has no rightful concern. In the Munn Case the question was whether the state of Illinois could fix, by law, the maximum of charges for the storage of grain in certain warehouses in that state-the private property of individual citizens. After quoting a remark attributed to Lord Chief Justice **HALE**, to the effect that when private property is "affected with a public interest it ceases to be juris privati only," the court says:

"Property does become clothed with a public interest when used in a manner to make it of public consequence and affect the community at large. When, therefore, one devotes his property to a use in which the public has an interest, he in effect grants to the public an interest in that use, and must submit to be controlled by the public for the common good to the extent of the interest he has thus created. He may withdraw his grant by discontinuing the use, but, so long as he maintains the use, he must submit to the control."

The doctrines of *Munn v. Illinois* have never been modified by this court, and I am justified, upon the authority of that case, in saying that places of public amusement, conducted under the authority of the law, are clothed with a public interest, because used in a manner to make them of public consequence and to affect the community at large. The law may therefore regulate, to some extent, the mode in which they shall be conducted, and consequently the public have rights in respect of such places which may be vindicated by the law. It is consequently not a matter purely of private concern.

Congress has not, in these matters, entered the domain of state control and supervision. It does not assume to prescribe the general conditions and limitations under which inns, public conveyances, and places of public amusement shall be conducted or managed. It simply declares in effect that since the nation has established universal freedom in this country for all time, there shall be no discrimination, based merely upon race or color, in respect of the legal rights in the accommodations [109 U.S. 3, 43] and advantages of public conveyances, inns, and places of public amusement.

I am of opinion that such discrimination is a badge of servitude, the imposition of which congress may prevent under its power, through appropriate legislation, to enforce the thirteenth amendment; and consequently, without reference to its enlarged power under the fourteenth amendment, the act of March 1, 1875, is not, in my judgment, repugnant to the constitution.

It remains now to consider these cases with reference to the power congress has possessed since the adoption of the fourteenth amendment.

Before the adoption of the recent amendments it had become, as we have seen, the established doctrine of this court that negroes, whose ancestors had been imported and sold as slaves, could not become citizens of a state, or even of the United States, with the rights and privileges guarantied to citizens by the national constitution; further, that one might have all the rights and privileges of a citizen of a state without being a citizen in the sense in which that word was used in the national constitution, and without being entitled to the privileges and immunities of citizens of the several states. Still further, between the adoption of the thirteenth amendment and the proposal by congress of the fourteenth amendment, on June 16, 1866, the statute-books of several of the states, as we have seen, had become loaded down with enactments which, under the guise of apprentice, vagrant, and contract regulations, sought to keep the colored race in a condition, practically, of servitude. It was openly announced that whatever rights persons of that race might have as freemen, under the guaranties of the national constitution, they could not become citizens of a state, with the rights belonging to citizens, except by the consent of such state; consequently, that their civil rights, as citizens of the state, depended entirely upon state legislation. To meet this new peril to the black race, that the [109 U.S. 3, 44] purposes of the nation might not be doubted or defeated, and by way of further enlargement of the power of congress, the fourteenth amendment was proposed for adoption.

Remembering that this court, in the *Slaughter-House Cases*, declared that the one pervading purpose found in all the recent amendments, lying at the foundation of each, and without which none of them would have been suggested, was "the freedom of the slave race, the security and firm establishment of that freedom, and the protection of the newly-made freeman and citizen from the oppression of those who had formerly exercised unlimited dominion over him;" that each amendment was addressed primarily to the grievances of that race,—let us proceed to consider the language of the fourteenth amendment. Its first and fifth sections are in these words:

"Section 1. All persons born or naturalized in the United States, and subject to the jurisdiction thereof, are citizens of the United States and of the state wherein they reside. No state shall make or enforce any law which shall abridge the privileges or immunities of citizens of the United States; nor shall any state deprive any person of life, liberty, or property without due process of law; nor deny to any person within its jurisdiction the equal protection of the laws.

...

"Sec. 5. That congress shall have power to enforce, by appropriate legislation, the provisions of this article."

It was adjudged in *Strauder v. West Virginia* and *Ex parte Virginia*, 100 U.S. 307 , 345, and my brethren concede, that positive rights and privileges were intended to be secured, and are in fact secured, by the fourteenth amendment.

But when, under what circumstances, and to what extent may congress, by means of legislation, exert its power to enforce the provisions of this amendment? The logic of the opinion of the majority of the court-the foundation upon which its whole reasoning seems to rest-is that the general government cannot, in advance of hostile state laws or hostile state [109 U.S. 3, 45] proceedings, actively interfere for the protection of any of the rights, privileges, and immunities secured by the fourteenth amendment. It is said that such rights, privileges, and immunities are secured by way of prohibition against state laws and state proceedings affecting such rights and privileges, and by power given to congress to legislate for the purpose of carrying such prohibition into effect; also, that congressional legislation must necessarily be predicated upon such supposed state laws or state proceedings, and be directed to the correction of their operation and effect.

In illustration of its position, the court refers to the clause of the constitution forbidding the passage by a state of any law impairing the obligation of contracts. The clause does not, I submit, furnish a proper illustration of the scope and effect of the fifth section of the fourteenth amendment. **No express power is given congress to enforce, by primary direct legislation, the prohibition upon state laws impairing the obligation of contracts.** Authority is, indeed, conferred to enact all necessary and proper laws for carrying into execution the enumerated powers of congress, and all other powers vested by the constitution in the government of the United States, or in any department or officer thereof. And, as heretofore shown, there is also, by necessary implication, power in congress, by legislation, to protect a right derived from the national constitution. **But a prohibition upon a state is not a power in congress or in the national government. It is simply a denial of power to the state. And the only mode in which the inhibition upon state laws impairing the obligation of contracts can be enforced, is, indirectly, through the courts, in suits where the parties raise some question as to the constitutional validity of such laws.** The judicial power of the United States extends to such suits, for the reason that they are suits arising under the constitution. The fourteenth amendment presents the first instance in our history of the investiture of congress with affirmative power, by legislation, to enforce an express prohibition upon the states. It is not said that the judicial power of the nation may be exerted for the enforcement of that amendment. No enlargement of the judicial power was required, for it is clear **[109 U.S. 3, 46]** that had the fifth section of the fourteenth amendment been entirely omitted, the judiciary could have stricken down all state laws and nullified all state proceedings in hostility to rights and privileges secured or recognized by that amendment. The power given is, in terms, by congressional legislation, to enforce the provisions of the amendment.

The assumption that this amendment consists wholly of prohibitions upon state laws and state proceedings in hostility to its provisions, is unauthorized by its language. The first clause of the first section—"all persons born or naturalized in the United States, and subject to the jurisdiction thereof, are citizens of the United States, and of the state wherein they reside"—is of a distinctly affirmative character. In its application to the colored race, previously liberated, it created and granted, as well citizenship of the United States, as citizenship of the state in which they respectively resided. It introduced all of that race, whose ancestors had been imported and sold as slaves, at once, into the political community known as the "People of the United States." They became, instantly, citizens of the United States, and of their respective states. Further, they were brought, by this supreme act of the nation, within the direct operation of that provision of the constitution which declares that "the citizens of each state shall be entitled to all privileges and immunities of citizens in the several states." Article 4, 2.

The citizenship thus acquired by that race, in virtue of an affirmative grant by the nation, may be protected, not alone by the judicial branch of the government, but by congressional legislation of a primary direct character; this, because the power of congress is not restricted to the enforcement of prohibitions upon state laws or state action. It is, in terms distinct and positive, to enforce "the provisions of this article" of amendment; not simply those of a prohibitive character, but the provisions,—all of the provisions,—affirmative and prohibitive, of the amendment. It is, therefore, a grave misconception to suppose that the fifth section of the amendment has reference exclusively to express prohibitions upon state laws or state action. If any right was created by that amendment, the **[109 U.S. 3, 47]** grant of power, through appropriate legislation, to enforce its provisions authorizes congress, by means of legislation operating throughout the entire Union, to guard, secure, and protect that right.

It is, therefore, an essential inquiry what, if any, right, privilege, or immunity was given by the nation to colored persons when they were made citizens of the state in which they reside? Did the national grant of state citizenship to that race, of its own force, invest them with any rights, privileges, and immunities whatever? That they became entitled, upon the adoption of the fourteenth amendment, "to all privileges and immunities of citizens in the several states," within the meaning of section 2 of article 4 of the constitution, no one, I suppose, will for a moment question. What are the privileges and immunities to which, by that clause of the constitution, they became entitled? To this it may be answered, generally, upon the authority of the adjudged cases, that they are those which are fundamental in citizenship in a free government, "common to the citizens in the latter states under their constitutions and laws by virtue of their being citizens." Of that provision it has been said, with the approval of this court, that no other one in the constitution has tended so strongly to constitute the citizens of the United States one people. *Ward v. Maryland,* 12 Wall. 430; *Corfield v. Coryell,* 4 Wash. C. C. 371; *Paul v. Virginia,* 8 Wall. 180; *Slaughter-House Cases,* 16 Wall. 77.

Although this court has wisely forborne any attempt, by a comprehensive definition, to indicate all the privileges and immunities to which the citizens of each state are entitled of right to enjoy in the several states, I hazard nothing, in view of former adjudications, in saying that no state can sustain her denial to colored citizens of other states, while within her limits, of privileges or immunities, fundamental in republican citizenship, upon the ground that she accords such privileges and immunities only to her white citizens and withholds them from her colored citizens. The colored citizens of other states, within the jurisdiction of that state, could claim, under the constitution, every privilege and immunity **[109 U.S. 3, 48]** which that state secures to her white citizens. Otherwise, it would be in the power of any state, by discriminating class legislation against its own citizens of a particular race or color, to withhold from citizens of other states, belonging to that proscribed race, when within her limits, privileges and immunities of the character regarded by all courts as fundamental in citizenship; and that, too, when the constitutional guaranty is that the citizens of each state shall be entitled to "all privileges and immunities of citizens of the several states." No state may, by discrimination against a portion of its own citizens of a particular race, in respect of privileges and immunities fundamental in citizenship, impair the constitutional right of citizens of other states, of whatever race, to enjoy in that state all such privileges and immunities as are there accorded to her most favored citizens. A colored citizen of Ohio or Indiana, being in the jurisdiction of Tennessee, is entitled to enjoy any privilege or immunity, fundamental in citizenship, which is given to citizens of the white race in the latter state. It is not to be supposed that any one will controvert this proposition.

But what was secured to colored citizens of the United States-as between them and their respective states-by the grant to them of state citizenship? With what rights, privileges, or immunities did this grant from the nation invest them? There is one, if there be no others-exemption from race discrimination in respect of any civil right belonging to citizens of the white race in the same state. That, surely, is their constitutional privilege when within the jurisdiction of other states. And such must be their constitutional right, in their own state, unless the recent amendments be "splendid baubles," thrown out to delude those who deserved fair and generous treatment at the hands of the nation. Citizenship in this country necessarily imports equality of civil rights among citizens of every race in the same state. It is fundamental in American citizenship that, in respect of such rights, there shall be no discrimination by the state, or its officers, or by individuals, or by corporations exercising public functions or authority, against any citizen because of his race or previous condition of servitude. In *U. S. v. Cruikshank,* 92 U.S. 555 , it was said **[109 U.S. 3, 49]** that "the equality of rights of citizens is a principle of republicanism." And in *Ex parte Virginia,* 100 U.S. 344 , the emphatic language of this court is that "one great purpose of these amendments was to raise the colored race from that condition of inferiority and servitude in which most of them had previously stood, into perfect equality of civil rights with all other persons within the jurisdiction of the states." So, in *Strauder v. West Virginia,* Id. 306, the court, alluding to the fourteenth amendment, said: "This is one of a series of constitutional provisions having a common purpose, namely, securing to a race recently emancipated, a race that through many generations had been held in slavery, all the civil rights that the superior race enjoy." Again, in *Neal v. Delaware*, 103 U.S. 386 , it was ruled that this amendment was designed, primarily, "to secure to the colored race, thereby invested with the rights, privileges, and responsibilities of citizenship, the enjoyment of all the civil rights that, under the law, are enjoyed by white persons."

Much light is thrown upon this part of the discussion by the language of this court in reference to the fifteenth amendment. In *U. S. v. Cruikshank* it was said:

"In U. S. v. Reese, 92 U.S. 214 , we held that the fifteenth amendment has invested the citizens of the United States with a new constitutional right, which is exemption from discrimination in the exercise of the elective franchise on account of race, color, or previous condition of servitude. From this it appears that the right of suffrage is not a necessary attribute of national citizenship, but that exemption from discrimination in the exercise of that right on account of race, etc., is. The right to vote in the states comes from the states; but the right of exemption from the prohibited discrimination comes from the United States. The first has not been granted or secured by the constitution of the United States, but the last has been."

Here, in language at once clear and forcible, is stated the principle for which I contend. It can hardly be claimed that exemption from race discrimination, in respect of civil rights, against those to whom state citizenship was granted by the **[109 U.S. 3, 50]** nation, is any less for the colored race a new constitutional right, derived from and secured by the national constitution, than is exemption from such discrimination in the exercise of the elective franchise. It cannot be that the latter is an attribute of national citizenship, while the other is not essential in national citizenship, or fundamental in state citizenship.

If, then, exemption from discrimination in respect of civil rights is a new constitutional right, secured by the grant of state citizenship to colored citizens of the United States, why may not the nation, by means of its own legislation of a primary direct character, guard, protect, and enforce that right? It is a right and privilege which the nation conferred. It did not come from the states in which those colored citizens reside. It has been the established doctrine of this court during all its history, accepted as vital to the national supremacy, that congress, in the absence of a positive delegation of power to the state legislatures, may by legislation enforce and protect any right derived from or created by the national constitution. It was so declared in *Prigg v. Com.* It was reiterated in *U. S. v. Reese*, 92 U.S. 214 , where the court said that "rights and immunities created by and dependent upon the constitution of the United States can be protected by congress. The form and manner of the protection may be such as congress, in the legitimate exercise of its discretion, shall provide. These may be varied to meet the necessities of the particular right to protected." It was distinctly reaffirmed in *Strauder v. West Virginia*, 100 U.S. 310, where we said that "a right or immunity created by the constitution or only guarantied by it, even without any express delegation of power, may be protected by congress." Will any one claim, in view of the declarations of this court in former cases, or even without them, that exemption of colored citizens within their states from race discrimination, in respect of the civil rights of citizens, is not an immunity created or derived from the national constitution?

This court has always given a broad and liberal construction to the constitution, so as to enable congress, by legislation, to **[109 U.S. 3, 51]** enforce rights secured by that instrument. The legislation congress may enact, in execution of its power to enforce the provisions of this amendment, is that which is appropriate to protect the right granted. Under given circumstances, that which the court characterizes as corrective legislation might be sufficient. Under other circumstances primary direct legislation may be required. But it is for congress, not the judiciary, to say which is best adapted to the end to be attained. In *U. S. v. Fisher*, 2 Cranch, 358, this court said that "congress must possess the choice of means, and must be empowered to use any means which are in fact conducive to the exercise of a power granted by the constitution." "The sound construction of the constitution," said Chief Justice **MARSHALL**, "must allow to the national legislature that discretion, with respect to the means by which the powers it confers are to be carried into execution, which will enable that body to perform the high duties assigned to it in the manner most beneficial to the people. Let the end be legitimate,—let it be within the scope of the constitution,—and all means which are appropriate, which are plainly adapted to that end, which are not prohibited, but consistent with the letter and spirit of the constitution, are constitutional." *McCulloch v. Maryland*, 4 Wheat. 423.

Must these rules of construction be now abandoned? Are the powers of the national legislature to be restrained in proportion as the rights and privileges, derived from the nation, are more valuable? Are constitutional provisions, enacted to secure the dearest rights of freemen and citizens, to be subjected to that rule of construction, applicable to private instruments, [109 U.S. 3, 52] which requires that the words to be interpreted must be taken most strongly against those who employ them? Or shall it be remembered that "a constitution of government, founded by the people for themselves and their posterity, and for objects of the most momentous nature,—for perpetual union, for the establishment of justice, for the general welfare, and for a perpetuation of the blessings of liberty,—necessarily requires that every interpretation of its powers should have a constant reference to these objects? No interpretation of the words in which those powers are granted can be a sound one which narrows down their ordinary import so as to defeat those objects." 1 Story, Const. 422.

The opinion of the court, as I have said, proceeds upon the ground that the power of congress to legislate for the protection of the rights and privileges secured by the fourteenth amendment cannot be brought into activity except with the view, and as it may become necessary, to correct and annul state laws and state proceedings in hostility to such rights and privileges. In the absence of state laws or state action, adverse to such rights and privileges, the nation may not actively interfere for their protection and security. Such I understand to be the position of my brethren. If the grant to colored citizens of the United States of citizenship in their respective states imports exemption from race discrimination, in their states, in respect of the civil rights belonging to citizenship, then, to hold that the amendment remits that right to the states for their protection, primarily, and stays the hands of the nation, until it is assailed by state laws or state proceedings, is to adjudge that the amendment, so far from enlarging the powers of congress,—as we have heretofore said it did,—not only curtails them, but reverses the policy which the general government has pursued from its very organization. Such an interpretation of the amendment is a denial to congress of the power, by appropriate legislation, to enforce one of its provisions. In view of the circumstances under which the recent amendments were incorporated into the constitution, and especially in view of the peculiar character of the new [109 U.S. 3, 53] rights they created and secured, it ought not to be presumed that the general government has abdicated its authority, by national legislation, direct and primary in its character, to guard and protect privileges and immunities secured by that instrument. Such an interpretation of the constitution ought not to be accepted if it be possible to avoid it. Its acceptance would lead to this anomalous result: that whereas, prior to the amendments, congress, with the sanction of this court, passed the most stringent laws-operating directly and primarily upon states, and their officers and agents, as well as upon individuals-in vindication of slavery and the right of the master, it may not now, by legislation of a like primary and direct character, guard, protect, and secure the freedom established, and the most essential right of the citizenship granted, by the constitutional amendments. I venture, with all respect for the opinion of others, to insist that the national legislature may, without transcending the limits of the constitution, do for human liberty and the fundamental rights of American citizenship, what it did, with the sanction of this court, for the protection of slavery and the rights of the masters of fugitive slaves. If fugitive slave laws, providing modes and prescribing penalties whereby the master could seize and recover his fugitive slave, were legitimate exertions of an implied power to protect and enforce a right recognized by the constitution, why shall the hands of congress be tied, so that-under an express power, by appropriate legislation, to enforce a constitutional provision, granting citizenship- it may not, by means of direct legislation, bring the whole power of this nation to bear upon states and their officers, and upon such individuals and corporations exercising public functions, as assume to abridge, impair, or deny rights confessedly secured by the supreme law of the land?

It does not seem to me that the fact that, by the second clause of the first section of the fourteenth amendment, the states are expressly prohibited from making or enforcing laws abridging the privileges and immunities of citizens of the United States, furnishes any sufficient reason for holding or maintaining that the amendment was intended to deny congress the power, by general, primary, and direct legislation, of **[109 U.S. 3, 54]** protecting citizens of the United States, being also citizens of their respective states, against discrimination, in respect to their rights as citizens, founded on race, color, or previous condition of servitude. Such an interpretation of the amendment is plainly repugnant to its fifth section, conferring upon congress power, by appropriate legislation, to enforce, not merely the provisions containing prohibitions upon the states, but all of the provisions of the amendment, including the provisions, express and implied, of the grant of citizenship in the first clause of the first section of the article. This alone is sufficient for holding that congress is not restricted to the enactment of laws adapted to counteract and redress the operation of state legislation, or the action of state officers of the character prohibited by the amendment. It was perfectly well known that the great danger to the equal enjoyment by citizens of their rights, as citizens, was to be apprehended, not altogether from unfriendly state legislation, but from the hostile action of corporations and individuals in the states. And it is to be presumed that it was intended, by that section, to clothe congress with power and authority to meet that danger. If the rights intended to be secured by the act of 1875 are such as belong to the citizen, in common or equally with other citizens in the same state, then it is not to be denied that such legislation is appropriate to the end which congress is authorized to accomplish, viz., to protect the citizen, in respect of such rights, against discrimination on account of his race. As to the prohibition in the fourteenth amendment upon the making or enforcing of state laws abridging the privileges of citizens of the United States, it was impossible for any state to have enforced laws of that character. The judiciary could have annulled all such legislation under the provision that the constitution shall be the supreme law of the land, anything in the constitution or laws of any state to the contrary notwithstanding. The states were **[109 U.S. 3, 55]** already under an implied prohibition not to abridge any privilege or immunity belonging to citizens of the United States as such. Consequently, the prohibition upon state laws hostile to the rights belonging to citizens of the United States, was intended only as an express limitation on the powers of the states, and was not intended to diminish, in the slightest degree, the authority which ten nation has always exercised, of protecting, by means of its own direct legislation, rights created or secured by the constitution. The purpose not to diminish the national authority is distinctly negatived by the express grant of power, by legislation, to enforce every provision of the amendment, including that which, by the grant of citizenship in the state, secures exemption from race discrimination in respect of the civil rights of citizens.

It is said that any interpretation of the fourteenth amendment different from that adopted by the court, would authorize congress to enact a municipal code for all the states, covering every matter affecting the life, liberty, and property of the citizens of the several states. Not so. Prior to the adoption of that amendment the constitutions of the several states, without, perhaps, an exception, secured all persons against deprivation of life, liberty, or property, otherwise than by due process of law, and, in some form, recognized the right of all persons to the equal protection of the laws. These rights, therefore, existed before that amendment was proposed or adopted. If, by reason of that fact, it be assumed that protection in these rights of persons still rests, primarily, with the states, and that congress may not interfere except to enforce, by means of corrective legislation, the prohibitions upon state laws or state proceedings inconsistent with those rights, it does not at all follow that privileges which have been granted by the nation may not be protected by primary legislation upon the part of congress. The rights and immunities of persons recognized in the prohibitive clauses of the amendments were always **[109 U.S. 3, 56]** under the protection, primarily, of the states, while rights created by or derived from the United States have always been, and, in the nature of things, should always be, primarily, under the protection of the general government. Exemption from race discrimination in respect of the civil rights which are fundamental in citizenship in a republican government, is, as we have seen, a new constitutional right, created by the nation, with express power in congress, by legislation, to enforce the constitutional provision from which it is derived. If, in some sense, such race discrimination is a denial of the equal protection of the laws, within the letter of the last clause of the first section, it cannot be possible that a mere prohibition upon state denial of such equal protection to persons within its jurisdiction, or a prohibition upon state laws abridging the privileges and immunities of citizens of the United States, takes from the nation the power which it has uniformly exercised of protecting, by primary direct legislation, those privileges and immunities which existed under the constitution before the adoption of the fourteenth amendment, or which have been created by that amendment in behalf of those thereby made citizens of their respective states. **[109 U.S. 3, 57]** It was said of *Dred Scott v. Sandford* that this court in that case overruled the action of two generations, virtually inserted a new clause in the constitution, changed its character, and made a new departure in the workings of the federal government. I may be permitted to say that if the recent amendments are so construed that congress may not, in its own discretion, and independently of the action or non-action of the states, provide, by legislation of a primary and direct character, for the security of rights created by the national constitution; if it be adjudged that the obligation to protect the fundamental privileges and immunities granted by the fourteenth amendment to citizens residing in the several states, rests, primarily, not on the nation, but on the states; if it be further adjudged that individuals and corporations exercising public functions may, without liability to direct primary legislation on the part of congress, make the race of citizens the ground for denying them that equality of civil rights which the constitution ordains as a principle of republican citizenship,— then, not only the foundations upon which the national supremacy has always securely rested will be materially disturbed, but we shall enter upon an era of constitutional law when the rights of freedom and American citizenship cannot receive from the nation that efficient protection which heretofore was accorded to slavery and the rights of the master.

But if it were conceded that the power of congress could not be brought into activity until the rights specified in the act of 1875 had been abridged or denied by some state law or state action, I maintain that the decision of the court is erroneous. There has been adverse state action within the fourteenth amendment as heretofore interpreted by this court. I allude to Ex parte Virginia, supra. It appears, in that case, that one Cole, judge of a county court, was charged with the duty, by the laws of Virginia, of selecting grand and petit jurors. The law of the state did not authorize or permit him, in making such selections, to discriminate against colored citizens because of their race. But he was indicted in the federal court, under the act of 1875, for making such discriminations. **[109 U.S. 3, 58]** The attorney general of Virginia contended before us that the state had done its duty, and had not authorized or directed that county judge to do what he was charged with having done, and consequently that the state had not denied to the colored race the equal protection of the laws, and the act of Cole must therefore be deemed his individual act, in contravention of the will of the state. Plausible as this argument was, it failed to convince this court, and after saying that the fourteenth amendment had reference to the political body denominated a state, "by whatever instruments or in whatever modes that action may be taken," and that a state acts by its legislative, executive, and judicial authorities, and can act in no other way, we proceeded:

"The constitutional provision, therefore, must mean that no agency of the state, or of the officers or agents by whom its powers are exerted, shall deny to any person within its jurisdiction the equal protection of the laws. Whoever, by virtue of public position under a state government, deprives another of property, life, or liberty without due process of law, or denies or takes away the equal protection of the laws, violates the constitutional inhibition; and, as he acts under the name and for the state, and is clothed with the state's power, his act is that of the state. This must be so, or the constitutional prohibition has no meaning. Then the state has clothed one of its agents with power to annul or evade it. But the constitutional amendment was ordained for a purpose. It was to secure equal rights to all persons, and, to insure to all persons the enjoyment of such rights, power was given to congress to enforce its provisions by appropriate legislation. Such legislation must act upon persons, not upon the abstract thing denominated a state, but upon the persons who are the agents of the state, in the denial of the rights which were intended to be secured." 100 U.S. 346 , 347.

In every material sense applicable to the practical enforcement of the fourteenth amendment, railroad corporations, keepers of inns, and managers of places of public amusement are agents of the state, because [109 U.S. 3, 59] amenable, in respect of their public duties and functions, to public regulation. It seems to me that, within the principle settled in *Ex parte Virginia*, a denial by these instrumentalities of the state to the citizen, because of his race, of that equality of civil rights secured to him by law, is a denial by the state within the meaning of the fourteenth amendment. If it be not, then that race is left, in respect of the civil rights under discussion, practically at the mercy of corporations and individuals wielding power under public authority.

But the court says that congress did not, in the act of 1866, assume, under the authority given by the thirteenth amendment, to adjust what may be called the social rights of men and races in the community. I agree that government has nothing to do with social, as distinguished from technically legal, rights of individuals. No government ever has brought, or ever can bring, its people into social intercourse against their wishes. Whether one person will permit or maintain social relations with another is a matter with which government has no concern. I agree that if one citizen chooses not to hold social intercourse with another, he is not and cannot be made amenable to the law for his conduct in that regard; for no legal right of a citizen is violated by the refusal of others to maintain merely social relations with him, even upon grounds of race. What I affirm is that no state, nor the officers of any state, nor any corporation or individual wielding power under state authority for the public benefit or the public convenience, can, consistently either with the freedom established by the fundamental law, or with that equality of civil rights which now belongs to every citizen, discriminate against freemen or citizens, in their civil rights, because of their race, or because they once labored under disabilities imposed upon them as a race. The rights which congress, by the act of 1875, endeavored to secure and protect are legal, not social, rights. The right, for instance, of a colored citizen to use the accommodations of a public highway upon the same terms as are permitted to white citizens is no more a social right than his right, under the law, to use the public streets of a city, or a town, or a turnpike road, or a public market, or a post-office, or his right to sit [109 U.S. 3, 60] in a public building with others, of whatever race, for the purpose of hearing the political questions of the day discussed. Scarcely a day passes without our seeing in this court-room citizens of the white and black races sitting side by side watching the progress of our business. It would never occur to any one that the presence of a colored citizen in a court-house or court-room was an invasion of the social rights of white persons who may frequent such places. And yet such a suggestion would be quite as sound in law-1 say it with all respect-as is the suggestion that the claim of a colored citizen to use, upon the same terms as is permitted to white citizens, the accommodations of public highways, or public inns, or places of public amusement, established under the license of the law, is an invasion of the social rights of the white race.

The court, in its opinion, reserves the question whether congress, in the exercise of its power to regulate commerce among the several states, might or might not pass a law regulating rights in public conveyances passing from one state to another. I beg to suggest that that precise question was substantially presented here in the only one of these cases relating to railroads,— *Robinson v. Memphis & C. R. Co.* In that case it appears that Mrs. Robinson, a citizen of Mississippi, purchased a railroad ticket entitling her to be carried from Grand Junction, Tennessee, to Lynchburg, Virginia. Might not the act of 1875 be maintained in that case, as applicable at least to commerce between the states, notwithstanding it does not, upon its face, profess to have been passed in pursuance of the power given to congress to regulate commerce? Has it ever been held that the judiciary should overturn a statute because the legislative department did not accurately recite therein the particular provision of the constitution authorizing its enactment? We have often enforced municipal bonds in aid of railroad subscriptions where they failed to recite the statute authorizing their issue, but recited one which did not sustain their validity. The inquiry in such cases has been, was there in any statute authority for the execution of the bonds? Upon this branch of the case it may be remarked that the state of Louisiana, in 1869, passed a statute **[109 U.S. 3, 61]** giving to passengers, without regard to race or color, equality of right in the accommodations of railroad and street cars, steam-boats, or other water-crafts, stage-coaches, omnibuses, or other vehicles. But in *Hall v. De Cuir,* 95 U.S. 487 , that act was pronounced unconstitutional so far as it related to commerce between the states, this court saying that "if the public good requires such legislation it must come from congress and not from the states." I suggest that it may become a pertinent inquiry whether congress may, in the exertion of its power to regulate commerce among the states, enforce among passengers on public conveyances equality of right without regard to race, color, or previous condition of servitude, if it be true—which I do not admit—that such legislation would be an interference by government with the social rights of the people.

My brethren say that when a man has emerged from slavery, and by the aid of beneficent legislation has shaken off the inseparable concomitants of that state, there must be some stage in the progress of his elevation when he takes the rank of a mere citizen, and ceases to be the special favorite of the laws, and when his rights as a citizen, or a man, are to be protected in the ordinary modes by which other men's rights are protected. It is, I submit, scarcely just to say that the colored race has been the special favorite of the laws. What the nation, through congress, has sought to accomplish in reference to that race is, what had already been done in every state in the Union for the white race, to secure and protect rights belonging to them as freemen and citizens; nothing more. The one underlying purpose of congressional legislation has been to enable the black race to take the rank of mere citizens. The difficulty has been to compel a recognition of their legal right to take that rank, and to secure the enjoyment of privileges belonging, under the law, to them as a component part of the people for whose welfare and happiness government is ordained. **[109 U.S. 3, 62]** At every step in this direction the nation has been confronted with class tyranny, which a contemporary English historian says is, of all tyrannies, the most intolerable, "for it is ubiquitous in its operation, and weighs, perhaps, most heavily on those whose obscurity or distance would withdraw them from the notice of a single despot." Today it is the colored race which is denied, by corporations and individuals wielding public authority, rights fundamental in their freedom and citizenship. At some future time it may be some other race that will fall under the ban. If the constitutional amendments be enforced, according to the intent with which, as I conceive, they were adopted, there cannot be, in this republic, any class of human beings in practical subjection to another class, with power in the latter to dole out to the former just such privileges as they may choose to grant. The supreme law of the land has decreed that no authority shall be exercised in this country upon the basis of discrimination, in respect of civil rights, against freemen and citizens because of their race, color, or previous condition of servitude. To that decree-for the due enforcement of which, by appropriate legislation, congress has been invested with express power-every one must bow, whatever may have been, or whatever now are, his individual views as to the wisdom or policy, either of the recent changes in the fundamental law, or of the legislation which has been enacted to give them effect.

For the reasons stated I feel constrained to withhold my assent to the opinion of the court.

United States Supreme Court
Colgate v. Harvey, 296 U.S. 404 (1935)

Argued Oct. 14, 15, 1935. Decided Dec. 16, 1935.
(headnotes omitted)

[**296 U.S. 404, 408**] Mr. E. J. Dimock, of New York City, for appellant.

[**296 U.S. 404, 410**] Mr. Guy M. Page, of Burlington, Vt., and Mr. Seymour P. Edgerton, of Rutland, Vt., for appellee.

[**296 U.S. 404, 416**]

Mr. Justice Sutherland delivered the opinion of the Court.

The Vermont Income and Franchise Tax Act of 1931, Public Laws of Vermont, 1933, 872 et seq. (the pertinent provisions of which are copied in the margin[1]), imposes [**296 U.S.**

---

[1] "Chapter 39.

"Sec. 873. *Rate; Exemptions*; Amount. —A tax is hereby imposed upon every resident of the state, which tax shall be levied, collected and paid annually, with respect to;

"I. His net income as herein defined, after deducting the exemptions provided in this chapter, at the rate of two per cent; and

"II. To the income received by him on account of the ownership or use of or interest in any stock, bond, note, agreement or other interest bearing security at the rate of four per cent; but the words 'income received by him on account of the ownership or use of or interest in any stock, bond, note, agreement or other interest bearing security' shall not include the following items which shall be exempt from taxation under this chapter:

"(a) Interest received on account of money loaned within this state, at a rate of interest not exceeding five per cent per annum evidenced by a promissory note, mortgage on real estate or a bond for a deed, including credits representing the purchase price, or any part thereof, of real estate within this state, sold or transferred, evidenced by a promissory note, mortgage or bond for a deed bearing a rate of interest not exceeding five per cent per annum. ...

"(e) Dividends on stocks of those corporations which are subject to taxation under chapter 40, but if a corporate franchise tax is not measured by the entire net income of such corporation, then a portion of the dividends paid by such corporation shall be taxable under this chapter, and such taxable portion shall be that proportion of the dividend as the income earned by the corporation from business done without the state of Vermont bears to the entire income of the corporation;

"(f). In case the income taxed in this section is derived wholly from ownership of or interest in any stock, bond, note or other interest bearing security, there shall be deducted from such income the following exemptions:

"1. In case of a single individual a personal exemption of four hundred dollars;

"2. In the case of the head of a family, or a married individual living with husband or wife, a personal exemption of eight hundred dollars; but if either a husband or wife shall receive any income other than that derived from the ownership of or interest in any stock, bond, note or other interest bearing security, then such personal exemption shall not be allowed. A husband and wife, living together, shall receive but one personal exemption of eight hundred dollars against their aggregate net income; and in case they make separate returns, the personal exemption of eight hundred dollars may be taken by either or divided between them. ...

"Chapter 40.

"Sec. 887. *Rate*. —For the privilege of exercising its franchise in this state in a corporate or organized capacity, every domestic corporation, and for the privilege of doing business in this state, every foreign corporation, liable to tax under this chapter shall annually pay to this state a franchise tax to be measured by its net income to be — (Continued on the following page)

155

404, 417] individual income taxes as follows: First, with respect to net income derived from salaries, wages, etc., denominated by the court below class A income, at the rate of 2 per cent.; second, with respect to income received on account of the ownership or use of or interest in any interest bearing security, denominated class B income, at the rate of 4 per cent., excluding, however, from such income (a) interest received **[296 U.S. 404, 418]** on account of money loaned within the state at a rate of interest not exceeding 5 per cent. per annum, evidenced by a promissory note, mortgage, or bond for a deed bearing a like rate of interest; (b) dividends on stocks of corporations subject to taxation under sections 887, 888 of the statute. If the income taxed is derived wholly from interest- bearing securities, there is allowed, in the case of a single individual, a personal exemption of $400, and, in the case of a head of a family or of a married individual living with husband or wife, a personal exemption of $ 800. If, however, either husband or wife shall receive any income other than that derived from such securities, then the personal exemption is not allowed. A distinct and larger personal exemption is allowed in the case of net income derived from salaries, wages, etc. (Section 880); namely, $1, 000 in the case of a single individual, and $2,000 in the case of a head of a family or a married individual living with husband or wife.

Appellant is a resident of Vermont, married, and living with his wife. During the taxable year in question, he received both class A and class B income; but his class A income, although large, was absorbed by allowable deductions, so that there was no net income from that source, and consequently nothing subject to taxation. His class B income amounted to a larger sum, part of which consisted of interest on notes, mortgages, etc., representing money loaned outside the state of Vermont at not exceeding 5 per cent. per annum, and another part from taxable dividends received from corporations other than Vermont corporations. Upon these two sums a tax was assessed against him at the rate of 4 per cent. Under the statute, he was allowed no personal exemption whatever.

The validity of the statute under the Federal Constitution was properly challenged. The grounds of attack, so far as necessary to be stated, are as follows: (1) The act imposes a tax upon dividends earned outside the state of **[296 U.S. 404, 419]** Vermont, while exempting from the tax dividends earned within the state, thereby denying petitioner the equal protection of the laws in violation of the Fourteenth Amendment; (2) the act, in violation of the same clause, discriminates in favor of money loaned within the state as against money loaned outside the state; (3) the act arbitrarily denies appellant the $ 800 exemption while giving it to other persons whose situation differed from his only in that they had no income from business, and thereby denies appellant the equal protection of the laws guaranteed by the Fourteenth Amendment; and in each of these three particulars the act abridges the privileges and immunities of appellant as a citizen of the United States in contravention of the same amendment.[2]

(Continued from the previous footnote.) computed in the manner hereinafter provided at the rate of two per cent upon the basis of its net income as herein computed, for the next preceding fiscal or calendar year.

"Sec. 888. *Basis on business within the state.* —If the entire business of the corporation be transacted within the state, the tax imposed shall be based upon the entire net income of such corporation for such fiscal or calendar year. If the entire business of the corporation be not transacted within the state and its gross income derived from business done both within and without the state, the determination of its net income shall be based upon the business done within the state and for the purpose of computing such net income the commissioner shall adopt such recommendations and regulations for the allocation of net income as will fairly and justly reflect the net income of that portion of the business done within the state."

[2] The further point is made that the discrimination in respect of dividends and interest upon loans is a regulation of interstate commerce and therefore void under the commerce clause of the Federal Constitution. But we mention this latter claim only to reject it as without merit, since clearly a tax upon income is not an interference with interstate commerce simply because the income is derived from a source within another state; and, moreover, if there be any tendency to interfere with such commerce, it is purely collateral and incidental. *Nathan v.*

The court below denied the contentions of appellant, and sustained the validity of the act in every particular. 107 Vt. 28, 175 A. 352.

First. Does the imposition of a tax upon dividends earned outside the state, from which tax dividends earned within the state are exempt, constitute, under the Fourteenth Amendment, an allowable classification? The basis of the classification rests in the consideration that by sections 887 and 888 a tax of 2 per cent., measured by net income, is imposed upon every corporation for the privilege of exercising **[296 U.S. 404, 420]** its franchise in the state and of doing business therein. If the entire business of the corporation be transacted within the state, the amount of the tax is fixed with regard to the entire net income. If the entire business be not so transacted, the net income is calculated with respect to that part of the business done within the state, to be allocated so as fairly and justly to reflect such net income. Dividends upon shares of corporations which are subjected to this tax are exempted from the income tax. In addition to the 2 per cent. franchise tax, all tangible corporate property lying within the state is subjected to a property tax. The evident aim of the classification, therefore, is to produce equality and not inequality; and, obviously, that aim will become effective in fact, to a greater or less extent, in the administration of the legislation.

The theory upon which the tax is laid upon dividends realized from out-of-state business while leaving dividends realized from domestic business untaxed, is that the 2 per cent. franchise tax, especially with the property tax added, has the effect of indirectly imposing a tax burden upon the latter measurably equivalent to that imposed directly upon the former. Thus, the tendency of the plan is to avoid taxing twice what is, in effect, the same thing. And conceding the power of the state to impose double or even multiple taxation, legislation which is calculated to avoid that undesirable result certainly cannot be condemned as arbitrary. Thus far, the question is settled in favor of the validity of the tax by prior decisions of this court. *Kidd v. Alabama*, 188 U.S. 730 , 23 S.Ct. 401; *Darnell v. Indiana*, 226 U.S. 390, 398 , 33 S.Ct. 120; *Travelers' Ins. Co. v. Connecticut*, 185 U.S. 364 , 22 S.Ct. 673; *Watson v. State Comptroller,* 254 U.S. 122, 124 , 125 S., 41 S.Ct. 43; *Lawrence v. State Tax Comm.*, 286 U.S. 276, 284 , 52 S.Ct. 556, 87 A.L.R. 374. True, it well may be assumed that similar franchise and property taxes are imposed upon the outside corporations by other states; but the assumption is immaterial **[296 U.S. 404, 421]** to the issue here involved. It is enough that such taxes are not imposed by the state of Vermont. It was so decided in *Kidd v. Alabama*, supra, where Mr. Justice Holmes, speaking for the court, said (188 U.S. 730 , page 732, 23 S.Ct. 401, 402): "The state of Alabama is not bound to make its laws harmonize in principle with those of other states. If property is untaxed by its laws, then for the purpose of its laws the property is not taxed at all." And see *Bacon v. Board of State Tax Com'rs,* 126 Mich. 22, 25, 26, 85 N.W. 307, 60 L.R.A. 321, 86 Am.St.Rep. 524.

Appellant urges that the franchise tax measured by the corporation's income is at the rate of 2 per cent., while the tax on dividends is at the rate of 4 per cent.; and concludes that this results in putting a burden on dividends directly taxed twice as great as that imposed indirectly by the franchise tax. But it is obvious that, since the 4 per cent. tax is imposed only upon such part of the corporate net income as passes to the shareholders in the form of dividends, and the 2 per cent. tax is measured by the entire net income of the corporation, this conclusion is erroneous. Corporations do not, at least as a general rule, pay out their entire net income in dividends. Something is reserved for future contingencies; and it may well result that a tax of 2 per cent. measured by the entire net income of the corporation will roughly approximate the amount imposed by a 4 per cent. tax on that part of the net income paid out as dividends. There is nothing in the equality clause of the Constitution which requires that the two sums shall be mathematically equivalent. *Concordia Fire Ins. Co. v. Illinois*, 292 U.S. 535, 547 , 54 S.Ct. 830.

Louisiana, 8 How. 73, 82; *Williams v. Fears*, 179 U.S. 270, 276 , 21 S.Ct. 128; *Diamond Glue Co. v. United States Glue Co.*, 187 U.S. 611, 616, 23 S. Ct. 206; *Anderson v. United States*, 171 U.S. 604, 616 , 19 S. Ct. 50; *Engel v. O'Malley*, 219 U.S. 128, 138 , 31 S.Ct. 190; *Moore v. N.Y. Cotton Exchange*, 270 U.S. 593, 604 , 46 S.Ct. 367, 45 A.L.R. 1370.

In *Klein v. Board of Supervisors*, 282 U.S. 19 , 51 S.Ct. 15, 73 A.L.R. 679, this court sustained an act exempting corporate shares from taxation where 75 per cent. of the total property of the corporation was taxable in the state and the taxes thereon were paid. It was said that this was plainly a reasonable effort to do justice to all in view of the way other assessments were made. **[296 U.S. 404, 422]** It is impossible to say from the record before us that there is a greater disproportion here than was presented in the *Klein* Case, or to conclude that the disproportion is so great as to stamp the classification as wholly arbitrary or capricious. Moreover, as a general thing, a corporation subject to the 2 per cent. franchise tax will pay also a tax upon property located within the state, with the effect of still further narrowing, if not altogether extinguishing, the difference.

This court has frequently said that absolute equality in taxation cannot be obtained, and is not required under the Fourteenth Amendment. This, of course, is not to say that, because some degree of inequality from the nature of things must be permitted, gross inequality must also be allowed. The boundary between what is permissible and what is forbidden by the constitutional requirement has never been precisely fixed, and is incapable of exact delimitation. In the great variety of cases which have arisen, decisions may seem to be difficult of reconcilement; but investigation will generally cause apparent conflicts to disappear when due weight is given to material circumstances which distinguish the cases. If the evident intent and general operation of the tax legislation is to adjust the burden with a fair and reasonable degree of equality, the constitutional requirement is satisfied. We think the provision now under consideration meets this test. Cf. *State Railroad Tax Cases*, 92 U.S. 575 , 612; *Tappan v. Merchants' National Bank*, 19 Wall. 490, 504; *Merchants' & Manufacturers' Nat. Bank v. Pennsylvania*, 167 U.S. 461, 464 , 17 S.Ct. 829.

Second. It is settled beyond the admissibility of further inquiry that the equal protection clause of the Fourteenth Amendment does pot preclude the states from resorting to classification for the purposes of legislation. *Royster Guano Co. v. Virginia*, 253 U.S. 412, 415, 40 S.Ct. 560, 561. And "the power of the state to classify for purposes of taxation is **[296 U.S. 404, 423]** of wide range and flexibility." *Louisville Gas & Electric Co. v. Coleman*, 277 U.S. 32, 37 , 48 S.Ct. 423, 425. But the classification "must be reasonable, not arbitrary, and must rest upon some ground of difference having a fair and substantial relation to the object of the legislation, so that all persons similarly circumstanced shall be treated alike." *Royster Guano Co. v. Virginia, supra; Air-Way Electric Appliance Corp. v. Day*, 266 U.S. 71, 85 , 45 S.Ct. 12; *Schlesinger v. Wisconsin*, 270 U.S. 230, 240 , 46 S.Ct. 260, 43 A.L.R. 1224. The classification, in order to avoid the constitutional prohibition, must be founded upon pertinent and real differences, as distinguished from irrelevant and artificial ones. The test to be applied in such cases as the present one is: Does the statute arbitrarily and without genuine reason impose a burden upon one group of taxpayers from which it exempts another group, both of them occupying substantially the same relation toward the subject-matter of the legislation? "Mere difference is not enough." *Louisville Gas & Electric Co. v. Coleman*, supra; *Frost v. Corporation Commission*, 278 U.S. 515, 522 , 49 S.Ct. 235.

The question depends here upon whether the income taxed and the income exempted from taxation reasonably can be assigned to different classes. As the Supreme Court of Vermont itself has pointed out, in all such cases it must appear not only that a classification has been made, but that it is one based on some reasonable ground. *State v. Hoyt,* 71 Vt. 59, 64-66, 42 A. 973. The decision in that case held invalid a state statute the effect of which was to impose a tax upon sales of goods manufactured in the state, while leaving sales of goods manufactured in other states free from taxation. It was held that the classification could not be based on any difference in the goods, because there was none; nor on the fact that they were made in different states, for that bore no just and proper relation to the classification, but was purely arbitrary; nor on the difference of residence of the manufacturers, for the same reason. And clearly the view of the court was that **[296 U.S. 404, 424]** a like discrimination against the products of another state would have been open to the same objections.

Let us apply these principles to the statute creating the exemption now in question. Upon the face of the statute the classification is based upon a difference having no substantial or fair relation to the object of the act, which, so far as this question is concerned, simply is to secure revenue. The statute itself suggests no other public purpose which will be served by the exemption. The language creating the exemption is: "(a) Interest received on account of money loaned within this state, at a rate of interest not exceeding five per cent per annum." The naked and complete test afforded by the statute is that the money shall be loaned within the state. What is to be done with the money, whether it is to be invested in the state or elsewhere, indeed, whether it is to be devoted to any useful purpose, are matters having nothing to do with the imposition of the tax or the exemption therefrom. If the statute had provided that interest on account of money so loaned when invested in property having a situs within the state shall be free from the tax, a different question as to classification might be presented. In that event the actual wealth of the state would be increased, and in addition, and as a consequence, opportunity to obtain additional revenue through taxation would result. But this exempting provision, we repeat, contains neither this qualification nor any other. Its terms are positive and all-inclusive, and will be fully satisfied whenever it appears that money has been loaned within the state. The Supreme Court of Vermont has not read into the statute a qualification that loans shall be deemed to be made within the state only if their proceeds be invested in the state. Obviously, this court cannot so read the provision, for that would be to amend and not to construe it. We are unable to find in the provision any public purpose which can be subserved by **[296 U.S. 404, 425]** making the taxation of income from loans dependent merely upon the adventitious circumstance as to the place of making the loan.

It is suggested, however, that, aside from anything in the statute, money loaned within the state generally will be invested therein. But there is nothing in the record to indicate that this will result; and for aught this court can know judicially, there is no warrant for saying either that it will or will not result. All we can say is that money so loaned may be invested in Vermont, or may be invested in some other state, for example, in property having a situs in New York, or may not be invested at all. If there be circumstances which will justify the exemption of any income derived from money loaned within the state while taxing the income from that loaned outside, it is for the state Legislature to point them out and limit the exemption accordingly. To import any such circumstances into the present situation is to indulge in pure speculation. *Compare Travis v. Yale & Towne Mfg. Co.*, 252 U.S. 60, 81 , 40 S.Ct. 228.

To assume that some unnamed public interest exists, which will sustain the discrimination, does not help the matter here; because the assumption can rest only upon surmise, with nothing concrete or explicit appearing to support it or to indicate a legislative intent to relate the exemption to any public purpose or to anything else beyond the mere fact that the favored loans are effected within the state. In principle, the classification is quite as arbitrary as that dealt with by this court in *Louisville Gas & Electric Co. v. Coleman*, supra, 277 U.S. 32 , pages 38, 39, 48 S.Ct. 423. If the exemption had been made to depend upon the time when the loan was made, instead of upon the locality where it was made, as, for example, a tax upon all income from loans except those made on Mondays, the arbitrary and capricious nature of the classification would scarcely be doubted, although a minute inspection of the field of **[296 U.S. 404, 426]** possibilities might persuade an anxious mind, bent on sustaining the tax at all events, to the view that in some far-fetched way a loan made on Monday would further some public purpose, other than that of revenue, which a loan made on another day of the week would not.

It is said that an exemption which may have for its aim the advancement of local interests can hardly be condemned under a Constitution which for a century has known a protective tariff. Considering the suggestion categorically, a pertinent answer to it is that while the general government may, for the benefit of national interests, exact impost duties which discriminate against foreign interests, one state, even for the advancement of its own interests, is not permitted to exact taxes discriminating against goods brought from a sister state. See, for example, *Welton v. State of Missouri*, 91 U.S. 275 ; cf. *Burnet v. Brooks*, 288 U.S. 378 , 401, et seq., 53 S.Ct. 457, 86 A.L.R. 747.

But, assuming that the state of Vermont is benefited by the exemption, the complete answer is that appellant is a citizen of the United States; and, quite apart from the equal protection of the laws clause, the suggestion is effectively met and overcome, and the fallacy of other attempts to sustain the validity of the exemption here under review clearly demonstrated, by reference to the privileges and immunities clause of the Fourteenth Amendment. "For all the great purposes for which the Federal government was formed," this court has said, "we are one people, with one common country." *Crandall v. State of Nevada*, 6 Wall. 35, 48, 49. As citizens of the United States we are members of a single great community consisting of all the states united, and not of distinct communities consisting of the states severally. No citizen of the United States is an alien in any state of the Union; and the very status of national citizenship connotes equality of rights and privileges, so far as they flow from such citizenship, everywhere within the limits of the **[296 U.S. 404, 427]** United States. This fact is obvious and vital, and no elaboration is required to establish it.

Section 2 of article 4 of the Constitution contains the provision, "The Citizens of each State shall be entitled to all Privileges and Immunities of Citizens in the several States." The Fourteenth Amendment, section 1, provides: "All persons born or naturalized in the United States, and subject to the jurisdiction thereof, are citizens of the United States and of the State wherein they reside. No State shall make or enforce any law which shall abridge the privileges or immunities of citizens of the United States."

Thus, the dual character of our citizenship is made plainly apparent. That is to say, a citizen of the United States is *ipso facto* and at the same time a citizen of the state in which he resides. And while the Fourteenth Amendment does not create a national citizenship, it has the effect of making that citizenship "paramount and dominant" instead of "derivative and dependent" upon state citizenship.[3] "In reviewing the subject," Chief Justice **WHITE** said, in the *Selective Draft Law Cases*, 245 U.S. 366, 377 , 388 S., 389, 38 S.Ct. 159, 165, L.R.A. 1918C, 361, Ann.Cas. 1918B, 856: "We have hitherto considered it as it has been argued from the point of view of the Constitution as it stood prior to the adoption of the Fourteenth Amendment. But to avoid all misapprehension we briefly direct attention to that (the fourteenth) amendment for the purpose of pointing out, as has been frequently done in the past, how completely it broadened the national scope of the government under the Constitution by causing citizenship of the United States to be paramount and dominant instead of being subordinate **[296 U.S. 404, 428]** and derivative, and therefore operating as it does upon all the powers conferred by the Constitution leaves no possible support for the contentions made if their want of merit was otherwise not to clearly made manifest."

The result is that whatever latitude may be thought to exist in respect of state power under the Fourth Article, a state cannot, under the Fourteenth Amendment, abridge the privileges of a citizen of the United States, albeit he is at the same time a resident of the state which undertakes to do so. This is pointed out by Mr. Justice Bradley in the *Slaughter House Case*, Fed.Cas. No. 8,408, 1 Woods, 21, 28:

"The "privileges and immunities" secured by the original constitution, were only such as each state gave to its own citizens. Each was prohibited from discriminating in favor of its own citizens, and against the citizens of other states.

"But the fourteenth amendment prohibits any state from abridging the privileges or immunities of the citizens of the United States, whether its own citizens or any others. It not merely requires equality of privileges; but it demands that the privileges and immunities of all citizens shall be absolutely unabridged, unimpaired."

The same distinction is made by this court in *Bradwell v. State of Illinois*, 16 Wall. 130, 138, where, speaking of the privileges and immunities provision of the Fourth Article, it was

---

[3] In *United States v. Hall,* 26 Fed.Cas. No. 15,282, page 79, 81, Judge **WOODS** said: "By the original constitution citizenship in the United States was a consequence of citizenship in a state. By this clause this order of things is reversed; ... and citizenship in a state is a result of citizenship in the United States."

said: "The protection designed by that clause, as has been repeatedly held, has no application to a citizen of the State whose laws are complained of. If the plaintiff was a citizen of the State of Illinois, that provision of the Constitution gave her no protection against its courts or its legislation."[4] **[296 U.S. 404, 429]** But the court added that with respect to the Fourteenth Amendment "there are certain privileges and immunities which belong to a citizen of the United States as such; otherwise it would be nonsense for the fourteenth amendment to prohibit a State from abridging them. ... We agree ... that there are privileges and immunities belonging to citizens of the United States, in that relation and character, and that it is these and these alone which a State is forbidden to abridge." The governments of the United States and of each of the several states are distinct from one another. The rights of a citizen under one may be quite different from those which he has under the other. To each he owes an allegiance; and, in turn, he is entitled to the protection of each in respect of such rights as fall within its jurisdiction. *United States v. Cruikshank*, 92 U.S. 542 , 549.

Under the Fourteenth Amendment, therefore, the simple inquiry is whether the privilege claimed is one which arises in virtue of national citizenship. If the privilege be of that character, no state can abridge it. No attempt has been made by the courts comprehensively to define or enumerate the privileges and immunities which the Fourteenth Amendment thus protects.[5] Among those privileges, however, undoubtedly is the right to pass freely from one state to another. Crandall v. State of Nevada, supra; *Williams v. Fears*, 179 U.S. 270, 274 , 21 S.Ct. 128. And that privilege, obviously, is as immune from abridgment by the state from which the citizen departs as it is from abridgment by the state which he seeks to enter. This results from the essential character of national citizenship. Cf. *In re Kemmler*, 136 U.S. 436, 448 , 10 S.Ct. 930; *Duncan v. Missouri*, 152 U.S. 377, 382 , 14 S.Ct. 570; *In re Quarles and Butler*, **[296 U.S. 404, 430]** 158 U.S. 532, 536 , 15 S.Ct. 959; *United States v. Cruikshank*, supra, 92 U.S. 542 , at page 552.

In the *Crandall* Case, while the court at least gravely doubted whether a capitation tax imposed by the state of Nevada upon persons leaving the state by railroad or stagecoach violated the commerce clause (6 Wall. 35, page 43), it was distinctly held that the tax did affect the rights of citizens under the federal government so as to invalidate the act imposing the tax. The doubt as to the first point has been resolved in later cases against the power of the state (*Helson and Randolph v. Kentucky*, 279 U.S. 245, 251 , 49 S.Ct. 279); but the ruling on the second point has never been doubted, and was definitely approved in the *Slaughter House Cases*, 16 Wall. 36, 79, and the right described in the *Crandall* Case placed among the partially enumerated privileges and immunities "which owe their existence to the Federal government, its National character, its Constitution, or its laws." The opinions in both cases were delivered by the same eminent justice; and it is not without significance that while the first opinion was delivered before the adoption of the Fourteenth Amendment, the second one was delivered afterwards and with direct reference to the privileges and immunities clause of that amendment. The fact that we have since decided, and should now hold, that the Nevada act was in violation of the commerce clause, in no way detracts from the view that it also violates the privileges and immunities clause; but simply demonstrates that the same act of state legislation may contravene more than one provision of the Federal Constitution.

The right of a citizen of the United States to engage in business, to transact any lawful business, or to make a lawful loan of money in any state other than that in which the citizen

---

[4] This does not mean that a state has unlimited power by law to abridge the privileges of its own citizens. It only means that in such case we must look elsewhere than to the language of the privileges and immunities clause of the Fourth Article of the Constitution for the constitutional infirmity of the statute, if it have any.

[5] For examples, however, see *Corfield v. Coryell*, Fed.Cas. No. 3,230, 4 Wash.C.C. 371, 380, 381; *Slaughter House Cases*, 16 Wall. 36, 79, 80; *Twining v. New Jersey*, 211 U.S. 78, 97 , 29 S.Ct. 14; *Ward v. Maryland*, 12 Wall. 418, 430; *Blake v. McClung*, 172 U.S. 239, 248 , 252 S., 19 S.Ct. 165; *United States v. Wheeler*, 254 U.S. 281 , 41 S.Ct. 133; *Paul v. Virginia*, 8 Wall. 168, 180.

resides is a privilege equally attributable to his national citizenship. A state law prohibiting the exercise of any of these rights in another state would, [296 U.S. 404, 431] therefore, be invalid under the Fourteenth Amendment. The imposition by one state of a discriminating tax upon a citizen resident in another state for trading in the territory of the former has been held invalid. *Ward v. Maryland,* 12 Wall. 418, 430. And, of course, conversely, a tax of that description is likewise void if imposed by one state upon a resident citizen of the United States for trading or doing business in the territory of another state. And such a tax is not justified because the taxing state will thereby help its domestic business.

The purpose of the pertinent clause in the Fourth Article was to require each state to accord equality of treatment to the citizens of other states in respect of the privileges and immunities of state citizenship. It has always been so interpreted. One purpose and effect of the privileges and immunities clause of the Fourteenth Amendment, read in the light of this interpretation, was to bridge the gap left by that article so as also to safeguard citizens of the United States against any legislation of their own states having the effect of denying equality of treatment in respect of the exercise of their privileges of national citizenship in other states. A provision which thus extended and completed the shield of national protection between the citizen and hostile and discriminating state legislation cannot be lightly dismissed as a mere duplication, or of subordinate or no value, or as an almost forgotten clause of the Constitution.

Reference has been made to numerous cases in which this court has rejected or ignored specific claims under the privileges and immunities clause; but since none of them relates to state legislation even remotely resembling the Vermont law here challenged, their collection and citation is without useful result, unless, as it seems to be thought, these numerous unsuccessful efforts to give the clause applications which fall outside its meaning show or tend to show that the clause itself has become a dead [296 U.S. 404, 432] letter. Such a conclusion is, of course, inadmissible; for as we have already said, referring to the Bradwell Case, there are privileges and immunities which belong to a citizen of the United States as such; otherwise it would be nonsense to prohibit a state from abridging them. Some of these privileges and immunities we have already pointed out; others are enumerated in the cases cited under note 5.

To these illustrations we may add another, which here is peculiarly pertinent. The business of insurance has grown to vast proportions. Insurance companies issuing policies are found in every state; and the activities of the larger companies overflow state lines and extend into every part of the country. But insurance is not commerce; and the right of a citizen to take out a policy in one state, insuring property in another where he resides, cannot be protected under the commerce clause. National protection, when appropriate, must be found in the Fourteenth Amendment. It well cannot be doubted that a citizen of the United States, residing and having property in Vermont, exercises a privilege of national citizenship when he negotiates and takes out in another state a policy insuring that property, or takes out in another state a policy insuring his life. There may be very cogent reasons, resting in the strength of the company, terms of the policy, and otherwise, making it desirable that he should do so. And it well cannot be doubted that legislation of one state denying the privilege or taxing the transaction when it occurs in another state, while leaving the transaction wholly free from taxation when it takes place in the former state, would abridge that privilege of citizenship. It would be no answer to say that thereby the former state was building up her local insurance companies and adding to the wealth of the state. Nor is it any answer to say that the citizen may resort to other clauses of the Fourteenth Amendment which will afford [296 U.S. 404, 433] protection. The right of a citizen of the United States resident in one state to contract in another may be a liberty safeguarded by the due process of law clause, and at the same time, none the less, a privilege protected by the privileges and immunities clause of the Fourteenth Amendment. It such case he may invoke either or both. This seems to be recognized in *Allgeyer v. Louisiana,* 165 U.S. 578 , 589-592, 17 S.Ct. 427, where the court evidently thought that under circumstances not unlike those just suggested the words "liberty" and "privilege" were interchangeable terms.

It follows from what has been said that when a citizen of the United States residing in Vermont goes into New Hampshire, he does not enter foreign territory, but passes from one field into another field of the same national domain. When he trades, buys, or sells, contracts or negotiates across the state line, when he loans money, or takes out insurance in New Hampshire, whether in doing so he remains in Vermont or not, he exercises rights of national citizenship which the law of neither state can abridge without coming into conflict with the supreme authority of the Federal Constitution.

The statute, as here applied, says that if a citizen resident in Vermont loan his money at 5 per cent. or less in another state, he must pay a tax upon the income; but if he loan money in Vermont at the same rate, no tax whatever shall be imposed. The power to tax income here asserted by Vermont is, in the final analysis, the power to tax so heavily as to preclude loans outside the state altogether. It reasonably is not open to doubt that the discriminatory tax here imposed abridges the privilege of a citizen of the United States to loan his money and make contracts with respect thereto in any part of the United States.

The tax on dividends, already discussed and upheld, rests in a different situation. Although dividends from outside investments are taxed, and those from state in- **[296 U.S. 404, 434]** vestments in terms are exempt, they are, as already appears, in substance and effect treated alike; the one by a tax falling directly upon the income of the individual stockholders, and the other falling indirectly but no less definitely upon that income, in the form of a tax which is first imposed upon the corporation as a franchise tax measured by income, but the burden of which ultimately is borne by the stockholders. The effect is the same as though the tax were imposed generally upon corporate dividends without exception or discrimination. *Travelers' Ins. Co. v. Connecticut*, 185 U.S. 364 , 369 et seq., 22 S.Ct. 673. The same would be true of the tax on income from loans, if it had been imposed in respect of all loans wherever made, or if there had been some form of equalizing tax which would have compensated for the burden cast upon loans made in other states. But such is not the case. Income from loans made outside the state is taxed directly, while income from loans made within the state is not taxed directly or in any indirect way so as to equalize the burden. *Woodruff v. Parham*, 8 Wall. 123, 140, dealt with a sales tax imposed upon all sales, whether made by a citizen of the state where the tax was imposed or a citizen of another state; and whether the goods sold were the product of the state enacting the law or of some other state. This court upheld the tax upon the ground that it did not discriminate against the products of other state or affect the privileges or immunities of their citizens; but the court clearly stated that if it had done so it would be an infringement of the provisions of the Constitution relating to those subjects. The principle of that case is applicable here and has the effect of sustaining the tax in respect of loans. *Compare Travis v. Yale & Towne Mfg. Co.*, supra.

Third. The statute, so far as it applies to appellant, provides that if the income taxed be derived wholly from ownership of or interest in interest-bearing securities, there shall be allowed an exemption of $800. If the in- **[296 U.S. 404, 435]** come be derived from other enumerated sources, an exemption is allowed of $ 2,000 against the "aggregate net income."

It is manifest that if the legislation had provided that where the taxpayer shall have income from both of these general sources he shall not be entitled to both exemptions, the provision would have been open to no constitutional objection. Such legislation might properly permit him, in that contingency, to select which of the exemptions he will take; or, on the other hand, might properly specify which of the two exemptions shall be accorded him. In effect, though not in terms, it is the latter alternative which the statute adopts. In terms, the statute provides that if the taxpayer receive any income other than that derived from interest- bearing securities, the personal exemption applicable to the latter class of income shall not be allowed. But the right to the $2,000 exemption allowed in respect of class A income remains unaffected. The taxpayer who receives both classes of income, while thus compelled to forego the smaller exemption, is accorded the larger one; and it is impossible reasonably to find in this situation anything arbitrary or capricious. It is true that during the taxable year in question appellant had no net income because his gross income derived from salaries, etc., amounting to about $70,000, was entirely absorbed by allowable deductions; but this was an incident of the particular year in question, and might never happen again. He failed to obtain the advantage of the exemption, not because of any hostile statutory intent or hostile enforcement of the tax, but because of the collateral circumstance, peculiar, perhaps, to him alone and to the taxable year in question, that his entire gross income was absorbed by deductions, allowed by the statute as a matter of grace as is the exemption itself, so that nothing remained from which the amount of the exemption or any part of it could be subtracted. **[296 U.S. 404, 436]** The question of equal protection must be decided in respect of the general classification rather than by the chance incidence of the tax in particular instances or with respect to particular taxpayers. "And inequalities that result not from hostile discrimination, but occasionally and incidentally in the application of a system that is not arbitrary in its classification, are not sufficient to defeat the law." *Maxwell v. Bugbee*, 250 U.S. 525, 543 , 40 S.Ct. 2, 7. "The operation of a general rule will seldom be the same for every one. If the accidents of trade lead to inequality or hardship, the consequences must be accepted as inherent in government by law instead of government by edict." *Fox v. Standard Oil Co.*, 294 U.S. 87, 102 , 55 S.Ct. 333, 339. Cf. *Packard v. Banton*, 264 U.S. 140, 145 , 44 S.Ct. 257; *Gant v. Oklahoma City*, 289 U.S. 98, 102 , 53 S.Ct. 530; *Storassli v. Minnesota*, 283 U.S. 57, 62 , 51 S.Ct. 354.

The general classification, namely, that the right to a partial exemption from a tax upon one class of income will depend upon whether the taxpayer is in receipt of income of another class with respect to which a different exemption applies, does not seem to us to be open to the objection that it is arbitrary or capricious, simply because, like any other general rule of taxation, its administration may involve incidental instances of inequality.

We conclude that the taxing act is valid in respect of the first and third points which we have discussed, but invalid in respect of the second.

Reversed and remanded for further proceedings not inconsistent with the foregoing opinion.

Mr. Justice **STONE** (dissenting in part).

I think that the exemption, from the tax, of net income from money loaned within the state at not more than 5 per cent., like the exemption of income from dividends of **[296 U.S. 404, 437]** corporations earned within the state, does not deny equal protection or infringe any privilege or immunity of citizens of the United States, and that the judgment should be affirmed in its entirety. Unless the constitutional validity of the exemptions is to turn upon the ground that we approve laws enacted to avoid taxing the same economic interest twice, but disapprove those to encourage residents to invest their funds at home, it would seem that the considerations which have led to upholding the one exemption would not admit of condemning the other. See *Southwestern Oil Co. v. Texas*, 217 U.S. 114, 127 , 30 S.Ct. 496.

1. It is not denied that the effect of both exemptions is to place a burden on income derived from sources or investments made without the state which they do not place on income derived from like sources or investments made within it. But that affords no ground for saying that either is invalid. The equal protection clause does not forbid inequalities in state taxation. A state may select the objects to be taxed, and selection, which is but the converse of exemption, involves the imposition of a tax burden on some which is not placed on others. As this Court has repeatedly held, inequalities resulting from the singling out of one particular class for taxation or exemption, regardless of the reason for the choice, or even if there is no discernible reason, are not to be pronounced invalid where there is no clear indication that the purpose or effect is a hostile or oppressive discrimination against particular persons or classes. *American Sugar Refining Co. v. Louisiana*, 179 U.S. 89 , 21 S.Ct. 43; *Board of Education v. Illinois*, 203 U.S. 553 , 27 S.Ct. 171, 8 Ann.Cas.157; *Beers v. Glynn (Lord v. Glynn)*, 211 U.S. 477 , 29 S.Ct. 186; *Southwestern Oil Co. v. Texas*, supra; *Quong Wing v. Kirkendall*, 223 U.S. 59 , 32 S.Ct. 192; *Citizens' Telephone Co. v. Fuller*, 229 U.S. 322 , 33 S.Ct. 833; *Heisler v. Thomas Colliery Co.*, 260 U.S. 245 , 43 S.Ct. 83; *Lawrence v. State Tax Commission*, 286 U.S. 276 , 52 S.Ct. 556, 87 A.L.R. 374; *Concordia Fire Insurance Co. v. Illinois*, 292 U.S. 535 , 54 S.Ct. 830. **[296 U.S. 404, 438]** The end sought by the classification is of significance in passing upon the constitutionality of the tax only in so far as it serves to show that the discrimination is not invidious. If it appears or may fairly be assumed that it is for the purpose of promoting a permissible public aim, it cannot be condemned because one class must pay a tax which another does not. Where the public interest is served, one business may be left untaxed and another taxed, in order to promote the one, *American Sugar Refining Co. v. Louisiana*, supra; *Heisler v. Thomas Colliery Co.*, supra; *Aero Mayflower Transit Co. v. Georgia Public Service Commission*, 295 U.S. 285 , 55 S.Ct. 709; or to restrict or suppress the other, *Maganano Co. v.*

Hamilton, 292 U.S. 40 , 54 S.Ct. 599; *Fox v. Standard Oil Co.*, 294 U.S. 87 , 55 S.Ct. 333; *Quong Wing v. Kirkendall*, supra; *Singer Sewing Machine Co. v. Brickell*, 233 U.S. 304 , 34 S.Ct. 493; *Alaska Fish Salting & By-Products Co. v. Smith*, 255 U.S. 44, 48 , 41 S.Ct. 219. But it is not necessary to go so far to support the present exemption. There is no serious contention that its purpose or effect is to suppress the lending of money without the state or to injure appellant or his fellow residents of Vermont who may prefer to invest their funds elsewhere. Nor can it be said that the exemption was not granted in furtherance of a permissible state policy, which was the legislative objective rather than an invidious discrimination against appellant and others similarly situated.

It seems to be conceded that if the statute had placed upon the tax gatherers the burden of ascertaining whether money loaned within the state is invested in property there, and had limited the exemption to money so loaned and invested, the tax would be sustained because of the benefit which would result from the increase of wealth in the state and the enlarged opportunity to obtain additional revenue. The attack is thus narrowed to the single objection that there are exempted loans, some of which, although made within the state, are or may be withdrawn and used elsewhere. It is assumed that money thus loaned **[296 U.S. 404, 439]** and withdrawn can be of no possible benefit to the state, and it is declared that since transactions may occur the Court cannot determine whether the exemption will have any beneficent effect and that it is therefore invalid.

But there are benefits other than the increase of its taxable wealth which a state is at liberty to stimulate by its taxing policy, and exemptions have been sustained on the broader ground that they foster some form of domestic industry. *People of State of New York ex rel. Parke, Davis & Co. v. Roberts*, 171 U.S. 658 , 19 S.Ct. 70; *Magnano Co. v. Hamilton*, supra; *Fox v. Standard Oil Co.*, supra; *Aero Mayflower Transit Co. v. Georgia Public Service Commission*, supra. If Vermont chooses to encourage, by tax exemption, loans at favorable rates of interest within the state, because it believes that local interests will be benefited, it can hardly be said for that reason to be contravening a Constitution that has known a protective tariff for more than 100 years. See *Alaska Fish Salting & By-Products Co. v. Smith*, supra, 255 U.S. 44, 48 , 41 S.Ct. 219; *Rast v. Van Deman & Lewis Co.*, 240 U.S. 342, 347 , 36 S.Ct. 370, L.R.A. 1917A, 421, Ann.Cas. 1917B, 455. It is true that a state may not lay taxes on imports or burden interstate commerce, *Welton v. Missouri*, 91 U.S. 275 , but it is too late for this Court to declare that a state may not favor domestic interests by granting exemptions in the exercise of its taxing power.

It is not for us to say that the Vermont Legislature was unmindful of these broader advantages, or to declare that the presence within the state of investment funds offered at 5 per cent. or less to borrowers there, including those who are carrying on the business and industry of the state, is not beneficial; or that if any loans made within the state are used elsewhere they are or ever would be more than negligible in amount; or if they were that they could not have a favorable effect on interest rates within the state, which is a matter of state concern. When the Vermont Legislature adopted the present exemption, it had before it the reports of two committees specially appointed to investigate **[296 U.S. 404, 440]** the tax system of the state, which clearly indicate their judgment, based on a study of conditions in the state, that the existing system was driving investment capital from the state or into secured and non-commercial loans, and that a tax exemption embracing both secured and commercial loans would tend to increase the supply of investment capital for both and to reduce interest rates in the state.[6]   This Court has no basis for saying that those committees were wrong and no

---

[6] The committee appointed in 1900 by the Governor of Vermont to investigate double taxation and to recommend measures for its relief found that the existing taxing system was driving capital from the state or into tax exempt savings banks, and suggested an exemption of loans secured by property returned for taxation in the state. Double Taxation in Vermont; Report of Special Committee Appointed to Report a Measure for its Relief to the Legislature of 1900, pp. 4, 15. In 1908, a similar committee recognized the same evils, but did not favor the exemption of secured loans alone, because it would increase interest rates on unsecured loans and cause a dearth of commercial credits. Vermont-Commission on Taxation- Report 1908, pp. 43 ff.

authority to say it. The state Supreme Court has stated in the present case that the Legislature did have in mind these broader advantages, for it rested its decision on the ground that the exemption was made "in the interests of thrift and state development" and "for the assistance of the agricultural and industrial interests of the state." 107 Vt. 28, 175 A, 352, 357.

If, in the face of so much which is persuasive of the legitimate purpose and effect of this legislation, we are to declare that we cannot say whether the benefits intended either will or will not result, it does not follow that the Vermont Legislature is similarly uninformed. We must assume that it is not, unless we are to discard the salutary principle of decision, that, out of a decent respect to an independent branch of the government, legislative acts must be taken to be based on facts which support their constitutional validity unless the contrary reasonably appears **[296 U.S. 404, 441]** . This Court, it is true, has held discriminations invalid where, upon the facts disclosed by the record or within the range of judicial notice, it has felt able to say that there could be no state of facts which could rationally support them. *Royster Guano Co. v. Virginia*, 253 U.S. 412 , 40 S.Ct. 560; *Heiner v. Donnan*, 285 U.S. 312 , 52 S. Ct. 358; *Louisville Gas & Electric Co. v. Coleman*, 277 U.S. 32 , 48 S.Ct. 423; *Liggett Co. v. Lee*, 288 U.S. 517 , 53 S.Ct. 481, 85 A.L.R. 699. But in no case has it rendered such a judgment where it has declared that it is unable to say that consequences which would justify the discrimination will not result. *Erb v. Morasch*, 177 U.S. 584, 586 , 20 S.Ct. 819; *Middleton v. Texas Power & Light Co.*, 249 U.S. 152, 158 , 39 S.Ct. 227; *Stebbins v. Riley*, 268 U.S. 137, 143 , 45 S.Ct. 424, 44 A.L.R. 1454; *Swiss Oil Corp. v. Shanks*, 273 U.S. 407, 413 , 414 S., 47 S.Ct. 393; Fort Smith *Light & Traction Co. v. Board of Improvement Paving Dist. No. 16*, 274 U.S. 387, 391 , 392 S., 47 S.Ct. 595; *State of Ohio ex rel. Clarke v. Deckebach*, 274 U.S. 392 , 47 S.Ct. 630; *Silver v. Silver*, 280 U.S. 117, 123 , 50 S.Ct. 57, 65 A.L.R. 939; *O'Gorman & Young, Inc. v. Hartford Fire Ins. Co.*, 282 U.S. 251, 257 , 258 S., 51 S.Ct. 130, 72 A.L.R. 1163; *State Board of Tax Commissioners v. Jackson*, 283 U.S. 527 , 537-541, 51 S.Ct. 540, 73 A.L.R. 1464; *Hardware Dealers Mut. Fire Insurance Co. v. Glidden Co.*, 284 U.S. 151, 158 , 52 S.Ct. 69; *Boston & Maine R.R. v. Armburg*, 285 U.S. 234, 240 , 52 S.Ct. 336; *Lawrence v. State Tax Commission*, supra, 286 U.S. 276, 283 , 52 S.Ct. 556, 87 A.L.R. 374; *Concordia Fire Insurance Co. v. Illinois*, supra, 292 U.S. 535, 547 , 548 S., 54 S.Ct. 830; *Metropolitan Casualty Insurance Co. of New York v. Brownell*, 292 U.S. 620 , 54 S.Ct. 780; *Fox v. Standard Oil Co.*, supra. Unless, as we profess not to do, *Standard Oil Co. v. City of Marysville*, 279 U.S. 582 , 49 S.Ct. 430, we are to sit as a Superlegislature, or as triers of the facts on which a Legislature is to say what shall and what shall not be taxed, we are not free to say that the exemption will not induce residents to offer to lend their funds within the state and at lower interest rates than they otherwise would, or that opportunities thus afforded will not be availed of by borrowers requiring funds for carrying on the commerce and industry of the state.

Even if we are to assume, in the absence of any actual knowledge, that money loaned in the state at favorable **[296 U.S. 404, 442]** rates would not benefit it if used elsewhere, and, further, that in fact some money is so loaned and used, there is no discernible reason why those circumstances should be deemed to invalidate the tax, and none is stated by the Court. It is irrelevant that the state, which has selected domestic loans for exemption in furtherance of a state policy, has not excluded from the exemption every transaction which conceivably might not advance its purpose. Whether the legislative object is completely achieved is of no concern to this Court, once it appears that the exemption is made for a permissible end and bears some reasonable relation to that end. Purpose or motive of the selection of the objects of taxation and exemption is material only so far as it is needful to ascertain whether the discrimination is invidious. If the choice is not condemned for that reason, it has never been held that an exemption must fail because it may benefit some who do not advance the legislative purpose. A classification for a permissible end is not to be condemned because it operates to prohibit transactions in themselves harmless, or fails to reach others which are harmful. *Powell v. Pennsylvania*, 127 U.S. 678 , 8 S.Ct. 992, 1257; *Purity Extract & Tonic Co. v. Lynch*, 226 U.S. 192 , 33 S.Ct. 44; *Hebe Co. v. Shaw*, 248 U.S. 297 , 39 S.Ct. 125; *Jacob Ruppert v. Caffey*, 251 U.S. 264 , 40 S.Ct. 141; *Miller v. Wilson*, 236 U.S. 373 , 35 S.Ct. 342, L.R.A. 1915F, 829;

Hawley v. Walker, 232 U.S. 718 , 34 S.Ct. 479.

All taxes must of necessity be levied by general rules capable of practical administration. In drawing the line between the taxed and the untaxed, the equal protection clause does not command the impossible or the impractical. Unless the line which the state draws is so wide of the mark as palpably to have no reasonable relation to the legitimate end, it is not for the judicial power to reject it and say that another must be substituted. *Citizens' Telephone Co. v. Fuller*, supra, 229 U.S. 322, 329 , 33 S.Ct. 833; *Miller v. Wilson*, 236 U.S. 373, 384 , 35 S.Ct. 342, L.R.A. 1915F, 829; *Clark v. Titusville*, 184 U.S. 329, 331 , 22 S.Ct. 382; *Metropolis Theatre Co. v. Chicago*, 228 U. S. **[296 U.S. 404, 443]** 61, 69, 70, 33 S.Ct. 441; see, also, *Salomon v. State Tax Commission*, 278 U.S. 484 , 49 S.Ct. 192; *McCray v. United States,* 195 U.S. 27 , 24 S.Ct. 769, 1 Ann.Cas. 561; *Quong Wing v. Kirkendall*, 223 U.S.59, 56, L.ed. 350, 32 S. Ct. 192, supra; *Bell's Gap R. Co. v. Pennsylvania*, 134 U.S. 232, 237 , 10 S.Ct. 533.

As the purpose of the exemption appears to be to encourage the lending of money within Vermont by its residents, at low rates of interest, and as it appears reasonably calculated to have that effect, and as we cannot say that such loans will not be of benefit to the state by tending to establish the interest rate at 5 per cent. or less, and by stimulating loans to borrowers for the purpose of carrying on business and industry within the state, the conclusion seems inescapable that the equal protection clause does not forbid it.

2. Feeble indeed is an attack on a statute as denying equal protection which can gain any support from the almost forgotten privileges and immunities clause of the Fourteenth Amendment. The notion that that clause could have application to any but the privileges and immunities peculiar to citizenship of the United States, as distinguished from those of citizens of states, has long since been rejected. *Slaughter House Cases*, 16 Wall. 36. It created no new privileges and immunities of United States citizenship, *Bartemeyer v. Iowa*, 18 Wall. 129, 133, and as they are derived exclusively from the Constitution and laws enacted under it, the states were powerless to abridge them before the adoption of the Fourteenth Amendment as well as after. See *Crandall v. Nevada*, 6 Wall. 35.

Before the amendment the privilege of passing from state to state for the purpose of approaching the seat of the national government, of transacting business with it, and of gaining access to its courts, its public offices, and its ports, was declared in *Crandall v. Nevada*, supra, 6 Wall. 35, 44, to be a right of national citizenship which could be exercised independently of the will of the state. Upon this **[296 U.S. 404, 444]** ground was placed he decision in that case that a state capitation tax on passengers transported out of the state by railroad or stagecoach infringed the Constitution. No one could doubt that if the decision had been made at any time after *Baltimore & Ohio Railroad Co. v. Maryland*, 21 Wall. 456, 472 (1874), and until the present moment, it would have been rested on the commerce clause. This Court has many times pointed out that movements of persons across state boundaries are a part of interstate commerce, subject to the regulation and entitled to the protection of the national government under the commerce clause. *Caminetti v. United States*, 242 U.S. 470 , 37 S.Ct. 192, L.R.A. 1917F, 502, Ann.Cas. 1917B, 1168; *Hoke v. United States*, 227 U.S. 308 , 33 S.Ct. 281, 43 L.R.A. (N.S.) 906, Ann.Cas. 1913E, 905; *Mayor of Vidalia v. McNeely*, 274 U.S. 676 , 47 S.Ct. 758; *Gloucester Ferry Co. v. Pennsylvania*, 114 U.S. 196 , 5 S.Ct. 826; cf. *Passenger Cases*, 7 How. 283. And it has specifically pointed out that *Crandall v. Nevada*, supra, is overruled so far as it referred the protection of such commerce to the privileges and immunities clause rather than to the commerce clause. *Helson and Randolph v. Kentucky*, 279 U.S. 245, 251 , 49 S.Ct. 279.

The privileges and immunities clause has consistently been construed as protecting only interests, growing out of the relationship between the citizen and the national government, created by the Constitution and federal laws. *Re Kemmler*, 136 U.S. 436, 448 , 10 S.Ct. 930; *McPherson v. Blacker*, 146 U.S. 1, 38 , 13 S.Ct. 3; *Giozza v. Tiernan*, 148 U.S. 657, 661 , 13 S.Ct. 721; *Duncan v. Missouri*, 152 U.S. 377, 382 , 14 S.Ct. 570. Appeals to this Court to extend the clause beyond these limitations have uniformly been rejected and even those basic privileges and immunities secured against federal infringement by the first eight amendments have been held not to be protected from state action by the privileges and immunities clause.

167

Walker v. Sauvinet, 92 U.S. 90 ; *Presser v. Illinois*, 116 U.S. 252 , 6 S.Ct. 580; *O'Neil v. Vermont*, 144 U.S. 323 , 12 S.Ct. 693; *Maxwell v. Dow*, 176 U.S. 581, 606 , 20 S.Ct. 448, 494; *Twining v. New Jersey*, 211 U.S. 78 , 29 S.Ct. 14; cf. *Hurtado v. California*, 110 U.S. 516 , 4 S.Ct. 111, 292; *West v. Louisiana*, **[296 U.S. 404, 445]** 194 U.S. 258 , 24 S.Ct. 650. The protection and control of intercourse between the states, not carried on in pursuance of the relationship between the citizen and the national government, has been left to the interstate commerce clause, to the due process and equal protection clauses of the Fourteenth Amendment, and to article 4, 2, guaranteeing to the citizens of each state the privileges and immunities of citizens in the several states. See *Williams v. Fears*, 179 U.S. 270 , 21 S.Ct. 128. In no case since the adoption of the Fourteenth Amendment has the privileges and immunities clause been held to afford any protection to movements of persons across state lines or other form of interstate transaction.

The reason for this reluctance to enlarge the scope of the clause has been well understood since the decision of the *Slaughter House Cases*, supra. If its restraint upon state action were extended more than is needful to protect relationships between the citizen and the national government, and it did more than duplicate the protection of liberty and property secured to persons and citizens by the other provisions of the Constitution, it would enlarge judicial control of state action and multiply restrictions upon it to an extent difficult to define, but sufficient to cause serious apprehension for the rightful independence of local government. That was the issue fought out in the *Slaughter House Cases*, supra, with the decision against the enlargement. Since the adoption of the Fourteenth Amendment, at least 44[7] cases have been **[296 U.S. 404, 446]** brought to this Court in which state statutes have been assailed as infringements of the privileges and immunities clause. Until today, none has held that state legislation infringed that clause.

If its sweep were now to be broadened to include protection of every transaction across state lines, regardless of its connection with any relationship between the citizen and the national government, a step would be taken, the gravity of which might well give us concern. But it is necessary to go much further before the present tax can be condemned. If protection

---

[7] *Slaughter House Cases*, 16 Wall. 36; *Bradwell v. State of Illinois*, 16 Wall. 130; *Bartemeyer v. Iowa*, 18 Wall. 129; *Minor v. Happersett*, 21 Wall. 162; *Walker v. Sauvinet*, 92 U.S. 90 ; *Kirtland v. Hotchkiss*, 100 U.S. 491 ; *Presser v. Illinois*, 116 U.S. 252 , 6 S.Ct. 580; *Mahon v. Justice*, 127 U.S. 700 , 8 S.Ct. 1204; *In re Kemmler*, 136 U.S. 436 , 10 S.Ct. 930; *Crowley v. Christensen*, 137 U.S. 86 , 11 S.Ct. 13; *McElvaine v. Brush*, 142 U.S. 155 , 12 S.Ct. 156; *McPherson v. Blacker*, 146 U.S. 1 , 13 S.Ct. 3; *Giozza v. Tiernan*, 148 U.S. 657 , 13 S.Ct. 1047; *Duncan v. Missouri*, 152 U.S. 377 , 14 S.Ct. 570; *Miller v. Texas*, 153 U.S. 535 , 14 S.Ct. 874; *Ex parte Lockwood*, 154 U.S. 116 , 14 S.Ct. 1082; *Iowa Central Ry. v. Iowa*, 160 U.S. 389 , 16 S. Ct. 344; *Plessy v. Ferguson*, 163 U.S. 537 , 16 S.Ct. 1138; *Orient Insurance Co. v. Daggs*, 172 U.S. 557 , 19 S.Ct. 281; *Cumming v. Board of Education*, 175 U.S. 528 , 20 S.Ct. 197; *Maxwell v. Dow*, 176 U.S. 581 , 20 S.Ct. 448, 494; *Williams v. Fears*, 179 U.S. 270 , 21 S.Ct. 128; *Orr v. Gilman*, 183 U.S. 278 , 22 S.Ct. 213; *Cox v. Texas*, 202 U.S. 446 , 26 S. Ct. 671; *Board of Education v. Illinois*, 203 U.S. 553 , 27 S. Ct. 171, 8 Ann.Cas. 157; *Ballard v. Hunter*, 204 U.S. 241 , 27 S.Ct. 261; *Western Turf Ass'n v. Greenberg*, 204 U.S. 359 , 27 S.Ct. 384; *Halter v. Nebraska*, 205 U.S. 34 , 27 S.Ct. 419, 10 Ann.Cas. 525; *Wilmington Star Mining Co. v. Fulton*, 205 U.S. 60, 73 , 27 S.Ct. 412; *Twining v. New Jersey*, 211 U.S. 78 , 29 S.Ct. 14; *Western Union Tel. Co. v. Com'l Mill. Co.*, 218 U.S. 406 , 31 S.Ct. 59, 36 L.R.A.(N.S.) 220, 21 Ann.Cas. 815; *Mo. Pacific Ry. Co. v. Castle*, 224 U.S. 541 , 32 S.Ct. 606; *Graham v. West Virginia*, 224 U.S. 616 , 32 S.Ct. 583; *Selover, Bates & Co. v. Walsh*, 226 U.S. 112 , 33 S.Ct. 69; *Rosenthal v. New York*, 226 U.S. 260 , 33 S.Ct. 27, Ann.Cas. 1914B, 71; *Waugh v. Board of Trustees*, 237 U.S. 589 , 35 S.Ct. 720; *Porter v. Wilson*, 239 U.S. 170 , 36 S.Ct. 91; *Crane v. Campbell*, 245 U.S. 304 , 38 S. Ct. 98; *Armour & Co. v. Virginia*, 246 U.S. 1 , 38 S.Ct. 267; *Omaechevarria v. Idaho*, 246 U.S. 343 , 38 S.Ct. 323; *Maxwell v. Bugbee*, 250 U.S. 525 , 40 S.Ct. 2; *Ownbey v. Morgan*, 256 U.S. 94 , 41 S.Ct. 433, 17 A.L.R. 873; *Prudential Ins. Co. v. Cheek*, 259 U.S. 530 , 42 S.Ct. 516, 27 A.L.R. 27; *Hamilton v. Regents*, 293 U.S. 245 , 55 S.Ct. 197.

of the freedom of the citizen to pass from state to state were the object of our solicitude, that privilege is adequately protected by the commerce clause, even though the purpose of his going be to effect insurance or transact any other kind of business which is in itself not commerce. But protection of the citizen's freedom of movement, whether by the privileges and immunities clause or by the commerce clause, will afford appellant no relief from the present tax. The record does not show that he was ever outside the state of Vermont, and for aught that appears he acquired his extra-state investments, which are in the form of negotiable [296 U.S. 404, 447] corporate securities, by gift or purchase in Vermont. Nor does it appear that the physical securities or payments of income of which appellant has had the benefit have crossed state lines. He can be saved from the tax only by the extension of the immunity to his income merely because the property from which it has been derived, or the corporation paying it, is located in another state.

Such is the contention now made; that the privilege of acquiring, owning, and receiving income from investments without the state is a privilege of federal citizenship. And the suggestion is that the privilege is infringed by taxing this income just as the commerce clause is infringed by state taxation burdening the privilege of carrying on commerce across state lines. In any case the privileges and immunities clause is said to be infringed by taxing this income at a different rate than income from investments made within the state.

The novel application thus given to the clause, and the arguments used to support it, leave one in doubt whether it is thought to preclude all differences of taxation of the two classes of income, or only to forbid such inequality as is in some sense arbitrary and unreasonable. If the former, the clause becomes an inexhaustible source of immunities, incalculable in their benefit to taxpayers and in their harm to local government, by imposing on the states the heavy burden of an exact equality of taxation wherever transactions across state lines may be involved. If the latter, it would seem to add nothing to the guarantee of the equal protection clause, which extends to all "persons," including citizens of the United States. In that case, discourse upon the privileges and immunities clause would appear to be a gratuitous labor of supererogation.

If the privilege of making investments without the state is one protected by the privileges and immunities clause [296 U.S. 404, 448] and a tax upon the income derived from them is analogous to a tax upon the privilege of carrying on interstate commerce, we must not only accept the view that the privilege is infringed by the present tax, but it would follow that any taxation of the income is forbidden. The answer is, of course, that a state tax on net income derived from interstate commerce has never been regarded as a burden on commerce or as an infringement of the commerce clause. See *United States Glue Co. v. Town of Oak Creek*, 247 U.S. 321 , 38 S.Ct. 499, Ann.Cas. 1918E, 748; *Shaffer v. Carter*, 252 U.S. 37 , 40 S.Ct. 221; cf. *Peck & Co. v. Lowe*, 247 U.S. 165 , 38 S.Ct. 432; *Wagner v. City of Covington*, 251 U.S. 95 , 40 S.Ct. 93. Far less could it be thought that a tax on property, or income from it, is an interference with commerce because the property had at some time been, or might some time become, the subject of such commerce. Cf. *Heisler v. Thomas Colliery Co.*, supra. In applying the privileges and immunities clause, as now interpreted, no ground is suggested, or well could be, for regarding a tax on income from investments without the state as infringing the privilege of carrying on interstate transactions, any more than a tax on net income derived from interstate commerce or from property which had at some time moved in interstate commerce infringes the commerce clause.

The contention that a state tax indirectly affecting transactions carried on across state lines, not forbidden by the commerce clause (art. 1, 8, cl. 3) or by article 4, 2, can be condemned under the privileges and immunities clause, was definitely rejected by this Court in *Williams v. Fears*, supra. There a state occupation tax upon those engaged in hiring laborers for employment outside the state was held not to infringe the privileges and immunities clause or the equal protection clause.

So far as the objection is addressed to bare inequality of taxation affecting interstate transactions, if valid, it must be accepted as compelling equality of taxation by [296 U.S. 404,

449] the state of the citizen's residence and as well by the state into which the transaction extends. More than this, since the exercise of the privilege involves both states, it would seem to be infringed not only by an unequal tax imposed by either, but by any tax imposed at the normal rate by both.

Starting with the dubious assumption that the protection of every movement of the citizen interstate, an acknowledged subject of the commerce clause, is independently a subject of the privileges and immunities clause, the protection afforded by the latter is expanded until it affords a refuge to the citizen from taxation which has no necessary relation to his movements interstate, and is in fact not shown to impose any restraint upon them. A tax immunity created avowedly for the protection of the citizen's privilege of movement from state to state is thus pressed far beyond the requirements of the interest put forward to justify it, and to a point which has never been thought needful or even desirable for the protection of the commerce of the nation. It is a transition effected only by ignoring the decision of this Court in *Williams v. Fears*, supra.

If mere difference in taxation is made the test of infringement, the iron rule of equality of taxation which the equal protection and due process clauses have failed to impose, see *Bell's Gap R. Co. v. Pennsylvania*, supra, 134 U.S. 232, 237 , 10 S.Ct. 533, is the first fruit of this expansion of the protection of the privileges and immunities clause. To gain the benefits of its shelter the citizen has only to acquire, by a transaction wholly intrastate, an investment outside his state. I can find in the language and history of the privileges and immunities clause no warrant for such a restriction upon local government and policy. Citizens of the United States are given no privilege not to pay taxes. It would seem that a subordination of state taxing power to the **[296 U.S. 404, 450]** interests of the individual, of such debatable wisdom, could be justified only by a pointed command of the Constitution of plain import.

If we turn from the reasoning by which this application of the privileges and immunities clause to state taxation is supported to the decision now actually made, it seems that the clause is thought to prohibit only these inequalities in taxation which are considered to be arbitrary and unreasonable. The exemption of dividends derived from corporate business carried on within the state, and the taxation of similar dividends from without the state, is held not to be an infringement of the clause. Exemption of income from investments in property within the state and taxation of like income from without the state is thought to be valid. But the privileges and immunities clause, it is declared, forbids any difference in the taxation of income from investment made within the state and income from investment made without, a conclusion which can only be attributed to the belief that this discrimination, as distinguished from the others, is arbitrary and unreasonable.

We are thus returned to the point of beginning, to a discussion of the question whether the exemption in the present tax is so unreasonable, so without support of a permissible state policy, as to infringe constitutional limitations. If the exemption does not merit condemnation as a denial of the equal protection which the Fourteenth Amendment extends to every person, nothing can be added to the vehemence or effectiveness of the denunciation by invoking the command of the privileges and immunities clause.

The judgment should be affirmed.

Mr. Justice **BRANDEIS** and Mr. Justice **CARDOZO** concur in this opinion.

Supreme Court of Indiana
Cory et al. v. Carter, 48 Ind. 327 (1874)

November Term 1874

1

[327] [328] [329] *(headnotes omitted)*

[329]

From the Marion Superior Court.

N.B. Taylor, F. Rand, and E. Taylor, for appellants.

J. W. Gordon, T. M. Browne, and R. N. Lamb, for appellee.

BUSKIRK, J.—This was a proceeding by mandate, on the part of the appellee against the appellants. The appellee, in his petition, alleged that he was a citizen of the State of Indiana and resided in school district number two, in Lawrence township, Marion county, in the said State, and was a taxpayer therein; that he was the father of two children, Mary and Edward Carter, and the grandfather of Lucy and John Carter, all of whom resided with him; that he was a negro of African descent, and that his said children and grandchildren were all negroes of the full blood and of the same descent; that his children and grandchildren were respectively of the age that entitled them to the benefits of the common schools in the said district; that there was a common school for white [330] children in progress in said district, and that his said children and grandchildren presented themselves at the school-house in said district and demanded admission and to be taught therein with the white children, but were refused admittance by the appellants Beaver and Craig, the director and teacher of said school, for the reason that the said school was a school for white children, and not for negro children; that after the refusal aforesaid, he caused to be served upon the appellants a written request and demand that his said children and grandchildren should ho received and taught in the said school with the white children of said district but they were refused admission solely upon the ground that they were negroes; that said appellants and all other persons have wholly neglected, failed, and refused, and still neglect, fail, and refuse, to provide any school in said district, or in any adjoining district, near enough for said children or grandchildren to attend as scholars; and that by reason of the premises his said children and grandchildren are denied all opportunity to attend any school in said district or elsewhere in the neighborhood, as in right and law they are entitled to do.

There is no allegation that the trustee of said school district number two had failed or refused to provide the means of education for such children within the district, outside of the said school for white children, to the extent of their proportion, according to number of the school revenues of the said district.

The aid of the court was requested to declare the right of admission of said negro children into the school for white children, and to compel the appellants to admit them.

An alternate writ was issued against the appellants, requiring them to admit such children into the school in said district for white children or appear and show cause why they should not so admit such children.

The appellants appeared and filed separate demurrers to the complaint, upon the ground that it did not state facts sufficient to constitute a cause of action, but the demurrers were overruled; and the appellants refusing to plead further, but electing [331] to stand by their exceptions to the rulings of the court, the court gave judgment for a peremptory writ of mandate.

The appellants appealed to the general term, where the judgment of the special term was affirmed.

The error assigned is, that the superior court, in general term, erred in affirming the judgment of the court in special term.

171

The question presented for our decision is, whether the court below erred in overruling the demurrer to the complaint, the correct solution of which will depend upon the proper construction to be placed upon the constitution and statutes of this State and the Constitution of the United States; and as preliminary to the consideration of the grave constitutional questions arising in the record, we proceed to inquire what provisions the legislature has made for the education of the white and colored children of the State.

The act of March 6th, 1865, provided for the annual assessment and collection of a tax on the property, real and personal, in the State (except that owned by negroes and mulattoes), for supporting a general system of common schools, in the State. It provided for the enumeration each year of the white children within the respective townships, towns, and cities in the State, between the ages of six and twenty-one years, exclusive of married persons. It provided the officers and agencies for the system, the mode and means of carrying it on, for locating and establishing schools, and carrying them on, for building school-houses, and employing teachers, etc. It was essentially white—none but white children between the named ages, and who were unmarried, were entitled to its privileges. 3 Ind. Stat. 440-472; *Draper v. Cambridge*, 20 Ind. 268.

At the session of the legislature of this State next after the ratification of the fourteenth amendment to the Constitution of the United States, an act was passed by the General Assembly of this State, entitled "an act to render taxation for common school purposes uniform, and to provide for the education [332] of the colored children of the State," which was approved May 13th, 1869, and is as follows:

"Section 1. Be it enacted by the General Assembly of the State of Indiana, that in assessing and collecting taxes for school purposes under existing laws, all property, real and personal, subject to taxation for State and county purposes, shall be taxed for the support common schools without regard to the race or color of the owner of the property.

"Sec. 2. All children of the proper age, without regard to the race or color, shall hereafter be included in the enumeration of the children of the respective school districts, townships, towns and cities of this State for school purposes; but in making such enumeration the officers charged by law with that duty shall enumerate the colored children of proper age, who may reside in any school district, in a separate and distinct list from that in which the other school children of such school district shall be enumerated.

"Sec. 3. The trustee or trustees of each township, town or city, shall organize the colored children into separate schools, having all the rights and privileges of other schools of the township: Provided, there are not a sufficient number within attending distance, the several districts may be consolidated and form one district. But if there arc not a sufficient number within reasonable distance to be thus consolidated, the trustee or trustees shall provide such other means of education for said children as shall use their proportion, according to numbers, of school revenue to the best advantage.

"Sec. 4. All laws relative to school matters, not inconsistent with this act, shall be deemed applicable to colored schools.

"Sec. 5. Whereas an emergency exists for the immediate taking effect of this act, the same shall be in force from and after its passage." 3 Ind. Stat. 472.

Prior to the passage of such act, the assessment of taxes for school purposes had been confined to the property white persons. The first section provided for the levy and collection [333] of a tax for school purposes upon all the property within the State subject to taxation, without regard to the race or color of the owner.

The second section adds to the enumeration directed in section 14 of the act of March 6th, 1865, all colored children of the proper age, within the State, and directs them to be enumerated at the same time with the white children; but in a separate list or class from that in which the white children are enumerated.

The third section commands the trustees of each township, town, or city in the State to organize the colored children therein into separate schools, with all the rights and privileges of white schools in the particular township, town, or city. But if the number of colored children within attending distance are not sufficient to organize a school, the trustees may consolidate several districts into one, for that purpose. And if the number of colored children within reasonable attending distance are not sufficient to be thus consolidated, the trustees shall provide such other means of education for such colored children as shall use their proportion, according to numbers, of the school revenue to the best advantage.

Tile fourth section makes all laws relative to school matters, not inconsistent with the provisions of the act, applicable to colored schools.

It is, in the first place, claimed that the act of May 13th, 1869, is in conflict, with section 19. of article 4 of our constitution, which provides, that every act shall "embrace but one subject and matters properly connected therewith; which subject shall be expressed in the title."

We think the subject of the act is common schools, and that the taxation of the property of all persons for school purposes and the enumeration of, and providing schools for, the colored children of the State are properly connected with the subject of the act. We have so frequently placed a construction upon the above quoted section that we do not deem it necessary to reexamine the question. We cite the late case of *The State*, **[334]** *ex rel. Pitman, v. Tucker*, 40 Ind. 355, where many of the cases are cited.

It is very plain and obvious to us, that by the supplemental act of May 13th, 1869, the legislature has provided for the education of the white and colored children of the State in separate schools, and the question presented for our decision is; whether such legislation is in conflict with the constitution of this State or the Constitution of the United States.

It is contended that the act in question is repugnant to section 23 of article 1, and section 1 of article 8, and they are: "Section 23. The General Assembly shall not grant to any citizen, or class of citizens, privileges or immunities which, upon the same terms, shall not equally belong to all citizens." 1 G. & II. 33.

Section 1, article 8 (1 G. & II. 48), declares, that "knowledge and learning, generally diffused throughout a community, being essential to the preservation of a free government, it shall be the duty of the General Assembly to encourage by all suitable means, moral, intellectual, scientific, and agricultural improvement; and to provide by law for a general and uniform system of common schools, wherein tuition shall be without charge, and equally open to all."

It is important that we should settle in advance the rules by which we are to be guided in placing a construction upon the constitutional provisions above quoted.

In The State v. Gibson, 36 Ind. 389, we held that it was settled by very high authority, that in placing a construction or any clause of part thereof, a court should look to the history of the times, and examine the state of things existing when the constitution, or any part thereof, was framed and adopted, to ascertain the old law, the mischief, and the remedy. The court should also look to the nature and objects of the particular powers, duties, and rights in question, with all the aids and lights of contemporary history, and give to the words of each provision just such operation and force, consistent with their legitimate meaning, as will fairly secure the end proposed. *Kendall v. The United* **[335]** *States*, 12 Peters, 524; *Prigg v. The Commonwealth of Pennsylvania*, 16 Peters, 539.

In the *Slaughter-House Cases*, 16 Wallace, 36, the same rules were laid down and illustrated with great force by reference to the history of the times and condition of things which brought about the recent amendments to the Constitution of the United States.

Judge **COOLEY**, in his great work on Constitutional Limitations, on page 54, says:

"A cardinal rule in dealing with written instruments is that they are to receive an unvarying interpretation, and that their practical construction is to be uniform. A constitution is not to be made to mean one thing at one time, and another at some subsequent time when the circumstances may have so changed as perhaps to make a different rule in the case seem desirable. A principal share of the benefit expected from written constitutions would be lost if the rules they established were so flexible as to bend to circumstances or be modified by public opinion. It is with special reference to the varying moods of public opinion, and with a view to putting the fundamentals of government beyond their control, that these instruments are framed; and there can be no such steady and imperceptible change in their rules as inheres in the principles of the common law. Those beneficent maxims of the common law which guard person and property have grown and expanded until they mean vastly more to us than they did to our ancestors, and are more minute, particular, and pervading in their protections; and we may confidently look forward in the future to still further modifications in the direction of improvement. Public sentiment and action effect such changes, and the courts recognize them; but a court or legislature which should allow a change in public sentiment to influence it in giving construction to a written constitution not warranted by the intention of it's founders, would, be justly chargeable with reckless disregard of official oath and public duty; and if its course could become a precedent, these instruments would be of little avail. The violence of public passion is quite as [336] likely to be in the direction of oppression as in any other; and the necessity for bills of rights in our fundamental laws lies mainly in the danger that the legislature will be influenced by temporary excitements and passions among the people to adopt oppressive enactment's. What a court is to do, therefore, is to declare the law as written, leaving it to the people themselves to make such changes as new circumstances may require. The meaning of the constitution is fixed when it is adopted, and it is not different at any subsequent time when a court has occasion to pass upon it."

Again, the learned author says:

"The object of construction, as applied to a written constitution, is to give effect to the intent of the people in adopting it. In the case of all written laws, it is the intent of the lawgiver that is to be enforced."

Another cardinal rule of construction laid down by this author is, that the whole instrument is to be examined in placing a construction upon any portion or clause thereof. He says:

"Nor is it lightly to be inferred that any portion of a written is so ambiguous as to require extrinsic aid in its construction. Every such instrument is adopted as a whole, and a clause which, standing by itself, might seen of doubtful import, may yet be made plain by comparison with other clauses or portions of the same law. It is therefore a rule of construction, that the whole is to be examine with a view to arriving at the true intention of each part; and this Sir Edward Coke regards the most natural and genuine method of expounding a statute. 'If any section [of a law] be intricate, obscure, or doubtful, the proper mode of discovering its true meaning is by comparing it with the other sections, and finding out the sense of one clause by the words or obvious intent of another.' And in making this comparison it is not to be supposed that any words have been employed without occasion, or without intent that they should have effect as to be of the law. The rule applicable here is, that effect is to be given, if possible, to the whole instrument, and to every section [337] and clause. If different portions seem to conflict, the courts must harmonize them, if practicable, and lean in favor of a construction which will render every word operative, rather than one which may make some idle and nugatory.

"This rule is especially applicable to written constitutions, in which the people will be presumed to have expressed themselves in careful and measured terms, corresponding with the immense importance of the powers delegated, leaving as little as possible to implication. It is scarcely conceivable that a case can arise where a court would be justifiable in declaring any portion of a written constitution nugatory because of ambiguity. One part may qualify another, so as to restrict its operation, or apply it otherwise than the natural construction would require if it stood by itself; but one part is not to be allowed to defeat another, if by any reasonable construction the two can be made to stand together."

In support of the above propositions, reference is made in the notes to the following authorities:

The *People v. Morrell*, 21 Wend. 563; *Newell v. The People*, 7 N.Y. 109; *McKoan v. Devries*, 3 Barb. 196; *The People v. Blodgett*, 13 Mich. 138; *United States v. Fisher*, 2 Cranch, 399; *Bosley v. Mattingly*, 14 B. Mon. 89 ; *Sturges v. Crowninshield*, 4 Wheat. 202; *Schooner Paulina's Cargo v. United States*, 7 Cranch, 60; *Ogden v. Strong*, 2 Paine C. C. 584; *United States v. Ragsdale*, Hemp. 497; *Southwark Bank v. The Commonwealth*, 20 Penn. St. 446;

174

Ingalls v. Cole, 47 Me. 530; *McCluskey v. Cromwell*, 11 N.Y. 593; *Furman v. City of New York*, 5 Sandf 16; *The People v. The New York Central R.R. Co.*, 24 N.Y. 492; *Bidwell v. Whittaker*, 1 Mich. 479; *Alexander v. Worthington*, 5 Md. 471; *Cantwell v. Owens*, 14 Md. 215; *Case v. Wildridge*, 4 Ind. 51; *Pitman v. Flint*, 10 Pick. 504; *Ludlow v. Johnson*, 3 Ohio, 553; *District Township v. The City of Dubuque*, 7 Iowa, 262; *Pattison v. Board*, etc., 13 Cal. 175; *Spencer v. The State*, 5 Ind. 41; *Denn v. Reid*, 10 Pet. 524; *Creencastle Township, etc., v. Black*, 5 Ind. 569; *Stowell . Lord Zouch*, Plow. 365; Broom Leg. Max. (5th Am. ed.) 551; Co. Lit. **[338]** 381, a.; *Attorney General v. Detroit, etc., Plank Road Co.*, 2 Mich. 138; *The People v. Burns*, 5 Mich. 114; *Manly v. The State*, 7 Md. 184; *Parkinson v. The State*, 14 Md. 184; *The Belleville, etc., R. R. Co., v. Gregory*, 15 Ill. 20; *Ryegate v. Wardsboro*, 30 Vt. 746; *Brooks v. Mobile School Comm'rs*, 31 Ala. 229; *Den v. Dubious*, 1 Harridan, 285; *Den v. Schnook*, 3 Halt. 34; *Walkout v. Widgeon*, 7 Ind. 44; *The People v. Purely*, 2 Hill N. Y. 36; *Green v. Welder*, 32 Miss. 650; *Warren v. Shaman*, 5 Texas, 441; *Quick v. White Water Township*, 7 Ind. 570; *Gibbons v. Olden*, 9 Wheat. 188; Smith Counts. Construct., sec. 502, 503; Sedge. Stat. Law, 229, 233, 251 ,and 252.

An examination of the above authorities shows that they are in point, and fully support the doctrines announced.

It is essential to a correct interpretation of the above provisions of our constitution, in the light of the above rules of construction, that we should look to the history of tile times and examine the condition of things existing prior to, and at the time of, the adoption and ratification of our present state constitution, and compare the sections in question with other portions and clauses of such constitution.

We will limit our inquiry into the political condition of the negroes in this State from the organization or our state government in 1816 down to the ratification of the thirteenth, fourteenth, and fifteenth amendments to the Constitution of the United States, and incidentally to their status in other states of the Union.

Prior to the act of May 13th, 1869, making taxation for common school purposes uniform, and providing for the education of the colored children of the State, 3 Ind. Stat. 472, no provision was made for their education in this State. As a race, their condition was one of marked and settled inferiority before the law, being reduced strictly to the enjoyment of the three primary rights only, and for a large portion of time legally precluded from their full exercise, viz., the right of personal security, the right of personal liberty, and the right of private property. But the power of exercising these rights was practically limited in degree as compared with the exercise and **[339]** enjoyment of the same rights by the white race. This was their most favorable condition in several states of the Union, they being admitted to the equal exercise of civil and political rights and privileges with the whites in but one state of the Union. In nearly one half of the states of the Union, as a race, they lived in a state of life-long servitude, having no control of their time or actions, no right to acquire property, no lawful power to follow the promptings of their own thoughts and judgments, their lives and limbs, their minds and strength, the property and subject to the will of their masters; and notwithstanding the proclamation of emancipation, this continued to be their condition, practically and in a large degree, until after the ratification of the thirteenth amendment to the Constitution of the United States, December 18th, 1865. 2 Kent Com., 7th ed., pp. 252, 258, and note *b* to *p.* 258; *Scott v. Sandford*, 19 How. 393; *Smith v Moody*, 26 Ind. 299; Rev. Stat. 1831, p. 375; Rev. Stat 1838, p. 418.

By sec. 7 of article 11 of the constitution of 1816, it is provided that there shall he neither slavery nor involuntary servitude in this State, otherwise than for the punishment of crimes, whereof the party shall have been duly convicted. Rev. Stat. 1838, 1). 50.

Sec. 2 of article 3 provided for an enumeration of all the
white male inhabitants above the age of twenty-one years. Rev. Stat. 1838, p 38.

See. 1 of article 6 limited the right of suffrage to the white male citizens of the United States of the age of twenty-one, and who had resided in the State one year immediately preceding the election. Rev. Stat. 1838, p.46.

By the act of February 10th, 1831, every such person, coming into or being brought into this State, was prohibited from residing therein, unless bond with good and sufficient security, to lie approved by the overseers of the poor of some township, was given on behalf of such person, payable to the State of Indiana, in the penal sum of five hundred dollars, conditioned that such person should not, at any time, become **[340]** a charge to the county in which such bond was given, nor to any other county in the State, as also for such person's good behavior, etc.

It provided penalties, likewise, for failure to comply with these provisions, consisting of hiring such person out and applying the proceeds to his benefit, and removal from the State; and by fine imposed and recovered by presentment or indictment, for harboring any such person failing to give the required bond.

This act remained upon the statute book of this State, and continued in force, for a period of over twelve years, and received the judicial sanction of the Supreme Court of the State. Rev. Stat. 1831, pp. 375, 376; Rev. Stat. 1838, pp 418, 419; *The State v. Cooper*, 5 Blackf. 258; *Baptiste v. The State*, 5 Blackf. 283; *Hickland v. The State*, 8 Blackf. 365.

Article 13 of the constitution of this State, which took effect on the 1st day of November, 1851, and superseded the constitution of 1816, prohibited negroes and mulattoes from coming into or settling in this State after its adoption, declared all contracts with such persons void, and made, it an offence punishable by fine of not less than ten nor more than five hundred dollars for any person to employ them; and this article was submitted, as a distinct proposition, to tile people of the State for their approval or disapproval, and was adopted by a vote of one hundred and nine thousand nine hundred and seventy-six to twenty-one thousand and sixty-six. 1 G. & H. 52; Dillon's Hist. Ind. 577.

Other provisions of this constitution excluded negroes and mulattoes from the elective franchise, from holding office in the State or any of its departments, from the enumeration for senatorial and representative purposes, and from participation in all of the privileges pertaining to full and active citizenship, making them a separate and distinct class of inferiors before the law, and placing them politically in a separate body, with no constitutional grant of privileges and immunities under the title of "citizen" or "citizens," but leaving them in possession only of the three primary rights heretofore **[341]** mentioned. 1 Opin. Att'y Gen. 506; 4 Opin. Att'y Gen. 147; *Smith v. Moody*, 20 Ind. 299.

This the constitution and subsequent recognized and decided constitutional legislation clearly establish. Acts June 18th, 1852, 1 G. & H. 443; *Hatwood v. The State*, 18 Ind. 492; *Barkshire v. The State*, 7 Ind. 389.

In the light of the foregoing history, constitutional provisions, legislative acts, and judicial constructions thereof, it is very plain and obvious to us, that persons of the African race were not in the minds or contemplation of the wise and thoughtful framers of our constitution, when they prepared and agreed upon the above quoted sections, or of the people of the State when they ratified and adopted the constitution containing such provisions.

In our opinion, the privileges and immunities secured by sec. 23 of article 1 were not intended for persons of the African race; for the section expressly limits the enjoyment of such privileges and immunities to citizens, and at that time negroes were neither citizens of the United States nor of this State. It was held by this court, in *Sears v. The Board of Commissioners Of Warren County*, 36 Ind. 267, that the privileges and immunities secured by the above quoted section were intended for citizens of this State.

Nor in view of the other provisions of our constitution, and in the light of the rules of construction before stated, can it be successfully maintained that the provisions of sec. 1 of article 8 were intended for the children of the African race. It is unreasonable to suppose that the framers of the constitution, who had denied to that race the right of citizenship, of suffrage, of holding office, of serving on juries, and of testifying as witnesses in any case where a white person was a party, and had prohibited, under heavy pains and penalties, the further immigration of that race into the State, intended to provide for the education of the children of that race in our common schools with the white children of the State.

The public sentiment of the State, at that time, was unfriendly to the African race and their participation in governmental [342] affairs, and demanded their exclusion from the State; and it is not for us to say, sitting here, whether such policy was wise or unwise, and we speak of it only as a matter of history having a bearing upon the construction of our Constitution.

An application of the rules of construction heretofore laid down to the various provisions of our constitution will conclusively demonstrate that the provisions of the sections under examination have no application to the children and grandchildren of the appellee.

One of the cardinal rules of construction is, that courts shall give effect to the intent of the framers of the instrument, and of the people in adopting it. Then, as it is manifest that neither the framers of the Constitution nor the people in adopting it intended that the children of the African race should participate in the advantages of a general and uniform system of common schools, we possess no power to adjudge to them what was not designated for them.

Another rule of Construction is, that in placing a construction upon one section or clause, courts are required to examine the whole instrument and to give effect, if possible, to the whole instrument; and if different portions seem to conflict, the courts must harmonize them, if practicable, and lean in favor of a construction which will render every word operative, rather than one which may make some idle and nugatory. There is but one construction which will preserve the unity, harmony, and consistency of our state constitution, and that is, to hold that it was made and adopted by and for the exclusive use and enjoyment of the white race. Any other construction would convict the members of the constitutional convention and the voters of the State of the grossest inconsistency, absurdity, and injustice. It would be monstrous to hold that the framers of the constitution in adopting, and the voters of the State in ratifying it, intended that the common schools of the State should be open to the children of the African race, when, by the same instrument, that portion of such race as then resided in the State Were denied all political rights, privileges, [343] and immunities, and the further immigration of that race into the State was prohibited by the thirteenth article of the constitution, which received the almost unanimous approval of the voters of the State.

Another important rule of construction is, that the meaning of a constitution is fixed when it is adopted, and it is not different at any subsequent time when a court has occasion to pass upon it. A constitution is inflexible and can not bend to circumstances or be modified by public opinion. It is, therefore, the duty of the court to declare the law as it is written, leaving to the people, in their sovereign capacity, to make such changes as new circumstances may require; and, in our opinion, using the appropriate and forcible language of Judge COOLEY, "a court or legislature which should allow a change in public sentiment to influence it in giving construction to a written constitution not warranted by the intention of its founders, would be justly chargeable with reckless disregard of official oath and public duty."

The views which we have expressed are greatly strengthened and enforced by the construction which this court placed upon a section of the constitution of 1816, and of an act passed while it was in force.

Section 1 of article 9 declares that "knowledge and learning, generally diffused through a community, being essential to the preservation of a free government, and spreading the opportunities and advantages of education through the various parts of the country being highly conducive to this end," etc. "the General Assembly shall, from time to time, pass such laws as shall be calculated to encourage intellectual, scientifical, and agricultural improvement, by allowing rewards and immunities for the promotion and improvement of arts, sciences, commerce, manufactures, and natural history; and to countenance and encourage the principles of humanity, industry, and morality."

Section 2 of said article provided, that "it shall be the duty of the General Assembly, as soon as circumstances will permit, to provide by law for a general system of education [344] ascending in a regular gradation from township schools to a state university, wherein tuition shall be gratis, and equally open to all." R.S. 1838, pp. 48, 49.

While the above constitution was in force, the legislature provided for a general common school system, the 102d section of which act was as follows:

"When any school is supported in any degree by the public school fund, or by taxation, so long as the money so derived shall be expending thereon, such school shall be open and free to all the white children resident within the district, over five and under twenty-one years or age." Chap. 15, R.S. 1843, p. 321.

In the case of *Lewis v. Henley*, 2 Ind. 332, this court was required to place a construction upon the above quoted section, and it was held that negro children were not entitled to admission to the schools with the white children, and that the legislature had the right, under the constitution, to exclude negro children from our public schools. It was further held that, although the negroes might be entitled to share in the funds derived from the sale of lands donated by Congress, yet they would have to do so in separate schools, and not in schools with white children.

Both constitutions provided for a general and uniform system of common schools; both provided that the tuition should be free and the schools equally open to all. Both constitutions deprived the negroes of all political rights. If the legislature, under the constitution of 1816, had the right to exclude the negroes from the public schools for white children, it is difficult to see why it may not be done under the present constitution.

Having reached the true construction of the constitution of this State, as it came from the hands of its framers and received the sanction of her qualified voters, the next stop is to find out the extent of its qualification or change by the Constitution of the United States.

Section 2 of article 4 of the Constitution of the United States declares, that "the citizens of each state shall be entitled [345] to all privileges and immunities of citizens in the several states."

This section, at an early date, received a construction in the case of *Corfield v. Coryell*, which has ever since been recognized and approved. It relates only to "those privileges and immunities which are fundamental," and which may all be comprehended under the following heads: "Protection by the government with the right to acquire and possess property of every kind, and to pursue and obtain happiness and safety, subject, nevertheless, to such restraints as the government may prescribe for the general good of the whole."

In the *Slaughter-House Cases*, the Supreme Court of the United States said: "Its sole purpose was to declare to the several states, that whatever those rights, as you grant or establish them to your own citizens, or as you limit or qualify, or impose restrictions on their exercise, the same, neither more nor less, shall be the measure of the rights of citizens of other states within your jurisdiction." It did not compel the state, into which the citizen of another state removed, to allow him the exercise of the same rights which he enjoyed in the state from which he removed. *Corfield v. Coryell*, 4 Wash. C. C. 371; *Slaughter-House Cases*, 16 Wal. 76, 77; *Bradwell v. The State*, 16 Wal. 130; *Ward v Maryland*, 12 Wal. 430; *Connor v. Elliott*, 18 How. 591; *Browne v. State of Md.*, 12 Wheat. 448, 449; *People v. Brady*, 40 Cal. 198; Story Const., secs. 1805, 1800; Cooley Const. Lim. 15, 16, 397; Potter's Dwarris on Stat. 525, 526; *Scars v. The Board*, etc., 36 Ind. 207; *The Jeffersonville, etc., R.R. Co. v. Hendricks*, 41 Ind. 48.

It is well settled by repeated decisions of the federal and state courts, that with the exception of the limitations imposed upon the powers of the states by section 10 of article 1 of the Constitution of the United States, the several states were left as before the Federal Union was formed, with full power to declare the rights of their citizens, without interference from the Federal Government.

It is a familiar rule of construction of the Constitution of the Union, that the sovereign powers vested in the state governments [346] by their respective constitutions, remain unaltered and unimpaired, except so far as they were granted to the government of the United States. In one of the states of the Union, colored children were entitled to admission into schools for white children, and to be taught with white children, and yet, if a person residing in such state should remove into some other state, where such right is denied, the right so exercised in the state from which the person removed would be lost, because it was not one of those fundamental rights which accompany the person, but a domestic regulation exclusively within the constitutional and legislative power of each state, and to be regarded in the nature of a domestic regulation necessary for the good of the whole people, or which the good of the people of one state, in their sovereign judgment, required to be different from the regulation in another, as best securing "the general comfort and prosperity of the state." Story Const., sees. 1853, 1409; Coolly Const. Lim. 572, 574; 2 Kent Com. 71; 2 Op. Att'y Gen'l, 426 ; *Commonwealth v. Alger*, 7 Cush. 84; *The City of New York v. Miln*, 11 Pet. 139; *Slaughter-House Cases*, 16 Wal. 62; *Bradwell v. The State*, 16 Wal. 130; *Thayer v. Hedges*, 22 Ind. 282; Potter's Dwarris on Stat. 352, 452, 455) 461.

It is very plain that the tenth amendment of the Constitution of the United States cannot receive such construction as will aid the claim of appellee. It declares, that "the powers not delegated to the United States by the Constitution, nor prohibited by it to the states, are reserved to the states respectively, or to the people;" and **the power to fix the qualifications of the citizen of the state, and to establish his rights in the state, is one of the powers expressly reserved to the state by this amendment**; for there is no express limitation of the power of the states in the Federal Constitution, in this respect, as it then stood, and such limitation could not exist without express mention. Rawle Const. 84, 87 ; Story Const., sec. 1904; Works of Webster, vol. 3, p. 322; Coolly Counts. Lim. 19; Federalist, 140; *Slaughter-House Cases, 16 Awl. 70*, 71, 72, 73; *Baron v. Mayor*, etc., 7 Pet. 243; *Smith v. State of Md.*, [347] 18 How. 71; *Pervear v. The Commonwealth*, 5 Wal. 475; *Barker v. The People*, 3 Cow. 686; *James v. The Commonwealth*, 12 S. & R. 220 ; *Jane v. Commonwealth*, 3 Met. Ky. 18; *Lincoln v. Smith*, 27 Vt. 336; *Warren v. Paul*, 22 Ind. 276; *The State, ex rel. Lakey, v. Garton*, 32 Ind. 1.

That the views hereinbefore expressed correctly represent the relative powers of the federal and state governments at the close of the great civil war, and until after the ratification of the amendments to the Constitution of the United States, which followed the termination of that contest cannot, we think, be successfully controverted.

We next proceed to determine whether such amendments, or either of them, have worked a change, and, if they have, to what extent.

The thirteenth amendment was proposed by Congress on the 1st day of February, 1865, and declared by the Secretary of State to have been ratified December 18th, 1865. It declares that "neither slavery nor involuntary servitude, except as a punishment for crime whereof the party shall have been duly convicted, shall exist within the United States, or any place subject to their jurisdiction;" and "Congress shall have power to enforce this article by appropriate legislation." 3 Ind. Stat. 579.

This amendment was to prevent any question in the future as to the effect of the war and the President's proclamation of emancipation upon slavery; and its obvious purpose was to forbid all shades and conditions of African slavery. *Slaughter-House Cases*, 16 Wal. 68, 69.

It had no other office, and its real effect was more for the future than the present. As to the matter of social and political rights, the African was left just where section 37, article 1, of our state constitution left him, and subject to all the inconveniences and burdens incident to his color and race, except his former one of servitude. He was a person whose place and office, in the body politic, was yet to be designated and established. He possessed no political rights, in the usual and [348] proper sense of that term, through, or had none conferred by, this enactment.

Following this constitutional amendment the civil rights bill of April 9th, 1866, was enacted by Congress, the first section of which declares who are citizens of the United States, and specifics certain rights which shall be accorded to such citizens in the states and territories, and the residue is made up of pains and penalties for violation of the rights sought to be conferred, and the machinery for enforcing its provisions.

It is not worth while to enquire into the effect of this act, or whether the Federal Constitution, which made citizens of the different states citizens of the United States, could be changed by a simple congressional enactment; for it is clear, admitting it to be valid, that it does not relate to or bear upon the right claimed in this case, for it purports only to confer upon negroes and mulattoes the right, in every state and territory, to make and enforce contracts, to sue, be parties and give evidence, to inherit, purchase, lease, sell, hold, and convey real and personal property, and the full and equal benefit of all laws and proceedings for the security of person and property as enjoyed by white citizens, and subjects them to like pains and penalties. 3 Ind. Stat. 589. In this nothing is left to inference. Every right intended is specified.

The fourteenth amendment to the Federal Constitution was proposed by Congress July 16th, 1866, and declared by the Secretary of State to have been ratified July 28th, 1868. It consists of several sections, but section 1 is the only one necessary to this examination. It declares, that "all persons born or naturalized in the United States, and subject to the jurisdiction thereof are citizens of the United States and of the state wherein they reside. No state shall make or enforce any law which shall abridge the privileges or immunities of citizens of the United States; nor shall any state deprive any person of life, liberty, or property, without due process of law, nor deny to any person within its jurisdiction the equal protection of the laws." [349]

This section can better be understood or construed, by dividing and considering it in four paragraphs or clauses, the last, however, being a mere re-statement of what precedes it:

First. "All persons born or naturalized in the United States, and subject to the jurisdiction thereof, are citizens of the United States and of the state wherein they reside."

In the *Slaughter-House Cases*, the Supreme Court of the United States say, this is a declaration "that persons may be citizens of the United States without regard to their citizenship of a particular state, and it overturns the Dred Scott decision by making all persons born within the United States and subject to its jurisdiction citizens of the United States. That its main purpose was to establish the citizenship of the negro can admit of no doubt. The phrase, 'subject to its jurisdiction,' was intended to exclude from its operation children of ministers, consuls, and citizens or subjects of foreign states born within the United States." It recognizes and establishes a "distinction between citizenship of the United States and citizenship of a state." "Not only may a man be a citizen of the United States without being a citizen of a state, but an important element is necessary to convert the former into the latter. He must reside within the state to make him a citizen of it, but it is only necessary that he should be born or naturalized in the United States to be a citizens of the Union. **It is quite clear, then, that there is a citizenship of the United States, and a citizenship of a state, which are distinct from each other, and which depend upon different characteristics or circumstances in the individual.**" Hence, a negro may be a citizen of the United States and reside without its territorial limits, or within some one of the territories; but he cannot be a citizen of a state until he becomes a *bona fide* resident of the state.

Second. "No state shall make or enforce any law which shall abridge the privileges or immunities of citizens of the United States."

This clause does not refer to citizens of the states. It *[350]* embraces only citizens of the United States. It leaves out the words "citizen of the state," which is so carefully used, and used in contradistinction to citizens of the United States, in the preceding sentence. It places the privileges and immunities of citizens of the United States under the protection of the Federal Constitution, and leaves the privileges and immunities of citizens of a state under the protection of the state constitution. This is fully shown by the recent decision of the Supreme Court of the United States in the *Slaughter-House Cases*, 16 Wal. 36.

Mr. Justice **MILLER**, in delivering the opinion of the court and in speaking in reference to the clause under examination, says:

"It is a little remarkable, if this clause was intended as a protection to the citizen of a state against the legislative power of his own state, that the word citizen of the state should be left out when it is so carefully used, and used in contradistinction to citizens of the United States, in the very sentence which precedes it. It is too clear for argument that the change in phraseology was adopted understandingly and with a purpose.

"Of the privileges and immunities of the citizen of the United States, and of the privileges and immunities of the citizen of the state, and what they respectively are, we will presently consider; but we wish to state here that it is only the former which are placed by this clause under the protection of the Federal Constitution, and that the latter, whatever they may be, are not intended to have any additional protection by this paragraph of the amendment.

"If, then, there is a difference between the privileges and immunities belonging to a citizen of the United States as such, and those belonging to the citizen of the state as such, the latter must rest for their security and protection Where they have heretofore rested; for they are not embraced by this paragraph of the amendment."

The same learned judge, in the further examination of the second clause, says: **[351]** "It would be the vainest show of learning to attempt to prove by citations of authority, that up to the adoption of the recent amendments, no claim or pretence was set up that those rights depended on the Federal Government for their existence or protection, beyond the very few express limitations which the Federal Constitution imposed upon the states—such, for instance, as the prohibition against *ex post facto* laws, bills of attainder, and laws impairing the obligation of contracts. But with the exception of these and a few other restrictions, the entire domain of the privileges and immunities of citizens of the states, as above defined, lay within the constitutional and legislative power of the states, and without that of the Federal Government. Was it the purpose of the fourteenth amendment, by the simple declaration that no state should make or enforce any law which shall abridge the privileges and immunities of citizens of the United States, to transfer the security and protection of all the civil rights which we have mentioned, from the states to the Federal Government? And where it is declared that Congress shall have the power to enforce that article, was it intended to bring within the power of Congress the entire domain of civil rights heretofore belonging exclusively to the states?

"All this and more must follow, if the proposition of the plaintiffs in error be sound. For not only are these rights subject to the control of Congress whenever in its discretion any of them are supposed to be abridged by state legislation, but that body may also pass laws in advance, limiting and restricting the legislative power of the states, in their most ordinary and usual functions, as in its judgment it may think proper on all such subjects. And still further, such a construction followed by the reversal of the judgments of the Supreme Court of Louisiana in these cases" (these judgments sustained the validity of the grant, by the legislature of Louisiana, of an exclusive right, guarded by certain limitations as to price, etc., to a corporation created by it, for twenty-five years, to build and maintain slaughter-houses, etc., and prohibited the right to all others, within a certain locality), **[352]** "would constitute this court a perpetual censor upon all legislation of the states, on the civil rights of their own citizens, with authority to nullify such as it did not approve as consistent with those rights, as they existed at the time of the adoption of this amendment.

"The argument we admit is not always the most conclusive which is drawn from the consequences urged against the adoption of a particular construction of an instrument. But when, as in the case before us, these consequences are so serious, so far-reaching and pervading, so great a departure from the structure and spirit of our institutions; when the effect is to fetter and degrade the state governments by subjecting them to the control of Congress, in the exercise of powers heretofore universally conceded to them of the most ordinary and fundamental character; when in fact it radically changes the whole theory of the relations of the state and Federal Governments to each other and of both these governments to the people; the argument has a force that is irresistible in the absence of language which expresses such a purpose too clearly to admit of doubt. WE are convinced that no such results were intended by the Congress which proposed these amendments, nor by the legislatures of the states which ratified them."

Third, "Nor shall any state deprive any person of life, liberty, or property, without due process of law."

This clause is the same contained in the fifth amendment to the Constitution of the United States, but there applied to the action of the Federal Government, and here placed as a check upon the states. But the constitution of our State contains, and perhaps those of all the states contain just such a provision, so that it expresses no new principle, but is the old rule in force since the foundation of the state governments. It prohibits the states from depriving any person of life, liberty, or property, except "in due course of legal proceedings, according to those rules and forms which have been established" by the state,

"for the protection of private rights." Cooley Const. Lim. 356, 357; *Westervelt v. Gregg*, 12 N. Y. 209. [353]

Fourth. "Nor deny to any person within its jurisdiction the equal protection of the laws." In regard to this clause, the Supreme Court of this State, in *The State v. Gibson*, 30 Ind. 389, say, it "seems to have been added in the abundance or caution, for it provides in express terms what was the fair, logical, and just implication from what had preceded it, and that was, that the persons made citizens by the amendment should be protected by the laws in the same manner, and to the same extent that white citizens were protected."

In the case of *The State v. Gibson*, supra, this court was called upon to place a construction upon the fourteenth amendment to the Constitution of the United States. It was claimed in that case, that such amendment had abolished the laws of this State prohibiting the intermarriage of negroes and whites. We held that marriage was a purely domestic institution, and subject to the exclusive control of the State; that such amendment had not conferred on the Federal Government any power to interfere with the institution of marriage, and that such amendment had not enlarged the powers of the Federal Government nor diminished those of the states. We then said:

"**The fourteenth amendment contains no new grant of power from the people, who are the inherent possessors of all power, to the Federal Government. It did not enlarge the powers of the Federal Government, nor diminish those of the states**. The inhibitions against the states doing certain things have no force or effect. They do not prohibit the states from doing any act that they could have done without them. * * * The only effect of the amendment under consideration was to extend the protection and blessings of the constitution and laws to a new class of persons. When they were made citizens they were as much entitled to the protection of the constitution and the laws as were the white citizens, and the states could no more deprive them of privileges and immunities than they could citizens of the white race. Citizenship entitled them to the protection of life, liberty, and property, and the [354] full and equal protection of the laws. Nor has the ratification of this amendment in any manner or to any extent impaired, weakened, or taken away any of the reserved rights of the states, as they had existed and been fully recognized by every department of the national government from its creation."

What was then intended to be expressed was, that the fourteenth amendment had not delegated to the Federal Government the power to regulate and control the domestic institutions of a state. As will be hereinafter shown, it imposes some limitations upon the powers of the states as to slavery and the equal protection of the rights of citizen of the United States and of the states.

We were then unaided by any judicial construction of the fourteenth amendment; and we are gratified to know that the views then expressed have been, in all substantial respects, sustained by the highest judicial tribunal in this country, and the one especially charged with the construction and interpretation of the Federal Constitution. By the solemn decision of that high court, the privileges and immunities belonging to the citizens of the states, as such, rest for their security and protection where they have heretofore rested, with the states themselves.

In *The Slate, ex rel, Garnes, v. McCann*, 21 Ohio St. 198, the Supreme Court of that state uses the following language:

"It would seem, then, that under the constitution and laws of this state, the right to classify the youth of the state for school purposes, on the basis of color, and to assign them to separate schools for education, both upon well recognized legal principles and the repeated adjudications of this court, is too firmly established to be now judicially disturbed.

"But it is claimed that the law authorizing the classification in question contravenes the provisions of the fourteenth amendment of the Constitution of the United States, and is, therefore, abrogated thereby.

"Unquestionably all doubts, whersoever they existed, as to the citizenship of colored persons, and their right to the 'equal protection of the laws,' are settled by this amendment.

[355] But neither of these was denied to them in this state before the adoption of the amendment. At all events, the statutes classifying the youth of the state for school purposes on the basis of color, and the decisions of this court in relation thereto, are not at all based on a denial that colored persons were citizens, or that they are entitled to the equal protection of the laws. It would seem, then, that these provisions of the amendment contain nothing conflicting with the statute authorizing the classification in question, nor the decisions heretofore made touching the point in controversy in this case. Nor do we understand that the contrary is claimed by counsel in this case. But the clause relied on, in behalf of the plaintiff; is that which forbids any state to 'make or enforce any law which shall abridge the privileges or immunities of citizens of the United States.'

"This involves the inquiry as to what privileges or immunities are embraced in the inhibition of this clause. We are not aware that this has been as yet judicially settled. The language of the clause, however, taken in connection with other provisions of the amendment, and of the constitution of which it forms a part, affords strong reasons for believing that it includes only such privileges or immunities as are derived from, or recognized by, the Constitution of the United States.

"A broader interpretation opens into a field of conjecture limitless as the range of speculative theories, and might work such limitations of the power of the states to manage and regulate their local institutions and affairs as were never contemplated by the amendment.

"If this construction be correct, the clause has no application to this case, for all the privileges or the school system of this state are derived solely from the constitution and laws of the state. If the General Assembly should pass a law repealing all laws creating and regulating the system, it can not be claimed that the fourteenth amendment could be interposed to prevent so grievous an abridgment of the privileges of the citizens of the state, for they would thereby be deprived of [356] privileges derived from the state, arid not of privileges derived from the United States.

"But we need not now further discuss this point, as the true meaning and exact limits of the clause in question are not necessarily involved in this case. For, conceding that the fourteenth amendment not only provides equal securities for all, but guarantees equality of rights to the citizens of a state, as one of the privileges or citizens of the United States, it remains to be seen whether this privilege has been abridged in the case before us. The law in question surely does not attempt to deprive colored persons of any rights. On the contrary, it recognizes their right, under the constitution of the state, to equal common school advantages, and secures to them their equal proportion of the school fund. It only regulates the mode and manner in which this right shall be enjoyed by all classes of persons. The regulation of this right arises from the necessity of the case. Undoubtedly it should be done in a manner to promote the best interests of all. But this task must, of necessity, be left to the wisdom and discretion of some proper authority. The people have committed it to the General Assembly, and the presumption is that it has discharged its duty in accordance with the best interests of all. At all events, the legislative action is conclusive, unless it clearly infringes the provisions of the constitution.

"At most, the fourteenth amendment only affords to colored citizens an additional guaranty of equality of rights to that already secured by the constitution of the state.

"The question, therefore, under consideration is the same that has, as we have seen, been heretofore determined in this state, that a classification of the youth of the state for school purposes, upon any basis which does not exclude either class from equal school advantage, is no infringement of the equal rights of citizens secured by the constitution of the state.

"We have seen that the law, in the case before us, works no substantial inequality of school privileges between the children of both classes in the locality of the parties. Under the [357] lawful regulation of equal educational privileges, the children of each class are required to attend the school provided for them, and to which they are assigned by those having the lawful official control of all.

"The plaintiff, then, can not claim that his privileges are abridged on the ground of inequality of school advantages for his children. Nor can he dictate where his children shall be instructed, or what teacher shall perform that office, without obtaining privileges not enjoyed by white citizens. Equality of rights does not involve the necessity of educating white and colored persons in the same school any more than it does that of educating children of both sexes in the same school, or that different grades of scholars must be kept in the same school. Any classification which preserves substantially equal school advantages is not prohibited by either the state or Federal Constitution, nor would it contravene the provisions of either. There is, then, no ground upon which the plaintiff can claim that his rights under the fourteenth amendment have been infringed?"

The foregoing opinion having been rendered since the ratification of the fourteenth amendment, is directly in point and is entitled to great weight and consideration, coming as it does from a court distinguished for its learning and ability.

How far, then, have the amendments operated to change the constitution of Indiana or imposed limitations or restrictions upon the sovereign power of the State? We answer, in the following particulars:

1. The State cannot in the future, while a member of the Federal Union, change her constitution so as to create or establish slavery or involuntary servitude; except as a punishment for crimes whereof the party shall have been convicted; thus protecting the new class of citizens, i. e., negroes and mulattoes, from being again reduced to slavery.

2. The State cannot deny to, or deprive a citizen of the United States, *i.e.*, any negro or mulatto, of, those national rights, privileges, or immunities which belong to him as such citizen. [358]

3. The State must recognize as its citizen any citizen of the United States, i.e., any negro or mulatto, who is or becomes a *bona fide* resident therein.

4. The State must give to such, *i.e.*, to such negro or mulatto, who is or who becomes a bona fide resident therein, the same rights, privileges, and immunities, secured by her constitution and laws to her other, *i.e.*, to the white citizens.

In our opinion, such amendments have not in any other respect imposed restrictions or limitations upon the sovereign power of the State. From this it results, that there is no limitation upon the power of the State, within the limits of her own constitution, to fix, secure, and protect the rights, privileges, and immunities of her citizens, as such, of whatever race or color they may be, so as to secure her own internal peace, prosperity, and happiness.

This will preserve in their purity and vigor the structure and spirit of our complex system of government, as it came from the hands of the great and illustrious men who achieved our independence and formed our matchless form of government. Anterior to the adoption of the Federal Constitution, the states existed as independent sovereignties, possessing supreme and absolute power over all questions of local and internal government. To the states the whole charge of interior regulation is left by the Federal Constitution; to them and to the people thereof all powers not expressly, or by necessary implication, delegated to the national government, and not prohibited to the states, are reserved to the states.

The Constitution of the United States is the bond which binds the states in one federal union. It forms and provides the agencies for the continuance and management of the federal government. It relates to and concerns matters of national import, and enables the states, represented by their federal head, as one of the independent and most powerful governments of the world, to enter into and manage its relations with the other independent powers of the earth. Under our constitution, our common school system must be general. That is, it must extend over and embrace every portion of the State. [359]

It must be uniform. The uniformity required has reference to the mode of government and discipline, the branches of learning taught, and the qualifications as to age and advancement in learning required of pupils as conditions of their admission. It does not mean that all the schools shall be of the same size and grade, or that all the branches of learning taught in one school shall be taught in all other schools, or that the qualifications as to age and advancement, which would admit a pupil in one school, would entitle such pupil to admission into all the other schools. Uniformity will be secured when all the schools of the same grade have the same system of government and discipline, the same branches of learning taught, and the same qualifications for admission.

The schools must be "equally open to all." This has reference to the persons who are entitled to receive instruction therein. The phrase, "equally open to all," is not to be taken in a literal sense, for this would embrace the whole people of the State, the infant, the middle-aged, the septuagenarian, and the married.

It is very obvious, that the common schools of the State are neither to be equally open to everybody, nor to every child; but that they are to be equally open to a class of persons, which class and their qualifications are to be designated and prescribed by the legislature.

The Federal Constitution does not provide for any system of education; to be conducted and controlled by the national government, nor does it vest in Congress any power to exercise a general or special supervision over the states on the subject of education. The Constitution gives to Congress the power to dispose of and make all needful rules and regulations respecting the territories and other property belonging to the United States, and by virtue of this power territorial governments are organized. It also confers on Congress the exclusive power to legislate in all cases whatever over the District of Columbia, and by virtue of this power Congress has established in such District a system of common schools. Con-[gress] **[360]** has also established and maintained military and naval schools at the expense of the government.

The system of common schools in this State has its origin in, and is provided for by, the constitution and laws of this State. It is purely a domestic institution, and is subject to the exclusive control of the constituted authorities of the State. The constitution does not provide the machinery, nor lay down its rule of government or discipline, nor define the terms and conditions of admission. It makes it the imperative duty of the legislature to provide by law the system, and imposes no limitations on the power of the legislature, except that tuition shall be free, and the schools shall be equally open to all; that is, to such classes of persons as the legislature may, in its wisdom, determine.

There being no further restriction upon the legislative power and discretion, it necessarily follows, that in providing for this system of schools, the legislature is left free to fix the qualifications of pupils to be admitted to its benefits, as respects age and capacity to learn; to classify them with reference to age, sex, advancement, and the branches of learning they are to pursue; to provide for the location and building of school-houses; and to designate to what schools and in what school-houses the different ages, sexes, and degrees of proficiency shall be assigned; for these all concern the good order and success of the system.

It must also follow, that this policy or framework of government for that system vitally concerns and blends itself with the internal affairs of the State, with its happiness and prosperity, its peace and good order, and depends upon the wisdom of the legislature and of the agencies provided by the legislature, acting under its established rules, and opines within the power possessed by every sovereign state, and is clearly without the grants or inhibitions of such amendments to the Constitution of the United States. *City of New York v. Miln*, 11 Pet. 139, 140; *License Tax Cases*, 5 Wal. 470, 471; *Lane County v. Oregon*, 7 Wal. 76; *United States v. Dewitt*, 9 Wal. 41; *The Collector v. Day*, 11 Wal. 124, 125; *The Slaughter-* **[361]** *House Cases*, supra; *Bartemeyer v. Iowa*, 18 Wal. 133; *The State v. Gibson*, 30 Ind. 389; *The West Chester, etc., R. R. Co. v. Miles*, 55 Pa. St. 209; Coolly Counts. Lim. 572, 574; *Elise v. The State*, 42 Ala. 525; *Fifield v. Close*, 15 Mich. 505.

This system of common schools must consist of many schools in different localities or geographical divisions; and these schools may be of different grades. In some of these localities or divisions there may be school-house; and in others none. In some the school-house or houses may not be sufficient to accommodate all, and the revenue may not be sufficient to provide for them.

In this system, there ought to be and must be a classification of the children. This classification ought to and will be with reference to some properties or characteristics common to or possessed by a certain number out of the whole; and these classes may be put into and taught in different parts of the same school, or different rooms in the same school-house, or different school-houses, as convenience and good policy may require.

This is too reasonable to admit of question; for it concerns the general good, and does not affect the quality of the privilege, but regulates the manner of its enjoyment.

This being settled, what is there to prevent the classification of children, equally entitled to the privileges of the system of common schools, with reference to difference of race or color, if the judgment of the legislature should hold such a classification to be most promotive of or conducive to, the good order and discipline of the schools in the system, and the interest of the public?

The legislature, under our state constitution as it existed without the limitation imposed upon the sovereign power of the State by the fourteenth amendment as hereinbefore stated, had the power to provide for the education only of the white children of the State; but since its ratification, no system of public schools would be general, uniform, and equally open to all which did not provide for the education of the colored children of the State. [362]

It being settled that the legislature must provide for the education of the colored children as well as for the white children, we are required to determine whether the legislature may classify such children, by color and race, and provide for their education in separate schools, or whether they must attend the same school without reference to race or color. In our opinion, the classification of scholars, on the basis of race or color, and their education in separate schools, involve questions of domestic policy which are within the legislative discretion and control, and do not amount to an exclusion of either class. In other words, the placing of the white children of the State in one class and the negro children of the State in another class, and requiring these classes to be taught separately, provision being made for their education in the same branches according to age, capacity, or advancement, with capable teachers, and to the extent of their pro rata share in the school revenue, does not amount to a denial of equal privileges of either, or conflict with the open character of the system required by the constitution. The system would be equally open to all. The tuition would be free. The privileges of the schools would be denied to none. The white children go to one school, or to certain of the schools in the system of common schools. The colored children go to another school, or to certain others of the schools in the system of the common schools. Or, if there are not a sufficient number of colored children within attending distance, the several districts may be consolidated and form one distinct. But if there are not a sufficient number within reasonable distance to be thus consolidated, the trustee or trustees shall provide such other means of education for said children as shall use their proportion, according to number, of school revenue to the best advantage. If there be cause of complaint, the white class has as much, if not greater cause than the colored class, for the later class receive their full share of the school revenue, although none of it may have been contributed by such class; and when districts can not be consolidated so as to form a school, such class is entitled to receive their full share of the school revenue, according [363] to number, which shall be expended for their benefit to the best advantage, a privilege which is not granted to the white class.

In our opinion, there would be as much lawful reason for complaint, by one scholar in the same school, that he could not occupy the seat of another scholar therein at the same time the latter occupied it, or by scholars in the different classes in the same school, that they were not all put in the same class, or by the scholars in different schools, that they were not all placed in one school, as there is that white and black children are placed in distinct classes and taught separately, or in separate schools. *The State v. The City of Cincinnati*, 19 Ohio, 178; *Van Camp v. The Board*, etc., 9 Ohio St. 406; *Baker v. The City of Cincinnati*, 11 Ohio St. 534; *The State, etc., v. McCann*, 21 Ohio St. 198; *Dallas v. Fosdick*, 40 How. Pr. 249.

It is to be noted that the appellee, in his petition for a mandate, complains only that his children and grandchildren were excluded from the school where the white children were taught. There are no allegations that there was not a sufficient number of colored children in attending distance to constitute a school, on that the trustee or trustees had failed to provide such other means of education for said children as would use their proportion, according to number, of school revenue to the best advantage. There is a general allegation that the defendants had neglected, failed, and refused to provide any school in said district, or in any adjoining district near enough for his said children and grandchildren to attend as scholars.

The question is, therefore, squarely presented, whether the children and grandchildren of the appellee were entitled to be admitted and taught in the same school with the white children of the district. The legislature has provided that a separate school shall be provided in each district for the education of the colored children therein, where there is a sufficient number of colored children, and where there is a deficiency of colored children to form one district, several districts shall be consolidated. But if separate schools can not be provided for the colored children on account of the smallness [364] of the number of such children, then, such other provision in to be made by the trustee for their education as the means in his hands will enable him to do.

The legislature has not pointed out or defined what other means shall be provided. There being no averment that the trustee has failed to provide for the education of the children and grandchildren of the appellee, outside of the school for white children, no question arises as to what would be a compliance with such requirement. But if such allegation had been made, it would not have entitled the children and grandchildren of appellee to admission into the white schools, because the legislature has not provided for the admission of colored children into the same schools with the white children, in any contingency; and even it, for the sake of the argument, we were to concede that colored children are, under and by force of the fourteenth amendment, so entitled, the courts cannot, in the absence of legislative authority, confer that right upon them. The legislature has declared that when schools can not be provided for the colored children, the trustee shall provide such other means for their education as will use up their full share, according to number, of the school revenue. If the trustee fails in the discharge of this duty, he may be compelled by mandate to discharge the duty imposed upon him by law,

The action of Congress, at the same session at which the fourteenth amendment was proposed to the states, and at a session subsequent to the date of its ratification, is worthy of consideration as evincing the concurrent and after-matured conviction of that body that there was nothing whatever in the amendment which prevented Congress from separating the white and colored races, and placing them, as classes, in different schools, and that such separation was highly proper and conducive to the well-being of the races, and calculated to secure the peace, harmony, and welfare of the public; and if no obligation was expected to be or was imposed upon Congress by the amendment, to place the two races and colors in the same school, with what show of reason can it be pretended [365] that it has such a compelling power upon the sovereign and independent states forming the Federal Union?

We refer to the legislation of Congress relative to schools in the District of Columbia, at the first session of the Thirty-Ninth Congress, and the third session of the Forty-Second Congress.

On the 23d day of July, 1866, the act of Congress, entitled "an act rating to public schools in the District of Columbia," took effect. It requires the cities of Washington and Georgetown to pay over to the trustees of colored schools of said cities such a proportionate part of all moneys received or expended for school or educational purposes in said cities, including the cost of sites, buildings, improvements, furniture, and books, and all other expenditures on account of schools, as the colored children between the ages of six and seventeen years; in the respective cities, bear to the whole number of children, white and colored, between the same ages. Acts sess. 1, 39th Cong. 222.

This was followed at the same session of Congress by an act, entitled "an act donating certain lots in the city of Washington for schools for colored children in the District of Columbia," approved July 28th, 1866, which authorized and required the Commissioner of Public Buildings to convey certain described lots, in the city of Washington which belonged to the United States, to the trustees for colored schools tor the cities of Washington and Georgetown in said District, for the sole use of schools for colored children in that District; the said lots having been designated and set apart by the Secretary of the Interior to be used for colored schools; and the said lots whenever converted to any other use to revert to the United States. Acts sess. 1, 29th Cong. 354.

At its 42d session an act was passed, entitled "an act to amend an act entitled 'An act governing the colored schools of the District of Columbia,'" approved March 3d, 1873, which fixes the number of the board of trustees of schools for colored children in the District of Columbia, their mode of [366] appointment, their duties, etc., and authorizes the Governor of the District to appoint a superindent of schools for colored children, who is to receive a salary of twenty-five hundred dollars annually, for his services, etc., and directs the proportion of school money then due, or afterward to become due, to the board of trustees of colored schools from the cities of Washington and Georgetown, to be paid to the treasurer of said board, and not to the trustees, as provided in the act of July 23d, 1866. Acts sess. 3, 42d Cong. 260.

This legislation of Congress continues in force, at the present time, as a legislative construction of the fourteenth amendment, and as a legislative declaration of what was thought to be lawful, proper, and expedient under such amendment, by the same body that proposed such amendment to the states for their approval and ratification.

We are very clearly of the opinion that the act of May 13th, 1869, is constitutional, and that while it remains in force colored children are not entitled to admission into the common schools which are provided for the education of the white children.

In our opinion, the court below erred in affirming the action of the court in special term; and the judgment is reversed, with costs, and the cause remanded to the court below, with directions to that court to overrule the judgment of the court in special term in overruling the demurrer to the petition for a mandate.

OSBORN, J.—I am inclined to think that the allegations in the complaint are not sufficient to entitle the appellee to a mandate, and that the judgment of the court below ought to be reversed. But there is very much in the foregoing opinion in which I do not concur.

If I desired to do so, I could not during the short time that I am to remain in my present position, properly and satisfactorily consider the questions discussed, and must therefore content myself with the qualified dissent. [367]

On Petition for a Rehearing

BUSKIRK, C. J.—The learned counsel for appellee has filed a very earnest, able, and elaborate brief in support of the petition for a rehearing. We have re-examined the questions involved and decided in the original opinion, and are entirely satisfied with the judgment rendered and the grounds upon which it was placed.

The petition is overruled.

Maryland Court of Appeals
Crosse v. Board of Elections,
243 Md. 555 (1966)

[555] Decided, per curiam, July 1, 1966. Opinion filed July 21, 1966.

CONSTITUTIONAL LAW — *State Citizenship — Appellant Held To Be A Qualified Candidate For Sheriff Of Baltimore City Where He Was A Resident Of The State For More Than Five Years But Was Not A United States Citizen For More Than Five Years — A Person Need Not Be A United States Citizen In Order To Be A Citizen Of His State.* In the instant case it was *held* that the appellant, who has been a resident of Maryland for more than five years preceding the election, was qualified to become a candidate for Sheriff of Baltimore City, although he was not a United States citizen for at least five years preceding the election. The Court stated that there is no express requirement in the Maryland Constitution that sheriffs be United States citizens. Article IV, Sec. 44, provides that a sheriff must be a resident in the county or city, where elected, and a citizen of the State at least five years preceding his election. It was pointed out that both before and after the Fourteenth Amendment to the federal Constitution, it has not been necessary for a person to be a citizen of the United States in order to be a citizen of his state. It was [556] further noted that the Maryland Constitution provides that the Governor, Judges and the Attorney General shall be qualified voters, and therefore, by necessary implication, citizens of the United States. The Court felt that the absence of a similar requirement as to the qualifications of sheriffs was significant. So also, was the absence of any period of residence for a sheriff except that he shall have been a citizen of the State for five years. The Governor, Judges and Attorney General in addition to being citizens of the State and qualified voters, must have been a resident of the State for various periods. The Court stated that the conjunction of the requisite period of residence with the state citizenship in the qualifications for sheriff strongly indicated that state citizenship, as used in the constitutional qualifications for this office, was meant to be synonymous with domicile, and that citizenship of the United States is not required, even by implication, as a qualification for this office. It was also noted that the office of sheriff, under our Constitution, is ministerial in nature; a sheriff's function and province is to execute duties prescribed by law. It was further pointed out that in this case, on the admitted facts, there could be no question of the appellant's undivided allegiance to this nation. And, in conclusion, the Court stated that it found nothing which requires that a citizen of a state must also be a citizen of the United States, if no question of federal rights or jurisdiction is involved. Absent any unconstitutional discrimination, a state has the right to extend qualifications for state office to its citizens, even though they are not citizens of the United States. This, it was *held* is what Maryland has done in fixing the constitutional qualifications for the office of sheriff.   pp. 557-563

H.C.

Decided, per curiam, July 1, 1966.
Opinion filed July 21, 1966.

Appeal from the Superior Court of Baltimore City (SODARO, J.).

Petition by St. George I. B. Crosse, III, for a writ of mandamus to compel the Board of Supervisors of Elections of Bal-[timore] [557] City to accept and certify his candidacy for Sheriff of Baltimore City. From an order denying the petition, plaintiff appeals.

Order reversed, with costs; the mandate, directing the granting of the writ of mandamus prayed for below, be issued forthwith.

The cause was argued before HAMMOND, HORNEY, MARBURY, OPPENHEIMER and BARNES, JJ.

St. George I. B. Crosse, III, in proper person, for appellant.

Edward L. Blanton, Jr., Assistant Attorney General, with whom was Thomas B. Finan, Attorney General, on the brief, for appellee.

OPPENHEIMER, J., delivered the opinion of the Court.

After argument, by per curiam order, we reversed the order of the Superior Court of Baltimore City which denied the appellant's petition for a writ of mandamus to compel the Board of Supervisors of Elections of Baltimore City, to accept and certify his candidacy for Sheriff of Baltimore City, and ordered that the mandate directing the writ of mandamus prayed for below be issued forthwith. The reasons for our order follow. The question involved is whether the appellant is qualified to become a candidate under the provisions of Article IV Section 44 of the Maryland Constitution. The material provisions of that Section are as follows:

> "There shall be elected in each county and in Baltimore City * * * one person, resident in said county, or City, above the age of twenty-five years and at least five years preceding his election, a citizen of the State, to the office of Sheriff."

The facts are not in dispute. The appellant was born in the West Indies and immigrated to the United States in June of 1957. He and his family established their residence in Crisfield, Maryland. Upon reaching his eighteenth birthday, and upon signing his Declaration of Intention to become a citizen [558] of the United States under the federal Naturalization law, he enlisted in the United States Army, served for approximately three years and was given an honorable discharge in 1960. He established his residence in Salisbury, Maryland, and matriculated at the Maryland State College from which he was graduated in 1964. He then entered the University of Maryland Law School and has successfully completed his first year. In May of 1964 he established his home in Baltimore City, where he has since resided. On April 29, 1966, he became a naturalized citizen of the United States and a registered voter of the State of Maryland. On May 26, 1966, the appellant filed his candidacy for the office of Sheriff of Baltimore City with the Board of Supervisors of Elections of Baltimore City. His Certificate of Nomination was notarized and accepted, as was his filing fee of $150. He received the usual material given to all candidates who file for public office. On June 4, 1966, he received a letter from the Board advising him that he did not qualify as a candidate for the office of Sheriff because he did not become a citizen of the United States until April 29, 1966, and that under the Fourteenth Amendment of the United States Constitution he did not become a citizen of the State of Maryland until that date. The Board acted on the advice of its counsel, the Attorney General of Maryland, and returned the application to the appellant together with the filing fee.

The court below held and the Board contends that the appellant did not become a citizen of Maryland, under the provisions of the Maryland Constitution, until he became a citizen of the United States, and is therefore ineligible to be Sheriff of Baltimore City because he was not a United States citizen at least five years preceding the election. We disagree.

Both before and after the Fourteenth Amendment to the federal Constitution, it has not been necessary for a person to be a citizen of the United States in order to be a citizen of his state. *United States v. Cruikshank,* 92 U.S. 542, 549 (1875); *Slaughter-House Cases,* 83 U.S. (16 Wall.) 36, 73-74 (1873); and see *Short v. State,* 80 Md. 392, 401-02, 31 A. 322 (1895). See also Spear, *State Citizenship,* 16 Albany L.J. 24 (1877). **Citizenship of the United States is defined by the Fourteenth Amendment** and federal statutes, but the requirements for cit-[izenship] [559] of a state generally depend not upon definition but the constitutional or statutory context in which the term is used. *Risewick v. Davis,* 19 Md. 82, 93 (1862); *Halaby v. Board of Directors of University of Cincinnati,* 162 Ohio St. 290, 293, 123 N.E.2d 3 (1954) and authorities therein cited.

The decisions illustrate the diversity of the term's usage. In *Field v. Adreon,* 7 Md. 209 (1854), our predecessors held that an unnaturalized foreigner, residing and doing business in this State, was a citizen of Maryland within the meaning of the attachment laws. The Court held that the absconding debtor was a citizen of the State for commercial or business purposes, although not necessarily for political purposes. *Dorsey v. Kyle*, 30 Md. 512, 518 (1869), is to the same effect. Judge Alvey, for the Court, said in that case, that "the term citizen, used in the formula of the affidavit prescribed by the 4th section of the Article of the Code referred to, is to be taken as synonymous with inhabitant or permanent resident."

Other jurisdictions have equated residence with citizenship of the state for political and other non-commercial purposes. *In re Wehlitz*, 16 Wis. 443, 446 (1863), held that the Wisconsin statute designating "all able-bodied, white, male citizens" as subject to enrollment in the militia included an unnaturalized citizen who was a resident of the state. "Under our complex system of government," the court said, "there may be a citizen of a state, who is not a citizen of the United States in the full sense of the term." *McKenzie v. Murphy*, 24 Ark. 155, 159 (1863), held that an alien, domiciled in the state for over ten years, was entitled to the homestead exemptions provided by the Arkansas statute to "every free white citizen of this state, male or female, being a householder or head of a family * * *" The court said: "The word 'citizen' is often used in common conversation and writing, as meaning only an inhabitant, a resident of a town, state, or county, without any implication of political or civil privileges; and we think it is so used in our constitution." *Halaby v. Board of Directors of University*, supra, involved the application of a statute which provided free university instruction to citizens of the municipality in which the university is located. The court held that the plaintiff, an alien minor whose parents were residents of and conducted a **[560]** business in the city, was entitled to the benefits of that statute, saying: "It is to be observed that the term, 'citizen,' is often used in legislation where 'domicile' is meant and where United States citizenship has no reasonable relationship to the subject matter and purpose of the legislation in question."

Closely in point to the interpretation of the constitutional provision here involved is a report of the Committee of Elections of the House of Representatives, made in 1823. A petitioner had objected to the right of a Delegate to retain his seat from what was then the Michigan Territory. One of the objections was that the Delegate had not resided in the Territory one year previous to the election in the status of a citizen of the United States. An act of Congress passed in 1819 provided that "every free white male citizen of said Territory, above the age of twenty-one years, who shall have resided therein one year next preceding" an election shall be entitled to vote at such election for a delegate to Congress. An act of 1823 provided that all citizens of the United States having the qualifications set forth in the former act shall be eligible to any office in the Territory. The Committee held that the statutory requirement of citizenship of the Territory for a year before the election did not mean that the aspirant for office must also have been a United States citizen during that period. The report said: "It is the person, the individual, the man, who is spoken of, and who is to possess the qualifications of residence, age, freedom, &c. at the time he offers to vote, or is to be voted for * * *". Upon the filing of the report, and the submission of a resolution that the Delegate was entitled to his seat, the contestant of the Delegate's election withdrew his protest, and the sitting Delegate was confirmed. *Biddle v. Richard*, Clarke and Hall, *Cases of Contested Elections in Congress* (1834) 407, 410.

There is no express requirement in the Maryland Constitution that sheriffs be United States citizens. Voters must be, under Article I, Section 1, but Article IV, Section 44 does not require that sheriffs be voters. A person does not have to be a voter to be a citizen of either the United States or of a state, as in the case of native-born minors. In Maryland, from 1776 to 1802, the Constitution contained requirements of property Page 561 ownership for the exercise of the franchise; there was no exception as to native-born citizens of the State. Steiner, *Citizenship and Suffrage in Maryland* (1895) 27, 31.

The Maryland Constitution provides that the Governor, Judges and the Attorney General shall be qualified voters, and therefore, by necessary implication, citizens of the United States. Article II, Section 5, Article IV, Section 2, and Article V, Section 4. The absence of a similar requirement as to the qualifications of sheriffs is significant. So also, in our opinion, is the absence of any period of residence for a sheriff except that he shall have been a citizen of the State for five years. The Governor, Judges and Attorney General in addition to being citizens of the State and qualified voters, must have been a resident of the State for various periods. The conjunction of the requisite period of residence with state citizenship in the qualifications for sheriff strongly indicates that, as in the authorities above referred to, state citizenship, as used in the constitutional qualifications for this office, was meant to be synonymous with domicile, and that citizenship of the United States is not required, even by implication, as a qualification for this office. The office of sheriff, under our Constitution, is ministerial in nature; a sheriff's function and province is to execute duties prescribed by law. See *Buckeye Dev. Corp. v. Brown & Schilling, Inc.*, 243 Md. 224, 220 A.2d 922 (1966), and the concurring opinion of Le Grand, C.J. in *Mayor & City Council of Baltimore v. State ex rel. Bd. of Police*, 15 Md. 376, 470, 488-90 (1860).

It may well be that the phrase, "a citizen of the State," as used in the constitutional provisions as to qualifications, implies that a sheriff cannot owe allegiance to another nation. By the naturalization act of 1779, the Legislature provided that, to become a citizen of Maryland, an alien must swear allegiance to the State. The oath or affirmation provided that the applicant renounced allegiance "to any king or prince, or any other State or Government." Act of July 1779, Ch. VI; Steiner, *op. cit.* 15. In this case, on the admitted facts, there can be no question of the appellant's undivided allegiance.

The court below rested its decision on its conclusion that, under the Fourteenth Amendment, no state may confer state **[562]** citizenship upon a resident alien until such resident alien becomes a naturalized citizen of the United States. The court relied, as does the Board in this appeal, upon *City of Minneapolis v. Reum*, 56 Fed. 576, 581 (8th Cir. 1893). In that case, an alien resident of Minnesota, who had declared his intention to become a citizen of the United States but had not been naturalized, brought a suit, based on diversity of citizenship, against the city in the Circuit Court of the United States for the District of Minnesota under Article III, Section 2 of the United States Constitution which provides that the federal judicial power shall extend to "Controversies between * * * a State, or the Citizens thereof, and foreign States, Citizens or Subjects." At the close of the evidence, the defendant moved to dismiss the action for want of jurisdiction, on the ground that the evidence failed to establish the allegation that the plaintiff was an alien. The court denied the motion, the plaintiff recovered judgment, and the defendant claimed error in the ruling on jurisdiction. The Circuit Court of Appeals affirmed. Judge Sanborn, for the court, stated that even though the plaintiff were a citizen of the state, that fact could not enlarge or restrict the jurisdiction of the federal courts over controversies between aliens and citizens of the state. The court said: "It is not in the power of a state to denationalize a foreign subject who has not complied with the federal naturalization laws, and constitute him a citizen of the United States or of a state, so as to deprive the federal courts of jurisdiction * * *".

Reum dealt only with the question of jurisdiction of federal courts under the diversity of citizenship clause of the federal Constitution. That a state cannot affect that jurisdiction by granting state citizenship to an unnaturalized alien does not mean it cannot make an alien a state citizen for other purposes. Under the Fourteenth Amendment all persons born or naturalized in the United States are citizens of the United States and of the state in which they reside, but we find nothing in Reum or any other case which requires that a citizen of a state must also be a citizen of the United States, if no question of federal rights or jurisdiction is involved. As the authorities referred to in the first portion of this opinion evidence, the law is to the contrary.

[563] Absent any unconstitutional discrimination, a state has the right to extend qualification for state office to its citizens, even though they are not citizens of the United States. This, we have found, is what Maryland has done in fixing the constitutional qualifications for the office of sheriff. The appellant meets the qualifications which our Constitution provides.

United States Supreme Court
Elk v. Wilkins, 112 U.S. 94 (1884)

November 3, 1884.
(headnotes omitted)

[94] A. J. Poppleton and J. L. Webster, for plaintiff in error.

G. M. Lamberton, for defendant in error.

GRAY, J.

This is an action brought by an Indian, in the circuit court of the United States for the district of Nebraska, against the registrar of one of the wards of the city of Omaha, for refusing to register him as a qualified voter therein. The petition was as follows: [112 U.S. 94, 95] 'John Elk, plaintiff, complains of Charles Wilkins, defendant, and avers that the matter in dispute herein exceeds the sum of five hundred dollars, to-wit, the sum of six thousand dollars, and that the matter in dispute herein arises under the constitution and laws of the United States; and, for cause of action against the defendant, avers that he, the plaintiff, is an Indian, and was born within the United States; that more than one year prior to the grievances hereinafter complained of he had severed his tribal relation to the Indian tribes, and had fully and completely surrendered himself to the jurisdiction of the United States, and still so continues subject to the jurisdiction of the United States; and avers that, under and by virtue of the fourteenth amendment to the constitution of the United States, he is a citizen of the United States, and entitled to the right and privilege of citizens of the United States. That on the sixth day of April, 1880, there was held in the city of Omaha (a city of the first class, incorporated under the general laws of the state of Nebraska, providing for the incorporation of cities of the first class) a general election for the election of members of the city council and other officers for said city. That the defendant, Charles Wilkins, held the office of and acted as registrar in the Fifth ward of said city, and that as such registrar it was the duty of such defendant to register the names of all persons entitled to exercise the elective franchise in said ward of said city at said general election. That this plaintiff was a citizen of and had been a bona fide resident of the state of Nebraska for more than six months prior to said sixth day of April, 1880, and had been a Bona fide resident of Douglas county, wherein the city of Omaha is situate, for more than forty days, and in the Fifth ward of said city more than ten days prior to the said sixth day of April, and was such citizen and resident at the time of said election, and at the time of his attempted registration, as hereinafter set forth, and was in every way qualified, under the laws of the state of Nebraska and of the city of Omaha, to be registered as a voter, and to cast a vote at said election, and complied with the laws of the city and state in that behalf. [112 U.S. 94, 96] That on or about the fifth day of April, 1880, and prior to said election, this plaintiff presented himself to said Charles Wilkins, as such registrar, at his office, for the purpose of having his name registered as a qualified voter, as provided by law, and complied with all the provisions of the statutes in that regard, and claimed that, under the fourteenth and fifteenth amendments to the constitution of the United States, he was a citizen of the United States, and was entitled to exercise the elective franchise, regardless of his race and color; and that said Wilkins, designedly, corruptly, willfully, and maliciously, did then and there refuse to register this plaintiff, for the sole reason that the plaintiff was an Indian, and therefore not a citizen of the United States, and not, therefore, entitled to vote, and on account of his race and color, and with the willful, malicious, corrupt, and unlawful design to deprive this plaintiff of his right to vote at said election, and of his rights, and all other Indians of their rights, under said fourteenth and fifteenth amendments to the constition of the United States, on account of his and their race and color. That on the sixth day of April this plaintiff presented himself at the place of voting in said ward, and presented a ballot, and requested the right to vote, where said Wilkins, who was then acting as one of the judges of said election in said ward,

193

in further carrying out his willful and malicious designs as aforesaid, declared to the plaintiff and to the other election officers that the plaintiff was an Indian, and not a citizen, and not entitled to vote, and said judges and clerks of election refused to receive the vote of the plaintiff, for that he was not registered as required by law. Plaintiff avers the fact to be that by reason of said willful, unlawful, corrupt, and mailcious refusal of said defendant to register this plaintiff, as provided by law, he was deprived of his right to vote at said election, to his damage in the sum of $6,000. Wherefore, plaintiff prays judgment against defendant for $6,000, his damages, with costs of suit.'

The defendant filed a general demurrer for the following causes: (1) That the petition did not state facts sufficient to **[112 U.S. 94, 97]** constitute a cause of action; (2) that the court had no jurisdiction of the person of the defendant; (3) that the court had no jurisdiction of the subject of the action. The demurrer was argued before Judge **MCCRARY** Judge **DUNDY**, and sustained; and, the plaintiff electing to stand by his petition, judgment was rendered for the defendant, dismissing the petition, with costs. The plaintiff sued out this writ of error.

By the constitution of the state of Nebraska, art. 7, 1, 'every male person of the age of twenty-one years or upwards, belonging to either of the following classes, who shall have resided in the state six months, and in the county, precinct, or ward for the term provided by law, shall be an elector: First, citizens of the United States; second, persons of foreign birth who shall have declared their intention to become citizens, conformably to the laws of the United States on the subject of naturalization, at least thirty days prior to an election.' By the statutes of Nebraska, every male person of the age of 21 years or upward, belonging to either of the two classes so defined in the constitution of the state, who shall have resided in the state 6 months, in the county 40 days, and in the precinct, township, or ward 10 days, shall be an elector; the qualifications of electors in the several wards of cities of the first class (of which Omaha is one) shall be the same as in precincts; it is the duty of the registrar to enter in the register of qualified voters the name of every person who applies to him to be registered, and satisfies him that he is qualified to vote under the provisions of the election laws of the state; and at all municipal, as well as county or state elections, the judges of election are required to check the name, and receive and deposit the ballot, of any person whose name appears on the register. Comp. St. Neb. 1881, c. 26, 3; c. 13, 14; c. 76, 6, 13, 19. **[112 U.S. 94, 98]** The plaintiff, in support of his action, relies on the first clause of the first section of the fourteenth article of amendment of the constitution of the United States, by which 'all persons born or naturalized in the United States, and subject to the jurisdiction thereof, are citizens of the United States and of the state wherein they reside;' and on the fifteenth article of amendment, which provides that 'the right of citizens of the United States to vote shall not be denied or abridged by the United States or by any state on account of race, color, or previous condition of servitude.' This being a suit at common law in which the matter in dispute exceeds $500, arising under the constitution of the United States, the circuit court had jurisdiction of it under the act of March 3, 1875, c. 137, 1, even if the parties were citizens of the same state. 18 St. 470; *Ames v. Kansas*, 111 U.S. 449; S. C. 4 SUP. CT. REP. 437. The judgment of that court, dismissing the action with costs, must have proceeded upon the merits, for if the dismissal had been for want of jurisdiction, no costs could have been awarded. *Mayor v. Cooper*, 6 Wall. 247; Mansfield, C. & L. M. Ry. v. Swan, 111 U.S. 379; S. C. 4 SUP. CT. REP. 510. And the only point argued by the defendant in this court is whether the petition sets forth facts enough to constitute a cause of action. The decision of this point, as both parties assume in their briefs, depends upon the question whether the legal conclusion, that under and by virtue of the fourteenth amendment of the constitution the plaintiff is a citizen of the United States, is supported by the facts alleged in the petition and admitted by the demurrer, to-wit: The plaintiff is an Indian, and was born in the United States, and has severed his tribal relation to the Indian tribes, and fully and completely surrendered himself to the jurisdiction of the United States, and still continues to be subject to the jurisdiction of the United States, and is a bona fide resident of the state of Nebraska and city of Omaha. The petition, while it does not show of what Indian tribe the plaintiff was a member, yet, by the allegations that he 'is **[112 U.S. 94, 99]** an Indian, and was born within the United States,' and that 'he had severed his tribal relations to the Indian tribes,' clearly implies that he was born a member of one of the Indian tribes within the limits of the United States which still exists and is recognized as a tribe by the government of the United States. Though the plaintiff alleges that he 'had fully and completely surrendered himself to the jurisdiction of the United States,' he does not allege that the United States accepted his surrender, or that he has ever been naturalized, or taxed, or in any way recognized or treated as a citizen by the state or by the United States. Nor is it contended by his counsel that there is any statute or treaty that makes him a citizen.

The question then is, whether an Indian, born a member of one of the Indian tribes within the United States, is, merely by reason of his birth within the United States, and of his afterwards voluntarily separating himself from his tribe and taking up his residence among white citizens, a citizen of the United States, within the meaning of the first section of the fourteenth amendment of the constitution. Under the constitution of the United States, as originally established, 'Indians not taxed' were excluded from the persons according to whose numbers representatives and direct taxes were apportioned among the several states; and congress had and exercised the power to regulate commerce with the Indian tribes, and the members thereof, whether within or without the boundaries of one of the states of the Union. The Indian tribes, being within the territorial limits of the United States, were not, strictly speaking, foreign states; but they were alien nations, distinct political communities, with whom the United States might and habitually did deal, as they thought fit, either through treaties made by the president and senate, or through acts of congress in the ordinary forms of legislation. The members of those tribes owed immediate allegiance to their several tribes, and were not part of the people of the United States. They were in a dependent condition, a state of pupilage, resembling that of a ward to his guardian. Indians and their property, exempt from taxation by treaty or statute of the United States, could not be taxed [**112 U.S. 94, 100**] by any state. General acts of congress did not apply to Indians, unless so expressed as to clearly manifest an intention to include them. Const. art. 1, 2, 8; art. 2, 2; *Cherokee Nation v. Georgia,* 5 Pet. 1; *Worcester v. Georgia,* 6 Pet. 515; *U. S. v. Rogers,* 4 How. 567; *U. S. v. Holliday,* 3 Wall. 407; *Case of the Kansas Indians,* 5 Wall. 737; *Case of the New York Indians,* Id. 761; *Case of the Cherokee Tobacco,* 11 Wall. 616; U. S. v. Whisky, 93 U.S. 188; *Pennock v. Commissioners,* 103 U.S. 44; *Crow Dog's Case,* 109 U.S. 556; S. C. 3 SUP. CT. REP. 396; *Goodell v. Jackson,* 20 Johns. 693; *Hastings v. Farmer,* 4 N. Y. 293.

The alien and dependent condition of the members of the Indian tribes could not be put off at their own will without the action or assent of the United States. They were never deemed citizens of the United States, except under explicit provisions of treaty or statute to that effect, either declaring a certain tribe, or such members of it as chose to remain behind on the removal of the tribe westward, to be citizens, or authorizing individuals of particular tribes to become citizens on application to a court of the United States for naturalization and satisfactory proof of fitness for civilized life; for examples of which see treaties in 1817 and 1835 with the Cherokees, and in 1820, 1825, and 1830 with the Choctaws, (7 St. 159, 211, 236, 335, 483, 488; Wilson v. Wall, 6 Wall. 83; Opinion of Atty. Gen. TANEY, 2 OP. Attys. Gen. 462;) in 1855 with the Wyandotts, (10 St. 1159; *Karrahoo v. Adams,* 1 Dill. 344, 346; *Gray v. Coffman,* 3 Dill. 393; Hicks v. Butrick, Id. 413;) in 1861 and in March, 1866, with the Pottawatomies, (12 st. 1192; 14 st. 763;) in 1862 with the Ottawas, (12 St. 1237;) and the Kickapoos, (13 St. 624;) and acts of congress of March 3, 1839, c. 83, 7, concerning the Brothertown Indians; and of March 3, 1843, c. 101, 7, August 6, 1846, c. 88, and March 3, 1865, c. 127, 4, concerning the Stockbridge Indians, (5 St. 351, 647; 9 St. 55; 13 St. 562.) See, also, treaties with the Stockbridge Indians in 1848 and 1856, (9 St. 955; 11 St. 667; 7 Op. Attys. Gen. 746.)

Chief Justice **TANEY,** in the passage cited for the plaintiff [**112 U.S. 94, 101**] from his opinion in *Scott v. Sandford,* 19 How. 393, 404, did not affirm or imply that either the Indian tribes, or individual members of those tribes, had the right, beyond other foreigners, to become citizens of their own will, without being naturalized by the United States. His words were: 'They' (the Indian tribes) 'may without doubt, like the subjects of any foreign government, be naturalized by the authority of congress, and become citizens of a state, and of the United States; and if an individual should leave his nation or tribe, and take up his abode among the white population, he would be entitled to all the rights and privileges which would belong to an emigrant from any other foreign people.' But an emigrant from any foreign state cannot become a citizen of the United States without a formal renunciation of his old allegiance, and an acceptance by the United States of that renunciation through such form of naturalization as may be required law.

The distinction between citizenship by birth and citizenship by naturalization is clearly marked in the provisions of the constitution, by which 'no person, except a natural-born citizen, or a citizen of the United States at the time of the adoption of this constitution, shall be eligible to the office of president;' and 'the congress shall have power to establish an uniform rule of naturalization.' Const. art. 2, 1; art. 1, 8. By the thirteenth amendment of the constitution slavery was prohibited. The main object of the opening sentence of the fourteenth amendment was to settle the question, upon which there had been a difference of opinion throughout the country and in this court, as to the citizenship of free negroes, (*Scott v. Sandford*, 19 How. 393;) and to put it beyond doubt that all persons, white or black, and whether formerly slaves or not, born or naturalized in the United States, and owing no allegiance to any alien power, should be citizens of the United States and of the state in which they reside. *Slaughter-House Cases*, 16 Wall. 36, 73; *Strauder v. West Virginia*, 100 U.S. 303, 306.

This section contemplates two sources of citizenship, and two sources only: birth and naturalization. The persons declared *[112 U.S. 94, 102]* to be citizens are 'all persons born or naturalized in the United States, and subject to the jurisdiction thereof.' The evident meaning of these last words is, not merely subject in some respect or degree to the jurisdiction of the United States, but completely subject to their political jurisdiction, and owing them direct and immediate allegiance. And the words relate to the time of birth in the one case, as they do to the time of naturalization in the other. Persons not thus subject to the jurisdiction of the United States at the time of birth cannot become so afterwards, except by being naturalized, either individually, as by proceedings under the naturalization acts; or collectively, as by the force of a treaty by which foreign territory is acquired. Indians born within the territorial limits of the United States, members of, and owing immediate allegiance to, one of the Indiana tribes, (an alien though dependent power,) although in a geographical sense born in the United States, are no more 'born in the United States and subject to the jurisdiction thereof,' within the meaning of the first section of the fourteenth amendment, than the children of subjects of any foreign government born within the domain of that government, or the children born within the United States, of ambassadors or other public ministers of foreign nations. This view is confirmed by the second section of the fourteenth amendment, which provides that 'representatives shall be apportioned among the several states according to their respective numbers, counting the whole number of persons in each state, excluding Indians not taxed.' Slavery having been abolished, and the persons formerly held as slaves made citizens, this clauses fixing the apportionment of representatives has abrogated so much of the corresponding clause of the original constitution as counted only three-fifths of such persons. But Indians not taxed are still excluded from the count, for the reason that they are not citizens. Their absolute exclusion from the basis of representation, in which all other persons are now included, is wholly inconsistent with their being considered citizens. So the further provision of the second section for a propor-[tionate] **[112 U.S. 94, 103]** reduction of the basis of the representation of any state in which the right to vote for presidential electors, representatives in congress, or executive or judicial officers or members of the legislature of a state, is denied, except for participation in rebellion or other crime, to 'any of the male inhabitants of such state, being twenty-one years of age and citizens of the United States,' cannot apply to a denial of the elective franchise to Indians not taxed, who form no part of the people entitled to representation.

It is also worthy of remark that the language used, about the same time, by the very congress which framed the fourteenth amendment, in the first section of the civil rights act of April 9, 1866, declaring who shall be citizens of the United States, is 'all persons born in the United States, and not subject to any foreign power, excluding Indians not taxed.' 14 St. 27; Rev. St. 1992. Such Indians, then, not being citizens by birth, can only become citizens in the second way mentioned in the fourteenth amendment, by being 'naturalized in the United States,' by or under some treaty or statute. The action of the political departments of the government, not only after the proposal of the amendment by congress to the states in June, 1866, but since the proclamation in July, 1868, of its ratification by the requisite number of states, accords with this construction. While the amendment was pending before the legislatures of the several states, treaties containing provisions for the naturalization of members of Indian tribes as citizens of the United States were made on July 4, 1866, with the Delawares, in 1867 with various tribes in Kansas, and with the Pottawatomies, and in April, 1868, with the Sioux. 14 St. 794, 796; 15 St. 513, 532, 533, 637.

The treaty of 1867 with the Kansas Indians strikingly illustrates the principle that no one can become a citizen of a nation without its consent, and directly contradicts the supposition that a member of an Indian tribe can at will be alternately a citizen of the United States and a member of the tribe. That treaty not only provided for the naturalization of mem-[bers] **[112 U.S. 94, 104]** of the Ottawa, Miami, Peoria, and other tribes, and their families, upon their making declaration, before the district court of the United States, of their intention to become citizens, (15 St. 517, 520, 521;) but, after reciting that some of the Wyandotts, who had become citizens under the treaty of 1855, were 'unfitted for the responsibilities of citizenship,' and enacting that a register of the whole people of this tribe, resident in Kansas or elsewhere, should be taken, under the direction of the secretary of the interior, showing the names of 'all who declare their desire to be and remain Indians and in a tribal condition,' and of incompetents and orphans as described in the treaty of 1855, and that such persons, and those only, should thereafter constitute the tribe, it provided that 'no one who has heretofore consented to become a citizen, nor the wife or children of any such person, shall be allowed to become members of the tribe, except by the free consent of the tribe after its new organization, and unless the agent shall certify that such party is, through poverty or incapacity, unfit to continue in the exercise of the responsibilities of citizenship of the United States, and likely to become a public charge.' 15 St. 514, 516.

Since the ratification of the fourteenth amendment, congress has passed several acts for naturalizing Indians of certain tribes, which would have been superfluous if they were, or might become without any action of the government, citizens of the United States. By the act of July 15, 1870, c. 296, 10, for instance, it was provided that if at any time thereafter any of the Winnebago Indians in the state of Minnesota should desire to become citizens of the United States, they should make application to the district court of the United States for the district of Minnesota, and in open court make the same proof, and take the same oath of allegiance as is provided by law for the naturalization of aliens, and should also make proof, to the satisfaction of the court, that they were sufficiently intelligent and prudent to control their affairs and interests, that they had adopted the habits of civilized life, and had for at least five years before been able to support themselves and their families; and there-[upon] **[112 U.S. 94, 105]** they should be declared by the court to be citizens of the United States, the declaration entered of record, and a certificate thereof given to the applicant; and the secretary of the interior, upon presentation of that certificate, might issue to them patents in fee-simple, with power of alienation, of the lands already held by them in severalty, and might cause to be paid to them their proportion of the money and effects of the tribe held in trust under any treaty or law of the United States; and thereupon such persons should cease to be members of the tribe; and the lands so patented to them should be subject to levy, taxation, and sale in like manner with the property of other citizens. 16 St. 361. By the act of March 3, 1873, c. 332, 3, similar provision was made for the naturalization of any adult members of the Miami tribe in Kansas, and of their minor children. 17 St. 632. And the act of March 3, 1865, c. 127, before referred to, making corresponding provision for the naturalization of any of the chiefs, warriors, or heads of families of the Stockbridge Indians, is re-enacted in section 2312 of the Revised Statutes.

The act of January 25, 1871, c. 38, for the relief of the Stockbridge and Munsee Indians in the state of Wisconsin, provided that 'for the purpose of determining the persons who are members of said tribes, and the future relation of each to the government of the United States,' two rolls should be prepared under the direction of the commissioner of Indian affairs, signed by the sachem and councilors of the tribe, certified by the person selected by the commissioner to superintend the same, and returned to the commissioner; the one, to be denominated the citizen roll, of the names of all such persons of full age, and their families, 'as signify their desire to separate their relations with said tribe and to become citizens of the United States,' and the other to be denominated the Indian roll, of the names of all such 'as desire to retain their tribal character and continue under the care and guardianship of the United States;' and that those rolls, so made and returned, should be held as a full surrender and relinquishment, on the part of all those of the first class, of all claims to be known or considered as members of the tribe, or to be interested **[112 U.S. 94, 106]** in any provision made or to be made by the United States for its benefit, 'and they and their descendants shall thenceforth be admitted to all the rights and privileges of citizens of the United States.' 16 St. 406.

The pension act exempts Indian claimants of pensions for service in the army or navy from the obligation to take the oath to support the constitution of the United States. Act of March 3, 1873, c. 234, 28, (17 St. 574; Rev. St. 4721.) The recent statutes concerning homesteads are quite inconsistent with the theory that Indians do or can make themselves independent citizens by living apart from their tribe. The act of March 3, 1875, c. 131, 15, allowed to 'any Indian born in the United States, who is the head of a family, or who has arrived at the age of twenty-one years, and who has abandoned, or may hereafter abandon, his tribal relations,' the benefit of the homestead acts, but only upon condition of his 'making satisfactory proof of such abandonment, under rules to be prescribed by the secretary of the interior;' and further provided that his title in the homestead should be absolutely inalienable for five years from the date of the patent, and that he should be entitled to share in all annuities, tribal funds, lands, and other property, as if he had maintained his tribal relations. 18 St. 420. And the act of March 3, 1884, c. 180, 1, while it allows Indians 'located on public lands' to 'avail themselves of the homestead laws as fully, and to the same extent, as may now be done by citizens of the United States,' provides that the form and the legal effect of the patent shall be that the United States does and will hold the land for twenty-five years in trust for the Indian making the entry, and his widow and heirs, and will then convey it in fee to him or them. 23 St. 96. The national legislation has tended more and more towards the education and civilization of the Indians, and fitting them to be citizens. But the question whether any Indian tribes, or any members thereof, have become so far advanced in civilization that they should be let out of the state of pupilage, and admitted to the privileges and responsibilities of citizenship, is a question to be decided by the nation whose wards they are **[112 U.S. 94, 107]** and whose citizens they seek to become, and not by each Indian for himself. There is nothing in the statutes or decisions, referred to by counsel, to control the conclusion to which we have been brought by a consideration of the language of the fourteenth amendment, and of the condition of the Indians at the time of its proposal and ratification.

The act of July 27, 1868, c. 249, declaring the right of expatriation to be a natural and inherent right of all people, and reciting that 'in the recognition of this principle this government has freely received emigrants from all nations, and invested them with the rights of citizenship,' while it affirms the right of every man to expatriate himself from one country, contains nothing to enable him to become a citizen of another without being naturalized under its authority. 15 St. 223; Rev. St. 1999. The provision of the act of congress of March 3, 1871, c. 120, that 'hereafter no Indian nation or tribe within the territory of the United States shall be acknowledged or recognized as an independent nation, tribe, or power with whom the United States may contract by treaty,' is coupled with a provision that the obligation of any treaty already lawfully made is not to be thereby invalidated or impaired; and its utmost possible effect is to require the Indian tribes to be dealt with for the future through the legislative and not through the treaty-making power. 16 St. 566; Rev. St. 2079.

In the case of *U. S. v. Elm*, 23 Int. Rev. Rec. 419, decided by Judge **WALLACE** in the district court of the United States for the Northern district of New York, the Indian who was held to have a right to vote in 1876 was born in the state of New York, one of the remnants of a tribe which had ceased to exist as a tribe in that state; and by a statute of the state it had been enacted that any native Indian might purchase, take, hold, and convey lands, and, whenever he should have become a freeholder to the value of $100, should be liable to taxation, and to the civil jurisdiction of the courts, in the same manner and to the same extent as a citizen. N. Y. St. 1843, c. 87. The condition of the tribe from which he **[112 U.S. 94, 108]** derived his origin, so far as any fragments of it remained within the state of New York, resembled the condition of those Indian nations of which Mr. Justice JOHNSON said in Fletcher v. Peck, 6 Cranch, 87, 146, that they 'have totally extinguished their national fire, and submitted themselves to the laws of the states;' and which Mr. Justice **MCLEAN** had in view when he observed in Worcester v. Georgia, 6 Pet. 515, 580, that in some of the old states 'where small remnants of tribes remain, surrounded by white population, and who, by their reduced numbers, had lost the power of self-government, the laws of the state have been extended over them, for the protection of their persons and property.' See, also, as to the condition of Indians in Massachusetts, remnants of tribes never recognized by the treaties or legislative or executive acts of the United States as distinct political communities, *Danzell v. Webquish*, 108 Mass. 133; *Pells v. Webquish*, 129 Mass. 469; Mass. St. 1862, c. 184; 1869, c. 463.

The passages cited as favorable to the plaintiff, from the opinions delivered in *Ex parte Kenyon*, 5 Dill. 385, 390, in *Ex parte Reynolds*, 5 Dill. 394, 397, and in *U. S. v. Crook*, 5 Dill. 453, 464, were obiter dicta. The Case of Reynolds was an indictment, in the circuit court of the United States for the Western district of Arkansas, for a murder in the Indian country, of which that court had jurisdiction if either the accused or the dead man was not an Indian, and was decided by Judge **PARKER** in favor of the jurisdiction, upon the ground that both were white men, and that, conceding the one to be an Indian by marriage, the other never was an Indian in any sense. 5 Dill. 397, 404. Each of the other two cases was a writ of habeas corpus; and any person, whether a citizen or not, unlawfully restrained of his liberty, is entitled to that writ. Case of the Hottentot Venus, 13 East, 195; *Case of Dos Santos*, 2 Brock. 493; *In re Kaine*, 14 How. 103. In Kenyon's Case, judge **PARKER** held that the court in which the prisoner had been convicted had no jurisdiction of the subject-matter, because the place of the commission of the act was beyond the territorial limits of its jurisdiction, and, as was truly said, 'this alone would be conclusive of this case.' 5 Dill. **[112 U.S. 94, 109]** 390. In *U. S. v. Crook*, the Ponca Indians were discharged by Judge Dundy because the military officers who held them were taking them to the Indian Territory by force and without any lawful authority, (5 Dill. 468;) and in the case at bar, as the record before us shows, that learned judge concurred in the judgment below for the defendant.

The law upon the question before us has been well stated by Judge Deady in the district court of the United States for the district of Oregon. In giving judgment against the plaintiff in a case resembling the case at bar, he said: 'Being born a member of 'an independent political community'-the Chinook-he was not born subject to the jurisdiction of the United States-not born in its allegiance.' *McKay v. Campbell*, 2 Sawy. 118, 134. And in a later case he said: 'But an Indian cannot make himself a citizen of the United States without the consent and co-operation of the government. The fact that he has abandoned his nomadic life or tribal relations, and adopted the habits and manners of civilized people, may be a good reason why he should be made a citizen of the United States, but does not of itself make him one. To be a citizen of the United States is a political privilege which no one, not born to, can assume without its consent in some form. The Indians in Oregon, not being born subject to the jurisdiction of the United States, were not born citizens thereof, and I am not aware of any law or treaty by which any of them have been made so since.' *U. S. v. Osborne*, 6 Sawy. 406, 409. Upon the question whether any action of a state can confer rights of citizenship on Indians of a tribe still recognized by the United States as retaining its tribal existence, we need not, and do not, express an opinion, because the state of Nebraska is not shown to have taken any action affecting the condition of this plaintiff. See *Chirac v. Chirac*, 2 Wheat. 259; *Fellows v. Blacksmith*, 19 How. 366; *U. S. v. Holliday*, 3 Wall. 407, 420; *U. S. v. Joseph*, 94 U.S. 614, 618. The plaintiff, not being a citizen of the United States under the fourteenth amendment of the constitution, has been deprived of no right secured by the fifteenth amendment, and cannot maintain this action. Judgment affirmed. **[112 U.S. 94, 110]**

HARLAN, J., dissenting.

Mr. Justice Woods and myself feel constrained to express our dissent from the interpretation which our brethren give to that clause of the fourteenth amendment which provides that 'all persons born or naturalized in the United States, and subject to the jurisdiction thereof, are citizens of the United States and of the state wherein they reside.' The case, as presented by the record, is this: John Elk, the plaintiff in error, is a person of the Indian race. He was born within the territorial limits of the United States. His parents were, at the time of his birth, members of one of the Indian tribes in this country. More than a year, however, prior to his application to be registered as a voter in the city of Omaha, he had severed all relations with his tribe, and, as he alleges, fully and completely surrendered himself to the jurisdiction of the United States. Such surrender was, of course, involved in his act of becoming, as the demurrer to the petition admits that he did become, a bona fide resident of the state of Nebraska. When he applied in 1880 to be registered as a voter, he possessed, as is also admitted, the qualifications of age and residence in state, county, and ward, required for electors by the constitution and laws of that state. It is likewise conceded that he was entitled to be so registered if, at the time of his application, he was a citizen of the United States; for, by the constitution and laws of Nebraska, every citizen of the United States, having the necessary qualifications of age and residence in state, county, and ward, is entitled to vote. Whether he was such citizen is the question presented by this writ of error.

It is said that the petition contains no averment that Elk was taxed in the state in which he resides, or had ever been treated by her as a citizen. It is evident that the court would not have held him to be a citizen of the United States, even if the petition had contained a direct averment that he was taxed; because its judgment, in legal effect, is that, although born within the territorial limits of the United States, he could not, if at his birth a member of an Indian tribe, acquire national citizenship **[112 U.S. 94, 111]** by force of the fourteenth amendment, but only in pursuance of some statute or treaty providing for his naturalization. It would, therefore, seem unnecessary to inquire whether he was taxed at the time of his application to be registered as a voter; for, if the words 'all persons born ... in the United States and subject to the jurisdiction thereof' were not intended to embrace Indians born in tribal relations, but who subsequently became bona fide residents of the several states, then, manifestly, the legal status of such Indians is not altered by the fact that they are taxed in those states. While denying that national citizenship, as conferred by that amendment, necessarily depends upon the inquiry whether the person claiming it is taxed in the state of his residence, or has property therein from which taxes may be derived, we submit that the petition does sufficiently show that the plaintiff was taxed, that is, belongs to the class which, by the laws of Nebraska, are subject to taxation. By the constitution and laws of Nebraska all real and personal property, in that state, are subject to assessment and taxation. Every person of full age and sound mind, being a resident thereof, is required to list his personal property for taxation. Const. Neb. art. 9, 1; Comp. St. Neb. c. 77, pp. 400, 401. Of these provisions upon the subject of taxation this court will take judicial notice. Good pleading did not require that they should be set forth, at large, in the petition. Consequently, an averment that the plaintiff is a citizen and bona fide resident of Nebraska implies, in law, that he is subject to taxation, and is taxed, in that state. Further: The plaintiff has become so far incorporated with the mass of the people of Nebraska that being, as the petition avers, a citizen and resident thereof, he constitutes a part of her militia. Comp. St. Neb. c. 56. He may, being no longer a member of an Indian tribe, sue and be sued in her courts. And he is counted in every apportionment of representation in the legislature; for the requirement of her constitution is that 'the legislature shall apportion the senators and representatives according to the number of inhabitants, excluding Indians not taxed, and soldiers and officers of the United States army.' Const. Neb. art. 3, 1. **[112 U.S. 94, 112]** At the adoption of the constitution there were, in many of the states, Indians, not members of any tribe, who constituted a part of the people for whose benefit the state governments were established. This is apparent from that clause of article 1, 3, which requires, in the apportionment of representatives and direct taxes among the several states 'according to their respective numbers,' the exclusion of 'Indians not taxed.' This implies that there were, at that time, in the United States, Indians who were taxed; that is, were subject to taxation by the laws of the state of which they were residents. Indians not taxed were those who held tribal relations, and therefore were not subject to the authority of any state, and were subject only to the authority of the United States, under the power conferred upon congress in reference to Indian tribes in this country. The same provision is retained in the fourteenth amendment; for, now, as at the adoption of the constitution, Indians in the several states, who are taxed by their laws, are counted in establishing the basis of representation in congress. By the act of April 9, 1866, entitled 'An act to protect all persons in the United States in their civil rights, and furnish means for their vindication,' (14 St. 27,) it is provided that 'all persons born in the United States, and not subject to any foreign power, excluding Indians not taxed, are hereby declared to be citizens of the United States.' This, so far as we are aware, is the first general enactment making persons of the Indian race citizens of the United States. Numerous statutes and treaties previously provided for all the individual members of particular Indian tribes becoming, in certain contingencies, citizens of the United States. But the act of 1866 reached Indians not in tribal relations. Beyond question, by that act, national citizenship was conferred directly upon all persons in this country, of whatever race, (excluding only 'Indians not taxed,') who were born within the territorial limits of the United States, and were not subject to any foreign power. Surely every one must admit that an Indian residing in one of the states, and subject to taxation there, became, by force alone of the act of 1866, a citizen of the United States, al-[though] **[112 U.S. 94, 113]** he may have been, when born, a member of a tribe. The exclusion of Indians not taxed evinced a purpose to include those subject to taxation in the state of their residence. Language could not express that purpose with more distinctness than does the act of 1866. Any doubt upon the subject, in respect to persons of the Indian race residing in the United States or territories, and not members of a tribe, will be removed by an examination of the debates, in which many distinguished statesmen and lawyers participated in the senate of the United States when the act of 1866 was under consideration.

In the bill as originally reported from the judiciary committee there were no words excluding 'Indians not taxed' from the citizenship proposed to be granted. Attention being called to this fact, the friends of the measure disclaimed any purpose to make citizens of those who were in tribal relations, with governments of their own. In order to meet that objection, while conforming to the wishes of those desiring to invest with citizenship all Indians permanently separated from their tribes, and who, by reason of their residence away from their tribes, constituted a part of the people under the jurisdiction of the United States, Mr. Trumbull, who reported the bill, modified it by inserting the words 'excluding Indians not taxed.' What was intended by that modification appears from the following language used by him in debate: 'Of course we cannot declare the wild Indians who do not recognize the government of the United States, who are not subject to our laws, with whom we make treaties, who have their own laws, who have their own regulations, whom we do not intend to interfere with or punish for the commission of crimes one upon the other, to be the subjects of the United States in the sense of being citizens. They must be excepted. The constitution of the United States excludes them from the enumeration of the population of the United States when it says that Indians not taxed are to be excluded. It has occurred to me that, perhaps, the amendment would meet the views of all gentlemen, which used these constitutional words, and said that all persons born in the United States, excluding **[112 U.S. 94, 114]** Indians not taxed, and not subject to any foreign power, shall be deemed citizens of the United States.' Cong. Globe, (1st Sess. 39th Congress,) p. 527. In replying to the objections urged by Mr. Hendricks to the bill even as amended, Mr. Trumbull said: 'Does the senator from Indiana want the wild roaming Indians, not taxed, not subject to our authority, to be citizens of the United States-persons that are not to be counted, in our government? If he does not, let him not object to this amendment that brings in even [only] the Indian when he shall have cast off his wild habits, and submitted to the laws of organized society and become a citizen.' Id. 528.

The entire debate shows, with singular clearness, indeed, with absolute certainty, that no senator who participated in it, whether in favor of or in opposition to the measure, doubted that the bill as passed admitted, and was intended to admit, to national citizenship Indians who abandoned their tribal relations and became residents of one of the states or territories, within the full jurisdiction of the United States. It was so interpreted by President Johnson, who, in his veto message, said: 'By the first section of the bill all persons born in the United States, and not subject to any foreign power, excluding Indians not taxed, are declared to be citizens of the United States. This provision comprehends the Chinese of the Pacific states, Indians subject to taxation, the people called gypsies, as well as the entire race designated as blacks, persons of color, negroes, mulattoes, and persons of African blood. Every individual of those races, born in the United States, is, by the bill, made a citizen of the United States.'

It would seem manifest, from this brief review of the history of the act of 1866, that one purpose of that legislation was to confer national citizenship upon a part of the Indian race in this country-such of them, at least, as resided in one of the states or territories, and were subject to taxation and other public burdens. And it is to be observed that, whoever was included within the terms of the grant contained in that act, became citizens of the United States without any record of [112 U.S. 94, 115] their names being made. The citizenship conferred was made to depend wholly upon the existence of the facts which the statute declared to be a condition precedent to the grant taking effect. At the same session of the congress which passed the act of 1866, the fourteenth amendment was approved and submitted to the states for adoption. Those who sustained the former urged the adoption of the latter. An examination of the debates, pending the consideration of the amendment, will show that there was no purpose on the part of those who framed it, or of those who sustained it by their votes, to abandon the policy inaugurated by the act of 1866, of admitting to national citizenship such Indians as were separated from their tribes and were residents of one of the states or territories outside of any reservation set apart for the exclusive use and occupancy of Indian tribes.

Prior to the adoption of the fourteenth amendment, numerous statutes were passed with reference to particular bodies of Indians, under which the individual members of such bodies, upon the dissolution of their tribal relations, or upon the division of their lands derived from the government, became, or were entitled to become, citizens of the United States by force alone of the statute, without observing the forms required by the naturalization laws in the case of a foreigner becoming a citizen of the United States. Such was the statute of March 3, 1839, (5 St. 349,) relating to the Brothertown Indians in the then territory of Wisconsin. Congress consented that the lands reserved for their use might be partitioned among the individuals composing the tribe. The act required the petition to be evidenced by a report and map to be filed with the secretary of the interior, by whom it should be transmitted to the president; whereupon the act proceeded: 'The said Brothertown Indians, and each and every of them, shall then be deemed to be, and from that time forth are hereby declared to be, citizens of the United States to all intents and purposes, and shall be entitled to all the rights, privileges, and immunities of such citizens,' etc. Similar legislation was enacted with [112 U.S. 94, 116] reference to the Stockbridge Indians. 5 St. 646, 647. Legislation of this character has an important bearing upon the present question, for it shows that prior to the adoption of the fourteenth amendment it had often been the policy of congress to admit persons of the Indian race to citizenship upon their ceasing to have tribal relations, and without the slightest reference to the fact that they were born in tribal relations. It shows, also, that the citizenship thus granted was not, in every instance, required to be evidenced by the record of a court. If it be said that the statutes prior to 1866, providing for the admission of Indians to citizenship, required in their execution that a record be made of the names of those who thus acquired citizenship, our answer is that it was entirely competent for congress to dispense, as it did in the act of 1866, with any such record being made in a court, or in any department of the government. And certainly it must be conceded that except in cases of persons 'naturalized in the United States,' (which phrase refers only to those who are embraced by the naturalization laws, and not to Indians,) the fourteenth amendment does not require the citizenship granted by it to be evidenced by the record of any court, or of any department of the government. Such citizenship passes to the person, of whatever race, who is embraced by its provisions, leaving the fact of citizenship to be determined, when it shall become necessary to do so in the course of legal inquiry, in the same way that questions as to one's nativity, domicile, or residence are determined.

If it be also said that, since the adoption of the fourteenth amendment, congress has enacted statutes providing for the citizenship of Indians, our answer is that those statutes had reference to tribes, the members of which could not, while they continued in tribal relations, acquire the citizenship granted by the fourteenth amendment. Those statutes did not deal with individual Indians who had severed their tribal connections and were residents within the states of the Union, under the complete jurisdiction of the United States. There is nothing in the history of the adoption of the fourteenth amendment which, in our opinion, justifies the conclusion **[112 U.S. 94, 117]** that only those Indians are included in its grant of citizenship who were, at the time of their birth, subject to the complete jurisdiction of the United States. As already stated, according to the doctrines of the court, in this case,—if we do not wholly misapprehend the effect of its decision,—the plaintiff, if born while his parents were members of an Indian tribe, would not be embraced by the amendment even had he been, at the time it was adopted, a permanent resident of one of the states, subject to taxation, and, in fact, paying property and personal taxes, to the full extent required of the white race in the same state.

When the fourteenth amendment was pending in the senate of the United States, Mr. Doolittle moved to insert after the words 'subject to the jurisdiction thereof,' the words 'excluding Indians not taxed.' His avowed object in so amending the measure was to exclude, beyond all question, from the proposed grant of national citizenship, tribal Indians who—since they were, in a sense, subject to the jurisdiction of the United States—might be regarded as embraced in the grant. The proposition was opposed by Mr. Trumbull and other friends of the proposed constitutional amendment, upon the ground that the words 'Indians not taxed' might be misconstrued, and also because those words were unnecessary, in that the phrase 'subject to the jurisdiction thereof' embraced only those who were subject to the complete jurisdiction of the United States, which could not be properly said of Indians in tribal relations. But it was distinctly announced by the friends of the amendment that they intended to include in the grant of national citizenship Indians who were within the jurisdiction of the states, and subject to their laws, because such Indians would be completely under the jurisdiction of the United States. Said Mr. Trumbull: 'It is only those who come completely within our jurisdiction, who are subject to our laws, that we think of making citizens; and there can be no objection to the proposition that such persons should be citizens.' Cong. Globe, pt. 4, (1st Sess. 39th Cong.) pp. 2890-2893. Alluding to the phrase 'Indians not taxed,' he remarked that the language of the proposed constitutional amendment was **[112 U.S. 94, 118]** better than that of the act of 1866 passed at the same session. He observed: 'There is a difficulty about the words 'Indians not taxed.' Perhaps one of the reasons why I think so is because of the persistency with which the senator from Indiana himself insisted that the phrase 'Indians not taxed,' the very words which the senator from Wisconsin wishes to insert here, would exclude everybody that did not pay a tax; that that was the meaning of it; we must take it literally. The senator from Maryland did not agree to that, nor did I; but, if the senator from Indiana was right, it would receive a construction which, I am sure, the senator from Wisconsin would not be for, for if these Indians come within our limits and within our jurisdiction and are civilized, he would just as soon make a citizen of a poor Indian as of the rich Indian.' Id. 2894.

A careful examination of all that was said by senators and representatives, pending the consideration by congress of the fourteenth amendment, justifies us in saying that every one who participated in the debates, whether for or against the amendment, believed that, in the form in which it was approved by congress, it granted, and was intended to grant, national citizenship to every person of the Indian race in this country who was unconnected with any tribe, and who resided, in good faith, outside of Indian reservations and within one of the states or territories of the Union. This fact is, we think, entitled to great weight in determining the meaning and scope of the amendment. *Lithographic Co. v. Sarony*, 111 U.S. 57; S. C. 4 SUP. CT. REP. 279. In this connection we refer to an elaborate report made by Mr. Carpenter, to the senate of the United States, in behalf of its judiciary committee, on the fourteenth of December,

1870. The report was made in obedience to an instruction to inquire as to the effect of the fourteenth amendment upon the treaties which the United States had with various Indian tribes of the country. The report says: 'For these reasons your committee do not hesitate to say that the Indian tribes within the limits of the United States, and the individuals, members of such tribes, while they adhere to and form a part of the tribes to which they belong, are not, within the meaning of the [112 U.S. 94, 119] fourteenth amendment, 'subject to the jurisdiction' of the United States, and therefore that such Indians have not become citizens of the United States by virtue of that amendment; and, if your committee are correct in this conclusion, it follows that the treaties heretofore made between the United States and the Indian tribes are not annulled by that amendment.' The report closes with this significant language: 'It is pertinent to say, in concluding this report, that treaty relations can properly exist with Indian tribes or nations only, and that, when the members of any Indian tribe are scattered, they are merged in the mass of our people, and become equally subject to the jurisdiction of the United States.'

The question before us has been examined by a writer upon constitutional law whose views are entitled to great respect. Judge COOLEY, referring to the definition of national citizenship as contained in the fourteenth amendment, says: 'By the express terms of the amendment, persons of foreign birth, who have never renounced the allegiance to which they were born, though they may have a residence in this country, more or less permanent, for business, instruction, or pleasure, are not citizens. Neither are the aboriginal inhabitants of the country citizens, so long as they preserve their tribal relations and recognize the headship of their chiefs, notwithstanding that, as against the action of our own people, they are under the protection of the laws, and may be said to owe a qualified allegiance to the government. When living within territory over which the laws, either state or territorial, are extended, they are protected by, and, at the same time, held amenable to, those laws in all their intercourse with the body politic, and with the individuals composing it; but they are also, as a quasi foreign people, regarded as being under the direction and tutelage of the general government, and subjected to peculiar regulations as dependent communities. They are 'subject to the jurisdiction' of the United States only in a much qualified sense; and it would be obviously inconsistent with the semi- independent character of such a tribe, and with the obedience they are expected to render to their tribal head, that they should be vested with the complete rights- or, on the other [112 U.S. 94, 120] hand, subjected to the full responsibilities-of American citizens. It would not for a moment be contended that such was the effect of this amendment. When, however, the tribal relations are dissolved, when the headship of the chief or the authority of the tribe is no longer recognized, and the individual Indian, turning his back upon his former mode of life, makes himself a member of the civilized community, the case is wholly altered. He then no longer acknowledges a divided allegiance; he joins himself to the body politic; he gives evidence of his purpose to adopt the habits and customs of civilized life; and, as his case is then within the terms of this amendment, it would seem that his right to protection, in person, property, and privilege, must be as complete as the allegiance to the government to which he must then be held; as complete, in short, as that of any other native-born inhabitant.' 2 Story, Const. (Cooley's Ed.) 1933, p. 654. To the same effect are *Ex parte Kenyon*, 5 Dill. 390; *Ex parte Reynolds*, Id. 397; U. S. v. Crook, Id. 454; *U. S. v. Elm*, Dist. Ct. U. S., N. D. N. Y. 23 Int. Rev. Rec. 419.

It seems to us that the fourteenth amendment, in so far as it was intended to confer national citizenship upon persons of the Indian race, is robbed of its vital force by a construction which excludes from such citizenship those who, although born in tribal relations, are within the complete jurisdiction of the United States. There were, in some of our states and territories at the time the amendment was submitted by congress, many Indians who had finally left their tribes and come within the complete jurisdiction of the United States. They were as fully prepared for citizenship as were or are vast numbers of the white and colored races in the same localities. Is it conceivable that the statesmen who framed, the congress which submitted, and the people who adopted that amendment intended to confer citizenship, national and state, upon the entire population in this country of African descent, (the larger part of which was shortly before held in slavery,) and, by the same constitutional provision, to exclude from such citizenship Indians [112 U.S. 94, 121] who had never been in slavery, and who, by becoming bona fide residents of states and territories within the complete jurisdiction of the United States, had evinced a purpose to abandon their former mode of life, and become a part of the people of the United States? If this question be answered in the negative, as we think it must be, then we are justified in withholding our assent to the doctrine which excludes the plaintiff from the body of citizens of the United States upon the ground that his parents were, when he was born, members of an Indian tribe; for, if he can be excluded upon any such ground, it must necessarily follow that the fourteenth amendment did not grant citizenship even to Indians who, although born in tribal relations, were, at its adoption, severed from their tribes, subject to the complete jurisdiction as well of the United States as of the state or territory in which they resided.

Our brethren, it seems to us, construe the fourteenth amendment as if it read: 'All persons born subject to the jurisdiction of, or naturalized in, the United States, are citizens of the United States and of the state in which they reside;' whereas the amendment, as it is, implies in respect of persons born in this country that they may claim the rights of national citizenship from and after the moment they become subject to the complete jurisdiction of the United States. This would not include the children born in this country of a foreign minister, for the reason that, under the fiction of extraterritoriality as recognized by international law, such minister, 'though actually in a foreign country, is considered still to remain within the territory of his own state,' and, consequently, he continues 'subject to the laws of his own country, both with respect to his personal status and his rights of property; and his children, though born in a foreign country, are considered as natives.' Halleck, Int. Law, c. 10, 12. Nor was plaintiff born without the jurisdiction of the United States in the same sense that the subject of a foreign state, born within the territory of that state, may be said to have been born without the jurisdiction of our government. For, according to the decision in *Cherokee* [112 U.S. 94, 122] *Nation v. Georgia*, 5 Pet. 17, the tribe of which the parents of plaintiff were members was not 'a foreign state, in the sense of the constitution,' but a domestic dependent people, 'in a state of pupilage,' and 'so completely under the sovereignty and dominion of the United States, that any attempt to acquire their lands, or to form a political connection with them, would be considered an invasion of our territory and an act of hostility.' They occupied territory which the court, in that case, said composed 'a part of the United States,' the title to which this nation asserted independent of their will. 'In all our intercourse with foreign nations,' said Chief Justice Marshall in the same case, 'in our commercial regulations, in any attempt at intercourse between Indians and foreign nations, they are considered as within the jurisdictional limits of the United States, subject to many of those restraints which are imposed upon our citizens. ... They look to our government for protection; rely upon its kindness and its power; appeal to it for relief to their wants; and address the president as their great father.' And, again, in *U. S. v. Rogers*, 4 How. 572, this court, speaking by Chief Justice Taney, said that it was 'too firmly and clearly established to admit of dispute that the Indian tribes, residing within the territorial limits of the United States, are subject to their authority.' *The Cherokee Tobacco*, 11 Wall. 616. Born, therefore, in the territory, under the dominion and within the jurisdictional limits of the United States, plaintiff has acquired, as was his undoubted right, a residence in one of the states, with her consent, and is subject to taxation and to all other burdens imposed by her upon residents of every race. If he did not acquire national citizenship on abandoning his tribe and becoming, by residence in one of the states, subject to the complete jurisdiction of the United States, then the fourteenth amendment has wholly failed to accomplish, in respect of the Indian race, what, we think, was intended by it there is; and still in this country a despised and rejected class of persons with no nationality whatever, who, born in our territory, owing no allegiance to any foreign power, and subject, as residents of the states, to all the burdens of government, [112 U.S. 94, 123] are yet not members of any political community, nor entitled to any of the rights, privileges, or immunities of citizens of the United States.

Supreme Court of California
Escobedo v. California, 35 Cal.2d 870 (1950)

September 13, 1950.
(headnotes omitted)

[870-872] PROCEEDING in mandamus to compel reissuance or reinstatement of a motor vehicle operator's license. Writ denied.

David C. Marcus for Petitioner.

Fred N. Howser, Attorney General, Walter L. Bowers, Assistant Attorney General, and E. G. Funke, Deputy Attorney General, for Respondents.

SCHAUER, J.—Petitioner asks that this court by mandate direct respondents, the Department of Motor Vehicles and the Director of Motor Vehicles of this state, to "re-issue, return or reinstate Petitioner's operator's license and/or driving privileges to operate a motor vehicle in this State." In September, 1948, respondents, without according petitioner a hearing, suspended his operator's license under the then provisions of sections 419 through 420.9 of the Vehicle Code (Stats. 1947, ch. 1235). These provisions constituted chapter 3 of division VII of the code, entitled "Security Following Accident"; they became operative July 1, 1948.[1] It is petitioner's position that the application of this law to him denied him due process and equal protection (U.S. Const., Amendment XIV, § 1; Cal. Const., art. I, §§ 11, 13) and vested judicial power in "a purely ministerial 'department' " in violation of the state Constitution (art. III, § 1; art. VI, § 1). We have concluded that petitioner's contentions should not be sustained and that upon the showing made the suspension of his license is legally tenable.

On July 1, 1948, petitioner held a valid license to drive a motor vehicle in California; on that date he operated a vehicle which was involved in a collision with another such vehicle at an intersection of public highways in this state. In August, 1948, petitioner received from respondents a written notice stating that because of the July 1 accident and because petitioner had "failed to otherwise meet the security requirements of Section 420 of the Vehicle Code," [35 Cal.2d 873] he was required to deposit with respondent department, on or before September 11, 1948, security in the sum of $2,800. The notice further stated that petitioner's "driving privilege and all licenses evidencing such privilege is [sic] hereby suspended as of" September 11, 1948, unless the deposit was made prior to that date, and that the suspension would "remain in effect until evidence satisfactory to the Department has been filed indicating that the security requirements of Section 420.2 of the Vehicle Code have been met." Petitioner is a gardener by occupation and "requires the use of his automobile" and his license to operate it in order to "transport himself and his tools between his different places of employment ... and to earn a livelihood for himself and his family [dependent wife and nine minor children]." He does not have $2,800 "or any like sum" to post as security, is unable to and did not post the security demanded by respondents and, pursuant to the provisions of section 420 of the Vehicle Code, his operator's license was and now is suspended. The Highway Patrol has notified petitioner "that they intend to arrest and prosecute" him under the provisions of subdivisions (a) and (d) of section 338 of the Vehicle Code, which forbid possession of, and failure to surrender to the department on lawful demand, a suspended license.

---

[1] Effective July 7, 1949, the chapter was completely recast (although its general plan remains the same) by amendment of section 419, repeal of sections 420 through 420.9, and addition of new sections 420 through 423.1 (Stats. 1949, ch. 834).

The applicable provisions of chapter 3 of division VII of the Vehicle Code (Stats. 1947, ch. 1235) which were in effect at the time of petitioner's accident and the suspension of his license are as follows:

Section 419 required that the operator of a motor vehicle involved in an accident in this state which resulted in personal injury, death or property damage exceeding $100 report the matter in writing to the Department of Motor Vehicles within 10 days after the accident. Section 420 (subd. (a)) provided that "The department shall, within 60 days after the receipt of a report of [such] a motor vehicle accident ... suspend the license of each operator ... involved in such accident ... unless such operator shall deposit security in a sum which shall be sufficient in the judgment of the department to satisfy any judgment or judgments for damages resulting from such accident as may be recovered against such operator. Notice of such suspension shall be sent by the department to such operator not less than 10 days prior to the effective date of such suspension and shall state the amount required as security." The deposit of security and suspension of license **[35 Cal.2d 874]** requirements did not apply if the operator or owner of the vehicle had an automobile or other public liability policy or bond covering $5,000 for injury or death of one person, $10,000 for injury or death of more than one person, and $1,000 property damage (Veh. Code, § 420, subds. (b), (c)), or to a person who had more than 25 vehicles registered in his name and qualified as a self-insurer (Veh. Code, § 420, subd. (b), par. (4), § 420.7); other situations in which the requirements did not apply are not here material. Suspension of license was to continue until security was deposited, or one year had passed without filing of an action for damages arising out of the accident, or until release from or satisfaction of liability, or final adjudication of nonliability. (Veh. Code, § 420.2.)

Specifically, petitioner urges that the above quoted or summarized sections of the Vehicle Code were unconstitutional in the following respects:

1. The statute violated the due process provisions of the federal Constitution (Amendment XIV, § 1) and the state Constitution (art. I, § 13) in that no provision was made for hearing before the department, or for recourse to the courts, before suspension of a license.

2. Judicial power was delegated to an administrative body in violation of the state Constitution (art. III, § 1; art. VI, § 1), in that no sufficient standard was provided to guide the department in determining the amount of security.

3. The effect of the statute was an arbitrary discrimination in violation of the equal protection clause of the federal Constitution (Amendment XIV, § 1) and the uniform operation of laws provision of the state Constitution (art. I, § 11) in that: (a) The posting of security by a driver who might not be culpable was required, before his liability was judicially determined. (b) Those who were financially able to carry insurance or post security were favored as against those who were not. (c) The provisions permitting any person in whose name more than 25 motor vehicles were registered to qualify as a self-insurer created an arbitrary classification.

Hearing, Due Process

There was no express provision in sections 419 through 420.9 of the Vehicle Code (Stats. 1947, ch. 1235) concerning hearing before determination by the department that security must be deposited or the operator's license suspended. At the time petitioner's license was suspended without hearing, **[35 Cal.2d 875]** section 315 of the Vehicle Code (Stats. 1947, ch. 431) provided that "A person shall be entitled to demand in writing a hearing before the director or his representative whenever the department ... [h]as given notice of the suspension ... of his privilege of operating a motor vehicle upon a highway or of an operator's ... license issued to such person," but it further provided that "The ... licensee shall not be entitled to a hearing under this section whenever such action by the department is made mandatory upon the department by the provisions of this code."[2] Since suspension of petitioner's license for failure

---

[2] In 1949 sections 314- 316 of the Vehicle Code, concerning notice, hearing, etc., were repealed and new provisions (§§ 314-319.1) concerning these subjects were enacted (Stats. 1949, ch. 1467

to deposit security was mandatory (Veh. Code, § 420) whenever it had been determined that a motor vehicle accident had occurred and damages exceeding $100 ensued which probably might result in "a judgment or judgments for damages ... recovered against such operator," it is apparent that it was not contemplated that the department necessarily should give an operator opportunity to be heard before it determined the amount of security required and notified him that his license would be suspended unless he deposited such sum. Thus we have for decision an aspect of the question expressly left open in *Ratliff v. Lampton* (1948), 32 Cal.2d 226, 233 [195 P.2d 792, 10 A.L.R.2d 826]: "Whether such summary procedure might be justified under the police power ... in some instances ..."

Fundamentally it must be recognized that in this country "Highways are for the use of the traveling public, and all have ... the right to use them in a reasonable and proper manner, and subject to proper regulations as to the manner of use." (13 Cal.Jur. 371, § 59.) "The streets of a city belong to the people of the state, and the use thereof is an inalienable right of every citizen, subject to legislative control or such reasonable regulations as to the traffic thereon or the manner of using them as the legislature may deem wise or proper to adopt and impose." (19 Cal.Jur. 54, § 407.) "Streets and highways are established and maintained primarily for purposes of travel and transportation by the public, and uses incidental thereto. Such travel may be for either business or pleasure ... The use of highways for purposes of travel and transportation is not a mere privilege, but a common and fundamental right, of which the public and [35 Cal.2d 876] individuals cannot rightfully be deprived ... [A]ll persons have an equal right to use them for purposes of travel by proper means, and with due regard for the corresponding rights of others." (25 Am.Jur. 456-457, § 163; see, also, 40 C.J.S. 244-247, § 233.) Notwithstanding such general principles characterizing the primary right of the individual, it is equally well established (as is recognized in the texts above cited) that usage of the highways is subject to reasonable regulation for the public good. In this connection, the constitutionality of various types of financial responsibility laws has been often upheld against contentions that they violated the due process clause of the Fourteenth Amendment. "The use of the public highways by motor vehicles, with its constant dangers, renders the reasonableness and necessity of regulation apparent. The universal practice is to register ownership of automobiles and to license their drivers. Any appropriate means adopted by the states to insure competence and care on the part of its licensees and to protect others using the highway is consonant with due process." (*Reitz v. Mealey* (1941), 314 U.S. 33, 36 [62 S.Ct. 24, 86 L.Ed. 21, 24]; see, also, *State v. Price* (1937), 49 Ariz. 19, 26 [63 P.2d 653, 108 A.L.R. 1156]; *Surtman v. Secretary of State* (1944), 309 Mich. 270 [15 N.W.2d 471, 474].)

The state, in the exercise of its police power, could constitutionally have required deposit of security by the owners of all vehicles as a condition to licensing them. (*Opinion of the Justices, In re* (1925), 81 N.H. 566 [129 A. 117, 39 A.L.R. 1023]; *Opinion of the Justices, In re* (1925), 251 Mass. 569 [147 N.E. 681]; *Brest v. Commissioner of Insurance* (1930), 270 Mass. 7 [169 N.E. 657]; *Ex parte Poresky* (1933), 290 U.S. 30 [54 S.Ct. 3, 78 L.Ed. 152].) Instead, the state chose to allow financially irresponsible licensed operators to drive until they became involved in an accident with the consequences described in sections 419 and 420 of the Vehicle Code and their financial irresponsibility was thus brought to the attention of the department, and then to require suspension of their licenses.

Suspension of the license without prior hearing but subject to subsequent judicial review did not violate due process if reasonably justified by a compelling public interest. (*Bourjois v. Chapman* (1937), 301 U.S. 183, 189 [57 S.Ct. 691, 81 L.Ed. 1027, 1032]; see also *Phillips v. Commissioner of Internal Rev.* (1931), 283 U.S. 589, 596-597 [51 S.Ct. 608, 75 L.Ed. 1289].) The compelling public interest here appears [35 Cal.2d 877] from the obvious carelessness and financial irresponsibility of a substantial number of drivers and from the following allegations of the petition: There are 3,879,931 motor vehicles registered in California. During the first four months after the effective date of the law now under consideration, 19,808 persons were ordered by the department to establish that they were adequately insured or deposit security.

More than 6,567 operators' licenses were suspended under the applicable law, and more than 1,300 "citations per month for suspension of license" were issued by the department. In these circumstances it is apparent that to require a hearing in every case before suspension of a license would have substantially burdened and delayed if not defeated the operation of the law. The requirement of due process was recognized and accepted by section 317 of the Vehicle Code, which declared that "Nothing in this code shall be deemed to prevent a review or other action as may be permitted by the Constitution and laws of this State by a court of competent jurisdiction with reference to any order of the department refusing, canceling, suspending or revoking a license." Such review can be had by application to the superior court for writ of mandate (Code Civ. Proc., §§ 1085, 1086). Also, an action for declaratory relief has been used in a comparable situation (*Ratliff v. Lampton* (1948), supra, 32 Cal.2d 226). General language concerning the requirement of a hearing in *Carroll v. California Horse Racing Bd.* (1940), 16 Cal.2d 164, 168 [105 P.2d 110]; *Ratliff v. Lampton* (1948), supra, p. 230 of 32 Cal.2d; and *People v. Noggle* (1935), 7 Cal.App.2d 14, 18 [45 P.2d 430], is not controlling here, for each of those cases concerned a statute which was construed to require opportunity to be heard before discretionary revocation of a license became effective.

Delegation of Power

Giving to the Department of Motor Vehicles the power and duty to find the facts on which suspension of license depended, and to exercise limited "judgment," did not violate section 1 of article III or section 1 of article VI of the state Constitution (see *Suckow v. Alderson* (1920), 182 Cal. 247, 250 [187 P. 965]; *Dominguez Land Corp. v. Daugherty* (1925), 196 Cal. 453, 483 [238 P. 697, 44 A.L.R. 1]). Although the Legislature did not provide detailed directions as to the manner in which the department was to reach a "judgment" as to the amount of security required, it specified as a guide **[35 Cal.2d 878]** the probable size of "any [court] judgment" which "may be recovered." (Veh. Code, § 420.) The facts and legal principles governing the recovery of judgments for damages are a matter of public knowledge and provide a reasonable, sufficiently certain standard to be followed by the department. (Cf. *Dominguez Land Corp. v. Daugherty* (1925), supra, pp. 485-486 of 196 Cal.; *Jersey Maid Milk Products Co. v. Brock* (1939), 13 Cal.2d 620, 652-657 [91 P.2d 577]; *Housing Authority v. Dockweiler* (1939), 14 Cal.2d 437, 461-462 [94 P.2d 794].)

Culpability

The statute did not require security of every operator who might be involved in an accident, but only of those against whom, in the opinion of the department, a judgment might be recovered. Inasmuch as the recovery of a judgment depends, in theory at least, upon culpability, it would seem that the statute, presumptively properly administered, was not open to the objection that under it the nonculpable were subject to arbitrary discrimination.

Financial Ability, Equal Protection

Financial responsibility laws such as this do not unconstitutionally discriminate against the poor. (See *Watson v. Division of Motor Vehicles* (1931), 212 Cal. 279, 284 [298 P. 481]; *Rosenblum v. Griffin* (1938), 89 N.H. 314, 319 [197 A. 701, 115 A.L.R. 1367].) Those damaged by the negligence of indigent drivers may be indigent also, and as little able as the drivers to bear the cost of such negligence. The fallacy of the argument that the law favored the rich over the poor "lies in the failure to distinguish between equality of opportunity and ability to take advantage of the opportunity which is offered to all. The equality of the Constitution is the equality of right, and not of enjoyment." (*Watson v. Division of Motor Vehicles* (1931), supra, p. 284 of 212 Cal.) Those who cannot afford to possess automobiles are as little able to enjoy the opportunity of driving on the public highways as those who cannot afford insurance or security.

Objection is made by petitioner that suspending his license after the accident did not make him more financially responsible; indeed, in his case, suspending his license made him less financially responsible, for it deprived him of his means of livelihood for himself, his wife and nine children. This contention constitutes no more than an argument that the Legislature

[35 Cal.2d 879] acted unwisely in selecting a financial responsibility law of a lock-the-barn-door-after-the-horse-is-stolen type instead of a compulsory preinsurance law or some other method of treating the problem (see 1 Stanf.L.Rev. 263). Our concern, however, is with the validity of the law under attack and not with whether a better law could be devised. (See *Watson v. Division of Motor Vehicles* (1931), supra, pp. 285-286 of 212 Cal.)

Self-Insurers

The provisions permitting persons in whose names more than 25 motor vehicles were registered to qualify as self-insurers (Veh. Code, § 420, subd. (b), par. (4), § 420.7) did not create an arbitrary discrimination. Inasmuch as the provisions were patently based upon the probable financial ability of such persons to respond in damages, the classification was one which the Legislature could reasonably make.

For the reasons above stated, the alternative writ of mandate heretofore issued is discharged, and the petition for the peremptory writ is denied.

Gibson, C.J., Shenk, J., Traynor, J., and Spence, J., concurred.

CARTER, J, Dissenting.—On the main issue, the majority hold (citing as authority *Bourjois v. Chapman*, 301 U.S. 183 [57 S.Ct. 691, 81 L.Ed. 1027]; *Phillips v. Commissioner of Internal Rev.*, 283 U.S. 589 [51 S.Ct. 608, 75 L.Ed. 1289]) that due process of law requiring notice and hearing is satisfied because a court review may be had after the suspension of a license without a hearing by the department. In the Bourjois case a Maine statute authorized the public official to issue permits for the sale of cosmetics and refuse such permits where they "... contain injurious substances in such amounts as to be poisonous, injurious or detrimental to the person." The court states: "And neither constitution requires that there must be a hearing of the applicant before the board may exercise a judgment under the circumstances and of the character here involved. The requirement of due process of law is amply safeguarded by sec. 2 of the statute, which provides: 'From the refusal of said department to issue a certificate of registration for any cosmetic preparation appeal shall lie to the superior court in the county of Kennebec or any other county in the state from which the same was offered for registration.' "

[35 Cal.2d 880] In the Phillips case the issue involved was the payment of taxes, and was based on the principle that: "Property rights must yield provisionally to governmental need. ... The underlying principle in that case was not such relation, but the need of the government promptly to secure its revenues." In the instant case it is said that the rule that a hearing in court after the suspension is sufficient to satisfy due process, is limited to cases where there is a "compelling public interest," and such interest in this case is: "... the *obvious carelessness* and financial irresponsibility of a substantial number of drivers and from the following allegations of the petition: There are 3,879,931 motor vehicles registered in California. During the first four months after the effective date of the law now under consideration, 19,808 persons were ordered by the department to establish that they were adequately insured or deposit security. More than 6,567 operators' licenses were suspended under the applicable law, and more than 1,300 'citations per month for suspension of license' were issued by the department. In these circumstances it is apparent that to require a hearing in every case before suspension of a license would have substantially burdened and delayed if not defeated the operation of the law." (Emphasis added.)

Assuming that the above rule stated by the majority is sound, there is no "compelling public interest" here. In *Bourjois v. Chapman*, supra, the vital interest was the necessity for immediate protection of the public health. In *Phillips v. Commissioner*, supra, it was the immediate necessity that the *government receive its tax revenue in order to function*. We have no comparable pressing need in the instant case. There is no issue of immediate danger to the public health involved nor is there any question of indispensable government revenue. *The sole need is that a private person shall have security for the payment of any damages caused to him by another individual.* Certainly that presents no urgency for immediate action which will justify depriving a person of the use of his automobile, his sole means of livelihood. The majority opinion states, as seen from the above quotation, that obviously careless persons' licenses were suspended for failure to post security. That is a *non sequitur*. It does not follow from the failure to post security that the drivers were careless. Nor does it follow from the fact that they were in accidents that they were careless drivers. They may have been wholly blameless. But even more important, there is no **[35 Cal.2d 881]** connection between careless drivers and posting of security, that is, the statute is not designed to keep seemingly careless drivers off the highways. *That is true because they are permitted to drive, careless or not, if they post security*. Hence the purpose of the statute is only security for payment of damages to the innocent person.

The recent U.S. Supreme Court case of *Ewing v. Mytinger & Cosselberry, Inc.*, 339 U.S. 594 [70 S.Ct. 870, 94 L.Ed. ___], involved a statute authorizing the administrator to determine whether probable cause existed for the seizure of goods on the basis that they were falsely labelled. That determination did not result in an immediate seizure. Such could only be accomplished if the attorney general, in his discretion, brought an action to seize and confiscate the goods. Only upon the commencement of such an action could the goods be seized pending the court proceeding. The court stated: "We have repeatedly held that no hearing at the preliminary stage is required by due process so long as the requisite hearing is held *before the final administrative order becomes effective*. (Emphasis added) ... But this case does not go as far. Here an administrative agency is merely determining whether a judicial proceeding should be instituted. Moreover, its finding of probable cause, while a necessary prerequisite to multiple seizures, has no effect in and of itself. All proceedings for the enforcement of the Act or to restrain violations of it must be brought by and in the name of the United States, sec. 307. Whether a suit will be instituted depends on the Attorney General, not on the administrative agency. He may or may not accept the agency's recommendation. If he does, seizures are made and libels are instituted. But the seizures and suits are dependent on the discretion of the Attorney General." In the instant case the person's license is suspended. Moreover, stress is laid upon the general public interest involved as distinguished from rights between individuals.

It should be noted that the United States Supreme Court has said since the Bourjois and Phillips cases: "The demands of due process do not require a hearing, at the initial stage or at any particular point or at more than one point in an administrative proceeding so long as the requisite hearing is held *before the final order becomes effective*." (Emphasis added.) (*Opp Cotton Mills v. Administrator of W. & H. Div.*, 312 U.S. 126, 152 [61 S.Ct. 524, 86 L.Ed. 624].) **[35 Cal.2d 882]**

In the case at bar no hearing has ever been accorded petitioner. His operator's license has been suspended.

Since his right to operate an automobile on the public highway is essential to his livelihood, I am constrained to hold that he has been deprived of property without due process of law, and the statute here involved is unconstitutional.

I would therefore issue the peremptory writ prayed for.

EDMONDS, J.—In my opinion, if the Department of Motor Vehicles may, without a hearing, summarily suspend the license of a person to operate a motor vehicle, the provisions of the Vehicle Code purporting to give that authority violate constitutional guarantees. As the court here construes the statute, one may lose a valuable property right without the opportunity even to show that the reported accident did not occur or, if there was such an accident, he was not the driver of an automobile causing personal injury or property damage.

The Vehicle Code, as it read in 1948 when Escobedo's license was suspended, provided that the Motor Vehicle Department shall "... within 60 days after the receipt of a report of a motor vehicle accident within this State which has resulted in bodily injury or death or damage to the property of any one person in excess of one hundred dollars ($100), suspend the license of each operator ... involved in such accident. ..." (Veh. Code, § 420(a).) The causes for suspension, therefore, are (1) the licensee was the operator of the vehicle involved in the accident; (2) less than 60 days have elapsed since the accident report was received; and (3) bodily injury resulted or property was damaged to an amount in excess of $100.

The license may not be suspended if the operator deposits security "in a sum which shall be sufficient in the judgment of the department to satisfy any judgment or judgments for damages resulting from such accident as may be recovered against such operator or owner." (Veh. Code, § 420(a).) An operator who alone suffers damage or injury or one who was driving a vehicle which was "... stopped, standing, or parked, whether attended or unattended ..." at the time of the accident, (unless he was doing so illegally or the vehicle lacked lighted lamps as required by law) does not have to meet this requirement. And suspension shall not be imposed upon one who has been released from liability, or has been finally adjudicated not liable, or has executed a confession of judgment or has executed an acknowledged agreement in [35 Cal.2d 883] writing providing for the payment of the amount of the damages resulting from the accident (§ 420.1).

Self-insurers are exempted from certain requirements of the law and other conditions are exacted of them (§ 420.7). Under some circumstances the license of a self-insured operator may not be suspended.

By these provisions, the Legislature has directed the Department of Motor Vehicles to suspend the license of an operator under specified circumstances or for certain causes, but only if his conduct, either at the time of the accident or subsequently, does not bring him within one of the stated exemptions which bars that action. This constitutes statutory authority to suspend an operator's license for enumerated causes only. Certainly the law contemplates a determination that the operator against whom action is proposed to be taken is the person who was involved in the accident reported as having occurred.

The administrative agency must also find whether personal injury occurred or property was damaged in extent of $100; whether the security demanded in the alternative to suspension is "sufficient in the judgment of the department"; whether any other policy or bond held by the driver is "... in the judgment of the department ..." sufficient; whether the vehicle was stopped, standing, or parked, and if so whether it was properly lighted; and finally, whether the operator is a self-insurer.

It is a well established principle that, under a statute providing for dismissal of an employee or revocation of a license "for cause," there must be notice and a hearing before such action may be taken. The rule has been applied to a teacher (*Keenan v. San Francisco Unified School Dist.*, 34 Cal.2d 708 [214 P.2d 382]); automobile operator (*Ratliff v. Lampton*, 32 Cal.2d 226 [195 P.2d 792, 10 A.L.R.2d 826]); liquor licensee (*Covert v. State Board of Equalization*, 29 Cal.2d 125 [173 P.2d 545]); horse trainer (*Carroll v. California Horse Racing Bd.*, 16 Cal.2d 164 [105 P.2d 110]); and civil servants generally (*La Prade v. Department of Water & Power*, 27 Cal.2d 47 [162 P.2d 13]; *Steen v. Board of Civil Service Commrs.*, 26 Cal.2d 716 [160 P.2d 816]). There is at least as much reason for requiring notice and hearing under a statute providing for deprivation of a license for any one of specifically enumerated causes as under legislation which allows such action "for cause" generally. Where the Legislature has [35 Cal.2d 884] enumerated the causes or conditions for which a license may be suspended, the requirement of notice and a hearing to determine the existence of those causes will be implied. Section 420(a) should be construed accordingly.

Moreover, section 420(a), under which Escobedo's license was suspended, should be read in conjunction with section 314, which is the general provision governing the suspension and revocation of an operator's license. The latter section provides for suspension or revocation of a license where, among other things, "... the licensee has been involved as a driver in any accident causing death or personal injury or serious damage to property ... [or where] ... the safety of ... persons upon the highway requires such action. ..."

Section 314 embodies express provision for notice and hearing, in that it requires an "investigation" and "reexamination of the licensee ... [upon] ... 10 days' written notice of the time and place thereof ..." and also provides for modification of any probation "... whenever good cause appears therefor." In *Ratliff v. Lampton*, supra, this court held that section 314 as

213

then worded required "... an investigation and hearing conducted by the department which would afford the licensee an opportunity to present evidence under the rule in the Carroll and Steen cases." At the time of the *Ratliff* decision, section 314 provided for a determination after investigation "that good cause exists" for suspension. The causes enumerated by the statute then, as now, included the determination that the licensee was "... involved as a driver in any accident causing death or personal injury or serious damage to property" and the rule of the Ratliff case in this regard remains unchanged. In fact, subsequent amendment providing for "reexamination" and "written notice" makes it all the more evident that the Legislature intended to continue in effect this court's construction of that section.

Cases such as *Surtman v. Secretary of State*, 309 Mich. 270 [15 N.W.2d 471]; *Nulter v. State Road Commission*, 119 W.Va. 312 [193 S.E. 549, 194 S.E. 270]; *LaPlante v. State Board of Public Roads*, 47 R. I. 258 [131 A. 641]; and *Sullins v. Butler*, 175 Tenn. 468 [135 S.W.2d 930], which hold that the operation of a motor vehicle upon a public highway is "merely a personal privilege, and is not a property right," either concerned that right in connection with the use of a pleasure vehicle or failed to recognize the evolution of modern transportation. Today the social and economic circumstances **[35 Cal.2d 885]** of many persons have placed a motor vehicle in the category of a necessity.

Escobedo's situation is a typical example of one in which the statute as now applied sweeps away established rights without opportunity for any defense of them. He is a gardener living at San Gabriel. By taking care of lawns and gardens there and in Pasadena, he supports himself, his wife and nine children. While driving his automobile from one place of his work to another, his vehicle collided with another one. The state can and does prescribe the qualifications which one must have to obtain a license allowing him to operate a motor vehicle. Failure to meet those requirements justifies denial of the license. But after it has been issued and one is relying upon it as a means of livelihood, a license to operate a motor vehicle attains the status of a property right. The suspension or revocation of such a license must meet the same requirements of procedural due process which have been applied in connection with a license to practice a profession.

The Motor Vehicle Department makes no claim that Escobedo was given a hearing. In an order of the department served upon him, he was told: "Since you have failed to otherwise meet the security requirements of section 420 of the Vehicle Code, you must now deposit security or have your driving privilege suspended." Such suspension was made effective 15 days after the date of the demand unless, in the meantime, security in the amount of $2,800 was deposited with the department. The attorney general does not contend that the department has made any determination of the respective liabilities of the operators of the two cars nor of the amount of damage caused by the crash. As far as the record shows, the order of suspension is based entirely upon the statements made in an "accident report" filed in one of its offices.

This is far from procedural due process. As succinctly stated in the *Ratliff* case, "It is contrary to commonly accepted principles of justice to revoke a license for cause without giving the person charged an opportunity to be heard before a decision is made, since the determination necessarily requires a fair consideration of any evidence offered by the licensee."

"Subsequent judicial review" of the department's action is no adequate substitute for a hearing in which the licensee would have an opportunity to present evidence tending to prove that he was not subject to the drastic sanction prescribed by the statute. This inadequacy is graphically illustrated by **[35 Cal.2d 886]** the present record. Escobedo was summarily ordered to surrender his license in September, 1948. When he declined to do so, he was advised that the authorities intended to arrest and prosecute him for having a revoked license in his possession. On January 18, 1949, he filed in this court his petition for writ of mandate. During the 20 months which have since elapsed, presumably he has been unable to carry on his work.

For these reasons, I would grant the writ of mandate

Supreme Court of California
Ex parte.—Frank Knowles, 5 Cal. 300 (1855)

July term
(headnotes omitted)

[300] HEYDENFELT, J., delivered the opinion of the Court. MURRAY, C J., and BRYAN, J., concurred.

This is an application on the part of an alien to become naturalized under provisions of the Constitution and laws of the United State. [301] It has been made directly to this Court, and has been resisted by several eminent members of the Bar, in the character of *amici curiæ*, on the ground that State Courts have no jurisdiction of the subject matter.

It might be a sufficient answer to the applicant to declare what is the settled decision of this Court, — that it is, under the State Constitution, an appellate tribunal, and can take no original jurisdiction, however conferred.

But the importance of the question which has been argued at the bar, and the learning and research which have been evinced in its examination, induce us, in departure from our usual habit to consider and determine the proper construction which should be given to the Constitution and laws of the United States, in respect to the question of naturalization. Two propositions which have been made by the counsel opposed to the applicant, will first be disposed of. These are: First — That the power to naturalize by virtue of the Act of Congress of 1802, is a judicial one; and Second — That Congress has no power to confer jurisdiction upon the Courts of a State. Upon both of these propositions we affirmatively concur. It is a judicial power; because upon evidence a conclusion has to be attained, resulting from the exercise of the judgment of the Court. This is simple and clear enough, without resorting to authority. But nevertheless, we will refer to the case of *Spratt v. Spratt*, 4 Peters, 406, where it is distinctly so settled by Chief Justice Marshall.

Congress has no power to confer jurisdiction upon the Courts of a State: because, First, the Constitution gives it no such power; and, Secondly the Constitution expressly declares that "the judicial power of the United States shall be vested in one Supreme Court and in such inferior Courts as the Congress may from time to time ordain and establish." See § 1, Art. 3, Const. U. S.

The Constitution having thus fixed where the judicial power shall be vested, it cannot be vested elsewhere.

There have been various adjudications maintaining this view, which it will be sufficient simply to cite. See *Martin v. Hunter's Lessee*, 1 Wheaton, 304. *The State of Maryland v. Thomas Butler*, reported [302] in 12 Niles' Register, p. 115; *United States v. Lathrop*, 17 Johnson

R., 4. *State v. McBride*, Rice R., 400.

It was urged in the course of the argument, and some authorities were cited, to the effect that although Congress could not confer jurisdiction on a State so as to compel its exercise, yet it would be legitimate if the Court was willing to accept it. This is to me a solecism. A court is a creature of the Constitution and laws under which it exists. To exercise any power not derived from such Constitution and laws, would necessarily be a usurpation. It sounds curious to say, Congress has no authority to give this power to the Court: yet the Court exercises this power by virtue of the authority of Congress."

I come now to the consideration of the main question, whether the State Courts of California, and if so, what State Courts, have the power to naturalize? —And I have come to the conclusion that this question is but little affected by the propositions which I have been already led to consider, on account of the seeming importance attached to them by the learned

215

counsel, and the able manner in which they were presented.

In §8, Art. I, of the Constitution, enumerating the powers of Congress, is the following separate clause: "To establish an uniform rule of naturalization and uniform laws on the subject of bankruptcy throughout the United States." By metaphysical refinement, in examining the form of our government it might be correctly said that there is no such thing as a citizen of the United States. But constant usage — arising from convenience, and perhaps necessity, and dating from the formation of the Confederacy — has given substantial existence to the idea which the term conveys. **A citizen of any one of the States of the Union, is held to be, and called a citizen of the United States, although technically and abstractly there is no such thing. To conceive a citizen of the United States who is not a citizen of some one of the States, is totally foreign to the idea, and inconsistent with the proper construction and common understanding of the expression as used in the Constitution, which must be deduced from its various other provisions.** The object then to be attained, by the exercise of the power of naturalization, was to make citizens of the respective States.

[303] At the time of the adoption of the Constitution, the States had power to make citizens of aliens. Does the clause of the Constitution above quoted deprive them of it?

The true rule of construction as to the exclusiveness of the power of Congress is, First — that it must be granted exclusively; Second — forbidden to the States; Third — from the nature of the power, its exercise by both must be incompatible and incongruous. Does the power under review come within either of these positions? If we examine the language closely, and according to the rules of rigid construction always applicable to delegated powers, we will find that the power to naturalize, in fact is not given to Congress, but simply the power to establish an uniform rule. The States are not forbidden to naturalize, nor is there anything in the exercise of the power by them, incongruous or incompatible with the power of Congress to establish an uniform rule. That the States, if they choose to exercise the power as an original one, must abide by the rule which Congress makes, there can not be the slightest difference of opinion. The power given to Congress was, according to my apprehension, intended to provide a rule for the action of the States, and not a rule for the action of the Federal Government. Else why was the term "uniform" made to qualify "rule?" If it was disigned simply to give the power of making citizens to Congress, simpler modes of expression might have been used, and ought to have been required, and surely there would have been no use for the term "uniform." Why should the rule be uniform, unless more than one had to execute the rule? It certainly could not have been imagined, that Congress would have made a rule for its own action or the action of its own officers, which could have operated without uniformity.

The States had the power to naturalize foreigners, and there was no necessity for this power to be surrendered to the General Government. But by another clause of the Constitution, § 1, Art. 4., it was determined that " the citizens of each State shall be entitled to the privileges and immunities of citizens in the several States." It might well have been apprehended, that in the feeble and sparsely populated condition of the States, a race would have been run for the acquisition of population, differing in its radicalism only according to the difference [304] of opinion as to the danger of the sudden introduction of too large a foreign element; and as, when once admitted to citizenship in one State, the alien would have all privileges in the other States, it would be in effect allowing one State to modify or break down the policy of another. This is made apparent by the discussions which then took place upon the subject Hence the necessity arose, not that Congress should have power to naturalize, but should have power to prescribe to the States a rule to be carried out by them, and which should be uniform in each. If this were not so, it follows conclusively that there is no mode by which a foreigner can be made expressly a citizen of a State, for I have already shown there is no such thing, technically as a citizen of the United States. **Consequently, one who is created a citizen of the United States, is certainly not made a citizen of any particular State. It follows, that as it is only the citizens of the State who are entitled to all privileges and immunities of citizens of the several States, if the process is left alone to the action of Congress through her federal tribunals, and in the form which they have adopted, then a distinction both in name and privileges**

216

is made to exist between citizens of the United States ex vi termini, and citizens of the respective States. To the former no privileges or immunities are granted; and it will hardly be contended, that political status can be derived by implication against express legal enactments. I cannot concede that such a result was ever contemplated, and yet it would be inevitable upon any other hypothesis, than that the "uniform rule," declared by the Constitution, was intended to be prescribed for the action of the States, and that by this rule they were left to exercise, or not, their original power of naturalization.

The next inquiry which is in proper order is, whether the State of California has determined, by her legislation, to admit foreigners to the rights of citizenship under the uniform rule established by the various Acts of Congress.

This question, in my opinion, is settled in the affirmative by an Act passed May 18, 1853, entitled "An Act to define the fees to be charged by the Clerks of Courts for the naturalization of foreigners." This Act after providing the amount of fees to be allowed the Clerks in **[305]** the process or making citizens, declares: "And said papers herein provided for shall be issued by the Court upon application of any individual entitled to receive them, and upon his complying with the provisions of the naturalization laws."

Much criticism might be indulged upon the form of this law; and upon the fact that its caption shows that it was intended only as a fee bill. But it must be conceded that in the construction of laws, the principal consideration is the intention of the law-maker. Governed by this rule, I have no hesitation in saying that the Act in question is equivalent to a direct and palpable declaration by the Legislature which enacted it, that it recognized the rule of naturalization prescribed for the States by Congress, and determined that the Courts of this State, of competent jurisdiction, should be vested with the power of carrying it out.

If this were not so, there was no reason whatever for passing the Act and Courts cannot decide an Act to be inoperative where a substantial meaning and design can be drawn from its expressions. In this Act the Courts are vested with jurisdiction: for they are required to issue the certificates of naturalization and to determine that the individual is entitled to receive them. The laws of Congress (the uniform rule) are recognized as the rule of action; for the term "Naturalization Laws," applies to none other, and their provisions are required, expressly, to be complied with.

What, however, are the Courts of competent jurisdiction? To answer this, we must turn to the Act of Congress of 1802, and be governed by the rule there established. Congress having power under the Constitution to make the rule, certainly had the right to make the exercise of it a judicial power, and fix upon the class of Courts which might be invested with the jurisdiction. This it could do as a part of the rule, although it might not directly confer the jurisdiction. **By the third section of the Act of 1802, it is enacted "that every Court of Record in any individual State, having common law jurisdiction and a seal, and clerk or prothonotary, shall be considered as a District Court within the meaning of this Act."**

We have already determined that this Court has not the jurisdiction: **[306]** because its powers are, exclusively, appellate. The District Courts of this State are Courts of original and common law jurisdiction; are Courts of Record; and have a seal and clerk, and consequently come fully within the description of the rule laid down by the Act of 1802; and, therefore, under the Act of this State of 1858, are fully invested with power and jurisdiction to naturalize foreigners who exhibit the qualifications fixed by the laws of the United States. The other Courts of this State are inferior and of limited powers. They are made Courts of Record by our statutes, but they have only statute and not common law jurisdiction; and, therefore, not coming within the class enumerated by the Act of Congress, have no power to grant naturalization, and any attempt of the kind would be necessarily *coram non judice* and void.

For the want of jurisdiction in this Court the application is denied

Supreme Court of Alabama
Gardina v. Board of Registrars,
160 Ala. 155, 48 S. Rep. 788 (1909)

July term
(headnotes omitted)

[788]
[789] William Conniff, for appellant Alexander K. Garber, Atty. Gen., for appellee.

MAYFIELD, J. We agree with counsel for appellant that there is but one question to be decided on this appeal, namely, can a man of foreign birth be registered as an elector of this state, on his mere declaration of intention to become a citizen of the state and the United States? The law regulating this subject is as follows:

Const. Ala. 1901, § 177:

"Every male citizen of this state who is a citizen of the United States, and every male resident of foreign birth, who, before the ratification of this Constitution, shall have legally declared his intention to become a citizen of the United States, twenty-one years old or upwards, not laboring under any of the disabilities named in this article, and possessing the qualifications required by it shall be an elector, and shall be entitled to vote at any election by the people: Provided, that all foreigners who have legally declared their intention to become citizens of the United States, shall, if they fail to become citizens thereof at the time they are entitled to become such, cease to have the right to vote until they become such citizens."

Const. Ala. 1875, § 2 art. 1:

"That all persons resident In this state, born in the United States, or naturalized, or who shall have legally declared their intention to become citizens of the United States, are hereby declared citizens of the state of Alabama, possessing equal civil and political rights."

Code Ala. 1907, §§ 290, 291:

"290. Qualification of Elector to Vote.— Every male citizen of this state who is a citizen of the United states, and every male resident of foreign birth, who, before the ratification of the present Constitution of the state, shall have legally declared his intention to become a citizen of the United States, twenty-one years old or upwards, not laboring under any of the disabilities named in section 293 (1557) of this Code, and who shall have resided in this state at least two years, In the county one year, and in the precinct or ward three months, immediately preceding the election at which be offers to vote, and who shall have been duly registered as an elector, and shall have paid on or before the first day of February next preceding the date of the election at which he offers to vote, all poll taxes due from him for the year 1901, and for each subsequent year, shall be an elector, and shall be entitled to vote at any election by the people.

"291. Foreigners, Right to Vote.— All foreigners, who shall have legally declared their intention to become citizens of the United States shall, if they fail to become citizens thereof at the time they are entitled to become such, cease to have the right to vote until they become such citizens."

Code of Alabama, 1907, § 312:

"Persons Qualified to Register.— The following persons, and no others, who, if their place of residence shall remain unchanged, will have, at the date of the next general election the qualifications as to residence prescribed by section 290 (1556) of this Code [790] shall be qualified to register as electors, provided they shall not be disqualified under section 293 (1557) of this Code," etc.

219

Elections are the machines through which the voice of the people acting in their sovereign capacity is transformed into law. These elections must be exercised at the time, place, and in the manner prescribed by the Constitution and statutes which the people, through their agents, have constituted. By means of elections the people choose these officers, and choose those who shall exercise the legislative, executive, and judicial functions of the government. The Constitutions of the various states contain provisions that certain specific propositions, such as amendments of Constitutions, removal of county seats, election of officers, etc., shall be determined by the vote of the electors, either by a majority or sometimes by two-thirds majority of the electors. While the sovereignty is in the people, theoretically speaking, practically considered it resides in those persons only who are permitted to exercise the right of elective franchise. Cooley, Const. Lim. 752.

The power to determine who are qualified electors and who are entitled to exercise the elective franchise is left to the several states. The federal Constitution does not prescribe the regulations as to this matter, except that the electors for Representatives in Congress shall have the qualifications requisite for electors of the most numerous branch of the State Legislature, and also the fifteenth amendment, which forbids the state from denying any citizen the right to vote on account of race, color, or previous condition of servitude. The exercise of elective franchise is a privilege, and not a right. The state may grant or deny the right. Aliens are denied the right. The fifteenth amendment does not deny the state the right to forbid any person from voting, but only provides that he shall not be excluded on account of his race, color, or previous condition of servitude. Minors and women may be and are usually excluded from the right to vote, and also those who have been convicted of infamous crimes, also idiots and lunatics, also nonresidents of the state, county or municipality, etc., in which the election is to be held; but these are not the only qualifications that the states may require. They may require any qualification, or exclude any person or class of persons, unless the federal Constitution or the state Constitution forbids it. The state may provide registration laws, and require that citizens conform thereto before they are entitled to vote. It is no excuse to the validity of such law that the registering officer may neglect to perform every duty and thereby disenfranchise the electors. The remedy would be for the elector to compel the performance of the duty. But regulations as to the elective franchise must be reasonable and uniform and impartial, and they should not deny or abridge the constitutional right of the citizen, nor unnecessarily impede its exercise. Statutes may prescribe the time and place of elections, and they may also prescribe the notice to be given of the election. Cooley, Const Lim. 757, 758.

It will be observed that the Constitution of 1901, and the election laws thereafter, wrought a complete change in the qualifications of electors and mode of registration as prerequisites to vote. It is also clear that only those foreigners who had declared their intention before the adoption of the Constitution of 1901 could register or vote thereafter, and they must have become citizens at the time they were entitled to become such, else they lost their right to vote or register until they did become citizens. The Code provisions on this subject were evidently intended to make these constitutional provisions perpetual, so as to apply to future cases.

The election laws, statute or Code, do not authorize these foreigners who have merely declared their intention to become citizens of the United States since the Constitution of 1901 was ratified, but who have not perfected their naturalization as required, to register or vote in this state, and it is doubtful if the Legislature could so authorize. It appearing that the appellant in this case had declared his intention of becoming a citizen since the ratification of the Constitution, and that he had not perfected his naturalization and was not a citizen at the time he applied for registration it follows that be cannot register until be perfects his naturalization, unless be is a "citizen of this state" within the meaning of the election laws of this state.

It will be observed that section 2, art 1, of the Constitution of 1875, defined or prescribed who were citizens of this state, and that appellant would be a citizen under that section; but it also appears that that section was not embraced in, or adopted as a part of, the Constitution of 1901, and there is no substitute for it in the new Constitution. We must therefore, resort to other sources for a definition of "citizen of this state." The word "citizen" has come to us from the Roman law. In Roman law it designated a person who had the freedom of the city of Rome and could exercise the political and civil privileges of the Roman government. 2 Kent Com. p.76, note. It was both an honor and a sacred privilege to be a Roman citizen. Paul, the great Apostle of the Gentiles, claimed and asserted the right of a Roman citizen when apprehended in Jerusalem. The chief captain answered him: "With a great sum obtained I this freedom: but Paul said, 'I was free born.'" Again this great Apostle is heard to say: "I am a man which am a Jew, of Tarsus, a city in Cilicia, a citizen of no mean city." Citizenship [791] has always been regarded as the most sacred right or privilege that the sovereign can confer. Mr. Webster defines "citizen" as "a person, native or naturalized, who has the privilege of voting for public officers and who is qualified to fill public offices in the gift of the people; also either native-born or naturalized persons who are entitled to full participation in the exercise and enjoyment of so-called private rights." Bouvier says a citizen, in American law, is one who, under the Constitution and law of the United States, has a right to vote for Representatives in Congress and other public officers and who is qualified to fill offices in the gift of the people; that all persons, born or naturalized, in the United States and subject to the jurisdiction thereof, are citizens of the United States and of the state where in they reside.

The Supreme Court of Nebraska has held that "citizen," as used in that Constitution, relative to the right to hold office, means a person who is an American citizen by birth or a person of foreign birth who has been naturalized. *State v. Boyd*, 31 Neb. 682, 48 N. W. 739, 51 N. W. 602. The Constitution of the United States provides; "All persons born or naturalized In the United States, and subject to the jurisdiction thereof, are citizens of the United States and of the State wherein they reside." Const Amend. 14. Congress of the United States has exclusive power to provide for naturalization, and is required to establish a uniform rule for all states, though it may provide for naturalization to be acquired by and through state courts. Const U.S. art 1, § 8, subd. 4. Naturalization is therefore a national right and privilege, rather than a matter of state concern. *Scott v. Strobach*, 49 Ala. 490.

There are, then, under our republican form of government, two classes of citizens, one of the United States and one of the state. One class of citizenship may exist in a person, without the other, as in the ease of a resident of the District of Columbia; but both classes usually exist in the same person. The federal Constitution, by this amendment, has undertaken to say who shall be citizens both of the states and United States. Prior to this amendment, the states could probably have determined, respectively, who were citizen, of each, though naturalization has been exclusively a national subject, rather than, a state, since the federal Constitution was first adopted. Consequently we find no authority, state or national, for registering appellant as an elector of this State.

The judgment of the lower court is affirmed.

Affirmed.

TYSON, C. J., and SIMPSON and DENSON, JJ., concur.

United States District Court
Jones v. Temmer, 829 F.Supp. 1226 (1993)

August 11, 1993.
(headnotes omitted)

[1226]
[1227]
[1228]

Paula Connely, Gorsuch, Kirgis, Campbell, Walker and Grover, Denver, CO, William H. Mellor III, Institute for Justice, Washington, DC, for plaintiffs.

Mana L. Jennin—Fader, Jeffrey A. Froeschle, Asst. Attys. Gen., Regulatory Law Section, Denver, C0, for defendants.

MEMORANDUM OPINION AND ORDER
BABCOCK, District Judge.

Plaintiffs Leroy Jones, Ani Ebong, Rowland Nwankwo, Girma Molalegne, and Quick Pick Cabs, Inc. (Quick Pick), have brought this action for injunctive and declaratory relief against Robert Temmer, Christine Alvarez, and Vincent Majowski (collectively, defendants or commissioners) claiming violation of rights protected by the Fourteenth Amendment to the Constitution. Specifically, in Count I plaintiffs allege violations of the privileges and immunities clause and deprivation of substantive due process. In Count II plaintiffs allege violations of the equal protection clause of the Fourteenth Amendment. Finally, in Count III plaintiff Tillman asserts a separate Fourteenth [1229] Amendment equal protection claim. Plaintiffs seek a judgment declaring that the system of Colorado state laws and regulations governing Denver taxicab business, as applied, effectively prohibits entry into the business, violates their substantive due process rights and is thus unconstitutional. In addition, plaintiffs seek to enjoin defendants from enforcing Colorado's state regulatory process and policies in a manner that unreasonably interferes with their right and opportunity to provide taxi service within the Denver metropolitan area.

Plaintiffs bring this action pursuant to the Fourteenth Amendment of the Constitution, 42 U.S.C. § 1983, and 28 U.S.C. § 2201. Jurisdiction is claimed pursuant to 28 U.S.C. §§ 1331 and 1343.

Defendants move to dismiss the amended complaint or, in the alternative, for summary judgment with respect to all counts of the amended complaint. They file this motion pursuant to Federal Rules of Civil Procedure 12(b)(1), 12(b)(6), 12(b)(7), and 56(b).

As the basis for this motion defendants state: 1) plaintiffs Quick Pick Cabs, Inc., Leroy Jones, Ani Ebong, and Rowland Nwankwo, and Girma Molalegne lack standing to bring a portion of the first claim for relief; 2) plaintiff Tillman lacks standing to bring the third claim for relief; 3) the applicable principles of abstention enunciated in *Colorado River Water Conservation Dist., v. U.S.*, 424 U.S. 800, 96 S.Ct 1236, 47 L.Ed.2d 483(1976), and in *Bufford v. Sun Oil Co.*, 319 U.S. 315, 63 S.Ct 1098, 87 L.Ed. 1424 (1943), require abstention in this case; 4) plaintiffs have failed to join necessary parties under Fed.R.Civ.P. 19; 5) plaintiffs have failed to state a cause or action upon which relief can be granted under any count in the amended complaint; and 6) summary judgment is appropriate in this case as there are no genuine issues of material fact and defendants are entitled to judgment as a matter of law.

For the reasons set forth below I conclude that 1) Quick pick Cabs, Inc., and Ani Ebong lack standing to bring a claim under the privileges and immunities clause; 2) Tillman lacks standing to bring the third claim for relief; 3)1 decline to abstain in this case; 4) taxicab companies operating in Denver are not necessary parties under Rule 19(a); 5) plaintiffs first and second claims will be dismissed for failure to state a cause of action under the privileges and immunities clause, substantive due process and equal protection; and 6) plaintiff Tillman's third claim will be dismissed for lack of standing and alternatively, for failure to state a claim. Because Rule 12 applies to resolve defendants' motions, I need not address their Rule 56 arguments.

I.

Under Colorado Revised Statutes § 40-10-102, taxicabs are deemed motor vehicle carriers, and as such are regulated as public utilities by the Public Utilities Commission (PUC). § 4O-10-102, 17 C.R.S. (1984). The PUC is a regulatory agency created pursuant to Article XXV of the Colorado Constitution. It regulates taxicabs pursuant to Articles 1 through 7, inclusive, Article 10 of Title 40 of the Colorado Revised Statutes, and pursuant to the rules and regulations found at 4 Code of Colorado Regulations 723, promulgated pursuant to statutory authority.

The regulatory scheme in Colorado for common carriers of passengers, including taxicabs, is regulated monopoly. This state policy is found in § 40-5-IO1, 17 C.R.S. (1984). The policy "was designed to prevent duplication of facilities and competition between utilities, and to authorize new utilities in a field only when existing ones are found to be inadequate." *Public Serv. Co. v. Public Utilities Comm'n of State of Colo.*, 765 P.2d 1015, 1021 (Colo.1988).

Anyone seeking to operate a taxicab business in Colorado must obtain a "certificate of public convenience and necessity" (CPCN) from the PUG. Under the current regulatory scheme, an applicant for a CPCN has the burden of demonstrating (1) that existing service in an area is substantially inadequate, and (2) that existing companies cannot provide adequate service. Once a CPCN is obtained no other utility may provide service in that territory unless it is established that the certified utility is unable or unwilling to provide adequate service. This exclusive right to serve an area is a **[1230]** property right which cannot be affected except by due process of law. Public Serv. Co., 785 P.2d at 1021. Until changed by the state General Assembly, the doctrine of regulated monopoly governs and restricts the PUC in exercising its discretion in the area of granting CPCNs to taxicabs. See *Rocky Mountain Airways Inc. v. Public Utilities Comm'n*, 181 Colo. 170, 509 P.2d 804, 807 (1973).

Plaintiffs Jones, Ebong, Nwankwo, and Molalegne formed Quick Pick, a Colorado corporation, and in July, 1992, Quick Pick filed an application with the PUC seeking a CPCN to operate a taxicab service in the Denver metro area. The existing Denver taxicab companies, along with 10 other companies operating elsewhere in Colorado, intervened to protest the application. At present, three companies, Yellow Cab, Zone Cab, and Metro Taxi, hold CPCNs and are authorized to provide taxicab service in the Denver metropolitan area. On November 23-24, 1992, the PUC conducted a hearing before an administrative law judge on Quick Pick Cabs' application. At the end of the hearing, the application was dismissed without prejudice.

II.

A. Abstention

As a preliminary matter, defendants move to dismiss the amended complaint based on the doctrine of abstention. The doctrine of abstention represents "an extraordinary and narrow exception to the duty of a district court to adjudicate a controversy properly before it." *Smith v. Paulk*, 705 F.2d 1279,1282 (10th Cir.1982) (quoting *Colorado River Water Conservation Dist. v. U.S.*, 424 U.S 800, 813, 96 S.Ct 1236, 1244, 47 L.Ed.2d 483 (1976)). The decision to abstain is largely committed to the discretion of the district court. *Ramos v. Lamm*, 639 F.2d 559, 564 n. 4 (10th Cir.1980), cert. denied, 450 U.S. 1041, 101 S.Ct. 1759, 68 L.Ed.2d 239 (1981).

Defendants argue that abstention is appropriate here because this case falls squarely within the principles enunciated in *Colorado River Conservation Dist. v. U.S.*, 424 U.S. 800,

96 S.Ct. 1236, 47 L.Ed.2d 483 (1978) and *Buford v. Sun Oil Co.*, 319 U.S. 315, 63 S.Ct 1098, 87 L.Ed. 1424 (1943). The principle distilled from these cases is that where timely and adequate state-court review is available, a federal court sitting in equity must decline to interfere with the proceedings or orders of state administrative agencies: (1) when there are "difficult questions of state law bearing on policy problems of substantial public import whose importance transcends the result in the case then at bar"; or (2) where the "exercise of federal review of the question in a case and in similar cases would be disruptive of state efforts to establish a coherent policy with respect to a matter of substantial public concern." *Colorado River Water Conservation Dist., v. U.S.*, 424 U.S. 800, 814, 96 S.Ct. 1236, 1245, 47 L.Ed.2d 483 (1976). Defendants argue that the applicable ground for abstention in this case is that the case presents difficult questions of state law bearing on policy problems of substantial public import with importance that transcends the result in this case. They assert that if this court were to modify either the basic nature of Colorado's regulatory policy or any part of the overall regulatory scheme, the modification would have ramifications and repercussions that would ripple throughout the reminder of the comprehensive and complex regulatory scheme established by the Colorado legislature and administered by the commission.

In *Buford v. Sun Oil*, a Federal District Court sitting in equity was confronted with a Fourteenth Amendment challenge to the reasonableness of the Texas Railroad Commission's grant of an oil drilling permit. The constitutional challenge was of minimal federal importance, involving solely the question whether the commission had properly applied Texas' complex oil and gas conservation regulations. 319 U.S. at 331 and n. 28, 63 S.Ct. at 1106 and n. 28. Abstention was appropriate in that case because the state courts had acquired a specialized knowledge of the regulations and industry. *Id.* at 327, 63 S.Ct. at 1104.

Here, plaintiffs seek relief for alleged violations of their constitutionally based civil rights under 42 U.S.C. § 1983. The obligation to exercise jurisdiction is particularly **[1231]** weighty when relief is sought pursuant to 42 U.S.C. § 1983. *San Francisco County Democratic Cent. Comm. v. Eu*, 826 F.2d 814, 825 n. 19 (9th Cir. 1987). This case does not involve a federal claim entangled in a complex state regulatory scheme. Although my inquiry in this case could result in an injunction against the enforcement of the state regulatory scheme as applies to these plaintiff's, abstention is not required merely because resolution of a federal question may result in the overturning of a state policy. *Zablocki V. Redhail*, 434 U.S. 374, 380 n. 5, 98 S.Ct 673, 678 n. 5, 54 L.Ed.2d 618 (1978). I decline to abstain from hearing plaintiffs' claims in this case.

B. Failure to Join Parties Under Rule 19

Defendants argue that taxicab companies operating in Colorado generally, and in the Denver area specifically, are necessary parties under Rule 19 and must be joined as defendants in this action, and if they cannot be joined, the action must be dismissed pursuant to Rule 12(b)(7).

To show that the taxicab companies are indispensable parties, defendants must establish that the companies fall within Rule 19(a)'s definition of necessary parties. Once a party has been found "necessary," Rule 19(b) provides factors to be considered to determine whether the suit should he dismissed if joinder of the party destroys jurisdiction. See Fed.R.Civ.P 19(a). A party is "necessary" under Rule 19(a) if:

(1) in the person's absence complete relief cannot be accorded among those already parties, or (2) the person claims an interest relating to the subject of the action and is so situated that the disposition of the action in the person's absence may (i) as a practical matter impair or impede the person's ability to protect that interest or (ii) leave any of the persons already parties subject to a substantial risk of incurring double, multiple, or otherwise inconsistent obligations by reason of the claimed interest.

Fed.R.Civ.P. 19(a).

There are at present 38 persons or entities in Colorado holding CPCNs to operate as taxicab companies. Defendants argue that current holders of CPCNs are necessary parties under both 19(a)(2)(i) and 19(a)(2)(ii). Defendants contend that the question of the constitutionality of the regulatory scheme governing taxicabs as applied to these plaintiffs raises the state law issue of protection of the property rights of the present taxicab CFCN holders. Defendants argue that the current holders of CPCNs are so situated that the disposition of this case in their absence may, as a practical matter, impair or impede their ability to protect that interest. See Fed.R.Civ.P. 19(a)(2)(i). Alternatively, defendants assert that because disposition of this case in the absence of these taxicabs companies may leave one or more of the present parties subject to a substantial risk of incurring inconsistent obligations, the CPCN holders must be joined as defendants. Fed.R.Civ.P. 19(a)(2)(ii). I find no merit in defendants arguments. Since I conclude that 19(a) does not apply 19(b) cannot be applied to dismiss the action.

C. Standards for Dismissal

Under Rule 12(b)(6), a district court may dismiss a complaint for failure to state a claim upon which relief can be granted if it appears beyond doubt that the plaintiff can prove no set of facts in support of his claim which would entitle him to relief. *Conley v. Gibson*, 355 U.S. 41, 45-46, 78 S.Ct. 99, 101-102, 2 L.Ed.2d 80 (1957). In reviewing the sufficiency of the complaint, all well-pled facts, as opposed to conclusory allegations, must be taken as true. *Weissmann v. Kirkland & Ellis*, 732 F.Supp. 1540, 1543 (D.Colo. 1990). All reasonable inferences must be liberally construed in the plaintiff's favor. *Id.*

D . Standing

Before the plaintiffs filed their amended complaint, the commission filed a motion to dismiss pursuant to Fed.R.Civ.P. 12(b)(1) asserting that this court lacks subject matter jurisdiction because plaintiffs lack standing to bring a portion of the first claim for relief and the entirety of the third claim for relief. Defendants renew this motion now.

[1232] The focus of an inquiry into standing "is whether the litigant is entitled to have the court decide the merits of the dispute or of particular issues. This inquiry involves both constitutional limitations on federal-court jurisdiction and prudential limitations on its exercise...." *Warth v. Seldin*, 422 U.S. 490, 498, 95 S.Ct 2197, 2205, 45 L.Ed.2d 343 (1975). The constitutional limitations of standing are derived from Article III, which limits judicial power to cases and controversies.

To overcome the Article III limitation on standing, often referred to as the "injury in fact" requirement, a plaintiff must at a minimum show an actual or threatened injury caused by the defendant and that a favorable judicial decision is likely to redress the injury. *Valley Forge Christian College v. American United for Separation of Church and State Inc.*, 454 U.S. 464, 472, 102 S.Ct. 752, 758, 70 L.Ed.2d 700 (1982). There are, in addition, prudential principles applying to standing that limit the class of persons who may invoke a courts' powers. Id. at 474, 102 S.Ct. at 759-6O. In *Valley Forge Christian College*, the court listed the three "prudential principles": (1) the plaintiff must assert his own rights and may not rely on the constitutional rights of third parties; (2) the court must not adjudicate "generalized grievances" that are more appropriately addressed by the executive or legislative branches of government; and (3) the plaintiff must come within the zone of interests to be protected or related by the statute or constitutional guarantee in question. *Id.* at 474-475, 102 S.Ct. at 759-60.

Defendants first argue that plaintiff Quick Pick has no standing to bring the first cause of action. According to paragraph 8 of the complaint, plaintiff Quick Pick is a corporation. The Tenth Circuit has held that a corporation has no standing to maintain a claim under the privileges and immunities clause of the Fourteenth Amendment. *Smith v. Paulk*, 705 F.2d 1279, 1282 (10th Cir. 1983). The privileges and immunities claim with respect to Quick Pick Cabs, Inc. will be dismissed for lack of standing.

Second, defendants argue that plaintiff Ebong has no standing to maintain a claim under the privileges and immunities clause because he is not a citizen of the United States. See *Banerjee v. Roberts*, 641 F.Supp. 1093, 1103 (D.Conn. 1985). By its terms, § 1 of the Fourteenth Amendment protects only "persons born or naturalized in the United States." By his own admission, plaintiff Ebong is neither; he is a "permanent resident of the United States."

(Complaint ¶ 5.) Thus, the privileges and immunities claim with respect to plaintiff Ebong will be dismissed for lack of standing.

Defendants further argue that all plaintiffs lack standing to bring the privileges and immunities portion of the first claim for relief because that clause protects nonresidents of Colorado from discrimination based on their nonresident status, and here, each plaintiff is a resident of Colorado. Plaintiffs respond that defendants have confused the privileges and immunities clause or the Fourteenth Amendment with the privileges and immunities clause under Article IV, section 2 of the Constitution. **The privileges and immunities clause of the Fourteenth Amendment protects very few rights because it neither incorporates any of the Bill of Rights nor protects all rights of individual citizens.** See *Slaughter-House Cases*, 83 U.S. (16 Wall.) 36, 21 L.Ed. 394 (1873). **Instead, this provision protects only those rights peculiar to being a citizen of the federal government; it does not protect those rights which relate to state citizenship.** *Id.* Accordingly, it is not necessary that plaintiffs have non-resident status in order to bring a claim under the privileges and immunities clause of the Fourteenth Amendment. As discussed below in section E(a), however, plaintiffs have failed to state a claim under the privileges and immunities clause or the Fourteenth Amendment.

Finally, defendants argue that plaintiff Tillman has no standing to bring the third claim for relief. In the third claim, Tillman alleges that: he is a member of the general public in Denver; he uses taxicabs in Denver; Colorado's regulatory scheme for taxicabs artificially limits the availability of taxicabs in Denver; and, as a result, he and **[1233]** other individuals in the neighborhood in which he lives and resides are denied "opportunities equal to those of other Denver residents to enjoy taxicab service." (Complaint at 14.) On these allegations, Tillman brings his claim of deprivation of his rights to equal protection under the Fourteenth Amendment.

Defendants argue that Tillman cannot prove a fairly traceable causal relationship between Colorado's regulatory scheme and his alleged injury. They also contend that Tillman has not shown, and cannot prove without engaging in gross speculation, that he will have any greater access to taxicab service in Denver if this court grants his request for declaratory and injunctive relief. Defendants further argue that Tillman asserts no special harm personal to him, but rather complains only about the general unavailability of taxicabs in some neighborhoods of Denver and complains that this has incidentally affected him.

As to defendants allegation that Tillman has alleged only a generalized grievance, Tillman need only allege a distinct and palpable injury to himself, even if it is an injury shared by a large class of other possible litigants. *Warth*, 422 U.S. at 501,95 S.Ct. at 2206. I find that Tillman has satisfied this requirement. I conclude, however, that defendants other arguments have merit.

Accepting his allegations as true, and construing the complaint in his favor, Tillman has failed to allege facts from which I can reasonably infer that, absent the defendants' restrictive regulatory scheme, there is a substantial probability that he would have access to taxicabs equal to that of other Denver residents. See *Warth v. Seldin*, 422 U.S. at 505-07, 95 S.Ct. at 2208-10. In addition, I am unable to infer that if I grant the relief requested, there is a substantial probability that the perceived inequity will be removed. See *Id.* I conclude, therefore, that Tillman lacks standing to bring the third claim for relief.

E. First Claim for Relief

The Supreme Court has established two necessary elements for recovery of damages under a 42 U.S.C. § 1983 civil rights claim. A plaintiff must prove that the defendant has deprived him of a right secured by the United States Constitution and, second, that the defendant deprived plaintiff of this right under color of state law. *Adickes v. S.H. Kress & Co.*, 398 U.S. 144, 150, 90 S.Ct. 1598, 1604, 26 L.Ed.2d 142 (1970).

Here, defendants do not dispute that all actions were taken under color of State law; the only issue is whether plaintiffs suffered a constitutional deprivation. Plaintiffs allege violations of their Fourteenth Amendment rights. I will address, seriatim, plaintiffs claims relating to privileges and immunities, substantive due process and equal protection.

a) Privileges and Immunities

Plaintiffs Jones, Ebong, Nwankwo, Molalegne, and Quick Pick Cabs, Inc. seek declaratory and injunctive relief based on the allegation that the Colorado regulatory regime for taxicabs deprives them of privileges and immunities of citizenship under the Fourteenth Amendment. That which plaintiffs seek to redress in this context is their "basic right to pursue their chosen livelihoods and to operate a legitimate business." Amended Complaint at 1.)

The privileges and immunities clause of the Fourteenth Amendment protects very few rights. To my knowledge, in the history of the United States Supreme Court, only one decision determined that a state violated this provision and that decision was overturned within a few years. *Colgate v. Harvey*, 296 U.S. 404, 56 S.Ct. 252, 80 L.Ed. 299 (1935), overruled in *Madden v. Commonwealth of Kentucky*, 309 U.S. 83, 60 S.Ct. 406, 84 L.Ed. 590 (1940). **In the** *Slaughter-House Cases*, **83 U.S. (16 Wall.) 36, 21 L.Ed. 394 (1873), the Supreme Court held that this clause neither incorporates the Bill of Rights nor protects all rights of individual citizens. Rather the provision protects only those rights peculiar to being a citizen of the United States; it does not protect those rights which relate to state citizenship.** As a court of this district noted, "the argument that the clause creates a substantive right to pursue one's lawful occupation or profession free from state limitations was laid to rest long **[1234]** ago by the United States Supreme Court." *Galahad v. Weinshienk*, 555 F.Supp. 1201, 1207 (D.Colo. 1983). Here, plaintiffs have failed to allege that defendants have eliminated a federal right protected by the privileges and immunities clause. I will dismiss the privileges and immunities claim against all defendants for failure to state a claim upon which relief can be granted.

b) Substantive Due Process

Plaintiffs Jones, Ebong, Nwankwo Molalegne, and Quick Pick Cabs, Inc., seek declaratory and injunctive relief claiming that Colorado's regulatory regime for taxicabs deprives them of due process under the Fourteenth Amendment. Plaintiffs make a substantive due process attack on the Colorado regulatory scheme.

The due process clause of the Fourteenth Amendment includes a substantive component which guards against arbitrary and capricious government action. *Sinaloa Lake Owners Ass'n v. City, of Simi Valley*, 882 F.2d 1398,140? (9th Cir. 1989), cert. denied, 494 U.S. 1016, 110 S.Ct. 1317, 108 L.Ed.2d 493 (1990). Substantive due process imposes limits on what a state may do regardless of what procedural protection is provided. *Harrington v. Almy*, 977 F.2d 37, 43 (1st Cir. 1992) (quoting *Pittsley v. Warish* 927 F.2d 3, 6 (1st Cir.) cert. denied — U.S. — ,112 S.Ct. 226, 116 L.Ed.2d 183 (1991).

The Tenth Circuit case law is unclear on what interest is required to trigger substantive due process guarantees. *Compare Harris v. Blake*, 798 F.2d 419, 424 (10th Cir. 1986), *cert. denied* 479 U.S. 1033, 107 S.Ct. 882, 93 L.Ed.2d 836 (1987) (claim for denial of substantive due process requires that plaintiff allege a liberty or property interest); *Brenna v. Southern Colorado State College*, 589 F.2d 475, 476 (10th Cir. 1978) (same); *Weathers v. West Ynina County School Dist.*, 536, F.2d 1335, 1342 (10th Cir. 1976) (same), with *Mangels v. Pena*, 789 F.2d 836, 839 (10th Cir. 1986) ("Rights or substantive due process are founded not upon state provisions but upon deeply rooted notions of fundamental personal interests derived from the Constitution.") The interest alleged by the plaintiffs, their liberty to pursue a chosen livelihood has not been treated as a fundamental right by the courts. *See City of New Orleans v. Dukes*, 427 U.S. 297, 303-04, 96 S.Ct. 2513. 2516-17, 49 L.Ed.2d 511(1976); Harper v. Lindsay, 616 F.2d 849, 854 (5th Cir.1980). Nor is the mere denial of a business or employment opportunity "without more," the deprivation of a liberty interest because plaintiffs ability to obtain future business or employment opportunities is not jeopardized. *Bannum, Inc. v. Town of Ashland*, 922 F.2d 197, 201 (4th Cir. 1990). The necessary "more" referred to by the court is provided when there is either public disparagement damaging to an individual's standing in the opportunity or a stigmatic injury to an employment interest likely to impair future work-related opportunities.

Schneeweis v. Jacobs, 771 F.Supp. 733, 737 (E.D.Va. 1991). aff'd 966 F.2d 1444 (4th Cir. 1992). Here, plaintiffs allege no public disparagement or stigmatic injury to their future ability to obtain employment.

Even assuming arguendo a protectable interest, I conclude that plaintiffs have failed to state a claim under substantive due process. The regulatory scheme at issue here is economic or business regulation based on the exercise of Colorado's police powers. Colorado's scheme for the regulation of motor vehicle carriers of passengers does not employ any classification based on a "suspect" category. Further, the regulatory scheme does not implicate any fundamental constitutionally-protected values. Thus, the substantive due process inquiry requires me to determine if the governmental action is rationally related to a legitimate state interest. *Allright Colorado, Inc., v. City and County of Denver*, 937 F.2d 1502, 1511 (10th Cir.), *cert. denied* — U.S. —, 112 S.Ct. 587, 116 L.Ed.2d 612 (1991).

Governmental bodies have "wide latitude in enacting social and economic legislation; the federal courts do not sit as arbiters of the wisdom or utility of these laws." *Allright Colorado*, 937 F.2d at 1512, quoting *Alamo Rent-A—Car, Inc.*, 825 F.2d at 370. I need not satisfy myself that the challenged rules will in fact further their articulated purposes; it is sufficient if the Colorado General Assembly could rationally have concluded that [1235] the purposes would be achieved. See *Allright Colorado*, 937 F.2d at 1512.

The Colorado Supreme Court has specifically identified the following as public health, welfare, and safety interests justifying public utility regulation: (1) prevention of, or reduction of, distinctive use of the public highways, *Public Utilities Comm. v. Manley*, 99 Colo. 153, 60 P.2d 913, 919 (1936); (2) increased safety of those traveling on or using the public highways, *McKay V. Public Utilities Comm'n*, 104 Colo. 402, 91 P.2d 965, 969 (1939): (3) coordination of commercial motor vehicle transportation on the public highways, Id.; and (4) prevention, "in the interest of the general public, [of] unnecessary duplication of facilities or systems for furnishing [service] to customers," *Public Serv. Co. v. Public Utilities Comm'n*, 142 Colo. 135, 350 P.2d 548, 550 (1960), *cert. denied*, 364 U.S. 820, 81 S.Ct. 53, 5 L.Ed.2d 50 (1960). Plaintiffs agree that a legitimate state interest exists in protecting the public health, safety, and welfare and contest only whether the regulatory scheme is rationally related to protecting these legitimate interests. I find and conclude that they clearly are rationally related to a legitimate Colorado state interest. I will, therefore, dismiss plaintiffs claim based on violation of substantive due process.

F. Second Claim for Relief-Equal Protection

The Equal Protection Clause requires that no state "deny to any person within its jurisdiction the equal protection of the laws." U.S. Const.Amend. XIV, § 1. A violation of equal protection occurs when the government treats someone differently than another who is similarly situated. *Jacobs Visconsi & Jacobs v City of Lawrence, Kan.*, 927 F.2d 1111, 1118 (10th Cir. 1991); *See also City of Cleburne, Tex. v. Cleburne Living Center, Inc.*, 473 U.S.. 432, 439,. 105 S.Ct. 3249, 3254, 87 L.Ed.2d 313 (1985); *Landmark Land Co. of Oklahoma, Inc., v. Buchanan*, 874 F.2d 717, 722 (10th Cir. 1989) In determining whether an equal protection violation has occurred, the court must (1) identify the questioned classification of groups, and (2) determine whether the classification is valid applying the appropriate standard of review. *See Allright Colorado v. City and County of Denver*, 937 F.2d 1502, 1511 (10th Cir. 1991). Plaintiffs bear the burden of demonstrating the unconstitutionality of the challenged classification and courts generally presume that the legislative act is valid. *Parham v. Hughes*, 441 U.S. 347, 351, 99 S.Ct. 1742, 1745-46, 60 L.Ed.2d 269. (1979).

The standard of review applicable when a plaintiff challenges economic or commercial legislation as violating the equal protection requires the state or municipal defendant to show that the classification has a rational basis. *Jacobs, Visconsi & Jacobs Co.*, 927 F.2d at 1119; *see also City of Cleburne Living Center*, 473 U.S. 432, 105 S.Ct. 3249, 87 L.Ed.2d 313 (1985); *Alamo Rent-A-Car, Inc., v. Saratota-Manatee Airport Auth.*, 825 F.2d 367 (11th Cir. 1987), cert. denied, 484 U.S. 1063, 108 S.Ct. 1022, 98 L.Ed.2d 987 (1988). The Supreme Court has recently reiterated this principle:

Whether embodied in the Fourteenth Amendment or inferred from the Fifth, equal protection is not a license for courts to judge the wisdom, fairness, or logic of legislative choices. In areas of social and economic policy, a statutory classification that neither proceeds along suspect lines nor infringes fundamental constitutional rights must be upheld against equal protection challenge *if* there *is any reasonably coneivable state of facts* that could provide a rational basis for the classification. [Citations omitted.] Where there are "plausible reasons" for [legislative] action, "our inquiry is at an end." [Citation omitted.]

Federal Communications Comm'n v. Beach Communications, Inc., — U.S. —, —, 113 S.Ct. 2096, 2101, 124 L.Ed.2d 211 (1993) (emphasis in original). The limitation in this analysis is that a State may not rely on a classification whose relationship to an asserted interest is so attenuated as to render the distinction arbitrary or irrational. *Cleborne*, 473 U.S. at 446, 105 S.Ct. at 3257-58.

Here, plaintiffs' claim is grounded in their objection to the policy choice made by the Colorado Central Assembly when it decided to regulate motor vehicle carriers of **[1236]** passengers under the doctrine or regulated monopoly. Plaintiffs identify three separate classification schemes. First, plaintiffs allege that there are two groups of common carriers by motor vehicle: one that transports property, and another that transports people. The transportation of property is regulated under the scheme of "regulated competition," while the transportation of people is regulated under the scheme of "regulated monopoly." Defendants do not dispute this classification, however, they argue there is a rational basis for it. Defendants have presented that the Colorado General Assembly could have determined the following: 1) that relaxed entry into the market for common carriers of property was acceptable as an experiment despite the possibility of the elimination of some carriers or an increase in the costs to carry the goods; 2) the availability of common carriers of passengers is an important means of public transportation and, thus, is too important to serve as a vehicle for an experiment in relaxed regulation; 3) public transportation of passengers is too important to risk the elimination of carriers, the disgruntlement of drivers who find their earnings decreasing, or the increase in the rates paid by passengers. I find and conclude, therefore, that a rational basis exists for this classification.

A second classification scheme alleged by plaintiffs is a difference in classification among transporters or passengers. Plaintiffs contend that while taxicab service is operated to impose an insurmountable barrier to entry, other passenger services, such as off-road scenic tours and charter buses seating over 32 passengers, impose no regulations that operate as barriers to entry. Defendants argue that a distinction between these two groups is justified because common carriers, such as taxicabs, are responsible for providing service in a designated service territory to any and all who seek its services while other passenger carriers are not. Defendants contend considerations such as wear and tear on the roads, control of traffic flow, and the need to assure the availability or different forms of transportation could have motivated the General Assembly. Again, defendants have presented a rational basis for this classification.

Plaintiffs claim a third classification scheme exists in the organization of the taxicab industry within the state. They contend that in almost every other market in Colorado the taxicab industry truly is a "regulated monopoly" in that there is only one certified taxicab company within a service are. In Denver, however, there is a "shared regulated monopoly" as a result of the existing companies being "grandfathered" into the regulated monopoly scheme decades ago resulting in three operating companies. I find and conclude that plaintiffs have failed to state how this "classification," works to deny them equal protection. Nevertheless, there is certainly a conceivable rational basis for grandfathering in existing companies at the time the regulatory scheme was enacted. Accordingly, plaintiffs claim based on violation of equal protection must fail.

G. Third Claim for Relief-Equal Protection, Tillman

Plaintiff Tillman argues that the effect of the PUC regulatory regime is to artificially limit the supply of taxicabs in Denver which results in poor service for low-income neighborhoods where Tillman resides and works. The effective ban on new companies denies individuals in these neighborhoods, including Tillman, opportunities equal to those of other Denver residents to enjoy taxicab services. Tillman argues that the regulatory regime affects his fundamental right to intra-state travel, requiring me to apply strict scrutiny in determining that the state regulations are necessary to achieve a compelling government interest.

I have held, above, that Tillman lacks standing to bring this third claim for relief. Even assuming Tillman's standing to assert this claim, dismissal is appropriate for failure to state a claim.

The strict scrutiny test is invoked in either of two situations: first, where there is a "suspect" classification based upon race, alienage or national origin; and second, where a fundamental interest is at stake. These fundamental interests include the right to vote, the right of access to the courts, and the right to interstate travel. **[1237]** *San Antonio Indep. School Dist. v. Rodriguez*, 411 U.S. 1, 18-20, 32-36, 93 S.Ct. 1278, 1288-90, 1296-98, 36 L.Ed.2d 16 (1973). The Supreme Court has never directly considered the right to intra-state travel. History teaches that the founding fathers were concerned with the former and not the later. I decline to recognize such a right under the facts presented here.

Accordingly, it is **ORDERED** that

1) defendants motion to dismiss the privileges and immunities claim brought by plaintiffs Quick Pick Cabs and Ebong for lack or standing is **GRANTED**;

2) defendants' motion to dismiss the privileges and immunities claim brought by plaintiffs Rowland Nwankwo and Girma Molalegne for lack of standing is **DENIED**;

3) defendants' motion to dismiss the third claim for relief because Tillman lacks standing, or alternatively for failure to state a claim, is **GRANTED**;

4) defendants' motion to join necessary parties pursuant to Rule 19(a) is **DENIED**;

5) defendants' request that I abstain from hearing this case is **DENIED**;

6) defendants' motion to dismiss plaintiffs' first and second claims based on privileges and immunities, substantive due process and equal protection, for failure to state a claim for which relief may be granted is **GRANTED**;

7) this action is dismissed and costs are awarded to defendants.

Supreme Court of California
K. Tashiro v. Jordan, 201 Cal. 236 (1927)

May 20, 1927.
(headnotes omitted)

[237] **APPLICATION** for a Writ of Mandate to compel the Secretary of State to file certain articles of incorporation. Writ granted. [238] The facts are stated in the opinion of the court.

J. Marion Wright for Petitioners.

U.S. Webb, Attorney-General, and Robert W. Harrison, Chief Deputy Attorney-General, for Respondents.

CURTIS, J.—This is an application for a writ of mandate to compel the respondents, as Secretary of State and Deputy Secretary of State, respectively, to file certain articles of incorporation prepared and executed by petitioners and presented by them to respondents as such officers, for the purpose of filing in the office of Secretary of State. The application also asks that the respondents be compelled to issue a certificate of incorporation and to certify and deliver to petitioners three copies of said articles of incorporation. It appears from said application that petitioners are residents of the state of California and county of Los Angeles, and are all Japanese subjects ineligible to become citizens of the United States or state of California; that they have voluntarily associated themselves together for the purpose of forming a corporation under the laws of the state of California to be known as the Japanese Hospital of Los Angeles; and that among the purposes for which this corporation is sought to be organized are those of maintaining a general hospital, to purchase the necessary equipment for the same and to lease land upon which the buildings necessary for the maintenance of said hospital may be erected. Respondents refuse to file these articles of incorporation or to take any official action thereon for the reason, as contended by them, that the treaty between this government and the Japanese government confers no right upon Japanese subjects residing in this country to form a corporation under the laws of this or of any other state of this country. Without this right is given to petitioners by the terms of said treaty., the respondents contend, petitioners are prohibited by the laws of this state, and particularly by the provisions of the Alien Land Law, from forming any corporation, one of the purposes of which is to possess, use, or occupy real property situated in this state.

[239] Section 1 of the Alien Land Law, as adopted by the electors of this state in 1920 and thereafter amended by the act of the legislature approved June 20, 1923 (Stats. 1923, p. 1020), deals with the rights of aliens eligible to citizenship and in no way relates to any matter involved in the present proceeding. Sections 2 and 3 of this act are as follows:

"Sec. 2. All aliens other than those mentioned in section one of this act may acquire, possess, enjoy, use, cultivate, occupy and transfer real property, or any interest therein, in this state, and have in whole or in part the beneficial use thereof, in the manner and to the extent, and for the purposes prescribed by any treaty now existing between the government of the United States and the nation or country of which such alien is a citizen or subject, and not otherwise.

"Sec. 3. Any company, association or corporation organized under the laws of this or any other state or nation, of which a majority of the members are aliens other than those specified in section one of this act, or in which a majority of the issued capital stock is owned by such aliens, may acquire, possess, enjoy, use, cultivate, occupy and transfer real property, or any interest therein, in this state, and have in whole or in part the beneficial use thereof, in the manner and to the extent and for the purposes prescribed by any treaty now existing between the government of the United States and the nation or country of which such members or

233

stockholders are citizens or subjects, and not otherwise. Hereafter all aliens other than those specified in section one hereof may become members of or acquire shares of stock in any company, association or corporation that is or may be authorized to acquire, possess, enjoy, use, cultivate, occupy and transfer real property, or any interest therein, in this state, in the manner and to the extent and for the purposes prescribed by any treaty now existing between the government of the United States and the nation or country of which such alien is a citizen or subject, and not otherwise."

It will be observed from a reading of the foregoing sections of the Alien Land Law that by the provisions of section 2 thereof the rights of aliens ineligible to citizenship to possess, use, or occupy real property in this state **[240]** are limited to such rights as are prescribed by the treaty between the country of which said aliens are subjects and this country. By section 3 of said act the rights of any corporation organized in this or any other state, of which a majority of the members thereof are aliens ineligible to citizenship, to possess, use, or occupy real property situated in this state are likewise limited and governed by the terms of the treaty existing between this government and the government of which such aliens are citizens or subjects. In other words, it was undoubtedly the object and purpose of the Alien Land Law of this state to accord to aliens ineligible to citizenship, either individually or as members of a corporation, in which a majority of the members thereof are ineligible to citizenship, the right to acquire and possess real property in this state "in the manner and to the extent and for the purposes prescribed by any treaty," and to deny to such aliens any and all other rights or privileges in or to the real property of this state. It is apparent, therefore, that the measure of petitioners' rights as asserted in this proceeding is to be determined by the terms and provisions of the treaty or treaties now in force between this government and the empire of Japan. Article I of the Treaty of Commerce and Navigation between this government and the empire of Japan, proclaimed April 5, 1911 (37 U.S. Stats. at Large, p. 1504), in so far as it is material to any question arising herein, provides that:

"The citizens or subjects of each of the High Contracting Parties shall have liberty to enter, travel and reside in the territories of the other to carry on trade, wholesale and retail, to own or lease and occupy houses, manufactories, warehouses and shops, to employ agents of their choice, to lease land for residential and commercial purposes, and generally to do anything incident to or necessary for trade upon the same terms as native citizens or subjects, submitting themselves to the laws and regulations there established."

It will be observed that by the terms of this article of said treaty, subjects of Japan are accorded the right, among others, to carry on trade, to lease land for commercial purposes, and "generally to do anything incident to or necessary for trade upon the same terms as native citizens" **[241]** of this country or state.

In the case of *State of California v. Tagami*, 195 Cal. 522 [234 P. 102], it was held that a lease of land to a subject of Japan, for the purpose of using and occupying the same as a health resort or sanatorium is for a "commercial purpose" within the terms of said treaty. It is not seriously contended by respondents that the use of land for the purpose of erecting and maintaining thereon a hospital is not a use for commercial purposes as the term is used in said treaty, nor is it contended that a subject of Japan or any number of them, either in their capacity as individuals or as members of a partnership, cannot under the terms of said treaty lease real property in this state for the purpose of maintaining thereon a hospital. The sole claim of respondents is that the treaty does not expressly or by reasonable inference confer upon Japanese subjects residing in this state the right to form a corporation, if one of the purposes thereof is to lease for commercial purposes real property situated in this state. In the case of *California v. Tagami*, supra, this court quoted with approval from the following language from the case of *De Geofroy v. Riggs*, 133 U.S. 258 [33 L.Ed. 642, 10 Sup. Ct. Rep. 295, see, also, Rose's U.S. Notes]: "It is a general principle of construction, with respect to treaties, that they shall be liberally construed, so as to carry out the apparent intention of the parties to secure equality and reciprocity between them. As they are contracts between independent nations, in their construction, words are to be taken in their ordinary meaning, as understood in the public law of nations, and not in any artificial or special sense impressed upon them by local law, unless such restricted sense is clearly intended. And it has been held by this court that where a treaty admits of two constructions, one restrictive of rights that may be claimed under it, and the other favorable to them, the latter is to be preferred." The principle thus enunciated appears to be accepted by the courts generally, and in 38 Ency. of Law and Procedure (Cyc.), 970, it is stated as follows: "Treaties should ordinarily be construed liberally, and so where the treaty admits of two constructions, one restrictive as to the rights that may be claimed under it and the other liberal, the latter is to be preferred." In **[242]** support of this text the following authorities are cited: *In re Wyman*, 191 Mass. 276 [114 Am. St. Rep. 601, 77 N.E. 379], *In re Stixrud's Estate*, 58 Wn. 339 [Ann. Cas. 1912A, 850, 33 L.R.A. (N.S.) 632, 109 P. 343], *Disconto Gesellschaft v. Umbreit*, 208 U.S. 570 [52 L.Ed. 625, 28 Sup. Ct. Rep. 337, see, also, Rose's U.S. Notes], *Scharpf v. Schmidt*, 172 Ill. 255 [50 N.E. 182], *Adams v. Akerlund*, 168 Ill. 632 [48 N.E. 454], and *De Geofroy v. Riggs*, 133 U.S. 258 [33 L.Ed. 642, 10 Sup. Ct. Rep. 295].

As we have already seen, section 1 of the Treaty of 1911 provides that subjects of Japan residing in this state shall have the right to carry on trade, wholesale and retail, to lease land for commercial purposes and generally do anything incident to or necessary for trade upon the same terms as native citizens or subjects. It is apparent from the reading of this section of the treaty that it was the intention of the high contracting parties thereto to give to the subjects of either country residing in the territory of the other the right to carry on trade therein upon the same terms as native subjects or citizens of the latter country. Yet this right to carry on trade is limited to such subjects and purposes as are enumerated in the treaty itself. Subjects of Japan residing in this country and subjects of our own country residing in Japan have only such rights in the country of their domicile as are expressly or by reasonable implication given to them by the treaty. The right to possess real property for agricultural purposes is not mentioned or referred to in the treaty. In fact, the treaty is silent upon this subject. Accordingly, it has been held that no right to possess real property for agricultural purposes is given to subjects of Japan residing in this country and, therefore, a statute prohibiting Japanese subjects residing in this state from possessing real property for agricultural purposes is valid and constitutional (*Porterfield v. Webb*, 195 Cal. 71 [231 P. 554]; *Porterfield v. Webb*, 263 U.S. 225 [68 L.Ed. 278, 44 Sup. Ct. Rep. 21]; *Webb v. O'Brien*, 263 U.S. 313 [68 L.Ed. 318, 44 Sup. Ct. Rep. 112]). It was further held that the right "to carry on trade" given by the treaty does not give to Japanese subjects residing in this state the privilege of acquiring stock in a corporation owning farm or agricultural land situated in this state (*Frick v. Webb*, 263 U.S. 326 [68 L.Ed. 323, 44 Sup. Ct. Rep. 115]). In this case the **[243]** court said: "The provisions of the act (Alien Land Law of California) were framed and intended for general application and to limit the privileges of all ineligible aliens in respect of agricultural lands to those prescribed by treaty between the United States and the nation or country of which such alien is a citizen or subject. The State has power, and the act evidences its purposes, to deny to ineligible aliens permission to own, lease, use or have the benefit of lands within its borders for agricultural purposes. . . . It may forbid indirect as well as direct ownership and control of agricultural land by ineligible aliens. The right 'to carry on trade' given by the treaty does not give the privilege to acquire the stock above described. To read the treaty to permit ineligible aliens to acquire such stock would be inconsistent with the intention and purpose of the parties."

But the right "to carry on trade" in the specific lines of business mentioned in the treaty, such as conducting manufactories, warehouses, and shops and leasing land for commercial purposes, is from the very terms of said treaty as extensive and complete as that employed by native citizens or subjects. It would be difficult to frame language much more comprehensive than that found in the following provision of article I of the treaty - "and generally to do anything incident to or necessary for trade upon the same terms as native citizens or subjects." This language follows the provision enumerating the different classes of trade or business in which resident aliens are authorized to engage and must be read in connection with such provision, and as so read it gives to such aliens an equal standing with native citizens or subjects in the conduct of those enumerated classes of business which may be carried on by such aliens.

If, then, Japanese subjects residing in this state are authorized to engage in certain lines of business, including that of leasing real property for commercial purposes, and under the terms of the treaty they are further authorized to do anything incident or necessary in the conduct of such business upon the same terms as native citizens or subjects, are they thereby empowered to form a corporation as one of the necessary incidents of transacting such business? The statutes of this state provide the terms under which native citizens of this country may enter into corporate [244] relations, and it is not questioned by respondents that petitioners have complied with the requirements of all such statutes, provided they are eligible to form a corporation under the terms of the treaty. It is hardly necessary to call attention to the extent to which corporations are formed and used by the citizens of this state, as well as by those of all other civilized countries, in the transaction of the various lines of trade carried on therein. There is scarcely a class of business of any consequence carried on in this state in which corporate interests do not play, if not a leading, at least an important part in its transaction. The extensive and widespread use of this means of carrying on trade or transacting business is convincing proof of the advantages to be derived therefrom. Why, then, should this method of carrying on trade as to the classes of business enumerated in the treaty be denied subjects of Japan residing in this state in the face of the plain provisions of the treaty conferring upon them as to such classes of business the right to do anything incident to such business upon the same terms as native citizens? A corporation, or the members thereof, in conducting any certain business do not thereby exercise any more extensive or different right or control over the property of said business than they would exercise over said property if they carried on the business as individuals. Should the petitioners as individuals decide to lease land and erect thereon and equip a hospital and maintain and operate the same, they could do so in the same manner and to the same extent as a corporation organized by them might do the same identical acts. As a corporation they would not be authorized to exercise any right over property which they do not now possess as individuals nor to transact any business nor engage in any line of trade which they could not transact or engage in as individuals. The corporation is simply the instrumentality through which the members thereof engage to carry on the business in which they have a common interest. It is simply incidental to the business just as an agreement of copartnership would be if a partnership were formed to perform the same acts. In view of these considerations, and mindful of the rule already referred to, requiring courts to give to treaties a liberal construction, we are of the opinion that the right of Japanese subjects residing in this state to form [245] a corporation for the purpose of leasing real property upon which to operate and maintain a hospital is within the reasonable intendment of the Treaty of 1911. Such right is therefore not within the prohibitions contained in the Alien Land Law of this state, but is expressly recognized by the terms thereof.

Respondents have directed our attention to the provisions of article VII of the Treaty of 1911, which was designed to confer certain rights upon corporations (therein referred to as limited-liability companies or associations) "organized in accordance with the laws of either High Contracting Party and domiciled in the territories of such Party." Following the granting of such rights said section of the treaty provides that: "The foregoing stipulation has no bearing upon the question whether a company or association organized in one of the two countries will or will not be permitted to transact its business or industry in the other, this permission remaining always subject to the laws and regulations enacted or established in the respective countries or in any part thereof." It is insisted by respondents that this provision argues most strongly against petitioners' contention in that it evinces no desire on the part of either party to the treaty of securing freedom of action in the territories of the other for corporations of its own creation. Therefore, say respondents, "How much less must it have been concerned in the creation by that other of corporations which were to act in this country of their creation?" We are not able to perceive the force of respondents' argument. The parties to the treaty evidently were not prepared to definitely bind themselves as to the rights of a corporation organized in one country and domiciled therein to transact and carry on business in the other. Hence, they left the question unaffected by the treaty and subject to be regulated by the respective countries.

They were, however, prepared to definitely fix and determine the rights of citizens and subjects of one country domiciled in the other, and to this end they set forth these rights distinctly and comprehensively in article I of the Treaty, the terms of which we have already considered and attempted to construe. Article XI of the Treaty also refers to corporations, but clearly this reference has no bearing upon the question to be considered in this proceeding.

[246] Finally, respondents contend that the words "native citizens" as used in the treaty in article I thereof, whereby it is sought to confer upon subjects of one country residing within the territory of the other the right "generally to do anything incident to or necessary for trade upon the same terms as native citizens," are employed in a restrictive sense, and that this provision of the treaty deals only with native citizens and subjects of the United States and their privileges and immunities as such and not with the privileges and immunities of the citizens and subjects of the several states. **That there is a citizenship of the United States and a citizenship of a state, and the privileges and immunities of one are not the same as the other is well established by the decisions of the courts of this country. The leading cases upon the subjects are those decided by the supreme court of the United States and reported in 16 Wall. 36, and known as the *Slaughter-House cases*.** However, to adopt the construction of the words "native citizens," as contended for by respondents, would be contrary not only to the spirit but to the express language of the rule applicable to the interpretation of treaties which we have already considered. We refer to the rule quoted with approval by this court in State of California v. Tagami, supra, and particularly to the following portion thereof: "words (of a treaty) are to be taken in their ordinary meaning, as understood in the public law of nations, and not in any artificial or special sense impressed upon them by local law, unless such restricted sense is clearly intended." There is nothing in the language of the treaty to indicate that the words "native citizens" used therein were employed in any restricted sense. On the other hand, we think it is plainly obvious from the terms of the treaty that the intent of the parties thereto in conferring upon the subjects of one country residing in the other the right to exercise certain privileges "upon the same terms as native citizens" was to extend to such foreign subjects all the rights that the native citizen enjoyed irrespective of the source of such rights.

It may be that the right to form a corporation such as that which petitioners desire to organize is governed by the local laws of each particular state, and that such right may not be conferred upon alien residents in this state, or, for that matter, upon any class of persons whatsoever, by treaty [247] or by any other act of the federal government. If this is so, then the state might disregard the treaty or any statute enacted by Congress which would infringe upon its exclusive jurisdiction in this particular and enact such laws in that regard as may meet the approval of the legislature or of the people of the state, irrespective of any treaty or federal statute. But in the enactment of the Alien Land Law the state of California has not attempted to run counter to the Treaty of 1911, or to any other treaty between this country and a foreign country. On the other hand, the provisions thereof relative to the right of aliens ineligible to citizenship to acquire and possess real property in this state expressly recognize such acquisition and possession "in the manner and to the extent and for the purpose prescribed by any treaty now existing between the government of the United States and the nation or country of which such alien is a citizen or subject." The provision found in section 3 of said act relative to corporations, a majority of whom are aliens not eligible to citizenship, acquiring or possessing real property in this state, contains a like reference to and recognition of the terms of any treaty between this government and any foreign nation. The fact, therefore, that the right to provide for and control the organization of corporations in this state may be within the exclusive jurisdiction of the state and not the national government is not decisive of any question arising in this proceeding for the reason that the action taken by the state in reference to such matters by the enactment of the Alien Land Law expressly limits the terms and provisions of said law to such rights as are not prescribed by any treaty.

Let the writ issue as prayed for. Langdon, J., Richards, J., Seawell, J., Preston, J., and Waste, C.J., concurred

237

United States Supreme Court
Madden v. Kentucky, 309 U.S. 83 (1940)

Argued Dec. 14, 1939. Decided Jan. 29, 1940.
(headnotes omitted)

[309 U.S. 83,84] Messrs. Leo T. Wolford and Wm. Marshall Bullitt, both of Louisville, Ky., for appellant.

[309 U.S. 84, 85] Mr. Samuel M. Rosenstein, of Frankfort, Ky., for appellee.

Mr. Justice REED delivered the opinion of the Court.

This is an appeal[1] brought here under Section 237(a) of the Judicial Code, 28 U.S.C.A. Section 344(a), from a judgment of the Court of Appeals of Kentucky sustaining the validity of a statute of that state against an attack by the appellant on the ground of its being repugnant to the due process, equal protection, [309 U.S. 83, 86] and privileges and immunities clauses of the Fourteenth Amendment of the Constitution of the United States, U.S.C.A.

The issue is whether a state statute which imposes on its citizens an annual ad valorem tax on their deposits in banks outside of the state at the rate of fifty cents per hundred dollars and at the same time imposes on their deposits in banks located within the state a similar ad valorem tax at the rate of ten cents per hundred dollars is obnoxious to the stated clauses of the Fourteenth Amendment. The relevant provisions of the Kentucky statutes for the period in question appear in the note below.[2]

The opinion of the Court of Appeals of Kentucky in this case construes the exception in Section 4019, limiting the tax on bank deposits to one-tenth of one per cent, as applicable only to depositors in local financial institutions organized under the laws of Kentucky or under the national [309 U.S. 83, 87] banking laws. This interpretation of the state laws is of course accepted by us.[3]

---

[1] See Act of January 31, 1928, 45 Stat. 54.

[2] Carroll's Kentucky Statutes, Baldwin Revision, 1930, 4019a-10, p. 2052 (Ky.Acts. 1924, Ch. 116, 3) provides:

> "All property subject to taxation for state purposes shall be subject also to taxation in the county, city, school, or other taxing district in which same has a taxable situs, except the following classes of property which shall be subject to taxation for state purposes only:
>
> "(4) Money in hand, notes, bonds, accounts and other credits, whether secured by mortgage, pledge, or otherwise, or unsecured, and shares of stock; ...."

Carroll's Kentucky Statutes, Baldwin's Revision 1930, 4019, p. 2048 (Ky.Acts 1924, Ch. 116, 1, p. 402, as reenacted in Ky.Acts 1926, Ch. 164, p. 739), provides as follows:

> "An annual ad valorem tax for state purposes of thirty cents (30ȼ) upon each one hundred dollars ($100.00) of value of all real estate directed to be assessed for taxation, as provided by law and fifty cents (50ȼ) upon each one hundred dollars ($100.00) of value of all other property directed to be assessed for taxation, as provided by law, shall be paid by the owner, person or corporation assessed; except a tax at the rate of one-tenth of one per cent. (0.1%) (i.e., 10 cents upon each $100) shall be paid annually upon the amount of deposits in any bank, trust company, or combined bank and trust company, organized under the laws of this State, or in any national bank of this State, as now provided by law; ...."

[3] *St. Louis Southwestern Ry. Co. v. Arkansas*, 235 U.S. 350, 362, 35 S. Ct. 99, 102; *Storaasli v. Minnesota*, 283 U.S. 57, 62, 51 S. Ct. 354, 355.

John E. Madden died in November, 1929, a citizen and resident of Fayette County, Kentucky. On several prior assessment dates, July 1 in Kentucky, Mr. Madden had on deposit in New York banks a considerable amount of funds. These deposits had not been reported for the purposes of taxation in Kentucky. That state brought suit against Mr. Madden's executor to have these deposits assessed as omitted property and to recover an ad valorem tax of 50 cents per hundred dollars as of July 1 of each year, together with interest and penalties. The executor used as one defense against this claim the contention that a tax on deposits in banks outside of Kentucky at a higher rate than the tax upon bank deposits within Kentucky would abridge decedent's privileges and immunities as a citizen of the United States, deprive him of his property right and the liberty to keep money on deposit outside of Kentucky without due process of law, and deny to him equal protection of the law in violation of the Fourteenth Amendment. The Court of Appeals passed upon the constitutional questions submitted because of the difference in taxing rate between Kentucky deposits and out-of-state deposits. It approved the classification as permissible under the due process and equal protection clauses and refused to accept the argument that its interpretation of the statutes violated the privileges and immunities clause.

I. Classification.—The broad discretion as to classification possessed by a legislature in the field of taxation **[309 U.S. 83, 88]** has long been recognized.[4] This Court fifty years ago concluded that "the fourteenth amendment was not intended to compel the states to adopt an iron rule of equal taxation,"[5] and the passage of time has only served to underscore the wisdom of that recognition of the large area of discretion which is needed by a legislature in formulating sound tax policies. Traditionally classification has been a device for fitting tax programs to local needs and usages in order to achieve an equitable distribution of the tax burden. It has, because of this, been pointed out that in taxation, even more than in other fields, legislatures possess the greatest freedom in classification.[6] Since the members of a legislature necessarily enjoy a familiarity with local conditions which this Court cannot have, the presumption of constitutionality can be overcome only by the most explicit demonstration that a classification is a hostile and oppressive discrimination against particular persons and classes.[7] The burden is on the one attacking the legislative arrangement to negative every conceivable basis which might support it.[8]

Paying proper regard to the scope of a legislature's powers in these matters, the insubstantiality of appellant's claim that he has been denied equal protection or due process of law by the classification is at once apparent. When these statutes were adopted in 1917 during a general revision of Kentucky's tax laws, the chief problem facing the legislature was the formulation of an **[309 U.S. 83, 89]** enforceable system of intangible taxation.[9] By placing the

---

[4] *New York Rapid Transit Corp. v. City of New York*, 303 U.S. 573, 58 S.Ct. 721, and cases there cited.

[5] *Bell's Gap R.R. Co. v. Com. of Pennsylvania*, 134 U.S. 232, 237, 10 S.Ct. 533, 535.

[6] *Citizens' Telephone Co. v. Fuller*, 229 U.S. 322, 329, 33 S.Ct. 833, 835.

[7] See the opinion of Mr. Justice Brandeis in *Louisville Gas & Electric Co. v. Coleman*, 277 U.S. 32, 42, 46, 47, 48 S.Ct. 423, 426, 428.

[8] *Lindsley v. Natural Carbonic Gas Co.*, 220 U.S. 61, 78, 79, 31 S.Ct. 337, 340, Ann.Cas.1912C, 160.

[9] Because of a prohibition in the Kentucky Constitution of 1891 against classification in taxation, the state and its political subdivisions taxed intangibles at the same rate as other property. This resulted in a total tax of about $2.65 per hundred dollars on intangibles, a tax which in the case of bank deposits almost equaled the interest on deposits. The high rate led to wide-spread evasion of the tax by concealment of intangibles; with bank deposits this took the form of withdrawals for deposits outside the state. The unequal burden which this evasion placed on other forms of property led to agitation for reform as early as 1908. Two special tax commissions reported on the need for a constitutional amendment and a general tax reform. After an amendment permitting classification was adopted in 1916, a third committee made specific proposals for revision, and most of the recommendations were adopted at a special

duty of collection on local banks, the tax on local deposits was made almost self-enforcing. The tax on deposits outside the state, however, still resembled that on investments in Watson v. State Comptroller, the collection of which was said to depend "either upon (the taxpayer's) will or upon the vigilance and discretion of the local assessors."[10] Here as in the Watson case the classification may have been "founded in 'the purposes **[309 U.S. 83, 90]** and policy of taxation.'" The treatment accorded the two kinds of deposits may have resulted from the differences in the difficulties and expenses of tax collection.[11]

II. Privileges and Immunities.—The appellant presses urgently upon us the argument that the privileges and immunities clause of the Fourteenth Amendment of the Constitution of the United States[12] forbids the enforcement by the Commonwealth of Kentucky of this enactment which imposes upon the testator taxes five times as great on money deposited in banks outside the State as it does on money of others deposited in banks within the State. The privilege or immunity which appellant contends is abridged is the right to carry on business beyond the lines of the State of his residence, a right claimed as appertaining to national citizenship.

There is no occasion to attempt again an exposition of the views of this Court as to the proper limitations of the privileges and immunities clause. There is a very recent discussion in *Hague v. Committee Industrial Organization.*[13] The appellant purports to accept as sound the position stated as the view of all the justices concurring in the Hague decision. This position is that the privileges and immunities clause protects all citizens against abridgement by states of rights of national citizenship as distinct from the fundamental or **[309 U.S. 83, 91]** natural rights inherent in state citizenship.[14] This Court declared in the *Slaughter-House Cases*[15] that

---

legislative session in 1917. See the message of Governor Stanley to the General Assembly of 1917, Kentucky Senate Journal of 1917, p. 13. In general the revision took the form of a drastic lowering of the rates on intangibles. An even lower rate was placed on bank deposits and almost complete collection assured by placing the duty of collection on the banks.

[10] 254 U.S. 122, 124, 41 S.Ct. 43, 44.

[11] *Carmichael v. Southern Coal & Coke Co.*, 301 U.S. 495, 511, 57 S.Ct. 868, 873, 109 A.L.R. 1327.

[12] The 14th Amendment, Section 1, provides: "All persons born or naturalized in the United States, and subject to the jurisdiction thereof, are citizens of the United States and of the State wherein they reside. No State shall make or enforce any law which shall abridge the privileges or immunities of citizens of the United States; ...."

[13] 307 U.S. 496, 59 S.Ct. 954. The prior cases are collected in Note 2 of the dissenting opinion in *Colgate v. Harvey*, 296 U.S. 404, 445, 56 S.Ct. 252, 266, 102 A.L.R. 54, and Note 1 of Mr. Justice Stone's opinion in the Hague case, 307 U.S. 496, 520, 59 S.Ct. 954, 966.

[14] Mr. Justice Roberts' opinion, 307 U.S. at page 512, 59 S.Ct. at page 962: "Although it has been held that the Fourteenth Amendment created no rights in citizens of the United States, but merely secured existing rights against state abridgement, it is clear that the right peaceably to assemble and to discuss these topics, and to communicate respecting them, whether orally or in writing, is a privilege inherent in citizenship of the United States which the Amendment protects." C Mr. Justice Stone's opinion, 307 U.S. at pages 519-521, 59 S.Ct. at pages 966, 967:

"Hence there is no occasion ... to revive the contention, rejected by this Court in the *Slaughter-House Cases*, supra, that the privileges and immunities of United States citizenship, protected by that clause, extend beyond those which arise or grow out of the relationship of United States citizens to the national government.

"That such is the limited application of the privileges and immunities clause seems now to be conceded by my brethren."

[15] 16 Wall. 36, at 71, 72: "We repeat, then, in the light of this recapitulation of events, almost too recent to be called history, but which are familiar to us all; and on the most casual examination of the language of these amendments, no one can fail to be impressed with the one pervading purpose found in them all, lying at the foundation of each, and without which none of them would have been even suggested; we mean the freedom of the slave race, the security and firm establishment of that freedom, and the protection of the newly-made freeman and citizen from the oppressions of those who had formerly exercised unlimited dominion over him...."

the Fourteenth Amendment as well as the Thirteenth and Fifteenth were adopted to protect the negroes in their freedom. This almost contemporaneous interpretation extended the benefits of the privileges and immunities clause to other rights which are inherent in national citizenship but denied it to those which spring from **[309 U.S. 83, 92]** state citizenship.[16] In applying this constitutional principle this Court has determined that the right to operate an independent slaughter-house,[17] to sell wine on terms of equality with grape growers[18] and to operate businesses free of state regulation[19] were not privileges and immunities protected by the Fourteenth Amendment. And a state inheritance tax statute which limited exemptions to charitable corporations within the state was held not to infringe any right protected by the privileges and immunities clause.[20] The Court has consistently refused to list completely the rights which are covered by the clause, though it has pointed out the type of rights protected.[21] **We think it quite clear that the right to carry out an incident to a trade, business or calling**[22] **such as the deposit** *[309 U.S. 83, 93]* **of money in banks is not a privilege of national citizenship.**

In the states, there reposes the sovereignty to manage their own affairs except only as the requirements of the Constitution otherwise provide. Within these constitutional limits the power of the state over taxation is plenary. An interpretation of the privileges and immunities clause which restricts the power of the states to manage their own fiscal affairs is a matter of gravest concern to them.[23] It is only the emphatic requirements of the Constitution which properly may lead the federal courts to such a conclusion.

Appellant relies upon *Colgate v. Harvey*, supra,[24] as a precedent to support his argument that the present statute is not within the limits of permissible classification and violates the privileges and immunities clause. In view of our conclusions, we look upon the decision in that case as repugnant to the line of reasoning adopted here. As a consequence, *Colgate v. Harvey*, supra, must be and is overruled.

"And so if other rights are assailed by the States which properly and necessarily fall within the protection of these articles, that protection will apply, though the party interested may not be of African descent. But what we do say, and what we wish to be understood is, that in any fair and just construction of any section or phrase of these amendments, it is necessary to look to the purpose which we have said was the pervading spirit of them all, the evil which they were designed to remedy, and the process of continued addition to the Constitution, until that purpose was supposed to be accomplished, as far as constitutional law can accomplish it."
[16] Id. 16 Wall. 78, 79

[17] *Slaughter-House Cases*, supra.

[18] Cox v. State of Texas, 202 U.S. 446, 26 S.Ct. 671; cf. Bartemeyer v. Iowa, 18 Wall. 129; Crowley v. Christensen, 137 U.S. 86, 11 S.Ct. 13; Giozza v. Tiernan, 148 U.S. 657, 13 S.Ct. 721; Crane v. Campbell, 245 U.S. 304, 38 S.Ct. 98.

[19] Holden v. Hardy, 169 U.S. 366, 18 S.Ct. 383; Wilmington Star Mining Co. v. Fulton, 205 U.S. 60, 27 S.Ct. 412; Western Union Telegraph Co. v. Commercial Milling Co., 218 U.S. 406, 31 S.Ct. 59, 36 L.R.A.,N.S., 220, 21 Ann.Cas. 815; Rosenthal v. People of New York, 226 U.S. 260, 33 S.Ct. 27, Ann.Cas.1914B, 71; Prudential Ins. Co. v. Cheek, 259 U.S. 530, 42 S.Ct. 516, 27 A.L.R. 27.

[20] Board of Education v. Illinois, 203 U.S. 553, 27 S.Ct. 171, 8 Ann.Cas. 157; cf. Ferry v. Spokane, P. & S. Ry., 258 U.S. 314, 42 S.Ct. 358, 20 A.L.R. 1326.

[21] They have been described as "privileges and immunities arising out of the nature and essential character of the national government, and granted or secured by the constitution of the United States." In re Kemmler, 136 U.S. 436, 448, 10 S.Ct. 930, 934. See also Slaughter-House Cases, supra, 16 Wall. at 79, 80; United States v. Cruikshank, 92 U.S. 542, 552; Williams v. Fears, 179 U.S. 270, 274, 21 S.Ct. 128, 129; Twining v. New Jersey, 211 U.S. 78, 97, 29 S.Ct. 14, 18.

[22] Cf. Twining v. New Jersey, 211 U.S. 78, 94, 29 S.Ct. 14, 17.

[23] Twining v. New Jersey, supra, 211 U.S. 92, 29 S.Ct. 16.

[24] 296 U.S. 404, 56 S.Ct. 252, 102 A.L.R. 54.

AFFIRMED

Mr. Chief Justice **HUGHES** concurs in the result upon the ground, as stated by the Court of Appeals of Kentucky, that the classification adopted by the legislature rested upon a reasonable basis.

Mr. Justice **ROBERTS**.

I think that the judgment should be reversed. Four years ago in *Colgate v. Harvey*, 296 U.S. 404, 56 S.Ct. 252, 102 A.L.R. 54, this court held that the equal protection clause and the privileges and immunities clause of the Fourteenth Amendment prohibit such a discrimination as results from the statute now under review. I adhere to the views expressed in **[309 U.S. 83, 94]** the opinion of the court in that case, and think it should be followed in this.

Mr. Justice **McREYNOLDS** joins in this opinion.

California Court of Appeal
O'Connell v. Judnich, 71 Cal.App 386 (1925)

February 24, 1925.
(headnotes ommitted)

[386]
David O'Connell, in pro per., for Appellant.
[387]
J.E. Manning and Wilford H. Tully, for Respondents.

TYLER, P. J. — Action for money had and received.

What is described as a bill of particulars forms a part of the complaint. Recitals contained therein allege Anna M. O'Connell to have been the owner of certain real property which, together with all her right, title, and interest thereto and therein, she assigned to the plaintiff. Other recitals are to the effect that with full knowledge of such facts defendants have collected certain rents and sold the property, in consequence of which there is in their hands a total sum of $4,321.91, to which plaintiff is entitled. The complaint concludes without a prayer.

Defendant Antone Judnich demurred upon numerous grounds; at the same time a motion was filed to strike the complaint from the files upon the ground that plaintiff was a disbarred attorney, and as such, under section 300 of the Code of Civil Procedure, had no right to prosecute the action. This motion was granted by reason of a judgment of disbarment at that time existing against plaintiff, who now appeals from the final judgment entered upon such order.

The section of the code invoked reads as follows: "No person who has been an attorney and counsellor [sic] shall, while a judgment of disbarment or suspension is in force, appear in his own behalf as plaintiff in the prosecution of any action where the subject of said action has been assigned to him subsequent to the entry of the judgment of disbarment or suspension." This act became effective August 17, 1923.

The original complaint, it is admitted, was filed prior to the time when the act took effect, but the amendment to the complaint was filed subsequent thereto and on the thirty-first day of August, 1923.

It is here urged that the judgment of dismissal was erroneous and void for the reason that the section involved is violative of several sections of the federal and state constitutions. In this contention we are of the opinion that appellant is correct.

Mr. Kerr, in an editorial note to the section in his Annotations to the Code of Civil Procedure, states that the provision is thought to be plainly unconstitutional (1) as class legislation and (2) as invading a fundamental right guaranteeing [388] to every citizen the right to personally conduct his own business if he so desires.

The very first section of the constitution of this state declares that all persons have certain inalienable rights, among which are the rights to acquire and protect property. The right to acquire and protect property must of necessity include the right to use all proper and legal means to accomplish those ends while the legislature may in its discretion, for the public good, regulate the pursuit of a remedy, it cannot thereby destroy the right. **One of the prime objects of the courts in to protect the constitutional rights of the citizen.** To say that one may not defend his own property is a usurpation of power by the legislature. **If by legislation a right vouchsafed by the constitution could be so abridged or limited, the right would not be an absolute or inalienable one but a mere privilege revocable at the will of the law-making body.**

It is suggested by respondent that to permit appellant to act as his own attorney in the

245

pursuit of his property is to permit him to do by indirection that which he has been directly forbidden to do.

While the right to practice law is not a constitutional right but rather a mere statutory privilege, the plaintiff here does not purport to be practicing law. He is not acting as an attorney. One acts as such only when he represents another, not when he appears for himself. Appellant, having the right to lawfully acquire property, has under the constitution the equal right to its perfect enjoyment, and, as a necessary incident to that right, the full power accorded to all of appearing in person to prosecute or defend all actions for its protection or preservation (*Philbrook v. Superior Court*, 111 Cal. 31 [43 Pac. 402). In so far, therefore, as the section purports to prevent one from personally appearing in a court of justice in pursuit or defense of a constitutional right—whether of person or property—it must be regarded as unconstitutional.

For the reasons given the judgment is reversed.

ST. SURE, J., and KNIGHT, J., concurred.

Supreme Court of California
People v. Brady, 40 Cal 198 (1870)

October term.

[198]
CONSTITUTIONAL CONSTRUCTION.— COMPETENCY OF WITNESS IN STATE COURTS. — The State Legislature has the power to declare who shall be competent to testify, and to regulate the production of evidence in the Courts of the State.

IDEM.—FOURTEENTH AMENDMENT.—CHINESE TESTIMONY.—**The Fourteenth Amendment to the Constitution of the United States does not conflict with the power of the Legislature in the exercise of its discretion to exclude Chinamen fro the right to testify in the State Courts.**

(remaining headnotes omitted)

[199]
Appeal from the County Court of the City and County of San Francisco.
The defendant appealed.
The other facts are stated in the opinion.

Hall & Dudley, for Appellant.

Jo Hamilton, Attorney-General, for Respondent.
Darwin & Murphy, of counsel.

The statutes of this State say, "Chinese shall not be witnesses in an action or proceeding wherein a white person is a party." And again: " No Chinese shell be permitted to give evidence in favor of or against any white person." These provisions are in force, unless in whole or in part repealed by a clause in the Fourteenth Amendment to the National Constitution, which provides: "Nor shall any State deprive any person of life, liberty or property, without due process of law, non deny to any person within its jurisdiction the equal protection of the laws." Now, if the denial of the power to testify, found in our statutes, amounts to a denial of an equal State protection, then such denial by our State law is made void by the superior force [200] of the Fourteenth Amendment. Or, let us put it this way: The United States Constitution, in its Fourteenth Amendment provides that no State shall deny to any person within its borders any legal protection which it accords to another — that its laws shall be so impersonal as to afford an equal protection to each. Now if our State, by excluding Chinese men from testifying in cases where white men are suffered to do so, deprives them of an equal legal protection, then such deprivation is in contravention of the higher law that of the National Constitution, and should be judicially disregarded. The question then to be answered is, whether a person who is deprived of the power of testifying is less protected than one, who amid the same surroundings, enjoys that power.

It is true that there are many cases in which the power of testifying is neither an object of desire, nor in any sense a right. Cases wherein it is but a burden, such are those in which the witness having no personal concern is summoned by another to illustrate that other's cause. But there are cases in which the dearest interests of the witness are involved, and must stand or not stand as the witness can stand or not stand in the tribunal which passes upon them. As to these I shall insist, that if the law allows one man to become a witness in his own cause, it is an unequal law, and distributes an unequal protection, unless it allows every other man the same

247

right. Were it not for the wonderful force of human prejudice, no argument would be needed to establish this proposition. Certainly to any number of white men similarly disfavored, the inequality would seem clear — would arouse the liveliest concern for their rights; and inflame just and instant resistance. Suppose one white man, unaided by other than his own proof could bring down the law upon his injurer, and thus punish a past and avert a future aggression, while another must stagger under repeated aggressions and could only invoke a tardy redress through the oath of one who might very much hesitate to be just and generous enough to incur the odium of seeming to take his part. The supposal in the case of white [201] men would be the strongest argument. Nor is it true, as urged by the objector, that to afford an equal protection by the laws means that the State shall stop in making an equal menace against the criminal, whether his victim be a white or a Chinaman. This the State has done. It means more. It demands that such other laws as shall be passed in aid of the menace, shall also apply equally. The menace may be a flaming sword for the protection of one because he call take and wield it, and it may sleep upon the wall within its sheath as to another, because he has been forbidden to take it down. To have equal protection of the laws, means to have equal protection of all the laws which contribute directly toward it. The State secures that protection by means of, first, a menace against the wrong doer; second, the enactment of means adequate to his discovery and conviction; and, third, the infliction of the menaced penalty. To constitute an equal protection to a Chinaman and white man, there must be an equality in each of these elements that go to afford it; and to deny equality in any one of these is to deny an equal protection. The State must not only utter an equal menace against and inflict an equal pain upon his aggressor, but it must also provide equal facilities and appliances for his conviction.

The deliberating aggressor is dissuaded, not by the menace, but by considerations touching the certainty of its execution. If this certainty is as great in the case of a Chinaman injured by a white man as it is in that of a white man injured by a Chinaman, then the restraining influences of the laws in each ease are also equal; and if this certainty be not as great in the case of the Chinaman, then the protection afforded him is not that equal protection demanded by the Fourteenth Amendment. If a man is kept at a disadvantage in the means of conviction, he cannot make equal avail either of the menace or its infliction. For his protection the menace bears less intimidation and its infliction a diminished assurance.

Equality of protection, demanding equality in the means of conviction, therefore, also demands that whether a Chinaman [202] or a white man be concerned, the modes of judicial investigation shall be the same. There shall be an equal right to the same instruments of proof; the same rower to compel their attendance; the same sanctions to insure their veracity; the same right for the party concerned, if he be cognizant of the facts to put hims4f and his oath into the judicial balance.

It is true, that when the law shall have announced equal opportunities in each of these means of self-protection, individual and national likings and loathings will yet, nevertheless, advance the conviction in one case and retard it in another, and an equality of protection wm not be exactly attained. But this failure will not be the fault of the law. The State will have done its duty. The law will have ceased to lend its support to the unfair denial. And until the law shall have done that, it will stand in conflict with the National Constitution. The natural consequence of the excluding law is, that more crimes against Chinamen than against white men go unwhipped of justice. The menace of the law is void, so far as regards all those injuries of which some friendly white man is not also cognizant. If a white man having malice enough, have also sufficient prescience, he may strike a Chinaman with every crime in the statute, without legal risk. True, a white man may also be struck at under conditions precluding discovery. But in his ease the impunity is accidental—is in spite of the law, and no law could prevent it. While in the case of a Chinaman, if not suggested by, it flows from, a defect in the law. The law does not equally mean to prevent it. It does not intend an equal protection. Let us emphasize the statement that there can be no equal protection unless there be equal facilities in making the legal menace productive of it; an equal power of pointing out the criminal, and of charging home his guilt. The Chinaman is mainly at the mercy of another for such protection as lie receives from the laws. The white man bears about with him his own protection. He cannot get beyond the reach of it. He is everywhere attended by a power which intimidates aggression by the menace of discovery. **[203]** He himself is the accredited messenger of the State to bear to its tribunals the story of his own wrongs, and may become their swift-winged avenger.

If it be conceded then, that one, denied the power of testifying against his aggressor, is less protected than one permitted to do so, it must also be conceded that the law of the State, which allows the white man to bear witness against his aggressor and denies a Chinaman the same right, in doing so, comes in conflict with the National Constitution, and to that extent is discharged of its force and becomes void. And our statutory exclusion of Chinamen in this sort of a case, should be legally held for naught; and in all those cases where white men may protect life or liberty or property by their own testimony, Chinamen should enjoy the same right.

It is objected that to be protected is a right, but to be a witness is not a right, but a privilege, which the State may confer or not.

1st. If to be protected be a right, then to be a witness is also a right, if being a witness be necessary to protection.

2d. To be a witness generally, may be a privilege or rather a duty which the officer conducting the prosecution may impose or not, in his discretion, under the law; but to be a witness in case of injury to one's self, against the aggressor, is not subject to such discretion, but a legal right of the injured party, if he claim to exercise it. Section 1416, Hittell's Digest, makes the injured party competent, and I claim, confers the right to enjoy the competency. Sections 1694 and 2195, the only ones on accusations or complaints, and Section 1740, seem to sustain this view.

But, no matter how that may be, it is practically true that whatever discretion the State Attorney possesses, he commonly uses it in favor of obtaining all the testimony he can, including that of the injured party, and that while he can, with or without right, decline to use a white party injured, he cannot in that discretion use a Chinaman, if a white man be the aggressor. So that even the presumed discretion does not help the objector's case; for that discretion **[204]** does not and cannot operate an equal protection. The deliberating aggressor, who agrees with the objector as to this discretion knows, at most, that the prosecutor, in an unusual exercise of power, may decline to testify the sufferer, even though a white man; but he also knows that the prosecutor cannot, in any contingency, testify him if a Chinaman. The fact remains, that in one case the injured party may be used, and in the other he cannot; and if power to testify is power to protect, there is higher protection where it may be, than where it cannot be exercised.

Again, it is argued that as those of our criminal laws which prohibit, are impersonal and general, that is all that is required by the amendment.

I have said that the mere utterance of a prohibition under a penalty, is but a small part of the legal machinery used in protecting from crime, and all that machinery must be applied, as well to the protection of the Chinaman, as; to that of the white man, else he has not equal protection. Suppose, while the menace of the law against robbery stood as now, it was declared that a Chinaman should not accuse, nor make complaint, nor have warrant nor subpoena, nor his witnesses sworn, nor the aid of an officer, nor of the State's Attorney. That the defendant should not be convicted save on the testimony of a dozen witnesses, nor even put upon his defense if he denied the accusation on oath. That, in case of his conviction, his punishment should be much smaller than if he had injured a white man. There are none but in such a case would see that the Chinaman had not equal protection, and also see that the protection does not come from the menace, but from the combined group of laws which bring it down upon the spoiler.

But among the group of protective laws — protective because conducing to conviction — there is none of so much direct value as that suffering the party injured to be a witness.

But the objector says, the testimony of the injured party does not secure conviction, and so is no sure protection. It **[205]** often does; it often aids it; is often the sole testimony to a technical point, which point has been made morally certain, but not been legally proved by other testimony. But it always tends, a priori, to make the conviction more likely, and so is a dissuading element in the mind of him who deliberates a crime. He can more safely strike a man legally dumb than one legally voiceful, and he prefers the former as a victim. The accident of non-punishment will always be possible, but in the one case it is reduced to a minimum, and in the other not. Only where this accident in both classes of cases possesses the same legal likelihood, will the protection be equal.

But the Chinaman would not be believed, for the law is only a popular conception of his unveracity, which would guide the jury were the law repealed.

Answer: The law is not a popular expression of his unveracity, as much as of our prejudice. If we held him unworthy of belief, we would not admit him as a witness in any case; but we do so when another Chinaman is concerned, and holding him credible when a Chinaman is concerned, we can only exclude him when a white man is, on the ground of prejudice. We really let him tell the truth, in case it hurts only a Chinaman, but not if it hurts a white man. To hold him capable of truly presenting his observations, in case of a Chinaman as actor and not in case of a white man, is an absurdity which can only be explained by prejudice.

The fact may be and probably is, that the Chinese, as a race, are not as credible as the whites, as a race. But there is no race absolut4y credible, and their lower grade of credibility is no reason for refusing the degree they possess. Then again, it is not the race, but an individual, that testifies, and we can apply to him, of whatsoever race, the same experimentum crucis, the same methods of verification we do in the case of a white witness. Credence is no more compulsory in the one than in the other case. Indeed, prejudice apart, the laws of belief are quite independent of reason, and dependent only on logic and conformity with known truths, and are the same in all cases.

[206] Some white men, not generally credible, are believed, in the particular case, because undoubted truths indorse them; we test their testimony by fixed canons and established liklihoods; we doubt or desbelieve in the case of disconformity. Submit the Chinaman to the same tests: the unveracious Chinaman is no more likely than the unveracious white man to steal away our faculties or misdirect our judgment.

But these considerations are rather on the reason of the law excluding, than to the effect of the amendment; and the logical answer is that, if the Chinaman testify, he may be more or less believed, and that chance of being believed, no matter how small, is a chance which might to that extent augment his protection by augmenting the risk of injuring him with impunity. If he is denied the value of that chance, be it ever so small, he has not as protection as the white man who enjoys the chance. The law which denies him ever so small a chance of protecting himself by his testimony, protects him less than it does the white man, to whom it accords the chance denied to him. It denies him thereby an equal protection.

The case of *People v. Washington*, (36 Cal. p. 658), was decided on the strength of the Civil Rights bill, but it decided a point or two which go in support of my argument. It decided (before the Fourteenth Amendment) that a white man in this State had the security of not being testified against by a Chinaman, and that the negro had the same right by virtue of the Civil Rights bill. Now, if exemption from being testified against be a security, or protection, capacity to testify in one's own behalf is also a security or protection. For testimony is decided to be a power to help or hurt, and its denial is the denial of a security or protection. Again, the Civil Rights bill guaranteed to negroes "the full and equal benefit of all laws and proceedings for the security of person," etc., and the Court, (in 36 Cal, 667,) said, "that in order to secure this, the rules of evidence must apply equally to all alike." Again, (on page 670,) the Court say: "The statutes of the State, regulating the competency of witnesses, are made applicable to all alike."

[207] Now, if this all follows from the terms of the Civil Rights bill, it quite as strenuously follows from those of the Fourteenth Amendment.

While citing this Washington case, I will add, that while we conceive the case in hand securely anchored on the Fourteenth Amendment, we yet, in the spirit of the suggestions of that case, urge that we are also sustained, and the Chinaman's admissibility is supported by Sections

1, 11, and 17, of our own State Constitution. (See Cooley, Const. Lim., p.255 and note, and pp. 392, 393, 369; *James v. Reynolds*, 2 Texas, 251; 2 Yerger, 269, 554; 44 Barb. 472; Cooley, pp. 368, 869.)

TEMPLE, J., delivered the opinion of the Court, WALLACE J., and SPRAGUE, J., concurring.

The defendant, a white man, was convicted of the crime of robbery, committed upon Hing Lee, a Chinaman, who was permitted to testify against the defendant on the trial.

The ruling of tile Court admitting this testimony against the defendant's objections is assigned as error, and is the only question raised on this appeal.

Section 14 of the Act of this State concerning crimes and punishments, as amended in 1863, reads as follows: "No Indian or person having one half or more Indian blood, or Mongolian or Chinese, shall be permitted to give evidence in favor of, or against, any white man."

This section is in full force, unless it is rendered inoperative in whole or in part by a clause in the Fourteenth Amendment to the Federal Constitution, which amendment, so far as material to this inquiry, reads as follows: "All persons born or naturalized in the United States, and subject to the jurisdiction thereof are citizens of the United States and of the State wherein they reside. No State shall make or enforce any law which stall abridge the privileges or immunities of citizens of the United States. Nor shall any State deprive any person of life, liberty or property without due process of law, nor deny to any within its jurisdiction the equal protection of the laws."

[208] It is claimed that the statute which denies to the Chinaman the right to testify against a white man is in conflict with this amendment, because it deprives the Chinaman of some degree of equal protection which it accords to the white man. That is to say, the ability to testify is a protection, because it tends to deter from crime against the person, by adding to the probability of conviction and punishment.

It is not charged that the law discriminates against the Chinaman, in affording a remedy to the white man for an injury, which upon the same state of facts is not afforded to the Chinaman. The facts being proven, the law pronounces the same judgment upon one as upon the other. The same facts being made to appear, the law provides for the Chinaman the same protection against threatened violence as for the white man. The protection of the whole police power of the State is afforded to them under the same circumstances, in the same way, and on precisely the same terms as to any other class of inhabitants. If a crime be committed against the person or property of a Chinaman, the same punishment is meted out to the criminal, when convicted, as though the crime had been committed upon a white man. But not only do the same consequences follow upon the same state of facts being proven, whether they affect Chinese or white men, but the law affords the Chinaman every means of bringing the facts to the knowledge of the Court for judicial action that is afforded to the white man. If a Chinaman be robbed, the commission of the crime may be proven by the same means as though he were a white man. If a white man be robbed by a white man, the fact cannot be established by Chinese testimony; and yet it may frequently happen that the fact cannot be proven in any other way. The same is true of a robbery committed upon a Chinaman by a white man. If a white man be robbed by a Chinaman, the fact may be proven by the evidence of white men or Chinese; and this is true as to a robbery committed upon a Chinaman by a Chinaman.

It is plain, therefore, that a crime is punished in the same way and may be proven by the same means in all cases [209] whether a white man or a Chinaman be the injured party. But it is said that if the general disqualification of Chinese to testify for or against a white man prevents them from testifying when a crime is committed upon them, the law is to that extent unequal and therefore void; that the right of the injured party to testify stands upon a very different footing from the right to call other witnesses. He may have a right to the use of the same species of evidence, but if he be the party concerned, he should also have the same right to offer himself as a witness. A crime may be committed under such circumstances that the party against whom it is committed is the only person by whom it can be proven. If the injured party be a white man, his testimony alone may be sufficient to cause the punishment of the wrongdoer, and by punishing a past wrong prevent a future wrong, and the Chinaman not being able to do this, is less protected. That although the law threatens the sane punishment for a crime committed upon the person of a Chinaman as when committed upon the person of a white man, the certainty of the punishment, and therefore the amount of protection afforded, is necessarily lessened by his exclusion as a witness.

I confess myself unable to see the force of this position, notwithstanding the confidence with which it is relied upon by the ingenious counsel who has made an interesting and able argument in the case on the part of the people. The white man is not permitted to testify because he is the injured party but because he is a competent witness on other grounds. The Chinaman is not excluded because he is the injured party and also a Chinaman, but because on other grounds he is an incompetent witness. The fact that he is the injured party is an immaterial circumstance in this discussion. His disadvantage is one shared, in a greater or lesser degree, by all who are so circumstanced as not to be surrounded by persons competent to testify. The fact that his countrymen, who are more likely to be his associates, are excluded, may be said to have an effect, in some degree in the same direction. But this is not owing to the inequality of the law. That affords to all the same instruments of [210] proof. All general laws operate more or less unequally — not on account of the partial provisions of the law, but from the various circumstances in which those upon whom they operate are #aced. The white man who employs Chinese as workmen upon his estate, is less likely to be able to prove offenses against his property than one who employs other laborers. He may, therefore, be said to be less protected; but this is the accident of his circumstances, and not the partiality of the law. He happens to be isolated from those who are competent to testify.

But it is contended that, although another may be so circumstanced as to be deprived of the equal protection of the laws, this is always accidental and not the necessary consequences of the provisions of law.

As to them the law is impersonal, and deprives them of no advantages afforded to others under the same circumstances; but the law excludes Mongolians, as a class, and itself creates the circumstance which places them at a disadvantage.

I think I have shown that there is no difference in principle — that the law does not cause them to be isolated from those competent to testify, although the fact of their exclusion may increase the chances that they will be so isolated. But if the position be admitted then the question resolves itself into this: Has the Legislature the power to declare classes of persons such as Indians and Mongolians incompetent to testify? That it may rightfully do so independently of the Fourteenth Amendment cannot be questioned. The Legislature of every State in the Union, so far as I know, and certainly of nearly every one, has continuously asserted and exercised this power during its entire history. To declare who shall be competent to testify and to regulate the production of evidence has always been considered a proper exercise of legislative power. It has excluded persons for nonconformity of religious belief, for inability to understand the nature of an oath, for having been convicted of an infamous crime, for having negro blood, for being an Indian or a Mongolia; and I am [211] not aware that the power of the Legislature to pass such laws has ever been questioned.

Now, in passing these laws, the Legislature does not act arbitrarily. It does not exclude a person because of his unbelief in popular theological dogmas, nor the Mongolian for being a Mongolian merely. The theory of the law and the idea upon which these laws are based is, that every person shall be permitted to testify who can aid the Court in coming to a correct conclusion as to the facts upon which it is to adjudicate. The reason why the testimony of such persons would be valueless in judicial investigations may be that they are incapable of testifying intelligently; that they are too unreliable to be of any service; that their admission would probably defeat justice by producing false testimony, or that they have particular prejudices against certain classes which would cause their evidence likely to do harm where the rights of such persons are concerned; such evidence, it is presumed, would impede rather than advance the cause of justice. It would not tend to protect any, but might cause the conviction of the innocent, or the acquittal of the guilty. Could counsel be convinced that Chinese testimony could never have any weight or that it would be more likely to cause the escape of the guilty than their punishment, and as likely to cause the conviction of the innocent as the guilty, he would not think their exclusion deprived them of any degree of protection to which they are fairly entitled; and yet this is what the legislature have decided, and had a right to decide, in enacting the law. I am not called upon to defend such legislation, or to deny that a more reasonable rule would be to allow the Courts to seek information from such sources as may be available, and to give to testimony such weight as it may deem it entitled to. The power of the Legislature to pass such laws is too well established to be called in question at this late day. (*Duffy v. Hobson*, October Term, 1870.)

If I am correct in the proposition that this is a proper subject to be regulated by legislative action, and that the [212] ground upon which the Legislature acts is that such evidence could not aid the Courts in their investigations, but would tend to defeat rather than promote the ends of justice, then it seems to me it must follow that the Fourteenth Amendment to the Federal Constitution can have no bearing upon the subject. It cannot be intended to compel the Courts to occupy their time in listening to evidence which cannot influence their judgment, or to deprive the State of the power to make such regulations as the cause of justice may absolutely require.

I am not called upon to say what should be the ruling if it were to appear that, under the pretense of regulating the production of evidence, the State has really deprived any person within its jurisdiction of any substantial means of protection afforded to others by its laws. There is no reason to suppose that the law in question was not passed in good faith, and with the honest purpose of promoting the cause of justice, even if that could be called in question here. The relation between the States and the Federal Government would forbid any such suspicion upon the motives of a State Legislature on the part of the Federal Government, and certainly this Court, a coordinate branch of the Government, cannot impugn their motives. And, independently of the comity which should exist between the departments of the Government, we can hardly conceive it possible that a legislative body in a Christian country would deliberately deprive its Courts and police of any proper means for the detection and prevention of crime; that it would willingly leave any class unprotected, so far as the commission of crimes against them are concerned; this would directly encourage crime, and lead inevitably to the demoralization of society, and consequently the insecurity of all. To withdraw from any class the protection of the police laws, through prejudice or from a desire to discourage their presence, would be inhuman and barbarous. We cannot attribute any such motives to a coordinate department of the Government, and we must conclude that the provisions of the law under consideration were supposed [213] by the Legislature to provide every means for the detection and punishment of crime consistent with justice and the safety of the community.

At the time the amendment was adopted similar laws existed in nearly every State of the Union. They had never been regarded as depriving any one of any degree of protection which the law afforded to others, or depriving the Courts of any proper assistance they could otherwise have had in their investigations. They were sustained on the ground that they were necessary that the guilty might be punished and the innocent escape. The amendment did not render such laws less appropriate or less necessary, and there is nothing in the principle established by it which conflicts with the theory of such laws. It cannot be supposed, therefore, that in adopting the amendment it was intended to deprive the State Legislature of their power over the subject.

I think I have shown that there is no inequality in the protective laws of this State; that the law interposes the same shield for the protection of the Chinaman as for the white man, and that it imposes the same punishment when he has been injured; that Upon the same facts it pronounces the same judgment, without regard to the person upon whom it may fall; that it dispenses equal justice to all; and further, that in the rules of evidence established by the

Legislature there is no inequality, or, if there is, it is made in furtherance of justice, and is unavoidable; that in excluding Chinamen the Legislature exercises a discretion properly entrusted to it, and that a proper exercise of it in the interests of justice, although it may exclude a Chinaman where another is allowed to testify, is not a violation of the Fourteenth Amendment I cannot think, however, that this last inquiry was necessary in this case. The inquiry should stop when it is ascertained that upon the same state of facts the same legal consequences follow to all. If the laws themselves are equal, imposing the same burdens upon and affording the same remedies to all, under the same ascertained circumstances, the requirement of equality is satisfied.

[214] Limitations upon the powers of the State Governments are appropriate in the Federal Constitution. It may he necessary to restrain the powers of the State that it may not interfere with the General Government in the exercise of the powers granted to it, or that a State may not, by its individual action, defeat any of the purposes for which the General Government exists. To the extent, however, of the powers not granted to the General Government or denied to the States, the power of the State is supreme. It enacts laws of its own right and should be allowed to execute them in its own way. The Federal Government cannot supervise its exercise of the powers it undoubtedly possesses. It is no part of purpose for which that Government was created, to stand guard over the States to see that they execute their laws in a manner not to oppress those who are subject to them The State Government is complete in itself, so far as matters of internal government are concerned, and contains in its own Constitution every necessary safeguard against improper use of its powers, and every protection to individual rights, which the people thought necessary.

Rules of evidence are a part of the contrivance by means of which the State executes its laws. They are always the means to an end, and if the law be one the State has a right to pass, I cannot think it was intended to interfere with the means the State may adopt to enforce it.

This view is sustained by a consideration of the particular purpose the amendment was designed to accomplish. Its chief purpose undoubtedly was to protect negroes in those States where slavery recently existed. Under those laws it sometimes happened that the law pronounced a different judgment upon a negro from that it pronounced upon a white man upon the same state of facts. The law provided a different punishment to the negro when convicted of crime from that which was provided for a white man when convicted of the same crime, and in other respects the law discriminated against the negro. The amendment was evidently intended to prevent these inequalities. It could [215] not have been intended to authorize the Federal Government to supervise the State in the exercise of its undoubted powers. Such a construction would reduce a State to condition of a mere municipality, exercising its meagre powers by sufferance, and render meaningless that clause of the Constitution which recognizes the possession of reserved powers by the States.

The counsel for The People cites the ease of *The People v. George Washington* (36 Cal., 658) as supporting his views, and it must be admitted that some of the positions taken in that case are inconsistent with the views I have expressed in this case. That case presented for consideration the constitutionality of the Act of Congress commonly caused the Civil Rights bill and its effect upon the fourteenth section or the Act of this State, concerning crimes and punishments, cited above. The Court decided the Act of Congress constitutional; that it was authorized by the Thirteenth Amendment to the Federal Constitution, which provides that "neither slavery nor involuntary servitude, except as a punishment for crime, whereof the party shall have been duly convicted, shall exist within the United States, or any place subject to their jurisdiction;" and also in the second section, that Congress may enforce the amendment by appropriate legislation.

I dissent, both from the reasoning used and conclusions arrived at in that case, for the reasons given by Mr. Justice Crockett in his dissenting opinion, and for reasons which will readily suggest themselves from what I have already stated. If I am correct as to the theory upon which legislation concerning the competency of evidence is based, it seems to me it must follow that the positions taken by the Court in that case are wrong. There is one reason why I disapprove of that case, however, which, as it has a direct bearing upon this case and differs a little from positions taken by Judge Crockett in that, and is, withal, an important matter, I propose to state.

It is stated in the opinion of the Court, in that case, that the object of the first section of the Thirteenth. Amendment **[216]** is not only to abolish slavery, but to deprive Congress and the States of the power to reduce any person within the jurisdiction of the United States to a state of slavery. That is to say, so far as its future operation is concerned it is a mere limitation upon the legislative power of the States and of the United States. That the second section confers upon Congress the power, by appropriate legislation, to secure all persons in the United States in the full enjoyment of that liberty contemplated by the first section; "or, in other words, the Thirteenth Amendment was at least intended to make all men born in the United States, without reference to race or color, equal before the law in respect to personal liberty one of the absolute rights of man — and to give Congress power to pass any and all laws necessary and proper to accomplish that end."

The first section is said by the Court and I think correctly, to be simply a limitation upon the power of the State to establish slavery or reduce any one to a state of slavery or involuntary servitude; and I cannot think that the second section which simply empowers Congress to enforce this limitation upon the legislative power of the State, confers upon Congress any power to establish a police system for the internal government of the State, or by its laws to annul the laws of a State, or to control their operation in any way whatever.

There is nothing in the language used in the first section of the amendment which can be construed into a grant of power. It is a restriction, and not an enlargement of the powers of the General Government, if it applies to the General Government at all. It is a limitation upon the States, depriving them of the power to establish slavery. If it were within the province of the Federal Government to establish a system of police laws for the protection of individuals within the States, the language is inappropriate to confer any power over the subject matter of the section. The apparent purpose of the amendment was not to prevent the illegal duress of individuals. It was aimed exclusively at the institution of slavery as established by the **[217]** laws of the States. It was directed to the States in their sovereign capacity as law-makers, and was not intended to afford relief to individuals unlawfully deprived of their liberty. Its purpose is satisfied when such restraint is rendered illegal. The right to personal liberty is secured by the amendment itself and it is not necessary that Congress should pass laws upon the subject, much less give to my one political rights which may add to their importance and enable them to maintain their state of freedom. This is absolutely secured by the Constitution itself, which renders void all laws for their enslavement. They are not to be armed that they may resist State laws, or given importance that they may influence State legislation.

The second section of the amendment certainly contains no substantive grant of power. It merely authorizes Congress to enforce the amendment by appropriate legislation. Its scope is limited by the first section. That is a mere limitation upon the powers 0£ the States. It authorizes Congress, therefore, to pass such laws as under our system of Government would be appropriate to enforce a limitation upon the legislative power of a State, and no other. It is not an affirmative grant of power before which State legislation must give way, like the power to establish uniform laws upon the subject of bankruptcy. The laws of the State must be tried by the language of the Constitutional inhibition and not by the laws of Congress. The power to enforce a limitation upon the power of a State cannot be construed to authorize Congress to enlarge the limitation if necessary to render it effectual. The State law in question ought, therefore, to have been tested by the language of the Constitution and not by the Civil Rights bill.

Nor is it appropriate legislation for Congress to nullify a law of the State, either directly or by preventing its execution. It could only do so when the law is unconstitutional, and to determine that question is the province of the judiciary. It would compel the people unnecessarily to sustain two police systems — one to execute the laws, and the other to control and, in certain cases, to prevent their execution. **[218]** It would interfere with efficiency of the police system of the State, and almost inevitably lead to conflicts between the two governments. The two governments, however, are not antagonistical, either in theory or interest. They are parts of one system, supplementary to each other, together supplying all the governmental wants of the people. They are both under the control of the people, but in their operation should be independent of and, therefore, a check upon each other.

Ever since the Federal Government has been in operation it has been, the practice to test the constitutionality of State laws, and enforce the limitations upon the powers of the States by judicial decisions. The claim on the part of the Supreme Court of the United States of the right to pass upon these questions, even when arising in the State Courts, though not always conceded, has been generally acquiesced in. Constitutional limitations, so far as they affect individual rights, have always under our system been enforced by judicial action, and I have no doubt a proper construction of the second section of the Thirteenth Amendment would confine legislation on the part of Congress to laws providing for judicial action in the premises.

But the claim on the part of Congress of the right to interfere with or control the operation of State Laws, is utterly repugnant to our system of Government. "The genius and character of the whole Government seems to be," said Chief Justice Marshall, in Gibbons v. Ogden, (9 Wheaton, 195) "that its action is to be applied to all the external concerns of the nation and to those internal concerns which affect the States generally, but not to those which are completely within a particular State, which do not affect other States, and with which it is not necessary to interfere, for the purpose of executing some of the general powers of the Government." The division of powers between the State and Federal Government, and the independence of the States within the sphere of their reserved powers, and their exclusive right of legislation as to most of the objects for which Governments exist, has always been considered the principal [219] and most valuable safeguard for civil liberty afforded by our system. The right of local legislation for each Colony is said by Mr. Madison to have been the fundamental idea of the Revolution. That the Colonies were with each other and with Great Britain co-ordinate members of one empire, under a common executive or sovereign, but not united by a legislative sovereign. The legislative power was maintained to be as complete in each American as in the British Parliament. (Madison's Virginia Report.)

The States, said Mr. Hamilton, can never lose their powers, till the whole people of America have lost their liberties. When the Federal Constitution was formed, no idea was more fixed than that the States should continue independent of Federal control as to all reserved powers, which were to include entire control over all matters exclusively appertaining to a particular State. The Colonies, with their local legislatures, had been the nurseries of civil liberty, and to the States, their legitimate successors, was intrusted the duty of maintaining it Chiefly to secure the continued existence of the States, to uphold and maintain them as independent States, and thereby to secure to the people and their posterity the blessings of liberty, the Constitution and the Union were formed.

At that time no writer was more popular with American statesmen than Montesquieu. From him was derived the idea of dividing the Government into three departments — the executive, legislative and judicial — as an essential security for the liberties of the people. Another idea advanced by him, which was very popular at that time, and often quoted, was that small States naturally gravitate to a republican form of government; larger States to a monarchical, and vast empires to a despotic government. The first was most favorable to individual liberty; the last, to national power. They claimed to have secured the advantages of the first by assuring the independence of the States, and the last by establishing the Federal Government as a common agent which, in the exercise of certain limited powers, should be supreme over all.

[220] It was more efficient than the Confederacy it displaced, for it executes its own laws To it was intrusted the control of the foreign relations of all the States. It could declare war, and, to carry it on, wield the entire military power of the Union. As to all the world, at least, except its own members, it presented us as one nation. Within the sphere of its limited authority it wielded the power of a vast empire with all the efficiency of the most despotic

Government, and yet it was supposed that it could not be dangerous to the liberties of the people, for its powers were limited and well defined, and could be used but for a few purposes, and those in which all the States had a common interest. The great mass of governmental powers were still reserved to the States. The absolute right of uncontrolled local legislation upon all objects most intimately connected with individual rights and most essential to the maintenance of personal liberty was reserved.

The Federal Government was created by the compact of sovereign States, and their continued existence in the uncontrolled exercise of their powers, is an essential element of the system. This is doubtless what Hamilton meant when he said that for the General Government to supersede or destroy the State Governments would be to commit suicide. It rests upon them as tile dome rests upon and yet upholds the columns which support it.

We cannot conclude from any doubtful language that it was intended to strike from the Constitution the fundamental idea upon which the Union was constructed — to rob the Government of its crowning glory and most beneficent principle; and had such been its apparent meaning, we ought to be diligent to find out some construction which would be less pernicious in its consequences; we should regard it as we would a law apparently legalizing murder or robbery; we could not conclude such a purpose was intended unless it is expressed in unmistakable language.

In this case, however, we are not forced to any such extremity. The most obvious construction is that which is [221] most in accord with the principles of our government, and which preserves beneficent features.

The judgment reversed and a new trial ordered.

By **CROCKET**t, J.: I concur in the judgment and in the opinion of Justice Temple, except in so far as it dissents from or questions the correctness of certain views expressed by me in the ease of The People v. Washington.

By **RHODES**, C. J.: I dissent. My views upon the questions involved in this case were to some extent expressed in *People v. George Washington* (36 Cal. 658); and I will hereafter, should time permit, more fully state the reasons which lead me to the conclusion that Section 14 of the Act concerning crimes and punishments was abrogated by the Fourteenth Amendment to the Constitution.

United States Supreme Court
The Slaughter-House Cases, 83 U.S. 36 (1872)

The Butcher's Benevolent Association of New Orleans v. The Crescent City Live-Stock Landing and Slaughter-House Company.

Paul Esteben, L. Ruch, J. P. Rouede, W. Maylie, S. Firmberg, B. Beaubay, William Fagan, J. D. Broderick, N. Seibel, M. Lannes, J. Gitzinger, J. P. Aycock, D. Verges, The Live-Stock Dealer's and Butcher's Association of New Orleans, and Charles Cavaroc v. The State of Louisiana, ex rel. S. Belden, Attorney-General.

The Butcher's Benevolent Association of New Orleans v. The Crescent City Live-Stock Landing and Slaughter-House Company.

December Term, 1872
(headnotes omitted)

[83 U.S. 36, 38] ERROR to the Supreme Court of Louisiana.

The three cases—the parties to which as plaintiffs and defendants in error, are given specifically as a sub-title, at the head of this report, but which are reported together also under the general name which, in common parlance, they had acquired-grew out of an act of the legislature of the State of Louisiana, entitled: *"An act to protect the health of the City of New Orleans, to locate the stock landings and slaughter-houses, and to incorporate 'The Crescent City Live-Stock Landing and Slaughter- House Company,'"* which was approved on the 8th of March, 1869, and went into operation on the 1st of June following; and the three cases were argued together.

The act was as follows:

"**SECTION** 1. *Be it enacted, &c.,* That from and after the first day of June, A.D. 1869, it shall not be lawful to land, keep, or slaughter any cattle, beeves, calves, sheep, swine, or other animals, or to have, keep, or establish any stock-landing, yards, pens, slaughter-houses, or abattoirs at any point or place within the city of New Orleans, *or the parishes of Orleans, Jefferson, and St. Bernard,* or at any point or place on the east bank of the Mississippi River within the corporate limits of the city of New Orleans, or at any point on the west bank of the Mississippi River, above the present depot of the New Orleans, Opelousas, and Great Western Railroad Company, *except* that the 'Crescent City Stock Landing and Slaughter-House Company' may establish *themselves* at any point or place as hereinafter provided. Any person or persons, or corporation or company carrying on any business or doing any act in contravention of this act, or landing, slaughtering or keeping any animal or animals in violation of this act, shall be liable to a fine of $250, for each and **[83 U.S. 36, 39]** every violation, the same to be recoverable, with costs of suit, before any court of competent jurisdiction."

The second section of the act created one Sanger and sixteen other persons named, a corporation, with the usual privileges of a corporation, and including power to appoint officers, and fix their compensation and term of office, and to fix the amount of the capital stock of the corporation and the number of shares thereof.

The act then went on:

"**SECTION** 3. *Be it further enacted, &c.,* That said company or corporation is hereby authorized to establish and erect at its own expense, at any point or place on the east bank of

259

the Mississippi River within the parish of St. Bernard, or in the corporate limits of the city of New Orleans, below the United States Barracks, or at any point or place on the west bank of the Mississippi River below the present depot of the New Orleans, Opelousas, and Great Western Railroad Company, wharves, stables, sheds, yards, and buildings necessary to land, stable, shelter, protect, and preserve all kinds of horses, mules, cattle, and other animals; and from and after the time such buildings, yards, &c., are ready and complete for business, and notice thereof is given in the official journal of the State, the said Crescent City Live-Stock Landing and Slaughter-House Company shall have the *sole and exclusive privilege of conducting and carrying on the live-stock landing and slaughter-house business within the limits and privileges granted by the provisions of this act*; and cattle and other animals destined for sale or slaughter in the city of New Orleans, or its environs, shall be landed at the live-stock landings and yards of said company, and shall be yarded, sheltered, and protected, if necessary, by said company or corporation; and said company or corporation shall be entitled to have and receive for each steamship landing at the wharves of the said company or corporation, $10; for each steamboat or other water craft, $5; and for each horse, mule, bull, ox, or cow landed at their wharves, for each and every day kept, 10 cents; for each and every hog, calf, sheep, or goat, for each and every day kept, 5 cents, all without including the feed; and said company or corporation shall be entitled to keep and detain each and all of said animals until said charges are fully paid. But **[83 U.S. 36, 40]** if the charges of landing, keeping, and feeding any of the aforesaid animals shall not be paid by the owners thereof after fifteen days of their being landed and placed in the custody of the said company or corporation, then the said company or corporation, in order to reimburse themselves for charges and expenses incurred, shall have power, by resorting to judicial proceedings, to advertise said animals for sale by auction, in any two newspapers published in the city of New Orleans, for five days; and after the expiration of said five days, the said company or corporation may proceed to sell by auction, as advertised, the said animals, and the proceeds of such sales shall be taken by the said company or corporation, and applied to the payment of the charges and expenses aforesaid, and other additional costs; and the balance, if any, remaining from such sales, shall be held to the credit of and paid to the order or receipt of the owner of said animals. Any person or persons, firm or corporation violating any of the provisions of this act, or interfering with the privileges herein granted, or landing, yarding, or keeping any animals in violation of the provisions of this act, or to the injury of said company or corporation, shall be liable to a fine or penalty of $250, to be recovered with costs of suit before any court of competent jurisdiction.

'The company shall, before the first of June, 1869, build and complete A GRAND SLAUGHTER-HOUSE of sufficient capacity to accommodate all butchers, and in which to slaughter 500 animals per day; also a sufficient number of sheds and stables shall be erected before the date aforementioned, to accommodate all the stock received at this port, all of which to be accomplished before the date fixed for the removal of the stock landing, as provided in the first section of this act, under penalty of a forfeiture of their charter.

"SECTION 4. *Be it further enacted, &c.*, That the said company or corporation is hereby authorized to erect, at its own expense, one or more landing-places for live stock, as aforesaid, at any points or places consistent with the provisions of this act, and to have and enjoy from the completion thereof, and after the first day of June, A.D. 1869, *the exclusive privilege of having landed at their wharves or landing-places all animals intended for sale or slaughter in the parishes of Orleans and Jefferson*; and are hereby also authorized (in connection) to erect at its own expense one or more slaughter-houses, at any points or places **[83 U.S. 36, 41]** consistent with the provisions of this act, and to have and enjoy, from the completion thereof, and after the first day of June, A.D. 1869, *the exclusive privilege of having slaughtered therein all animals, the meat of which is destined for sale in the parishes of Orleans and Jefferson.*

"SECTION 5. *Be it further enacted, &c.*, That whenever said slaughter-houses and accessory buildings shall be completed and thrown open for the use of the public, said company or corporation shall immediately give public notice for thirty days, in the official journal of the State, and within said thirty days' notice, and within, from and after the first day of June, A.D. 1869, *all other stock landings and slaughter-houses within the parishes of Orleans, Jefferson, and St. Bernard shall be closed, and it will no longer be lawful to slaughter cattle, hogs, calves, sheep, or goats, the meat of which is determined for sale within the parishes aforesaid, under a penalty of $100, for each and every offence, recoverable, with costs of suit, before any court of competent jurisdiction; that all animals to be slaughtered, the meat whereof is determined for sale in the parishes of Orleans or Jefferson, must be slaughtered in the slaughter-houses erected by the said company or corporation*; and upon a refusal of said company or corporation to allow and animal or animals to be slaughtered after the same has been certified by the inspector, as hereinafter provided, to be fit for human food, the said company or corporation shall be subject to a fine in each case of $ 250, recoverable, with costs of suit, before any court of competent jurisdiction; said fines and penalties to be paid over to the auditor of public accounts, which sum or sums shall be credited to the educational fund.

"SECTION 6. *Be it further enacted, &c.*, That the governor of the State of Louisiana shall appoint a competent person, clothed with police powers, to act as inspector of all stock that is to be slaughtered, and whose duty it will be to examine closely all animals intended to be slaughtered, to ascertain whether they are sound and fit for human food or not; and if sound and fit for human food, to furnish a certificate stating that fact, to the owners of the animals inspected; and without said certificate no animals can be slaughtered for sale in the slaughter-houses of said company or corporation. The owner of said animals so inspected to pay the inspector 10 cents for each and every animal so inspected, one- half of which fee the said inspector shall retain for his services, and the other half of said fee shall be **[83 U.S. 36, 42]** paid over to the auditor of public accounts, said payment to be made quarterly. Said inspector shall give a good and sufficient bond to the State, in the sum of $5000, with sureties subject to the approval of the governor of the State of Louisiana, for the faithful performance of his duties. Said inspector shall be fined for dereliction of duty $50 for each neglect. Said inspector may appoint as many deputies as may be necessary. The half of the fees collected as provided above, and paid over to the auditor of public accounts, shall be placed to the credit of the educational fund.

"SECTION 7. *Be it further enacted, &c.*, That all persons slaughtering or causing to be slaughtered, cattle or other animals in said slaughter- houses, shall pay to the said company or corporation the following rates or perquisites, viz.: For all beeves, $1 each; for all hogs and calves, 50 cents each; for all sheep, goats, and lambs, 30 cents each; *and the said company or corporation shall be entitled to the head, feet, gore, and entrails of all animals excepting hogs, entering the slaughter-houses and killed therein,* it being understood that the heart and liver are not considered as a part of the gore and entrails, and that the said heart and liver of all animals slaughtered in the slaughter-houses of the said company or corporation shall belong, in all cases, to the owners of the animals slaughtered.

"SECTION 8. *Be it further enacted, &c.*, That all the fines and penalties incurred for violations of this act shall be recoverable in a civil suit before any court of competent jurisdiction, said suit to be brought and prosecuted by said company or corporation in all cases where the privileges granted to the said company or corporation by the provisions of this act are violated or interfered with; that one-half of all the fines and penalties recovered by the said company or corporation [*Sic* in copy—REP.], in consideration of their prosecuting the violation of this act, and the other half shall be paid over to the auditor of public accounts, to the credit of the educational fund.

"SECTION 9. *Be it further enacted, &c.*, That said Crescent City Live-Stock Landing and Slaughter-House Company shall have the right to construct a railroad from their buildings to the limits of the city of New Orleans, and shall have the right to run cars thereon, drawn by horses or other locomotive power, as they may see fit; said railroad to be built on either of the public roads running along the levee on each side of the

Mississippi [83 U.S. 36, 43] River. The said company or corporation shall also have the right to establish such steam ferries as they may see fit to run on the Mississippi River between their buildings and any points or places on either side of said river.

"**SECTION** 10. *Be it further enacted, &c.*, That at the expiration of twenty-five years from and after the passage of this act the privileges herein granted shall expire."

The parish of Orleans containing (as was said[1]) an area of 150 square miles; the parish of Jefferson of 384; and the parish of St. Bernard of 620; the three parishes together 1154 square miles, and they having between two and three hundred thousand people resident therein, and prior to the passage of the act above quoted, about 100 persons employed daily in the business of procuring, preparing, and selling animal food, the passage of the act necessarily produced great feeling. Some hundreds of suits were brought on the one side or on the other; the butchers, not included in the 'monopoly' as it was called, acting sometimes in combinations, in corporations, and companies, and sometimes by themselves; the same counsel, however, apparently representing pretty much all of them. The ground of the opposition to the slaughter-house company's pretensions, so far as any cases were finally passed on in this court was, that the act of the Louisiana legislature made a monopoly and was a violation of the most important provisions of the thirteenth and fourteenth Articles of Amendment to the Constitution of the United States. The language relied on of these articles is thus:

AMENDMENT XIII.

"Neither slavery nor *involuntary servitude* except as a punishment for crime, whereof the party shall have been duly convicted, shall exist within the United States, nor any place subject to their jurisdiction."

AMENDMENT XIV.

"All persons born or naturalized in the United States, and subject to the jurisdiction thereof, *are citizens of the United States* and of the State wherein they reside. [83 U.S. 36, 44] "No State shall make or enforce any law which shall abridge the *privileges or immunities of citizens of the United States*, nor shall any State deprive any person of *life, liberty, or property*, without due process of law, nor deny to any person within its jurisdiction the *equal protection of the laws*."

The Supreme Court of Louisiana decided in favor of the company, and five of the cases came into this court under the 25th section of the Judiciary Act in December, 1870; where they were the subject of a preliminary motion by the plaintiffs in error for an order in the nature of a supersedeas. After this, that is to say, in March, 1871, a compromise was sought to be effected, and certain parties professing, apparently, to act in a representative way in behalf of the opponents to the company, referring to a compromise that they assumed had been effected, agreed to discontinue "all writs of error concerning the said company, now pending in the Supreme Court of the United States;" stipulating further "that their agreement should be sufficient authority for any attorney to appear and move for the dismissal of all said suits." Some of the cases were thus confessedly dismissed. But the three of which the names are given as a sub- title at the head of this report were, by certain of the butchers, asserted not to have been *dismissed*. And *Messrs. M. H. Carpenter, J. S. Black, and T. J. Durant, in behalf of the new corporation*, having moved to dismiss them also as embraced in the agreement, affidavits were filed on the one side and on the other; the affidavits of the butchers opposed to the "monopoly" affirming that they were plaintiffs in error in these three cases, and that they never consented to what had been done, and that no proper authority had been given to do it. This matter was directed to be heard with the merits. The case being advanced was first heard on these, January 11th, 1872; Mr. Justice Nelson being indisposed and not in his seat. Being ordered for reargument, it was heard again, February 3[d], 4th, and 5th, 1873.

---

[1] See infra, pp. 85, 86.

Mr. John A. Campbell, and also Mr. J. Q. A. Fellows, argued the case at much length and on the authorities, in behalf of **[83 U.S. 36, 45]** the plaintiffs in error. The reporter cannot pretend to give more than such an abstract of the argument as may show to what the opinion of the court was meant to be responsive.

I. The learned counsel quoting Thiers[2], contended that "the right to one's self, to one's own faculties, physical and intellectual, one's own brain, eyes, hands, feet, in a word to his soul and body, was an incontestable right; one of whose enjoyment and exercise by its owner no one could complain, and one which no one could take away. More than this, the obligation to labor was a duty, a thing ordained of God, and which if submitted to faithfully, secured a blessing to the human family." Quoting further from Turgot, De Tocqueville, Buckle, Dalloz, Leiber, Sir G. C. Lewis, and others, the counsel gave a vivid and very interesting account of the condition and grievances of the lower orders in various countries of Europe, especially in France, with its *banalités* and "*seigneurs justiciers,*" during those days when "the prying eye of the government followed the butcher to the shambles and the baker to the oven;" when "the peasant could not cross a river without paying to some nobleman a toll, nor take the produce which he raised to market until he had bought leave to do so; nor consume what remained of his grain till he had sent it to the lord's mill to be ground, nor full his cloths on his own works, nor sharpen his tools at his own grindstone, nor make wine, oil, or cider at his own press;" the days of monopolies; monopolies which followed men in their daily avocations, troubled them with its meddling spirit, and worst of all diminished their responsibility to themselves. Passing from Scotland, in which the cultivators of each barony or regality were obliged to pay a "multure" on each stack of hay or straw reaped by the farmer—"thirlage" or "thraldom," as it was called—and when lands were subject to an "astriction" astricting them and their inhabitants to particular mills for the grinding of grain that was raised on them, and coming to Great Britain, the counsel adverted to the reigns of Edward III, and Richard **[83 U.S. 36, 46]** II, and their successors, when the price of labor was fixed by law, and when every able-bodied man and woman, not being a merchant or craftsman, was "bounden" to serve at the wages fixed, and when to prevent the rural laborer from seeking the towns he was forbidden to leave his own village. It was in England that the earliest battle for civil liberty had been made. Macaulay thus described it:[3]

"It was in the Parliament of 1601, that the opposition which had, during forty years, been silently gathering and husbanding strength, fought its first great battle and won its first victory. The ground was well chosen. The English sovereigns had always been intrusted with the supreme direction of commercial police. It was their undoubted prerogative to regulate coins, weights, measures, and to appoint fairs, markets, and ports. The line which bounded their authority over trade, had, as usual, been but loosely drawn. They therefore, as usual, encroached on the province which rightfully belonged to the legislature. The encroachment was, as usual, patiently borne, till it became serious. But at length the Queen took upon herself to grant patents of monopoly by scores. There was scarcely a family in the realm that did not feel itself aggrieved by the oppression and extortion which the abuse naturally caused. Iron, oil, vinegar, coal, lead, starch, yarn, leather, glass, could be bought only at exorbitant prices. The House of Commons met in an angry and determined mood. It was in vain that a courtly minority blamed the speaker for suffering the acts of the Queen's highness to be called in question. The language of the discontented party was high and menacing, and was echoed by the voice of the whole nation. The coach of the chief minister of the crown was surrounded by an indignant populace, who cursed *monopolies*, and exclaimed that the prerogative should not be allowed to touch the old liberties of England."

Macaulay proceeded to say that the Queen's reign was in danger of a shameful and disgraceful end, but that she, with admirable judgment, declined the contest and redressed the

---

[2] De la Propriété, 36, 47.
[3] History of England, vol. 1, p. 58.

grievance, and in touching language thanked the Commons for their tender care of the common weal. [**83 U.S. 36, 47**] The great grievance of our ancestors about the time that they largely left England, was this very subject. Sir John Culpeper, in a speech in the Long Parliament, thus spoke of these monopolies and pollers of the people:

"They are a nest of wasps-a swarm of vermin which have overcrept the land. Like the frogs of Egypt they have gotten possession of our dwellings, and we have scarce a room free from them. They sup in our cup; they dip in our dish; they sit by our fire. We find them in the dye-fat, wash-bowl, and powdering-tub. They share with the butler in his box. They will not bait us a pin. We may not buy our clothes without their brokage. These are the leeches that have sucked the commonwealth so hard that it is almost hectical. Mr. Speaker! I have echoed to you the cries of the Kingdom. I will tell you their hopes. They look to Heaven for a blessing on this Parliament."

Monopolies concerning wine, coal, salt, starch, the dressing of meat in taverns, beavers, belts, bone-lace, leather, pins, and other things, to the gathering of rags, are referred to in this speech.

But more important than these discussions in Parliament were the solemn judgments of the courts of Great Britain. The great and leading case was that reported by Lord Coke, *The Case of Monopolies*.[4] The patent was granted to Darcy to buy beyond the sea all such playing-cards as he thought good, and to utter and sell them within the kingdom, and that he and his agents and deputies should have the whole trade, traffic, and merchandise of playing-cards, and that another person and none other should have the making of playing-cards within the realm. A suit was brought against a citizen of London for selling playing-cards, and he pleaded that being a citizen free of the city he had a right to do so. And—

"Resolved (Popham, C.J.) per totam Curiam, that the said grant of the plaintiff of the sole making of cards within the realm, was utterly void, and for two reasons: [**83 U.S. 36, 48**]

"1. That it is a monopoly and against the common law.

"2. That it is against divers acts of Parliament."

[The learned counsel read Sir Edward Coke's report of the judgment in this case, which was given fully in the brief at length, seeking to apply it to the cases before the court.]

It was from a country which had been thus oppressed by monopolies that our ancestors came. And a profound conviction of the truth of the sentiment already quoted from M. Thiers— that every man has a right to his own faculties, physical and intellectual, and that this is a right, one of which no one can complain, and no one deprive him-was at the bottom of the settlement of the country by them. Accordingly, free competition in business, free enterprise, the absence of all exactions by petty tyranny, of all spoliation of private right by public authority-the suppression of sinecures, monopolies, titles of nobility, and exemption from legal duties- were exactly what the colonists sought for and obtained by their settlement here, their long contest with physical evils that attended the colonial condition, their struggle for independence, and their efforts, exertions, and sacrifices since.

Now, the act of the Louisiana legislature was in the face of all these principles; it made it unlawful for men to use their own land for their own purposes; made it unlawful to any except the seventeen of this company to exercise a lawful and necessary business for which others were as competent as they, for which at least one thousand persons in the three parishes named had qualified themselves, had framed their arrangements in life, had invested their property, and had founded all their hopes of success on earth. The act was a pure MONOPOLY; as such against common right, and void at the common law of England. And it was equally void by our own law. The case of *The Norwich Gaslight Company v. The Norwich City Gaslight Company*,[5] a case in Connecticut, and more pointedly still, *The City of Chicago v. Rumpff*,[6] a case in Illinois, and *The Mayor of the City of Hudson v. Thorne*,[7] [**83 U.S. 36, 49**] a case in New York, were in

---

[4] 11 Reports, 85.
[5] 25 Connecticut, 19.
[6] 45 Illinois, 90.
[7] 7 Paige, 261.

entire harmony with Coke's great case, and declared that monopolies are against common right.[8]

How, indeed, do authors and inventors maintain a monopoly in even the works of their own brain? in that which in a large sense may be called their own. Only through a provision of the Constitution preserving such works to them. Many State constitutions have denounced monopolies by name, and it is certain that every species of exclusive privilege is an offence to the people, and that popular aversior to them does but increase the more largely that they are granted.

II. But if this monopoly were not thus void at common law, would be so under both the thirteenth and the fourteenth amendments.

The thirteenth amendment prohibits "slavery and involuntary *servitude.*" The expressions are ancient ones, and were familiar even before the time when they appeared in the great Ordinance of 1787, for the government of our vast Northwestern Territory; a territory from which great States were to arise. In that ordinance that are associated with enactments affording comprehensive protection for life, liberty, and property; for the spread of religion, morality, and knowledge; for maintaining the inviolability of contracts, the freedom of navigation upon the public rivers, and the unrestrained conveyance of property by contract and devise, and for equality of children in the inheritance of patrimonial estates. The ordinance became a law after Great Britain, in form the most popular government in Europe, had been expelled from that territory because of "injuries and usurpations having in direct object the establishment of an absolute tyranny over the States." Feudalism at that time prevailed in nearly all the kingdoms of Europe, and serfdom and servitude and feudal service depressed their people to the level of slaves. The prohibition of "slavery and involuntary servitude" in every form and degree, except as a **[83 U.S. 36, 50]** sentence upon a conviction for crime, comprises much more than the abolition or prohibition of African slavery. Slavery in the annals of the world had been the ultimate solution of controversies between the creditor and debtor; the conqueror and his captive; the father and his child; the state and an offender against its laws. The laws might enslave a man to the soil. The whole of Europe in 1787 was crowded with persons who were held as vassals to their landlord, and serfs on his dominions. The American constitution for that great territory was framed to abolish slavery and involuntary servitude in all forms, and in all degrees in which they have existed among men, except as a punishment for crime duly proved and adjudged.

Now, the act of which we complain has made of three parishes of Louisiana "enthralled ground." "The seventeen" have *astricted* not only the inhabitants of those parishes, but of all other portions of the earth who may have cattle or animals for sale or for food, to land them at the wharves of that company (if brought to that territory), to keep them in their pens, yards, or stables, and to prepare them for market in their abattoir or slaughter-house. Lest some competitor may present more tempting or convenient arrangements, the act directs that all of these shall be closed on a particular day, and prohibits any one from having, keeping, or establishing any other; and a peremptory command is given that all animals shall be sheltered, preserved, and protected by this corporation, and by none other, under heavy penalties.

Is not this "a servitude?" Might it not be so considered in a strict sense? It is like the "thirlage" of the old Scotch law and the *banalités* of seignioral France; which were servitudes undoubtedly. But, if not strictly a servitude, it is certainly a servitude in a more popular sense, and, being an enforced one, it is an involuntary servitude. Men are surely subjected to a servitude when, throughout three parishes, embracing 1200 square miles, every man and every woman in them is compelled to refrain from the use of their own land and exercise of their own industry and the improvement **[83 U.S. 36, 51]** of their own property, in a way confessedly lawful and necessary in itself, and made unlawful and unnecessary only because, at their cost, an exclusive privilege is granted to seventeen other persons to improve and exercise it for them. We have here the "servients" and the "dominants" and the "thraldom" of the old seignioral

---

[8] The statement of these cases being made, infra, pp. 106-109, in the dissenting opinion of Mr. Justice Field, is not here given.

system. The servients in this case are all the inhabitants in any manner using animals brought to the markets for sale or for slaughter. The dominants are "the seventeen" made into a corporation, with these seignioral rights and privileges. The masters are these seventeen, who alone can admit or refuse other members to their corporation. The abused persons are the community, who are deprived of what was a common right and bound under a thraldom.

III. *The act is even more plainly in the face of the fourteenth amendment.* That amendment was a development of the thirteenth, and is a more comprehensive exposition of the principles which lie at the foundation of the thirteenth.

Slavery had been abolished as the issue of the civil war. More than three millions of a population lately servile, were liberated without preparation for any political or civil duty. Besides this population of emancipated slaves, there was a large and growing population who came to this country without education in the laws and constitution of the country, and who had begun to exert a perceptible influence over our government. There were also a large number of unsettled and difficult questions of State and National right that had no other settlement or solution but what the war had afforded. It had been maintained from the origin of the Constitution, by one political party-men of a high order of ability, and who exerted a great influence-that the State was the highest political organization in the United States; that through the consent of the separate States the Union had been formed for limited purposes; that there was no social union except by and through the States, and that in extreme cases the several States might cancel the obligations to the Federal government and reclaim the allegiance and fidelity of its members. Such were the doctrines of Mr. **[83 U.S. 36, 52]** Calhoun, and of others; both those who preceded and those who have followed him. It is nowhere declared in the Constitution what "a citizen" is, or what constitutes citizenship; and what ideas were entertained of citizenship by one class in our country may be seen in the South Carolina case of Hunt v. The State, where Harper, J., referring to the arguments of Messrs. Petigru, Blanding, McWillie, and Williams-men eminent in the South as jurists-who were opposing nullification, says:

> "It has been *admitted* in argument by all the counsel except one, that in case of a secession by the State from the Union, the citizens and constituted authorities would be bound to obey and give effect to the act."

But the fourteenth amendment does define citizenship and the relations of citizens to the State and Federal government. It ordains that "all persons born or naturalized in the United States and subject to the jurisdiction thereof are citizens of the United States and of the State where they reside." Citizenship in a State is made by residence and without reference to the consent of the State. Yet, by the same amendment, when it exists, no State can abridge its privileges or immunities. The doctrine of the "States-Rights party," led in modern times by Mr. Calhoun, was, that there was no citizenship in the whole United States, except sub modo and by the permission of the States. According to their theory the United States had no integral existence except as an incomplete combination among several integers. The fourteenth amendment struck at, and forever destroyed, all such doctrines. It seems to have been made under an apprehension of a destructive faculty in the State governments. It consolidated the several "integers" into a consistent whole. Were there Brahmans in Massachusetts, "the chief of all creatures, and with the universe held in charge for them," and Soudras in Pennsylvania, "who simply had life through the benevolence of the other," this amendment places them on the same footing. By it the national principle has received an indefinite enlargement. **[83 U.S. 36, 53]** The tie between the United States and every citizen in every part of its own jurisdiction has been made intimate and familiar. To the same extent the confederate features of the government have been obliterated. The States in their closest connection with the members of the State, have been placed under the oversight and restraining and enforcing hand of Congress. The purpose is manifest, to establish through the whole jurisdiction of the United States ONE PEOPLE, and that every member of the empire shall understand and appreciate the fact that his privileges and immunities cannot be abridged by State authority; that State laws must be so framed as to secure life, liberty, property from arbitrary violation and secure protection of law to all. Thus, as the great personal rights of each and every person were established and guarded, a reasonable confidence that there would be good government might seem to be justified. The amendment embodies all that the statesmanship of the country has conceived for accommodating the Constitution and the institutions of the country to the vast additions of territory, increase of the population, multiplication of States and Territorial governments, the annual influx of aliens, and the mighty changes produced by revolutionary events, and by social, industrial, commercial development. It is an act of Union, an act to determine the reciprocal relations of the millions of population within the bounds of the United States-the numerous State governments and the entire United States administered by a common government-that they might mutually sustain, support, and co-operate for the promotion of peace, security, and the assurance of property and liberty.

Under it the fact of citizenship does not depend upon parentage, family, nor upon the historical division of the land into separate States, some of whom had a glorious history, of which its members were justly proud. Citizenship is assigned to nativity in any portion of the United States, and every person so born is a citizen. The naturalized person acquires citizenship of the same kind without any action of the State at all. So either may by this title of citizenship **[83 U.S. 36, 54]** make his residence at any place in the United States, and under whatever form of State administration, he must be treated as a citizen of that State. His "privileges and immunities" must not be impaired, and all the privileges of the English Magna Charta in favor of freemen are collected upon him and overshadow him as derived from this amendment. The States must not weaken nor destroy them. The comprehensiveness of this amendment, the natural and necessary breadth of the language, the history of some of the clauses; their connection with discussions, contests, and domestic commotions that form landmarks in the annals of constitutional government, the circumstances under which it became part of the Constitution, demonstrate that the weighty import of what it ordains is not to be misunderstood.

From whatever cause originating, or with whatever special and present or pressing purpose passed, the fourteenth amendment is not confined to the population that had been servile, or to that which had any of the disabilities or disqualifications arising from race or from contract. The vast number of laborers in mines, manufactories, commerce, as well as the laborers on the plantations, are defended against the unequal legislation of the States. Nor is the amendment confined in its application to laboring men. The mandate is universal in its application to persons of every class and every condition. There are forty millions of population who may refer to it to determine their rank in the United States, and in any particular State. There are thirty-seven governments among the States to which it directs command, and the States that may be hereafter admitted, and the persons hereafter to be born or naturalized will find here declarations of the same weighty import to them all. To the State governments is says: "Let there be no law made or enforced to diminish one of the privileges and immunities

of the people of the United States;" nor law to deprive them of their life, liberty, property, or protection without trial. To the people the declaration is: "Take and hold this your certificate of status and of **[83 U.S. 36, 55]** capacity, the Magna Charta of your rights and liberties." To the Congress it says: "Take care to enforce this article by suitable laws."

The only question then is this: "When a State passes a law depriving a thousand people, who have acquired valuable property, and who, through its instrumentality, are engaged in an honest and necessary business, which they understand, of their right to use such their own property, and to labor in such their honest and necessary business, and gives a monopoly, embracing the whole subject, including the right to labor in such business, to seventeen other persons-whether the State has abridged any of the privileges or immunities of these thousand persons?"

Now, what are "privileges and immunities" in the sense of the Constitution? They are undoubtedly the personal and civil rights which usage, tradition, the habits of society, written law, and the common sentiments of people have recognized as forming the basis of the institutions of the country. The first clause in the fourteenth amendment does not deal with any interstate relations, nor relations that depend in any manner upon State laws, nor is any standard among the States referred to for the ascertainment of these privileges and immunities. It assumes that there were privileges and immunities that belong to an American citizen, and the

State is commanded neither to make nor to enforce any law that will abridge them.

The case of *Ward v. Maryland*[9] bears upon the matter. That case involved the validity of a statute of Maryland which imposed a tax in the form of a license to sell the agricultural and manufactured articles of other States than Maryland by card, sample, or printed lists, or catalogue. The purpose of the tax was to prohibit sales in the mode, and to relieve the resident merchant from the competition of these itinerant or transient dealers. This court decided that the power to carry on commerce in this form was "a privilege or immunity" of the sojourner. **[83 U.S. 36, 56]**

2. The act in question is equally in the face of the fourteenth amendment in that it denies to the plaintiffs the equal protection of the laws. By an act of legislative partiality it enriches seventeen persons and deprives nearly a thousand others of the same class, and as upright and competent as the seventeen, of the means by which they earn their daily bread.

3. *It is equally in violation of it, since it deprives them of their property without due process of law.* The right to labor, the right to one's self physically and intellectually, and to the product of one's own faculties, is past doubt property, and property of a sacred kind. Yet this property is destroyed by the act; destroyed not by due process of law, but by charter; a grant of privilege, of monopoly; which allows such rights in this matter to no one but to a favored "seventeen."

It will of course be sought to justify the act as an exercise of the police power; a matter confessedly, in its general scope, within the jurisdiction of the States. Without doubt, in that general scope, the subject of sanitary laws belong to the exercise of the power set up; but it does not follow there is no restraint on State power of legislation in police matters. The police power was invoked in the case of *Gibbons v. Ogden*.[10] New York had granted to eminent citizens a monopoly of steamboat navigation in her waters as compensation for their enterprise and invention. They set up that Gibbons should not have, keep, establish, or land with a steamboat to carry passengers and freight on the navigable waters of New York. Of course the State had a great jurisdiction over its waters for all purposes of police, but none to control navigation and intercourse between the United States and foreign nations, or among the States. Suppose the grant to Fulton and Livingston had been that all persons coming to the United States, or from the States around, should, because of their services to the State, land on one of their lots and pass through their gates. This would abridge the rights secured in the fourteenth amendment. **[83 U.S. 36, 57]** The right to move with freedom, to choose his highway, and to be exempt from impositions, belongs to the citizen. He must have this power to move freely to perform his duties as a citizen.

The *Passenger Cases*, in 7 Howard, are replete with discussions on the police powers of the States. The arguments in that case appeal to the various titles in which the freedom of State action had been supposed to be unlimited. Immigrants, it was said, would bring pauperism, crime, idleness, increased expenditures, disorderly conduct. The acts, it was said, were in the nature of health acts. But the court said that the police power would not be invoked to justify even the small tax there disputed.

Messrs. M. H. Carpenter and J. S. Black (a brief of Mr. Charles Allen being filed on the same side), and Mr. T. J. Durant, representing in addition the State of Louisiana, contra.

Mr. Justice **MILLER**, now, April 14th, 1873, delivered the opinion of the court.

These cases are brought here by writs of error to the Supreme Court of the State of Louisiana. They arise out of the efforts of the butchers of New Orleans to resist the Crescent City Live-Stock Landing and Slaughter-House Company in the exercise of certain powers conferred by the charter which created it, and which was granted by the legislature of that State.

The cases named on a preceding page,[11] with others which have been brought here and dismissed by agreement, were all decided by the Supreme Court of Louisiana in favor of the

---

[9] 12 Wallace, 419.
[10] 9 Wheaton, 203.

Slaughter-House Company, as we shall hereafter call it for the sake of brevity, and these writs are brought to reverse those decisions.

The records were filed in this court in 1870, and were argued before it as length on a motion made by plaintiffs in error for an order in the nature of an injunction or supersedeas, [83 U.S. 36, 58] pending the action of the court on the merits. The opinion on that motion is reported in 10 Wallace, 273.

On account of the importance of the questions involved in these cases they were, by permission of the court, taken up out of their order on the docket and argued in January, 1872. At that hearing one of the justices was absent, and it was found, on consultation, that there was a diversity of views among those who were present. Impressed with the gravity of the questions raised in the argument, the court under these circumstances ordered that the cases be placed on the calendar and reargued before a full bench. This argument was had early in February last.

Preliminary to the consideration of those questions is a motion by the defendant to dismiss the cases, on the ground that the contest between the parties has been adjusted by an agreement made since the records came into this court, and that part of that agreement is that these writs should be dismissed. This motion was heard with the argument on the merits, and was much pressed by counsel. It is supported by affidavits and by copies of the written agreement relied on. It is sufficient to say of these that we do not find in them satisfactory evidence that the agreement is binding upon all the parties to the record who are named as plaintiffs in the several writs of error, and that there are parties now before the court, in each of the three cases, the names of which appear on a preceding page,[11] who have not consented to their dismissal, and who are not bound by the action of those who have so consented. They have a right to be heard, and the motion to dismiss cannot prevail.

The records show that the plaintiffs in error relied upon, and asserted throughout the entire course of the litigation in the State courts, that the grant of privileges in the charter of defendant, which they were contesting, was a violation of the most important provisions of the thirteenth and fourteenth articles of amendment of the Constitution of the United States. The jurisdiction and the duty of this court [83 U.S. 36, 59] to review the judgment of the State court on those questions is clear and is imperative.

The statute thus assailed as unconstitutional was passed March 8th, 1869, and is entitled "An act to protect the health of the city of New Orleans, to locate the stock-landings and slaughter-houses, and to incorporate the Crescent City Live-Stock Landing and Slaughter-House Company."

The first section forbids the landing or slaughtering of animals whose flesh is intended for food, within the city of New Orleans and other parishes and boundaries named and defined, or the keeping or establishing any slaughter-houses or *abattoirs* within those limits except by the corporation thereby created, which is also limited to certain places afterwards mentioned. Suitable penalties are enacted for violations of this prohibition.

The second section designates the corporators, gives the name to the corporation, and confers on it the usual corporate powers.

The third and fourth sections authorize the company to establish and erect within certain territorial limits, therein defined, one or more stock-yards, stock-landings, and slaughter-houses, and imposes upon it the duty of erecting, on or before the first day of June, 1869, one grand slaughter-house of sufficient capacity for slaughtering five hundred animals per day.

It declares that the company, after it shall have prepared all the necessary buildings, yards, and other conveniences for that purpose, shall have the sole and exclusive privilege of conducting and carrying on the live-stock landing and slaughter-house business within the limits and privilege granted by the act, and that all such animals shall be landed at the stock-landings and slaughtered at the slaughter-houses of the company, and nowhere else. Penalties

---

[11] See supra, p. 36, sub-title.
[12] See subtitle, supra, p. 36.—REP.

are enacted for infractions of this provision, and prices fixed for the maximum charges of the company for each steamboat and for each animal landed.

Section five orders the closing up of all other stock-landings **[83 U.S. 36, 60]** and slaughter-houses after the first day of June, in the parishes of Orleans, Jefferson, and St. Bernard, and makes it the duty of the company to permit any person to slaughter animals in their slaughter-houses under a heavy penalty for each refusal. Another section fixes a limit to the charges to be made by the company for each animal so slaughtered in their building, and another provides for an inspection of all animals intended to be so slaughtered, by an officer appointed by the governor of the State for that purpose.

These are the principal features of the statute, and are all that have any bearing upon the questions to be decided by us.

This statute is denounced not only as creating a monopoly and conferring odious and exclusive privileges upon a small number of persons at the expense of the great body of the community of New Orleans, but it is asserted that it deprives a large and meritorious class of citizens-the whole of the butchers of the city-of the right to exercise their trade, the business to which they have been trained and on which they depend for the support of themselves and their families, and that the unrestricted exercise of the business of butchering is necessary to the daily subsistence of the population of the city.

But a critical examination of the act hardly justifies these assertions.

It is true that it grants, for a period of twenty-five years, exclusive privileges. And whether those privileges are at the expense of the community in the sense of a curtailment of any of their fundamental rights, or even in the sense of doing them an injury, is a question open to considerations to be hereafter stated. But it is not true that it deprives the butchers of the right to exercise their trade, or imposes upon them any restriction incompatible with its successful pursuit, or furnishing the people of the city with the necessary daily supply of animal food.

The act divides itself into two main grants of privilege,—the one in reference to stock-landings and stock-yards, and **[83 U.S. 36, 61]** the other to slaughter-houses. That the landing of livestock in large droves, from steamboats on the bank of the river, and from railroad trains, should, for the safety and comfort of the people and the care of the animals, be limited to proper places, and those not numerous, it needs no argument to prove. Nor can it be injurious to the general community that while the duty of making ample preparation for this is imposed upon a few men, or a corporation, they should, to enable them to do it successfully, have the exclusive right of providing such landing-places, and receiving a fair compensation for the service.

It is, however, the slaughter-house privilege, which is mainly relied on to justify the charges of gross injustice to the public, and invasion of private right.

It is not, and cannot be successfully controverted, that it is both the right and the duty of the legislative body-the supreme power of the State or municipality-to prescribe and determine the localities where the business of slaughtering for a great city may be conducted. To do this effectively it is indispensable that all persons who slaughter animals for food shall do it is those places *and nowhere else.*

The statute under consideration defines these localities and forbids slaughtering in any other. It does not, as has been asserted, prevent the butcher from doing his own slaughtering. On the contrary, the Slaughter-House Company is required, under a heavy penalty, to permit and person who wishes to do so, to slaughter in their houses; and they are bound to make ample provision for the convenience of all the slaughtering for the entire city. The butcher then is still permitted to slaughter, to prepare, and to sell his own meats; but he is required to slaughter at a specified place and to pay a reasonable compensation for the use of the accommodations furnished him at that place.

The wisdom of the monopoly granted by the legislature may be open to question, but it is difficult to see a justification for the assertion that the butchers are deprived of the right to labor in their occupation, or the people of their daily service in preparing food, or how this statute, with the **[83 U.S. 36, 62]** duties and guards imposed upon the company, can be said to destroy the business of the butcher, or seriously interfere with its pursuit.

270

The power here exercised by the legislature of Louisiana is, in its essential nature, one which has been, up to the present period in the constitutional history of this country, always conceded to belong to the States, however it may now be questioned in some of its details.

"Unwholesome trades, slaughter-houses, operations offensive to the senses, the deposit of powder, the application of steam power to propel cars, the building with combustible materials, and the burial of the dead, may all," says Chancellor Kent,[13] "be interdicted by law, in the midst of dense masses of population, on the general and rational principle, that every person ought so to use his property as not to injure his neighbors; and that private interests must be made subservient to the general interests of the community." This is called the police power; and it is declared by Chief Justice Shaw[14] that it is much easier to perceive and realize the existence and sources of it than to mark its boundaries, or prescribe limits to its exercise.

This power is, and must be from its very nature, incapable of any very exact definition or limitation. Upon it depends the security of social order, the life and health of the citizen, the comfort of an existence in a thickly populated community, the enjoyment of private and social life, and the beneficial use of property. "It extends," says another eminent judge,[15] "to the protection of the lives, limbs, health, comfort, and quiet of all persons, and the protection of all property within the State; . . . and persons and property are subject to all kinds of restraints and burdens in order to secure the general comfort, health, and prosperity of the State. Of the perfect right of the legislature to do this no question ever was, or, upon acknowledged general principles, ever can be made, so far as natural persons are concerned." **[83 U.S. 36, 63]** The regulation of the place and manner of conducting the slaughtering of animals, and the business of butchering within a city, and the inspection of the animals to be killed for meat, and of the meat afterwards, are among the most necessary and frequent exercises of this power. It is not, therefore, needed that we should seek for a comprehensive definition, but rather look for the proper source of its exercise.

In *Gibbons v. Ogden*,[16] Chief Justice Marshall, speaking of inspection laws passed by the States, says: "They form a portion of that immense mass of legislation which controls everything within the territory of a State not surrendered to the General Government-all which can be most advantageously administered by the States themselves. Inspection laws, quarantine laws, health laws of every description, as well as laws for regulating the internal commerce of a State, and those which respect turnpike roads, ferries, &c., are component parts. No direct general power over these objects is granted to Congress; and consequently they remain subject to State legislation."

The exclusive authority of State legislation over this subject is strikingly illustrated in the case of the *City of New York v. Miln*.[17] In that case the defendant was prosecuted for failing to comply with a statute of New York which required of every master of a vessel arriving from a foreign port, in that of New York City, to report the names of all his passengers, with certain particulars of their age, occupation, last place of settlement, and place of their birth. It was argued that this act was an invasion of the exclusive right of Congress to regulate commerce. And it cannot be denied that such a statute operated at least indirectly upon the commercial intercourse between the citizens of the United States and of foreign countries. But notwithstanding this it was held to be an exercise of the police power properly within the control of the State, and unaffected by the clause of the Constitution which conferred on Congress the right to regulate commerce. **[83 U.S. 36, 64]** To the same purpose are the recent cases of [the] *The License Tax*,[18] and *United States v. De Witt*.[19] In the latter case an act of

---

[13] 2 Commentaries, 340.
[14] Commonwealth v. Alger, 7 Cushing, 84.
[15] Thorpe v. Rutland and Burlington Railroad Co., 27 Vermont, 149.
[16] 9 Wheaton, 203.
[17] 11 Peters, 102.
[18] 5 Wallace, 471.
[19] 9 Id. 41.

Congress which undertook as a part of the internal revenue laws to make it a misdemeanor to mix for sale naphtha and illuminating oils, or to sell oil of petroleum inflammable at less than a prescribed temperature, was held to be void, because as a police regulation the power to make such a law belonged to the States, and did not belong to Congress.

It cannot be denied that the statute under consideration is aptly framed to remove from the more densely populated part of the city, the noxious slaughter-houses, and large and offensive collections of animals necessarily incident to the slaughtering business of a large city, and to locate them where the convenience, health, and comfort of the people require they shall be located. And it must be conceded that the means adopted by the act for this purpose are appropriate, are stringent, and effectual. But it is said that in creating a corporation for this purpose, and conferring upon it exclusive privileges-privileges which it is said constitute a monopoly-the legislature has exceeded its power. If this statute had imposed on the city of New Orleans precisely the same duties, accompanied by the same privileges, which it has on the corporation which it created, it is believed that no question would have been raised as to its constitutionality. In that case the effect on the butchers in pursuit of their occupation and on the public would have been the same as it is now. Why cannot the legislature confer the same powers on another corporation, created for a lawful and useful public object, that it can on the municipal corporation already existing? That wherever a legislature has the right to accomplish a certain result, and that result is best attained by means of a corporation, it has the right to create such a corporation, and to endow it with the powers necessary to effect the desired and lawful purpose, seems hardly to admit of debate. The proposition is ably discussed and affirmed in the case of *McCulloch v. The State of Maryland,*[20] in relation to the power of Congress to organize **[83 U.S. 36, 65]** the Bank of the United States to aid in the fiscal operations of the government.

It can readily be seen that the interested vigilance of the corporation created by the Louisiana legislature will be more efficient in enforcing the limitation prescribed for the stock-landing and slaughtering business for the good of the city than the ordinary efforts of the officers of the law.

Unless, therefore, it can be maintained that the exclusive privilege granted by this charter to the corporation, is beyond the power of the legislature of Louisiana, there can be no just exception to the validity of the statute. And in this respect we are not able to see that these privileges are especially odious or objectionable. The duty imposed as a consideration for the privilege is well defined, and its enforcement well guarded. The prices or charges to be made by the company are limited by the statute, and we are not advised that they are on the whole exorbitant or unjust.

The proposition is, therefore, reduced to these terms: Can any exclusive privileges be granted to any of its citizens, or to a corporation, by the legislature of a State?

The eminent and learned counsel who has twice argued the negative of this question, has displayed a research into the history of monopolies in England, and the European continent, only equaled by the eloquence with which they are denounced.

But it is to be observed, that all such references are to monopolies established by the monarch in derogation of the rights of his subjects, or arise out of transactions in which the people were unrepresented, and their interests uncared for. The great *Case of Monopolies,* reported by Coke, and so fully stated in the brief, was undoubtedly a contest of the commons against the monarch. The decision is based upon the ground that it was against common law, and the argument was aimed at the unlawful assumption of power by the crown; for whoever doubted the authority of Parliament to change or modify the common law? The discussion in the House of Commons cited from Macaulay clearly **[83 U.S. 36, 66]** establishes that the contest was between the crown, and the people represented in Parliament.

But we think it may be safely affirmed, that the Parliament of Great Britain, representing

---

[20] 4 Wheaton, 316.

the people in their legislative functions, and the legislative bodies of this country, have from time immemorial to the present day, continued to grant to persons and corporations exclusive privileges-privileges denied to other citizens-privileges which come within any just definition of the word monopoly, as much as those now under consideration; and that the power to do this has never been questioned or denied. Nor can it be truthfully denied, that some of the most useful and beneficial enterprises set on foot for the general good, have been made successful by means of these exclusive rights, and could only have been conducted to success in that way.

It may, therefore, be considered as established, that the authority of the legislature of Louisiana to pass the present statute is ample, unless some restraint in the exercise of that power be found in the constitution of that State or in the amendments to the Constitution of the United States, adopted since the date of the decisions we have already cited.

If any such restraint is supposed to exist in the constitution of the State, the Supreme Court of Louisiana having necessarily passed on that question, it would not be open to review in this court.

The plaintiffs in error accepting this issue, allege that the statute is a violation of the Constitution of the United States in these several particulars:

That it creates an involuntary servitude forbidden by the thirteenth article of amendment;

That it abridges the privileges and immunities of citizens of the United States;

That it denies to the plaintiffs the equal protection of the laws; and,

That it deprives them of their property without due process of law; contrary to the provisions of the first section of the fourteenth article of amendment. **[83 U.S. 36, 67]** This court is thus called upon for the first time to give construction to these articles.

We do not conceal from ourselves the great responsibility which this duty devolves upon us. No questions so far-reaching and pervading in their consequences, so profoundly interesting to the people of this country, and so important in their bearing upon the relations of the United States, and of the several States to each other and to the citizens of the States and of the United States, have been before this court during the official life of any of its present members. We have given every opportunity for a full hearing at the bar; we have discussed it freely and compared views among ourselves; we have taken ample time for careful deliberation, and we now propose to announce the judgments which we have formed in the construction of those articles, so far as we have found them necessary to the decision of the cases before us, and beyond that we have neither the inclination nor the right to go.

Twelve articles of amendment were added to the Federal Constitution soon after the original organization of the government under it in 1789. Of these all but the last were adopted so soon afterwards as to justify the statement that they were practically contemporaneous with the adoption of the original; and the twelfth, adopted in eighteen hundred and three, was so nearly so as to have become, like all the others, historical and of another age. But within the last eight years three other articles of amendment of vast importance have been added by the voice of the people to that now venerable instrument.

The most cursory glance at these articles discloses a unity of purpose, when taken in connection with the history of the times, which cannot fail to have an important bearing on any question of doubt concerning their true meaning. Nor can such doubts, when any reasonably exist, be safely and rationally solved without a reference to that history; for in it is found the occasion and the necessity for recurring again to the great source of power in this country, the people of the States, for additional guarantees of human rights; **[83 U.S. 36, 68]** additional powers to the Federal government; additional restraints upon those of the States. Fortunately that history is fresh within the memory of us all, and its leading features, as they bear upon the matter before us, free from doubt.

The institution of African slavery, as it existed in about half the States of the Union, and the contests pervading the public mind for many years, between those who desired its curtailment and ultimate extinction and those who desired additional safeguards for its security and perpetuation, culminated in the effort, on the part of most of the States in which slavery existed, to separate from the Federal government, and to resist its authority. This constituted the war of the rebellion, and whatever auxiliary causes may have contributed to bring about this war, undoubtedly the overshadowing and efficient cause was African slavery.

In that struggle slavery, as a legalized social relation, perished. It perished as a necessity of the bitterness and force of the conflict. When the armies of freedom found themselves upon the soil of slavery they could do nothing less than free the poor victims whose enforced servitude was the foundation of the quarrel. And when hard pressed in the contest these men (for they proved themselves men in that terrible crisis) offered their services and were accepted by thousands to aid in suppressing the unlawful rebellion, slavery was at an end wherever the Federal government succeeded in that purpose. The proclamation of President Lincoln expressed an accomplished fact as to a large portion of the insurrectionary districts, when he declared slavery abolished in them all. But the war being over, those who had succeeded in re-establishing the authority of the Federal government were not content to permit this great act of emancipation to rest on the actual results of the contest or the proclamation of the Executive, both of which might have been questioned in after times, and they determined to place this main and most valuable result in the Constitution of the restored Union as one of its fundamental articles. Hence the thirteenth article of amendment of that instrument. **[83 U.S. 36, 69]** Its two short sections seem hardly to admit of construction, so vigorous is their expression and so appropriate to the purpose we have indicated.

"1. Neither slavery nor involuntary servitude, except as a punishment for crime, whereof the party shall have been duly convicted, shall exist within the United States or any place subject to their jurisdiction.

"2. Congress shall have power to enforce this article by appropriate legislation."

To withdraw the mind from the contemplation of this grand yet simple declaration of the personal freedom of all the human race within the jurisdiction of this government-a declaration designed to establish the freedom of four millions of slaves-and with a microscopic search endeavor to find in it a reference to servitudes, which may have been attached to property in certain localities, requires an effort, to say the least of it.

That a personal servitude was meant is proved by the use of the word "involuntary," which can only apply to human beings. The exception of servitude as a punishment for crime gives an idea of the class of servitude that is meant. The word servitude is of larger meaning than slavery, as the latter is popularly understood in this country, and the obvious purpose was to forbid all shades and conditions of African slavery. It was very well understood that in the form of apprenticeship for long terms, as it had been practiced in the West India Islands, on the abolition of slavery by the English government, or by reducing the slaves to the condition of serfs attached to the plantation, the purpose of the article might have been evaded, if only the word slavery had been used. The case of the apprentice slave, held under a law of Maryland, liberated by Chief Justice Chase, on a writ of habeas corpus under this article, illustrates this course of observation.[21] And it is all that we deem necessary to say on the application of that article to the statute of Louisiana, now under consideration. **[83 U.S. 36, 70]** The process of restoring to their proper relations with the Federal government and with the other States those which had sided with the rebellion, undertaken under the proclamation of President Johnson in 1865, and before the assembling of Congress, developed the fact that, notwithstanding the formal recognition by those States of the abolition of slavery, the condition of the slave race would, without further protection of the Federal government, be almost as bad as it was before. Among the first acts of legislation adopted by several of the States in the legislative bodies which claimed to be in their normal relations with the Federal government, were laws which imposed upon the colored race onerous disabilities and burdens, and curtailed their rights in the pursuit of life, liberty, and property to such an extent that their freedom was of little value, while they had lost the protection which they had received from their former owners from motives both of interest and humanity.

They were in some States forbidden to appear in the towns in any other character than

---

[21] Matter of Turner, 1 Abbott United States Reports, 84.

menial servants. They were required to reside on and cultivate the soil without the right to purchase or own it. They were excluded from many occupations of gain, and were not permitted to give testimony in the courts in any case where a white man was a party. It was said that their lives were at the mercy of bad men, either because the laws for their protection were insufficient or were not enforced.

These circumstances, whatever of falsehood or misconception may have been mingled with their presentation, forced upon the statesmen who had conducted the Federal government in safety through the crisis of the rebellion, and who supposed that by the thirteenth article of amendment they had secured the result of their labors, the conviction that something more was necessary in the way of constitutional protection to the unfortunate race who had suffered so much. They accordingly passed through Congress the proposition for the fourteenth amendment, and they declined to treat as restored to their full participation in the government of the Union the States which had been in insurrection, until they **[83 U.S. 36, 71]** ratified that article by a formal vote of their legislative bodies.

Before we proceed to examine more critically the provisions of this amendment, on which the plaintiffs in error rely, let us complete and dismiss the history of the recent amendments, as that history relates to the general purpose which pervades them all. A few years' experience satisfied the thoughtful men who had been the authors of the other two amendments that, notwithstanding the restraints of those articles on the States, and the laws passed under the additional powers granted to Congress, these were inadequate for the protection of life, liberty, and property, without which freedom to the slave was no boon. They were in all those States denied the right of suffrage. The laws were administered by the white man alone. It was urged that a race of men distinctively marked as was the negro, living in the midst of another and dominant race, could never be fully secured in their person and their property without the right of suffrage.

Hence the fifteenth amendment, which declares that "the right of a citizen of the United States to vote shall not be denied or abridged by any State on account of race, color, or previous condition of servitude." The negro having, by the fourteenth amendment, been declared to be a citizen of the United States, is thus made a voter in every State of the Union.

We repeat, then, in the light of this recapitulation of events, almost too recent to be called history, but which are familiar to us all; and on the most casual examination of the language of these amendments, no one can fail to be impressed with the one pervading purpose found in them all, lying at the foundation of each, and without which none of them would have been even suggested; we mean the freedom of the slave race, the security and firm establishment of that freedom, and the protection of the newly-made freeman and citizen from the oppressions of those who had formerly exercised unlimited dominion over him. It is true that only the fifteenth amendment, in terms, **[83 U.S. 36, 72]** mentions the negro by speaking of his color and his slavery. But it is just as true that each of the other articles was addressed to the grievances of that race, and designed to remedy them as the fifteenth.

We do not say that no one else but the negro can share in this protection. Both the language and spirit of these articles are to have their fair and just weight in any question of construction. Undoubtedly while negro slavery alone was in the mind of the Congress which proposed the thirteenth article, it forbids any other kind of slavery, now or hereafter. If Mexican peonage or the Chinese coolie labor system shall develop slavery of the Mexican or Chinese race within our territory, this amendment may safely be trusted to make it void. And so if other rights are assailed by the States which properly and necessarily fall within the protection of these articles, that protection will apply, though the party interested may not be of African descent. But what we do say, and what we wish to be understood is, that in any fair and just construction of any section or phrase of these amendments, it is necessary to look to the purpose which we have said was the pervading spirit of them all, the evil which they were designed to remedy, and the process of continued addition to the Constitution, until that purpose was supposed to be accomplished, as far as constitutional law can accomplish it.

The first section of the fourteenth article, to which our attention is more specially invited, opens with a definition of citizenship-not only citizenship of the United States, but citizenship of the States. No such definition was previously found in the Constitution, nor had any attempt been made to define it by act of Congress. It had been the occasion of much discussion in the courts, by the executive departments, and in the public journals. It had been said by eminent judges that no man was a citizen of the United States, except as he was a citizen of one of the States composing the Union. Those, therefore, who had been born and resided always in the District of Columbia or in the Territories, though within the United States, were not citizens. Whether **[83 U.S. 36, 73]** this proposition was sound or not had never been judicially decided. But it had been held by this court, in the celebrated *Dred Scott* case, only a few years before the outbreak of the civil war, that a man of African descent, whether a slave or not, was not and could not be a citizen of a State or of the United States. This decision, while it met the condemnation of some of the ablest statesmen and constitutional lawyers of the country, had never been overruled; and if it was to be accepted as a constitutional limitation of the right of citizenship, then all the negro race who had recently been made freemen, were still, not only not citizens, but were incapable of becoming so by anything short of an amendment to the Constitution.

To remove this difficulty primarily, and to establish a clear and comprehensive definition of citizenship which should declare what should constitute citizenship of the United States, and also citizenship of a State, the first clause of the first section was framed.

"All persons born or naturalized in the United States, and subject to the jurisdiction thereof, are citizens of the United States and of the State wherein they reside."

The first observation we have to make on this clause is, that it puts at rest both the questions which we stated to have been the subject of differences of opinion. It declares that persons may be citizens of the United States without regard to their citizenship of a particular State, and it overturns the Dred Scott decision by making *all persons* born within the United States and subject to its jurisdiction citizens of the United States. **That its main purpose was to establish the citizenship of the negro can admit of no doubt.** The phrase, "subject to its jurisdiction" was intended to exclude from its operation children of ministers, consuls, and citizens or subjects of foreign States born within the United States.

The next observation is more important in view of the arguments of counsel in the present case. It is, that **the distinction between citizenship of the United States and citizenship of a State is clearly recognized and established. [83 U.S. 36, 74]** Not only may a man be a citizen of the United States without being a citizen of a State, but an important element is necessary to convert the former into the latter. He must reside within the State to make him a citizen of it, but it is only necessary that he should be born or naturalized in the United States to be a citizen of the Union.

It is quite clear, then, that there is a citizenship of the United States, and a citizenship of a State, which are distinct from each other, and which depend upon different characteristics or circumstances in the individual.

We think this distinction and its explicit recognition in this amendment of great weight in this argument, because the next paragraph of this same section, which is the one mainly relied on by the plaintiffs in error, speaks only of privileges and immunities of citizens of the United States, and does not speak of those of citizens of the several States. The argument, however, in favor of the plaintiffs rests wholly on the assumption that the citizenship is the same, and the privileges and immunities guaranteed by the clause are the same.

The language is, "No State shall make or enforce any law which shall abridge the privileges or immunities of citizens of *the United States*." It is a little remarkable, if this clause was intended as a protection to the citizen of a State against the legislative power of his own State, that the word citizen of the State should be left out when it is so carefully used, and used in contradistinction to citizens of the United States, in the very sentence which precedes it. It is too clear for argument that the change in phraseology was adopted understandingly and with a purpose.

Of the privileges and immunities of the citizen of the United States, and of the privileges and immunities of the citizen of the State, and what they respectively are, we will presently consider; but we wish to state here that it is only the former which are placed by this clause under the protection of the Federal Constitution, and that the latter, whatever they may be, are not intended to have any additional protection by this paragraph of the amendment. **[83 U.S. 36, 75]** If, then, there is a difference between the privileges and immunities belonging to a citizen of the United States as such, and those belonging to the citizen of the State as such the latter must rest for their security and protection where they have heretofore rested; for they are not embraced by this paragraph of the amendment.

The first occurrence of the words "privileges and immunities" in our constitutional history, is to be found in the fourth of the articles of the old Confederation.

It declares "that the better to secure and perpetuate mutual friendship and intercourse among the people of the different States in this Union, the free inhabitants of each of these States, paupers, vagabonds, and fugitives from justice excepted, shall be entitled to all the privileges and immunities of free citizens in the several States; and the people of each State shall have free ingress and regress to and from any other State, and shall enjoy therein all the privileges of trade and commerce, subject to the same duties, impositions, and restrictions as the inhabitants thereof respectively."

In the Constitution of the United States, which superseded the Articles of Confederation, the corresponding provision is found in section two of the fourth article, in the following words: "The citizens of each State shall be entitled to all the privileges and immunities of citizens of the several States."

There can be but little question that the purpose of both these provisions is the same, and that the privileges and immunities intended are the same in each. In the article of the Confederation we have some of these specifically mentioned, and enough perhaps to give some general idea of the class of civil rights meant by the phrase.

Fortunately we are not without judicial construction of this clause of the Constitution. The first and the leading case on the subject is that of *Corfield v. Coryell,* decided by Mr. Justice Washington in the Circuit Court for the District of Pennsylvania in 1823.[22] **[83 U.S. 36, 76]** "The inquiry," he says, "is, what are the privileges and immunities of citizens of the several States? We feel no hesitation in confining these expressions to those privileges and immunities which are fundamental; which belong of right to the citizens of all free governments, and which have at all times been enjoyed by citizens of the several States which compose this Union, from the time of their becoming free, independent, and sovereign. What these fundamental principles are, it would be more tedious than difficult to enumerate. They may all, however, be comprehended under the following general heads: protection by the government, with the right to acquire and possess property of every kind, and to pursue and obtain happiness and safety, subject, nevertheless, to such restraints as the government may prescribe for the general good of the whole."

This definition of the privileges and immunities of citizens of the States is adopted in the main by this court in the recent case of *Ward v. The State of Maryland,*[23] while it declines to undertake an authoritative definition beyond what was necessary to that decision. The description, when taken to include others not named, but which are of the same general character, embraces nearly every civil right for the establishment and protection of which organized government is instituted. They are, in the language of Judge Washington, those rights which the fundamental. Throughout his opinion, they are spoken of as rights belonging to the individual as a citizen of a State. They are so spoken of in the constitutional provision which he was construing. And they have always been held to be the class of rights which the State governments were created to establish and secure.

In the case of *Paul v. Virginia,*[24] the court, in expounding this clause of the Constitution, says that "the privileges and immunities secured to citizens of each State in the several States,

---

[22] 4 Washington's Circuit Court, 371.
[23] 12 Wallace, 430.
[24] 8 Id. 180.

by the provision in question, are those privileges and immunities which are common to the citizens in the latter [83 U.S. 36, 77] States under their constitution and laws by virtue of their being citizens."

The constitutional provision there alluded to did not create those rights, which it called privileges and immunities of citizens of the States. It threw around them in that clause no security for the citizen of the State in which they were claimed or exercised. Nor did it profess to control the power of the State governments over the rights of its own citizens.

Its sole purpose was to declare to the several States, that whatever those rights, as you grant or establish them to your own citizens, or as you limit or qualify, or impose restrictions on their exercise, the same, neither more nor less, shall be the measure of the rights of citizens of other States within your jurisdiction.

It would be the vainest show of learning to attempt to prove by citations of authority, that up to the adoption of the recent amendments, no claim or pretence was set up that those rights depended on the Federal government for their existence or protection, beyond the very few express limitations which the Federal Constitution imposed upon the States-such, for instance, as the prohibition against ex post facto laws, bills of attainder, and laws impairing the obligation of contracts. But with the exception of these and a few other restrictions, the entire domain of the privileges and immunities of citizens of the States, as above defined, lay within the constitutional and legislative power of the States, and without that of the Federal government. Was it the purpose of the fourteenth amendment, by the simple declaration that no State should make or enforce any law which shall abridge the privileges and immunities of citizens of the United States, to transfer the security and protection of all the civil rights which we have mentioned, from the States to the Federal government? And where it is declared that Congress shall have the power to enforce that article, was it intended to bring within the power of Congress the entire domain of civil rights heretofore belonging exclusively to the States?

All this and more must follow, if the proposition of the [83 U.S. 36, 78] plaintiffs in error be sound. For not only are these rights subject to the control of Congress whenever in its discretion any of them are supposed to be abridged by State legislation, but that body may also pass laws in advance, limiting and restricting the exercise of legislative power by the States, in their most ordinary and usual functions, as in its judgment it may think proper on all such subjects. And still further, such a construction followed by the reversal of the judgments of the Supreme Court of Louisiana in these cases, would constitute this court a perpetual censor upon all legislation of the States, on the civil rights of their own citizens, with authority to nullify such as it did not approve as consistent with those rights, as they existed at the time of the adoption of this amendment. The argument we admit is not always the most conclusive which is drawn from the consequences urged against the adoption of a particular construction of an instrument. But when, as in the case before us, these consequences are so serious, so far-reaching and pervading, so great a departure from the structure and spirit of our institutions; **when the effect is to fetter and degrade the State governments by subjecting them to the control of Congress, in the exercise of powers heretofore universally conceded to them of the most ordinary and fundamental character; when in fact it radically changes the whole theory of the relations of the State and Federal governments to each other and of both these governments to the people; the argument has a force that is irresistible, in the absence of language which expresses such a purpose too clearly to admit of doubt.**

We are convinced that no such results were intended by the Congress which proposed these amendments, nor by the legislatures of the States which ratified them.

Having shown that the privileges and immunities relied on in the argument are those which belong to citizens of the States as such, and that they are left to the State governments for security and protection, and not by this article placed under the special care of the Federal government, we may hold ourselves excused from defining the privileges [83 U.S. 36, 79] and immunities of citizens of the United States which no State can abridge, until some case involving those privileges may make it necessary to do so.

But lest it should be said that no such privileges and immunities are to be found if those we have been considering are excluded, we venture to suggest some which own their existence to the Federal government, its National character, its Constitution, or its laws.

One of these is well described in the case of *Crandall v. Nevada*.[25] It is said to be the right of the citizen of this great country, protected by implied guarantees of its Constitution, "to come to the seat of government to assert any claim he may have upon that government, to transact any business he may have with it, to seek its protection, to share its offices, to engage in administering its functions. He has the right of free access to its seaports, through which all operations of foreign commerce are conducted, to the subtreasuries, land offices, and courts of justice in the several States." And quoting from the language of Chief Justice Taney in another case, it is said "that for all the great purposes for which the Federal government was established, we are one people, with one common country, we are all citizens of the United States;" and it is, as such citizens, that their rights are supported in this court in *Crandall v. Nevada*.

Another privilege of a citizen of the United States is to demand the care and protection of the Federal government over his life, liberty, and property when on the high seas or within the jurisdiction of a foreign government. Of this there can be no doubt, nor that the right depends upon his character as a citizen of the United States. The right to peaceably assemble and petition for redress of grievances, the privilege of the writ of habeas corpus, are rights of the citizen guaranteed by the Federal Constitution. The right to use the navigable waters of the United States, however they may penetrate the territory of the several States, all rights secured to our citizens by treaties with foreign nations, [83 U.S. 36, 80] are dependent upon citizenship of the United States, and not citizenship of a State. One of these privileges is conferred by the very article under consideration. It is **that a citizen of the United States can, of his own volition, become a citizen of any State of the Union by a *bonâ fide* residence therein, with the same rights as other citizens of that State**. To these may be added the rights secured by the thirteenth and fifteenth articles of amendment, and by the other clause of the fourteenth, next to be considered.

But it is useless to pursue this branch of the inquiry, since we are of opinion that the rights claimed by these plaintiffs in error, if they have any existence, are not privileges and immunities of citizens of the United States within the meaning of the clause of the fourteenth amendment under consideration.

"All persons born or naturalized in the United States, and subject to the jurisdiction thereof, are citizens of the United States and of the State wherein they reside. No State shall make or enforce any law which shall abridge the privileges or immunities of citizens of the United States; nor shall any State deprive any person of life, liberty, or property without due process of law, nor deny to any person within its jurisdiction the equal protection of its laws."

The argument has not been much pressed in these cases that the defendant's charter deprives the plaintiffs of their property without due process of law, or that it denies to them the equal protection of the law. The first of these paragraphs has been in the Constitution since the adoption of the fifth amendment, as a restraint upon the Federal power. It is also to be found in some form of expression in the constitutions of nearly all the States, as a restraint upon the power of the States. This law then, has practically been the same as it now is during the existence of the government, except so far as the present amendment may place the restraining power over the States in this matter in the hands of the Federal government.

We are not without judicial interpretation, therefore, both State and National, of the meaning of this clause. And it [83 U.S. 36, 81] is sufficient to say that under no construction of that provision that we have ever seen, or any that we deem admissible, can the restraint imposed by the State of Louisiana upon the exercise of their trade by the butchers of New Orleans be held to be a deprivation of property within the meaning of that provision.

"Nor shall any State deny to any person within its jurisdiction the equal protection of the laws."

---

[25] 6 Wallace, 36.

In the light of the history of these amendments, and the pervading purpose of them, which we have already discussed, it is not difficult to give a meaning to this clause. The existence of laws in the States where the newly emancipated negroes resided, which discriminated with gross injustice and hardship against them as a class, was the evil to be remedied by this clause, and by it such laws are forbidden.

If, however, the States did not conform their laws to its requirements, then by the fifth section of the article of amendment Congress was authorized to enforce it by suitable legislation. We doubt very much whether any action of a State not directed by way of discrimination against the negroes as a class, or on account of their race, will ever be held to come within the purview of this provision. It is so clearly a provision for that race and that emergency, that a strong case would be necessary for its application to any other. But as it is a State that is to be dealt with, and not alone the validity of its laws, we may safely leave that matter until Congress shall have exercised its power, or some case of State oppression, by denial of equal justice in its courts, shall have claimed a decision at our hands. We find no such case in the one before us, and do not deem it necessary to go over the argument again, as it may have relation to this particular clause of the amendment.

In the early history of the organization of the government, its statesmen seem to have divided on the line which should separate the powers of the National government from those of the State governments, and though this line has **[83 U.S. 36, 82]** never been very well defined in public opinion, such a division has continued from that day to this.

The adoption of the first eleven amendments to the Constitution so soon after the original instrument was accepted, shows a prevailing sense of danger at that time from the Federal power. And it cannot be denied that such a jealousy continued to exist with many patriotic men until the breaking out of the late civil war. It was then discovered that the true danger to the perpetuity of the Union was in the capacity of the State organizations to combine and concentrate all the powers of the State, and of contiguous States, for a determined resistance to the General Government.

Unquestionably this has given great force to the argument, and added largely to the number of those who believe in the necessity of a strong National government.

But, however pervading this sentiment, and however it may have contributed to the adoption of the amendments we have been considering, we do not see in those amendments any purpose to destroy the main features of the general system. Under the pressure of all the excited feeling growing out of the war, our statesmen have still believed that the existence of the State with powers for domestic and local government, including the regulation of civil rights-the rights of person and of property-was essential to the perfect working of our complex form of government, though they have thought proper to impose additional limitations on the States, and to confer additional power on that of the Nation.

But whatever fluctuations may be seen in the history of public opinion on this subject during the period of our national existence, we think it will be found that this court, so far as its functions required, has always held with a steady and an even hand the balance between State and Federal power, and we trust that such may continue to be the history of its relation to that subject so long as it shall have duties to perform which demand of it a construction of the Constitution, or of any of its parts. **[83 U.S. 36, 83]** The judgments of the Supreme Court of Louisiana in these cases are

AFFIRMED.

Mr. Justice **FIELD**, dissenting:

I am unable to agree with the majority of the court in these cases, and will proceed to state the reasons of my dissent from their judgment.

The cases grow out of the act of the legislature of the State of Louisiana, entitled "An act to protect the health of the city of New Orleans, to locate the stock-landings and slaughter-houses, and to incorporate 'The Crescent City Live-Stock Landing and Slaughter-House Company,'" which was approved on the eighth of March, 1869, and went into operation on the first of June following. The act creates the corporation mentioned in its title, which is composed of seventeen persons designated by name, and invests them and their successors with the powers usually conferred upon corporations in addition to their special and exclusive privileges. It first declares that it shall not be lawful, after the first day of June, 1869, to "land, keep, or slaughter any cattle, beeves, calves, sheep, swine, or other animals, or to have, keep, or establish any stock-landing, yards, slaughter-houses, or abattoirs within the city of New Orleans or the parishes of Orleans, Jefferson, and St. Bernard," except as provided in the act; and imposes a penalty of two hundred and fifty dollars for each violation of its provisions. It then authorizes the corporation mentioned to establish and erect within the parish of St. Bernard and the corporate limits of New Orleans, below the United States barracks, on the east side of the Mississippi, or at any point below a designated railroad depot on the west side of the river, "wharves, stables, sheds, yards, and buildings, necessary to land, stable, shelter, protect, and preserve all kinds of horses, mules, cattle, and other animals," and provides that cattle and other animals, destined for sale or slaughter in the city of New Orleans or its environs, shall be landed at the landings and yards of the company, and be there [83 U.S. 36, 84] yarded, sheltered, and protected, if necessary; and that the company shall be entitled to certain prescribed fees for the use of its wharves, and for each animal landed, and be authorized to detain the animals until the fees are paid, and if not paid within fifteen days to take proceedings for their sale. Every person violating any of these provisions, of any of these provisions, or elsewhere, is subjected to a fine of two hundred and fifty dollars.

The act then requires the corporation to erect a grand slaughter-house of sufficient dimensions to accommodate all butchers, and in which five hundred animals may be slaughtered a day, with a sufficient number of sheds and stables for the stock received at the port of New Orleans, at the same time authorizing the company to erect other landing-places and other slaughter-houses at any points consistent with the provisions of the act.

The act then provides that when the slaughter-houses and accessory buildings have been completed and thrown open for use, public notice thereof shall be given for thirty days, and within that time "all other stock-landings and slaughter-houses within the parishes of Orleans, Jefferson, and St. Bernard shall be closed, and it shall no longer be lawful to slaughter cattle, hogs, calves, sheep, or goats, the meat of which is determined [destined] for sale within the parishes aforesaid, under a penalty of one hundred dollars for each and every offence."

The act then provides that the company shall receive for every animal slaughtered in its buildings certain prescribed fees, besides the head, feet, gore, and entrails of all animals except of swine.

Other provisions of the act require the inspection of the animals before they are slaughtered, and allow the construction of railways to facilitate communication with the buildings of the company and the city of New Orleans.

But it is only the special and exclusive privileges conferred by the act that this court has to consider in the cases before it. These privileges are granted for the period of twenty-five years. Their exclusive character not only follows [83 U.S. 36, 85] from the provisions I have cited, but it is declared in express terms in the act. In the third section the language is that the corporation "shall have the *sole and exclusive privilege* of conducting and carrying on the live-stock, landing, and slaughter-house business within the limits and privileges granted by the provisions of the act." And in the fourth section the language is, that after the first of June, 1869, the company shall have "the exclusive privilege of having landed at their landing-places all animals intended for sale or slaughter in the parishes of Orleans and Jefferson," and "the exclusive privilege of having slaughtered" in its slaughter-houses all animals, the meat of which is intended for sale in these parishes.

In order to understand the real character of these special privileges, it is necessary to know the extent of country and of population which they affect. The parish of Orleans contains an area of country of 150 square miles; the parish of Jefferson, 384 square miles; and the parish of St. Bernard, 620 square miles. The three parishes together contain an area of 1154 square miles, and they have a population of between two and three hundred thousand people.

The plaintiffs in error deny the validity of the act in question, so far as it confers the special and exclusive privileges mentioned. The first case before us was brought by an association of butchers in the three parishes against the corporation, to prevent the assertion and enforcement of these privileges. The second case was instituted by the attorney-general of the State, in the name of the State, to protect the corporation in the enjoyment of these privileges, and to prevent an association of stock-dealers and butchers from acquiring a tract of land in the same district with the corporation, upon which to erect suitable buildings for receiving, keeping, and slaughtering cattle, and preparing animal food for market. The third case was commenced by the corporation itself, to restrain the defendants from carrying on a business similar to its own, in violation of its alleged exclusive privileges.

The substance of the averments of the plaintiffs in error [83 U.S. 36, 86] is this: That prior to the passage of the act in question they were engaged in the lawful and necessary business of procuring and bringing to the parishes of Orleans, Jefferson, and St. Bernard, animals suitable for human food, and in preparing such food for market; that in the prosecution of this business they had provided in these parishes suitable establishments for landing, sheltering, keeping, and slaughtering cattle and the sale of meat; that with their association about four hundred persons were connected, and that in the parishes named about a thousand persons were thus engaged in procuring, preparing, and selling animal food. And they complain that the business of landing, yarding, and keeping, within the parishes named, cattle intended for sale or slaughter, which was lawful for them to pursue before the first day of June, 1869, is made by that act unlawful for any one except the corporation named; and that the business of slaughtering cattle and preparing animal food for market, which it was lawful for them to pursue in these parishes before that day, is made by that act unlawful for them to pursue afterwards, except in the buildings of the company, and upon payment of certain prescribed fees, and a surrender of a valuable portion of each animal slaughtered. And they contend that the lawful business of landing, yarding, sheltering, and keeping cattle intended for sale or slaughter, which they in common with every individual in the community of the three parishes had a right to follow, cannot be thus taken from them and given over for a period of twenty-five years to the sole and exclusive enjoyment of a corporation of seventeen persons or of anybody else. And they also contend that the lawful and necessary business of slaughtering cattle and preparing animal food for market, which they and all other individuals had a right to follow, cannot be thus restricted within this territory of 1154 square miles to the buildings of this corporation, or be subjected to tribute for the emolument of that body.

No one will deny the abstract justice which lies in the position of the plaintiffs in error; and I shall endeavor to [83 U.S. 36, 87] show that the position has some support in the fundamental law of the country.

It is contended in justification for the act in question that it was adopted in the interest of the city, to promote its cleanliness and protect its health, and was the legitimate exercise of what is termed the police power of the State. That power undoubtedly extends to all regulations affecting the health, good order, morals, peace, and safety of society, and is exercised on a great variety of subjects, and in almost numberless ways. All sorts of restrictions and burdens are imposed under it, and when these are not in conflict with any constitutional prohibitions, or fundamental principles, they cannot be successfully assailed in a judicial tribunal. With this power of the State and its legitimate exercise I shall not differ from the majority of the court. But under the pretence of prescribing a police regulation the State cannot be permitted to encroach upon any of the just rights of the citizen, which the Constitution intended to secure against abridgment.

In the law in question there are only two provisions which can properly be called police regulations-the one which requires the landing and slaughtering of animals below the city of New Orleans, and the other which requires the inspection of the animals before they are slaughtered. When these requirements are complied with, the sanitary purposes of the act are accomplished. In all other particulars the act is a mere grant to a corporation created by it of special and exclusive privileges by which the health of the city is in no way promoted. It is plain that if the corporation can, without endangering the health of the public, carry on the business of landing, keeping, and slaughtering cattle within a district below the city embracing an area of over a thousand square miles, it would not endanger the public health if other persons were also permitted to carry on the same business within the same district under similar conditions as to the inspection of the animals. The health of the city might require the removal from its limits and suburbs of all buildings for keeping and slaughtering cattle, but no such [83 U.S. 36, 88] object could possibly justify legislation removing such buildings from a large part of the State for the benefit of a single corporation. The pretence of sanitary regulations for the grant of the exclusive privileges is a shallow one, which merits only this passing notice.

It is also sought to justify the act in question on the same principle that exclusive grants for ferries, bridges, and turnpikes are sanctioned. But it can find no support there. Those grants are of franchises of a public character appertaining to the government. Their use usually requires the exercise of the sovereign right of eminent domain. It is for the government to determine when one of them shall be granted, and the conditions upon which it shall be enjoyed. It is the duty of the government to provide suitable roads, bridges, and ferries for the convenience of the public, and if it chooses to devolve this duty to any extent, or in any locality, upon particular individuals or corporations, it may of course stipulate for such exclusive privileges connected with the franchise as it may deem proper, without encroaching upon the freedom or the just rights of others. The grant, with exclusive privileges, of a right thus appertaining to the government, is a very different thing from a grant, with exclusive privileges, of a right to pursue one of the ordinary trades or callings of life, which is a right appertaining solely to the individual.

Nor is there any analogy between this act of Louisiana and the legislation which confers upon the inventor of a new and useful improvement an exclusive right to make and sell to others his invention. The government in this way only secures to the inventor the temporary enjoyment of that which, without him, would not have existed. It thus only recognizes in the inventor a temporary property in the product of his own brain.

The act of Louisiana presents the naked case, unaccompanied by any public considerations, where a right to pursue a lawful and necessary calling, previously enjoyed by every citizen, and in connection with which a thousand persons were daily employed, is taken away and vested exclusively [83 U.S. 36, 89] for twenty-five years, for an extensive district and a large population, in a single corporation, or its exercise is for that period restricted to the establishments of the corporation, and there allowed only upon onerous conditions.

If exclusive privileges of this character can be granted to a corporation of seventeen persons, they may, in the discretion of the legislature, be equally granted to single individual. If they may be granted for twenty-five years they may be equally granted for a century, and in perpetuity. If they may be granted for the landing and keeping of animals intended for sale or slaughter they may be equally granted for the landing and storing of grain and other products of the earth, or for any article of commerce. If they may be granted for structures in which animal food is prepared for market they may be equally granted for structures in which farinaceous or vegetable food is prepared. They may be granted for any of the pursuits of human industry, even in its most simple and common forms. Indeed, upon the theory on which the exclusive privileges granted by the act in question are sustained, there is no monopoly, in the most odious form, which may not be upheld.

The question presented is, therefore, one of the gravest importance, not merely to the parties here, but to the whole country. It is nothing less than the question whether the recent amendments to the Federal Constitution protect the citizens of the United States against the deprivation of their common rights by State legislation. In my judgment the fourteenth amendment does afford such protection, and was so intended by the Congress which framed and the States which adopted it.

The counsel for the plaintiffs in error have contended, with great force, that the act in question is also inhibited by the thirteenth amendment.

That amendment prohibits slavery and involuntary servitude, except as a punishment for crime, but I have not supposed it was susceptible of a construction which would cover the enactment in question. I have been so accustomed to regard it as intended to meet that form of slavery which had **[83 U.S. 36, 90]** previously prevailed in this country, and to which the recent civil war owed its existence, that I was not prepared, nor am I yet, to give to it the extent and force ascribed by counsel. Still it is evidence that the language of the amendment is not used in a restrictive sense. It is not confined to African slavery alone. It is general and universal in its application. Slavery of white men as well as of black men is prohibited, and not merely slavery in the strict sense of the term, but involuntary servitude in every form.

The words "involuntary servitude" have not been the subject of any judicial or legislative exposition, that I am aware of, in this country, except that which is found in the Civil Rights Act, which will be hereafter noticed. It is, however, clear that they include something more than slavery in the strict sense of the term; they include also serfage, vassalage, villenage, peonage, and all other forms of compulsory service for the mere benefit or pleasure of others. Nor is this the full import of the terms. The abolition of slavery and involuntary servitude was intended to make every one born in this country a freeman, and as such to give to him the right to pursue the ordinary avocations of life without other restraint than such as affects all others, and to enjoy equally with them the fruits of his labor. A prohibition to him to pursue certain callings, open to others of the same age, condition, and sex, or to reside in places where others are permitted to live, would so far deprive him of the rights of a freeman, and would place him, as respects others, in a condition of servitude. A person allowed to pursue only one trade or calling, and only in one locality of the country, would not be, in the strict sense of the term, in a condition of slavery, but probably none would deny that he would be in a condition of servitude. He certainly would not possess the liberties nor enjoy the privileges of a freeman. The compulsion which would force him to labor even for his own benefit only in one direction, or in one place, would be almost as oppressive and nearly as great an invasion of his liberty as the compulsion which would force him to labor for the benefit or pleasure of another, **[83 U.S. 36, 91]** and would equally constitute an element of servitude. The counsel of the plaintiffs in error therefore contend that "wherever a law of a State, or a law of the United States, makes a discrimination between classes of persons, which deprives the one class of their freedom or their property, or which makes a caste of them to subserve the power, pride, avarice, vanity, or vengeance of others," there involuntary servitude exists within the meaning of the thirteenth amendment.

It is not necessary, in my judgment, for the disposition of the present case in favor of the plaintiffs in error, to accept as entirely correct this conclusion of counsel. It, however, finds support in the act of Congress known as the Civil Rights Act, which was framed and adopted upon a construction of the thirteenth amendment, giving to its language a similar breadth. That amendment was ratified on the eighteenth of December, 1865,[26] and in April of the following year the Civil Rights Act was passed.[27] Its first section declares that all persons born in the United States, and not subject to any foreign power, excluding Indians not taxed, are "citizens of the United States," and that "such citizens, of every race and color, without regard to any previous condition of slavery, or involuntary servitude, except as a punishment for crime, whereof the party shall have been duly convicted, shall have the same right in every State and Territory in the United States, to make and enforce contracts, to sue, be parties, and give evidence, to inherit, purchase, lease, sell, hold, and convey real and personal property, and to full and equal benefit of all laws and proceedings for the security of person and property, as enjoyed by white citizens."

This legislation was supported upon the theory that citizens of the United States as such were entitled to the rights and privileges enumerated, and that to deny to any such citizen equality in these rights and privileges with others, was, to the extent of the denial, subjecting him to an involuntary **[83 U.S. 36, 92]** servitude. Senator Trumbull, who drew the act and who was its earnest advocate in the Senate, stated, on opening the discussion upon it in that body, that the measure was intended to give effect to the declaration of the amendment, and to secure to all persons in the United States practical freedom. After referring to several statutes passed

---

[26] The proclamation of its ratification was made on that day (13 Stat. at Large, 774).
[27] 14 Id. 27.

in some of the Southern States, discriminating between the freedmen and white citizens, and after citing the definition of civil liberty given by Blackstone, the Senator said: "I take it that any statute which is not equal to all, and which deprives any citizen of civil rights, which are secured to other citizens, is an unjust encroachment upon his liberty; and it is in fact a badge of servitude which by the Constitution is prohibited."[28]

By the act of Louisiana, within the three parishes named, a territory exceeding one thousand one hundred square miles, and embracing over two hundred thousand people, every man who pursues the business of preparing animal food for market must take his animals to the buildings of the favored company, and must perform his work in them, and for the use of the buildings must pay a prescribed tribute to the company, and leave with it a valuable portion of each animal slaughtered. Every man in these parishes who has a horse or other animal for sale, must carry him to the yards and stables of this company, and for their use pay a like tribute. He is not allowed to do his work in his own buildings, or to take his animals to his own stables or keep them in his own yards, even though they should be erected in the same district as the buildings, stables, and yards of the company, and that district embraces over eleven hundred square miles. The prohibitions imposed by this act upon butchers and dealers in cattle in these parishes, and the special privileges conferred upon the favored corporation, are similar in principle and as odious in character as the restrictions imposed in the last century upon the peasantry in some parts of France, where, as says a French [83 U.S. 36, 93] writer, the peasant was prohibited "to hunt on his own lands, to fish in his own waters, to grind at his own mill, to cook at his own oven, to dry his clothes on his own machines, to whet his instruments at his own grindstone, to make his own wine, his oil, and his cider at his own press , . . . or to sell his commodities at the public market." The exclusive right to all these privileges was vested in the lords of the vicinage. "The history of the most execrable tyranny of ancient times," says the same writer, "offers nothing like this. This category of oppressions cannot be applied to a free man, or to the peasant, except in violation of his rights."

But if the exclusive privileges conferred upon the Louisiana corporation can be sustained, it is not perceived why exclusive privileges for the construction and keeping of ovens, machines, grindstones, wine- presses, and for all the numerous trades and pursuits for the prosecution of which buildings are required, may not be equally bestowed upon other corporations or private individuals, and for periods of indefinite duration.

It is not necessary, however, as I have said, to rest my objections to the act in question upon the terms and meaning of the thirteenth amendment. The provisions of the fourteenth amendment, which is properly a supplement to the thirteenth, cover, in my judgment, the case before us, and inhibit any legislation which confers special and exclusive privileges like these under consideration. The amendment was adopted to obviate objections which had been raised and pressed with great force to the validity of the Civil Rights Act, and to place the common rights of American citizens under the protection of the National government. It first declares that "all persons born or naturalized in the United States, and subject to the jurisdiction thereof, are citizens of the United States and of the State wherein they reside." It then declares that "no State shall make or enforce any law which shall abridge the privileges or immunities of citizens of the United States, nor shall any State deprive any person of life, liberty, or property, without due [83 U.S. 36, 94] process of law, nor deny to any person within its jurisdiction the equal protection of the laws."

The first clause of this amendment determines who are citizens of the United States, and how their citizenship is created. Before its enactment there was much diversity of opinion among jurists and statesmen whether there was any such citizenship independent of that of the State, and, if any existed, as to the manner in which it originated. With a great number the opinion prevailed that there was no such citizenship independent of the citizenship of the State. Such was the opinion of Mr. Calhoun and the class represented by him. In his celebrated speech in the Senate upon the Force Bill, in 1833, referring to the reliance expressed by a senator upon the fact that we are citizens of the United States, he said: "If by citizen of the United States he

---

[28] Congressional Globe, 1st Session, 39th Congress, part 1, page 474.

means a citizen at large, one whose citizenship extends to the entire geographical limits of the country without having a local citizenship in some State or Territory, a sort of citizen of the world, all I have to say is that such a citizen would be a perfect nondescript; that not a single individual of this description can be found in the entire mass of our population. Notwithstanding all the pomp and display of eloquence on the occasion, every citizen is a citizen of some State or Territory, and as such, under an express provision of the Constitution, is entitled to all privileges and immunities of citizens in the several States; and it is in this and no other sense that we are citizens of the United States."[29]

In the *Dred Scott* case this subject of citizenship of the United States was fully and elaborately discussed. The exposition in the opinion of Mr. Justice Curtis has been generally accepted by the profession of the country as the one containing the soundest views of constitutional law. And he held that, under the Constitution, citizenship of the United States in reference to natives was dependent upon citizenship in the several States, under their constitutions and laws. [83 U.S. 36, 95] The Chief Justice, in that case, and a majority of the court with him, held that the words "people of the United States" and "citizens" were synonymous terms; that the people of the respective States were the parties to the Constitution; that these people consisted of the free inhabitants of those States; that they had provided in their Constitution for the adoption of a uniform rule of naturalization; that they and their descendants and persons naturalized were the only persons who could be citizens of the United States, and that it was not in the power of any State to invest any other person with citizenship so that he could enjoy the privileges of a citizen under the Constitution, and that therefore the descendants of persons brought to this country and sold as slaves were not, and could not be citizens within the meaning of the Constitution.

The first clause of the fourteenth amendment changes this whole subject, and removes it from the region of discussion and doubt. It recognizes in express terms, if it does not create, citizens of the United States, and it makes their citizenship dependent upon the place of their birth, or the fact of their adoption, and not upon the constitution or laws of any State or the condition of their ancestry. A citizen of a State is now only a citizen of the United States residing in that State. The fundamental rights, privileges, and immunities which belong to him as a free man and a free citizen, now belong to him as a citizen of the United States, and are not dependent upon his citizenship of any State. The exercise of these rights and privileges, and the degree of enjoyment received from such exercise, are always more or less affected by the condition and the local institutions of the State, or city, or town where he resides. They are thus affected in a State by the wisdom of its laws, the ability of its officers, the efficiency of its magistrates, the education and morals of its people, and by many other considerations. This is a result which follows from the constitution of society, and can never be avoided, but in no other way can they be affected by the action of the State, or by the residence of the citizen therein. They do not derive [83 U.S. 36, 96] their existence from its legislation, and cannot be destroyed by its power.

The amendment does not attempt to confer any new privileges or immunities upon citizens, or to enumerate or define those already existing. It assumes that there are such privileges and immunities which belong of right to citizens as such, and ordains that they shall not be abridged by State legislation. If this inhibition has no reference to privileges and immunities of this character, but only refers, as held by the majority of the court in their opinion, to such privileges and immunities as were before its adoption specially designated in the Constitution or necessarily implied as belonging to citizens of the United States, it was a vain and idle enactment, which accomplished nothing, and most unnecessarily excited Congress and the people on its passage. With privileges and immunities thus designated or implied no State could ever have interfered by its laws, and no new constitutional provision was required to inhibit such interference. The supremacy of the Constitution and the laws of the United States always controlled any State legislation of that character. But if the

---

[29] Calhoun's Works, vol. 2, p. 242.

amendment refers to the natural and inalienable rights which belong to all citizens, the inhibition has a profound significance and consequence.

What, then, are the privileges and immunities which are secured against abridgment by State legislation?

In the first section of the Civil Rights Act Congress has given its interpretation to these terms, or at least has stated some of the rights which, in its judgment, these terms include; it has there declared that they include the right "to make and enforce contracts, to sue, be parties and give evidence, to inherit, purchase, lease, sell, hold, and convey real and personal property, and to full and equal benefit of all laws and proceedings for the security of person and property." That act, it is true, was passed before the fourteenth amendment, but the amendment was adopted, as I have already said, to obviate objections to the act, or, speaking more accurately, I should say, to obviate objections to legislation [83 U.S. 36, 97] of a similar character, extending the protection of the National government over the common rights of all citizens of the United States. Accordingly, after its ratification, Congress re-enacted the act under the belief that whatever doubts may have previously existed of its validity, they were removed by the amendment.[30]

The terms, privileges and immunities, are not new in the amendment; they were in the Constitution before the amendment was adopted. They are found in the second section of the fourth article, which declares that "the citizens of each State shall be entitled to all privileges and immunities of citizens in the several States," and they have been the subject of frequent consideration in judicial decisions. In *Corfield v. Coryell*,[31] Mr. Justice Washington said he had "no hesitation in confining these expressions to those privileges and immunities which were, in their nature, fundamental; which belong of right to citizens of all free governments, and which have at all times been enjoyed by the citizens of the several States which compose the Union, from the time of their becoming free, independent, and sovereign;" and, in considering what those fundamental privileges were, he said that perhaps it would be more tedious than difficult to enumerate them, but that they might be "all comprehended under the following general heads: protection by the government; the enjoyment of life and liberty, with the right to acquire and possess property of every kind, and to pursue and obtain happiness and safety, subject, nevertheless, to such restraints as the government may justly prescribe for the general good of the whole." This appears to me to be a sound construction of the clause in question. The privileges and immunities designated are those *which of right belong to the citizens of all free governments*. Clearly among these must be placed the right to pursue a lawful employment in a lawful manner, without other restraint than such as equally affects all persons. In the discussions [83 U.S. 36, 98] in Congress upon the passage of the Civil Rights Act repeated reference was made to this language of Mr. Justice Washington. It was cited by Senator Trumbull with the observation that it enumerated the very rights belonging to a citizen of the United States set forth in the first section of the act, and with the statement that all persons born in the United States, being declared by the act citizens of the United States, would thenceforth be entitled to the rights of citizens, and that these were the great fundamental rights set forth in the act; and that they were set forth "as appertaining to every freeman."

The privileges and immunities designated in the second section of the fourth article of the Constitution are, then, according to the decision cited, those which of right belong to the citizens of all free governments, and they can be enjoyed under that clause by the citizens of each State in the several States upon the same terms and conditions as they are enjoyed by the citizens of the latter States. No discrimination can be made by one State against the citizens of other States in their enjoyment, nor can any greater imposition be levied than such as is laid upon its own citizens. It is a clause which insures equality in the enjoyment of these rights between citizens of the several States whilst in the same State.

---

[30] May 31st, 1870; 16 Stat. at Large, 144.
[31] 4 Washington's Circuit Court, 380.

Nor is there anything in the opinion in the case of *Paul v. Virginia*,[32] which at all militates against these views, as is supposed by the majority of the court. The act of Virginia, of 1866, which was under consideration in that case, provided that no insurance company, not incorporated under the laws of the State, should carry on its business within the State without previously obtaining a license for that purpose; and that it should not receive such license until it had deposited with the treasurer of the State bonds of a specified character, to an amount varying from thirty to fifty thousand dollars. No such deposit was required of insurance companies incorporated by the State, for carrying on **[83 U.S. 36, 99]** their business within the State; and in the case cited the validity of the discriminating provisions of the statute of Virginia between her own corporations and the corporations of other States, was assailed. It was contended that the statute in this particular was in conflict with that clause of the Constitution which declares that "the citizens of each State shall be entitled to all privileges and immunities of citizens in the several States." But the court answered, that corporations were not citizens within the meaning of this clause; that the term citizens as there used applied only to natural persons, members of the body politic owing allegiance to the State, not to artificial persons created by the legislature and possessing only the attributes which the legislature had prescribed; that though it had been held that where contracts or rights of property were to be enforced by or against a corporation, the courts of the United States would, for the purpose of maintaining jurisdiction, consider the corporation as representing citizens of the State, under the laws of which it was created, and to this extent would treat a corporation was a citizen within the provision of the Constitution extending the judicial power of the United States to controversies between citizens of different States, it had never been held in any case which had come under its observation, either in the State or Federal courts, that a corporation was a citizen within the meaning of the clause in question, entitling the citizens of each State to the privileges and immunities of citizens in the several States. And the court observed, that the privileges and immunities secured by that provision were those privileges and immunities which were common to the citizens in the latter States, under their constitution and laws, by virtue of their being citizens; that special privileges enjoyed by citizens in their own States were not secured in other States by the provision; that it was not intended by it to give to the laws of one State any operation in other States; that they could have no such operation except by the permission, expressed or implied, of those States; and that the special privileges which they conferred must, therefore, be enjoyed at home unless the assent **[83 U.S. 36, 100]** of other States to their enjoyment therein were given. And so the court held, that a corporation, being a grant of special privileges to the corporators, had no legal existence beyond the limits of the sovereignty where created, and that the recognition of its existence by other States, and the enforcement of its contracts made therein, depended purely upon the assent of those States, which could be granted upon such terms and conditions as those States might think proper to impose.

The whole purport of the decision was, that citizens of one State do not carry with them into other States any special privileges or immunities, conferred by the laws of their own States, of a corporate or other character. That decision has no pertinency to the questions involved in this case. The common privileges and immunities which of right belong to all citizens, stand on a very different footing. These the citizens of each State do carry with them into other States and are secured by the clause in question, in their enjoyment upon terms of equality with citizens of the latter States. This equality in one particular was enforced by this court in the recent case of *Ward v. The State of Maryland*, reported in the 12th of Wallace. A statute of that State required the payment of a larger sum from a non-resident trader for a license to enable him to sell his merchandise in the State, than it did of a resident trader, and the court held, that the statute in thus discriminating against the non-resident trader contravened the clause securing to the citizens of each State the privileges and immunities of citizens of the several States. The privilege of disposing of his property, which was an essential incident to his ownership, possessed by the non-resident, was subjected by the statute of Maryland to a greater burden than was imposed upon a like privilege of her own citizens. The privileges of the non-

---

[32] 8 Wallace, 168.

resident were in this particular abridged by that legislation.

What the clause in question did for the protection of the citizens of one State against hostile and discriminating legislation of other States, the fourteenth amendment does for [83 U.S. 36, 101] the protection of every citizen of the United States against hostile and discriminating legislation against him in favor of others, whether they reside in the same or in different States. If under the fourth article of the Constitution equality of privileges and immunities is secured between citizens of different States, under the fourteenth amendment the same equality is secured between citizens of the United States.

It will not be pretended that under the fourth article of the Constitution any State could create a monopoly in any known trade or manufacture in favor of her own citizens, or any portion of them, which would exclude an equal participation in the trade or manufacture monopolized by citizens of other States. She could not confer, for example, upon any of her citizens the sole right to manufacture shoes, or boots, or silk, or the sole right to sell those articles in the State so as to exclude non-resident citizens from engaging in a similar manufacture or sale. The non-resident citizens could claim equality of privilege under the provisions of the fourth article with the citizens of the State exercising the monopoly as well as with others, and thus, as respects them, the monopoly would cease. If this were not so it would be in the power of the State to exclude at any time the citizens of other States from participation in particular branches of commerce or trade, and extend the exclusion from time to time so as effectually to prevent any traffic with them.

Now, what the clause in question does for the protection of citizens of one State against the creation of monopolies in favor of citizens of other States, the fourteenth amendment does for the protection of every citizen of the United States against the creation of any monopoly whatever. The privileges and immunities of citizens of the United States, of every one of them, is secured against abridgment in any form by any State. The fourteenth amendment places them under the guardianship of the National authority. All monopolies in any known trade or manufacture are an invasion of these privileges, for they encroach upon the liberty of citizens to acquire property and pursue happiness, and were [83 U.S. 36, 102] held void at common law in the great *Case of Monopolies*, decided during the reign of Queen Elizabeth.

A monopoly is defined "to be an institution or allowance from the sovereign power of the State by grant, commission, or otherwise, to any person or corporation, for the sole buying, selling, making, working, or using of anything, whereby any person or persons, bodies politic or corporate, are sought to be restrained of any freedom or liberty they had before, or hindered in their lawful trade." All such grants relating to any known trade or manufacture have been held by all the judges of England, whenever they have come up for consideration, to be void at common law as destroying the freedom of trade, discouraging labor and industry, restraining persons from getting an honest livelihood, and putting it into the power of the grantees to enhance the price of commodities. The definition embraces, it will be observed, not merely the sole privilege of buying and selling particular articles, or of engaging in their manufacture, but also the sole privilege of using anything by which others may be restrained of the freedom or liberty they previously had in any lawful trade, or hindered in such trade. It thus covers in every particular the possession and use of suitable yards, stables, and buildings for keeping and protecting cattle and other animals, and for their slaughter. Such establishments are essential to the free and successful prosecution by any butcher of the lawful trade of preparing animal food for market. The exclusive privilege of supplying such yards, buildings, and other conveniences for the prosecution of this business in a large district of country, granted by the act of Louisiana to seventeen persons, is as much a monopoly as though the act had granted to the company the exclusive privilege of buying and selling the animals themselves. It equally restrains the butchers in the freedom and liberty they previously had, and hinders them in their lawful trade.

The reasons given for the judgment in the *Case of Monopolies* apply with equal force to the case at bar. In that case a patent had been granted to the plaintiff giving him the sole [83 U.S. 36, 103] right to import playing-cards, and the entire traffic in them, and the sole right to make such cards within the realm. The defendant, in disregard of this patent, made and sold some gross of such cards and imported others, and was accordingly sued for infringing upon the exclusive privileges of the plaintiff. As to a portion of the cards made and sold within the realm, he pleaded that he was a haberdasher in London and a free citizen of that city, and as such had a right to make and sell them. The court held the plea good and the grant void, as against the common law and divers acts of Parliament. "All trades," said the court, "as well mechanical as others, which prevent idleness (the bane of the commonwealth) and exercise men and youth in labor for the maintenance of themselves and their families, and for the increase of their substance, to serve the queen when occasion shall require, are profitable for the commonwealth, and therefore the grant to the plaintiff to have the sole making of them is *against the common law and the benefit and liberty of the subject.*"[33] The case of Davenant and Hurdis was cited in support of this position. In that case a company of merchant tailors in London, having power by charter to make ordinances for the better rule and government of the company, so that they were consonant to law and reason, made an ordinance that any brother of the society who should have any cloth dressed by a cloth-worker, not being a brother of the society, should put one-half of his cloth to some brother of the same society who exercised the art of a cloth-worker, upon pain of forfeiting ten shillings, "and it was adjudged that the ordinance, although it had the countenance of a charter, was against the common law, because it was against the liberty of the subject; for every subject, by the law, has freedom and liberty to put his cloth to be dressed by what cloth-worker he pleases, and cannot be restrained to certain persons, for that in effect would be a monopoly, and, therefore, such ordinance, by color of a charter or any grant by charter to such effect, would be void." **[83 U.S. 36, 104]** Although the court, in its opinion, refers to the increase in prices and deterioration in quality of commodities which necessarily result from the grant of monopolies, the main ground of the decision was their interference with the liberty of the subject to pursue for his maintenance and that of his family any lawful trade or employment. This liberty is assumed to be the natural right of every Englishman.

The struggle of the English people against monopolies forms one of the most interesting and instructive chapters in their history. It finally ended in the passage of the statute of 21st James I, by which it was declared "that all monopolies and all commissions, grants, licenses, charters, and letters-patent, to any person or persons, bodies politic or corporate, whatsoever, of or for the sole buying, selling, making, working, or using of anything" within the realm or the dominion of Wales were altogether contrary to the laws of the realm and utterly void, with the exception of patents for new inventions for a limited period, and for printing, then supposed to belong to the prerogative of the king, and for the preparation and manufacture of certain articles and ordnance intended for the prosecution of war.

The common law of England, as is thus seen, condemned all monopolies in any known trade or manufacture, and declared void all grants of special privileges whereby others could be deprived of any liberty which they previously had, or be hindered in their lawful trade. The statute of James I, to which I have referred, only embodied the law as it had been previously declared by the courts of England, although frequently disregarded by the sovereigns of that country.

The common law of England is the basis of the jurisprudence of the United States. It was brought to this country by the colonists, together with the English statutes, and was established here so far as it was applicable to their condition. That law and the benefit of such of the English statutes as existed at the time of their colonization, and which they had by experience found to be applicable to their circumstances, were claimed by the Congress of the United Colonies in 1774 as a part of their "indubitable rights and liberties."[34] **[83 U.S. 36, 105]** Of the statutes, the benefits of which was thus claimed, the statute of James I against monopolies was one of the most important. And when the Colonies separated from the mother country no privilege was more fully recognized or more completely incorporated into the fundamental law of the country than that every free subject in the British empire was entitled to pursue his

---

[33] Coke's Reports, part 11, page 86.
[34] Journals of Congress, vol. i, pp. 28-30.

happiness by following any of the known established trades and occupations of the country, subject only to such restraints as equally affected all others. The immortal document which proclaimed the independence of the country declared as self-evident truths that the Creator had endowed all men "with certain inalienable rights, and that among these are life, liberty, and the pursuit of happiness; and that to secure these rights governments are instituted among men."

If it be said that the civil law and not the common law is the basis of the jurisprudence of Louisiana, I answer that the decree of Louis XVI, in 1776, abolished all monopolies of trades and all special privileges of corporations, guilds, and trading companies, and authorized every person to exercise, without restraint, his art, trade, or profession, and such has been the law of France and of her colonies ever since, and that law prevailed in Louisiana at the time of her cession to the United States. Since then, notwithstanding the existence in that State of the civil law as the basis of her jurisprudence, freedom of pursuit has been always recognized as the common right of her citizens. But were this otherwise, the fourteenth amendment secures the like protection to all citizens in that State against any abridgment of their common rights, as in other States. That amendment was intended to give practical effect to the declaration of 1776 of inalienable rights, rights which are the gift of the Creator, which the law does not confer, but only recognizes. If the trader in London could plead that he was a free citizen of that city against the enforcement to his injury of monopolies, surely under the fourteenth amendment every **[83 U.S. 36, 106]** citizen of the United States should be able to plead his citizenship of the republic as a protection against any similar invasion of his privileges and immunities.

So fundamental has this privilege of every citizen to be free from disparaging and unequal enactments, in the pursuit of the ordinary avocations of life, been regarded, that few instances have arisen where the principle has been so far violated as to call for the interposition of the courts. But whenever this has occurred, with the exception of the present cases from Louisiana, which are the most barefaced and flagrant of all, the enactment interfering with the privilege of the citizen has been pronounced illegal and void. When a case under the same law, under which the present cases have arisen, came before the Circuit Court of the United States in the District of Louisiana, there was no hesitation on the part of the court in declaring the law, in its exclusive features, to be an invasion of one of the fundamental privileges of the citizen. The presiding justice, in delivering the opinion of the court, observed that it might be difficult to enumerate or define what were the essential privileges of a citizen of the United States, which a State could not by its laws invade, but that so far as the question under consideration was concerned, it might be safely said that "it is one of the privileges of every American citizen to adopt and follow such lawful industrial pursuit, not injurious to the community, as he may see fit, without unreasonable regulation or molestation, and without being restricted by any of those unjust, oppressive, and odious monopolies or exclusive privileges which have been condemned by all free governments." And again: "There is no more sacred right of citizenship than the right to pursue unmolested a lawful employment in a lawful manner. It is nothing more nor less than the sacred right of labor."

In the *City of Chicago v. Rumpff*,[35] which was before the Supreme Court of Illinois, we have a case similar in all its **[83 U.S. 36, 107]** features to the one at bar. That city being authorized by its charter to regulate and license the slaughtering of animals within its corporate limits, the common council passed what was termed an ordinance in reference thereto, whereby a particular building was designated for the slaughtering of all animals intended for sale or consumption in the city, the owners of which were granted the exclusive right for a specified period to have all such animals slaughtered at their establishment, they to be paid a specific sum for the privilege of slaughtering there by all persons exercising it. The validity of this action of the corporate authorities was assailed on the ground of the grant of exclusive privileges, and

---

[35] 45 Illinois, 90.

the court said: "The charter authorizes the city authorities to license or regulate such establishments. Where that body has made the necessary regulations, required for the health or comfort of the inhabitants, all persons inclined to pursue such an occupation should have an opportunity of conforming to such regulations, otherwise the ordinance would be unreasonable and tend to oppression. Or, if they should regard it for the interest of the city that such establishments should be licensed, the ordinance should be so framed that all persons desiring it might obtain licenses by conforming to the prescribed terms and regulations for the government of such business. We regard it neither as a regulation nor a license of the business to confine it to one building or to give it to one individual. Such an action is oppressive, and creates a monopoly that never could have been contemplated by the General Assembly. It impairs the rights of all other persons, and cuts them off from a share in not only a legal, but a necessary business. Whether we consider this as an ordinance or a contract, it is equally unauthorized, as being opposed to the rules governing the adoption of municipal by-laws. The principle of equality of rights to the corporators is violated by this contract. If the common council may require all of the animals for the consumption of the city to be slaughtered in a single building, or on a particular lot, and the owner be paid a specific sum for the privilege, what would prevent the making a **[83 U.S. 36, 108]** similar contract with some other person that all of the vegetables, or fruits, the flour, the groceries, the dry goods, or other commodities should be sold on his lot and he receive a compensation for the privilege? We can see no difference in principle."

It is true that the court in this opinion was speaking of a municipal ordinance and not of an act of the legislature of a State. But, as it is justly observed by counsel, a legislative body is no more entitled to destroy the equality of rights of citizens, nor to fetter the industry of a city, than a municipal government. These rights are protected from invasion by the fundamental law.

In the case of the *Norwich Gaslight Company v. The Norwich City Gas Company*,[36] which was before the Supreme Court of Connecticut, it appeared that the common council of the city of Norwich had passed a resolution purporting to grant to one Treadway, his heirs and assigns, for the period of fifteen years, the right to lay gas-pipes in the streets of that city, declaring that no other person or corporation should, by the consent of the common council, lay gas-pipes in the streets during that time. The plaintiffs having purchased of Treadway, undertook to assert an exclusive right to use the streets for their purposes, as against another company which was using the streets for the same purposes. And the court said: "As, then, no consideration whatever, either of a public or private character, was reserved for the grant; and as the business of manufacturing and selling gas is an ordinary business, like the manufacture of leather, or any other article of trade in respect to which the government has no exclusive prerogative, we think that so far as the restriction of other persons than the plaintiffs from using the streets for the purpose of distributing gas by means of pipes, can fairly be viewed as intended to operate as a restriction upon its free manufacture and sale, it comes directly within the definition and description of a monopoly; and although we have no direct constitutional provision against a monopoly, **[83 U.S. 36, 109]** yet the whole theory of a free government is opposed to such grants, and it does not require even the aid which may be derived from the Bill of Rights, the first section of which declares 'that no man or set of men are entitled to exclusive public emoluments or privileges from the community,' to render them void."

In the *Mayor of the City of Hudson v. Thorne*,[37] an application was made to the chancellor of New York to dissolve an injunction restraining the defendants from erecting a building in the city of Hudson upon a vacant lot owned by them, intended to be used as a hay-press. The common council of the city had passed an ordinance directing that no person should erect, or construct, or cause to be erected or constructed, any wooden or frame barn, stable, or hay-press of certain dimensions, within certain specified limits in the city, without its permission. It

---

[36] 25 Connecticut, 19.
[37] 7 Paige, 261.

292

appeared, however, that there were such buildings already in existence, not only in compact parts of the city, but also within the prohibited limits, the occupation of which for the storing and pressing of hay the common council did not intend to restrain. And the chancellor said: "If the manufacture of pressed hay within the compact parts of the city is dangerous in causing or promoting fires, the common council have the power expressly given by their charter to prevent the carrying on of such manufacture; but as all by-laws must be reasonable, the common council cannot make a by-law which shall permit one person to carry on the dangerous business and prohibit another who has an equal right from pursuing the same business."

In all these cases there is a recognition of the equality of right among citizens in the pursuit of the ordinary avocations of life, and a declaration that all grants of exclusive privileges, in contravention of this equality, are against common right, and void.

This equality of right, with exemption from all disparaging and partial enactments, in the lawful pursuits of life, **[83 U.S. 36, 110]** throughout the whole country, is the distinguishing privilege of citizens of the United States. To them, everywhere, all pursuits, all professions, all avocations are open without other restrictions than such as are imposed equally upon all others of the same age, sex, and condition. The State may prescribe such regulations for every pursuit and calling of life as will promote the public health, secure the good order and advance the general prosperity of society, but when once prescribed, the pursuit or calling must be free to be followed by every citizen who is within the conditions designated, and will conform to the regulations. This is the fundamental idea upon which our institutions rest, and unless adhered to in the legislation of the country our government will be a republic only in name. The fourteenth amendment, in my judgment, makes it essential to the validity of the legislation of every State that this equality of right should be respected. How widely this equality has been departed from, how entirely rejected and trampled upon by the act of Louisiana, I have already shown. And it is to me a matter of profound regret that its validity is recognized by a majority of this court, for by it the right of free labor, one of the most sacred and imprescriptible rights of man, is violated.[38] As stated by the Supreme Court of Connecticut, in **[83 U.S. 36, 111]** the case cited, grants of exclusive privileges, such as is made by the act in question, are opposed to the whole theory of free government, and it requires no aid from any bill of rights to render them void. That only is a free government, in the American sense of the term, under which the inalienable right of every citizen to pursue his happiness is unrestrained, except by just, equal, and impartial laws.[39]

---

[38] 'The property which every man has in his own labor,' says Adam Smith, 'as it is the original foundation of all other property, so it is the most sacred and inviolable. The patrimony of the poor man lies in the strength and dexterity of his own hands; and to hinder him from employing this strength and dexterity in what manner he thinks proper, without injury to his neighbor, is a plain violation of this most sacred property. It is a manifest encroachment upon the just liberty both of the workman and of those who might be disposed to employ him. As it hinders the one from working at what he thinks proper, so it hinders the others from employing whom they think proper.' (Smith's Wealth of Nations, b. 1, ch. 10, part 2.)

In the edict of Louis XVI, in 1776, giving freedom to trades and professions, prepared by his minister, Turgot, he recites the contributions that had been made by the guilds and trade companies, and says: 'It was the allurement of these fiscal advantages undoubtedly that prolonged the illusion and concealed the immense injury they did to industry and their infraction of natural right. This illusion had extended so far that some persons asserted that the right to work was a royal privilege which the king might sell, and that his subjects were bound to purchase from him. We hasten to correct this error and to repel the conclusion. God in giving to man wants and desires rendering labor necessary for their satisfaction, conferred the right to labor upon all men, and this property is the first, most sacred, and imprescriptible of all.' . . . He, therefore, regards it 'as the first duty of his justice, and the worthiest act of benevolence, to free his subjects from any restriction upon this inalienable right of humanity.'

[39] 'Civil liberty, the great end of all human society and government, is that state in which each individual has the power to pursue his own happiness according to his own views of his interest, and the dictates of his conscience, unrestrained, except by equal, just, and impartial laws.' (1 Sharswood's Blackstone, 127, note 8.)

I am authorized by the **CHIEF JUSTICE**, Mr. Justice **SWAYNE**, and Mr. Justice **BRADLEY**, to state that they concur with me in this dissenting opinion.

Mr. Justice BRADLEY, also dissenting:

I concur in the opinion which has just been read by Mr. Justice Field; but desire to add a few observations for the purpose of more fully illustrating my views on the important question decided in these cases, and the special grounds on which they rest.

The fourteenth amendment to the Constitution of the United States, section 1, declares that no State shall make or enforce any law which shall abridge the privileges and immunities of citizens of the United States.

The legislature of Louisiana, under pretence of making a police regulation for the promotion of the public health, passed an act conferring upon a corporation, created by the act, the exclusive right, for twenty-five years, to have and maintain slaughter-houses, landings for cattle, and yards for [83 U.S. 36, 112] confining cattle intended for slaughter, within the parishes of Orleans, Jefferson, and St. Bernard, a territory containing nearly twelve hundred square miles, including the city of New Orleans; and prohibiting all other persons from building, keeping, or having slaughter-houses, landings for cattle, and yards for confining cattle intended for slaughter within the said limits; and requiring that all cattle and other animals to be slaughtered for food in that district should be brought to the slaughter- houses and works of the favored company to be slaughtered, and a payment of a fee to the company for such act.

It is contended that this prohibition abridges the privileges and immunities of citizens of the United States, especially of the plaintiffs in error, who were particularly affected thereby; and whether it does so or not is the simple question in this case. And the solution of this question depends upon the solution of two other questions, to wit:

First. Is it one of the rights and privileges of a citizen of the United States to pursue such civil employment as he may choose to adopt, subject to such reasonable regulations as may be prescribed by law?

Secondly. Is a monopoly, or exclusive right, given to one person to the exclusion of all others, to keep slaughter-houses, in a district of nearly twelve hundred square miles, for the supply of meat for a large city, a reasonable regulation of that employment which the legislature has a right to impose?

The first of these questions is one of vast importance, and lies at the very foundations of our government. The question is now settled by the fourteenth amendment itself, that citizenship of the United States is the primary citizenship in this country; and that State citizenship is secondary and derivative, depending upon citizenship of the United States and the citizen's place of residence. The States have not now, if they ever had, any power to restrict their citizenship to any classes or persons. A citizen of the United States has a perfect constitutional right to go to and reside in any State he chooses, and to claim citizenship therein, [83 U.S. 36, 113] and an equality of rights with every other citizen; and the whole power of the nation is pledged to sustain him in that right. He is not bound to cringe to any superior, or to pray for any act of grace, as a means of enjoying all the rights and privileges enjoyed by other citizens. And when the spirit of lawlessness, mob violence, and sectional hate can be so completely repressed as to give full practical effect to this right, we shall be a happier nation, and a more prosperous one than we now are. Citizenship of the United States ought to be, and, according to the Constitution, is, a sure and undoubted title to equal rights in any and every States in this Union, subject to such regulations as the legislature may rightfully prescribe. If a man be denied full equality before the law, he is denied one of the essential rights of citizenship as a citizen of the United States.

Every citizen, then, being primarily a citizen of the United States, and, secondarily, a citizen of the State where he resides, what, in general, are the privileges and immunities of a citizen of the United States? Is the right, liberty, or privilege of choosing any lawful employment one of them?

294

If a State legislature should pass a law prohibiting the inhabitants of a particular township, county, or city, from tanning leather or making shoes, would such a law violate any privileges or immunities of those inhabitants as citizens of the United States, or only their privileges and immunities as citizens of that particular State? Or if a State legislature should pass a law of caste, making all trades and professions, or certain enumerated trades and professions, hereditary, so that no one could follow any such trades or professions except that which was pursued by his father, would such a law violate the privileges and immunities of the people of that State as citizens of the United States, or only as citizens of the State? Would they have no redress but to appeal to the courts of that particular State?

This seems to me to be the essential question before us for consideration. And, in my judgment, the right of any citizen to follow whatever lawful employment he chooses to adopt (submitting himself to all lawful regulations) is one of [83 U.S. 36, 114] his most valuable rights, and one which the legislature of a State cannot invade, whether restrained by its own constitution or not.

The right of a State to regulate the conduct of its citizens is undoubtedly a very broad and extensive one, and not to be lightly restricted. But there are certain fundamental rights which this right of regulation cannot infringe. It may prescribe the manner of their exercise, but it cannot subvert the rights themselves. I speak now of the rights of citizens of any free government. Granting for the present that the citizens of one government cannot claim the privileges of citizens in another government; that prior to the union of our North American States the citizens of one State could not claim the privileges of citizens in another State; or, that after the union was formed the citizens of the United States, as such, could not claim the privileges of citizens in any particular State; yet the citizens of each of the States and the citizens of the United States would be entitled to certain privileges and immunities as citizens, at the hands of their own government-privileges and immunities which their own governments respectively would be bound to respect and maintain. In this free country, the people of which inherited certain traditional rights and privileges from their ancestors, citizenship means something. It has certain privileges and immunities attached to it which the government, whether restricted by express or implied limitations, cannot take away or impair. It may do so temporarily by force, but it cannot do so by right. And these privileges and immunities attach as well to citizenship of the United States as to citizenship of the States.

The people of this country brought with them to its shores the rights of Englishmen; the rights which had been wrested from English sovereigns at various periods of the nation's history. One of these fundamental rights was expressed in these words, found in Magna Charta: "No freeman shall be taken or imprisoned, or be disseized of his freehold or liberties or free customs, or be outlawed or exiled, or any otherwise destroyed; nor will we pass upon him or condemn [83 U.S. 36, 115] him but by lawful judgment of his peers or by the law of the land." English constitutional writers expound this article as rendering life, liberty, and property inviolable, except by due process of law. This is the very right which the plaintiffs in error claim in this case. Another of these rights was that of habeas corpus, or the right of having any invasion of personal liberty judicially examined into, at once, by a competent judicial magistrate. Blackstone classifies these fundamental rights under three heads, as the absolute rights of individuals, to wit: the right of personal security, the right of personal liberty, and the right of private property. And of the last he says: "The third absolute right, inherent in every Englishman, is that of property, which consists in the free use, enjoyment, and disposal of all his acquisitions, without any control or diminution save only by the laws of the land."

The privileges and immunities of Englishmen were established and secured by long usage and by various acts of Parliament. But it may be said that the Parliament of England has unlimited authority, and might repeal the laws which have from time to time been enacted. Theoretically this is so, but practically it is not. England has no written constitution, it is true; but it has an unwritten one, resting in the acknowledged, and frequently declared, privileges of Parliament and the people, to violate which in any material respect would produce a revolution in an hour. A violation of one of the fundamental principles of that constitution in the Colonies, namely, the principle that recognizes the property of the people as their own, and which, therefore, regards all taxes for the support of government as gifts of the people through their representatives, and regards taxation without representation as subversive of free government, was the origin of our own revolution.

This, it is true, was the violation of a political right; but personal rights were deemed equally sacred, and were claimed by the very first Congress of the Colonies, assembled in 1774, as the undoubted inheritance of the people of this country; and the Declaration of Independence, which [83 U.S. 36, 116] was the first political act of the American people in their independent sovereign capacity, lays the foundation of our National existence upon this broad proposition: "That all men are created equal; that they are endowed by their Creator with certain inalienable rights; that among these are life, liberty, and the pursuit of happiness." Here again we have the great threefold division of the rights of freemen, asserted as the rights of man. Rights to life, liberty, and the pursuit of happiness are equivalent to the rights of life, liberty, and property. These are the fundamental rights which can only be taken away by due process of law, and which can only be interfered with, or the enjoyment of which can only be modified, by lawful regulations necessary or proper for the mutual good of all; and these rights, I contend, belong to the citizens of every free government.

For the preservation, exercise, and enjoyment of these rights the individual citizen, as a necessity, must be left free to adopt such calling, profession, or trade as may seem to him most conducive to that end. Without this right he cannot be a freeman. This right to choose one's calling is an essential part of that liberty which it is the object of government to protect; and a calling, when chosen, is a man's property and right. Liberty and property are not protected where these rights are arbitrarily assailed.

I think sufficient has been said to show that citizenship is not an empty name, but that, in this country at least, it has connected with it certain incidental rights, privileges, and immunities of the greatest importance. And to say that these rights and immunities attach only to State citizenship, and not to citizenship of the United States, appears to me to evince a very narrow and insufficient estimate of constitutional history and the rights of men, not to say the rights of the American people.

On this point the often-quoted language of Mr. Justice Washington, in *Corfield v. Coryell*,[40] is very instructive. Being [83 U.S. 36, 117] called upon to expound that clause in the fourth article of the Constitution, which declares that "the citizens of each State shall be entitled to all the privileges and immunities of citizens in the several States," he says: "The inquiry is, what are the privileges and immunities of citizens in the several States? We feel no hesitation in confining these expressions to those privileges and immunities which are, in their nature, fundamental; which belong, of right, to the citizens of all free governments, and which have at all times been enjoyed by the citizens of the several States which compose this Union from the time of their becoming free, independent, and sovereign. What these fundamental privileges are it would perhaps be more tedious than difficult to enumerate. They may, however, be all comprehended under the following general heads: Protection by the government; the enjoyment of life and liberty, with the right to acquire and possess property of every kind, and to pursue and obtain happiness and safety, subject, nevertheless, to such restraints as the government may justly prescribe for the general good of the whole; the right of a citizen of one State to pass through, or to reside in, any other State for purposes of trade, agriculture, professional pursuits, or otherwise; to claim the benefit of the writ of habeas corpus; to institute and maintain actions of any kind in the courts of the State; to take, hold, and dispose of property, either real or personal; and an exemption from higher taxes or impositions than are paid by the other citizens of the State, may be mentioned as some of the particular privileges and immunities of citizens which are clearly embraced by the general description of privileges deemed to be fundamental."

---

[40] 4 Washington, 380.

It is pertinent to observe that both the clause of the Constitution referred to, and Justice Washington in his comment on it, speak of the privileges and immunities of citizens *in* a State; not of citizens *of* a State. It is the privileges and immunities of citizens, that is, of citizens as such, that are to be accorded to citizens of other States when they are found in any State; or, as Justice Washington says, "privileges and immunities which are, in their nature, fundamental; [83 U.S. 36, 118] which belong, of right, to the citizens of all free governments."

It is true the courts have usually regarded the clause referred to as securing only an equality of privileges with the citizens of the State in which the parties are found. Equality before the law is undoubtedly one of the privileges and immunities of every citizen. I am not aware that any case has arisen in which it became necessary to vindicate any other fundamental privilege of citizenship; although rights have been claimed which were not deemed fundamental, and have been rejected as not within the protection of this clause. Be this, however, as it may, the language of the clause is as I have stated it, and seems fairly susceptible of a broader interpretation than that which makes it a guarantee of mere equality of privileges with other citizens.

But we are not bound to resort to implication, or to the constitutional history of England, to find an authoritative declaration of some of the most important privileges and immunities of citizens of the United States. It is in the Constitution itself. The Constitution, it is true, as it stood prior to the recent amendments, specifies, in terms, only a few of the personal privileges and immunities of citizens, but they are very comprehensive in their character. The States were merely prohibited from passing bills of attainder, *ex post facto* laws, laws impairing the obligation of contracts, and perhaps one or two more. But others of the greatest consequence were enumerated, although they were only secured, in express terms, from invasion by the Federal government; such as the right of *habeas corpus*, the right of trial by jury, of free exercise of religious worship, the right of free speech and a free press, the right peaceably to assemble for the discussion of public measures, the right to be secure against unreasonable searches and seizures, and above all, and including almost all the rest, the right of *not being deprived of life, liberty, or property, without due process of law*. These, and still others are specified in the original Constitution, or in the early amendments of it, as among the privileges and immunities [83 U.S. 36, 119] of citizens of the United States, or, what is still stronger for the force of the argument, the rights of all persons, whether citizens or not.

But even if the Constitution were silent, the fundamental privileges and immunities of citizens, as such, would be no less real and no less inviolable than they now are. It was not necessary to say in words that the citizens of the United States should have and exercise all the privileges of citizens; the privilege of buying, selling, and enjoying property; the privilege of engaging in any lawful employment for a livelihood; the privilege of resorting to the laws for redress of injuries, and the like. Their very citizenship conferred these privileges, if they did not possess them before. And these privileges they would enjoy whether they were citizens of any State or not. Inhabitants of Federal territories and new citizens, made such by annexation of territory or naturalization, though without any status as citizens of a State, could, nevertheless, as citizens of the United States, lay claim to every one of the privileges and immunities which have been enumerated; and among these none is more essential and fundamental than the right to follow such profession or employment as each one may choose, subject only to uniform regulations equally applicable to all.

II. The next question to be determined in this case is: Is a monopoly or exclusive right, given to one person, or corporation, to the exclusion of all others, to keep slaughter-houses in a district of nearly twelve hundred square miles, for the supply of meat for a great city, a reasonable regulation of that employment which the legislature has a right to impose?

The keeping of a slaughter-house is part of, and incidental to, the trade of a butcher-one of the ordinary occupations of human life. To compel a butcher, or rather all the butchers of a large city and an extensive district, to slaughter their cattle in another person's slaughter-house and pay him a toll therefor, is such a restriction upon the trade as materially to interfere with its prosecution. It is onerous, unreasonable, arbitrary, and unjust. It has none of the [83 U.S. 36,

120] qualities of a police regulation. If it were really a police regulation, it would undoubtedly be within the power of the legislature. That portion of the act which requires all slaughter-houses to be located below the city, and to be subject to inspection, &c., is clearly a police regulation. That portion which allows no one but the favored company to build, own, or have slaughter-houses is not a police regulation, and has not the faintest semblance of one. It is one of those arbitrary and unjust laws made in the interest of a few scheming individuals, by which some of the Southern States have, within the past few years, been so deplorably oppressed and impoverished. It seems to me strange that it can be viewed in any other light.

The granting of monopolies, or exclusive privileges to individuals or corporations, is an invasion of the right of others to choose a lawful calling, and an infringement of personal liberty. It was so felt by the English nation as far back as the reigns of Elizabeth and James. A fierce struggle for the suppression of such monopolies, and for abolishing the prerogative of creating them, was made and was successful. The statute of 21st James, abolishing monopolies, was one of those constitutional landmarks of English liberty which the English nation so highly prize and so jealously preserve. It was a part of that inheritance which our fathers brought with them. This statute abolished all monopolies except grants for a term of years to the inventors of new manufactures. This exception is the groundwork of patents for new inventions and copyrights of books. These have always been sustained as beneficial to the state. But all other monopolies were abolished, as tending to the impoverishment of the people and to interference with their free pursuits. And ever since that struggle no English-speaking people have ever endured such an odious badge of tyranny.

It has been suggested that this was a mere legislative act, and that the British Parliament, as well as our own legislatures, have frequently disregarded it by granting exclusive privileges for erecting ferries, railroads, markets, and other establishments of a public kind. It requires but a slight **[83 U.S. 36, 121]** acquaintance with legal history to know that grants of this kind of franchises are totally different from the monopolies of commodities or of ordinary callings or pursuits. These public franchises can only be exercised under authority from the government, and the government may grant them on such conditions as it sees fit. But even these exclusive privileges are becoming more and more odious, and are getting to be more and more regarded as wrong in principle, and as inimical to the just rights and greatest good of the people. But to cite them as proof of the power of legislatures to create mere monopolies, such as no free and enlightened community any longer endures, appears to me, to say the least, very strange and illogical.

Lastly: Can the Federal courts administer relief to citizens of the United States whose privileges and immunities have been abridged by a State? Of this I entertain no doubt. Prior to the fourteenth amendment this could not be done, except in a few instances, for the want of the requisite authority.

As the great mass of citizens of the United States were also citizens of individual States, many of their general privileges and immunities would be the same in the one capacity as in the other. Having this double citizenship, and the great body of municipal laws intended for the protection of person and property being the laws of the State, and no provision being made, and no machinery provided by the Constitution, except in a few specified cases, for any interference by the General Government between a State and its citizens, the protection of the citizen in the enjoyment of his fundamental privileges and immunities (except where a citizen of one State went into another State) was largely left to State laws and State courts, where they will still continue to be left unless actually invaded by the unconstitutional acts or delinquency of the State governments themselves.

Admitting, therefore, that formerly the States were not prohibited from infringing any of the fundamental privileges and immunities of citizens of the United States, except **[83 U.S. 36, 122]** in a few specified cases, that cannot be said now, since the adoption of the fourteenth amendment. In my judgment, it was the intention of the people of this country in adopting that amendment to provide National security against violation by the States of the fundamental rights of the citizen.

The first section of this amendment, after declaring that all persons born or naturalized in the United States, and subject to its jurisdiction, are citizens of the United States and of the State wherein they reside, proceeds to declare further, that "no State shall make or enforce any law which shall abridge the privileges or immunities of citizens of the United States; nor shall any State deprive any person of life, liberty, or property, without due process of law, nor deny to any person within its jurisdiction the equal protection of the laws;" and that Congress shall have power to enforce by appropriate legislation the provisions of this article.

Now, here is a clear prohibition on the States against making or enforcing any law which shall abridge the privileges or immunities of citizens of the United States.

If my views are correct with regard to what are the privileges and immunities of citizens, it follows conclusively that any law which establishes a sheer monopoly, depriving a large class of citizens of the privilege of pursuing a lawful employment, does abridge the privileges of those citizens.

The amendment also prohibits any State from depriving any person (citizen or otherwise) of life, liberty, or property, without due process of law.

In my view, a law which prohibits a large class of citizens from adopting a lawful employment, or from following a lawful employment previously adopted, does deprive them of liberty as well as property, without due process of law. Their right of choice is a portion of their liberty; their occupation is their property. Such a law also deprives those citizens of the equal protection of the laws, contrary to the last clause of the section.

The constitutional question is distinctly raised in these cases; the constitutional right is expressly claimed; it was **[83 U.S. 36, 123]** violated by State law, which was sustained by the State court, and we are called upon in a legitimate and proper way to afford redress. Our jurisdiction and our duty are plain and imperative.

It is futile to argue that none but persons of the African race are intended to be benefited by this amendment. They may have been the primary cause of the amendment, but its language is general, embracing all citizens, and I think it was purposely so expressed.

The mischief to be remedied was not merely slavery and its incidents and consequences; but that spirit of insubordination and disloyalty to the National government which had troubled the country for so many years in some of the States, and that intolerance of free speech and free discussion which often rendered life and property insecure, and led to much unequal legislation. The amendment was an attempt to give voice to the strong National yearning for that time and that condition of things, in which American citizenship should be a sure guaranty of safety, and in which every citizen of the United States might stand erect on every portion of its soil, in the full enjoyment of every right and privilege belonging to a freeman, without fear of violence or molestation.

But great fears are expressed that this construction of the amendment will lead to enactments by Congress interfering with the internal affairs of the States, and establishing therein civil and criminal codes of law for the government of the citizens, and thus abolishing the State governments in everything but name; or else, that it will lead the Federal courts to draw to their cognizance the supervision of State tribunals on every subject of judicial inquiry, on the plea of ascertaining whether the privileges and immunities of citizens have not been abridged.

In my judgment no such practical inconveniences would arise. Very little, if any, legislation on the part of Congress would be required to carry the amendment into effect. Like the prohibition against passing a law impairing the obligation of a contract, it would execute itself. The point would **[83 U.S. 36, 124]** be regularly raised, in a suit at law, and settled by final reference to the Federal court. As the privileges and immunities protected are only those fundamental ones which belong to every citizen, they would soon become so far defined as to cause but a slight accumulation of business in the Federal courts. Besides, the recognized existence of the law would prevent its frequent violation. But even if the business of the National courts should be increased, Congress could easily supply the remedy by increasing their number and efficiency. The great question is, What is the true construction of the amendment? When once we find that, we shall find the means of giving it effect. The argument from inconvenience ought not to have a very controlling influence in questions of this sort. The National will and National interest are of far greater importance.

In my opinion the judgment of the Supreme Court of Louisiana ought to be reversed.

Mr. Justice **SWAYNE**, dissenting:

I concur in the dissent in these cases and in the views expressed by my brethren, Mr. Justice Field and Mr. Justice Bradley. I desire, however, to submit a few additional remarks.

The first eleven amendments to the Constitution were intended to be checks and limitations upon the government which that instrument called into existence. They had their origin in a spirit of jealousy on the part of the States, which existed when the Constitution was adopted. The first ten were proposed in 1789 by the first Congress at its first session after the organization of the government. The eleventh was proposed in 1794, and the twelfth in 1803. The one last mentioned regulates the mode of electing the President and Vice-President. It neither increased nor diminished the power of the General Government, and may be said in that respect to occupy neutral ground. No further amendments were made until 1865, a period of more than sixty years. The thirteenth amendment was proposed by Congress on the 1st of February, 1865, the fourteenth on **[83 U.S. 36, 125]** the 16th of June, 1866, and the fifteenth on the 27th of February, 1869. These amendments are a new departure, and mark an important epoch in the constitutional history of the country. They trench directly upon the power of the States, and deeply affect those bodies. They are, in this respect, at the opposite pole from the first eleven.[41]

Fairly construed these amendments may be said to rise to the dignity of a new Magna Charta. The thirteenth blotted out slavery and forbade forever its restoration. It struck the fetters from four millions of human beings and raised them at once to the sphere of freemen. This was an act of grace and justice performed by the Nation. Before the war it could have been done only by the States where the institution existed, acting severally and separately from each other. The power then rested wholly with them. In that way, apparently, such a result could never have occurred. The power of Congress did not extend to the subject, except in the Territories.

The fourteenth amendment consists of five sections. The first is as follows: "All persons born or naturalized within the United States, and subject to the jurisdiction thereof, are citizens of the United States and of the State wherein they reside. No State shall make any law which shall abridge the privileges or immunities of citizens of the United States, nor shall any State deprive any person of life, liberty, or property, without due process of law, nor deny to any person within its jurisdiction the equal protection of the laws."

The fifth section declares that Congress shall have power to enforce the provisions of this amendment by appropriate legislation.

The fifteenth amendment declares that the right to vote shall not be denied or abridged by the United States, or by any State, on account of race, color, or previous condition of servitude. Until this amendment was adopted the subject [83 U.S. 36, 126] to which it relates was wholly within the jurisdiction of the States. The General Government was excluded from participation.

The first section of the fourteenth amendment is alone involved in the consideration of these cases. No searching analysis is necessary to eliminate its meaning. Its language is intelligible and direct. Nothing can be more transparent. Every word employed has an established signification. There is no room for construction. There is nothing to construe. Elaboration may obscure, but cannot make clearer, the intent and purpose sought to be carried out.

(1.) Citizens of the States and of the United States are defined.

(2.) It is declared that no State shall, by law, abridge the privileges or immunities of citizens of the United States.

---

[41] Barron v. Baltimore, 7 Peters, 243; Livingston v. Moore, Ib. 551; Fox v. Ohio, 5 Howard, 429; Smith v. Maryland, 18 Id. 71; Pervear v. Commonwealth, 5 Wallace, 476; Twitchell v. Commonwealth, 7 Id. 321.

(3.) That no State shall deprive *any person*, whether a citizen or not, of life, liberty, or property, without due process of law, nor deny to any person within its jurisdiction the equal protection of the laws.

A citizen of a State is *ipso facto* a citizen of the United States. No one can be the former without being also the latter; but the latter, by losing his residence in one State without acquiring it in another, although he continues to be the latter, ceases for the time to be the former. "The privileges and immunities" of a citizen of the United States include, among other things, the fundamental rights of life, liberty, and property, and also the rights which pertain to him by reason of his membership of the Nation. The citizen of a State has the same fundamental rights as a citizen of the United States, and also certain others, local in their character, arising from his relation to the State, and in addition, those which belong to the citizen of the United States, he being in that relation also. There may thus be a double citizenship, each having some rights peculiar to itself. It is only over those which belong to the citizen of the United States that the category here in question throws the shield of its protection. All those which belong to the citizen of a State, except as a bills of attainder, *ex post facto* **[83 U.S. 36, 127]** laws, and laws impairing the obligation of contracts,[42] are left to the guardianship of the bills of rights, constitutions, and laws of the States respectively. Those rights may all be enjoyed in every State by the citizens of every other State by virtue of clause 2, section 4, article 1, of the Constitution of the United States as it was originally framed. This section does not in anywise affect them; such was not its purpose.

In the next category, obviously *ex industriâ*, to prevent, as far as may be, the possibility of misinterpretation, either as to persons or things, the phrases "citizens of the United States" and "privileges and immunities" are dropped, and more simple and comprehensive terms are substituted. The substitutes are "any person," and "life," "liberty," and "property," and "the equal protection of the laws." Life, liberty, and property are forbidden to be taken "without due process of law," and "equal protection of the laws" is guaranteed to all. Life is the gift of God, and the right to preserve it is the most sacred of the rights of man. Liberty is freedom from all restraints but such as are justly imposed by law. Beyond that line lies the domain of usurpation and tyranny. Property is everything which has an exchangeable value, and the right of property includes the power to dispose of it according to the will of the owner. Labor is property, and as such merits protection. The right to make it available is next in importance to the rights of life and liberty. It lies to a large extent at the foundation of most other forms of property, and of all solid individual and national prosperity. "Due process of law" is the application of the law as it exists in the fair and regular course of administrative procedure. "The equal protection of the laws" places all upon a footing of legal equality and gives the same protection to all for the preservation of life, liberty, and property, and the pursuit of happiness."[43] **[83 U.S. 36, 128]** It is admitted that the plaintiffs in error are citizens of the United States, and persons within the jurisdiction of Louisiana. The cases before us, therefore, present but two questions.

(1.) Does the act of the legislature creating the monopoly in question abridge the privileges and immunities of the plaintiffs in error as citizens of the United States?

(2.) Does it deprive them of liberty or property without due process of law, or deny them the equal protection of the laws of the State, they being persons "within its jurisdiction?"

Both these inquiries I remit for their answer as to the facts to the opinions of my brethren, Mr. Justice Field and Mr. Justice Bradley. They are full and conclusive upon the subject. A more flagrant and indefensible invasion of the rights of many for the benefit of a few has not occurred in the legislative history of the country. The response to both inquiries should

---

[42] Constitution of the United States, Article I, Section 10.
[43] *Corfield v. Coryell*, 4 Washington, 380; *Lemmon v. The People*, 26 Barbour, 274, and 20 New York, 626; *Conner v. Elliott*, 18 Howard, 593; *Murray v. McCarty*, 2 Mumford, 399; *Campbell v. Morris*, 3 Harris & McHenry, 554; Towles's Case, 5 Leigh, 748; *State v. Medbury*, 3 Rhode Island, 142; 1 Tucker's Blackstone, 145; 1 Cooley's Blackstone, 125, 128.

be in the affirmative. In my opinion the cases, as presented in the record, are clearly within the letter and meaning of both the negative categories of the sixth section. The judgments before us should, therefore, be reversed.

These amendments are all consequences of the late civil war. The prejudices and apprehension as to the central government which prevailed when the Constitution was adopted were dispelled by the light of experience. The public mind became satisfied that there was less danger of tyranny in the head than of anarchy and tyranny in the members. The provisions of this section are all eminently conservative in their character. They are a bulwark of defence, and can never be made an engine of oppression. The language employed is unqualified in its scope. There is no exception in its terms, and there can be properly none in their application. By the language "citizens of the United States" was meant all such citizens; and by "any person" [83 U.S. 36, 129] was meant all persons within the jurisdiction of the State. No distinction is intimated on account of race or color. This court has no authority to interpolate a limitation that is neither expressed nor implied. Our duty is to execute the law, not to make it. The protection provided was not intended to be confined to those of any particular race or class, but to embrace equally all races, classes, and conditions of men. It is objected that the power conferred is novel and large. The answer is that the novelty was known and the measure deliberately adopted. The power is beneficent in its nature, and cannot be abused. It is such an should exist in every well-ordered system of polity. Where could it be more appropriately lodged than in the hands to which it is confided? It is necessary to enable the government of the nation to secure to every one within its jurisdiction the rights and privileges enumerated, which, according to the plainest considerations of reason and justice and the fundamental principles of the social compact, all are entitled to enjoy. Without such authority any government claiming to be national is glaringly defective. The construction adopted by the majority of my brethren is, in my judgment, much too narrow. It defeats, by a limitation not anticipated, the intent of those by whom the instrument was framed and of those by whom it was adopted. To the extent of that limitation it turns, as it were, what was meant for bread into a stone. By the Constitution, as it stood before the war, ample protection was given against oppression by the Union, but little was given against wrong and oppression by the States. That want was intended to be supplied by this amendment. Against the former this court has been called upon more than once to interpose. Authority of the same amplitude was intended to be conferred as to the latter. But this arm of our jurisdiction is, in these cases, stricken down by the judgment just given. Nowhere, than in this court, ought the will of the nation, as thus expressed, to be more liberally construed or more cordially executed. This determination of the majority seems to me to lie far in the other direction. [83 U.S. 36, 130] I earnestly hope that the consequences to follow may prove less serious and far-reaching than the minority fear they will be.

United States Supreme Court
Twining v. New Jersey, 211 U.S. 78 (1908)

Argued March 19, 20, 1908. — Decided November 9, 1908.
(headnotes omitted)

[211 U.S. 78, 79] Albert C. Twining and David C. Cornell, the plaintiffs in error, hereafter called the defendants, were indicted by the grand jury of Monmouth county, in the state of New Jersey. The indictment charged that the defendants, being directors of the Monmouth Trust & Safe Deposit Company, knowingly exhibited a false paper to Larue Vreedenberg, an examiner of the state banking department, with intent to deceive him as to the condition of the company. Such an act is made a misdemeanor by a statute of the state (P. L. 1899, p. 450, at 461), which is as follows:

"Every director, officer, agent, or clerk of any trust company who willfully and knowingly subscribes or makes any false statement of facts or false entries in the books of such trust company, or knowingly subscribes or exhibits any false paper, with intent to deceive any person authorized to examine as to the condition of such trust company, or willfully or knowingly subscribes to or makes any false report, shall be guilty of a high misdemeanor and punished accordingly."

The defendants were found guilty on March 1, 1904, by the verdict of a jury, and judgment upon the verdict, that the defendants be imprisoned for six and four years, respectively, was affirmed successively by the supreme court and the court [211 U.S. 78, 80] of errors and appeals. There needs to be stated here only such part of what occurred at the trial as will describe the questions on which this court is authorized to pass. It appeared that in February, 1903, the company closed its doors. The bank examiner came at once to the place of business for the purpose of examining the affairs of the company, and found there Twining and Cornell, who were respectively president and treasurer as well as directors. Having soon discovered that, according to a book entry, there had been a recent payment of $44,875, for 381 shares of stock, the examiner inquired of the defendants by what authority this had been done, and was informed that it was done by authority of the board of directors, and the following paper was produced to him as a record of the transaction:

Monmouth Trust & Safe Deposit Company, Asbury Park, N. J.

A special meeting of the board of directors of this company was held at the office of the company on Monday, Feb. 9th, 1903

There were present the following directors: George F. Kroehl, S. A. Patterson, G. B. M. Harvey, A. C. Twining, D. C. Cornell.

The minutes of the regular meeting held Jan. 15th, 1903, were read, and on motion duly approved.

All loans taken since the last meeting were gone over carefully, and, upon motion duly seconded, were unanimously approved.

A resolution that this company buy 381 shares of the stock of the First National Bank at $44,875 was adopted.

On motion the meeting adjourned.

This was the paper referred to in the indictment, and it was incumbent on the prosecution to prove that it was false and that it was "knowingly" exhibited by the defendants to the examiner. There was evidence on the part of the prosecution tending to prove both these propositions. The defendants called no witnesses and did not testify themselves, although the law of New Jersey gave them the right to do so if they chose. In his charge to the jury the presiding judge said:

"Now, gentlemen, was this paper false? In the first place, [211 U.S. 78, 81] the paper charged in the indictment certifies in effect that a special meeting of the board of directors of this company was held at the office of the company on Monday, February 9, 1903. There were present the following directors: George F. Kroehl, S. A. Patterson, G. B. M. Harvey, A. C. Twining, D. C. Cornell.

"Among other things appears a resolution of this company to buy 381 shares of the stock of the First National Bank at $44,875, which was adopted.

"Now, was that meeting held or not?

"That paper says that at this meeting were present, among others, Patterson, Twining, and Cornell.

"Mr. Patterson has gone upon the stand and has testified that there was no such meeting to his knowledge; that he was not present at any such meeting; that he had no notice of any such meeting; and that he never acquiesced, as I understand, in any way, in the passage of a resolution for the purchase of this stock.

"Now, Twining and Cornell, this paper says, were present. They are here in court and have seen this paper offered in evidence, and they know that this paper says that they were the two men, or two of the men, who were present. Neither of them has gone upon the stand to deny that they were present or to show that the meeting was held. "Now, it is not necessary for these men to prove their innocence. It is not necessary for them to prove that this meeting was held. But the fact that they stay off the stand, having heard testimony which might be prejudicial to them, without availing themselves of the right to go upon the stand and contradict it, is sometimes a matter of significance.

"Now, of course, in this action, I do not see how that can have much weight, because these men deny that they exhibited the paper, and if one of these men exhibited the paper and the other did not, I do not see how you could say that the person who claims he did not exhibit the paper would be under any obligation at all to go upon the stand. Neither is under any [211 U.S. 78, 82] obligation. It is simply a right they have to go upon the stand, and, consequently the fact that they do not go upon the stand to contradict this statement in the minutes, they both denying, through their counsel and through their plea, that they exhibited the paper, I do not see that that can be taken as at all prejudicial to either of them. They simply have the right to go upon the stand, and they have not availed themselves of it, and it may be that there is no necessity for them to go there. I leave that entirely to you."

Further, in that part of the charge relating to the exhibition of the paper to the examiner, the judge said:

"Now, gentlemen, if you believe that that is so; if you believe this testimony, that Cornell did direct this man's attention to it,—Cornell has sat here and heard that testimony and not denied it,—nobody could misunderstand the import of that testimony, it was a direct accusation made against him of his guilt,—if you believe that testimony beyond a reasonable doubt, Cornell is guilty. And yet he has sat here and not gone upon the stand to deny it. He was not called upon to go upon the stand and deny it, but he did not go upon the stand and deny it, and it is for you to take that into consideration.

"Now Twining has also sat here and heard this testimony, but you will observe there is this distinction as to the conduct of these two men in this respect: the accusation against Cornell was specific by Vreedenberg. It is rather inferential, if at all, against Twining, and he might say,—it is for you to say whether he might say,—'Well, I don't think the accusation against me is made with such a degree of certainty as to require me to deny it, and I shall not; nobody will think it strange if I do not go upon the stand to deny it, because Vreedenberg is uncertain as to whether I was there; he won't swear that I was there." So consequently the fact that Twining did not go upon the stand can have no significance at all.

"You may say that the fact that Cornell did not go upon the stand has no significance. You may say so, because the circumstances may be such that there should be no inference [211 U.S. 78, 83] drawn of guilt or anything of that kind from the fact that he did not go upon the stand. Because a man does not go upon the stand you are not necessarily justified in drawing an inference of guilt. But you have a right to consider the fact that he does not go upon the stand where a direct accusation is made against him."

The question duly brought here by writ of error is whether the parts of the charge set forth, affirmed, as they were, by the court of last resort of the state, are in violation of the 14th Amendment of the Constitution of the United States.

[211 U.S. 78, 84-89] *(The listing of the attorney's and statements of their arguments are ommitted here.)*

[211 U.S. 78, 90] Mr. Justice **MOODY**, after making the foregoing statement, delivered the opinion of the court:

In the view we take of the case we do not deem it necessary to consider whether, with respect to the Federal question, there is any difference in the situation of the two defendants. It is assumed, in respect of each, that the jury were instructed that they might draw an unfavorable inference against him from his failure to testify, where it was within his power, in denial of the evidence which tended to incriminate him. The law of the state, as declared in the case at bar, which accords with other decisions (*Parker v. State*, 61 N. J. L. 308, 39 Atl. 651; *State v. Wines*, 65 N. J. L. 31, 46 Atl. 702; *State v. Zdanowicz*, 69 N. J. L. 619, 55 Atl. 743; *State v. Banusik* (N. J.) 64 Atl. 994), permitted such an inference to be drawn. The judicial act of the highest court of the **[211 U.S. 78, 91]** state, in authoritatively construing and enforcing its laws, is the act of the state. *Ex parte Virginia*, 100 U.S. 339 , 25 L. ed. 676; *Scott v. McNeal*, 154 U.S. 34 , 38 L. ed. 896, 14 Sup. Ct. Rep. 1108; *Chicago, B. & Q. R. Co. v. Chicago*, 166 U.S. 226 , 41 L. ed. 979, 17 Sup. Ct. Rep. 581. The general question, therefore, is, whether such a law violates the 14th Amendment, either by abridging the privileges or immunities of citizens of the United States, or by depriving persons of their life, liberty, or property without due process of law. In order to bring themselves within the protection of the Constitution it is incumbent on the defendants to prove two propositions: First, that the exemption from compulsory self-incrimination is guaranteed by the Federal Constitution against impairment by the states; and, second, if it be so guaranteed, that the exemption was in fact impaired in the case at bar. The first proposition naturally presents itself for earlier consideration. If the right here asserted is not a Federal right, that is the end of the case. We have no authority to go further and determine whether the state court has erred in the interpretation and enforcement of its own laws.

The exemption from testimonial compulsion, that is, from disclosure as a witness of evidence against oneself, forced by any form of legal process, is universal in American law, though there may be differences as to its exact scope and limits. At the time of the formation of the Union the principle that no person could be compelled to be a witness against himself had become embodied in the common law and distinguished it from all other systems of jurisprudence. It was generally regarded then, as now, as a privilege of great value, a protection to the innocent, though a shelter to the guilty, and a safeguard against heedless, unfounded, or tyrannical prosecutions. Five of the original thirteen states (North Carolina, 1776; Pennsylvania, 1776; Virginia, 1776; Massachusetts, 1780; New Hampshire, 1784) had then guarded the principle from legislative or judicial change by including it in Constitutions or Bills of Right; Maryland had provided in her Constitution (1776) that "no man ought to be compelled to give evidence against **[211 U.S. 78, 92]** himself, in a common court of law, or in any other court, but in such cases as have been usually practised in this state or may hereafter be directed by the legislature;" and in the remainder of those states there seems to be no doubt that it was recognized by the common law. The privilege was not included in the Federal Constitution as originally adopted, but was placed in one of the ten amendments which were recommended to the states by the first Congress, and by them adopted. Since then all the states of the Union have, from time to time, with varying form, but uniform meaning, included the privilege in their Constitutions, except the states of New Jersey and Iowa, and in those states it is held to be part of the existing law. *State v. Zdanowicz*, supra; *State v. Height*, 117 Iowa, 650, 59 L.R.A. 437, 94 Am. St. Rep. 323, 91 N. W. 935. It is obvious from this short statement that it has been supposed by the states that, so far as the state courts are concerned, the privilege had its origin in the Constitutions and laws of the states, and that persons appealing to it must look to the state for their protection. Indeed, since, by the unvarying decisions of this court, the first ten Amendments of the Federal Constitution are restrictive only of national action, there was nowhere else to look up to the time of the adoption of the 14th Amendment, and the state, at least until then, might give, modify, or withhold the privilege at its will. The 14th Amendment withdrew from the states powers theretofore enjoyed by them to an extent not yet fully ascertained, or rather, to speak more accurately, limited those powers and restrained their exercise. There is no doubt of the duty of this court to enforce the limitations and restraints whenever they exist, and there has been no hesitation in the performance of the duty. But, whenever a new limitation or restriction is declared, it is a matter of grave import, since, to that extent, it diminishes the authority of the state, so necessary to the perpetuity of our dual form of government, and changes its relation to its people and to the Union. The question in the case at bar has been twice before us, and been left undecided, as the cases were disposed of on other grounds. *Adams v. New* **[211 U.S. 78, 93]** *York*, 192 U.S. 585 , 48 L. ed. 575, 24 Sup. Ct. Rep. 372; *Consolidated Rendering Co. v. Vermont*, 207 U.S. 541 , 52 L. ed. 327, 28 Sup. Ct. Rep. 178. The defendants contend, in the first place, that the exemption from self-incrimination is one of the privileges and immunities of citizens of the United States which the 14th Amendment forbids the states to abridge. It is not argued that the defendants are protected by that part of the 5th Amendment which provides that "no person . . . shall be compelled in any criminal case to be a witness against himself," for it is recognized by counsel that, by a long line of decisions, the first ten Amendments are not operative on the states. *Barron v. Baltimore*, 7 Pet. 243, 8 L. ed. 672; *Spies v. Illinois*, 123 U.S. 131 , 31 L. ed. 80, 8 Sup. Ct. Rep. 21, 22; *Brown v. New Jersey*, 175 U.S. 172 , 44 L. ed. 119, 20 Sup. Ct. Rep. 77; *Barrington v. Missouri*, 205 U.S. 483 , 51 L. ed. 890, 27 Sup. Ct. Rep. 582. But it is argued that this privilege is one of the fundamental rights of national citizenship, placed under national protection by the 14th Amendment, and it is specifically argued that the "privileges and immunities of citizens of the United States," protected against state action by that Amendment, include those fundamental personal rights which were protected against national action by the first eight Amendments; that this was the intention of the framers of the 14th Amendment, and that this part of it would otherwise have little or no meaning and effect. These arguments are not new to this court and the answer to them is found in its decisions. The meaning of the phrase "privileges and immunities of citizens of the United States," as used in the 14th Amendment, came under early consideration in the *Slaughter-House Cases*, 16 Wall. 36, 21 L. ed. 394. A statute of Louisiana created a corporation and conferred upon it the exclusive privilege, for a term of years, of establishing and maintaining within a fixed division of the city of New Orleans stock yards and slaughterhouses. The act provided that others might use these facilities for a prescribed price, forbade the landing for slaughter or the slaughtering of animals elsewhere or otherwise, and established a system of inspection. Those persons who were driven out of independent business by this law denied its validity in suits which came to this **[211 U.S. 78, 94]** court by writs of error to the supreme court of the state, which had sustained the act. It was argued, inter alia, that the statute abridged the privileges and immunities of the plaintiffs in error as citizens of the United States, and the particular privilege which was alleged to be violated was that of pursuing freely their chosen trade, business, or calling. The majority of the court were not content with expressing the opinion that the act did not in fact deprive the plaintiffs in error of their right to exercise their trade (a proposition vigorously disputed by four dissenting justices), which would have disposed of the case, but preferred to rest the decision upon the broad ground that the right asserted in the case was not a privilege or immunity belonging to persons by virtue of their national citizenship, but, if existing at all, belonging to them only by virtue of their state citizenship. The 14th Amendment, it is observed by Mr. Justice Miller, delivering the opinion of the court, removed the doubt whether there could be a citizenship of the United States independent of citizenship of the state, by recognizing or creating and defining the former. "It is quite clear, then," he proceeds to say (p. 74), "that there is a citizenship of the United States and a citizenship of a state, which are distinct from each other and which depend upon different characteristics or circumstances in the individual." The description of the privileges and immunities of state citizenship, given by Mr. Justice Washington in *Corfield v. Coryell*, 4 Wash. C. C. 371, Fed. Cas. No. 3,230, is then quoted, approved, and said to include "those rights which are fundamental," to embrace "nearly every civil right for the establishment and protection of which organized government is instituted," and "to be the class of rights which the state governments were created to establish and secure." This part of the opinion then concludes with the holding that the rights relied upon in the case are those which belong to the citizens of states, as such, and are under the sole care and protection of the state governments. The conclusion is preceded by the important declaration that the civil rights theretofore appertaining to citizenship of the states **[211 U.S. 78, 95]** and under the protection of the states were not given the security of national protection by this clause of the 14th Amendment. The exact scope and the momentous consequence of this decision are brought into clear light by the dissenting opinions. The view of Mr. Justice Field, concurred in by Chief Justice Chase and Justices Swayne and Bradley, was that the fundamental rights of citizenship, which, by the opinion of the court, were held to be rights of state citizenship, protected only by the state government, became, as the result of the 14th Amendment, rights of national citizenship, protected by the national Constitution. Said Mr. Justice Field (p. 95):

"The fundamental rights, privileges, and immunities which belong to him as a free man and a free citizen, now belong to him as a citizen of the United States, and are not dependent upon his citizenship of any state . . . . The Amendment does not attempt to confer any new privileges or immunities upon citizens, or to enumerate or define those already existing. It assumes that there are such privileges and immunities, which belong of right to citizens as such, and ordains that they shall not be abridged by state legislation. If this inhibition has no reference to privileges and immunities of this character, but only refers, as held by the majority of the court in their opinion, to such privileges and immunities as were, before its adoption, specially designated in the Constitution, or necessarily implied as belonging to citizens of the United States, it was a vain and idle enactment, which accomplished nothing, and most unnecessarily excited Congress and the people on its passage. With privileges and immunities thus designated or implied no state could ever have interfered by its laws, and no new constitutional provision was required to inhibit such interference. The supremacy of the Constitution and the laws of the United States always controlled any state legislation of that character. But, if the Amendment refers to the natural and inalienable rights which belong to all citizens, the inhibition has a profound significance and consequence." **[211 U.S. 78, 96]**

In accordance with these principles it is said by the learned justice that the privileges and immunities of state citizenship, described by Mr. Justice Washington, and held by the majority of the court still to pertain exclusively to state citizenship, and to be protected solely by the state government, have been guaranteed by the 14th Amendment as privileges and immunities of citizens of the United States. And see the concurring opinions of Mr. Justice Field and Mr. Justice Bradley in *Bartemeyer v. Iowa*, 18 Wall. 129, 21 L. ed. 929; and in *Butchers' Union S. H. & L. S. L. Co. v. Crescent City L. S. L. & S. H. Co.* 111 U.S. 746 , 28 L. ed. 585, 4 Sup. Ct. Rep. 652. There can be no doubt, so far as the decision in the *Slaughter-House Cases* has determined the question, that the civil rights sometimes described as fundamental and inalienable, which, before the War Amendments, were enjoyed by state citizenship and protected by state government, were left untouched by this clause of the 14th Amendment. Criticism of this case has never entirely ceased, nor has it ever received universal assent by members of this court. Undoubtedly, it gave much less effect to the 14th Amendment than some of the public men active in framing it intended, and disappointed many others. On the other hand, if the views of the minority had prevailed, it is easy to see how far the authority and independence of the states would have been diminished, by subjecting all their legislative and judicial acts to correction by the legislative and review by the judicial branch of the national government. But we need not now inquire into the merits of the original dispute. This part, at least, of the *Slaughter-House Cases*, has been steadily adhered to by this court, so that it was said of it, in a case where the same clause of the Amendment was under consideration (*Maxwell v. Dow*, 176 U.S. 581, 591 , 44 S. L. ed. 597, 601, 20 Sup. Ct. Rep. 448, 494): "The opinion upon the matters actually involved and maintained by the judgment in the case has never been doubted or overruled by any judgment of this court." The distinction between national and state citizenship and their respective privileges there drawn has come to be firmly established. And so it was held that the right of peaceable assembly **[211 U.S. 78, 97]** for a lawful purpose (it not appearing that the purpose had any reference to the national government) was not a right secured by the Constitution of the United States, although it was said that the right existed before the adoption of the Constitution of the United States, and that "it is and always has been one of the attributes of citizenship under a free government." *United States v. Cruikshank*, 92 U.S. 542, 551 , 23 S. L. ed. 588, 591. And see *Hodges v. United States*, 203 U.S. 1 , 51 L. ed. 65, 27 Sup. Ct. Rep. 6. In each case the *Slaughter-House Cases* were cited by the court, and in the latter case the rights described by Mr. Justice Washington were again treated as rights of state citizenship, under state protection. **If, then, it be assumed, without deciding the point, that an exemption from compulsory self-incrimination is what is described as a fundamental right belonging to all who live under a free government, and incapable of impairment by legislation or judicial decision, it is, so far as the states are concerned, a fundamental right inherent in state citizenship, and is a privilege or immunity of that citizenship only. Privileges and immunities of citizens of the United States, on the other hand, are only such as arise out of the nature and essential character of the national government**, or are specifically granted or secured to all citizens or persons by the Constitution of the United States. *Slaughter-House Cases*, supra, p. 79; *Re Kemmler*, 136 U.S. 436, 448 , 34 S. L. ed. 519, 524, 10 Sup. Ct. Rep. 930; *Duncan v. Missouri*, 152 U.S. 377, 382 , 38 S. L. ed. 485, 487, 14 Sup. Ct. Rep. 570.

Thus, among the rights and privileges of national citizenship recognized by this court are the right to pass freely from state to state (*Crandall v. Nevada*, 6 Wall. 35, 18 L. ed. 745); **the right to petition Congress for a redress of grievances** (*United States v. Cruikshank*, supra); **the right to vote for national officers** (*Ex parte Yarbrought*, 110 U.S. 651 , 28 L. ed. 274, 4 Sup. Ct. Rep. 152; *Wiley v. Sinkler*, 179 U.S. 58 , 45 L. ed. 84, 21 Sup. Ct. Rep. 17); **the right to enter the public lands** (*United States v. Waddell*, 112 U.S. 76 , 28 L. ed. 673, 5 Sup. Ct. Rep. 35); **the right to be protected against violence while in the lawful custody of a United States marshal** (*Logan v. United States*, 144 U.S. 263 , 36 L. ed. 429, 12 Sup. Ct. Rep. 617); **and the right to inform the United States authorities of violation of its laws.** (*Re Quarles*, 158 U.S. 532 , 39 L. ed. 1080, 15 Sup. Ct. Rep. 959). **[211 U.S. 78, 98]** Most of these cases were indictments against individuals for conspiracies to deprive persons of rights secured by the Constitution of the United States, and met with a different fate in this court from the indictments in *United States v. Cruikshank* and *Hodges v. United States*, because the rights in the latter cases were rights of state, and not of national, citizenship. But assuming it to be true that the exemption from self-incrimination is not, as a fundamental right of national citizenship, included in the privileges and immunities of citizens of the United States, counsel insist that, as a right specifically granted or secured by the Federal Constitution, it is included in them. This view is based upon the contention which must now be examined, that the safeguards of personal rights which are enumerated in the first eight articles of amendment to the Federal Constitution, sometimes called the Federal Bill of Rights, though they were by those Amendments originally secured only against national action, are among the privileges and immunities of citizens of the United States, which this clause of the 14th Amendment protects against state action. This view has been, at different times, expressed by justices of this court (Mr. Justice Field in *O'Neil v. Vermont*, 144 U.S. 323, 361 , 36 S. L. ed. 450, 466, 12 Sup. Ct. Rep. 693; Mr. Justice Harlan in the same case, 370, and in *Maxwell v. Dow*, supra, 606, 671), and was undoubtedly that entertained by some of those who framed the Amendment. It is, however, not profitable to examine the weighty arguments in its favor, for the question is no longer open in this court. **The right of trial by jury in civil cases, guaranteed by the 7th Amendment** (*Walker v. Sauvinet*, 92 U.S. 90 , 23 L. ed. 678), **and the right to bear arms, guaranteed by the 2d Amendment** (*Presser v. Illinois,* 116 U.S. 252 , 29 L. ed. 615, 6 Sup. Ct. Rep. 580), **have been distinctly held not to be privileges and immunities of citizens of**

the United States, guaranteed by the 14th Amendment against abridgment by the states, and in effect the same decision was made in respect of the guaranty against prosecution, except by indictment of a grand jury, contained in the 5th Amendment (*Hurtado v. California*, 110 U.S. 516 , 28 L. ed. 232, 4 Sup. Ct. Rep. 111, 292), **[211 U.S. 78, 99] and in respect of the right to be confronted with witnesses, contained in the 6th Amendment** (*West v. Louisiana*, 191 U.S. 258 , 48 L. ed. 965, 24 Sup. Ct. Rep. 650). In *Maxwell v. Dow*, supra, where the plaintiff in error had been convicted in a state court of a felony upon an information, and by a jury of eight persons, it was held that the indictment, made indispensable by the 5th Amendment, and the trial by jury, guaranteed by the 6th Amendment, were not privileges and immunities of citizens of the United States, as those words were used in the 14th Amendment. The discussion in that case ought not to be repeated. All the arguments for the other view were considered and answered, the authorities were examined and analyzed, and the decision rested upon the ground that this clause of the 14th Amendment did not forbid the states to abridge the personal rights enumerated in the first eight Amendments, because those rights were not within the meaning of the clause "privileges and immunities of citizens of the United States." If it be possible to render the principle which governed the decision more clear, it is done so by the dissent of Mr. Justice Harlan. **We conclude, therefore, that the exemption from compulsory self-incrimination is not a privilege or immunity of national citizenship guaranteed by this clause of the 14th Amendment against abridgment by the states.**

The defendants, however, do not stop here. They appeal to another clause of the 14th Amendment, and insist that the self-incrimination which they allege the instruction to the jury compelled was a denial of due process of law. This contention requires separate consideration, for it is possible that some of the personal rights safeguarded by the first eight Amendments against national action may also be safeguarded against state action, because a denial of them would be a denial of due process of law. *Chicago, B. & Q. R. Co. v. Chicago*, 166 U.S. 226 , 41 L. ed. 979, 17 Sup. Ct. Rep. 581. If this is so, it is not because those rights are enumerated in the first eight Amendment, but because they are of such a nature that they are included in the conception of due process of law. Few **[211 U.S. 78, 100]** phrases of the law are so elusive of exact apprehension as this. Doubtless the difficulties of ascertaining its connotation have been increased in American jurisprudence, where it has been embodied in constitutions and put to new uses as a limit on legislative power. This court has always declined to give a comprehensive definition of it, and has preferred that its full meaning should be gradually ascertained by the process of inclusion and exclusion in the course of the decisions of cases as they arise. There are certain general principles, well settled, however, which narrow the field of discussion, and may serve as helps to correct conclusions. These principles grow out of the proposition universally accepted by American courts on the authority of Coke, that the words "due process of law" are equivalent in meaning to the words "law of the land," contained in that chapter of Magna Charta which provides that "no freeman shall be taken, or imprisoned, or disseized, or outlawed, or exiled, or any wise destroyed; nor shall we go upon him, nor send upon him, but by the lawful judgment of his peers or by the law of the land." Den ex dem. *Murray v. Hoboken Land & Improv. Co.* 18 How. 272, 15 L. ed. 372; *Davidson v. New Orleans*, 96 U.S. 97 , 24 L. ed. 616; *Jones v. Robbins*, 8 Gray, 329; *Cooley, Const. Lim.* 7th ed. 500; *McGehee, Due Process of Law*, 16. From the consideration of the meaning of the words in the light of their historical origin this court has drawn the following conclusions:

First. What is due process of law may be ascertained by an examination of those settled usages and modes of proceedings existing in the common and statute law of England before the emigration of our ancestors, and shown not to have been unsuited to their civil and political condition by having been acted on by them after the settlement of this country. This test was adopted by the court, speaking through Mr. Justice Curtis, in Den ex dem. *Murray v. Hoboken Land & Improv. Co.* 18 How. 272, 280, 15 L. ed. 372, 376 (approved in *Hallinger v. Davis*, 146 U.S. 314, 320 , 36 S. L. ed. 986, 989, 13 Sup. Ct. Rep. 105; *Holden v. Hardy*, 169 U.S. 366, 390 , 42 S. L. ed. 780, 790, 18 Sup. Ct. Rep. 383; but see *Lowe v. Kansas*, 163 U.S. 81, 85 , 41 S. L. ed. 78, 79, 16 Sup. Ct. Rep. 1031). Of course, the part of the Constitution then **[211 U.S.**

78, 101] before the court was the 5th Amendment. If any different meaning of the same words, as they are used in the 14th Amendment, can be conceived, none has yet appeared in judicial decision. "A process of law," said Mr. Justice Matthews, commenting on this statement of Mr. Justice Curtis, "which is not otherwise forbidden, must be taken to be due process of law, if it can show the sanction of settled usage both in England and in this country." *Hurtado v. California*, 110 U.S. 516, 528 , 28 S. L. ed. 232, 236, 4 Sup. Ct. Rep. 111, 117, 292.

Second. It does not follow, however, that a procedure settled in English law at the time of the emigration, and brought to this country and practised by our ancestors, is an essential element of due process of law. If that were so, the procedure of the first half of the seventeenth century would be fastened upon the American jurisprudence like a straight jacket, only to be unloosed by constitutional amendment. That, said Mr. Justice Matthews, in the same case, p. 529, "would be to deny every quality of the law but its age, and to render it incapable of progress or improvement." *Holden v. Hardy*, 69 U.S. 366, 388 , 42 S. L. ed. 780, 789, 18 Sup. Ct. Rep. 383; Brown v. New Jersey, 175 U.S. 172, 175 , 44 S. L. ed. 119, 120, 20 Sup. Ct. Rep. 77.

Third. But, consistently with the requirements of due process, no change in ancient procedure can be made which disregards those fundamental principles, to be ascertained from time to time by judicial action, which have relation to process of law, and protect the citizen in his private right, and guard him against the arbitrary action of government. This idea has been many times expressed in differing words by this court, and it seems well to cite some expressions of it. The words "due process of law" "were intended to secure the individual from the arbitrary exercise of the powers of government, unrestrained by the established principles of private rights and distributive justice." *Bank of Columbia v. Okely*, 4 Wheat. 235, 244, 4 L. ed. 559, 561 (approved in *Hurtado v. California*, 110 U.S. 516, 527 , 28 S. L. ed. 232, 235, 4 Sup. Ct. Rep. 111, 292; Leeper v. Texas, 139 U.S. 462, 468 , 35 S. L. ed. 225, 227, 11 Sup. Ct. Rep. 577; Scott v. McNeal, 154 U.S. 34, 45 , 38 S. L. ed. 896, 901, 14 Sup. Ct. Rep. 1108). "This court has never attempted to define **[211 U.S. 78, 102]** with precision the words 'due process of law.' . . . It is sufficient to say that there are certain immutable principles of justice which inhere in the very idea of free government which no member of the Union may disregard." *Holden v. Hardy*, 169 U.S. 366, 389 , 42 S. L. ed. 780, 790, 18 Sup. Ct. Rep. 383, 387. "The same words refer to that law of the land in each state, which derives its authority from the inherent and reserved powers of the state, exerted within the limits of those fundamental principles of liberty and justice which lie at the base of all our civil and political institutions." *Re Kemmler*, 136 U.S. 436, 448 , 34 S. L. ed. 519, 524, 10 Sup. Ct. Rep. 930, 934. "The limit of the full control which the state has in the proceedings of its courts, both in civil and criminal cases, is subject only to the qualification that such procedure must not work a denial of fundamental rights or conflict with specific and applicable provisions of the Federal Constitution." *West v. Louisiana*, 194 U.S. 258, 263 , 48 S. L. ed. 965, 969, 24 Sup. Ct. Rep. 650, 652.

The question under consideration may first be tested by the application of these settled doctrines of this court. If the statement of Mr. Justice Curtis, as elucidated in *Hurtado v. California*, is to be taken literally, that alone might almost be decisive. For nothing is more certain, in point of historical fact, than that the practice of compulsory self-incrimination in the courts and elsewhere existed for four hundred years after the granting of Magna Charta, continued throughout the reign of Charles I. (though then beginning to be seriously questioned), gained at least some foothold among the early colonists of this country, and was not entirely omitted at trials in England until the eighteenth century. Wigmore, Ev. 2250 (see for the Colonies, note 108); Hallam's Constitutional History of England, chapter 8, Widdleton's American ed. vol. 2, p. 37 (describing the criminal jurisdiction of the court of star chamber); Bentham's Rationale of Judicial Evidence, book 9, chap. 3, 4.

Sir James Fitzjames Stephen, in his studies of the reports of English trials for crime, has thrown much light on the existence of the practice of questioning persons accused of **[211 U.S. 78, 103]** crime, and its gradual decay. He considers, first, a group of trials which occurred between 1554 and 1637. Speaking of the trial before the jury, he says:

"The prisoner, in nearly every instance, asked, as a favor, that he might not be overpowered by the eloquence of counsel denouncing him in a set speech, but, in consideration of the weakness of his memory, might be allowed to answer separately to the different matters which might be alleged against him. This was usually granted, and the result was that the trial became a series of excited altercations between the prisoner and the different counsel opposed to him. Every statement of counsel operated as a question to the prisoner, and indeed they were constantly thrown into the form of questions, the prisoner either admitting or denying or explaining what was alleged against him. The result was that, during the period in question, the examination of the prisoner, which is at present scrupulously and I think even pedantically avoided, was the very essence of the trial, and his answers regulated the production of the evidence; the whole trial, in fact, was a long argument between the prisoner and counsel for the Crown, in which they questioned each other and grappled with each other's arguments with the utmost eagerness and closeness of reasoning." Stephen, History of the Crim. Law, 325.

This description of the questioning of the accused and the meeting of contending arguments finds curious confirmation in the report of the trial, in 1637, of Ann Hutchinson (which resulted in banishment) for holding and encouraging certain theological views which were not approved by the majority of the early Massachusetts rulers. 1 Hart's American History Told by Contemporaries, 382. The trial was presided over and the examination very largely conducted by Governor Winthrop, who had been, for some years before his emigration, an active lawyer and admitted to the Inner Temple. An examination of the report of this trial will show that he was not aware of any privilege against self-incrimination or conscious of **[211 U.S. 78, 104]** any duty to respect it. Stephen says of the trials between 1640 and 1660 (Id. 358): "In some cases the prisoner was questioned, but never to any greater extent than that which it is practically impossible to avoid when a man has to defend himself without counsel. When so questioned the prisoners usually refused to answer." He further says (Id. 440): "Soon after the Revolution of 1688 the practice of questioning the prisoner died out." But committing magistrates were authorized to take the examination of persons suspected, which, if not under oath, was admissible against him on his trial, until by the 11 & 12 Vict. chap. 2, the prisoner was given the option whether he would speak, and warned that what he said might be used against him. But even now there seems to be a very well-recognized and important exception in English law to the rule that no person can be compelled to furnish evidence against himself. A practice in bankruptcy has existed from ancient times, and still exists, which would not be constitutionally possible under our national bankruptcy law or under the insolvency law of any state whose Constitution contains the customary prohibition of compulsory self-incrimination. The bankruptcy act of 1 James I., chap. 15, 7 (1603), authorized the commissioners of bankruptcy to compel, by commitment, if necessary, the bankrupt to submit to an examination touching his estate and dealings. The provision was continued in the subsequent acts, and in 1820, in *Ex parte Cossens, Buck,* Bankr. Cas. 531, 540, Lord Eldon, in the course of a discussion of the right to examine a bankrupt, held that he could be compelled to disclose his violations of law in respect of his trade and estate, and, while recognizing the general principle of English law, that no one could be compelled to incriminate himself, said: "I have always understood the proposition to admit of a qualification with respect to the jurisdiction in bankruptcy." The act of 6 Geo. IV., chap. 16, 36 (1825), authorized the compulsory examination of the bankrupt "touching all matters relating either to his trade, dealings, or estate, or which may tend to disclose any **[211 U.S. 78, 105]** secret grant, conveyance, or concealment of his lands." The act of 12 & 13 Vict. chap. 106, 117 (1849), contained the same provision. Construing these acts, it was held that the bankrupt must answer, though his answer might furnish evidence of his crime, and even if an indictment were pending against him; and that the evidence thus compelled was admissible on his trial for crime. *Re Heath*, 2 Deacon & C. 214; *Re Smith*, 2 Deacon & C. 230, 235; *Reg. v. Scott*, Dears. & B. C. C. 47; *Reg. v. Cross*, 7 Cox, C. C. 226; *Queen v. Widdop*, L. R. 2 C. C. 3. The act of 46 & 47 Vict. chap. 52, 17 (1883), which we understand to be (with some amendment, not material here) the present law, passed after the decisions cited, expressly provided that the examination shall be taken in writing and signed by the debtor, "and may thereafter be used in evidence against him." It has since been held that other evidence of his testimony than that written and signed by him may be used. *Queen v. Erdheim* [1896] 2 Q. B. 260, and see *King v. Pike* [1902] 1 K. B. 552. It is to be observed that not until 1883 did Parliament, which has an unlimited legislative power, expressly provide that the evidence compelled from the bankrupt could be used in proof of an indictment against him. The rule had been previously firmly established by judicial decisions upon statutes simply authorizing a compulsory examination. If the rule had been thought to be in conflict with "the law of the land" of Magna Charta, "a sacred text, the nearest approach to an irrepealable 'fundamental statute' that England has ever had" (1 Pollock & M. History of English Law, 152), it is inconceivable that such a consideration would not have received some attention from counsel and judges. We think it is manifest, from this review of the origin, growth, extent, and limits of the exemption from compulsory self- incrimination in the English law, that it is not regarded as a part of the law of the land of Magna Charta or the due process of law, which

In certain offenses, which may be generally described as embezzlements, the evidence compelled from a bankrupt cannot be used against him. 24 & 25 Vict. chap. 96, 85; 53 & 54 Vict. chap. 71, 27. **[211 U.S. 78, 106]** has been deemed an equivalent expression, but, on the contrary, is regarded as separate from and independent of due process. It came into existence not as an essential part of due process, but as a wise and beneficent rule of evidence developed in the course of judicial decision. This is a potent argument when it is remembered that the phrase was borrowed from English law, and that to that law we must look at least for its primary meaning.

But, without repudiating or questioning the test proposed by Mr. Justice Curtis for the court, or rejecting the inference drawn from English law, we prefer to rest our decision on broader grounds, and inquire whether the exemption from self-incrimination is of such a nature that it must be included in the conception of due process. Is it a fundamental principle of liberty and justice which inheres in the very idea of free government and is the inalienable right of a citizen of such a government? If it is, and if it is of a nature that pertains to process of law, this court has declared it to be essential to due process of law. In approaching such a question it must not be forgotten that in a free representative government nothing is more fundamental than the right of the people, through their appointed servants, to govern themselves in accordance with their own will, except so far as they have restrained themselves by constitutional limits specifically established, and that, in our peculiar dual form of government, nothing is more fundamental than the full power of the state to order its own affairs and govern its own people, except so far as the Federal Constitution, expressly or by fair implication, has withdrawn that power. The power of the people of the states to make and alter their laws at pleasure is the greatest security for liberty and justice, this court has said in *Hurtado v. California*, 110 U.S. 516, 527 , 28 S. L. ed. 232, 235, 4 Sup. Ct. Rep. 111, 292. We are not invested with the jurisdiction to pass upon the expediency, wisdom, or justice of the laws of the states as declared by their courts, but only to determine their conformity with the Federal Constitution and the paramount laws enacted pursuant to it. Under the guise of interpreting the Constitution we must **[211 U.S. 78, 107]** take care that we do not import into the discussion our own personal views of what would be wise, just, and fitting rules of government to be adopted by a free people, and confound them with constitutional limitations. The question before us is the meaning of a constitutional provision which forbids the states to deny to any person due process of law. In the decision of this question we have the authority to take into account only those fundamental rights which are expressed in that provision; not the rights fundamental in citizenship, state or national, for they are secured otherwise; but the rights fundamental in due process, and therefore an essential part of it. We have to consider whether the right is so fundamental in due process that a refusal of the right is a denial of due process. One aid to the solution of the question is to inquire how the right was rated during the time when the meaning of due process was in a formative state, and before it was incorporated in American constitutional law. Did those who then were formulating and insisting upon the rights of the people entertain the view that the right was so fundamental that there could be no due process without it? It has already appeared that, prior to the formation of the American Constitutions, in which the exemption from compulsory self-incrimination was specifically secured, separately, independently, and side by side with the requirement of due process, the doctrine was formed, as other doctrines of the law of evidence have been formed, by the course of decision in the courts, covering a long period of time. Searching further, we find nothing to show that it was then thought to be other than a just and useful principle of law. None of the great instruments in which we are accustomed to look for the declaration of the fundamental rights made reference to it. The privilege was not dreamed of for hundreds of years after Magna Charta (1215), and could not have been implied in the "law of the land" there secured. The Petition of Right (1629), though it insists upon the right secured by Magna Charta to be condemned only by the law of the land, and sets forth, by way of grievance, divers violations of **[211 U.S. 78, 108]** it, is silent upon the practice of compulsory self-incrimination, though it was then a matter of common occurrence in all the courts of the realm. The Bill of Rights of the first year of the reign of William and Mary (1689) is likewise silent, though the practice of questioning the prisoner at his trial had not then ceased. The negative argument which arises out of the omission of all reference to any exemption from compulsory self- incrimination in these three great declarations of English liberty (though it is not supposed to amount to a demonstration) is supported by the positive argument that the English courts and Parliaments, as we have seen, have dealt with the exemption as they would have dealt with any other rule of evidence, apparently without a thought that the question was affected by the law of the land of Magna Charta, or the due process of law which is its equivalent.

We pass by the meager records of the early colonial time, so far as they have come to our attention, as affording light too uncertain for guidance. See Wigmore, Ev. 2250, note 108; 2 Hening's Stat. at L. 422 (1676) Va.; 1 Winthrop's History of New England, 47, provincial act, 4 Wm. & Mary, Ancient Charters, Massachusetts, 214. Though it is worthy of note that neither the declaration of rights of the Stamp Act Congress (1765) nor the declaration of rights of the Continental Congress (1774) nor the ordinance for the government of the Northwestern territory included the privilege in their enumeration of fundamental rights.

But the history of the incorporation of the privilege in an amendment to the national Constitution is full of significance in this connection. Five states-Delaware, Pennsylvania, New Jersey, Georgia, and Connecticut- ratified the Constitution without proposing amendments. Massachusetts then followed with a ratification, accompanied by a recommendation of nine amendments, none of which referred to the privilege; Maryland with a ratification without proposing amendments; South Carolina with a ratification accompanied by a recommendation of four amendments, none of which referred to the privilege, **[211 U.S. 78, 109]** and New Hampshire with a ratification accompanied by a recommendation of twelve amendments, none of which referred to the privilege. The nine states requisite to put the Constitution in operation ratified it without a suggestion of incorporating this privilege. Virginia was the tenth state to ratify, proposing, by separate resolution, an elaborate bill of rights under twenty heads, and, in addition, twenty amendments to the body of the Constitution. Among the rights enumerated as "essential and inalienable" is that no man "can be compelled to give evidence against himself," and "no freeman ought to be deprived of his life, liberty, or property but by the law of the land." New York ratified with a proposal of numerous amendments and a declaration of rights which the convention declared could not be violated and were consistent with the Constitution. One of these rights was that "no person ought to be taken, imprisoned or deprived of his freehold, or be exiled or deprived of his privileges, franchises, life, liberty, or property but by due process of law;" and another was that, "in all criminal prosecutions, the accused . . . should not be compelled to give evidence against himself." North Carolina and Rhode Island were the last to ratify, each proposing a large number of amendments, including the provision that no man "can be compelled to give evidence against himself;" and North Carolina, that "no freeman ought to be . . . deprived of his life, liberty, or property but by the law of the land;" and Rhode Island, that "no freeman ought to be . . . deprived of his life, liberty, or property but by the trial by jury, or by the law of the land."

Thus it appears that four only of the thirteen original state insisted upon incorporating the privilege in the Constitution, and they separately and simultaneously with the requirement of due process of law, and that three states proposing amendments were silent upon this subject. It is worthy of note that two of these four states did not incorporate the privilege in their own Constitutions, where it would have had a much wider field of usefulness, until many years after. New York **[211 U.S. 78, 110]** in 1821 and Rhode Island in 1842 (its first Constitution). This survey does not tend to show that it was then in this country the universal or even general belief that the privilege ranked among the fundamental and inalienable rights of mankind; and what is more important here, it affirmatively shows that the privilege was not conceived to be inherent in due process of law, but, on the other hand, a right separate, independent, and outside of due process. Congress, in submitting the Amendments to the several states, treated the two rights as exclusive of each other. Such also has been the view of the states in framing their own Constitutions, for in every case, except in New Jersey and Iowa, where the due process clause or its equivalent is included, it has been thought necessary to include separately the privilege clause. Nor have we been referred to any decision of a state court save one (*State v. Height*, 117 Iowa, 650, 59 L.R. A. 437, 94 Am. St. Rep. 323, 91 N. W. 935), where the exemption has been held to be required by due process of law. The inference is irresistible that it has been the opinion of constitution makers that the privilege, if fundamental in any sense, is not fundamental in due process of law, nor an essential part of it. We believe that this opinion is proved to have been correct by every historical test by which the meaning of the phrase can be tried.

The decisions of this court, though they are silent on the precise question before us, ought to be searched to discover if they present any analogies which are helpful in its decision. The essential elements of due process of law, already established by them, are singularly few, though of wide application and deep significance. We are not here concerned with the effect of due process in restraining substantive laws, as, for example, that which forbids the taking of private property for public use without compensation. We need notice now only those cases which deal with the principles which must be observed in the trial of criminal and civil causes. Due process requires that the court which assumes to determine the rights of parties shall have jurisdiction (*Pennoyer v. Neff*, 95 U.S. 714, 733 , 24 S. L. ed. 565, 572; *Scott v. McNeal*, 154 U.S. 34 , 38 L. ed. 896, 14 Sup. Ct. Rep. 1108; *Old Wayne Mut. Life Asso* **[211 U.S. 78, 111]** *v. McDonough*, 204 U.S. 8 , 51 L. ed. 345, 27 Sup. Ct. Rep. 236), and that there shall be notice and opportunity for hearing given the parties. (*Hovey v. Elliott*, 167 U.S. 409 , 42 L. ed. 215, 17 Sup. Ct. Rep. 841; *Roller v. Holly*, 176 U.S. 398 , 44 L. ed. 520, 20 Sup. Ct. Rep. 410; and see *Londoner v. Denver*, 210 U.S. 373 , 52 L. ed. 1103, 28 Sup. Ct. Rep. 708). Subject to these two fundamental conditions, which seem to be universally prescribed in all systems of law established by civilized countries, this court has, up to this time, sustained all state laws, statutory or judicially declared, regulating procedure, evidence, and methods of trial, and held them to be consistent with due process of law. *Walker v. Sauvinet*, 92 U.S. 90 , 23 L. ed. 678; *Re Converse*, 137 U.S. 624 , 34 L. ed. 796, 11 Sup. Ct. Rep. 191; *Caldwell v. Texas*, 137 U.S. 692 , 34 L. ed. 816, 11 Sup. Ct. Rep. 224; *Leeper v. Texas*, 139 U.S. 462 , 35 L. ed. 225, 11 Sup. Ct. Rep. 577; *Hallinger v. Davis*, 146 U.S. 314 , 36 L. ed. 986, 13 Sup. Ct. Rep. 105; *McNulty v. California*, 149 U.S. 645 , 37 L. ed. 882, 13 Sup. Ct. Rep. 959; *McKane v. Durston*, 153 U.S. 684 , 38 L. ed. 867, 14 Sup. Ct. Rep. 913; *Iowa C. R. Co. v. Iowa*, 160 U.S. 389 , 40 L. ed. 467, 16 Sup. Ct. Rep. 344; *Lowe v. Kansas*, 163 U.S. 81 , 41 L. ed. 78, 16 Sup. Ct. Rep. 1031; *Allen v. Georgia*, 166 U.S. 138 , 41 L. ed. 949, 17 Sup. Ct. Rep. 525; *Hodgson v. Vermont*, 168 U.S. 262 , 42 L. ed. 461, 18 Sup. Ct. Rep. 80; *Brown v. New Jersey*, 175 U.S. 172 , 44 L. ed. 119, 20 Sup. Ct. Rep. 77; *Bolln v. Nebraska*, 176 U.S. 83 , 44 L. ed. 382, 20 Sup. Ct. Rep. 287; *Maxwell v. Dow*, 176 U.S. 581 , 44 L. ed. 597, 20 Sup. Ct. Rep. 448, 494; *Simon v. Craft*, 182 U.S. 427 , 45 L. ed. 1165, 21 Sup. Ct. Rep. 836; *West v. Louisiana*, 194 U.S. 258 , 48 L. ed. 965, 24 Sup. Ct. Rep. 650; *Marvin v. Trout*, 199 U.S. 212 , 50 L. ed. 157, 26 Sup. Ct. Rep. 31; *Rogers v. Peck*, 199 U.S. 425 , 50 L. ed. 256, 26 Sup. Ct. Rep. 87; *Howard v. Kentucky*, 200 U.S. 164 , 50 L. ed. 421, 26 Sup. Ct. Rep. 189; *Rawlins v. Georgia*, 201 U.S.

638 , 50 L. ed. 899, 26 Sup. Ct. Rep. 560; *Felts v. Murphy*, 201 U.S. 123 , 50 L. ed. 689, 26 Sup. Ct. Rep. 366.

Among the most notable of these decisions are those sustaining the denial of jury trial both in civil and criminal cases, the substitution of informations for indictments by a grand jury, the enactment that the possession of policy slips raises a presumption of illegality, and the admission of the deposition of an absent witness in a criminal case. The cases proceed upon the theory that, given a court of justice which has jurisdiction, and acts, not arbitrarily, but in conformity with a general law, upon evidence, and after inquiry made with notice to the parties affected and opportunity to be heard, then all the requirements of due process, so far as it relates to procedure in court and methods of trial and character and effect of evidence, are complied with. Thus it was said in *Iowa C. R. Co. v. Iowa*, supra, p. 393: "But it is clear that the 14th Amendment in no way undertakes to control the [211 U.S. 78, 112] power of a state to determine by what process legal rights may be asserted or legal obligations be enforced, provided the method of procedure adopted for these purposes gives reasonable notice and accords fair opportunity to be heard before the issues are decided;" and in *Louisville & N. R. Co. v. Schmidt*, 177 U.S. 236 , 44 L. ed. 750, 20 Sup. Ct. Rep. 622: "It is no longer open to contention that the due process clause of the 14th Amendment to the Constitution of the United States does not control mere forms of procedure in state courts or regulate practice therein. All its requirements are complied with, provided in the proceedings which are claimed not to have been due process of law the person condemned has had sufficient notice, and adequate opportunity has been afforded him to defend;" and in *Hooker v. Los Angeles*, 188 U.S. 314, 318 , 47 S. L. ed. 487, 491, 63 L.R.A. 471, 479, 23 Sup. Ct. Rep. 395, 397: "The 14th Amendment does not control the power of a state to determine the form of procedure by which legal rights may be ascertained, if the method adopted gives reasonable notice and affords a fair opportunity to be heard;" and if *Rogers v. Peck*, supra, p. 435: "Due process of law guaranteed by the 14th Amendment does not require the state to adopt a particular form of procedure, so long as it appears that the accused has had sufficient notice of the accusation and an adequate opportunity to defend himself in the prosecution." It is impossible to reconcile the reasoning of these cases and the rule which governed their decision with the theory that an exemption from compulsory self-incrimination is included in the conception of due process of law. Indeed, the reasoning for including indictment by a grand jury and trial by a petit jury in that conception, which has been rejected by this court in *Hurtado v. California* and *Maxwell v. Dow*, was historically and in principle much stronger. Clearly appreciating this, Mr. Justice Harlan, in his dissent in each of these cases, pointed out that the inexorable logic of the reasoning of the court was to allow the states, so far as the Federal Constitution was concerned, to compel any person to be a witness against himself. In *Missouri v. Lewis* (*Bowman v. Lewis*) 101 U.S. 22 , 25 L. ed. 989, Mr. Justice Bradley, speaking [211 U.S. 78, 113] for the whole court, said, in effect, that the 14th Amendment would not prevent a state from adopting or continuing the Civil Law instead of the common law. This dictum has been approved and made an essential part of the reasoning of the decision in *Holden v. Hardy*, 169 U.S. 387, 389 , 42 S. L. ed. 789, 790, 18 Sup. Ct. Rep. 383, and *Maxwell v. Dow*, supra, 598. The statement excludes the possibility that the privilege is essential to due process, for it hardly need be said that the interrogation of the accused at his trial is the practice in the Civil Law.

Even if the historical meaning of due process of law and the decisions of this court did not exclude the privilege from it, it would be going far to rate it as an immutable principle of justice which is the inalienable possession of every citizen of a free government. Salutary as the principle may seem to the great majority, it cannot be ranked with the right to hearing before condemnation, the immunity from arbitrary power not acting by general laws, and the inviolability of private property. The wisdom of the exemption has never been universally assented to since the days of Bentham, many doubt it to-day, and it is best defended not as an unchangeable principle of universal justice, but as a law proved by experience to be expedient. See Wigmore, Ev. 2251. It has no place in the jurisprudence of civilized and free countries outside the domain of the common law, and it is nowhere observed among our own people in the search for truth outside the administration of the law. It should, must, and will be rigidly observed where it is secured by specific constitutional safeguards, but there is nothing in it which gives it a sanctity above and before constitutions themselves. Much might be said in favor of the view that the privilege was guaranteed against state impairment as a privilege and immunity of national citizenship, but, as has been shown, the decisions of this court have foreclosed that view. There seems to be no reason whatever, however, for straining the meaning of due process of law to include this privilege within it, because, perhaps, we may think it of great value. The states had guarded the privilege **[211 U.S. 78, 114]** to the satisfaction of their own people up to the adoption of the 14th Amendment. No reason is perceived why they cannot continue to do so. The power of their people ought not to be fettered, their sense of responsibility lessened, and their capacity for sober and restrained self- government weakened, by forced construction of the Federal Constitution. If the people of New Jersey are not content with the law as declared in repeated decisions of their courts, the remedy is in their own hands. They may, if they choose, alter it by legislation, as the people of Maine did when the courts of that state made the same ruling. *State v. Bartlett*, 55 Me. 200; i, 57 Me. 574; *State v. Cleaves,* 59 Me. 298, 8 Am. Rep. 422; *State v. Banks*, 78 Me. 492, 7 Atl. 269; Rev. Stat. chap. 135, 19.

We have assumed only for the purpose of discussion that what was done in the case at bar was an infringement of the privilege against self- incrimination. We do not intend, however, to lend any countenance to the truth of that assumption. The courts of New Jersey, in adopting the rule of law which is complained of here, have deemed it consistent with the privilege itself, and not a denial of it. The reasoning by which this view is supported will be found in the cases cited from New Jersey and Maine, and see Queen v. Rhodes [1899] 1 Q. B. 77; Ex parte Kops [1894] A. C. 650. The authorities upon the question are in conflict. We do not pass upon the conflict, because, for the reasons given, we think that the exemption from compulsory self-incrimination in the courts of the states is not secured by any part of the Federal Constitution.

Judgment affirmed.

Mr. Justice **HARLAN**, dissenting:

I feel constrained by a sense of duty to express my nonconcurrence in the action of the court in this case.

Twining and Cornell were indicted for a criminal offense in a New Jersey court, and, having been found guilty by a jury, were sentenced, respectively, to imprisonment for six and **[211 U.S. 78, 115]** four years. The judgment of conviction was affirmed, first in the supreme court of the state, afterwards in the court of errors and appeals. The case was brought here for review, and the accused assigned for error that the mode of proceeding during the trial was such as to deny them a right secured by the Constitution of the United States,—namely, the right of an accused not to be compelled to testify against himself.

Upon this point the court, in the opinion just delivered, says: "We have assumed, only for the purpose of discussion, that what was done in the case at bar was an infringement of the privilege against self-incrimination." But the court takes care to add immediately: "We do not intend, however, to lend any countenance to the truth of that assumption. The courts of New Jersey, in adopting the rule of law which is complained of here, have deemed it consistent with the privilege itself."

It seems to me that the first inquiry on this writ of error should have been whether, upon the record before us, that which was actually done in the trial court amounted, in law, to a violation of that privilege. If the court was not prepared to hold, upon the record before it, that the privilege of immunity from self-incrimination had been actually violated, then, I submit, it ought not to have gone further and held it to be competent for a state, despite the granting of immunity from self- incrimination by the Federal Constitution, to compel one accused of crime to be a witness against himself. Whether a state is forbidden by the Constitution of the United States to violate the principle of immunity from self-incrimination is a question which it is clearly unnecessary to decide now, unless what was, in fact, done at the trial, was inconsistent with that immunity. But, although expressly declaring that it will not lend any countenance to the truth of the assumption that the proceedings below were in disregard of the maxim, Nemo tenetur seipsum accusare, and without saying whether there was, in fact, any substantial violation of the privilege [211 U.S. 78, 116] of immunity from self-incrimination, the court, for the purpose only of discussion, has entered upon the academic inquiry whether a state may, without violating the Constitution of the United States, compel one accused of crime to be a witness against himself,—a question of vast moment, one of such transcendent importance that a court ought not to decide it unless the record before it requires that course to be adopted. It is entirely consistent with the opinion just delivered that the court thinks that what is complained of as having been done at the trial of the accused was not, in law, an infringement of the privilege of immunity from self-incrimination. Yet, as stated, the court, in its wisdom, has forborne to say whether, in its judgment, that privilege was, in fact, violated in the state court, but simply, for the purpose of discussion, has proceeded on the assumption that the privilege was disregarded at the trial.

As a reason why it takes up first the question of the power of a state, so far as the Federal Constitution is concerned, to compel self- incrimination, the court says that if the right here asserted is not a Federal right that is an end of the case, and it must not go further. It would, I submit, have been more appropriate to say that, if no ground whatever existed, under the facts disclosed by the record, to contend that a Federal right had been violated, this court would be without authority to go further and express its opinion on an abstract question relating to the powers of the states under the Constitution.

What I have suggested as to the proper course of procedure in this court is supported by our action in *Shoener v. Pennsylvania*, 207 U.S. 188, 195 , 52 S. L. ed. 163, 166, 28 Sup. Ct. Rep. 110. That was a criminal case, brought here from the supreme court of Pennsylvania,— the accused, who was convicted, insisting that the proceeding against him in the state court was in violation of the clause of the Federal Constitution declaring that no person shall be subject for the same offense to be twice put in jeopardy of life or limb. Upon looking into the record of that case we found that the accused had not been, previously, put in legal jeopardy for [211 U.S. 78, 117] the same offense. We went no further, but dismissed the writ of error, declining to consider the grave constitutional question pressed upon our attention, namely, whether the jeopardy clause of the Federal Constitution operated as a restraint upon the states in the execution of their criminal laws. But as a different course has been pursued in this case, I must of necessity consider the sufficiency of the grounds upon which the court bases its present judgment of affirmance.

The court, in its consideration of the relative rights of the United States and of the several states, holds, in this case, that, without violating the Constitution of the United States, a state can compel a person accused of crime to testify against himself. In my judgment, immunity from self-incrimination is protected against hostile state action, not only by that clause in the 14th Amendment declaring that "no state shall make or enforce any law which shall abridge the privileges or immunities of citizens of the United States," but by the clause, in the same Amendment, "nor shall any state deprive any person of life, liberty, or property, without due process of law." No argument is needed to support the proposition that, whether manifested by statute or by the final judgment of a court, state action, if liable to the objection that it abridges the privileges or immunities of national citizenship, must also be regarded as wanting in the due process of law enjoined by the 14th Amendment, when such state action substantially affects life, liberty, or property.

At the time of the adoption of the 14th Amendment immunity from self- incrimination was one of the privileges or immunities belonging to citizens, for the reason that the 5th Amendment, speaking in the name of the people of the United States, had declared, in terms, that no person "shall be compelled, in any criminal case, to be a witness against himself; nor be deprived of life, liberty, or property, without due process of law." That Amendment, it was long ago decided, operated as a restriction on the exercise of powers by the United States or by Federal tribunals and agencies, but [211 U.S. 78, 118] did not impose any restraint upon a state or upon a state tribunal or agency. The original Amendments of the Constitution had their origin, as all know, in the belief of many patriotic statesmen in the states then composing the Union, that, under the Constitution, as originally submitted to the people for adoption or rejection, the national government might disregard the fundamental principles of Anglo-American liberty, for the maintenance of which our fathers took up arms against the mother country.

What, let me inquire, must then have been regarded as principles that were fundamental in the liberty of the citizen? Every student of English history will agree that, long before the adoption of the Constitution of the United States, certain principles affecting the life and liberty of the subject had become firmly established in the jurisprudence of England, and were deemed vital to the safety of freemen, and that among those principles was the one that no person accused of crime could be compelled to be a witness against himself. It is true that at one time in England the practice of "questioning the prisoner" was enforced in star chamber proceedings. But we have the authority of Sir James Fitzjames Stephen, in his History of the Criminal Law of England, for saying that, soon after the Revolution of 1688, the practice of questioning the prisoner died out. Vol. 1, p. 440. The liberties of the English people had then been placed on a firmer foundation. Personal liberty was thenceforward jealously guarded. Certain it is, that when the present government of the United States was established it was the belief of all liberty-loving men in America that real, genuine freedom could not exist in any country that recognized the power of government to compel persons accused of crime to be witnesses against themselves. And it is not too much to say that the wise men who laid the foundations of our constitutional government would have stood aghast at the suggestion that immunity from self-incrimination was not among the essential, fundamental principles of English law. An able writer on English and American constitutional **[211 U.S. 78, 119]** law has recently well said: "When the first Continental Congress of 1774 claimed to be entitled to the benefit, not only of the common law of England, but of such of the English statutes as existed at the time of the colonization, and which they had by experience found to be applicable to their several local and other circumstances, they simply declared the basic principle of English law that English subjects, going to a new and uninhabited country, carry with them, as their birthright, the laws of England existing when the colonization takes place. . . . English law, public and private, continued in force in all the states that became sovereign in 1776, each state declaring for itself the date from which it would recognize it." Taylor, Science of Jurisprudence, 436, 437. It is indisputably established that, despite differences in forms of government, the people in the colonies were a unit as to certain leading principles, among which was the principle that the people were entitled to "enjoy the rights and privileges of British-born subjects and the benefit of the common laws of England" (1 Story, Const. 163), and that (to use the words of the Continental Congress of 1774) "by immigration to the colonies, the people by no means forfeited, surrendered, or lost any of those rights, but that they were then, and their descendants are now, entitled to the exercise and enjoyment of them as their local and other circumstances enable them to exercise and enjoy."

Can there be any doubt that, at the opening of the War of Independence, the people of the colonies claimed as one of their birthrights the privilege of immunity from self-incrimination? This question can be answered in but one way. If, at the beginning of the Revolutionary War, any lawyer had claimed that one accused of crime could lawfully be compelled to testify against himself, he would have been laughed at by his brethren of the bar, both in England and America. In accordance with this universal view as to the rights of freemen, Virginia, in its convention of May, 1776,—in advance, be it observed, of the Declaration of Independence,—made a **[211 U.S. 78, 120]** declaration (drawn entirely by the celebrated George Mason) which set forth certain rights as pertaining to the people of that state and to their posterity "as the basis and foundation of government." Among those rights (that famous declaration distinctly announced) was the right of a person not to be compelled to give evidence against himself. Precisely the same declaration was made in Pennsylvania by its convention assembled at Philadelphia on the 15th of July 1776. Vermont, by its convention of 1777, said "Nor can he [a man accused of crime] be compelled to give evidence against himself." Maryland, in 1776, declared that "no man ought to be compelled to give evidence against himself, in a court of criminal law." Massachusetts, in its Constitution of 1780, provided that "no subject shall be . . . compelled to accuse, or to furnish evidence against, himself." The same provision was made by New Hampshire in its Constitution of 1784. And North Carolina as early as 1776 recognized the privilege of immunity from self-incrimination by declaring, in its Constitution, that a man "shall not be compelled to give evidence against himself." These explicit declarations in the Constitutions of leading colonies, before the submission of the national Constitution to the people for adoption or rejection, caused patriotic men, whose fidelity to American liberty no one doubted, to protest that that instrument was defective, in that it furnished no express guaranty against the violation by the national government of the personal rights that inhered in liberty. Nothing is made clearer by the history of our country than that the Constitution would not have been accepted by the requisite number of states, but for the understanding, on all sides, that it should be promptly amended so as to meet this objection. So, when the first Congress met, there was entire unanimity among statesmen of that day as to the necessity and wisdom of having a national Bill of Rights which would, beyond all question, secure against Federal encroachment all the rights, privileges, and immunities which, everywhere and by everybody in America, were then recognized as **[211 U.S. 78, 121]** fundamental in Anglo-American liberty. Hence the prompt incorporation into the supreme law of the land of the original Amendments. By the 5th Amendment, as already stated, it was expressly declared that no one should be compelled, in a criminal case, to be a witness against himself. Those Amendments being adopted by the nation, the people no longer feared that the United States or any Federal agency could exert power that was inconsistent with the fundamental rights recognized in those Amendments. It is to be observed that the Amendments introduced no principle not already familiar to liberty-loving people. They only put in the form of constitutional sanction, as barriers against oppression, the principles which the people of the colonies, with entire unanimity, deemed vital to their safety and freedom.

Still more. At the close of the late Civil War, which had seriously disturbed the foundations of our governmental system, the question arose whether provision should not be made by constitutional Amendments to secure against attack by the states the rights, privileges, and immunities which, by the original Amendments, had been placed beyond the power of the United States or any Federal agency to impair or destroy. Those rights, privileges, and immunities had not then, in terms, been guarded by the national Constitution against impairment or destruction by the states, although, before the adoption of the 14th Amendment, every state, without, perhaps, an exception, had, in some form, recognized, as part of its fundamental law, most, if not all, the rights and immunities mentioned in the original Amendments, among them immunity from self-incrimination. This is made clear by the opinion of the court in the present case. The court says: "The exemption from testimonial compulsion, that is, from disclosure as a witness of evidence against one's self, forced by any form of legal process, is universal in American law, though there may be a difference as to its exact scope and limits. At the time of the formation of the Union, the principle that no person could be compelled to be a witness against himself **[211 U.S. 78, 122]** had become embodied in the common law and distinguished it from all other systems of jurisprudence. It was generally regarded then, as now, as a privilege of great value, a protection to the innocent, though a shelter to the guilty, and a safeguard against heedless, unfounded, or tyrannical prosecutions." Such was the situation, the court concedes, at the time the 14th Amendment was prepared and adopted. That Amendment declared that all persons born or naturalized in the United States and subject to its jurisdiction are citizens of the United States, "and of the state wherein they reside." Momentous as this declaration was, in its political consequences, it was not deemed sufficient for the complete protection of the essential rights of national citizenship and personal liberty. Although the nation was restrained by existing constitutional provisions from encroaching upon those rights, yet, so far as the Federal Constitution was concerned, the states could, at that time, have dealt with those rights upon the basis entirely of their own Constitution and laws. It was therefore deemed necessary that the 14th Amendment should, in the name of the United States, forbid, as it expressly does, any state from making or enforcing a law that will abridge the privileges or immunities of citizens of the United States, or deprive any person of life, liberty, or property without due process of law. The privileges and immunities mentioned in the original Amendments, and universally regarded as our heritage of liberty from the common law, were thus secured to every citizen of the United States, and placed beyond assault by any government, Federal or state; and due process of law, in all public proceedings affecting life, liberty, or property, was enjoined equally upon the nation and the states.

What, then, were the privileges and immunities of citizens of the United States which the 14th Amendment guarded against encroachment by the states? Whatever they were, that Amendment placed them beyond the power of any state to abridge. And what were the rights of life and liberty which the Amendment protected? Whatever they were, that Amendment **[211 U.S. 78, 123]** guarded them against any hostile state action that was wanting in due process of law.

I will not attempt to enumerate all the privileges and immunities which at that time belonged to citizens of the United States. But I confidently assert that among such privileges was the privilege of immunity from self-incrimination which the people of the United States, by adopting the 5th Amendment, had placed beyond Federal encroachment. Can such a view be deemed unreasonable in the face of the fact, frankly conceded in the opinion of the court, that, at common law, as well at the time of the formation of the Union and when the 14th Amendment was adopted, immunity from self-incrimination was a privilege "universal in American law," was everywhere deemed "of great value, a protection to the innocent, though a shelter to the guilty, and a safeguard against heedless, unfounded, or tyrannical prosecutions?" Is it conceivable that a privilege or immunity of such a priceless character, one expressly recognized in the supreme law of the land, one thoroughly interwoven with the history of Anglo-American liberty, was not in the mind of the country when it declared, in the 14th Amendment, that no state shall abridge the privileges or immunities of citizens of the United States? The 14th Amendment would have been disapproved by every state in the Union if it had saved or recognized the right of a state to compel one accused of crime, in its courts, to be a witness against himself. We state the matter in this way because it is common knowledge that the compelling of a person to criminate himself shocks or ought to shock the sense of right and justice to everyone who loves liberty. Indeed, this court has not hesitated thus to characterize the star chamber method of compelling an accused to be a witness against himself. In *Boyd v. United States*, 116 U.S. 616, 631 , 633 S., 29 L. ed. 746, 751, 752, 6 Sup. Ct. Rep. 524, 533, 534, will be found some weighty observations by Mr. Justice Bradley, delivering the judgment of the court, as to the scope and meaning of the 4th and 5th Amendments. The court, speaking by that eminent jurist, said: **[211 U.S. 78, 124]** "Now, it is elementary knowledge, that one cardinal rule of the court of chancery is never to decree a discovery which might tend to convict the party of a crime, or to forfeit his property. And any compulsory discovery by extorting the party's oath, or compelling the production of his private books and papers, to convict him of crime, or to forfeit his property, is contrary to the principles of a free government. It is abhorrent to the instincts of an Englishman; it is abhorrent to the instincts of an American. It may suit the purposes of despotic power, but it cannot abide the pure atmosphere of political liberty and personal freedom." Again: "We have already noticed the intimate relation between the two Amendments. They throw great light on each other. For the 'unreasonable searches and seizures' condemned in the 4th Amendment are almost always made for the purpose of compelling a man to give evidence against himself, which, in criminal cases, is condemned in the 5th Amendment; and compelling a man 'in a criminal case to be a witness against himself,' which is condemned in the 5th Amendment, throws light on the question as to what is an 'unreasonable search and seizure' within the meaning of the 4th Amendment. And we have been unable to perceive that the seizure of a man's private books and papers, to be used in evidence against him, is substantially different from compelling him to be a witness against himself." These observations were referred to approvingly in *Counselman v. Hitchcook*, 142 U.S. 547, 580 , 581 S., 35 L. ed. 1110, 1120, 3 Inters. Com. Rep.

816, 12 Sup. Ct. Rep. 195.

I am of opinion that, as immunity from self-incrimination was recognized in the 5th Amendment of the Constitution, and placed beyond violation by any Federal agency, it should be deemed one of the immunities of citizens of the United States which the 14th Amendment, in express terms, forbids any state from abridging,—as much so, for instance, as the right of free speech (1st Amend.) or the exemption from cruel or unusual punishments (8th Amend.), or the exemption from being put twice in jeopardy of life or limb for the same offense (5th Amend.), or the exemption from unreasonable searches **[211 U.S. 78, 125]** and seizures of one's person, house, papers, or effects (4th Amend.). Even if I were anxious or willing to cripple the operation of the 14th Amendment by strained or narrow interpretations, I should feel obliged to hold that, when that Amendment was adopted, all these last-mentioned exemptions were among the immunities belonging to citizens of the United States, which, after the adoption of the 14th Amendment, no state could impair or destroy. But, as I read the opinion of the court, it will follow from the general principles underlying it, or from the reasoning pursued therein, that the 14th Amendment would be no obstacle whatever in the way of a state law or practice under which, for instance, cruel or unusual punishments (such as the thumbscrew, or the rack, or burning at the stake) might be inflicted. So of a state law which infringed the right of free speech, or authorized unreasonable searches or seizures of persons, their houses, papers, or effects, or a state law under which one accused of crime could be put in jeopardy twice or oftener, at the pleasure of the prosecution, for the same offense.

It is my opinion, also, that the right to immunity from self- incrimination cannot be taken away by any state consistently with the clause of the 14th Amendment that relates to the deprivation by the state of life or liberty without due process of law. This view is supported by what Mr. Justice Miller said for the court in *Davidson v. New Orleans*, 96 U.S. 97, 101 , 102 S., 24 L. ed. 616, 618, 619. That great judge, delivering the opinion in that case said: "The prohibition against depriving the citizen or subject of his life, liberty, or property without due process of law, is not new in the constitutional history of the English race. It is not new in the constitutional history of this country, and it was not new in the Constitution of the United States when it became a part of the 14th Amendment, in the year 1866." After observing that the equivalent of the phrase "due process of law," according to Lord Coke, is found in the words, "law of the land," in the Great Charter, in connection with the guaranties of the rights of the subject **[211 U.S. 78, 126]** against the oppression of the Crown, the court said: "In the series of amendments to the Constitution of the United States, proposed and adopted immediately after the organization of the government, which were dictated by the jealousy of the states as further limitations upon the power of the Federal government, it is found in the fifth, in connection with other guaranties of personal rights of the same character." Among these guaranties this court distinctly said was protection against being twice tried for the same offense, and protection "against the accused being compelled, in a criminal case, to testify against himself." Again, said the court: "It is easy to see that when the great barons of England wrung from King John, at the point of the sword, the concession that neither their lives nor their property should be disposed of by the Crown, except as provided by the law of the land, they meant by "law of the land" the ancient and customary laws of the English people, or laws enacted by the Parliament, of which those barons were a controlling element. It was not in their minds, therefore, to protect themselves against the enactment of laws by the Parliament of England. But when, in the year of grace 1866, there is placed in the Constitution of the United States a declaration that "no state shall deprive any person of life, liberty, or property without due process of law," can a state make anything due process of law which, by its own legislation, it chooses to declare such? To affirm this is to hold that the prohibition to the states is of no avail or has no application where the invasion of private rights is affected under the forms of state legislation."

I cannot support any judgment declaring that immunity from self- incrimination is not one of the privileges or immunities of national citizenship, nor a part of the liberty guaranteed by the 14th Amendment against hostile state action. The declaration of the court, in the opinion just delivered that immunity from self-incrimination is of great value, a protection to the innocent, and a safeguard against unfounded and tyrannical prosecutions, meets my cordial **[211 U.S. 78, 127]** approval. And the court having heretofore, upon the fullest consideration, declared that the compelling of a citizen of the United States, charged with crime, to be a witness against himself, was a rule abhorrent to the instincts of Americans, was in violation of universal American law, was contrary to the principles of free government, and a weapon of despotic power which could not abide the pure atmosphere of political liberty and personal freedom, I cannot agree that a state may make that rule a part of its law and binding on citizens, despite the Constitution of the United States. No former decision of this court requires that we should now so interpret the Constitution

United States Supreme Court
U.S. v. Cruikshank, 92 U.S. 542 (1875)

October Term, 1875
(headnotes omitted)

[542-544]

[92 U.S. 542, 544] ERROR to the Circuit Court of the United States for the District of Louisiana.

This was an indictment for conspiracy under the sixth section of the act of May 30, 1870, known as the Enforcement Act (16 Stat. 140), and consisted of thirty-two counts.

The *first* count was for banding together, with intent 'unlawfully and feloniously to injure, oppress, threaten, and intimidate' two citizens of the United States, 'of African descent and persons of color,' 'with the unlawful and felonious intent thereby' them 'to hinder and prevent in their respective free [92 U.S. 542, 545] exercise and enjoyment of their lawful right and privilege to peaceably assemble together with each other and with other citizens of the said United States for a peaceable and lawful purpose.'

The *second* avers an intent to hinder and prevent the exercise by the same persons of the 'right to keep and bear arms for a lawful purpose.'

The *third* avers an intent to deprive the same persons 'of their respective several lives and liberty of person, without due process of law.'

The *fourth* avers an intent to deprive the same persons of the 'free exercise and enjoyment of the right and privilege to the full and equal benefit of all laws and proceedings for the security of persons and property' enjoyed by white citizens.

The *fifth* avers an intent to hinder and prevent the same persons 'in the exercise and enjoyment of the rights, privileges, immunities, and protection granted and secured to them respectively as citizens of the said United States, and as citizens of the said State of Louisiana, by reason of and for and on account of the race and color' of the said persons.

The *sixth* avers an intent to hinder and prevent the same persons in 'the free exercise and enjoyment of the several and respective right and privilege to vote at any election to be thereafter by law had and held by the people in and of the said State of Louisiana.'

The *seventh* avers an intent 'to put in great fear of bodily harm, injure, and oppress' the same persons, 'because and for the reason' that, having the right to vote, they had voted.

The *eighth* avers an intent 'to prevent and hinder' the same persons 'in their several and respective free exercise and enjoyment of every, each, all, and singular and several rights and privileges granted and secured' to them 'by the constitution and laws of the United States.'

The next eight counts are a repetition of the first eight, except that, instead of the words 'band together,' the words 'combine, conspire, and confederate together' are used. Three of the defendants were found guilty under the first sixteen counts, and not guilty under the remaining counts. [92 U.S. 542, 546] The parties thus convicted moved in arrest of judgment on the following grounds:—

1. Because the matters and things set forth and charged in the several counts, one to sixteen inclusive, do not constitute offences against the laws of the United States, and do not come within the purview, true intent, and meaning of the act of Congress, approved 31st May, 1870, entitled *'An Act to enforce the right of citizens of the United States,'* & c.

2. Because the matters and things in the said indictment set forth and charged do not constitute offences cognizable in the Circuit Court, and do not come within its power and jurisdiction.

3. Because the offences created by the sixth section of the act of Congress referred to, and upon which section the aforesaid sixteen counts are based, are not constitutionally within the jurisdiction of the courts of the United States, and because the matters and things therein

323

referred to are judicially cognizable by State tribunals only, and legislative action thereon is among the constitutionally reserved rights of the several States.

4. Because the said act, in so far as it creates offences and imposes penalties, is in violation of the Constitution of the United States, and an infringement of the rights of the several States and the people.

5. Because the eighth and sixteenth counts of the indictment are too vague, general, insufficient, and uncertain, to afford the accused proper notice to plead and prepare their defence, and set forth no specific offence under the law.

6. Because the verdict of the jury against the defendants is not warranted or supported by law.

On this motion the opinions of the judges were divided, that of the presiding judge being that the several counts in question are not sufficient in law, and do not contain charges of criminal matter indictable under the laws of the United States; and that the motion in arrest of judgment should be granted. The case comes up at the instance of the United States, on certificate of this division of opinion.

Sect. 1 of the Enforcement Act declares, that all citizens of the United States, otherwise qualified, shall be allowed to vote at all elections, without distinction of race, color, or previous servitude.

[92 **U.S.** 542, 547] Sect. 2 provides, that, if by the law of any State or Territory a prerequisite to voting is necessary, equal opportunity for it shall be given to all, without distinction, &c.; and any person charged with the duty of furnishing the prerequisite, who refuses or knowingly omits to give full effect to this section, shall be guilty of misdemeanor.

Sect. 3 provides, that an offer of performance, in respect to the prerequisite, when proved by affidavit of the claimant, shall be equivalent to performance; and any judge or inspector of election who refuses to accept it shall be guilty, &c.

Sect. 4 provides, that any person who, by force, bribery, threats, intimidation, or other unlawful means, hinders, delays, prevents, or obstructs any citizen from qualifying himself to vote, or combines with others to do so, shall be guilty, &c.

Sect. 5 provides, that any person who prevents, hinders, controls, or intimidates any person from exercising the right of suffrage, to whom it is secured by the fifteenth amendment, or attempts to do so, by bribery or threats of violence, or deprivation of property or employment, shall be guilty, &c.

The sixth section is as follows:—

'That if two or more persons shall band or conspire together, or go in disguise upon the public highway, or upon the premises of another, with intent to violate any provisions of this act, or to injure, oppress, threaten, or intimidate any citizen with intent to prevent or hinder his free exercise and enjoyment of any right or privilege granted or secured to him by the constitution or laws of the United States, or because of his having exercised the same, such persons shall be held guilty of felony, and, on conviction thereof, shall be fined or imprisoned, or both, at the discretion of the court,-the fine not to exceed $5,000, and the imprisonment not to exceed ten years; and shall, moreover, be thereafter ineligible to, and disabled from holding, any office or place of honor, profit, or trust created by the constitution or laws of the United States.'

This case was argued at the October Term, 1874, by Mr. Attorney-General Williams and Mr. Solicitor-General Phillips for the plaintiff in error; and by Mr. Reverdy Johnson, Mr. David Dudley Field, Mr. Philip Phillips, and Mr. R. H. Marr for the defendants in error. [92 **U.S.** 542, 548]

Mr. Chief Justice **WAITE** delivered the opinion of the court.

This case comes here with a certificate by the judges of the Circuit Court for the District of Louisiana that they were divided in opinion upon a question which occurred at the hearing. It presents for our consideration an indictment containing sixteen counts, divided into two series of eight counts each, based upon sect. 6 of the Enforcement Act of May 31, 1870. That section is as follows:—

'That if two or more persons shall band or conspire together, or go in disguise upon the public highway, or upon the premises of another, with intent to violate any provision of this act, or to injure, oppress, threaten, or intimidate any citizen, with intent to prevent or hinder his free exercise and enjoyment of any right or privilege granted or secured to him by the constitution or laws of the United States, or because of his having exercised the same, such persons shall be held guilty of felony, and, on conviction thereof, shall be fined or imprisoned, or both, at the discretion of the court,-the fine not to exceed $5,000, and the imprisonment not to exceed ten years; and shall, moreover, be thereafter ineligible to, and disabled from holding, any office or place of honor, profit, or trust created by the constitution or laws of the United States.' 16 Stat. 141.

The question certified arose upon a motion in arrest of judgment after a verdict of guilty generally upon the whole sixteen counts, and is stated to be, whether 'the said sixteen counts of said indictment are severally good and sufficient in law, and contain charges of criminal matter indictable under the laws of the United States.'

The general charge in the first eight counts is that of 'banding,' and in the second eight, that of 'conspiring' together to injure, oppress, threaten, and intimidate Levi Nelson and Alexander Tillman, citizens of the United States, of African descent and persons of color, with the intent thereby to hinder and prevent them in their free exercise and enjoyment of rights and privileges 'granted and secured' to them 'in common with all other good citizens of the United States by the constitution and laws of the United States.'

The offences provided for by the statute in question do not consist in the mere 'banding' or 'conspiring' of two or **[92 U.S. 542, 549]** more persons together, but in their banding or conspiring with the intent, or for any of the purposes, specified. To bring this case under the operation of the statute, therefore, it must appear that the right, the enjoyment of which the conspirators intended to hinder or prevent, was one granted or secured by the constitution or laws of the United States. If it does not so appear, the criminal matter charged has not been made indictable by any act of Congress.

We have in our political system a government of the United States and a government of each of the several States. Each one of these governments is distinct from the others, and each has citizens of its own who owe it allegiance, and whose rights, within its jurisdiction, it must protect. The same person may be at the same time a citizen of the United States and a citizen of a State, but his rights of citizenship under one of these governments will be different from those he has under the other. *Slaughter-House Cases*, 16 Wall. 74.

Citizens are the members of the political community to which they belong. They are the people who compose the community, and who, in their associated capacity, have established or submitted themselves to the dominion of a government for the promotion of their general welfare and the protection of their individual as well as their collective rights. In the formation of a government, the people may confer upon it such powers as they choose. The government, when so formed, may, and when called upon should, exercise all the powers it has for the protection of the rights of its citizens and the people within its jurisdiction; but it can exercise no other. The duty of a government to afford protection is limited always by the power it possesses for that purpose.

Experience made the fact kno3wn to the people of the United States that they required a national government for national purposes. The separate governments of the separate States, bound together by the articles of confederation alone, were not sufficient for the promotion of the general welfare of the people in respect to foreign nations, or for their complete protection as citizens of the confederated States. For this reason, the people of the United States, 'in order to form a more perfect union, establish justice, insure domestic tranquillity, provide for **[92 U.S. 542, 550]** the common defence, promote the general welfare, and secure the blessings of liberty' to themselves and their posterity (Const. Preamble), ordained and established the government of the United States, and defined its powers by a constitution, which they adopted as its fundamental law, and made its rule of action.

The government thus established and defined is to some extent a government of the States in their political capacity. It is also, for certain purposes, a government of the people. Its powers are limited in number, but not in degree. Within the scope of its powers, as enumerated and defined, it is supreme and above the States; but beyond, it has no existence. It was erected for special purposes, and endowed with all the powers necessary for its own preservation and the accomplishment of the ends its people had in view. It can neither grant nor secure to its citizens any right or privilege not expressly or by implication placed under its jurisdiction.

The people of the United States resident within any State are subject to two governments: one State, and the other National; but there need be no conflict between the two. The powers which one possesses, the other does not. They are established for different purposes, and have separate jurisdictions. Together they make one whole, and furnish the people of the United States with a complete government, ample for the protection of all their rights at home and abroad. True, it may sometimes happen that a person is amenable to both jurisdictions for one and the same act. Thus, if a marshal of the United States is unlawfully resisted while executing the process of the courts within a State, and the resistance is accompanied by an assault on the officer, the sovereignty of the United States is violated by the resistance, and that of the State by the breach of peace, in the assault. So, too, if one passes counterfeited coin of the United States within a State, it may be an offence against the United States and the State: the United States, because it discredits the coin; and the State, because of the fraud upon him to whom it is passed. This does not, however, necessarily imply that the two governments possess powers in common, or bring them into conflict with each other. It is the natural consequence of a citizenship [92 U.S. 542, 551] which owes allegiance to two sovereignties, and claims protection from both. The citizen cannot complain, because he has voluntarily submitted himself to such a form of government. He owes allegiance to the two departments, so to speak, and within their respective spheres must pay the penalties which each exacts for disobedience to its laws. In return, he can demand protection from each within its own jurisdiction.

The government of the United States is one of delegated powers alone. Its authority is defined and limited by the Constitution. All powers not granted to it by that instrument are reserved to the States or the people. No rights can be acquired under the constitution or laws of the United States, except such as the government of the United States has the authority to grant or secure. All that cannot be so granted or secured are left under the protection of the States.

We now proceed to an examination of the indictment, to ascertain whether the several rights, which it is alleged the defendants intended to interfere with, are such as had been in law and in fact granted or secured by the constitution or laws of the United States.

The first and ninth counts state the intent of the defendants to have been to hinder and prevent the citizens named in the free exercise and enjoyment of their 'lawful right and privilege to peaceably assemble together with each other and with other citizens of the United States for a peaceful and lawful purpose.' The right of the people peaceably to assemble for lawful purposes existed long before the adoption of the Constitution of the United States. In fact, it is, and always has been, one of the attributes of citizenship under a free government. It 'derives its source,' to use the language of Chief Justice Marshall, in *Gibbons v. Ogden*, 9 Wheat. 211, 'from those laws whose authority is acknowledged by civilized man throughout the world.' It is found wherever civilization exists. It was not, therefore, a right granted to the people by the Constitution. The government of the United States when established found it in existence, with the obligation on the part of the States to afford it protection. As no direct power over it was granted to Congress, it remains, according to the ruling in *Gibbons v. Ogden*, id. 203, subject to State jurisdiction. [92 U.S. 542, 552] Only such existing rights were committed by the people to the protection of Congress as came within the general scope of the authority granted to the national government.

The first amendment to the Constitution prohibits Congress from abridging 'the right of the people to assemble and to petition the government for a redress of grievances.' This, like the other amendments proposed and adopted at the same time, was not intended to limit the powers of the State governments in respect to their own citizens, but to operate upon the National government alone. *Barron v. The City of Baltimore,* 7 Pet. 250; *Lessee of Livingston v. Moore,* id. 551; Fox v. Ohio, 5 How. 434; *Smith v. Maryland,* 18 id. 76; *Withers v. Buckley,* 20 id. 90; *Pervear v. The Commonwealth,* 5 Wall. 479; *Twitchell v. The Commonwealth,* 7 id. 321; *Edwards v. Elliott,* 21 id. 557. It is now too late to question the correctness of this construction. As was said by the late Chief Justice, in *Twitchell v. The Commonwealth,* 7 Wall. 325, 'the scope and application of these amendments are no longer subjects of discussion here.' They left the authority of the States just where they found it, and added nothing to the already existing powers of the United States.

The particular amendment now under consideration assumes the existence of the right of the people to assemble for lawful purposes, and protects it against encroachment by Congress. The right was not created by the amendment; neither was its continuance guaranteed, except as against congressional interference. For their protection in its enjoyment, therefore, the people must look to the States. The power for that purpose was originally placed there, and it has never been surrendered to the United States.

The right of the people peaceably to assemble for the purpose of petitioning Congress for a redress of grievances, or for any thing else connected with the powers or the duties of the national government, is an attribute of national citizenship, and, as such, under the protection of, and guaranteed by, the United States. The very idea of a government, republican in form, implies a right on the part of its citizens to meet peaceably for consultation in respect to public affairs and to petition for a redress of grievances. If it had been alleged in **[92 U.S. 542, 553]** these counts that the object of the defendants was to prevent a meeting for such a purpose, the case would have been within the statute, and within the scope of the sovereignty of the United States. Such, however, is not the case. The offence, as stated in the indictment, will be made out, if it be shown that the object of the conspiracy was to prevent a meeting for any lawful purpose whatever.

The second and tenth counts are equally defective. The right there specified is that of 'bearing arms for a lawful purpose.' This is not a right granted by the Constitution. Neither is it in any manner dependent upon that instrument for its existence. The second amendment declares that it shall not be infringed; but this, as has been seen, means no more than that it shall not be infringed by Congress. This is one of the amendments that has no other effect than to restrict the powers of the national government, leaving the people to look for their protection against any violation by their fellow-citizens of the rights it recognizes, to what is called, in *The City of New York v. Miln,* 11 Pet. 139, the 'powers which relate to merely municipal legislation, or what was, perhaps, more properly called internal police,' 'not surrendered or restrained' by the Constitution of the United States.

The third and eleventh counts are even more objectionable. They charge the intent to have been to deprive the citizens named, they being in Louisiana, 'of their respective several lives and liberty of person without due process of law.' This is nothing else than alleging a conspiracy to falsely imprison or murder citizens of the United States, being within the territorial jurisdiction of the State of Louisiana. The rights of life and personal liberty are natural rights of man. 'To secure these rights,' says the Declaration of Independence, 'governments are instituted among men, deriving their just powers from the consent of the governed.' The very highest duty of the States, when they entered into the Union under the Constitution, was to protect all persons within their boundaries in the enjoyment of these 'unalienable rights with which they were endowed by their Creator.' Sovereignty, for this purpose, rests alone with the States. It is no more the duty or within the power of the United States to punish for a conspiracy **[92 U.S. 542, 554]** to falsely imprison or murder within a State, than it would be to punish for false imprisonment or murder itself.

The fourteenth amendment prohibits a State from depriving any person of life, liberty, or property, without due process of law; but this adds nothing to the rights of one citizen as against another. It simply furnishes an additional guaranty against any encroachment by the

States upon the fundamental rights which belong to every citizen as a member of society. As was said by Mr. Justice Johnson, in *Bank of Columbia v. Okely*, 4 Wheat. 244, it secures 'the individual from the arbitrary exercise of the powers of government, unrestrained by the established principles of private rights and distributive justice.' These counts in the indictment do not call for the exercise of any of the powers conferred by this provision in the amendment.

The fourth and twelfth counts charge the intent to have been to prevent and hinder the citizens named, who were of African descent and persons of color, in 'the free exercise and enjoyment of their several right and privilege to the full and equal benefit of all laws and proceedings, then and there, before that time, enacted or ordained by the said State of Louisiana and by the United States; and then and there, at that time, being in force in the said State and District of Louisiana aforesaid, for the security of their respective persons and property, then and there, at that time enjoyed at and within said State and District of Louisiana by white persons, being citizens of said State of Louisiana and the United States, for the protection of the persons and property of said white citizens.' There is no allegation that this was done because of the race or color of the persons conspired against. When stripped of its verbiage, the case as presented amounts to nothing more than that the defendants conspired to prevent certain citizens of the United States, being within the State of Louisiana, from enjoying the equal protection of the laws of the State and of the United States.

The fourteenth amendment prohibits a State from denying to any person within its jurisdiction the equal protection of the laws; but this provision does not, any more than the one which precedes it, and which we have just considered, add any thing **[92 U.S. 542, 555]** to the rights which one citizen has under the Constitution against another. The equality of the rights of citizens is a principle of republicanism. Every republican government is in duty bound to protect all its citizens in the enjoyment of this principle, if within its power. That duty was originally assumed by the States; and it still remains there. The only obligation resting upon the United States is to see that the States do not deny the right. This the amendment guarantees, but no more. The power of the national government is limited to the enforcement of this guaranty.

No question arises under the Civil Rights Act of April 9, 1866 (14 Stat. 27), which is intended for the protection of citizens of the United States in the enjoyment of certain rights, without discrimination on account of race, color, or previous condition of servitude, because, as has already been stated, it is nowhere alleged in these counts that the wrong contemplated against the rights of these citizens was on account of their race or color.

Another objection is made to these counts, that they are too vague and uncertain. This will be considered hereafter, in connection with the same objection to other counts.

The sixth and fourteenth counts state the intent of the defendants to have been to hinder and prevent the citizens named, being of African descent and, colored, 'in the free exercise and enjoyment of their several and respective right and privilege to vote at any election to be thereafter by law had and held by the people in and of the said State of Louisiana, or by the people of and in the parish of Grant aforesaid.' In *Minor v. Happersett*, 21 Wall. 178, we decided that the Constitution of the United States has not conferred the right of suffrage upon any one, and that the United States have no voters of their own creation in the States. In *United States v. Reese* et al., supra, p. 214, we hold that the fifteenth amendment has invested the citizens of the United States with a new constitutional right, which is, exemption from discrimination in the exercise of the elective franchise on account of race, color, or previous condition of servitude. From this it appears that the right of suffrage is not a necessary attribute of national citizenship; but that exemption from discrimination in the exercise of that right on **[92 U.S. 542, 556]** account of race, &c., is. The right to vote in the States comes from the States; but the right of exemption from the prohibited discrimination comes from the United States. The first has not been granted or secured by the Constitution of the United States; but the last has been.

Inasmuch, therefore, as it does not appear in these counts that the intent of the defendants was to prevent these parties from exercising their right to vote on account of their race, &c., it does not appear that it was their intent to interfere with any right granted or secured by the constitution or laws of the United States. We may suspect that race was the cause of the hostility; but it is not so averred. This is material to a description of the substance of the offence, and cannot be supplied by implication. Every thing essential must be charged positively, and not inferentially. The defect here is not in form, but in substance.

The seventh and fifteenth counts are no better than the sixth and fourteenth. The intent here charged is to put the parties named in great fear of bodily harm, and to injure and oppress them, because, being and having been in all things qualified, they had voted 'at an election before that time had and held according to law by the people of the said State of Louisiana, in said State, to wit, on the fourth day of November, A.D. 1872, and at divers other elections by the people of the State, also before that time had and held according to law.' There is nothing to show that the elections voted at were any other than State elections, or that the conspiracy was formed on account of the race of the parties against whom the conspirators were to act. The charge as made is really of nothing more than a conspiracy to commit a breach of the peace within a State. Certainly it will not be claimed that the United States have the power or are required to do mere police duly in the States. If a State cannot protect itself against domestic violence, the United States may, upon the call of the executive, when the legislature cannot be convened, lend their assistance for that purpose. This is a guaranty of the Constitution (art. 4, sect. 4); but it applies to no case like this.

We are, therefore, of the opinion that the first, second, third, fourth, sixth, seventh, ninth, tenth, eleventh, twelfth, fourteenth, **[92 U.S. 542, 557]** and fifteenth counts do not contain charges of a criminal nature made indictable under the laws of the United States, and that consequently they are not good and sufficient in law. They do not show that it was the intent of the defendants, by their conspiracy, to hinder or prevent the enjoyment of any right granted or secured by the Constitution.

We come now to consider the fifth and thirteenth and the eighth and sixteenth counts, which may be brought together for that purpose. The intent charged in the fifth and thirteenth is 'to hinder and prevent the parties in their respective free exercise and enjoyment of the rights, privileges, immunities, and protection granted and secured to them respectively as citizens of the United States, and as citizens of said State of Louisiana,' 'for the reason that they, . . . being then and there citizens of said State and of the United States, were persons of African descent and race, and persons of color, and not white citizens thereof;' and in the eighth and sixteenth, to hinder and prevent them 'in their several and respective free exercise and enjoyment of every, each, all, and singular the several rights and privileges granted and secured to them by the constitution and laws of the United States.' The same general statement of the rights to be interfered with is found in the fifth and thirteenth counts.

According to the view we take of these counts, the question is not whether it is enough, in general, to describe a statutory offence in the language of the statute, but whether the offence has here been described at all. The statute provides for the punishment of those who conspire 'to injure, oppress, threaten, or intimidate any citizen, with intent to prevent or hinder his free exercise and enjoyment of any right or privilege granted or secured to him by the constitution or laws of the United States.' These counts in the indictment charge, in substance, that the intent in this case was to hinder and prevent these citizens in the free exercise and enjoyment of 'every, each, all, and singular' the rights granted them by the Constitution, &c. There is no specification of any particular right. The language is broad enough to cover all.

In criminal cases, prosecuted under the laws of the United States, the accused has the constitutional right 'to be informed **[92 U.S. 542, 558]** of the nature and cause of the accusation.' Amend. VI. In *United States v. Mills*, 7 Pet. 142, this was construed to mean, that the indictment must set forth the offence 'with clearness and all necessary certainty, to apprise the accused of the crime with which he stands charged;' and in *United States v. Cook*, 17 Wall. 174, that 'every ingredient of which the offence is composed must be accurately and clearly alleged.' It is an elementary principle of criminal pleading, that where the definition of an offence, whether it be at common law or by statute, 'includes generic terms, it is not sufficient that the indictment shall charge the offence in the same generic terms as in the definition; but it must state the species,-it must descend to particulars. 1 Arch. Cr. Pr. and Pl., 291. The object of the indictment is, first, to furnish the accused with such a description of the charge against him as will enable him to make his defence, and avail himself of his conviction or acquittal for protection against a further prosecution for the same cause; and, second, to inform the court of the facts alleged, so that it may decide whether they are sufficient in law to support a conviction, if one should be had. For this, facts are to be stated, not conclusions of law alone. A crime is made up of acts and intent; and these must be set forth in the indictment, with reasonable particularity of time, place, and circumstances.

It is a crime to steal goods and chattels; but an indictment would be bad that did not specify with some degree of certainty the articles stolen. This, because the accused must be advised of the essential particulars of the charge against him, and the court must be able to decide whether the property taken was such as was the subject of larceny. So, too, it is in some States a crime for two or more persons to conspire to cheat and defraud another out of his property; but it has been held that an indictment for such an offence must contain allegations setting forth the means proposed to be used to accomplish the purpose. This, because, to make such a purpose criminal, the conspiracy must be to cheat and defraud in a mode made criminal by statute; and as all cheating and defrauding has not been made criminal, it is necessary for the indictment to state the means proposed, in order that the court **[92 U.S. 542, 559]** may see that they are in fact illegal. *State v. Parker*, 43 N. H. 83; *State v. Keach*, 40 Vt. 118; *Alderman v. The People*, 4 Mich. 414; *State v. Roberts*, 34 Me. 32. In Maine, it is an offence for two or more to conspire with the intent unlawfully and wickedly to commit any crime punishable by imprisonment in the State prison (State v. Roberts); but we think it will hardly be claimed that an indictment would be good under this statute, which charges the object of the conspiracy to have been 'unlawfully and wickedly to commit each, every, all, and singular the crimes punishable by imprisonment in the State prison.' All crimes are not so punishable. Whether a particular crime be such a one or not, is a question of law. The accused has, therefore, the right to have a specification of the charge against him in this respect, in order that he may decide whether he should present his defence by motion to quash, demurrer, or plea; and the court, that it may determine whether the facts will sustain the indictment. So here, the crime is made to consist in the unlawful combination with an intent to prevent the enjoyment of any right granted or secured by the Constitution, &c. All rights are not so granted or secured. Whether one is so or not is a question of law, to be decided by the court, not the prosecutor. Therefore, the indictment should state the particulars, to inform the court as well as the accused. It must be made to appear-that is to say, appears from the indictment, without going further-that the acts charged will, if proved, support a conviction for the offence alleged.

But it is needless to pursue the argument further. The conclusion is irresistible, that these counts are too vague and general. They lack the certainty and precision required by the established rules of criminal pleading. It follows that they are not good and sufficient in law. They are so defective that no judgment of conviction should be pronounced upon them.

The order of the Circuit Court arresting the judgment upon the verdict is, therefore, affirmed; and the cause remanded, with instructions to discharge the defendants.

Mr. Justice **CLIFFORD** dissenting.

0I concur that the judgment in this case should be arrested, but for reasons quite different from those given by the court. **[92 U.S. 542, 560]** Power is vested in Congress to enforce by appropriate legislation the prohibition contained in the fourteenth amendment of the Constitution; and the fifth section of the Enforcement Act provides to the effect, that persons who prevent, hinder, control, or intimidate, or who attempt to prevent, hinder, control, or intimidate, any person to whom the right of suffrage is secured or guaranteed by that amendment, from exercising, or in exercising such right, by means of bribery or threats; of depriving such person of employment or occupation; or of ejecting such person from rented house, lands, or other property; or by threats of refusing to renew leases or contracts for labor;

or by threats of violence to himself or family,-such person so offending shall be deemed guilty of a misdemeanor, and, on conviction thereof, shall be fined or imprisoned, or both, as therein provided. 16 Stat. 141.

Provision is also made, by sect. 6 of the same act, that, if two or more persons shall band or conspire together, or go in disguise, upon the public highway, or upon the premises of another, with intent to violate any provision of that act, or to injure, oppress, threaten, or intimidate any citizen with intent to prevent or hinder his free exercise and enjoyment of any right or privilege granted or secured to him by the constitution and laws of the United States, or because of his having exercised the same, such persons shall be deemed guilty of felony, and, on conviction thereof, shall be fined or imprisoned, or both, and be further punished as therein provided.

More than one hundred persons were jointly indicted at the April Term, 1873, of the Circuit Court of the United States for the District of Louisiana, charged with offences in violation of the provisions of the Enforcement Act. By the record, it appears that the indictment contained thirty-two counts, in two series of sixteen counts each: that the first series were drawn under the fifth and sixth sections of the act; and that the second series were drawn under the seventh section of the same act; and that the latter series charged that the prisoners are guilty of murder committed by them in the act of violating some of the provisions of the two preceding sections of that act.

Eight of the persons named in the indictment appeared on **[92 U.S. 542, 561]** the 10th of June, 1874, and went to trial under the plea of not guilty, previously entered at the time of their arraignment. Three of those who went to trial-to wit, the three defendants named in the transcript-were found guilty by the jury on the first series of the counts of the indictment, and not guilty on the second series of the counts in the same indictment.

Subsequently the convicted defendants filed a motion for a new trial, which motion being overruled they filed a motion in arrest of judgment. Hearing was had upon that motion; and the opinions of the judges of the Circuit Court being opposed, the matter in difference was duly certified to this court, the question being whether the motion in arrest of judgment ought to be granted or denied.

Two only of the causes of arrest assigned in the motion will be considered in answering the questions certified: (1.) Because the matters and things set forth and charged in the several counts in question do not constitute offences against the laws of the United States, and do not come within the purview, true intent, and meaning of the Enforcement Act. (2.) Because the several counts of the indictment in question are too vague, insufficient, and uncertain to afford the accused proper notice to plead and prepare their defence, and do not set forth any offence defined by the Enforcement Act.

Four other causes of arrest were assigned; but, in the view taken of the case, it will be sufficient to examine the two causes above set forth.

Since the questions were certified into this court, the parties have been fully heard in respect to all the questions presented for decision in the transcript. Questions not pressed at the argument will not be considered; and, inasmuch as the counsel in behalf of the United States confined their arguments entirely to the thirteenth, fourteenth, and sixteenth counts of the first series in the indictment, the answers may well be limited to these counts, the others being virtually abandoned. Mere introductory allegations will be omitted as unimportant, for the reason that the questions to be answered relate to the allegations of the respective counts describing the offence.

As described in the thirteenth count, the charge is, that the **[92 U.S. 542, 562]** defendants did, at the time and place mentioned, combine, conspire, and confederated together, between and among themselves, for and with the unlawful and felonious intent and purpose one Levi Nelson and one Alexander Tillman, each of whom being then and there a citizen of the United States, of African descent, and a person of color, unlawfully and feloniously to injure, oppress, threaten, and intimidate, with the unlawful and felonious intent thereby the said persons of color, respectively, then and there to hinder and prevent in their respective and several free exercise and enjoyment of the rights, privileges, and immunities, and protection, granted and secured to them respectively as citizens of the United States and citizens of the State, by reason of their race and color; and because that they, the said persons of color, being then and there citizens of the State and of the United States, were then and there persons of African descent and race, and persons of color, and not white citizens thereof; the same being a right or privilege granted or secured to the said persons of color respectively, in common with all other good citizens of the United States, by the Federal Constitution and the laws of Congress.

Matters of law conceded, in the opinion of the court, may be assumed to be correct without argument; and, if so, then discussion is not necessary to show that every ingredient of which an offence is composed must be accurately and clearly alleged in the indictment, or the indictment will be bad, and may be quashed on motion, or the judgment may be arrested before sentence, or be reversed on a writ of error. *United States v. Cook*, 17 Wall. 174.

Offences created by statute, as well as offences at common law, must be accurately and clearly described in an indictment; and, if the offence cannot be so described without expanding the allegations beyond the mere words of the statute, then it is clear that the allegations of the indictment must be expanded to that extent, as it is universally true that no indictment is sufficient which does not accurately and clearly allege all the ingredients of which the offence is composed, so as to bring the accused within the true intent and meaning of the statute defining the offence. Authorities of great weight, besides those referred to by me, in the dissenting opinion just read, **[92 U.S. 542, 563]** may be found in support of that proposition. 2 East, P. C. 1124; *Dord v. People*, 9 Barb. 675; *Ike v. State*, 23 Miss. 525; *State v. Eldridge*, 7 Eng. 608.

Every offence consists of certain acts done or omitted under certain circumstances; and, in the indictment for the offence, it is not sufficient to charge the accused generally with having committed the offence, but all the circumstances constituting the offence must be specially set forth. Arch. Cr. Pl., 15th ed., 43.

Persons born on naturalized in the United States, and subject to the jurisdiction thereof, are citizens thereof; and the fourteenth amendment also provides, that no State shall make or enforce any law which shall abridge the privileges or immunities of citizens of the United States. Congress may, doubtless, prohibit any violation of that provision, and may provide that any person convicted of violating the same shall be guilty of an offence, and be subject to such reasonable punishment as Congress may prescribe.

Conspiracies of the kind described in the introductory clause of the sixth section of the Enforcement Act are explicitly forbidden by the subsequent clauses of the same section; and it may be that if the indictment was for a conspiracy at common law, and was pending in a tribunal having jurisdiction of common-law offences, the indictment in its present form might be sufficient, even though it contains no definite allegation whatever of any particular overt act committed by the defendants in pursuance of the alleged conspiracy.

Decided cases may doubtless be found in which it is held that an indictment for a conspiracy, at common law, may be sustained where there is an unlawful agreement between two or more persons to do an unlawful act, or to do a lawful act by unlawful means; and authorities may be referred to which support the proposition, that the indictment, if the conspiracy is well pleaded, is sufficient, even though it be not alleged that any overt act had been done in pursuance of the unlawful combination.

Suffice it to say, however, that the authorities to that effect are opposed by another class of authorities equally respectable, and even more numerous, which decide that the indictment is **[92 U.S. 542, 564]** bad unless it is alleged that some overt act was committed in pursuance of the intent and purpose of the alleged conspiracy; and in all the latter class of cases it is held, that the overt act, as well as the unlawful combination, must be clearly and accurately alleged.

Two reasons of a conclusive nature, however, may be assigned which show, beyond all doubt, that it is not necessary to enter into the inquiry which class of those decisions is correct.

1. Because the common law is *not a source of jurisdiction* in the circuit courts, nor in any other Federal court.

Circuit Courts have no common-law jurisdiction of offences of any grade or description; and it is equally clear that the appellate jurisdiction of the Supreme Court does not extend to any case or any question, in a case not within the jurisdiction of the subordinate Federal courts. *State v. Wheeling Bridge Co.*, 13 How. 503; *United States v. Hudson et al.*, 7 Cranch, 32.

2. Because it is conceded that the offence described in the indictment is an offence created and defined by an act of Congress.

Indictments for offences created and defined by statute must in all cases follow the words of the statute: and, where there is no departure from that rule, the indictment is in general sufficient, except in cases where the statute is elliptical, or where, by necessary implication, other constituents are component parts of the offence; as where the words of the statute defining the offence have a compound signification, or are enlarged by what immediately precedes or follows the words describing the offence, and in the same connection. Cases of the kind do arise, as where, in the dissenting opinion in *United States v. Reese et al.*, supra, p. 222, it was held, that the words *offer to pay a capitation tax* were so expanded by a succeeding clause of the same sentence that the word 'offer' necessarily included readiness to perform what was offered, the provision being that the offer should be equivalent to actual performance if the offer failed to be carried into execution by the wrongful act or omission of the party to whom the offer was made.

Two offences are in fact created and defined by the sixth section of the Enforcement Act, both of which consist of a **[92 U.S. 542, 565]** conspiracy with an intent to perpetrate a forbidden act. They are alike in respect to the conspiracy; but differ very widely in respect to the act embraced in the prohibition.

1. Persons, two or more, are forbidden to band or conspire together, or go in disguise upon the public highway, or on the premises of another, with *intent to violate* any provision of the Enforcement Act, which is an act of twenty-three sections.

Much discussion of that clause is certainly unnecessary, as no one of the counts under consideration is founded on it, or contains any allegations describing such an offence. Such a conspiracy with intent to injure, oppress, threaten, or intimidate any person, is also forbidden by the succeeding clause of that section, if it be done with intent to prevent or hinder his free exercise and enjoyment of *any right or privilege* granted or secured to him by the constitution or laws of the United States, or because of having exercised the same. Sufficient appears in the thirteenth count to warrant the conclusion, that the grand jury intended to charge the defendants with the second offence created and defined in the sixth section of the Enforcement Act.

Indefinite and vague as the description of the offence there defined, is, it is obvious that it is greatly more so as described in the allegations of the thirteenth count. By the act of Congress, the prohibition is extended to *any right or privilege* granted or secured by the constitution or laws of Congress; leaving it to the pleader to specify the particular right or privilege which had been invaded, in order to give the accusation that certainty which the rules of criminal pleading everywhere require in an indictment; but the pleader in this case, overlooking any necessity for any such specification, and making no attempt to comply with the rules of criminal pleading in that regard, describes the supposed offence in terms much more vague and indefinite than those employed in the act of Congress.

Instead of specifying the particular right or privilege which had been invaded, the pleader proceeds to allege that the defendants, with all the others named in the indictment, did combine, conspire, and confederate together, with the unlawful intent and purpose the said persons of African descent and **[92 U.S. 542, 566]** persons of color then and there to injure, oppress, threaten, and intimidate, and thereby then and there to hinder and prevent them in the free exercise and enjoyment of the *rights, privileges, and immunities and protection* granted and secured to them as citizens of the United States and citizens of the State, without any other specification of the rights, privileges, immunities, and protection which had been violated or invaded, or which were threatened, except what follows; to wit, the same being a right or privilege granted or secured in common with all other good citizens by the constitution and laws of the United States.

Vague and indefinite allegations of the kind are not sufficient to inform the accused in a criminal prosecution of the nature and cause of the accusation against him, within the meaning of the sixth amendment of the Constitution.

Valuable rights and privileges, almost without number, are granted and secured to citizens by the constitution and laws of Congress; none of which may be, with impunity, invaded in violation of the prohibition contained in that section. Congress intended by that provision to protect citizens in the enjoyment of all such rights and privileges; but in affording such protection in the mode there provided Congress never intended to open the door to the invasion of the rule requiring certainty in criminal pleading, which for ages has been regarded as one of the great safeguards of the citizen against oppressive and groundless prosecutions.

Judge Story says the indictment must charge the time and place and nature and circumstances of the offence with clearness and certainty, so that the party may have full notice of the charge, and be able to make his defence with all reasonable knowledge and ability. 2 Story, Const., sect. 1785

Nothing need be added to show that the fourteenth count is founded upon the same clause in the sixth section of the Enforcement Act as the thirteenth count, which will supersede the necessity of any extended remarks to explain the nature and character of the offence there created and defined. Enough has already been remarked to show that that particular clause of the section was passed to protect citizens in the free exercise and enjoyment of every right or privilege granted [**92 U.S. 542, 567**] or secured to them by the constitution and laws of Congress, and to provide for the punishment of those who band or conspire together, in the manner described, to injure, oppress, or intimidate any citizen, to prevent or hinder him from the free exercise and enjoyment of all such rights or privileges, or because of his having exercised any such right or privilege so granted or secured.

What is charged in the fourteenth count is, that the defendants did combine, conspire, and confederate the said citizens of African descent and persons of color to injure, oppress, threaten, and intimidate, with intent the said citizens thereby to prevent and hinder in the free exercise and enjoyment of the right and privilege to vote *at any election to be thereafter had and held* according to law by the people of the State, or by the people of the parish; they, the defendants, well knowing that the said citizens were lawfully qualified to vote at any such election thereafter to be had and held.

Confessedly, some of the defects existing in the preceding count are avoided in the count in question; as, for example, the description of the particular right or privilege of the said citizens which it was the intent of the defendants to invade is clearly alleged; but the difficulty in the count is, that it does not allege for what purpose the election or elections were to be ordered, nor when or where the elections were to be had and held. All that is alleged upon the subject is, that it was the intent of the defendants to prevent and hinder the said citizens of African descent and persons of color in the free exercise and enjoyment of the right and privilege to vote *at any election thereafter to be had and held*, according to law, by the people of the State, or by the people of the parish, without any other allegation whatever as to the purpose of the election, or any allegation as to the time and place when and where the election was to be had and held.

Elections thereafter to be held must mean something different from pending elections; but whether the pleader means to charge that the intent and purpose of the alleged conspiracy extended only to the next succeeding elections to be held in the State or parish, or to all future elections to be held in the State or parish during the lifetime of the parties, may admit of [**92 U.S. 542, 568**] a serious question, which cannot be easily solved by any thing contained in the allegations of the count.

Reasonable certainty, all will agree, is required in criminal pleading; and if so it must be conceded, we think, that the allegation in question fails to comply with that requirement. Accused persons, as matter of common justice, ought to have the charge against them set forth in such terms that they may readily understand the nature and character of the accusation, in order that they, when arraigned, may know what answer to make to it, and that they may not be embarrassed in conducting their defence; and the charge ought also to be laid in such terms that, if the party accused is put to trial, the verdict and judgment may be pleaded in bar of a second accusation for the same offence.

Tested by these considerations, it is quite clear that the fourteenth count is not sufficient to warrant the conviction and sentence of the accused.

Defects and imperfections of the same kind as those pointed out in the thirteenth count also exist in the sixteenth count, and of a more decided character in the latter count than in the former; conclusive proof of which will appear by a brief examination of a few of the most material allegations of the charge against the defendants. Suffice it to say, without entering into details, that the introductory allegations of the count are in all respects the same as in the thirteenth and fourteenth counts. None of the introductory allegations allege that any overt act was perpetrated in pursuance of the alleged conspiracy; but the jurors proceed to present that the unlawful and felonious intent and purpose of the defendants were to prevent and hinder the said citizens of African descent and persons of color, by the means therein described, in the free exercise and enjoyment *of each, every, all, and singular the several rights and privileges* granted and secured to them by the constitution and laws of the United States in common with all other good citizens, without any attempt to describe or designate any particular right or privilege which it was the purpose and intent of the defendants to invade, abridge, or deny.

Descriptive allegations in criminal pleading are required to be reasonably definite and certain, as a necessary safeguard **[92 U.S. 542, 569]** to the accused against surprise, misconception, and error in conducting his defence, and in order that the judgment in the case may be a bar to a second accusation for the same charge. Considerations of the kind are entitled to respect; but it is obvious, that, if such a description of the ingredient of an offence created and defined by an act of Congress is held to be sufficient, the indictment must become a snare to the accused; as it is scarcely possible that an allegation can be framed which would be less certain, or more at variance with the universal rule that every ingredient of the offence must be clearly and accurately described so as to bring the defendant within the true intent and meaning of the provision defining the offence. Such a vague and indefinite description of a material ingredient of the offence is not a compliance with the rules of pleading in framing an indictment. On the contrary, such an indictment is insufficient, and must be held bad on demurrer or in arrest of judgment.

Certain other causes for arresting the judgment are assigned in the record, which deny the constitutionality of the Enforcement Act; but, having come to the conclusion that the indictment is insufficient, it is not necessary to consider that question.

United States Court of Appeal
U.S. v. Prudden, 424 F.2d 1021 (1970)

April 10, 1970.

(headnotes omitted)

[1021]
[1022]

Samuel S. Forman, Asst. U. S. Atty., Jacksonville, Fla., Joseph M. Walters, Asst. Atty. Gen., Joseph M. Howard, John M. Brant, Attys., Tax Div., U. S. Dept. of Justice, Washington D. C., Edward F. Boardman, U. S. Atty., John L. Briggs, U. S. Atty., Middle District of Florida, for plaintiff-appellant.

C. Harris Dittmar, Chester Bedell, Charles, P. Pillans, Jacksonville, Florida, for defendant-appellee; Bedell, Bedell, Dittmar, Smith & Zihmer, Jacksonville, Fla., of counsel.

Before John R. Brown, Chief Judge, and Coleman and Clark, Circuit Judges.

CLARK, Circuit Judge:

Horton R. Prudden was indicted on seventeen counts of evading taxes due the United States. On taxpayer's motion made prior to trial, the court below in a blanket order suppressed all statements made and all corporate and personal documents furnished by Prudden to a special agent of the Internal Revenue Service, together with all evidence obtained through or as a result of such statements or documentary evidence. Suppression was based on a finding that the Internal Revenue Service had obtained such statements and documents by engaging in a deliberate scheme to deceive Prudden in order to prevent his understanding that an investigation originally commenced by a revenue agent had materially altered at the time the special agent entered the case.[1] The United States chose to appeal the suppression order rather than to proceed to trial without the evidence thus suppressed. Since the record does not clearly and convincingly demonstrate a deliberate scheme to deceive and we reject the taxpayer's contention that be was entitled to *Miranda* warnings, we reverse.

The following facts are either undisputed or are stated most favorably to the taxpayer. On May 10, 1968, certain returns of The Florida Corporation of America (FCA) and [1023] its subsidiaries were assigned to Revenue Agent Lexow for the purpose of determining the correctness of the tax reported. At this time Lexow had been with the Internal Revenue Service about one year—he was still in training and was not a full-grade agent. Prudden was 50 years of age, a law school graduate and then employed as a security analyst for a member firm of the New York Stock Exchange. After learning that FCA was to be examined, Prudden telephoned Lexow at the Palm Beach office of the Internal Revenue Service from his home in Connecticut, stating that he was a director of FCA. He inquired if Lexow's examination was to cover FCA alone or its subsidiaries also and further asked if the examination was routine. Lexow replied that the examination would cover both FCA and its subsidiaries and that it was not routine; that the returns had been selected in Jacksonville to be examined and had been assigned to Lexow from there.

---

[1] 305 F.Supp 110 (M.D.Fla.1969)

The examination actually commenced on May 31 when Lexow contacted Mrs. Anne G. Smith, who was indicated on the returns to be the president of these corporations.[2] All of Lexow's subsequent examinations were made under the supervision of Mrs. Smith either with or without Prudden present. Prudden and Mrs. Smith were cooperative with Agent Lexow, furnishing him most of the documents he wished to examine and making copies for him at his request. By June 17 Lexow's examinations had disclosed what he considered to be possible indications of fraud. It appeared to Lexow that a Nassau based corporation, Research and Development, Ltd., might be skimming profits off one of FCA's subsidiaries. He further noted there was no indication as required on the return, that the Bahamian and American corporations were related. Lexow had also discovered information concerning a sale of stock which gave the appearance of having produced a large capital gain, but had been reported as a loss. By this time Lexow's investigation had also broadened to cover Prudden's personal returns. Lexow made no report of these suspicions to his superiors at this juncture because he wanted to pursue the examination further. A number of times during Lexow's audit Prudden told him that if they found anything wrong, he, Prudden, wished that Lexow would let him know so that it could be corrected and any tax due could be paid. Prudden was particularly insistent that Lexow advise him on how to handle several details of a particular stock sale. Lexow testified that it was possible that he did tell Prudden that when all the facts were known to him he would advise Prudden how a 52,000 dollar escrow item connected with the stock sale should be handled, but Prudden admits he never got this advice.

When a revenue agent discovers indicia of fraud in the course of an examination, the routine procedure requires that he refer a complete report of his findings to the Intelligence Division of the revenue service, which then determines whether it will assign a special agent to take charge of the case. On June 27, while Lexow's examination was continuing, he had his first discussions with other persons in his office about the possibility of referring the case to the Intelligence Division. Lexow began to write his referral report on July 3 and completed it on July 15. On July 9 he wrote Prudden requesting bank statements and canceled checks of Research and Development, Ltd., urging him to forward these documents to Lexow in order to save time and enable Lexow to proceed with his examination of FCA and its subsidiaries. He also complimented Prudden on his cooperation. A copy of this letter is set out in the margin.[3] It was not shown that Prudden ever furnished the documents requested to Lexow or his successors.

Lexow did not meet with Prudden or Mrs. Smith after July 9. On August 14, Lexow received advice from the Intelligence Division that it had decided to [1024] make a full-scale investigation. On August 29, after a telephone conversation with Mrs. Smith indicated that Prudden wanted a written request, Lexow wrote Prudden requesting that copies be made available to him of papers previously furnished but inadvertently left in the corporation's office. He also asked for a schedule which computed losses incurred from acts of an unfaithful employee. In this letter Lexow advised Prudden that he was being transferred at his own request, to an assignment that would permit him to return to college, and that Agent Lewis E. Stanley was to become the agent on the case. Lexow's letter requested Prudden to continue to

---

[2] Prudden testified that Mrs. Smith had merely been a statistician and at the time of these examinations she was not a corporate officer but was acting as an independent agent on an hourly pay basis. The ownership of substantially all the FCA stock was held in trusts, of which Prudden was co-trustee for his sons.

[3] "Dear Mr. Prudden: I presume that you have retrieved from storage the bank statements and canceled checks of Research and Development Ltd.'s two bank accounts. Please forward them to me in care of this office. By doing so, we will both benefit in that you will be saved a considerable amount of time upon your return to Florida and prior to your return, I will be able to proceed with my examination of F C A and subsidiaries. You have been most cooperative in furnishing information and in giving of your time in connection with this examination; therefore, I feel sure that you will give your immediate attention to this matter.

Sincerely,"

cooperate with Agent Stanley. A copy of this letter is set out in the margin.[4] On the date of this letter Lexow knew that Special Agent Edward M. Cohen was then in charge of the Prudden investigation, but his name was not mentioned to Prudden or Mrs. Smith.[5]

In several instances, Prudden refused to give Lexow requested documents which Prudden felt were outside the proper scope of Lexow's examination. Lexow once told Prudden that the Internal Revenue Service would never leave him alone until he produced some records for Research and Development, Ltd. Prudden took the position that such records did not have to be produced and, as stated, he never produced them. On one occasion when Lexow raised a question as to constructive ownership with Prudden, Prudden told Lexow not to attempt to tell him about the rules of constructive ownership, that that subject had been his specialty in law school and be had studied it for three years. On several occasions Prudden told Lexow that he, Lexow, was simply on a fishing expedition—trying only to gather facts that would support Lexow's preconceived conclusions. In his final letter to Lexow, Prudden stated that he was left with the impression that items were being singled out of context in order to attack his intentions as unfair and not forthright. He pointed out that he had frequently asked for the Internal Revenue Service's views but had never received a stable answer of any kind. He further offered to review with Agent Stanley "whatever context he may wish to go over," expressly including the summary of losses sustained due to activities of the unfaithful employee, which Lexow had previously requested.

On September 13, 1963, Revenue Agent Lewis E. Stanley wrote Prudden confirming a meeting on October 1, 1963 in Palm Beach. Although the letter did not mention him, Special Agent Cohen intended to and did meet with Prudden and Stanley. When Cohen and Stanley **[1025]** opened the meeting they identified themselves to Prudden as a special agent and a revenue agent respectively, and showed him their written credentials, which he examined. Cohen's credentials plainly carried the legend "Intelligence Division". Prudden testified that he did not know the significance of Cohen's designation as a special agent. They informed Prudden that they were there to make an audit and examination of his returns, the returns of his three sons and the returns of FCA and its eight subsidiaries. He was also told that the examination would include any other corporation or gift tax returns that be had filed. Neither Stanley nor Cohen ever stated to Prudden that a criminal investigation was being conducted or that the investigation they were making was being made to determine the possibility of fraud. Prudden was never given any warning nor was he ever advised that he had a right to remain silent or that any information furnished by him could be used against him in any subsequent

---

[4] "Dear Mr. Prudden:

Before you left on the 9th of August you made copies of some papers for me which I left in your office by mistake. I would appreciate it if you would have your Secretary, Mrs. Smith, make them available to me. It is necessary that I have them to properly verify your returns, The copies were of tine following three items: 1) a note from H. B. Bradford, CPA advising you on the proper way to handle costs relative to the sale of 1st S. E. stock which were incurred after the sale; 2) a list of 1st 8. B. subsidiaries with addresses and locations; and a) your letter to Kent, re: $52.800.00 escrowed money (it 18 not absolutely necessary that I have this).

A fourth item which I need but failed to ask for (during your last visit is a copy of the schedule you recently prepared showing a computation of the Palmer Fidelity loss.

At my request the Government is moving me to our Ocala, Florida office, in order that my wife and I can take advantage of the educational facilities at the University of Florida. Your return along with the others under examination are being transferred to Agent Lewis F. Stanley of this office. Please address all future correspondence to hint.

You have been most cooperative in this examination to date, I trust that you will extend the same courtesies to Agent Stanley.

Sincerely."

[5] Lexow testified that the information was sought to make his final report on the matter complete and that he did not withhold tile disclosure of Cohen's assignment because of any fear such disclosure would cut off the flow of information.

proceedings. All actions and procedures followed by Stanley and Cohen were in accord with what was then the Internal Revenue Service's standard procedure in such cases.

On December 21, 1964, Revenue Agent Stanley and Special Agent Cohen interviewed Prudden at the Internal Revenue Service Intelligence Division office. Prudden answered the questions asked him but refused to allow the conversation to be recorded. All other meetings between Prudden and the IRS agents were at Prudden's office at his convenience during regular business hours. The work of Special Agent Cohen and Agent Stanley extended over a period of some fifteen months. Prudden persisted in refusing records of the Bahamian corporation and records outside the years he felt were properly open. He continued to complain that the agents were fishing and criticized third-party investigations, but he also continued to cooperate within these limits with the agents' requests for information and records during the entire period.

I. NECESSARY WARNINGS AND ADVICE

Prudden contends that the evidence obtained after Special Agent Cohen entered the investigation must be suppressed because he, Prudden, was not warned and advised of his rights according to *Miranda v. Arizona*, 384 U.S. 436, 86 S.Ct. 1602, 16 L.Ed.2d 694 (1966).[6] We adhere to our prior rulings and reject this contention. However, the Supreme Court's ruling in *Mathis v. United States*, 391 U.S. 1, 88 S.Ct. 1503, 20 L.Ed.2d 381 (1968) reversing this court and holding that routine tax investigations are not immune from the Miranda requirements for warnings to be given to a person in custody, and two recent decisions from the Seventh Circuit which reach a result contrary to ours here,[7] indicate that we make a detailed review of this issue.

[1026] A recurrence to the constitutional foundation is always an appropriate beginning point. The Fifth Amendment's mandate is that no person shall be "compelled in any criminal case to be a witness against himself * * *."

Compulsion, a requisite to the invocation of the Amendment's protection against self-incrimination, was not attenuated in *Miranda*. The majority opinion in *Miranda* is complex and lengthy but the following pertinent extracts highlight the problem presented and explain the controlling principles. In the preface the court epitomized the decision's meaning thusly:

"Our holding will be spelled out with some specificity in the pages which follow but briefly stated it is this: the prosecution may not use statements, whether exculpatory or inculpatory, stemming from custodial interrogation of the defendant unless it demonstrates the use of procedural safeguards effective to secure the privilege against self-incrimination. By custodial interrogation, we mean questioning initiated by law enforcement officers after a person has been taken into custody or otherwise deprived of his freedom of action in any significant way."

(384 U.S. at 444, 86 S.Ct at 1612)

Part I began with the following paragraph:

"The constitutional issue we decide in each of these cases is the admissibility of

---

[6] Although the evidence in question was obtained prior to the decision in Miranda, the Supreme Court applied that decision to persons whose trials had not begun as of June 13, 1966, regardless of when the alleged constitutional infirmity occurred. Johnson v. New Jersey, 884 U.S. 719, 734, 86 S.Ct. 1772, 1781, 16 L.Ed.2d 882 (1966). In Jenkins v. Delaware, 395 U.S. 213, 89 S.Ct. 1677, 23 L.Ed.2d 253 (1969), the Court limited the retroactivity of the rule by refusing to apply it to retrials commenced after the date of the decision even though the original trial preceded Miranda. It is appropriate to here note that the District Court was under the impression that Prudden did not rely on Miranda and the order suppressing evidence was expressly declared to be independent of any application of Miranda to the instant case. The constitutional dimensions of that rule and the fact that this cause must be remanded for further proceedings where the point might be raised, indicate that we should rule on it now.

[7] United States v. Dickerson, 413 F.2d 1111 (7th Cir. 1969), and United States v. Habig, 413 F.2d 1108 (7th Cir. 1969), cert. den., 398 U.S. 1014, 90 S.Ct. 559, 24 L.Ed.2d 506 (1970) (The Miranda issue was not presented to the Court in the Application for Writ of Certiorari,). See also United States v. Campione, 416 F.2d 486 (7th Cir. 1969).

statements obtained from a defendant questioned while in custody or otherwise deprived of his freedom of action in any significant way. In each, the defendant was questioned by police officers, detectives, or a prosecuting attorney in a room in which he was cut off from the outside world. In none of these cases was the defendant given a full and effective warning of his rights at the outset of the interrogation process. In all the cases, the questioning elicited oral admissions, and in three of them, signed statements as well which were admitted at their trials. They all thus share salient features—incommunicado interrogation of individuals in a police-dominated atmosphere, resulting in self-incriminating statements without full warnings of constitutional rights." (384 U.S. at 445, 86 S.Ct. at 1612)

The Court continued by pointing out that sophisticated psychological techniques had been developed by police to supplant the oft condemned use of physical force to extort confessions, the key to which called for isolating suspects from familiar surroundings and friends. It distilled the new techniques this way:

"From these representative samples of interrogation techniques, the setting prescribed by the manuals and observed in practice becomes clear. In essence, it is this: To be alone with the subject is essential to prevent distraction and to deprive him of any outside support. The aura of confidence in his guilt undermines his will to resist."

(384 U.S. at 455, 86 S.Ct. at 1617)

and concluded thusly:

"In each of the cases, the defendant was thrust into an unfamiliar atmosphere and run through menacing police interrogation procedures. The potentiality for compulsion is forcefully apparent, * * *. It is obvious that such an interrogation environment is created for no purpose other than to subjugate the individual to the will of his examiner. This atmosphere carries its own badge of intimidation."

(384 U.S. at 457, 86 S.Ct. at 1618)

Part II traced the history of the privilege, its embodiment in our Constitution and its subsequent court implementations down through Escobedo v. Illinois, 378 U.S. 479, 84 S.Ct. 1758, 12 L.Ed.2d 977 (1964), with this application of the latter's rationale:

"The entire thrust of police interrogation there, as in all the cases today, was to put the defendant in such an emotional state as to impair his capacity for rational judgment. The abdication [1027] of the constitutional privilege the choice on his part to speak to the police was not made knowingly or competently because of the failure to apprise him of his rights; the compelling atmosphere of the in-custody interrogation, and not an independent decision on his part, caused the defendant to speak."

(384 U.S. at 465, 86 S.Ct. at 1623)

Part III demonstrated how the rule announced was to be employed and detailed the justification for tendering an attorney's advice. It closed with this caveat:

"Our decision is not intended to hamper the traditional function of police officers in investigating crime. See Escobedo V. State of Illinois, 378 U.S. 478, 492, 84 S.Ct 1758, 1765. When an individual is in custody on probable cause, the police may, of course, seek out evidence in the field to be used at trial against him. Such investigation may include inquiry of persons not under restraint. General on-the-scene questioning as to facts surrounding a crime or other general questioning of citizens the fact-finding process is not affected by our holding. It is an act of responsible citizenship for individuals to give whatever information they may have to aid in law enforcement. In such situations the compelling atmosphere inherent in the process of in-custody interrogation is not necessarily present.46

46. "The distinction and its significance has been aptly described in the opinion of a Scottish court:

'In former times such questioning, if undertaken, would be conducted by police officers visiting the house or place of business of the suspect and there questioning him, probably in the presence of a relation or friend. However convenient the modern practice may be, it must normally create a situation very unfavorable to the suspect.' Chalmers v. H. M. Advocate [1954] Sess.Cas. 66, 78 (J.C.)."

"In dealing with statements obtained through interrogation, we do not purport to find al confessions inadmissible. Confessions remain a proper element in law enforcement. Any statement given freely and voluntary without any compelling influences is, of course, admissible in evidence. The fundamental import of the privilege while an individual is in custody is not whether he is allowed to talk to the police without the benefit of warnings and counsel, but whether he can be interrogated. There is no requirement that police stop a person who enters a police station and states that he wishes to confess to a crime, or a person who calls the police to offer a confession or any other statement he desires to make. Volunteered statements of any kind are not barred by the Fifth Amendment and their admissibility is not affected by our holding today." (364 U.S. at 477, 478, 86 S.Ct. at 1629-1630), Cf. *United States V. Robertson*, 425 F.2d 1386 (8th Cir. 1970).

In *Mathis V. United States*, supra, the taxpayer was convicted of tax fraud on the basis of evidence elicited by a regular revenue agent on a routine investigation made while the taxpayer was in prison for an unrelated crime. The Supreme Court reversed our affirmance of the conviction because the prisoner had not been given the *Miranda* warnings. Although Mathis makes it clear that *Miranda* is potentially applicable to any tax investigation, it most definitely does not require *Miranda* warnings in all tax investigations. Mathis in no way diminishes the necessity for showing actual or inherent compulsion to self-incrimination. Mathis was not merely at the station house, he was imprisoned for a fixed term. He was deprived of his liberty in a most positive way. Thus when the court established that the type of inquiry there present was not determinative, the result was necessarily a finding of Fifth Amendment violation. **[1028]**

In our view, the Seventh Circuit's recent opinion in *United States V. Dickerson*, supra, which petitioner urges we now adopt, is an unwarranted extension of the *Miranda* decision. *Dickerson* held that *Miranda* warnings must be given a taxpayer at the inception of first contact with him following the transfer of a tax case to the Intelligence Division. The facts recited in that opinion show no element of custody or restraint—no deprivation of freedom—no compelling atmosphere—only a visit by a regular and a special agent of the Internal Revenue Service to defendant at his place of business. The opinion stated:

"We understand the teaching of Miranda to be that one confronted with governmental authority in an adversary situation should be accorded the opportunity to make an intelligent decision as to the assertion or relinquishment of those constitutional rights designed to protect him under precisely such circumstances." 413 F.2d at 1114.

Thus, the court inferred compulsion from the fact that the investigators represented "governmental authority in an adversary situation." Such a rule is over broad and we expressly decline to follow it.

We cannot agree that every administrative official who confronts a citizen with a request for information that might disclose criminal conduct, thereby exerts a compulsion on the citizen that must be dispelled by the *Miranda* placebo. In today's vast and complex network of widespread daily administrative contacts between citizens and government officials, such a holding would open a veritable Pandora's box. When a census taker returns to recheck information he has received or a building inspector comes to investigate a report of noncompliance with provisions of the city housing code or a game warden who hears shooting out-of-season stops a man he finds in the woods or a bank examiner questions a teller whose figures are out of balance, would each then have to give the *Miranda* warnings? In each case a governmental official is confronting a citizen and criminal charges may result. There are a thousand and one administrative inquiries routinely made every day in every city which could evoke responses that might form a part of the basis in proof for a charge of perjury, falsification

---

[8] We held that routine tax investigations were not criminal in nature, and thus were beyond the protection of the Fifth Amendment without regard to the presence or absence of compulsion. *Mathis v. United States*, 376 F.2d 595 (5th Cir. 1967).

of records, failure to file a report or perform a legal duty or other criminal conduct. Most of these routine administrative confrontations would be rendered ineffective to the citizen and his government by imposing *Miranda* requirements. Indeed, if the warning became too commonplace, the very purpose of its requirement could be undermined. If "authority" were allowed to supplant custody—the deprivation of freedom—as the determinant of compulsion, even these routine field investigations which *Miranda* expressly exempted must fall. Under such a rule a policeman upon stopping a motorist could not ask to see his license without warning him and advising him in full.[9] It is not for this Court to so extend *Miranda*, and we are particularly unwilling to extend it to an adult experienced businessman, a law school graduate, who for over a year voluntarily furnished selected corporate and personal records to tax agents—not claimed to be overbearing but over kind.[10] **[1029]**

The record shows that Prudden's interviews with all the agents were on generally amicable terms — what Prudden described as a "normal business arrangement." He limited the information he gave the agents, specifically refusing to give them requested information from years not under examination and the records of the Bahamian subsidiary. He testified that he was never threatened. He even testified that Lexow once told him that the Internal Revenue Service would not leave him alone unless he produced the Bahamian company records, yet he never produced them. There was simply no factual support for a contention that Prudden was put in such an emotional state as to impair his capacity for rational judgment.

Moreover, there is no evidence that the incriminating evidence was coerced as a matter of law; i.e., was the result of in-custody interrogation or anything approaching comparable pressures.[11] None of the evidence that Prudden seeks to suppress was obtained while he was under arrest or under any sort of actual or implied restraint. In fact, Prudden's fraud, deceit and trickery contentions strongly militate against any thought of pressure. The basic thrust of this other contention is that the agents were too nice to him. He was never deprived of his freedom in any significant way during the questioned interviews, all but one of which took place at his own office at his convenience during regular office hours.[12] The one interview which occurred

---

[9] Cf, *United States v. Marlow*, 428 F.2d 1064 (5th Cir. 1970), where a routine request for a driver's license made without *Miranda* warnings produced a wrongfully acquired credit card that led to the driver's conviction for obstructing the mails.

[10] There are other incongruities in *Dickerson*. It purports to apply *Mathis* but admittedly does not use *Mathis'* standard. In *Mathis* a routine examination by a regular revenue agent prior to any reference of the case to the Intelligence Division of the Revenue Service, was voided. Dickerson does not apply this rule, it admits incriminations by the taxpayer produced by the regular agent and only suppresses information obtained after the case had been transferred to the Intelligence Division. Since *Mathis* did not recognize any distinction between the regular and special agent, the compulsive effect of the agent's official status is identical. Unless the regulations of the Internal Revenue Service are changed or United States v. Heffner infra. n. 12, is not followed, *Dickerson* will have no effect as precedent. Prior to its rendition, the Revenue Service adopted a relation requiring special agents to give *Miranda* type warnings on their first contact with taxpayers. In recognition of the fact that *Dickerson* represented a departure from the present state of the law, the court determined that its holding would only apply to interrogations taking place after the date of the decision. Thus only *Dickerson* and the taxpayer in the companion case of *Habig* will be affected. If Prudden's ease were now presented to that circuit ht would get no benefit from that ruling since the investigations here involved took place in 1963 and 1964.

[11] The Supreme Court in *Miranda*, defined custodial interrogation to mean questioning a initiated by law enforcement officers after a person has been taken into custody or otherwise deprived of his freedom in any significant way. The Court also emphasized that the "salient features" of the cases there decided showed "incommunicado interrogation of individuals in a police-dominated atmosphere." 348 U.S. at 445, 86 S.Ct. at 1612.

[12] We recognize that custodial interrogation can occur beyond the confines of the station house. For example, in Orozco v. Texas, 394 U.S. 324, 89 S.Ct 1095, 22 L.Ed.2d 311 (1960), the Court applied Miranda to incriminating evidence obtained by questioning the suspect in his own room in a boarding house. The suspect was alone and in the custody of four police officers who questioned him. Under those circumstances, Orozco was held to be significantly deprived of his freedom. But Orozco merely

in the Internal Revenue Service office is of no consequence. He came to the office voluntarily and was not restrained from leaving whenever he chose. The courts have uniformly held that such office interviews are neither custodial nor do they impose any significant restraints of freedom.[13] **[1030]**

In applying *Miranda's* rule, this Circuit has taken a case-by-case approach on the theory that "to foster proper development of controlling precedent * * * each case must be examined to determine whether there were present the compulsive factors with which *Miranda* was concerned." *United States v. Montos*, 421 F.2d 215, 223 (5th Cir. 1970). All of our case-by-case holdings have uniformly applied one concept—that *Miranda* warnings are not constitutionally required in tax investigation cases where the taxpayer is not deprived of his freedom and is not actually compelled or coerced to furnish statements or documents. Such holdings and our ruling here are also consistent with other circuits.[14] Our most recent decisions have maintained a similar consistency of approach. In *Agoranos v. United States*, 409 F.2d 833 (5th Cir.), cert. den., 396 U.S. 824, 90 S.Ct. 67, 24 L.Ed.2d 75 (1969) the taxpayer sought reversal of a tax fraud conviction because he had not been given Miranda warnings. We refused to reverse because at the time the taxpayer was questioned by the special agent he "was not in custody and the Miranda doctrine applies only to in-custody interrogation."[15] Prudden seeks to distinguish *Agoranos* because the special agent did not know at the time of the questioning that the taxpayer was being investigated, but such an attempted distinction misses the true thrust of that holding—the taxpayer was not in custody or under compulsion when the interview took place. In *United States v. Jernigan*, 411 F.2d 471 (5th Cir.), cert. den., 396 U.S. 927, 90 S.Ct. 262, 24 L.Ed.2d 225 (1969) we again refused to require *Miranda* warnings. Prudden's attempt to distinguish this case because the agent was a regular and not a special agent not only conflicts with *Mathia* but is not apropos to the point he makes. Regular agents

---

stands for the rule that "a compelling atmosphere" can exist outside of the station house, it does not hold that any inquiry by a government official carries such an element of intimidation as amounts to compulsion to self-incrimination. The majority opinion emphatically states: "We do not, as the dissent implies, expand or extend to the slightest extent our *Miranda* decision." See also *United States v. Lackey*, 413 F.2d 655 (7th Cir. 1969), where a recorded courthouse basement interrogation of the taxpayer alone was held to be within *Miranda's* ambit. No comparable significant deprivation of freedom or compelling atmosphere ever existed in the case now before us.

[13] See e.g., *Ping v. United States*, 407 F.2d 157 (8th Cir.), cert. den., 395 U.S. 926, 89 S.Ct. 1784, 23 L.Ed.2d 244 (1969); *Spinney v. United States,* 385 F.2d 908 (1st Cir.), cert. den., 390 U.S, 921, 88 S.Ct. 854, 19 L.Ed.2d 981 (1967); *Schlinsky v. United States*, 379 F.2d 735 (1st Cir.), cert. den., 389 U.S. 920, 88 S.Ct. 236, 19 L.Ed.2d 265 (1967).

[14] An exhaustive collection of such authorities is set out in United States v. Squeri. 398 F.2d 785, 789-790 (2d Cir. 1968). See also *United States v. White*, 417 F.2d 89, 91 (2d Cir, 1969), cert. den, 397 U.S. 912, 90 S.Ct. 910, 25 L.Ed.2d 92 (1970) in which the Second Circuit explicitly refused to follow *Dickerson*, and the cases there cited, and *Spahr v, United States*, 409 F.2d 1303 (9th Cir.), cert. den. 396 U.S. 840. 90 S.Ct 102, 24 L.Ed.2d 91 (1969). The only contrary authorities are the decisions of the Seventh Circuit in *United States v. Dickerson* and *United States v. Habig*, supra, and the District Court rulings noted in *Dickerson*, 413 F.2d at 1114, n. 6. See also *United States v. Casias*, 306 F.Supp. 166 (D.Colo.1969). Though not as circumscribed as *Dickeson*. our holding here may have limited effect as precedent for the same reason mentioned in note 8, supra. Since May of 1967 the Internal Revenue Service has required Special Agents to give the taxpayer all essential *Miranda* warnings and advice at their initial conference. See I.R.S. News Release IR-949 (1969 CCH Fed. Tax Rptr. 6946). The Fourth Circuit has recently held that in tax investigations occurring after the inception of this policy the IRS is required to comply with its own rule on the basis of *United States ex rel. Accardi v. Shaughnessy*, 347 U.S. 260, 74 S.Ct. 499, 98 L.Ed. 681 (1954). *United States v. Heffner,* 420 F.2d 809 (4th Cir. 1969). Since this question is not presented by this appeal, we refrain from expressing any direct opinion on it. It is appropriate, however, that we now note that our holding here accords no retroactive significance to the promulgation of this administrative policy. That the Internal Revenue Service has voluntarily taken upon itself to now give a taxpayer *Miranda* type warnings and advice at the Special Agent's first meeting with him, does not give taxpayers questioned before the promulgation of this order additional constitutional rights.

[15] 409 F.2d at 835.

frequently obtain evidence which later forms one or more links in the chain which affixes criminality to the acts of a tax evader.

Marcus v. United States, 422 F.2d 752 (5th Cir, 1970) is our latest decision which discusses this question. Marcus was convicted for failing to file individual tax returns. One ground of his appeal was that he had not been given *Miranda* warnings nor expressly told of the criminal nature of the investigation by special agents of the Internal Revenue Service until after he had supplied records [1031] and made damaging admissions.[16] Marcus contended, as Prudden now does, that Miranda applied to noncustodial tax fraud investigations. We rejected this contention with the statement: "In a criminal tax fraud case, this Court has recently held that the Miranda doctrine applies only to in-custody interrogation. *Agoranos v. United States*, 5 Cir., 1969, 409 F.2d 833. Since [the taxpayer] was at no time in custody during the Internal Revenue Service investigation, the contention is without merit."[17] Two recent cases before this court, *United States v, Roundtree*, 420 F.2d 845 (5th Cir, 1969) and *Stuart v. United States*, 416 F.2d 459 (5th Cir. 1969), concerned a related but distinguishable question. Those taxpayers claimed that enforcement of an Internal Revenue Service administrative summons would compel them to incriminate themselves. In those cases we recognized that a routine tax investigation may be criminal in nature. In *Roundtree* we stated that if the taxpayer can show that the proceeding had become an inquiry with dominant criminal overtones, he would be entitled to raise Fifth Amendment objections. Compulsion was present in *Roundtree* and *Stuart* in the form of the subpoena and the single remaining element necessary to invoke the Fifth Amendment's protection was the claim of self-incrimination. Even if Prudden could show that the inquiry into the tax liability of the corporation, himself and his family was one with dominant criminal overtones, be would fail to bring himself within *Miranda's* ambit because he cannot show compulsion.

II. THE CLAIM OF FRAUD, DECEIT AND TRICKERY

The trial judge suppressed all evidence obtained on or after the day when Lexow referred the case to the Intelligence Division because he found that the Internal Revenue Service agents engaged in a deliberate scheme to deceive Prudden in order to prevent his suspecting that the nature of the investigation had altered materially.[18] Here the ultimate fact determination was reached by a process of reasoning from undisputed evidentiary facts. After a careful review of the entire record, we conclude that ultimate fact finding—fraud, deceit and trickery by the agents—is a mistaken one.[19] We are left with the definite and firm conviction that this finding is in error.[20]

Because of the holding we make here it is unnecessary to discuss the breadth of the suppression order, reaching as it did not just persona records but corporate records in

---

[16] The facts in *Marcus*, which was decided after the instant appeal was argued, do differ from the case sub judice. In the words of that opinion:
"There is testimony in the record * * * that at the first interview the Internal Revenue agents informed Marcus that they were Special Agents attached to the Intelligence Division, which handles only criminal investigations, that he had a right to remain silent, and that any thing he said could be used against him. Likewise, it is undisputed that the agents failed to inform Marcus that he had a right to an attorney, as they were required to do if Marcus was entitled to a Miranda warning." 422 F.2d at 756.
These factual differences do not serve to distinguish *Marcus*, The rights protected by *Miranda* are constitutional in nature and if *Miranda* warnings and advices are required at all. They are all required for unconstitutionality knows no gradations.

[17] 422 F.2d at 756

[18] 305 F.Supp. at 111

[19] *Galena Oaks Corporation v. Scofield*, 218 F.2d. 217 (5th Cir 1954) *Mayo v. Pioneer Bank & Trust Co.*, 297 F.2d 392 (5th Cir. 1961).

[20] *United States v. United States Gypsum Co.*, 333 U.S. 364, 394-395, 68 S.Ct. 525, 541-542, 92 L.Ed. 746 (1948); *United States v. Singer Mfg. Co.*, 374 U.S. 174,194 n. 9, 88 S.Ct 1773, 1784 n. 9, 10 L.Ed.2d 823 (1968); *Minneapolis-Moline, Inc. v. Bryan*, 415 F.2d 841 (5th Cir.1969).

corporations with which Prudden was connected only as a director or an employee. No claim of privilege as to self-incrimination relative **[1032]** to this type of third party records has previously been recognized. See, e. g., *Hale v. Henkel*, 201 U.S 43, 26 S.Ct. 370, 50 L.Ed. 652 (1906); *Fineberg v. United States*, 393 F.2d 417 (9th Cir. 1968); *Hensley v. United States*, 406 F.2d 481 (10th Cir. 1968).

If the evidence obtained subsequent to Special Agent Cohen's entry into the investigation were the result of an unreasonable search in violation of the Fourth Amendment, then it would have to be suppressed. Prudden also asserts violation of Fifth and Sixth Amendment rights. Since all claimed violations depend upon a showing of the existence of fraud, deceit or trickery, it is not necessary to discuss each constitutional claim separately. Prudden postulates that the search was unreasonable because his consent to examine the records was obtained by fraud, deceit and trickery. While we recognize that fraud, deceit or trickery in obtaining access to incriminating evidence can make an otherwise lawful search unreasonable.[21] Prudden, as the moving party in the motion to suppress, did not sustain the burden that was his of demonstrating that fraud, deceit or trickery were present.[22]

The essence of Prudden's contention and the finding of the trial court is that the circumstances surrounding the transformation of the investigation into one with increased possibilities of resultant criminal charges without Prudden's knowledge, required suppression of the evidence.[23] Just how Prudden was defrauded, deceived or tricked is what we fail to perceive. Certainly, if the agents had given Prudden the full panoply of Miranda warnings, and advice, he could not make such a claim. *Miranda* warnings, however, were not required. So what were the agents required to do or leave undone or say or let go unsaid that discloses the fraud, deceit and trickery? They told him they wanted to audit and examine records in his possession relating to tar returns. They pursued this announced intention in what Prudden describes as a businesslike way at intervals over many months, despite his occasional expressions of discontent. We are unable to say that they had a duty to do more or less under the circumstances disclosed by this record.

Prudden points to the failure of Special Agent Cohen to tell him that his function was to investigate for criminal fraud. All Cohen was required to do by the then existing Internal Revenue Service requirements was to tell Prudden that he was a Special Agent and show Prudden his credentials. This he did. He in no way concealed his true identity. He could not have affirmatively mislead Prudden as to the function of the Intelligence Division or as to the duties of a special agent, since neither of these subjects were ever discussed. **Silence can only be equated with fraud where there is a legal or moral duty to speak or where an inquiry left unanswered would be intentionally misleading.**[24] None of these factors were present here.

In *Spahr v. United States*, supra note 21, one ground of taxpayer's appeal of **[1033]** his conviction for corporate tax evasion was that incriminating evidence was procured through guile and fraud. Allegedly the revenue agents fraudulently concealed the true purpose of their investigation. As in the instant case, two agents merely identified themselves as a special agent and a revenue agent, respectively, without giving any additional warnings. The Ninth Circuit

---

[21] *Gouled v. United States*, 255 U.S. 298, 41 S.Ct. 261, 65 L.Ed. 647 (1921); *Spahr v. United States*, 409 F.2d 1303 (9th Cir. 1959), cert. den., 396 U.S. 840, 90 S.Ct. 102, 24 L.Ed.2d 91 (1969): United States v. Sclafani, 265 F.2d 408 (2d Cir.), cert. den., 360 U.S. 918,79 S.Ct. 1436, 3 L.Ed. 2d 1584 (1959). We explicitly reject the government's contention that the agents were free to use fraud, deceit or trickery. In cases where the IRS agents are obtaining consent to examine documents, they cannot gain such consent by affirmatively misrepresenting the nature of the search.
[22] *Nardone v. United States*, 308 U.S. 338, 60 S.Ct. 266, 84 L.Ed.2d 307 (1939) *Deer Guardian v. United States*, 872 F.2d 697 (5th Cir. 1967)
[23] 305 F.Supp. at 111
[24] See *United States v. Sclafani*, 265 F.2d 408 (2d Cir.), cert. den., 360 U.S. 918, 79 S.Ct. 1436, 3 L.Ed.2d 1534 (1959); c. f., Avery v. Cleary, 132 U.S. 604, 10 S.Ct. 220, 38 L.Ed. 469 (1890); *Atilus v. United States*, 406 F.2d 694, 698 (5th Cir. 1969); *American Nat'l Ins. Co., etc. v. Murray*, 383 F.2d 81 (5th Cir. 1987)

found no deception. Quoting the Second Circuit's opinion in United States V. Sclafani, Supra note 21, they said:[25]

"A 'routine' tax investigation openly commenced as such is devoid of stealth or deceit because the ordinary taxpayer surely knows that there is inherent in it a warning that the government's agents will pursue evidence of misreporting without regard to the shadowy line between avoidance and evasion, mistake and willful omission."

In *Sclafani*, as in the instant case, the taxpayer objected that records obtained from him after the "routine audit" commenced by a revenue agent was turned over to a special agent should have been suppressed because they were obtained through stealth and deceit. The court found no fraud or deceit and stated:[26]

"The Fourth Amendment does not require more than this, that when his consent is sought the taxpayer be apprised of the government's concern with the accuracy of his reports, and therefore of such hazards as may be incident to a voluntary disclosure. We hold that Sclafani was so apprised by the warning inherent in the request when Agent Sonkin identified himself and disclosed his purpose to audit certain returns of the corporation."

We conclude that the mere failure of a revenue agent (be he regular or special) to warn the taxpayer that the investigation may result in criminal charges, absent any acts by the agent which materially misrepresent the nature of the inquiry, do not constitute fraud, deceit and trickery. Therefore, the record here must disclose some affirmative misrepresentation to establish the existence of fraud, and this showing must be clear and convincing.[27]

Prudden points to several incidents to establish the existence of affirmative misrepresentations by the Internal Revenue Service agents. He does not in any of these, however, establish fraud by clear and convincing proof, rather the evidence tends to show that fraud was not present.

Audit and Examination. Prudden seeks to distinguish Spahr and Sclafani because in those cases no affirmative acts of misrepresentation were shown. On the other hand, Prudden claims that Cohen's statement at the hearing that "we informed Mr. Prudden that we had come for an audit and examination of his returns—his son's returns, and the returns of the Florida Corporation of America and its eight subsidiaries" was affirmative misrepresentation in the case at bar. Telling Prudden that an audit and examination were to take place is not deceptive. That is exactly what the agents did. They audited and examined his books. That in so doing they uncovered incriminating evidence does not change the character of the investigation they undertook. Audit and examination is but one means of gathering evidence in a tax fraud case. Since the agents did not have to warn him directly that they were undertaking a criminal investigation, then telling him the means by which they were to gather evidence in no way is misleading. **[1034]**

Letters from Lexow to Prudden. Prudden contends that the two letters from Lexow fraudulently misrepresented the nature of the inquiry. The July 9th letter, which was written before the Intelligence Division came into the case but while Lexow was preparing to refer it to them, asked Prudden to send records of one of FCA's subsidiaries to him in order to facilitate big examination and to save Prudden time.[28] There are no misrepresentations of fact in the letter. Even if the letter had been misleading, Prudden complains of no evidence obtained as a result of it. In fact, the record does not show that he ever complied with the letter's request. Furthermore, the trial court's suppression order only applied to evidence obtained on or after August 14, a full month after the writing of the letter.

---

[25] 409 F.2d at 1306, quoting, 265 F.2d at 414-415
[26] 265 F.2d at 415. See *United States v. Squeri*, 398 F.2d 785, 788 (2d Cir. 1968): "[T]he information that a taxpayer's returns are under audit gives notice of the possibility of criminal prosecution regardless of whether the agents contemplate civil or criminal action when they speak to him."
[27] *Jett v. Zink*, 362 F.2d 723, 729 (5th Cir. 1066). cert. den., *Chaimberlain v. Zink*, 385 U.S. 987, 87 S.Ct. 597, 17 L.Ed.2d 448 (1967).
[28] This letter is set out at note 3 supra.

The second letter was written on August 28, two weeks after the referral of the case to the Intelligence Division without advising him of any change in the nature of the investigation. There is no evidence of guile by Lexow. He testified that he was only conscientiously trying to leave a complete record of all the facts he had previously accumulated for his successor. The documents he requested were those which Prudden had already authorized him to copy, but he had inadvertently left them in Prudden's office. Thus, nothing new was added to the government's case. Furthermore, the evidence received pursuant to this letter was exempted from the suppression order by the trial court, to which Prudden did not object. Secondly, Prudden contends that the letter was deceptive since Lexow's reference to the transfer of the case to Revenue Agent Stanley was calculated to raise no suspicion and specific mention that Special Agent Cohen of the Intelligence Division would henceforth be in charge of the investigation was omitted. Lexow testified that his omission of the Special Agent's assignment to the case was not made because he was afraid of the flow of information would be cut off. The only possible harm in this letter would be that Prudden would think that the entry into the case of a different agent was of no significance. Whatever momentary misapprehension in this direction that was left in Prudden's mind by the letter should have been quickly dispelled by the actual appearance not only of Revenue Agent Stanley but also Special Agent Cohen. In place of one neophyte, two experienced agents appeared and persisted in an examination and audit for fifteen months. At any rate, this contention falls far short of persuading us that the letter was fraudulent.

Friendliness of the Agents. Prudden argues that the nature of the investigation was concealed because of the friendliness and cordiality of the relationship between himself and the agents. Most of the evidence he cites as proof of deceit through cordiality is with regard to Lexow. Here again we are reminded that none of the information gathered by Lexow is subject to suppression. Even with regard to the more businesslike attitudes adopted by Cohen and Stanley, we perceive no possible subterfuge. We can see no reason why civil servants should be required in their daily dealings to assume an uncivil character just because they are in a position to discover criminality on the part of a citizen. That would be a poor form of warning at best. If direct warnings are unnecessary, then requiring circuitous warnings by the manner of action of the agents is irrational. Furthermore, the tone of every interpersonal relationship is subject to the control of all the parties. Prudden's own conduct was a necessary ingredient of the amicable relationship of which he now complains. It may well be that kindness on a taxpayer's part could be calculated to dispel an agent's suspicions or to help to persuade him to see the results of his investigation in the most favorable light. By this we only mean to observe that "it takes two to tango".

Promises and Advice. Prudden further argues that promised advice from [1035] the agents, another manifestation of their "deceptive" cordiality, was fraudulent. He first claims that Lexow said that he would advise him on how to handle one feature of a particular stock sale involving a 52,800 dollar escrow account Lexow promised Prudden an answer when he knew all the facts. But Lexow left the investigation without giving Prudden any answer. So Lexow's promise was not deceitful. Prudden also pressed Cohen and Stanley for advice in regard to the same transaction but admits that he got no "recognizable answer." The long and short of this is that none of the agents ever gave him any advice on the escrow transaction. How could this deceive him? Prudden also claims that the failure of the agents to advise him that he should file an amended return in 1963 was misleading. He asked Cohen if he should file an amended return and was told that the agents would consider only his original return in preparing their report. This is no more than a factual statement. It was not shown to be false or deceitful.

Cumulative Misrepresentations. The explication of a case in factual and legal segments can distort the overall picture of what really happened. Therefore, we have carefully reviewed the record as a whole but still cannot find that Prudden sustained his burden of proving fraud, deceit and trickery. *Goodman v. United States*, 285 F.Supp. 245 (C.D.Cal.1968), which was

---

[29] This letter is set out in note 4 supra.

relied on by the District Court is distinguishable. Most noticeably, in that case the taxpayer had only a grammar school education and was affirmatively led to believe that the information which he was giving the revenue agents was part of the investigation of another taxpayer. That is not near this case on either count.

Any reasonable person is bound to be aware that the filing of an incorrect tax return may result in a charge of wrongdoing. If common sense and knowledge are not enough, then the warning at the bottom of every tax form which the taxpayer must sign before filing, should suffice.[30] The appearance of the revenue agent at the door, in itself, ought in no way to dispel this knowledge of a potential criminal charge. Rather, when the agent says he is there to examine the taxpayer's books, the taxpayer's concern should intensify. We find it entirely implausible for Prudden, a well-educated businessman with a law degree and experience in the tax field, to claim that he did not know that the investigation could lead to criminal charges and that after fifteen months of investigation by numerous special agents of his affairs in New York and Florida, he was surprised or shocked to find himself in a criminal case. When the record is taken most favorably to Prudden's position it falls markedly short of demonstrating by clear and convincing evidence that he was the victim of fraud, deceit or trickery. The suppression order is reversed and the case is remanded to the district court for further proceedings not inconsistent with this opinion.

Reversed and remanded.

ON PETITION FOR REHEARING AND PETITION FOR REHEARING EN BANC

PER CURIAM:

The Petition for Rehearing is denied and no member of this panel nor Judge in regular active service on the Court having requested that the Court be polled on rehearing en banc, (Rule 85 Federal Rules of Appellate Procedure; Local

Fifth Circuit Rule 12) the Petition for Rehearing En Banc is denied.

---

[30] The warning states: "Under penalties of perjury, I declare that I have examined this return, including accompanying schedules and statements, and to the best of my knowledge and belief it is true, correct, and complete."

Supreme Court of California
Van Valkenburg v. Brown, 43 Cal. 43 (1872)

January 1872

[43]

(headnotes omitted)

[44]
Appeal from the District Court of the Third Judicial District, County of Santa Cruz.

The facts are stated in the opinion.

[45]
Albert Hagan, for Appellant.
Albert Heath, for Respondents.
By the Court, **WALLACE**, C. J.:

The plaintiff applied to the Court below for a writ of mandamus against the defendant, who is the County Clerk of the county of Santa Cruz, to compel him to inscribe her name in the Great Register, and enroll her as a legal voter of said county. Judgment having been rendered refusing the writ, she brings appeal.

[46] It appears that she is "a white female resident and citizen of the United States and of the State of California, over the age of twenty-one years, and for more than one year last past a resident of Santa Cruz County," and was born within the limits and subject to the jurisdiction of the United States.

The Court below held that by reason of her sex she was disqualified to exercise the elective franchise; and it is admitted that if her claim in that respect is to be determined alone by the Constitution and laws of this State, excluding, as they do, persons of her sex from the exercise of the elective franchise, the judgment below is correct, and should be affirmed here.

But it is claimed that she is entitled to registration as a voter by reason of the first section of the recent amendment to the Federal Constitution of July 20th, 1868, known as the Fourteenth Amendment. That section is in the following words:

"Article 14, Section 1. All persons born or naturalized in the United States, and subject to the jurisdiction thereof, are citizens of the United States and of the State wherein they reside. No State shall make or enforce any law which shall abridge the privileges and immunities of citizens' of the United States, nor shall any State deprive any person of life, liberty, or property, without due process of law, nor deny to any person within its jurisdiction the equal protection of the laws."

1. It is claimed that the plaintiff is a citizen of the United States and of this State. Undoubtedly she is. It is argued that she became such by force of the first section of the Fourteenth Amendment, already recited. This, however, is a mistake. It could as well be claimed that she became free by the effect of the Thirteenth Amendment, by which slavery was abolished; for she was no less a citizen [47] than she was free before the adoption of either of these amendments. **No white person born within the limits of the United States, and subject to their jurisdiction, or born without those limits, and subsequently naturalized under their laws, owes the status of citizenship to the recent amendments to the Federal Constitution. The history and aim of the Fourteenth Amendment is well known, and the purpose had in view in its adoption well understood. That purpose was to confer the status of citizenship upon a numerous class of persons domiciled within the limits of the**

United States, who could not be brought within the operation of the naturalization laws because native horn, and whose birth, though native, had at the same time left them without the status of citizenship. These persons were not white persons, but were, in the main, persons of African descent, who had been held in slavery in this country, or, if having themselves never been held in slavery, were the native born descendants of slaves. Prior to the adoption of the Fourteenth Amendment it was settled that neither slaves, nor those who had been such, nor the descendants of these, though native and free born, were capable of becoming citizens of the United States. (*Dred Scott v. Sanford*, 19 Row. 893.) The Thirteenth Amendment, though conferring the boon of freedom upon native-born persons of African blood, had yet left them under an insuperable bar as to citizenship; and it was mainly to remedy this condition that the Fourteenth Amendment was adopted.

This is recent history—familiar to all.

2. It is next claimed that, by whatever means the plaintiff became a citizen of the United States, her privileges and immunities as such citizen cannot be abridged by State laws; and this is true. The purpose and the effect of the amendment, in this respect, is to place the privileges and immunities of citizens of the United States beyond the operation of State legislation. Those immunities and privileges, whatever [48] they may be, are guaranteed and protected in every State by this clause in the Federal Constitution.

3. It is urged that, among these privileges and immunities, is included the privilege of the plaintiff to exercise the elective franchise within the limits of this State, even in disregard of the Constitution and laws of the State, which unquestionably exclude persons of her sax. And this brings us to inquire what is meant by the phrase "privileges or immunities of citizens of the United States," as used in this amendment.

This phraseology was known in our history anterior to the formation of the present Federal Union. In the articles of confederation between the American States it was provided "that the free inhabitants of each of these States (paupers, vagabonds, and fugitives from justice excepted) shall be entitled to all privileges and immunities of free citizens of the several States, and the people of each State shall, in every other, enjoy all the privileges of trade and commerce, subject to the same duties, impositions, and restrictions as the inhabitants thereof respectively," etc. (Art IV.) The term "privileges and immunities" was therefore not a new one when, in the second section of the fourth article of the Federal Constitution, as originally ratified, it was declared that "the citizens of each State shall be entitled to all privileges and immunities of the citizens in the several States." The words *"privileges and immunities"* had at that time acquired a distinctive meaning and a well-known signification. They comprehended the enjoyment of life and liberty, and the right to acquire and possess property, and to demand and receive the protection of the Government in aid of these. They included the right to sue and defend in the Courts, to have the benefit of the writ of habeas corpus, and an exemption from higher taxes or heavier impositions than were to be borne by other persons under like conditions and circumstances.

[49] The Federal Constitution went into operation in March, 1789, and within a few years thereafter — in 1797 — a question came before the General Court in Maryland in respect to the meaning of the words "privileges and immunities" as thus employed in that instrument. The question was argued by the most eminent counsel in the State, and among them was the celebrated Luther Martin, then Attorney General. Upon this point the Court said: "Privilege and immunity are synonymous, or nearly so. Privilege signifies a peculiar advantage, exemption, immunity; immunity signifies exemption, privilege. The peculiar advantages and exemptions contemplated under this part of the Constitution may be ascertained, if not with precision and accuracy, yet satisfactorily. By taking a retrospective view of our situation antecedent to the formation of the first General Government, or the Confederation, in which the same clause is used verbatim, one of the great objects must occur to every person, which was the enabling of the citizens of the several States to acquire and hold real property in any of the States, and deemed necessary, as each State was a sovereign and independent State, and the States had confederated only for the purposes of general defense and security, and to promote

the genera l welfare. It seems agreed from the manner of expounding or defining the words 'immunities and privileges' by the counsel on both sides, that a particular and limited operation is to be given to those words and not a full and comprehensive one. It is agreed it does not mean the right of election, the right of holding office, the right of being elected. The Court are of opinion it means that the citizens of all the States shall have the peculiar advantage of acquiring and holding real as well as personal property, and that such property shall be protected and secured by the laws of the State in the same manner as the property of the citizens [50] of the State is protected," etc. (*Campbell V. Morris*, 3 Harr. & McH. 554.)

The expression, "privileges and immunities," had been found in the Constitution for a period of nearly eighty years prior to the adoption of the Fourteenth Amendment, and had never been supposed to include the right to the exercise of the elective franchise. Notwithstanding the citizens of each State were, during all that time, entitled to all the privileges and immunities of citizens in the several States, it was never supposed that the citizen of any State might, upon his removal into any other State, lawfully claim to vote there because he had exercised that privilege in the State from which he had just emigrated.

In point of fact the States have generally conferred the privilege of the elective franchise upon such of their male inhabitants as had become citizens of the United States, if of the requisite age, etc. This circumstance has given rise to a notion in some quarters that the privilege of voting and the status of citizenship are necessarily connected in some way—so that the existence of the one argues that of the other. But the history of the country shows that there was never any foundation for such a view. Thus citizens of the United States, resident in the State of Virginia, were prevented by State law from voting there, unless seized of a freehold estate; and citizens of the United States, resident in Massachusetts, were by the laws of that State denied the privileges of the elective franchise, unless owners of personal property to a designated amount. While the privilege of voting was thus, by State laws, withheld in those States from persons who were citizens of the United States, the elective franchise was in other States of the Union conferred by State laws upon persons who were not citizens. In New York and North Carolina, for instance, at an early day the privilege of voting was conferred upon negroes, persons of African descent, under certain conditions. These were not [51] citizens of the United States, nor then even capable of becoming such. In Wisconsin and Michigan, though negroes were excluded, persons of the Indian blood were admitted; and in Indiana, Illinois, Minnesota, and other States, unnaturalized foreigners were by State laws allowed to vote — following in this respect the early policy of the Federal Government, who, in the ordinance of 1787, for the government of the Northwestern Territory, had permitted the elective franchise to the unnaturalized French and Canadians, of whom the population of that Territory was then largely composed. It will be found that from the earliest periods of our history the State laws regulated the privilege of the elective franchise within their respective limits, and that these laws were exactly such as local interests, peculiar conditions, or supposed policy dictated, and that it was never asserted that the exclusion of any class of inhabitants from the privilege of voting amounted to an interference with the privileges of the excluded class as citizens. As was well said by Judge MILLS, of the Court of Appeals of Kentucky: "The mistake on the subject arises from not attending to a sensible distinction between political and civil rights. The latter constitute the citizen, while the former are not necessary ingredients. A State may deny all her political rights to an individual, and yet he may be a citizen. The rights of office and suffrage are political purely, and are denied by some or all the States to part of their population, who are still citizens. A citizen, then, is one who owes the Government allegiance, service, and money by way of taxation, and to whom the Government in turn, grants and guarantees liberty of person and of conscience, the right of acquiring and possessing property, of marriage and the social relations, of suit and defense, and security of person, estate, and reputation. These, with some others which might be enumerated, being guaranteed and secured by Government, constitute a citizen. To aliens we [52] extend these privileges by courtesy; to others we secure them — to male as well as female— to the infant as well as the person of hoary hairs" (1 Litt. R. 342.)

4. But the language of the second section of tile Fourteenth Amendment itself demonstrates that the elective franchise is not one of the " privileges or immunities mentioned in the first section, and as such not to be abridged or taken away by State laws.

The second section of the amendment (so far as material upon this point) is in the following words:

" Section 2. Representatives shall be apportioned among the several States, according to their respective numbers. But when the right to vote * * * is denied to any of the male inhabitants of such State, being twenty-one years of age, and citizens of the United States * * * the basis of representation therein shall be reduced" * * * etc.

It will thus be seen that by this second section of the Fourteenth Amendment it is expressly provided that if the State law shall deny the elective franchise to the citizens of the United States therein mentioned, the basis of Federal representation to which such State would otherwise be entitled shall be thereupon and in consequence of such denial readjusted and reduced in a designated ratio. If the power of the State to deny the elective franchise to a citizen of the United States had been absolutely taken away by the first section, then a State law enacted for that purpose would necessarily be absolutely void — as a bill of attainder passed or cx post facto law enacted, would he void, as being in contravention of the prohibitions of Article I, Section 10, of the Federal Constitution. But by the second section of the amendment under consideration it is provided that the action of the State authority denying the right of citizens of the United States to vote, so far from being null and void, shall [53] furnish a new basis of Federal numbers in the State, upon which a new apportionment of representation in Congress is to follow. It is inconceivable that such constitutional consequences are to follow the doing of an act which the Constitution had just forbidden to be done at all.

5. The Fifteenth Amendment to the Constitution was adopted nearly two years after the Fourteenth. It provides that the right of a citizen of the United States to vote shall not be denied on account of race, color, or previous condition of servitude. If, under the Fourteenth Amendment already adopted, the right of a citizen to vote was not to be denied upon any ground whatsoever; what necessity or propriety in subsequently providing that it should not be denied upon either of three enumerated grounds? It will be seen that the construction claimed for the Fourteenth Amendment by the counsel for the plaintiff would leave nothing for the Fifteenth to operate upon.

Many other and hardly less cogent reasons might be mentioned going to show that the elective franchise is not one of the immunities or privileges secured by the first section of the Fourteenth Amendment. The mere power of the State to determine the class of inhabitants who may vote within her limits was not curtailed in the Fourteenth Amendment.

The Fifteenth Amendment took away her authority to discriminate against citizens of the United States on account of either race, color, or previous condition of servitude; but the power of exclusion upon all other grounds, including that of sex, remains intact.

Judgment affirmed.

Supreme Court of California
Walther v. Rabolt, 30 Cal. 185 (1866)

July 1866

[185]

(headnotes omitted)

APPEAL from the County Court, Eleventh Judicial District, Amador County.

[186]
H. H. Hartley, for Appellant.
[187]
Badgley & Tilden, for Respondents.

[188]
By the Court, SAWYER, J.:

The evidence is sufficient to justify the finding that the defendent [*sic*] is an alien. (*Jackson v. Wright*, 4 John. 79.)

The only other question is, whether an alien is eligible to the office of County Treasurer. It may be said, generally, that the right to vote and of eligibility to office, are political, and in some sense correlative rights. At common law an alien had no recognized political rights. He was permitted to enjoy certain civil rights, but even these were hedged in by many restrictions and limitations. The English common and statutory law was very chary of extending political privileges to those who were alien born; so much so, that when an alien was naturalized by Act of Parliament, a proviso was appended excluding him from holding office—a consequence which would otherwise follow as a matter of course from the naturalization. Indeed, so important was this exclusion considered, that there was a statute expressly prohibiting the introduction into Parliament of any bill for the naturalization of an alien unless it contained such a proviso. When it was considered advisable to grant this great boon—the capacity to hold office—as a matter of especial favor to some distinguished foreigner about to be naturalized, it was accomplished in this wise: An Act was first. passed, repealing, as to the party designed to be thus honored, the clause of the statute inhibiting the introduction of a proper bill for the purpose; and an Act was then passed without exceptions. Thus, then, it appears that neither a citizen at common law, nor a naturalized denizen under the general statutory law of England can hold office. A *fortiori*, an alien cannot. (*Rex v. De Mierre*, 7 Burr. 2,788; 1 Bac. Abgt, Let. B. p. 200 and note; 1 Black. Com. 374.) And such we understand to be the common law in force in the other States in respect to aliens, where not in any particular modified by constitutional or statutory provisions. And such we also understand the law to be with reference to political rights in all civilized countries. (Cushing's Law. Legis. Ass., Secs. 24, 32, 56; Vattel's Law of N. 1, Chap. 19, Sec. 214, 2 [189] Kent's Com. 84; Bouv. Law Dic., title "Alien;" *Dorst v. Beecker*, 6 John. 332; *Searcy v. Grove*, 15 Cal. 117.) We know of no constitutional or statutory modification of the common law in this State as to the political rights of aliens. But the question is so well discussed under the second head in respondent's brief that, without repeating the argument, upon the reasons there stated and authorities cited, in addition to what has already been said, we hold the defendant to be ineligible.

It follows that the judgment must be affirmed, and it is so ordered.

SANDERSON, J., concurring:

"All political power is inherent in the people," (Art. I, Sec. 2, of the Constitution) and those who are not of the people can have no share in it. **The people are such as are horn upon the soil, by whom and for whom in the first place the Government was ordained**, and such persons of foreign birth as may elect to assume the obligations of a citizen by complying with the laws of naturalization as enacted by Congress. If they desire to secure political rights they must cease to be aliens and become citizens in the mode there prescribed. Until then they can neither vote nor hold office; they can neither choose nor be chosen, for that is to exercise political power, and they are not of the people, who alone may exercise it. In the nature of things this must be so, and cannot be otherwise, except by force of some positive law. None such exists. By Section 17 of Article I of the Constitution, foreigners who were then or might thereafter become *bona fide* residents of the State, are vested with the civil rights of native born citizens as to the possession, enjoyment and inheritance of property; but neither there nor elsewhere are they clothed with a share of the political power which is inherent in the people, or allowed upon any terms other than those of allegiance to participate in the management of public affairs.

I concur in the judgment

Thomas Marvin; Maxwell v. Steven Grouley

1	Thomas Marvin; Maxwell Post Office Box 9655	**ORIGINAL FILED**
2	at the United States Post Office Canoga Park, California	
3	818-846-1482/fax 818-842-0561	APR 1 2 2000
4		LOS ANGELES
5	Thomas Marvin; Maxwell In *propria persona*; not PRO SE	SUPERIOR COURT
6		
7		

In the superior court[1]
for Los Angeles county, California

B C228126

Thomas Marvin; Maxwell, one of the people[2])
of California)   Case No. _____

Plaintiff)

      vs.)   **Verified Complaint in the nature of**
                                              Declaratory Relief

Steven Grouley, Director of Motor Vehicles)

Defendant _____)

1.   I, **Thomas Marvin; Maxwell**, hereby allege:

2.   I am now, and at all times mentioned in this Verified Complaint have been, one of the people of California, a citizen of state, and a ***national*** as defined in the Nationality Act of 1940 at 54 stat 1137 §101(a) and 8 U.S.C. §1101(a)(21), and specifically not welfare enumerated; in *propria persona* and not PRO SE, living on the Land within the boundaries of Los Angeles county, in California, one of the united states of America by an act of Congress at 9 Stat 452; with express and explicit reservation of all Vested Natural, Inherent, and Common Law Rights, whether enumerated or not in the Constitution for the State of California of 1849; specifically and

---

[1]Concurrent with and equivalent to the *district court* as created in the Constitution for the State of California of 1849, and the *seventeenth judicial district*. see Stats 1872. ch. CXIV. p. 116
[2]"The people are such as are born upon the soil, by whom and for whom in the first place the Government was ordained...." *Walther v. Rabolt*, 30 Cal. 185, 189 (1866)

1

357

1   expressly not within the venue and/or jurisdiction of the quasi-constitution of 1879 based on the

2   document entitled "Affidavit in Support of Verified Complaint in the nature of Declaratory

3   Relief" filed concurrently with this Verified Complaint and incorporated as if fully restated

4   herein; without representation of any attorney-at-law.

5   3.   **Steven Grouley,** Director of Motor Vehicles, is now, and at all times mentioned

6   in this Verified Complaint has been, a civil executive officer, appointed by the governor to have

7   control over the Department of Motor Vehicles, and holds said office at the pleasure of the

8   governor.

9   **Statement of Facts**

10   4.   I have had personal involvement in research of the law in California, from its

11   beginning as one of the united states of America in 1850 to the present. I have discovered

12   changes that have taken place in the law, and the "policy" of how the laws are enforced that

13   have slowly and silently deceived the people of California into waiving access to their

14   common law inalienable rights that are acknowledged and protected by the state constitution,

15   and also thereby waiving access to the Bill of Rights amended to the federal constitution.

16   5.   I believe that one of the key methods of creating this silent and undisclosed

17   waiving of rights is accomplished by the "Driver License Application", DMV form "DL 44

18   (REV. 9/98)". The Driver License Application must be signed under penalty of perjury. An

19   applicant must also declare that they "have made no false statements".

20   6.   I canceled a previous Driver License on 06-30-93 (see Exhibit A) after

21   discovering the initial indications in my research that there were problems with having the

22   Driver License pursuant to current DMV policy.

23   7.   Due to the knowledge that I now have as a result of the research that I have

24   done, in order to reapply for a Driver License, I must make changes on the standard Driver

25   License Application in order to be able to sign it under penalty of perjury, thereby claiming

26   that I have made no false statements.

27

28

8.   I did make changes and alterations to a DMV form "DL 44" with a bar code/serial number of A678839534, on December 3, 1999 (see Exhibit B), and submitted said form to the Department of Motor Vehicles at the office in Glendale, California.

9.   The changes that I made are as follows:

A.   In section 2, the space marked "birth date" was changed to "date born".

B.   In section 2, the space marked "residence address" was changed to "home location".

C.   On the back of the form, in the area labeled "Certifications", the third sentence after the third "bullet" which says, "I agree to accept service of process at this mailing address according to §415.20(b), §415.30(a) and §416.90 of the Civil Procedure Code." was changed to say, "(This copy is deleted because I cannot and will not waive constitutionally protected right to due process.)".

D.   On the back of the form, in the area labeled "Certifications", the sentence after the fourth "bullet" which says, "I certify that I am a U.S. citizen or a qualified alien ... " was changed to say, "I certify that I am a national as defined in the Nationality Act of 1940, 54 Stat. 1137, and 8 U.S.C. §1101(a)(21), and that I am expressly not a citizen of the United States as created by and defined in the Fourteenth Amendment to the federal constitution.".

E.   On the back of the form, in the area labeled "Disclosure Statement", after the bold type at the first bullet I added the following, "(A "national" is not authorized to have an SSN.)".

Facts Establishing a Cause of Action for Declaratory Relief

10.   It is a fact that there are two distinct classes of citizenship in the united states of America. This fact is evidenced by the following.

A.   In *Cory v. Carter,* 48 Ind. 327, 328, and 349 (1874) the Supreme Court of Indiana gave a detailed ruling clarifying the distinction between the "citizen of the United States" and the "citizen of state":

3

"The First Clause of the 14th Amendment made negroes citizens of the United States, and citizens of the state in which they reside, and thereby created **two classes of citizens, one of the United States and the other of the state.** ... This [second] clause places the privileges and immunities of citizens of the United States under the protection of the Federal Constitution, and leaves the privileges and immunities of citizens of a state under the protection of the constitution and laws of the state. ... It is quite clear, then, that there is a citizenship of the United States, and a citizenship of state, **which are distinct from each other,** and which depend upon different characteristics or circumstances in the individual. ... The only effect of the amendment under consideration was to extend the protection and blessings of the constitution and laws to **a new class of persons.**"

B. In *Crosse v. Board of Supervisors of Elections,* 221 A.2d 431, 433. (1966) it is clearly shown that a citizen of one of the several states is not required to be a "U.S. citizen".

"**Both before and after the Fourteenth Amendment** to the federal Constitution, it has not been necessary for a person to be a **citizen of the United States** in order to be a **citizen of his state**. United States v. Cruikshank, 92 U.S. 542, 549, 23 L.Ed. 588 **(1875)**", [emphasis added]

C. In *Jones v. Temmer,* 829 F.Supp. 1226 (D.Colo. 1993) it is clearly shown that the rights of a "citizen of the United States", i.e. a "citizen of the federal government", are very different from the citizen of state:

"The privileges and immunities clause of the **Fourteenth Amendment protects very few rights** because it neither incorporates any of the Bill of Rights nor protects all rights of individual citizens. *See Slaughter-House Cases,* 83 U.S. (16 Wall.) 36, 21 L.Ed. 394 (1873). Instead, this provision **protects only those rights peculiar to being a citizen of the federal government**; it does not protect those rights which relate to state citizen. ... Rather the provision **protects only those rights peculiar to being a citizen of the United States**; it does not protect those rights which relate to state citizenship." [emphasis added]

D. *Van Valkenburg v. Brown,* 43 Cal. 43, 47, leaves no doubt that the Fourteenth Amendment to the federal constitution has an extremely limited scope.

"The history and aim of the Fourteenth Amendment is well known, and the purpose had in view well understood. That purpose was to confer the status of citizenship upon a numerous class of persons[3] ... of African descent, who had been held in slavery in this country, or, if having themselves never been held in slavery, were native born descendants of slaves."

---

[3]Note the use of the word "persons" rather that "people".

4

11.   It is a fact that the distinction between these two classes of citizenship is still expressed in current law:

    A.   The Nationality Act of 1940, 54 Stat. 1137, Title I, Section 1, Chapter I -- Definitions
        Sec. 101. For the purposes of this Act--
(a) The term "national" means a person owing permanent allegiance to a state.
(b) the term "national of the United States" means (1) a citizen of the United States, or (2) a person, who though not a citizen of the United States, owes permanent allegiance to the United States. It does not include an alien.

    B.   8 U.S.C. §1101 - Definitions
        (a) As used in this chapter -
(21) The term "national" means a person owing permanent allegiance to a state.
(22) the term "national of the United States" means (A) a citizen of the United States, or (B) a person, who though not a citizen of the United States, owes permanent allegiance to the United States.

12.   It is a fact that the California Vehicle Code alleges that "No person shall drive a motor vehicle upon a highway, unless the person then holds a valid driver's license ... " VC §12500(a).

13.   The foregoing appears to be consistent with the Statutes of California:

Stats 1923, ch. 266
    Section 18. "Operator." Every person who drives, operates or is in actual physical control of a motor vehicle upon a public highway.
    Section 58. Operators and chauffeurs must be licensed. It shall be unlawful for any person to drive any motor vehicle upon any public highway in this state whether as an operator or a chauffeur unless licensed as an operator or chauffeur, ..."

14.   Notwithstanding the foregoing, it must be noted that there are some exceptions in the Statutes of California that remain ambiguous as to the actual application in conjunction with the foregoing:

Stats 1933, ch. 339 as amended by Stats 1939 ch 944
    Section 1(a) The term "operator" ..... shall not mean or include the following: (1) Any person transporting his own property in a motor vehicle owned or operated by him; ..."

15.   Notwithstanding the fact that there are two classes of citizenship in this country, the Defendant does not provide an application for the "national", i.e. the citizen of state, to apply for a Driver License. Form "DL 44 (REV. 9/98)" is restricted to applicants who can

1 truthfully "certify" that they are a "U.S. citizen", i.e. the "national of the United States", or a

2 qualified alien (see Exhibit C). When the Department of Motor Vehicles offers form "DL 44

3 (REV.9/98)" to a "national" of California, said form is a **privy token**[4].

4   16. In an attempt to comply by means of removing the fraudulent aspects of the

5 form, I presented an altered "DL 44 (REV. 9/98)" to the Department of Motor Vehicles on

6 December 3, 1999, at the field office located in Glendale, California (see Exhibit B).

7   17. Though the Department of Motor Vehicles did in fact accept the altered applica-

8 tion which correctly identifies me as a "national", the DMV will still not issue the final Driver

9 License until I provide a "Social Security Number" (see Exhibit D).

10   18. The alleged "requirement" of a "Social Security Number" **again** restricts me as a

11 "national" from receiving the Driver License. An application for a "Social Security Number"

12 is evidence of this fact (see Exhibit E). In section 3 of an SSN application, there are only four

13 categories under which a "Social Security Number" can be applied for: "U.S. citizen", "Legal

14 alien allowed to work", "Legal alien not allowed to work", and "Other". The instructions for

15 the "Other" category make it clear that it is only referring to those who would be trying to

16 acquire a government "benefit or service"[5].

17   19. It is a fact, based upon the Social Security Application itself, that as a "national"

18 I would not even be qualified to apply for a "Social Security Number". Only the "citizen of

19 the federal government", i.e. the "citizen of the United States" or "US citizen" is qualified to

20 apply for and receive a federal benefit.

21   20. Therefore, I hereby allege the following:

22   A. That it is unlawful to restrict me from receiving a Driver License for

23 failure to provide a number which I am not authorized to have or use.

24   B. That any requirement that I misidentify myself as a US citizen in order to

25 receive a Driver License due to policy requirements imposed by the Defendant, is a felony

26 known as "subornation of perjury".

27

---

[4]"... used to deceive persons, and thereby fraudulently obtain possession of property."
[5]For example, an illegal alien who is applying for AFDC for a child who is a U.S. citizen.

28

6

Demand for Judgment

21.　Based upon all the foregoing, and the evidence and argument to be presented at trial, I hereby demand a judgment in the nature of declaratory relief including but not necessarily limited to the following:

A.　That the Defendant be order by the court to issue a Driver License to me which properly identifies me as a "national";

B.　That such a Driver License must, upon the face thereof, expressly state that there is "No Social Security Number on file", in order to provide that the issuance thereof does not create a false presumption that I have a valid SSN.

C.　That such a Driver License must, upon the face thereof, pursuant to the United States Government Printing Office Style Manual, ¶3.2, have my Proper Name spelled with "initial capitals" only and all other letters in lower case i.e., Thomas Marvin Maxwell rather than THOMAS MARVIN MAXWELL. I can in fact find no law requiring that a citizens name be spelled in "all CAPITAL letters".

D.　That such a Driver License must, upon the face thereof, expressly state that I am a "national" as defined in the Nationality Act of 1940, 54 Stat. 1137 §101(a), and currently expressed in 8 U.S.C. §1101(a)(21).

Verification

I, Thomas Marvin; Maxwell, hereby swear under penalty of perjury, under the law of the Land in California, one of the united states of America, that the foregoing is true and correct and so done in good faith to the best of my knowledge and belief.

Subscribed and sworn this sixth day of the fourth month, in the year A.D. two thousand.

L.S.] *Thomas Marvin; Maxwell*
Thomas Marvin; Maxwell

7

363

DATE:07-25-96 TIME:13:04*
DL/NO:N5664650*B/D:12-16-50 NAME:MAXWELL THOMAS MARVIN*
ADDR AS OF 11-08-91:21821 SATICOY ST 11, CANOGA PARK 91304*CC:19*
OTH/ADDR AS OF 12-04-87:PO BX 6631, THOUSAND OAKS *

PULL NOTICE:NONE*

P&M CODE:NONE*

REVIEW DT:NONE*

COMMENT:
    NO:MM PURGE:11-11 637110891221821 SATICOY ST 11   CANOGA
    PARK CA91304000063711089106500? *
STATUS:
LIC/ISS:11-08-91 LIC/MLD:00-00-00 EXP:CANC*RBM2*RESTR:MUST WEAR
    CORRECTIVE LENSES WHEN DRIVING**
CLASS:C NON-COMMERCIAL*HEALTH QUESTIONNAIRE EXPIRES:NONE*
PREV LIC:CL3 EXP/BD:95*CERT:NONE*
                    **** M O R E ****

LATEST APP:RENEWAL*ISS/DATE:11-08-91 OFF:WKA*BATES:MAG*
LIC/LOC:5,RSN:0*
PHOTO INFO:
    :A- DL PHOTO ON VENDOR FILE*
LEGAL HISTORY:

HNG/ ACTION	RSN	HNG/MAIL DATE	MOD/EFF DATE	LOC&RSLT/ AUTH SEC	THRU DATE	SERV ORD/ BRIEF	COR ORD	CC
CANC	640	06-30-93	06-09-93	13100		S:A/06-30-93		10

ABSTRACTS:NONE*

FTP:NONE*

FTA:NONE*
ACCIDENTS:NONE*
END

365

**DRIVER LICENSE OR
IDENTIFICATION CARD
APPLICATION**

A678839534

44

1. PURPOSE FOR YOUR VISIT ✓ the appropriate box(es)

DO NOT DUPLICATE

DRIVER LICENSE (DL)	IDENTIFICATION CARD (ID)	NAME CHANGE	FOR DMV USE ONLY
☐ DL/Permit ☐ Change/Add Class	☐ ID Card/Renewal	☐ DL	BD/LP Code
☐ Duplicate ☐ Add CDL Endorsement	☐ Senior ID Card (Age 62+)	☐ ID CARD	Initials
☒ Renewal ☐ Remove Restriction	☐ Duplicate	Complete Parts 2, 4, & 5 only.	LE Code
Complete Parts 2 through 6.	Complete Parts 2, 4A, & 5 only.		Initials

2. PLEASE TELL US ABOUT YOURSELF (Use your full name)

DRIVER LICENSE OR ID CARD NUMBER	STATE OR COUNTRY	EXPIRES	date born	SOCIAL SECURITY NUMBER
N5664650	California	canceled 6/30/93	MO 12/16/1950	N/A for "national"
FIRST NAME	MIDDLE NAME		LAST NAME	SUFFIX (JR, SR)
Thomas	Marvin		Maxwell	
MAILING ADDRESS (Include St. Ave., Rd., Ct., Blvd., Way, etc.)	APT/SPACE NO	home location		APT/SPACE NO
PO Box 9655		1723 Thurber Place		
CITY	STATE	ZIP CODE	CITY	STATE
Canoga Park	California	91309	Burbank	California
gender	HAIR COLOR	EYE COLOR	HEIGHT	WEIGHT
☒ M ☐ F	brown	brown	5'6"	145 lbs.

3. LICENSING NEED: ✓ all boxes that you need. See explanation in California Driver Handbook.

BASIC LICENSE
☒ Basic Class C
☐ Motorcycle

If basic license only, go to Part 4.

NON-COMMERCIAL LICENSE
☐ Class A

FIRE FIGHTER
☐ Class A
☐ Class B

☐ Ambulance Certificate
☐ Verification of Transit Training

COMMERCIAL DRIVER ONLY
(SSN is verified before any original commercial driver license application is started.)

COMMERCIAL LICENSE   **Endorsements**
☐ Class A   ☐ Passenger Transport   ☐ Tank
☐ Class B   ☐ Hazardous Materials/Waste ☐ Air Brakes
☐ Class C   ☐ Doubles/Triples

I certify that the motor vehicle in which I am taking the driving skills test is representative of the type of motor vehicle I expect to operate. I am not subject to any disqualification, suspension, revocation, or cancellation as contained in Title 49 of Federal Regulations, Part 383.51, and I do not have a driver license from more than one state or jurisdiction.

ACCORDING TO PART 391 OF THE FEDERAL MOTOR CARRIER SAFETY REGULATIONS
☐ I plan to operate in foreign or interstate commerce and I meet the qualifications.
☐ I do not plan to operate in foreign or interstate commerce and I am not subject to Part 391.

4. QUESTIONS: Please answer the following questions.

A Have you ever applied for a driver license or ID card under a different name(s)? ☒ No ☐ Yes If yes, list name(s) here _____

Question B is for the confidential use of the DMV. *Please review the "Medical Information" on the back of this form before answering.*
B Have you had any health or vision problems that could affect your ability to drive safely? ☒ No ☐ Yes If yes, briefly explain _____

5. DO YOU WISH TO REGISTER TO VOTE OR CHANGE YOUR VOTER ADDRESS?

CHECK ONE BOX ONLY. Complete the attached form if you check box "Y" or "C" only.
Y ☐ First-time voter registration or a voter registration change (i.e., name change or political party change)
N ☒ I do not wish to register to vote or to change my voter registration address.
C ☐ Please update my voter registration address record to a new county.
S ☐ Please update my voter registration address record within the same county.

6. FOR DRIVER UNDER 18, PARENT/GUARDIAN SIGNATURES REQUIRED: If both parents/guardians have joint custody, *BOTH MUST* sign. I/We accept liability for this minor.

MOTHER'S/GUARDIAN'S SIGNATURE	DATE	DAYTIME PHONE NUMBER
FATHER'S/GUARDIAN'S SIGNATURE	DATE	DAYTIME PHONE NUMBER

7. CERTIFICATION: I have read and agree to all the certifications on the back of this form and I have made no false statements. I certify under penalty of perjury under the laws of the State of California that the foregoing is true and correct.

STOP   Do not sign until instructed to do so by a DMV employee.

SIGNATURE OF APPLICANT	DATE	DAYTIME PHONE NUMBER
X		

DL 44 (REV 8/98)

DMV A Public Service Agency

IT IS IMPORTANT THAT YOU READ AND UNDERSTAND
THE FOLLOWING INFORMATION.

MEDICAL INFORMATION

Within the last three years have you:
- experienced, on one or more occasions, a loss of consciousness; or
- had any episode of marked confusion caused by any condition which may bring about recurring lapses; or
- had any disease, disorder, or disability which affects your ability to operate a motor vehicle safely upon a highway. If so, check "Yes" and explain in Question 4B.

Examples of the above are:
- epilepsy   • diabetes   • stroke   • drug or alcohol addiction

CERTIFICATIONS

- I agree to submit to a chemical test of my blood, breath, or urine for the purpose of determining the alcohol or drug content of my blood when testing is requested by a peace officer acting in accordance with Vehicle Code §23157.
- Signing this application tells DMV that you were notified that if you are under 21 years of age, you cannot legally drive with a blood alcohol concentration (BAC) of 0.01% or more. Driving with a BAC of 0.01% or more, or refusing to take, or failing to complete an alcohol screening or drug test, results in a one-year suspension of your driving privilege.
- I am the person whose name appears on the front of this form. The mailing address shown is valid, existing, and accurate. (This copy is deleted because I cannot and will not waive constitutionally protected right to due process.)
- I certify that I am a national as defined in the Nationality Act of 1940, 54 Stat 1137, and 8 U.S.C. §1101(a)(21), and that I am expressly not a citizen of the United States as created by and defined in the Fourteenth Amendment to the federal constitution.

DISCLOSURE STATEMENTS

- **SOCIAL SECURITY NUMBER COLLECTION DISCLOSURE — You are required by law to provide your social security number or your application will be denied.** (A "national" is not authorized to have a SSN.) Authority to collect the social security number is 42 U.S.C. 405 and California Vehicle Code §1653.5, §4150, §4150.2, §12800, and §12801. It will be used in the administration of driver license laws and motor vehicle registration laws and to respond to requests for information from the Franchise Tax Board for tax administration and from any agency operating pursuant to 42 U.S.C. 601 et seq. It will be used to aid in the collection of monies owed in connection with failure to pay fines or failure to appear in court by an applicant, and to aid in the collection of monies owed by an applicant in connection with Aid to Families with Dependent Children, Child Support, and/or Establishment of Paternity.
- The mailing address listed on the front of this application will be the address shown on your driver license or identification card.

ADVISORY STATEMENT

The information required on this form pertains to eligibility for and issuance of a driver license. It is required under the authority of Division 6 of the Vehicle Code. Failure to provide the information is cause for refusal to issue a driver license, or, in some cases, cancellation or withdrawal of the driving privilege.

Except as made confidential (medical information is confidential by law) or exempted under the Public Records Act, this information is a public record and is regularly used by law enforcement agencies and insurance companies. Access to address information is now restricted, and will be available to various authorized requesters for limited use. Individuals can obtain copies of their own information during regular office hours.

- Any person who uses false documents to conceal his or her true citizenship or resident alien status is guilty of a felony pursuant to California Penal Code §114.

REFUNDS

Once this application form and fee have been submitted, no refunds will be made.

DL 44 (REV 9/98)

367

DRIVER LICENSE OR
IDENTIFICATION CARD
APPLICATION

A678839545

44

1. PURPOSE FOR YOUR VISIT: ✔ the appropriate box(es).

DO NOT DUPLICATE

DRIVER LICENSE (DL)	IDENTIFICATION CARD (ID)	NAME CHANGE	FOR DMV USE ONLY
☐ DL/Permit ☐ Change/Add Class	☐ ID Card/Renewal	☐ DL	BD/LP Code _____
☐ Duplicate ☐ Add CDL Endorsement	☐ Senior ID Card (Age 62+)	☐ ID CARD	Initials _____
☐ Renewal ☐ Remove Restriction	☐ Duplicate	*Complete Parts 2, 4, & 5 only.*	LE Code _____
Complete Parts 2 through 6.	*Complete Parts 2, 4A, & 5 only.*		Initials _____

2. PLEASE TELL US ABOUT YOURSELF: Use your true full name.

DRIVER LICENSE OR ID CARD NUMBER	STATE OR COUNTRY	EXPIRES	BIRTH DATE	SOCIAL SECURITY NUMBER
			MO ___ DAY ___ YR ___	
FIRST NAME	MIDDLE NAME		LAST NAME	SUFFIX (JR., SR., III)
MAILING ADDRESS (include St., Ave., Rd., Ct., Blvd., Way, etc.)	APT/SPACE NO.	RESIDENCE ADDRESS (if different from mailing address)		APT/SPACE NO.
CITY	STATE	ZIP CODE	CITY	STATE	ZIP CODE
SEX ☐ M ☐ F	HAIR COLOR	EYE COLOR	HEIGHT	WEIGHT

3. LICENSING NEED: ✔ all boxes that you need. See explanation in California Driver Handbook.

BASIC LICENSE
☐ Basic Class C
☐ Motorcycle
If basic license only, go to Part 4.

NON-COMMERCIAL LICENSE
☐ Class A

FIRE FIGHTER
☐ Class A
☐ Class B

☐ Ambulance Certificate
☐ Verification of Transit Training

COMMERCIAL DRIVER ONLY
(SSN is verified before any original commercial driver license application is started.)

COMMERCIAL LICENSE
☐ Class A
☐ Class B
☐ Class C

Endorsements
☐ Passenger Transport
☐ Hazardous Materials/Waste
☐ Doubles/Triples
☐ Tank
☐ Air Brakes

I certify that the motor vehicle in which I am taking the driving skills test is representative of the type of motor vehicle I expect to operate. I am not subject to any disqualification, suspension, revocation, or cancellation as contained in Title 49 of Federal Regulations, Part 383.51, and I do not have a driver license from more than one state or jurisdiction.

ACCORDING TO PART 391 OF THE FEDERAL MOTOR CARRIER SAFETY REGULATIONS
☐ I plan to operate in foreign or interstate commerce and I meet the qualifications.
☐ I do **not** plan to operate in foreign or interstate commerce and I am **not** subject to Part 391.

4. QUESTIONS: Please answer the following questions.

A. Have you ever applied for a driver license or ID card under a different name(s): ☐ No ☐ Yes If yes, list name(s) here _____

Question B is for the confidential use of the DMV. *Please review the "Medical Information" on the back of this form before answering.*
B. Have you had any health or vision problems that could affect your ability to drive safely? ☐ No ☐ Yes If yes, briefly explain: _____

5. DO YOU WISH TO REGISTER TO VOTE OR CHANGE YOUR VOTER ADDRESS?

CHECK ONE BOX ONLY. Complete the attached form if you check box "Y" or "C" only.
Y ☐ First-time voter registration or a voter registration change (i.e., name change or political party change).
N ☐ I do not wish to register to vote or to change my voter registration address.
C ☐ Please update my voter registration address record to a **new** county.
S ☐ Please update my voter registration address record within the **same** county.

6. FOR DRIVER UNDER 18, PARENT/GUARDIAN SIGNATURES REQUIRED: If both parents/guardians have joint custody, *BOTH MUST* sign. I/We accept liability for this minor.

MOTHER'S/GUARDIAN'S SIGNATURE	DATE	DAYTIME PHONE NUMBER
FATHER'S/GUARDIAN'S SIGNATURE	DATE	DAYTIME PHONE NUMBER

7. CERTIFICATION: I have read and agree to all the certifications on the back of this form and I have made no false statements. I certify under penalty of perjury under the laws of the State of California that the foregoing is true and correct.

STOP Do not sign until instructed to do so by a DMV employee.

SIGNATURE OF APPLICANT	DATE	DAYTIME PHONE NUMBER
X		

DL 44 (REV. 9/98)

DMV A Public Service Agency

IT IS IMPORTANT THAT YOU READ AND UNDERSTAND THE FOLLOWING INFORMATION.

MEDICAL INFORMATION

Within the last three years have you:
* experienced, on one or more occasions, a loss of consciousness; or
* had any episode of marked confusion caused by any condition which may bring about recurring lapses; or
* had any disease, disorder, or disability which affects your ability to operate a motor vehicle safely upon a highway. If so, check "Yes" and explain in Question 4B.

Examples of the above are:
* epilepsy   • diabetes   • stroke   • drug or alcohol addiction

CERTIFICATIONS

* I agree to submit to a chemical test of my blood, breath, or urine for the purpose of determining the alcohol or drug content of my blood when testing is requested by a peace officer acting in accordance with Vehicle Code §23157.
* Signing this application tells DMV that you were notified that if you are under 21 years of age, you cannot legally drive with a blood alcohol concentration (BAC) of 0.01% or more. Driving with a BAC of 0.01% or more, or refusing to take, or failing to complete an alcohol screening or drug test, results in a one-year suspension of your driving privilege.
* I am the person whose name appears on the front of this form. The mailing address shown is valid, existing, and accurate. I agree to accept service of process at this mailing address according to §415.20(b), §415.30(a), and §416.90 of the Civil Procedure Code.
* I certify that I am a U.S. citizen or a qualified alien pursuant to the Personal Responsibility and Work Opportunity Reconciliation Act of 1996 (8 U.S.C. §1621 et seq.) and therefore eligible for a commercial license, a noncommercial fire fighter license, a special certificate, a training document, or a clearance document.

DISCLOSURE STATEMENTS

* **SOCIAL SECURITY NUMBER COLLECTION DISCLOSURE — You are required by law to provide your social security number or your application will be denied.**
  Authority to collect the social security number is 42 U.S.C. 405 and California Vehicle Code §1653.5, §4150, §4150.2, §12800, and §12801. It will be used in the administration of driver license laws and motor vehicle registration laws and to respond to requests for information from the Franchise Tax Board for tax administration and from any agency operating pursuant to 42 U.S.C. 601 et seq. It will be used to aid in the collection of monies owed in connection with failure to pay fines or failure to appear in court by an applicant, and to aid in the collection of monies owed by an applicant in connection with Aid to Families with Dependent Children, Child Support, and/or Establishment of Paternity.
* The mailing address listed on the front of this application will be the address shown on your driver license or identification card.

ADVISORY STATEMENT

The information required on this form pertains to eligibility for and issuance of a driver license. It is required under the authority of Division 6 of the Vehicle Code. Failure to provide the information is cause for refusal to issue a driver license, or, in some cases, cancellation or withdrawal of the driving privilege.

Except as made confidential (medical information is confidential by law) or exempted under the Public Records Act, this information is a public record and is regularly used by law enforcement agencies and insurance companies. Access to address information is now restricted, and will be available to various authorized requesters for limited use. Individuals can obtain copies of their own information during regular office hours.

* Any person who uses false documents to conceal his or her true citizenship or resident alien status is guilty of a felony pursuant to California Penal Code §114.

REFUNDS

Once this application form and fee have been submitted, no refunds will be made.

DL 44 (REV. 9/98)

TEMPORARY DRIVER LICENSE

N5664650   CLASS C

ISSUED:12-03-99   510   C2/   EXPIRES:01-31-00

THOMAS MARVIN MAXWELL   SEX:M   HAIR:BRN   EYES:BRN
PO BOX 9655   HT:5-06 WT:145   DOB:12-16-50
CANOGA PARK   CA 91309

THIS LICENSE IS ISSUED AS A LICENSE TO DRIVE A MOTOR VEHICLE;
IT DOES NOT ESTABLISH ELIGIBILITY FOR EMPLOYMENT, VOTER
REGISTRATION, OR PUBLIC BENEFITS.

*** SOCIAL SECURITY NUMBER REQUIRED ***
X *Thomas Marvin Maxwell*
510   12-03-99   48/501

TEMPORARY DRIVER LICENSE

N5664650   CLASS C

ISSUED:01-31-00   510   H4/   EXPIRES:05-08-00

THOMAS MARVIN MAXWELL   SEX:M   HAIR:BRN   EYES:BRN
PO BOX 9655   HT:5-06 WT:145   DOB:12-16-50
CANOGA PARK   CA 91309

THIS LICENSE IS ISSUED AS A LICENSE TO DRIVE A MOTOR VEHICLE;
IT DOES NOT ESTABLISH ELIGIBILITY FOR EMPLOYMENT, VOTER
REGISTRATION, OR PUBLIC BENEFITS.

*** SOCIAL SECURITY NUMBER REQUIRED ***
X *Thomas Marvin Maxwell*
510   12-03-99   48/501

SOCIAL SECURITY ADMINISTRATION
Application for a Social Security Card

Applying for a Social Security Card is easy AND it is FREE!

If you DO NOT follow these instructions, we CANNOT process your application!

STEP 1   Complete and sign the application with BLUE or BLACK ink.
Do NOT use pencil! Follow instructions below.

STEP 2   See Page 2 to determine what evidence we need.

STEP 3   Submit the application and evidence to any Social Security office. Follow instructions below.

HOW TO COMPLETE THE APPLICATION

Most items on the form are self-explanatory. Those that need explanation are discussed below. The numbers match the numbered items on the form. If you are completing this form for someone else, please complete the items as they apply to that person.

2. Show an address where you can receive the card 10 to 14 days from now.

3. If you check "other" for CITIZENSHIP, provide a document from the Federal/State or local agency explaining why you need a Social Security number and that you meet all the requirements for the benefit or service except for a number.

5. You do not have to complete this item about race/ethnic background. We use this information for statistical reports on how Social Security programs affect people. We do not reveal the identities of individuals.

6. Show the month, day, and full (4-digit) year of birth, for example, "1998" for year of birth.

8. You **must** enter the mother's Social Security number in item 8B. if you are applying for a number for a child under age 18.

9. You **must** enter the father's Social Security number in item 9B. if you are applying for a number for a child under age 18.

13. If the date of birth you show in item 6 is different from the date of birth you used on a prior application for a Social Security number card, show the date of birth you used on the prior application and submit evidence of age to support the date of birth in item 6.

16. You **must** sign the application if you are age 18 or older and are physically and mentally capable. If you are under age 18, you may also sign the application if you are physically and mentally capable. If you cannot sign your name, you should sign with an "X" mark and have two people sign as witnesses in the space beside the mark. If you are physically or mentally incapable, generally a parent, close relative, or legal guardian may sign the application. Call us if you need clarification about who can sign.

HOW TO SUBMIT THE APPLICATION

Mail the form and your evidence documents to the nearest Social Security office. We will return your documents to you. If you do not want to mail your original documents, take them to the nearest Social Security office with this application.

If you are age 18 or older and have never been assigned a number before, you must apply in person.

Form **SS-5** (2-98) Destroy Prior Editions   Page 1   Printed on recycled paper

371

EVIDENCE WE NEED

CAUTION: We cannot accept photocopies of documents. You must submit original documents or copies certified by the custodian of the record. **Notarized copies are not acceptable.** If your documents do not meet this requirement, we cannot process your application. We will return your documents. IF YOU DO NOT WANT TO MAIL YOUR ORIGINAL DOCUMENTS, TAKE THEM TO ANY SOCIAL SECURITY OFFICE.

If you need an **ORIGINAL CARD** (you have NEVER been assigned a Social Security number before), you must show us proof of :

> **AGE,**
> **IDENTITY, and**
> **U.S. CITIZENSHIP or LAWFUL ALIEN STATUS**

If you need a **DUPLICATE CARD** (no name change), you must show us proof of **IDENTITY**.

IMPORTANT: If you were born outside the U.S., you must also show us proof of **U.S. CITIZENSHIP or LAWFUL ALIEN STATUS.**

If you need a **CORRECTED CARD** because of a name change, you must show us proof of **IDENTITY**.

To **CHANGE YOUR NAME** on our records, we need one or more documents identifying you by your OLD NAME on our records and your NEW NAME.

IMPORTANT: If you were born outside the U.S., you must also show us proof of **U.S. CITIZENSHIP or LAWFUL ALIEN STATUS.**

AGE: We prefer to see your birth certificate. However, we can accept other documents such as a hospital record of your birth made before you were age 5 or a religious record made before you were three months old. If you were born outside the U.S., we can accept your passport. Call us for advice if you cannot obtain any of these documents.

IDENTITY: We must see a document in the name you want shown on the card. We can generally accept a current document that has enough information to identify you (e.g., signature, name, age, date of birth, parents' names). **We CANNOT ACCEPT a BIRTH CERTIFICATE, HOSPITAL BIRTH RECORD, SSN CARD, SSN CARD STUB, OR SSA RECORD.** Some documents that we can accept are:

- Driver's license
- Employer ID card
- Passport

- Marriage or divorce record
- Adoption record
- Health Insurance card (not a Medicare card)

- Military records
- Insurance policy
- School ID card

IMPORTANT: If you are applying for a card on behalf of someone else, we must see proof of identity for both you and the person to whom the card will be issued.

NAME CHANGE: If your name is now different from the name shown on your card, we need an identity document that identifies you by BOTH your old name AND your new name. Examples include a marriage certificate, divorce decree, or a court order that changes your name. Or we can accept two identity documents—one in your old name and one in your new name. (See IDENTITY for examples of identity documents.)

U.S. CITIZENSHIP: We can accept most documents that show you were born in the U.S. If you are a U.S. citizen born outside the U.S., show us a U.S. consular report of birth, a U.S. passport, a Certificate of Citizenship, or a Certificate of Naturalization.

ALIEN STATUS: We need to see a current document issued to you by the U.S. Immigration and Naturalization Service (INS), such as Form I-551, I-94, I-688B, or I-766. We CANNOT accept a receipt showing you applied for the document. If you are not authorized to work in the U.S., we can issue you a Social Security card if you are lawfully here and need the number for a valid nonwork reason. Your card will be marked to show you cannot work, and, if you do, we will notify INS.

IF YOU HAVE ANY QUESTIONS: If you have any questions about this form, or about the documents you need to show us, please contact any Social Security office. A telephone call will help you make sure you have everything you need to apply for a card.

THE PAPERWORK/PRIVACY ACT AND YOUR APPLICATION

The Privacy Act of 1974 requires us to give each person the following notice when applying for a Social Security number.

Sections 205(c) and 702 of the Social Security Act allow us to collect the facts we ask for on this form.

We use the facts you provide on this form to assign you a Social Security number and to issue you a Social Security card. You do not have to give us these facts, however, without them we cannot issue you a Social Security number or a card. Without a number, you may not be able to get a job and could lose Social Security benefits in the future.

The Social Security number is also used by the Internal Revenue Service for tax administration purposes as an identifier in processing tax returns of persons who have income which is reported to the Internal Revenue Service and by persons who are claimed as dependents on someone's Federal income tax return.

We may disclose information as necessary to administer Social Security programs, including to appropriate law enforcement agencies to investigate alleged violations of Social Security law; to other government agencies for administering entitlement, health, and welfare programs such as Medicaid, Medicare, veterans benefits, military pension, and civil service annuities, black lung, housing, student loans, railroad retirement benefits, and food stamps; to the Internal Revenue Service for Federal tax administration; and to employers and former employers to properly prepare wage reports. We may also disclose information as required by Federal law, for example, to the Department of Justice, Immigration and Naturalization Service, to identify and locate aliens in the U.S.; to the Selective Service System for draft registration; and to the Department of Health and

Human Services for child support enforcement purposes. We may verify Social Security numbers for State motor vehicle agencies that use the number in issuing drivers licenses, as authorized by the Social Security Act. Finally, we may disclose information to your Congressional representative if they request information to answer questions you ask him or her.

We may use the information you give us when we match records by computer. Matching programs compare our records with those of other Federal, State, or local government agencies to determine whether a person qualifies for benefits paid by the Federal government. The law allows us to do this even if you do not agree to it.

Explanations about these and other reasons why information you provide us may be used or given out are available in Social Security offices. If you want to learn more about this, contact any Social Security office.

The **Paperwork Reduction Act of 1995** requires us to notify you that this information collection is in accordance with the clearance requirements of section 3507 of the Paperwork Reduction Act of 1995. We may not conduct or sponsor, and you are not required to respond to, a collection of information unless it displays a valid OMB control number. We estimate that it will take you about 8.5 to 9 minutes to complete this form. This includes the time it will take to read the instructions, gather the necessary facts and fill out the form.

SOCIAL SECURITY ADMINISTRATION
Application for a Social Security Card

Form Approved
OMB No. 0960-0066

1	**NAME** TO BE SHOWN ON CARD ⟶	First	Full Middle Name	Last
	FULL NAME AT BIRTH IF OTHER THAN ABOVE ⟶	First	Full Middle Name	Last
	OTHER NAMES USED ⟶			

2 **MAILING ADDRESS** ⟶ Do Not Abbreviate

Street Address. Apt. No., PO Box, Rural Route No.

City | State | Zip Code

3 **CITIZENSHIP** (Check One) ⟶
☐ U.S. Citizen ☐ Legal Alien Allowed To Work ☐ Legal Alien Not Allowed To Work ☐ Other (See Instructions On Page 1)

4 **SEX** ⟶ ☐ Male ☐ Female

5 **RACE/ETHNIC DESCRIPTION** (Check One Only—Voluntary) ⟶
☐ Asian Asian-American or Pacific Islander ☐ Hispanic ☐ Black (Not Hispanic) ☐ North American Indian or Alaskan Native ☐ White (Not Hispanic)

6 **DATE OF BIRTH** Month, Day, Year

7 **PLACE OF BIRTH** (Do Not Abbreviate) City | State or Foreign Country | FCI   Office Use Only

8
A. **MOTHER'S MAIDEN NAME** ⟶ First | Full Middle Name | Last Name At Her Birth
B. **MOTHER'S SOCIAL SECURITY NUMBER** (Complete only if applying for a number for a child under age 18.) ⟶ ☐☐☐-☐☐-☐☐☐☐

9
A. **FATHER'S NAME** ⟶ First | Full Middle Name | Last
B. **FATHER'S SOCIAL SECURITY NUMBER** (Complete only if applying for a number for a child under age 18.) ⟶ ☐☐☐-☐☐-☐☐☐☐

10 Has the applicant or anyone acting on his/her behalf ever filed for or received a Social Security number card before?
☐ Yes (If "yes", answer questions 11-13.) ☐ No (If "no", go on to question 14.) ☐ Don't Know (If "don't know", go on to question 14.)

11 Enter the Social Security number previously assigned to the person listed in item 1. ⟶ ☐☐☐-☐☐-☐☐☐☐

12 Enter the name shown on the most recent Social Security card issued for the person listed in item 1. ⟶ First | Middle | Last

13 Enter any different date of birth if used on an earlier application for a card. ⟶ Month, Day, Year

14 **TODAY'S DATE** Month, Day, Year

15 **DAYTIME PHONE NUMBER** ( ) Area Code Number

DELIBERATELY FURNISHING (OR CAUSING TO BE FURNISHED) FALSE INFORMATION ON THIS APPLICATION IS A CRIME PUNISHABLE BY FINE OR IMPRISONMENT, OR BOTH.

16 **YOUR SIGNATURE** ▶

17 **YOUR RELATIONSHIP TO THE PERSON IN ITEM 1 IS:**
☐ Self ☐ Natural or Adoptive Parent ☐ Legal Guardian ☐ Other (Specify)

DO NOT WRITE BELOW THIS LINE (FOR SSA USE ONLY)

NPN			DOC	NTI	CAN		ITV
PBC	EVI	EVA	EVC	PRA	NWR	DNR	UNIT

EVIDENCE SUBMITTED

SIGNATURE AND TITLE OF EMPLOYEE(S) REVIEWING EVIDENCE AND/OR CONDUCTING INTERVIEW

DATE

DCL   DATE

Form SS-5 (2-98) Destroy Prior Editions   Page 5

375

```
 1  BILL LOCKYER, Attorney General       NO FEE - GOV. CODE § 6103
       of the State of California
 2  DANA T. CARTOZIAN, (State Bar No. 76011)
       Deputy Attorney General
 3  300 South Spring Street, Fifth Floor
    Los Angeles, California  90013-1204
 4  Tel: (213) 897-2091; FAX: (213) 897-1071

 5  Attorneys for Defendant:
    Steven Grouley, Director of Motor Vehicles
 6

 7

 8          SUPERIOR COURT OF THE STATE OF CALIFORNIA

 9             FOR THE COUNTY OF LOS ANGELES

10

11

12  Thomas Marvin; Maxwell, one of )  CASE NO. BC 228126
    the people of California,      )
13                                 )  NOTICE OF DEMURRER AND
                       Plaintiff,  )  DEMURRER TO COMPLAINT
14                                 )  (Code of Civ. Proc. § 430.10)
         v.                        )
15                                 )  (Assigned to Judge Gregory
    Steven Grouley, Director of    )  O'Brien, Dept. 21)
16  Motor Vehicles,                )
                                   )  Date: June 27, 2000
17                     Defendant.  )  Time: 8:30 a.m.
                                   )  Dept: 21
18  _____)

19

20       TO PLAINTIFF Thomas Marvin; Maxwell, PLAINTIFF IN PROPRIA

21  PERSONA:

22       PLEASE TAKE NOTICE that on June 27, 2000, at 8:30 a.m. or as

23  soon thereafter as the matter may be heard, in Department 21 of

24  the above-entitled Court, located at 111 North Hill Street, Los

25  Angeles, California, defendant Steven Grouley, Director of Motor

26  Vehicles (hereinafter "DMV" or "defendant") will demurrer to

27  plaintiff's Complaint as follows:

28
                               1.
```

1   To the entirety of the Complaint on the grounds that the

2   Complaint does not state facts sufficient to constitute a cause

3   of action. (Code Civ. Proc. § 430.10, subd. (e).)

4   The demurrer is based on this notice; the attached

5   memorandum of points and authorities; and the complete files and

6   records of this action.

7   WHEREFORE, it is prayed that the demurrer be sustained and

8   that an order issue dismissing this action.

9   Dated: May 2 4, 2000.

10

11   BILL LOCKYER, Attorney General
                        of the State of California

12   DANA T. CARTOZIAN,
                        Deputy Attorney General

13

14   By: _____

15   DANA T. CARTOZIAN

16   Attorneys for Defendant:
                  Steven Grouley, Director of Motor

17   Vehicles

18

19

20

21

22

23

24

25

26

27

28

INTRODUCTION

The gravamen of the Complaint brought by plaintiff Thomas Marvin; Maxwell (hereinafter "Maxwell" or "plaintiff") is his objection to the California Department of Motor Vehicles, i.e., "DMV", requiring him to provide a social security number as a condition to the DMV issuing him a California driver's license.

The Complaint is identified as one for declaratory relief. However, the plaintiff does not appear to be seeking a declaration of any legal obligation or the definition of the nature of any relationship between the parties.

Rather, the plaintiff prays for relief from this Court in the form of an order commanding the DMV to issue him a driver's license pursuant to specified conditions, prominent among them the absence of any requirement of his providing a social security number. Thus, this Complaint - its title notwithstanding - effectively resembles a petition for writ of mandate brought pursuant to Code of Civil Procedure section 1085.

In determining whether a section 1085 writ of mandate should issue against an administrative agency, a court must review the challenged agency action in accordance with certain settled rules of law. For the writ to issue, there must be a clear, present, and ministerial duty imposed by law on the agency to do what the petitioner seeks to compel the agency to do. (See Sullivan v. State Board of Control (1985) 176 Cal.App.3d 1059, 1062-1063.)

"A writ of mandate should not issue to enforce an abstract or moot right." (Slater v. City Council (1965) 238 Cal.App.2d 864, 868.)

3.

1   If this action is construed in fact, as well as in name, as
2 a request for declaratory relief, it is left to this Court's
3 discretion whether to entertain the request. (<u>Code Civ. Proc. §
4 1060</u>.)

5   Code of Civil Procedure 1060 contains the requirement that
6 there be an "actual controversy" for a declaratory judgment
7 action to be entertained.

8   "'Actual controversy' referred to in the declaratory
relief statute is one which 'admits of definitive and
9 conclusive relief by judgment within the field of
judicial administration, as distinguished from an advisory
10 opinion upon a particular or hypothetical state of facts.'"
(<u>Winter</u> v. <u>Gnaizda</u> (1979) 90 Cal.App.3d 750, 755.)
11

12   "As repeatedly pointed out, the fact that an issue
raised in an action for declaratory relief is of broad
13 general interest is not enough for the courts to grant
such relief in the absence of a true justiciable
14 controversy". (Citations omitted.)

15   "Under an established line of authorities, a
difference of opinion as to the interpretation of a
16 statute as between a citizen and a government agency
does not give rise to a justiciable controversy."
17 (<u>Winter</u>, supra, 90 Cal.App.3d 756.)

18   **ARGUMENT**

19   As alleged in the Complaint, the single impediment to the
20 DMV issuing Maxwell a driver's license is the DMV's requirement
21 that Maxwell provide to the DMV - as part of the application
22 process - a social security number. (Complaint, p. 6, ¶ 17.)

23   The statutory authority for the DMV requiring a social
24 security number as part of the driver's license application or
25 renewal process can be found in Vehicle Code section 1653.5,
26 subdivision (a).
27 ///
28

4.

1　　　This provision expressed in Vehicle Code section 1653.5

2　regarding providing a social security number has been upheld by

3　Courts of Appeal in recent decisions: Nowlin v. Department of

4　Motor Vehicles (1997) 53 Cal.App.4th 1529; Lauderbach v. Zolin

5　(1995) 35 Cal.App.4th 578. An exception to this general

6　requirement of providing a social security number to the DMV has

7　to do with that category of persons whose presence in the United

8　States is authorized by federal law, but who are ineligible for a

9　social security account number. (Lauderbach, supra, 35

10　Cal.App.4th 585.)

11　　　A demurrer, like its counterpart - a motion for judgment on

12　the pleadings - admits the truth of all material facts pleaded.

13　(Consolidated Fire Protection Dist. v. Howard Jarvis Taxpayers'

14　Assn. (1998) 63 Cal.App.4th 211, 219.)

15　　　However, a demurrer does not concede to contentions,

16　deductions, or conclusions of fact or law. (See Serrano v. Priest

17　(1971) 5 Cal.3d 584, 591.) Thus, this Court is not obliged to

18　accept uncritically Maxwell's conclusory assertion that he is not

19　qualified, i.e., not eligible, to apply for and be issued a

20　social security number. (Complaint, p. 6, ¶ 19.)

21　　　Notably, the plaintiff does not allege that he has never

22　been issued a social security number, or that a previously issued

23　social security number was revoked by the Social Security

24　Administration because of a (subsequent) determination of his

25　ineligibility. Nor does he allege that he has applied to the

26　Social Security Administration for a number and has been denied

27　issuance of it due to ineligibility.

28

5.

381

SUMMARY

Arguably Maxwell may have stated facts sufficient to support a petition for writ of mandate pursuant to Code of Civil Procedure section 1085 if he had alleged with factual specificity that the DMV was requiring him to provide a social security number as part of a driver's license application - despite a determination by the Social Security Administration of his ineligibility for a social security number. He provides no such factual allegations.

Within in the context of a declaratory relief action, if the purpose of this Complaint is solely to obtain a declaration that persons whose presence in the United States is authorized by federal law - but who are ineligible for social security account numbers - may still obtain a driver's license, then this Court should exercise its discretion in declining to entertain the Complaint - for that issue has already been adjudicated.

Maxwell has not pleaded facts establishing 1) he does not have a social security number to provide to the DMV; and 2) the Social Security Administration has determined that he is not eligible to receive one. Absent such factual allegations, the Complaint does not present an "actual controversy" to be adjudicated.

///
///
///
///
///

6.

1 **CONCLUSION**

2 By reason of the foregoing the demurrer should be sustained.

3 Leave to amend may properly be denied unless the plaintiff

4 represents to this Court that he can cure the defects in his

5 pleading, i.e., that he can allege in an amended complaint:

6 1) he has never been issued a social security number or - if

7 he ever did have one, it was revoked by the Social Security

8 Administration; and

9 2) he has recently submitted a completed application to the

10 Social Security Administration seeking issuance of a social

11 security number and has been denied said issuance on the grounds

12 of ineligibility.

13 Absent such a representation the Court should proceed to

14 order the dismissal of this action.

15 Dated: May 2⅃, 2000.

16 Respectfully submitted,

17 BILL LOCKYER, Attorney General
    of the State of California

18 DANA T. CARTOZIAN,
    Deputy Attorney General

19

20 By: _____

21 DANA T. CARTOZIAN

22 Attorneys for Defendant:
    Steven Grouley, Director of Motor

23 Vehicles

24

25

26

27

28

7.

1 | **Thomas Marvin;** Maxwell
Post Office Box 9655
2 | Canoga Park, California
818-846-1482/fax 818-842-0561
3

4 | **Thomas Marvin;** Maxwell
In *propria persona*; not PRO SE
5

6

7

8 | **In the superior court[1]
for Los Angeles county, California**

9

10

11 | Thomas Marvin; Maxwell, one of the people[2])
of California)
12 |)   **Case No. B C228126**
Plaintiff)
13 |)   **Opposition to Demurrer;**
)   **Memorandum of Points**
14 | vs.)   **and Authorities**
)
15 |)   **Date: June 27, 2000**
Steven Grouley,)   **Time: 8:30 am**
16 | **Director of Motor Vehicles**)   **Department 21**
)
17 | Defendant_____)

18

19

20 | I, **Thomas Marvin;** Maxwell, hereby oppose the Demurrer of Defendant Steven

21 | Grouley, Director of Motor Vehicles (hereinafter "Defendant"), filed on or about May 24,

22 | 2000.

23 | The solitary ground alleged in the demurrer is erroneous. The Defendant misstates

24 | and/or misunderstands the issues raised in the complaint. The Verified Complaint does

25 | expressly state facts sufficient to constitute a cause of action.

26

27 | [1]Concurrent with and equivalent to the *district court* as created in the Constitution for the State of California of 1849, and the *seventeenth judicial district*, see Stats 1872, ch. CXIV, p. 116

28 | [2]"The people are such as are born upon the soil, by whom and for whom in the first place the Government was ordained...." *Walther v. Rabolt*, 30 Cal. 185, 189 (1866)

1

385

1   This opposition is based on and supported by the Memorandum of Points and
2 Authorities attached hereto and filed herewith and such oral argument as may be presented at
3 the hearing.

4

5   Submitted this fifteenth day of the eleventh month, in the year A.D. nineteen hundred
6 ninety nine.

7

8

9

10 L.S.] *Thomas Marvin;*
    Thomas Marvin; Maxwell

11

12

13

14

15

16

17

18

19

20

21

22

23

24

25

26

27

28

2

Opposition to Demurrer; Memorandum of Points and Authorities

1 <u>**Memorandum of Points and Authorities**</u>

2   **The Defendant Attempts to Mischaracterize the Cause of Action**

3   On page 3, lines 7 through 27, the Defendant attempts to convince the Court that the

4 Complaint resembles a Petition for Writ of Mandate. This is either an intentional "red

5 herring" to try to confuse the issues, or it is a blatant demonstration of the ignorance of the

6 Defendant. The Defendant states at page 3, lines 8 through 10 that "the plaintiff does not

7 appear to be seeking a declaration of any legal obligation or the definition of the nature of any

8 relationship between parties." The Complaint does in fact expressly seek a declaration of **any**

9 legal obligation or the definition of the nature of any relationship between parties. The Defen-

10 dant's failure to understand the Complaint does not change the content of the Complaint.

11

12   **The Defendant Does Not Clarify VC §1653.5**

13   On page 4, lines 25 and 26, the Defendant refers to Vehicle Code §1653.5(a), but does

14 not cite the actual language thereof. The exact language is important and must be reviewed.

15   1653.5(a) Every form prescribed by the department for use by an applicant for
the issuance or renewal by the department of a driver's license or identification
16 card pursuant to Division 6 (commencing with Section 12500) shall contain a
section for the applicant's social security account number.
17

18   Thus VC §1653.5(a) in fact only alleges to require the Driver License **form** to contain a

19 space for a Social Security Number. But since VC §1653.5 does not end with subdivision a,

20 we must also review more of the text.

21   1653.5(c) Any person who submits to the department a form that, pursuant to
subdivision (a), contains a section for the applicant's social security account
22 number, or pursuant to subdivision (b), the applicant's driver's license or identification card number, if any, shall furnish the **appropriate** number in the space
23 provided. (**emphasis** added)

24   The exact language of the foregoing **does not require a social security number.** The

25 exact language expressly alleges to require an **appropriate** number. This bring us to the cause

26 of action stated within the Verified Complaint, in that I do not have an **appropriate** number,

27 nor can I lawfully obtain one.

28

3

A fact admitted to by the Defendant– **"Both before and after the Fourteenth Amendment** to the federal Constitution, it has not been necessary for a person to be a **citizen of the United States** in order to be a **citizen of his state.** United States v. Cruikshank, 92 U.S. 542, 549, 23 L.Ed. 588 **(1875)"**, In *Crosse v. Board of Supervisors of Elections*, 221 A.2d 431, 433. **(1966)** [emphasis added]

The foregoing **are not** my contentions, deductions, or conclusions of fact or law. They are **facts** supported by case law.

The following case law expressly clarifies the **fact** of **what** the "citizen of the United States" **is.**

A fact admitted to by the Defendant -- "The history and aim of the Fourteenth Amendment is well known, and the purpose had in view well understood. That purpose was to confer the status of citizenship upon a numerous class of persons[3] ... of African descent, who had been held in slavery in this country, or, if having themselves never been held in slavery, were native born descendants of slaves." *Van Valkenburg v. Brown*, 43 Cal. 43, 47

Based upon the foregoing case law, **it is a fact admitted to by the Defendant**, that the Driver License application provided by the Defendant (see Exhibit C to the Verified Complaint) requires that the applicant (unless the applicant is an alien) to declare under penalty of perjury that he is a U.S. citizen, i.e., a descendant of a former slave pursuant to the Fourteenth Amendment to the federal constitution. Without altering the form such as I did, the Driver License form **does not provide an option** for a national of California to apply for a Driver License.

On the back of the Driver License application #A678839534, I properly identified myself as a "national as defined in the Nationality Act of 1940, 54 Stat 1137, and 8 U.S.C. §1101(a)(21), and that I am expressly not a citizen of the United States as created and defined in the Fourteenth Amendment to the federal constitution."

A fact admitted to by the Defendant -- A.   The Nationality Act of 1940, 54 Stat. 1137, Title I, Section 1, Chapter I -- Definitions
      Sec. 101. For the purposes of this Act--
(a) The term "national" means a person owing permanent allegiance to a state.
(b) the term "national of the United States" means (1) a citizen of the United States, or (2) a person, who though not a citizen of the United States, owes permanent allegiance to the United States. It does not include an alien.

---

[3]Note the use of the word **"persons"** rather that **"people"**.

5

388

1   (d) The department shall not complete any application that does not include the applicant's social security account number or driver's license or identification
2   card number as required by subdivision (c).

3   The exact language of the foregoing is very important. The foregoing **does not** allege

4   any **mandatory requirement** for each applicant to have or obtain a social security number. It

5   merely presumes that an applicant might have one, and if the applicant does have a social

6   security number, he must disclose that number on the form. Subsection (d) does not allege that

7   an applicant **must** first obtain a social security number before he can apply for a driver license.

8   If an applicant does not have a social security number, and cannot lawfully even apply for a

9   social security number, the applicant cannot provide an **appropriate number.**

10   This is the actual controversy. *Lauderbach v. Zolin,* 35 Cal.App.4th 578, does not

11   apply to me since I am not an alien, nor does it apply to the issues raised in the Verified

12   Complaint. The fact is that the Defendant does not provide for, or even consider the possibility

13   of, an applicant who does not have an **appropriate** social security number to disclose. Both

14   *Lauderbach,* supra., and *Nowlin v DMV,* 53 Cal.App.4th 1529, can not be applied to this cause

15   of action in that **neither of them address the issues that I have raised.**

16

17   **The Defendant Acknowledges the Truth of All Material Facts**

18   Based on the following, the Defendant admits that there are two classes of citizenship

19   within the united states of America, and thus within California, which is one of the united

20   states of America pursuant to 9 Stat 452.

21   *A fact admitted to by the Defendant* -- There are two classes of citizen-
     ship in this country. "The First Clause of the 14th Amendment made negroes
22   citizens of the United States, and citizens of the state in which they reside, and
     thereby created **two classes of citizens, one of the United States and the other**
23   **of the state.** ... This [second] clause places the privileges and immunities of
     citizens of the United States under the protection of the Federal Constitution, and
24   leaves the privileges and immunities of citizens of a state under the protection of
     the constitution and laws of the state. ... It is quite clear, then, that there is a
25   citizenship of the United States, and a citizenship of state, **which are distinct**
     from each other, and which depend upon different characteristics or circum-
26   stances in the individual. ... The only effect of the amendment under considera-
     tion was to extend the protection and blessings of the constitution and laws to **a**
27   **new class of persons.**" *Cory v. Carter,* 48 Ind. 327, 328, and 349 (1874)

28

4

389

B.   8 U.S.C. §1101 - Definitions
   (a) As used in this chapter -
(21) The term "national" means a person owing permanent allegiance to a state.
(22) the term "national of the United States" means (A) a citizen of the United States, or (B) a person, who though not a citizen of the United States, owes permanent allegiance to the United States.

The Defendant Does Not Address the Main Issue

The **fact** that both federal statutes and various case law support the **fact** that there are two classes of citizenship, coupled with the **fact** that the Defendant does not make any reference to that issue, much less make any attempt to controvert the effect of it, is a fatal flaw to the demurrer because the existence of the two classes of citizenship is a key factor for the foundation of my cause of action.   How can a demurrer make a valid claim that there are not sufficient facts to constitute a cause of action, when the demurrer does not address or controvert the key issue which supports the cause of action? Obviously, it cannot.

Conclusion

Based upon all the foregoing, the Defendant's demurrer must be overruled, and the Defendant must be ordered to Answer the Verified Complaint.

Submitted this sixth day of the sixth month, in the year A.D. two thousand

[L.S.] *Thomas Marvin; Maxwell*
Thomas Marvin; Maxwell

6

```
 1 | BILL LOCKYER, Attorney General        NO FEE - GOV. CODE § 6103
   | of the State of California
 2 | DANA T. CARTOZIAN, (State Bar No. 76011)
   | Deputy Attorney General
 3 | 300 South Spring Street, Fifth Floor
   | Los Angeles, California  90013-1204
 4 | Tel: (213) 897-2091; FAX: (213) 897-1071
 5 | Attorneys for Defendant:
   | Steven Grouley, Director of Motor Vehicles
 6 |
 7 |
 8 |          SUPERIOR COURT OF THE STATE OF CALIFORNIA
 9 |             FOR THE COUNTY OF LOS ANGELES
10 |
11 |
12 | Thomas Marvin; Maxwell, one of  ) CASE NO. BC 228126
   | the people of California,        )
13 |                                  ) DEFENDANT'S REPLY TO
   |                  Plaintiff,      ) PLAINTIFF'S OPPOSITION TO
14 |                                  ) DEFENDANT'S DEMURRER
   |       v.                         )
15 |                                  ) (Assigned to Judge Gregory
   | Steven Grouley, Director of      ) O'Brien, Dept. 21)
16 | Motor Vehicles,                  )
   |                                  ) Date: June 27, 2000
17 |                  Defendant.      ) Time: 8:30 a.m.
   | _____  ) Dept: 21
18 |
19 |
20 |      Defendant Steven Grouley, Director of Motor Vehicles
21 | (hereinafter "DMV" or "defendant") submits the following in reply
22 | to the opposition of plaintiff Thomas Marvin; Maxwell's
23 | (hereinafter "Maxwell" or "plaintiff") to defendant's demurrer.
24 | ///
25 | ///
26 | ///
27 | ///
28 |
   |                              1.
```

DISCUSSION

Notably, the plaintiff has not responded to the demurrer by requesting leave to amend his complaint in the event the demurrer is sustained. This Court should therefore presume that the plaintiff has no additional material facts to allege beyond that provided in the initial complaint. Accordingly, should the demurrer be sustained, there is no apparent purpose served by providing leave to file an amended complaint.

In his complaint the plaintiff alleges that he is not "qualified" to apply for a social security number; that he is not "authorized" to have or use a social security number. (Compl., p. 6, ¶¶ 19, 20A.) In his opposition to the demurrer he implies that he cannot "lawfully" apply for a social security number; that he cannot provide to the DMV an "appropriate" number in response to the inquiry regarding a social security number. (Oppos., p. 4: 8-9.) This Court, however, is not obliged to accept these conclusions asserted by the plaintiff; _factual_ allegations are necessary. (See <u>Serrano</u> v. <u>Priest</u> (1971) 5 Cal.3d 584, 591.)[1]

The plaintiff has not alleged - and apparently does not seek leave to amend his complaint in order to allege - the following:

He does not have currently a social security number and either:

///

///

---

1. That which is implied in plaintiff's opposition, of course, is not allegations of the Complaint. Arguably, these implications can be read into the Complaint, but are still only conclusions, not facts.

2.

1   1) he had previously been issued a social security number
2   but it was revoked by the social security administration because
3   the social security administration determined that the plaintiff
4   was not eligible to have a number; or

5   2) he has applied for a social security number but his
6   application was denied by the social security administration
7   because the social security administration determined that the
8   plaintiff was not eligible to be issued a number.

9   Without such allegations there is no "actual controversy" to
10 be adjudicated. (Code Civ. Proc. § 1060; Winter v. Gnaizda (1979)
11 90 Cal.App.3d 750, 755.) As discussed in the demurrer (p. 4: 19-
12 26; p. 5: 1-10), the validity of the requirement to provide a
13 social security number as part of the driver's license
14 application process is already well established. The demurrer
15 should be sustained and leave to amend should be denied.[2/]

16   Dated: June 15, 2000.

17   Respectfully submitted,

18   BILL LOCKYER, Attorney General
                                of the State of California
19   DANA T. CARTOZIAN,
                                Deputy Attorney General
20

21   By: _____
                                  DANA T. CARTOZIAN
22

23   Attorneys for Defendant:
                              Steven Grouley, Director of Motor
                              Vehicles
24

25   2. The DMV is prepared to have both the demurrer - and
    plaintiff's motion to strike the demurrer - be decided on the
26 basis of the pleadings, being of the opinion that the matters are
    sufficiently briefed. However, absent instructions from the Court
27 to the contrary, an appearance on the DMV's behalf at the 27 June
    hearing is intended.
28

                                  3.

Thomas Marvin; Maxwell
Post Office Box 9655
at the United States Post Office
Canoga Park, California

818-846-1482/fax 818-842-0561

Thomas Marvin; Maxwell
In *propria persona*; not PRO SE

ORIGINAL FILED

JUN 0 6 2000

LOS
SUPERIOR COURT

In the superior court[1]
for Los Angeles county, California

Thomas Marvin; Maxwell, one of the people[2] of California Plaintiff vs. Steven Grouley, Director of Motor Vehicles Defendant	Case No. B C228126 Notice of Motion and Motion to Strike Demurrer; Memorandum of Points and Authorities Date: June 27, 2000 Time: 8:30 am Dept. 21 [In the nature of C.C.P. § 435(b)(3)]

I, Thomas Marvin; Maxwell, one of the people of California and plaintiff in this matter,
Hereby Give Notice that a Motion to Strike Demurrer will be heard in Department 21 of the
superior court[1] for Los Angeles county, located at 111 North Hill Street, Los Angeles,
California, on Tuesday, June 27, 2000 at 8:30 am or as soon thereafter as possible in the nature
of CCP §435(b)(3) which states that "A notice of motion to strike a demurrer, or a portion
thereof, shall set the hearing thereon concurrently with the hearing on the demurrer.

I, Thomas Marvin; Maxwell, one of the people of California and plaintiff in this matter,
hereby move this court to strike the demurrer of the Defendant on the following grounds:

---

[1]Concurrent with and equivalent to the *district court* as created in the Constitution for the State of California of 1849, and the *seventeenth judicial district*, see Stats 1872, ch. CXIV, p. 116

[2]"The people are such as are born upon the soil, by whom and for whom in the first place the Government was ordained...." *Walther v. Rabolt*, 30 Cal. 185, 189 (1866)

1

395

1. The Defendant's demurrer does not identify the court in which this action was filed.

2. The Defendant's demurrer does not accurately reflect the case number under which this case is identified in the Court's file.

This motion is based upon the Notice of Motion as stated hereinabove, brought in the nature of Code of Civil Procedure §435(b)(3) and is supported by the Memorandum of Points and Authorities attached hereto and filed herewith.

Submitted this sixth day of the sixth month, in the year A.D. two thousand.

L.S.] *Thomas Marvin; Maxwell* [Seal]
Thomas Marvin; Maxwell

1   **Memorandum of Points and Authorities**

2

3   **The Venue Within Which the Complaint was Filed**

4   When the Clerk of the superior court certified the Summons, the identification of the

5   issuing superior court was placed upon the face of the summons, to wit:

6

7   "superior court, Los Angeles county, California"

8

9

10

11

12

13

14   **District Court changed to Superior Court**

15   Stats 1880 ch. IV renamed the courts in California. At §2 thereof , it states:

16   "The Superior Court **of each county** in this State shall, **for all purposes**,
    be considered the successor of the District, County, and Probate Courts
17   thereof,..." (**emphasis** included)

18   The foregoing statute created and authorized a superior court **of each county**.   Said

19   statute did not create a "SUPERIOR COURT **OF THE STATE OF CALIFORNIA**".   And

20   correctly so, the seal of this court identifies a "superior court for Los Angeles county", and I

21   have so named the court on the face of my Verified Complaint.

22   Within the text of Stats 1880 ch. IV, the words "for all purposes", would then of neces-

23   sity, include the venue and jurisdiction of the original district court.   On the face of the

24   complaint and all other papers filed by me, I have expressly included the language, footnoted

25   after the words "superior court" on the caption page, "Concurrent with and equivalent to the

26   *district court* as created in the Constitution for the State of California of 1849".   The venue and

27   jurisdiction of the original *district court* in Los Angeles county was of course "on the land"

28

3

1 within the boundaries of Los Angeles county, with Los Angeles county being created pursuant

2 by statute pursuant to the Constitution of the State of California, and California being one of the

3 united states of America pursuant to 9 Stat 452.   The venue of this superior court must, of

4 necessity, still be in that same venue.

5

6 **The Defendant Has Named a Different Court**

7 The Defendant renamed the court, i.e., "SUPERIOR COURT OF THE STATE OF

8 CALIFORNIA FOR THE COUNTY OF LOS ANGELES". No such entitled court has ever

9 been created by any valid Statute of California.

10

11 **The Defendant Has Changed the Case Number**

12 This Verified Complaint was assigned a case number of "B C288126". The Defendant

13 has changed the case number by changing the space between the "B" and the "C" to a space

14 between "BC" and "228126, to wit., "BC 228126".   This could be construed as being a differ-

15 ent number. I cannot and will not acquiesce to a change of the case number.

16

17 **Conclusion**

18 The venue of any court must be expressly identified in order to determine jurisdiction

19 and the proper application of the law within that venue. I am informed and believe that the

20 "renaming of the court" creates an undisclosed change of venue. I cannot and will not acqui-

21 esce to any such change of venue with regard to this matter.

22 Based on all the foregoing, this Court must Order the following:

23 1.   The demurrer filed by the Defendant must be Ordered stricken from the record.

24 The Court must further Order the Defendant to properly identify the Court as designated by the

25 plaintiff on the face of the Verified Complaint and in conformity with that language on the

26 seal of this Court.

27

28

4

2.   In the alternative, this Court must issue a ruling expressly stating that the venue of this Court is actually equivalent to and concurrent with the venue to which the superior court became the successor of pursuant to Stats 1880 ch. IV and that the manner in which the Defendant has entitled the Court, and the manner in which the Defendant has changed the case number, does not effect any undisclosed change of the venue.

Submitted this sixth day of the sixth month, in the year A.D. two thousand.

L.S.] *Thomas Marvin; Maxwell*
Thomas Marvin; Maxwell

5

1 | BILL LOCKYER, Attorney General   NO FEE - GOV. CODE § 6103
   of the State of California
2 | DANA T. CARTOZIAN, (State Bar No. 76011)
   Deputy Attorney General
3 | 300 South Spring Street, Fifth Floor
Los Angeles, California 90013-1204
4 | Tel: (213) 897-2091; FAX: (213) 897-1071

5 | Attorneys for Defendant:
Steven Grouley, Director of Motor Vehicles

6

7

8 | **SUPERIOR COURT OF THE STATE OF CALIFORNIA**

9 | **FOR THE COUNTY OF LOS ANGELES**

10

11

12 | Thomas Marvin; Maxwell, one of)   CASE NO. BC 228126
the people of California,   )
13 |)   DEFENDANT'S OPPOSITION TO
)   PLAINTIFF'S MOTION TO STRIKE
14 | Plaintiff,   )   DEFENDANT'S DEMURRER
)
15 | v.   )   (Assigned to Judge Gregory
)   O'Brien, Dept. 21)
16 | Steven Grouley, Director of   )
Motor Vehicles,   )   Date: June 27, 2000
17 | Defendant.   )   Time: 8:30 a.m.
)   Dept: 21
18 | _____)

19

20 | Defendant Steven Grouley, Director of Motor Vehicles

21 | (hereinafter "DMV" or "defendant") submits the following in

22 | opposition to plaintiff Thomas Marvin; Maxwell's (hereinafter

23 | "Maxwell" or "plaintiff") motion to strike defendant's demurrer.

24 | ///

25 | ///

26 | ///

27 | ///

28 | 1.

401

DISCUSSION

The plaintiff moves to strike the entirety of defendant's demurrer. Yet, the motion to strike fails to specify any portion of the demurrer containing "irrelevant, false, or improper matter", or which was drawn or filed other than "in conformity with the laws of this state, a court rule, or an order of the court", so as to warrant the striking of the demurrer. (<u>Code Civ. Proc. § 436, subds. (a) & (b)</u>.)

Accordingly, the motion to strike should be denied and this Court should proceed to consider the merits of the demurrer.

Dated: June 15 , 2000.

Respectfully submitted,

BILL LOCKYER, Attorney General
of the State of California
DANA T. CARTOZIAN,
Deputy Attorney General

By: _Dana T. Cartozian_
DANA T. CARTOZIAN

Attorneys for Defendant:
Steven Grouley, Director of Motor Vehicles

2.

```
 1 │ BILL LOCKYER, Attorney General        NO FEE - GOV. CODE § 6103
   │    of the State of California
 2 │ DANA T. CARTOZIAN, (State Bar No. 76011)
   │    Deputy Attorney General
 3 │ 300 South Spring Street, Fifth Floor
   │ Los Angeles, California  90013-1204
 4 │ Tel: (213) 897-2091; FAX: (213) 897-1071
   │
 5 │ Attorneys for Defendant:
   │ Steven Grouley, Director of Motor Vehicles
 6 │
   │
 7 │
   │
 8 │        SUPERIOR COURT OF THE STATE OF CALIFORNIA
   │
 9 │            FOR THE COUNTY OF LOS ANGELES
   │
10 │
   │
11 │
   │
12 │ Thomas Marvin; Maxwell, one of  )  CASE NO. BC 228126
   │ the people of California,        )
13 │                                  )  NOTICE OF RULING
   │              Plaintiff,          )
14 │                                  )  (Assigned to Judge Gregory
   │     v.                           )  O'Brien, Dept. 21)
15 │                                  )
   │ Steven Grouley, Director of      )  Date: June 27, 2000
16 │ Motor Vehicles,                  )  Time: 8:30 a.m.
   │                                  )  Dept: 21
17 │              Defendant.          )
   │                                  )
18 │ ─────────────────────────────────
   │
19 │
   │
20 │     TO PLAINTIFF Thomas Marvin; Maxwell, PLAINTIFF IN PROPRIA
   │
21 │ PERSONA:
   │
22 │     PLEASE TAKE NOTICE that on June 27, 2000 Judge Gregory C.
   │
23 │ ///
   │
24 │ ///
   │
25 │ ///
   │
26 │ ///
   │
27 │ ///
   │
28 │
   │                          1.
```

1 | O'Brien ruled as follows in the above-captioned matter:

2 | Defendant's demurrer was sustained. Leave to amend was

3 | denied. Plaintiff's motion to strike the demurrer was viewed as

4 | moot given the ruling regarding defendant's demurrer.

5 | Dated: June 27, 2000.

                  BILL LOCKYER, Attorney General
                    of the State of California
                  DANA T. CARTOZIAN,
                    Deputy Attorney General

                  By: _____
                       DANA T. CARTOZIAN

                  Attorneys for Defendant:
                  Steven Grouley, Director of Motor
                  Vehicles

2.

SUPERIOR COURT OF THE STATE OF CALIFORNIA

FOR THE COUNTY OF LOS ANGELES

Thomas Marvin; Maxwell, one of the people of California,
 	
            Plaintiff,
 	
    v.
 	
Steven Grouley, Director of Motor Vehicles,
 	
            Defendant.
	CASE NO. BC 228126
	
	(PROPOSED) ORDER:
	
	1. SUSTAINING DEFENDANT'S DEMURRER;
	
	2. DISMISSING COMPLAINT

The demurrer of defendant Steven Grouley, Director of Motor Vehicles ("defendant") to the complaint of plaintiff Thomas Marvin; Maxwell ("plaintiff"), and the motion to strike defendant's demurrer brought by the plaintiff, both came on regularly for hearing June 27, 2000, in Department 21 of the above-entitled court, Gregory C. O'Brien, Judge presiding.

    Plaintiff appeared in propria persona. Defendant was represented by Dana T. Cartozian, Deputy Attorney General.

1.

405

1 The Court, having considered the pleadings submitted and
2 having entertained oral argument, now HEREBY ORDERS AND DECREES
3 as follows:
4   1. Defendant's demurrer is sustained. Leave to to amend is
5 denied.
6   2. Plaintiff's motion to strike defendant's demurrer is
7 considered moot given the adjudication of defendant's demurrer.
8   3. This action is dismissed.
9
10 Dated:_____   _____
11   GREGORY C. O'BRIEN
12   Judge of the Los Angeles County
                                 Superior Court
13
14
15
16
17
18
19
20
21
22
23
24
25
26
27
28

                                    2.

1

SUPERIOR COURT OF THE STATE OF CALIFORNIA

FOR THE COUNTY OF LOS ANGELES

DEPARTMENT 21   HON. GREGORY C. O'BRIEN, JR., JUDGE

THOMAS MARVIN,   )
)
          PLAINTIFF,   )
)
     VS.   ) NO. BC228126
)
STEVEN GROULEY,   )
)
          DEFENDANT.   )
_____)

REPORTER'S TRANSCRIPT OF PROCEEDINGS

TUESDAY, JUNE 27, 2000

APPEARANCES:
FOR PLAINTIFF: IN PROPRIA PERSONA
                     THOMAS MARVIN; MAXWELL
                     P.O. BOX 9655
                     CANOGA PARK, CALIFORNIA

FOR DEFENDANT: DEPARTMENT OF JUSTICE,
                     OFFICE OF THE ATTORNEY GENERAL
                     BY: DANA T. CARTOZIAN,
                     DEPUTY ATTORNEY GENERAL
                     300 SOUTH SPRING STREET
                     SUITE 500
                     LOS ANGELES, CALIFORNIA 90013

                     MARLA ALECK, CSR NO. 9511
                     OFFICIAL REPORTER

407

2

```
 1        LOS ANGELES, CALIFORNIA; TUESDAY, JUNE 27, 2000

 2                           8:55 A.M.

 3    DEPARTMENT 21        HON. GREGORY C. O'BRIEN, JR., JUDGE

 4                            -oOo-

 5

 6        THE COURT:  NUMBER 3, MARVIN VERSUS GROULEY.

 7        MR. MAXWELL:  GOOD MORNING, YOUR HONOR.  I AM THOMAS

 8    MARVIN MAXWELL, PLAINTIFF IN PROPRIA PERSONA.

 9        MR. CARTOZIAN:  GOOD MORNING, YOUR HONOR.  DAVID

10    CARTOZIAN, DEPUTY ATTORNEY GENERAL, FOR THE DEFENDANT.

11        THE COURT:  GOOD MORNING.

12            AND YOUR LAST NAME IS MAXWELL?

13        MR. MAXWELL:  YES.

14        THE COURT:  I'M SORRY.

15            MR. MAXWELL, YOU SAW THE COURT'S TENTATIVE

16    THIS MORNING?  YOU SAW THE COURT'S TENTATIVE RULING,

17    HANDWRITTEN RULING?

18        MR. MAXWELL:  I SAW A TENTATIVE ON THE DEMURRER.  I

19    DIDN'T SEE A TENTATIVE ON THE MOTION TO STRIKE.

20        THE COURT:  WELL, THE MOTION TO STRIKE IS MOOT

21    BECAUSE THE DEMURRER IS SUSTAINED WITHOUT LEAVE TO AMEND.

22        MR. MAXWELL:  WOULDN'T THE MOTION TO STRIKE THE

23    DEMURRER HAVE TO BE HEARD BEFORE THE DEMURRER CAN EVEN BE

24    RULED ON?

25        THE COURT:  WELL, WHEN YOU BECOME A JUDGE, IF YOU

26    WANT TO DO IT THAT WAY, THAT WOULD BE FINE.  I RULE ON THE

27    DEMURRERS FIRST.  THEY USUALLY MOOT THE MOTION TO STRIKE.

28        MR. MAXWELL:  WELL, THE ISSUE THAT I HAVE RAISED IN
```

408

3

1   THE MOTION TO STRIKE IS RAISING CONCERNS OF EXACTLY WHAT

2   THE VENUE OF THIS COURTROOM IS. AND UNTIL THE VENUE OF

3   THIS COURTROOM IS IDENTIFIED, I DON'T SEE HOW THIS

4   COURTROOM CAN EVEN TAKE JURISDICTION OVER THIS CASE.

5   BECAUSE WHAT MY CONCERN IS IS THE COURT SEAL ON THE

6   SUMMONS THAT WAS SERVED WITH THIS CASE IDENTIFIES THE

7   COURT AS "SUPERIOR COURT, LOS ANGELES COUNTY,

8   CALIFORNIA." THE DEFENDANT IDENTIFIES SOME COURT THAT

9   GOES BY THE NAME OF "SUPERIOR COURT OF THE STATE OF

10 CALIFORNIA FOR THE COUNTY OF LOS ANGELES." I CAN FIND NO

11 STATUTE THAT HAS EVER CREATED A COURT THAT GOES BY THAT

12 NAME. AND MY CONCERN IS THAT EVEN THIS COURT WEBSITE AND

13 THE HISTORY OF THIS COURT IDENTIFIES THE DATE OF WHEN THE

14 NAME OF THE COURT WAS CHANGED TO SUPERIOR COURT IN 1880.

15   AND HERE'S A COPY OF THE STATUTE RIGHT

16 THERE. "SUPERIOR COURT OF EACH COUNTY IN THIS STATE SHALL

17 FOR ALL PURPOSES BE CONSIDERED THE SUCCESSOR OF THE

18 DISTRICT COUNTY AND PROBATE COURTS THEREOF."

19   SO MY CONCERN IS, IS THE VENUE OF THIS

20 COURTROOM CONCURRENT AND EQUIVALENT TO THE VENUE THAT THE

21 SUPERIOR COURT BECAME SUCCESSOR TO IN THIS STATUTE AND

22 STAT 1880, CHAPTER FOUR? AND IF THIS COURT CANNOT ANSWER

23 YES TO THAT QUESTION, YOU CAN'T TAKE JURISDICTION OF THE

24 CASE BECAUSE THIS IS THE VENUE IN WHICH I FILED MY CASE.

25   THE COURT. ANYTHING ELSE?

26   ALL RIGHT. THE DEMURRER IS SUSTAINED WITHOUT

27 LEAVE TO AMEND. THE ATTORNEY GENERAL WILL GIVE NOTICE.

28   MR. CARTOZIAN: YES. THANK YOU, YOUR HONOR.

4

```
 1        MR. MAXWELL:  AND I WOULD LIKE THE RECORD TO NOTE
 2   THAT THE JUDGE HAS USURPED JURSIDICTION WITHOUT
 3   IDENTIFYING THE VENUE OF THE COURTROOM.
 4            AND I WILL REQUEST A COPY OF THE TRANSCRIPT
 5   TO BE PREPARED, AND I GIVE THE COURT --
 6        THE COURT:  ALL RIGHT.  SIR, YOU MAY DO ALL OF THAT,
 7   ARRANGE ALL OF THAT, AFTER THE COURT IS IN RECESS.  YOU
 8   MAY ASK FOR A TRANSCRIPT.  TALK TO THE COURT REPORTER.
 9   BUT WAIT UNTIL WE'RE IN RECESS.
10            (THE PROCEEDINGS CONCLUDED AT 9:55 A.M.)
11
12
13
14
15
16
17
18
19
20
21
22
23
24
25
26
27
28
```

```
                                                          5
 1              SUPERIOR COURT OF THE STATE OF CALIFORNIA
 2                   FOR THE COUNTY OF LOS ANGELES
 3
 4   DEPARTMENT 21         HON. GREGORY C. O'BRIEN, JR., JUDGE
 5
     THOMAS MARVIN,                  )
 6                                   )
                   PLAINTIFF,        )
 7                                   )
            VS.                      )  NO. BC228126
 8                                   )
     STEVEN GROULEY,                 )
 9                                   )
                   DEFENDANT.        )
10   _____)
11   STATE OF CALIFORNIA     )
                             ) SS
12   COUNTY OF LOS ANGELES   )
13
14        I, MARLA ALECK, CSR NO. 9511, OFFICIAL COURT
15   REPORTER OF THE SUPERIOR COURT OF THE STATE OF CALIFORNIA,
16   FOR THE COUNTY OF LOS ANGELES, DO HEREBY CERTIFY THAT THE
17   FOREGOING PAGES, 2 THROUGH 4, COMPRISE A FULL, TRUE AND
18   CORRECT TRANSCRIPT OF THE TESTIMONY TAKEN AND PROCEEDINGS
19   HELD IN THE ABOVE-ENTITLED MATTER ON TUESDAY, JUNE 27,
20   2000.
21        DATED THIS 1ST DAY OF JULY, 2000.
22
23
24
25
                   _____, CSR NO. 9511
26                 OFFICIAL COURT REPORTER
27
28
```

(proposed) Amendment XXVII

SECTION 1. The first section of the fourteenth article of amendment to the Constitution of the United States is hereby repealed.

SECTION 2. We hold these truths to be self-evident, that all people are created equal, that they are endowed by their Creator with certain unalienable rights, that among these are life, liberty, privacy, and the pursuit of happiness.

All people born or naturalized in one of the several states are expressly so endowed with these unalienable rights, and shall enjoy citizenship of the state in which they are born or make their permanent abode, with rights protected by the constitution and laws of that state, as well as the Bill of Rights amended to this constitution, and with all other rights preserved to the states or to the people by this constitution, subject to the provisions of Section 3 of this Amendment.

SECTION 3. Upon reaching the age of majority, all people born or naturalized in one of the several states shall have the right to a voluntary choice of either: a) citizenship of the state in which he or she is born or makes his or her permanent abode; or, b) national citizenship of the United States whose rights shall be exclusively protected by this constitution and applicable federal law.

SECTION 4. All people born within the boundaries of District of Columbia shall be deemed as citizens of one of the states which ceded the land to form the seat of the federal government.

SECTION 5. All people born within the boundaries of Puerto Rico, Guam, the Virgin Islands of the United States or any other applicable federal territory, shall have national citizenship of the United States, and shall be qualified to apply for naturalization as a citizen of one of the several states upon establishing permanent residency therein.

SECTION 6. Each of the several states shall retain sovereign control over the protection of the rights of its citizens. No state shall make or enforce any law that abridges the privileges and immunities of national citizenship of the United States, although particular privileges and immunities of national citizenship, as may be established by law, shall of necessity depend upon the establishment of permanent residency within a particular state.

SECTION 7. No state shall make any law respecting any race, creed, ethnic background, or gender, so that each citizen of any one of the several states shall have equal protection under the laws of that state, including unfettered access to any declaration of rights or bill of rights applicable within that state, as well as unfettered access to all rights protected in this constitution within the federal jurisdiction where they are applicable.

SECTION 8. Nothing in this Amendment shall be construed as amending or altering the effect of Article IV, Section 2, clause 1, of this constitution. The provisions of this Amendment shall apply to all people to whom it expressly applies that are born or naturalized after the ratification thereof as well as those who are alive at the time of its ratification. Congress shall have power to enforce, by appropriate legislation, the provisions of this article.

Index

Need more copies of **Identity Fraud?**

Send your Order to:

Thomas Marvin; Maxwell
Blaquemoor Productions
Post Office Box 396
Arvin, California   93203

name _____

address _____

city/state _____

                                   zip _____

qty   price

____ $19.95 @ $ _____

shipping & handling $ _____
$4.00 for one
$1.50 each additional book

Total $ _____